SERGEI O. PROKOFIEFF (1954–2014) studied Fine Arts and Painting at the Moscow School of Art. He encountered the work of Rudolf Steiner in his youth, and quickly decided to devote his life to it. He became active as an author and lecturer in 1982, and helped found the Anthroposophical Society in his native Russia in 1991. In Easter 2001, he was appointed as a member of the Executive Council of the General Anthroposophical Society in Dornach, Switzerland, a position he held until his death. A popular speaker, he wrote numerous books and articles that are published in many languages.

D1109086

Rudolf Steiner and the Founding of the New Mysteries

Sergei O. Prokofieff

TEMPLE LODGE

Translated from the Russian by Paul King
(Introduction, Afterword and author's revisions and additions to the
second edition translated by Simon Blaxland de Lange)

Temple Lodge Publishing
Hillside House, The Square
Forest Row RH18 5ES

www.templelodge.com

First English edition by Rudolf Steiner Press, 1986
Second edition with additional material published by Temple Lodge, 1994
Reprinted 2017

Originally published in German under the title *Rudolf Steiner und die Grundlegung der neuen Mysterien* by Verlag Freies Geistesleben, Stuttgart in 1982

A catalogue record for this book is available from the British Library

ISBN 978 1 912230 04 4

The publishers wish to express their gratitude to Karla Kiniger for her work on the translated text

Typeset by DP Photosetting, Aylesbury, Bucks
Printed and bound in Great Britain by 4Edge Ltd., Essex

*'This anthroposophical movement is not an earthly service;
this anthroposophical movement, in every detail of its totality,
is a divine service, a service of the Gods.'*

From Rudolf Steiner's opening lecture
of the Christmas Conference,
24 December 1923.

Contents

Foreword

Humanity is approaching the end of the century and therefore also those events of which Rudolf Steiner spoke as being of the greatest significance for the whole future development of the Earth. Looking towards the end of this century, it is an awareness of the acute urgency of the work facing the Anthroposophical Society and every individual anthroposophist that has led the author to write this book, which is intended for members of the Anthroposophical Society only.

It is the profound conviction of the author that the practical realization of these tasks, which *must be accomplished in our century*, and the role that falls particularly to the anthroposophist, are directly connected with the realization of the spiritual impulse that came into the world with the Christmas Conference of 1923–24.

A significant step on the way to this goal for every anthroposophist can be the knowledge that the Christmas Conference is a Mystery-event. It is the beginning of the New Mysteries, the Michael Mysteries of esoteric Christianity, the development of which will be decisive for the destiny of all future spiritual culture.

Particularly important in this connection are two books published in recent years dealing with this theme: *The Christmas Foundation; Beginning of a New Cosmic Age* by Rudolf Grosse, and *Mystery Streams in Europe and the New Mysteries* by B.C.J. Lievegoed. Together with the earlier publication of *The Foundation Stone* by F.W. Zeylmans van Emmichoven, these books place the Christmas Conference at the very centre of anthroposophical spiritual life in an endeavour to communicate to as many anthroposophists as possible a true understanding of its Mystery-character. They were written out of a realization that only our understanding of the esoteric nature of the Christmas Conference and our commitment to it can give the Anthroposophical Society, as the bearer of the anthroposophical movement, the strength it needs at the present time to fulfil the tasks conferred upon it.

In writing this book an attempt has been made to look at the founding of the New Mysteries in relation to the path of Rudolf Steiner's life and its culmination—the Christmas Conference of 1923–24—and to view this in such a way as to deepen further our understanding of that Conference. It is based on four talks given by the author at Christmas 1979, wherein the aim was to present the Christmas Conference as the climax of the path of

Rudolf Steiner's life and also as the most important event to occur in the twentieth century *on the physical plane*. Subsequent work on these talks in a written form led to a considerable broadening of their content which, nevertheless, seemed to the author in the course of time to take on more and more the character of a unified whole developing organically into seven chapters.

This book is addressed to anyone who has established a working basis in Anthroposophy and who wishes to penetrate more deeply into its esoteric being and essence. Knowledge is assumed of a whole series of books and lectures by Rudolf Steiner (in particular the Christological and Karma lectures), of the most important stages of his life, the history of the development of the anthroposophical movement and the Anthroposophical Society, and also of the books about the Christmas Conference mentioned above. Thus, for example, in the description in the first chapter of the activity of Rudolf Steiner in the world, the main emphasis is not placed so much on the outer events—for these may well be sufficiently known to the reader from other sources—as on the nature of the inner, occult events that stand behind them.

In order not to weigh down the main text too much, further aspects which arose naturally in the course of the work have been dealt with separately in the relatively extensive supplementary Notes, the aim of which is intended to stimulate the reader to a deepening and further study of related questions.

Seen as a whole, it is hoped that the words at the beginning of Zeylmans van Emmichoven's book may also hold good for this work: 'Some things it will only be possible to hint at. The most important matters cannot be expressed concretely at all, since they concern a process which is still going on and can only reveal itself fully in the distant future. Nevertheless, some picture of this future may perhaps emerge from between the lines.'

All that remains to be said is that the significance and complexity of the questions to be examined demanded the working through of such a breadth of material that it has not been possible to bring every detail to a final form. The fundamental content of the ideas, however, seems to the author to have been expressed sufficiently clearly, and for this reason he believes that in its existing form the present work will be of sufficient help to every anthroposophist who is seeking a *personal* and *living* relationship to the Christmas Conference as the true centre of the anthroposophical movement in the world, and to its founder—Rudolf Steiner.

Sergei O. Prokofieff
Easter 1981/Easter 1986

Introduction

How I came to write the book
Rudolf Steiner and the Founding of the New Mysteries *

When in the autumn of this year (1986) the Stuttgart publishing house, Verlag Freies Geistesleben, suggested that I write a short article for an anthology commemorating its 40 years of existence about how I found my way to the ideas which form the content of my book *Rudolf Steiner and the Founding of the New Mysteries*, my initial conviction was to decline. For on the one hand I have always endeavoured to exclude from my work everything of a 'personal' nature. On the other hand, the background to and the writing of this book was no smooth and even process but associated with certain spiritual and occult experiences that would have no place in an article written for the general public. Nevertheless, after further lengthy consideration, I decided to make the attempt through what follows to point towards some underlying themes in my life that ultimately led to the arising of the book in question. The fundamental reason why I eventually came to this conclusion was the feeling that the *objective* aspect of what underlies the spiritual guidance of *every* human destiny can, under certain circumstances, have some significance for others as well, especially for those who have come to the Earth in the second half of the twentieth century with similar inner impulses. For such people, the story of how one human being of our time, who was born and grew up in very difficult spiritual circumstances in Eastern Europe and who nevertheless not only found his way to Anthroposophy in general but also to those questions which in a certain sense are of central importance in it and which have their focal point in the event of the founding of the New Mysteries at the Christmas Conference of 1923, may be of some interest.

Of course, the life of each human individual has many layers and consists of a number of different streams and impulses. What follows is, therefore, a description only of what can make the inner and outer motives that led me to write my book more comprehensible.

There are two themes, two childhood experiences, from my earliest days that particularly stand out. In the first place I always—as far as I can recall—

---

* This essay has been included in this new edition at the suggestion of the present publishers.

1

inwardly felt myself to be a Christian. Not that I had any particular influence in this respect from my family. Although it was highly cultured—almost all the arts and exact sciences being represented amongst the occupations of its members—my family's spiritual views were of a very diverse kind. There were some idealists and even those who professed a faith, but there were also confirmed materialists. Thus to preserve the peace and also to maintain a harmonious coexistence between the various spiritual trends, 'ideological questions' were as a rule not discussed. And so I was in this respect from the very start left entirely to myself. All the same, there was one circumstance that was of considerable significance for me, something that was quite a rarity in the country where I was born; from my earliest days I had access to the Gospels, to the New Testament. For this Book was in an altogether non-confessional way—as an essential part of the cultural heritage of humanity—also part of the life of our family, on a par with the other works of world literature, music and painting.

The second element that can be traced back to my earliest childhood was the dim awareness that I was not living on Earth for the first time, an awareness which was connected with the constant feeling that I had been living before my birth in a completely different world, one that was radiant and immeasurably sublime. In the verses that I wrote in my childhood and youth I tried to express in a clumsy poetic form both these fundamental moods which lived at that time unspoken in my soul.

A further aspect that should be mentioned here is that in our family virtually everyone adored the music of Richard Wagner, and the day when one of the older members of the family translated the whole of the libretto of Wagner's *Parsifal* for me at sight was one of the great events of my childhood. With this, the theme that was to accompany me spiritually throughout all subsequent years first entered my soul. It made so strong an impression on me that I even tried to write a 'Parsifal' of my own in the form of a broadly conceived drama in verse, where the idea of reincarnation played a significant part. Thus it was that I had my first contact with the stream of esoteric Christianity, and the consequence of my becoming imbued with this impulse was that a question came to fill my entire being: where is it possible to find the modern continuation of this spiritual stream today?

This new inner yearning—and the constant search for an answer—was subsequently further strengthened as a result of my acquaintance with certain elements of eastern, and in particular Indian, wisdom. Here—or so I felt—was a body of deep esoteric knowledge, but it lacked a centre, it lacked Christ. In the official church, where I went on several occasions in search of answers to the questions that tormented me, I did not find any continuation of that spiritual stream which had opened up to me through the content of Wagner's *Parsifal*. In the East—so I felt at the time, though I would probably not have been able to express this in such a clearly conceptual form—there were vast treasures of spiritual wisdom, of which the exoteric Christianity of the church was almost completely bereft. However, if Christianity really was what I felt it to be in my soul, it must contain still higher and more all-encompassing treasures of wisdom than the religions and philosophical systems of the East. This feeling that lived in me can best be expressed through the following words of Rudolf Steiner, which, if I had read them at the time, I could have fully related to myself: 'It is not the Christ that we lack; the knowledge of Christ, the Isis of Christ, the Sophia of Christ is what fails us' (lecture of 24 December 1920, GA 202). The question of *esoteric Christianity* lived in my soul at that time with considerable power.

Several years later, in the first of Rudolf Steiner's lecture-cycles that fell into my hands, I found in the introductory lecture words which state that in esoteric Rosicrucian Christianity 'absolutely all' of the ancient wisdom of the East has been preserved but it has been 'newly born from the rejuvenating spring of the Christ-impulse' (lecture of 12 April 1909, GA 110).

The guidance of destiny, of which every individual can be aware as he inwardly reviews his own past, is perhaps especially clearly apparent where outward circumstances would seem to oppose it. Thus it happened that approximately in my fourteenth year I first came across Rudolf Steiner's book *Knowledge of the Higher Worlds*. From the start it was for me not only a guide and source of help on the inner path but was above all a first answer to my great question about modern 'esoteric Christianity'. For although the name of Christ is hardly mentioned at all in the book itself, it was completely clear to me after the first reading that I held in my hands a description of that path of the human soul to Christ that had been given out of the spirit of our time.

It was, however, the last two chapters, which called forth in me utterly different feelings, that made the strongest impression on me. One of these feelings was an experience of my own deep inner imperfection, which was brought about through reading the description of the spirit-pupil's meeting with the Lesser Guardian of the Threshold, while the other was the certainty that was evoked upon reading those words spoken by the Greater Guardian of the Threshold to the pupil that only Christ Himself can address a human being in this way! That means that the book *Knowledge of the Higher Worlds* is a central work of modern esoteric Christianity. (At the time I as yet knew virtually nothing about the personality of Rudolf Steiner, the Anthroposophical Society, the Goetheanum etc.) This rev-

3

elation was subsequently fully confirmed through reading *Occult Science*. But for me personally the fact that I became aware of who it is that is revealed in the figure of the Greater Guardian of the Threshold not through *Occult Science* but solely through intensively living with the inner content of *Knowledge of the Higher Worlds* was of considerable significance.

My first acquaintance with *Occult Science* also came about in a quite distinctive way. It first came into my hands in French. At the time, I could only read French very slowly and with a dictionary; there was therefore no question of reading the *whole* of the book. As I was most familiar with the theme of the 'path of knowledge', I looked at this chapter and almost immediately found there the description of the Rose Cross Meditation. This exercise was the first that I got to know from *Occult Science*. The fundamental significance of this exercise—which consists in purifying the human blood from lower desires and the human ego from egoism—and its imaginative form made a considerable impression on me; and since then the exercise has become an inseparable part of my inner life. It was also a confirmation of an intuition that I had that the Rosicrucian path of spiritual knowledge described in this book has a certain relationship to the Grail Mysteries. Only half a year later, when I acquired *Occult Science* in Russian and read the whole book, was I able to find complete confirmation of my intuition; for the spiritual path described in this book was not only the path of esoteric or Rosicrucian Christianity but also the modern form of the Mysteries of the Holy Grail, the most important spiritual heritage of the Christian world.

The main impression that I received from reading *Occult Science* (it was the third anthroposophical book that I read, the second being *Theosophy*), and in particular from becoming familiar with the spirit-imbued nature of world evolution of which it speaks, can best be expressed through the following words that Rudolf Steiner spoke in his lecture of 30 June 1909 (GA 112): 'Thus the anthroposophical view of the whole panorama of reincarnation, the nature of man and the cosmos, and so forth, regards the Christ Being as a focal point. And anyone who rightly studies this anthroposophical view of the world will say to himself: I can contemplate all that, but I can understand it only if the whole picture is related to the great focal point of the Christ. I have depicted in various ways the doctrine of reincarnation, teachings about the various human races, planetary evolution and so on; but the Being of Christ is here painted from a single point of view, and this sheds light on everything else. It is a picture with a principal figure to which everything else is related, and I can only understand the significance and expression of the other figures if I have understood the principal figure. The anthroposophical way is that we first project a great picture of the various phenomena of the spiritual world, but then we concentrate on the principal figure and only then do the details of the picture become intelligible.'

Thus as a result of reading *Occult Science* I was not only introduced to a new spiritual cosmos, which in its majesty and sublimity excelled everything that I had experienced before, but above all to a cosmos which had as its centre, as its 'great focal point', the figure of the Cosmic Christ. To the inner sense of the indisputable truth of such a state of affairs, which had lived within me since my earliest childhood, there was now added the pure and all-embracing *knowledge* that it was so.

Finally, a further theme which clarified for me the occult connection between historical Christianity and the eastern teaching of the Bodhisattvas was the comparison of the spiritual paths of Christ and Buddha that is to be found at the end of the sixth chapter of the book *Christianity as Mystical Fact and the Mysteries of Antiquity* (GA 8). It became clear from what was said in this chapter that it was precisely at the radiant heights at which the Buddha's life-path culminated that the spiritual path of Christ Jesus *began*. In other words: where the path of one of the highest initiates of mankind ended was where the divine-human path of Christ had its beginning. (This theme subsequently acquired a conclusive form in my mind when I became familiar with the last lecture of the cycle *The East in the Light of the West. The Children of Lucifer and the Brothers of Christ*, GA 113, and with the lecture 'The Sphere of the Bodhisattvas' from GA 116.)

These particular themes from my gradual acquaintance with the fundamental works of Rudolf Steiner are cited here for two reasons. The first was because these were the themes that from the very start gave rise to the clear feeling: everything that Rudolf Steiner is saying here is already familiar to me, though I had not been able to formulate it conceptually before now. What had been living in my soul as a general vague feeling has now been permeated by the clarity of intellectual consciousness. (Much later I came to realize that a similar sense of 'inner recollection' upon reading spiritual–scientific material has also been the experience of many other anthroposophists.) The second reason was that I was later to find all these themes, in a more elevated and concentrated form, in the *Foundation Stone Meditation*.

Because of certain family connections, it happened that I was taken at the age of 14 to a house on the shores of the Black Sea in Eastern Crimea which had belonged to a well-known poet,* who just before the First World War had taken part in the building of the First Goetheanum (then

* Maximilian Voloshin (1877–1932). His wife was Maria Stepanovna Voloshina (1887–1976). The house was at Koktebel in Eastern Crimea.

known as the 'Johannes Bau', the 'St John's Building'). In this house, where the whole atmosphere was strongly reminiscent of the beginning of our present century, there was amongst much else an extensive occult library in Russian and in French containing almost all Rudolf Steiner's basic books, which had been published in Russian before the Revolution by a press belonging to the Russian Anthroposophical Society, 'Dukhovnoye Znanie' ('Spiritual Life'). Thus in the period between my fourteenth and nineteenth years I was able to familiarize myself with Rudolf Steiner's fundamental works and also with many other spiritual and occult authors belonging to eastern, theosophical and mystically ecclesiastical streams.

I actually spent these five years in complete spiritual solitude, for none of the people around me were interested in Anthroposophy. Nevertheless, this time was for me an important period of probation. These solitary years were the time when, sustained only by my own inner forces and my yearning to find answers to the vital questions that confronted me, I was to choose Anthroposophy—or, as I said to myself at that time, the spiritual stream represented by Rudolf Steiner—as my life's task, as my higher calling in this world. And only when this inner decision was taken, when I experienced with all my strength that my whole life had acquired a new meaning and a new purpose with the beginning of my conscious *service* of those ideals which had formerly resided within my soul but had only become a conscious reality through spiritual science, was I led by destiny out of my initial state of solitude.

This happened as follows. In the house of some friends whom I had come to know in the Crimea, a cycle of lectures by Rudolf Steiner fell quite 'by chance' into my hands for the first time. It should be said that until then I did not know that such lecture-cycles existed, or, to be more precise, I knew that individual lectures had been given but I had no idea whether any record of them had been preserved. And now I held in my hands the cycle of ten lectures entitled *The Spiritual Hierarchies and their Reflection in the Physical World. Zodiac, Planets, Cosmos* (GA 110). Their history was briefly as follows. They had been translated out of French by a lady who had returned in the middle of the fifties to Russia after a period of emigration. In Paris, where she had spent a number of years, she had discovered Rudolf Steiner shortly before her return home and brought some of his books with her. On arriving in Russia, she had to settle in one of the central towns in the Ukraine. But as none of the people around her were interested in spiritual questions, she would when she visited her friends simply leave behind copies of her translations, for the most part of Rudolf Steiner. In this way my friends acquired one of these copies.

Through this lecture-cycle a completely new world opened up. I felt as

6

though the higher spiritual reality standing behind Rudolf Steiner's various descriptions had now come much closer to me. When I heard from my friends that it *appeared* that the translator had other cycles I immediately resolved to go and visit her. What did it matter to me if I had to journey 900 kilometres to a town I did not know and to completely strange people if I might acquire thereby *even one* lecture-cycle. At that time I was ready to overcome any obstacle in order to obtain them, for Anthroposophy had become more important than anything else in my life!

Everything turned out better than I dared hope. The meeting was very warm and developed into a deep friendship, which lasted for four years until the premature death of this woman. After this initial visit I returned home with four or five more cycles, mostly studies of the Gospels.

At approximately the same time, destiny—again as though 'fortuitously'—granted me a further acquaintance. It, too, was enacted in the Crimea, in the house of the Russian poet. In August 1973 a young man (somewhat older than I) came on a visit to this house. He wished to become more closely acquainted with the life and creative work of its former owner, since he knew that he had personally taken part in the building of the First Goetheanum. The young man was an anthroposophist. We got to know one another. He hailed from a large town in the north-west of Russia. At the end of the conversation we exchanged addresses. Six months later I made a first visit to my new acquaintance. This was the beginning of a real anthroposophical friendship.

This first anthroposophical friend of mine put further 'cycles' at my disposal, and also various meditative texts and dicta of Rudolf Steiner (from GA 40 and GA 245★ in Russian translation. Over the course of three years I visited my new friend two or three times a year and so entered more deeply into the world of Rudolf Steiner's lectures.

It should be said that I am now, as I look back at the way my destiny has led me, deeply grateful that it allowed me first to familiarize myself in quiet concentration with the basic *books* and only then with the lectures of Rudolf Steiner. Only much later did I realize that this order represents the best way of entering into the spiritual cosmos of Anthroposophy.

From the various experiences of this three-year period there is one that I should like especially to mention, inasmuch as it has a direct connection with the theme of the present essay. During one of my visits my anthroposophical friend suggested one evening that we read a short cycle of three lectures, observing with a somewhat mysterious air that these lectures had something very important to say about the karma of anthroposophists, that is, about *our own* karma. These were the famous

★ Translated as *Verses and Meditations* and *Guidance in Esoteric Training*.

Arnhem lectures from the sixth volume of *Karmic Relationships* (GA 240). The whole night through I did not close my eyes for a moment. Only at dawn did I go to sleep. Only my unwillingness to rouse the whole household restrained me from waking my friend and telling him about the new feelings that now filled me, feelings that so overwhelmed me as to render me almost speechless.

Only later in another karma lecture, where Rudolf Steiner speaks about the 'cosmic thunderstorms' that took place in the spiritual world at the beginning of the fifteenth century, when with spiritual thunder and lightning the First Hierarchy transmitted the Cosmic Intelligence from the bosom of the Second Hierarchy to the heads of men on Earth, and where he also describes how this 'cosmic thunderstorm' was beheld by the souls gathered around Michael in his supersensible School, did I find at the end of this description the following words: 'This should be understood, for these thunders and lightnings must become enthusiasm in the hearts and minds of anthroposophists!' (GA 237, lecture of 28 July 1924). It was this higher spiritual enthusiasm, which springs from the soul's deeply hidden memory of events that had been spiritually experienced and is able utterly to fill both heart and soul if these memories are brought into everyday waking consciousness, that I experienced in that memorable night.

It was as though a curtain had been torn asunder before my inner sight. Now I knew the spiritual Being whom I served and to whom I henceforth wanted to dedicate my whole being—'the Countenance of Christ', Michael, the inspirer of modern spiritual science.

For me personally, this experience was also an inner answer to the requirement expressed by Rudolf Steiner at the beginning of the first of the Arnhem lectures that it was necessary to 'stand in life as true representatives of the anthroposophical movement', to 'represent Anthroposophy in the world through one's [whole] personality' (lecture of 18 July 1924, GA 240).* When I read these lines, I did not have any clear idea of what the First Class of the Esoteric School mentioned in the lecture was about, but I felt with absolute clarity that this requirement proceeded not from Rudolf Steiner but *through* Rudolf Steiner *from Michael himself* and that in this moment it was above all directed personally towards me.

Such moments in life are moments of inner commitment or 'pledging'. And in a remarkable way Rudolf Steiner goes on to speak in this Arnhem lecture about *his* 'pledge' to the spiritual world and to the spiritual powers guiding him, and about his 'unswerving' loyalty to the spiritual obligation that he had taken upon himself.

* The relevant portion of the lecture has been omitted from the English edition (Translator's note).

8

At that time I was as yet unable to formulate in words what Rudolf Steiner had in mind by his 'pledge', but I dimly felt that my pledge was in some mysterious way connected with *his*, albeit only as a microcosm to a macrocosm, just as great and small worlds are despite all their differences related to one another. That this 'pledge' of Rudolf Steiner was a commitment of faithfulness to the *spiritual impulse* brought by him to the Earth through the Christmas Conference I understood only later. Thus in the introductory address to the lecture of 23 May 1924 (GA 239) he speaks about 'the forces behind the alliance we were able to establish *through the Christmas Conference* with good spiritual powers...' Rudolf Steiner wished to remain—and remained—true to this new alliance established with the higher powers guiding the anthroposophical movement in the spiritual world until the end of his earthly life and beyond in his supersensible existence. At the time I as yet knew too little outwardly about the Christmas Conference to be able to judge, but nevertheless—even without being fully conscious of it—the 'night' experience described above was my first contact with its esoteric being.

After the Christmas Conference—said Rudolf Steiner in the Arnhem lectures—everything in the anthroposophical movement and the Anthroposophical Society becomes different. 'Behold, I make all things new' (Revelation 21: 5)—this motif sounded forth with particular power from these lectures and evoked a deep echo in my soul. Henceforth, I felt, everything in my life too had to become new, for I had 'made a pledge', the first conscious pledge of my life.

On three subsequent occasions I had similar inner experiences. These were on reading the lectures given in Christiania on the Fifth Gospel (GA 148), on becoming acquainted with the so-called 'Michael Letters' (GA 26) and on reading the Neuchâtel lectures on Christian Rosenkreutz (GA 130). Thus by this time I had acquired an initial idea of the spiritual beings inspiring Rudolf Steiner. I pictured this as a mighty spiritual ascent reaching from Christian Rosenkreutz, the leading Master-individuality of western (Christian) humanity, to the Spirit of our time, Michael, and from him to the spiritual focus of our cosmos, to Christ, the bearer of the Divine Logos.

From this same time I began to make considerable efforts to bring order to my meditative life. After various more or less short-lived attempts I now tried to find the path to a more purposeful and rhythmically ordered meditative work, first once and then twice a day, as Rudolf Steiner directed all the pupils of the esoteric school which he founded and which continued to exist until 1914 (see GA 245).

All this took place shortly before my twenty-first birthday.

★

9

A further year and a half passed by. Then it came about that, in the course of one of his visits to the town where I was living, my anthroposophical friend offered to acquaint me with some other anthroposophical friends in the same town. I consented. And so it happened that at Easter 1976 I found myself for the first time in a small circle of people whose anthroposophical work was accompanied on every occasion by reading the *Foundation Stone Meditation* line by line in two languages, German and Russian.

It should be pointed out here that although I had already had the opportunity of familiarizing myself with a Russian translation of the *Foundation Stone Meditation*, nevertheless despite the reverence with which I read it I did not become fully aware of what it was that I had encountered.

In order rightly to understand what follows, something should be said about my initial relationship to the German language, or, to be more precise, about the absence of any relationship to it; for that language which I heard from time to time by chance on the radio or in television films tended rather to repel me through its outer coarseness (I did not know at the time that *this* strange German language had really no right to be called 'German'). At school I learnt French and then tried to learn English. Although I had by then read quite a lot of Rudolf Steiner's books and lectures in Russian, I had scarcely any interest in the language in which they were originally written or spoken. Only the *content* was important and this filled me completely, nourishing my entire soul and spiritual life. This reading was at the time the most important aspect of my life (I knew German literature only in translation).★

And then a miracle occurred that was comparable only with awakening from a deep sleep. When I heard the German text of the *Foundation Stone Meditation*, a whole world of completely new spirituality opened up to me for the first time. The language that I heard was a language as rich and as inspired as the sublime meaning which it conveyed. Language and content appeared for the first time in their indissoluble unity. For not only was the German language revealed to me at that moment as the sole possible bearer of the full wisdom of the new Christian esotericism but also the *content* of the *Foundation Stone Meditation* appeared for the first time in all its cosmic-earthly power before my soul. Thus only when I heard the *Foundation Stone Meditation* 'from mouth to ear', that is, as it rang out for the first time at the Christmas Conference on 25 December 1923, was I able to experience what it was as regards its esoteric essence from the very beginning: the modern revelation of the Cosmic Word, that is, of Christ

★ My sole acquaintance with the German language 'from the other side', so to speak, was through music. Wagner's operas, Bach's *Passions* and Schumann's song-cycles had been my companions since childhood.

Himself ('... heard coming from the Cosmic Word' [26 December 1923], as I later realized Rudolf Steiner said of it).

These are words of Christ, which are directed now from the spiritual world to every 'human soul' of modern times through the ninefold choir of the divine-spiritual Hierarchies; and they reveal in the mysteries of the ego, which have their source in the events of the Turning-point of Time, the past, present and future of man-anthropos, the future Tenth Hierarchy.

The ensuing period was devoted to daily work with the *Meditation*, though now in both languages. In the course of the next holidays I was able to undertake a journey to south-west Siberia with one of my new anthroposophical friends. There during our wanderings in the mountains I continued working with the original text of the *Meditation* (my companion read a little German), and by the time we returned home I knew the German text by heart.

Thus through the guidance of destiny it came about that the first work in German that really entered my life was the *Foundation Stone Meditation*. From this time the German language became the principal language of my spiritual life. Now I no longer had any doubts: I had to learn—and as soon as possible—*this language*, the language of the new Christian revelation, the language of Rudolf Steiner, the great Christian initiate, the modern ambassador of Michael-Christ.

If after ten years I were to give expression to what lived in my soul at that time, I would do this with the help of an image which is for me no mere comparison but a deeply experienced reality. I felt at the time with my whole soul that there was only one work written in a human tongue which could in a spiritual sense be placed alongside the *Foundation Stone Meditation*: the Gospel of St John or, to be more precise, its prologue and the farewell discourses of Christ-Jesus. In other words, it was clear to me from the start that both originated from the same divine source, from the same universal sphere of the Cosmic Logos, from the direct revelation of the living Christ. And I would today clothe this knowledge, which lived unspoken within me at that time, in the following image. As we turn inwardly to the central event of the Turning-point of Time, to the Mystery of Golgotha, we see at the foot of the Cross 'the Lord's beloved disciple', the only *conscious witness* of this greatest of events in the whole of earthly history. While if in our time of the new supersensible appearance of Christ in the etheric body, which was—according to the testimony of spiritual science—preceded by a repetition of the Mystery of Golgotha in the higher worlds (see the lecture of 2 May 1913, GA 152⋆), we seek the person who similarly stands as a conscious witness and proclaimer on Earth

⋆ The crucial part of this lecture does not appear in the English edition (Translator's note).

of this principal spiritual event of modern times, of the supersensible Mystery of Golgotha and the new appearance of Christ, we find such a person in *Rudolf Steiner.*

Thus these two great teachers of esoteric Christianity stand like two guardians at the gates of the two most important events in the evolution of mankind. And they stand beside one another in the spiritual worlds today as the leading spirit-guardians of modern Christian-Rosicrucian esotericism.

Before I move on to describing *how* I found my way to the theme of the Christmas Conference, and through it to the writing of my book, I should mention that the first lecture-cycle that I read in German was *Christ and the Spiritual World. The Search for the Holy Grail* (GA 149), which was at the time not yet translated into Russian. This cycle, in addition to considerably deepening my knowledge of the esoteric stream of the Grail, brought me something completely new, namely, a further revelation of the mysteries of the Nathan Soul, which are connected with the most important events in the spiritual evolution of mankind. I had already been prepared for this theme by reading the cycle of lectures devoted to the Gospel of St Luke (GA 114), but only now, after becoming acquainted with the description of the three pre-earthly stages of the Mystery of Golgotha in the lecture of 30 December 1913, did the picture become complete, and since then the theme of the Nathan Soul, especially in its relationship to the Second Coming of Christ in the etheric body, became one of the principal themes of my further spiritual quest.

My next reading in German, after the cycle to which I have referred, consisted of the six volumes of *Karmic Relationships,* and immediately after this volume GA 260 (*The Christmas Conference for the Foundation of the General Anthroposophical Society, 1923–1924*).

After my first spiritual encounter with the *Foundation Stone Meditation,* which thenceforth became the cornerstone of my inner life, I naturally wanted to know everything about its origin, about the history of its arising, about where and under what conditions it was first given to humanity. All this led me directly to the theme of the Christmas Conference. My path lay from working with the 'Karma lectures' to the book *The Christmas Conference.*

Thus my encounter with the *Foundation Stone Meditation* and the stirring of my interest in the theme of the Christmas Conference came about in a somewhat similar way to my initial acquaintance with Anthroposophy approximately seven years before.

To begin with, being left altogether to my own devices, taking as a starting-point only my inner experiences connected with the *Foundation*

Stone Meditation and without any outside influence, I had to find my own *personal* relationship to the Christmas Conference as the most important spiritual event that had taken place on the physical plane in the twentieth century. And only when this relationship had been established out of my own cognitive forces and, moreover, transformed into an unshakable inner certainty did my further investigations lead to three books about the Christmas Conference falling into my hands one after the other (this was at the end of 1978 and the beginning of 1979).⋆ These were Bernard Lievegoed's *Mystery Streams in Europe and the New Mysteries*, which had at the time just been translated from Dutch; Rudolf Grosse's *The Christmas Foundation; Beginning of a New Cosmic Age*; and somewhat later Zeylmans van Emmichoven's *The Foundation Stone*. These three books were not only a testimony that I was not alone in my spiritual quests and aspirations but they also became for me very important examples of independent work with this central theme.

In Bernard Lievegoed's book I was aware of a lofty flight of thought, encompassing in a single picture all the various Mystery streams of humanity and their culmination, their final uniting in the single channel of the New Mysteries at the Christmas Conference. With Grosse I was especially struck by the intimate and heartfelt quality of his insight into the more hidden aspects of the events of Christmas 1923. With Zeylmans van Emmichoven's book, which came more from the will sphere, what was important to me was the methodological way of working with the material, and the first indication of the necessity and possibility of working with the text, of the Foundation Stone Meditation and, in particular, with the rhythms of the Christmas Conference. The two latter books I read in German, and I myself translated the second of them into Russian (Rudolf Grosse's book was also soon translated).

Marie Steiner's Foreword to the first edition of the stenographical material relating to the Christmas Conference (GA 260) made a very strong impression on me in this respect. Here there appeared before me with full clarity the whole tragic aspect of the Christmas Conference, or, to be more precise, the deep polarity between its 'divine' and 'human' elements. Thus Marie Steiner wrote on the one hand of an 'atmosphere of the most lofty spirituality, which was an offering of gratitude and supplication to the higher powers', and, on the other, she gave very clear indications of the flimsiness and inadequacy of the earthly human forces: 'We have not

---

⋆ Shortly before this I had also become familiar with a lecture, translated from German, that was directed against the Christmas Conference. However, its content, which was based on purely speculative and external arguments, was unable to exert any particular influence on what had by then become a matter of *personal experience*.

proved equal to the call, as further developments have shown.'

The events of the last day of the Christmas Conference, Rudolf Steiner's sudden illness and its occult foundations (which had to do with his having taken upon himself the karma of the Anthroposophical Society), became more comprehensible to me from an altogether different standpoint soon after I had read this Foreword. For owing to a particular concurrence of circumstances, what I had read could become to a certain extent a personal experience, enabling me, *albeit only as a very dim intuition*, to have an awareness out of my own life of the deeply tragic reality that stood behind the words: 'The outcome [of the Christmas Conference] revealed what it meant for Dr Steiner to take our karma upon himself' and '. . . our human karma and that of the Society burst upon him . . .'

Shortly after my first acquaintance with the materials of the Christmas Conference another book fell into my hands, where the history of all the difficulties and conflicts within the Anthroposophical Society after Rudolf Steiner's departure from the physical plane, together with the tragedy of its culmination in 1935, is analysed step by step in all its details. This book made such an impression on me that for several days I was *physically ill*. This difficult experience, as I have said, enabled me in a very small way to gain a real idea of what it meant at the time, in 1923, for Rudolf Steiner to take upon himself the karma of the Society. Thus as a result of my own experience I learnt what it really means to become a pupil of Rudolf Steiner also in this sphere. In any case, having once experienced this even to a physical degree, I also understood the impossibility of arriving at simple solutions to such questions through an outward search for the 'guilty' and 'innocent' parties in these events of the past. The true reality of what happened lay much deeper, and it has to be *endured* if one is to be freed from the urge to resolve the problems associated with it through abstractly intellectual means alone.

This tormenting experience did, however, have another side to it. For immediately afterwards I had the feeling that the spiritual form of the teacher had become even closer than before and that only after this experience was I fully able to consider myself his esoteric pupil.

One thing was in any case completely clear after reading Marie Steiner's foreword. Out of this pain, an echo of which I now also bore in my soul, a power of corresponding magnitude must be born to fight for the fulfilment of the impulse of the Christmas Conference, the most significant spiritual impulse of our time. 'This pain must lead us to *take hold of our tasks* with a will that is all the stronger'—these words of Marie Steiner became for me a kind of leitmotif of my life, a call to exert all my strength to 'take hold of our tasks', which were none other than the tasks placed by Rudolf Steiner before the members of the General Anthroposophical Society at the

Christmas Conference. At the time I understood these words as a summons to work further towards the fulfilment of the goals and tasks of the Christmas Conference. That is how I understand them today.

There was another passage in Marie Steiner's Foreword that was of very great importance to me. She wrote: 'Now it is our task to let the Christmas Conference speak for itself through the talks and lectures given by Rudolf Steiner and preserved for us in shorthand reports.' How grateful I was then (and still am now) to Marie Steiner for this indication that we should direct our inner eye not only to the human weaknesses and inadequacies of these, and subsequent, years but above all to its spiritual essence, to what lived in it as its undying core, as the 'mystic fact' that we can understand only in the sense of the words of Christ which Rudolf Steiner so often quoted: 'My kingdom is not of this world, my followers would have fought on my behalf...; but my kingdom is not from the world' (John 18: 36).*

Such an experience of the Christmas Conference, which originates in its spiritual or, one could also say, esoteric essence, cannot be conveyed outwardly, whether in words or on paper, to those people who have not had such an experience, still less to those who through a variety of *human opinions* have erected insurmountable obstacles for themselves towards what Marie Steiner really wanted to say to the members of the Anthroposophical Society when she decided shortly before her death to publish all the materials relating to the Christmas Conference. It was not a case of letting the various opinions of individuals have their say but rather of allowing the Christmas Conference itself to speak forth, and that means enabling it to speak not merely through shorthand reports and the minutes of meetings but as 'the voice from the Spirit-land' (GA 260, 1 January 1924) which is directed towards every anthroposophist, and then apprehending this voice in an altogether unprejudiced and deeply reverential way, truly standing at this moment solely before the spiritual world and the spiritual powers guiding the anthroposophical movement.

I would now like to cite some observations of Rudolf Steiner about the Christmas Conference as an indication of that region where alone *the spiritual reality of the Christmas Conference can be experienced*. These observations must be intensely *meditated upon* if they are to become a path towards the *experience* of the higher reality that stands behind them. The first two observations were made by Rudolf Steiner after the Christmas conference: 'Thus as far as Anthroposophy is concerned, the Christmas Conference is either everything or nothing' (lecture of 6 February 1924, GA 240). And from the fact that, according to the oft-repeated testimony of Rudolf

---

* See Rudolf Steiner's elucidation of these words at the end of the lecture of 19 November 1922 (GA 218).

Steiner, the stream of supersensible revelations and the participation of spiritual powers in the unfolding of the anthroposophical movement *since* the Christmas Conference have become considerably stronger, we can conclude with absolute certainty that *for Rudolf Steiner himself,* in the sense of his words quoted above, *the Christmas Conference was everything!* A further observation: '... If you think back to this Christmas Conference, you will have to acknowledge that something was present there which issued from the spiritual world itself... and that for such an event as our Christmas Conference one should not dwell upon what is going on within the earthly realm' (18 January 1924, GA 260a). And now from words spoken at the Christmas Conference itself. Regarding the initial sounding of the Foundation Stone Meditation on 25 December 1923: '... I should like once more to repeat before you at least a part of those words which were spoken to you yesterday *in accordance with the will of the spiritual world*... We can enter into a right relationship with words such as these, *which are heard coming from the Cosmic Word,* if we so make them a part of our own souls that they cannot depart from us again' (GA 260, 26 December 1923). And on the last day of the Christmas Conference, 1 January 1924: 'For this purpose we have immersed ourselves in those words with which I began, in those words with which I wish to close this Christmas Conference, this Christmas Conference which *is to be for us a festival of consecration* not merely of the beginning of a new year but *for the beginning of a cosmic Turning-point of Time* to which we want to devote ourselves in dedicated cultivation of the life of the spirit.' The 'beginning of a cosmic Turning-point of Time'—if we would but truly ponder what Rudolf Steiner had in mind when he said these words, whole worlds would unfold before our inner eye.

These and many other observations of Rudolf Steiner are a clear testimony that the Christmas Conference took place *in two worlds,* which is to say that a real judgement of it—that is, one that corresponds to its true nature—cannot be made if it is judged from the standpoint of the earthly world *alone,* however tragic the events that have taken place there since that time have been.

Thus when people said of my book that it is too idealistic and reflects everything in too 'cloudless' a way (even though I take the view that I have given a sufficient indication of the tragedy associated with the events of the last years of Rudolf Steiner's earthly life), I can only answer: yes, but surely true idealism is none other than 'the way to the Christ through the will' that is appropriate for our time (see the lecture of 11 February 1919, GA 193).

Now a few words about the composition of the book, *Rudolf Steiner and the Founding of the New Mysteries.* After an intensely experienced Michaelmas time in 1979, the thoughts that lie at the foundation of the fifth and sixth chapters of my book germinated in the period between Michaelmas and Christmas. Thus as I worked with the rhythms of the Christmas Conference in association with my experience of their origin in the spiritual world itself, I became aware that their inner structure is an expression of the sevenfold path of Christian-Rosicrucian initiation and also incorporates the seven principal stages of the life of the human soul after death in the spiritual world. On the other hand, I found in the *Foundation Stone Meditation* a union of *all* the principal occult streams out of the amalgamation of which through the earthly activity of Rudolf Steiner Anthroposophy could arise in the world of today: the Rosicrucian stream; the Grail stream, which has from the outset been connected with the Mysteries of the Nathan Soul; the spiritual stream that originates from the sphere of the Bodhisattvas; the supersensible stream of Michael; and, finally, as the culmination of them all, the modern revelation of the Etheric Christ—all of these various spiritual streams and impulses were for me united in the single whole of the spiritual substance of the *Foundation Stone Meditation*.

By Christmas these themes had acquired so clear a conceptual form in my soul that in the period of the twelve Holy Nights of 1979/1980 I was able to decide to present the results of my work in four lectures.

When at the beginning of the following year a friend turned to me with the suggestion to present their content in written form, I became aware after an initial attempt of the complete impossibility of achieving this to any degree of satisfaction without bringing these two themes (the theme of the Christmas Conference and the theme of the *Foundation Stone Meditation*) into a relationship with the path of Rudolf Steiner's life, and without indicating the place that the Christmas Conference has within it.

Thus the chapters on the Christmas Conference and the *Foundation Stone Meditation* had to be preceded by a description of Rudolf Steiner's life path, viewed *from the standpoint of the Christmas Conference*, that is, from a position lying in a certain sense beyond the threshold. Looked at in such a way this life's path, illuminated in a certain sense by the spiritual light of the Christmas Conference, stood before me as the profoundest Christian Mystery of the twentieth century.

A further theme which, as was clarified in the course of the book, also had to precede the two central chapters was that of the First Goetheanum and the Mystery-deed of its founding on 20 September 1913. For the description of the higher spiritual metamorphosis through which its imaginative forms passed, forms that were sacrificed to the flames on New Year's Eve 1922 in order that they might rise anew out of the cosmic sphere of Michael in the inspired form of the words of the *Foundation Stone Meditation*, had by virtue of an inner necessity to be preceded by the chapters devoted to the laying of the Foundation Stone of the General Anthroposophical Society.

Finally, it proved to be necessary to add to the six chapters that had been written a concluding seventh chapter, which brought together the spiritual tasks of the beginning and end of our century and pointed towards the significance of the impulse of the Christmas Conference for the future.

As was already indicated at the beginning of this essay, the writing of the book itself, which took some three years, was connected for me with certain inner experiences. I should like to allude to just two of these, inasmuch as they have in a certain sense found expression in the book. One of these experiences can briefly be expressed as follows: never have I felt the spiritual presence, the soul support and the inner closeness of Rudolf Steiner, as occult teacher and older friend, so intensely and with so strong a degree of reality as at the time when I was thinking about and working with the themes directly or indirectly related to the Christmas Conference.

A second experience, which relates to the content of the final chapter, should also be mentioned here. For the moment when—in the course of my writing of the book—the essential nature of the 'dodecahedral Stone of Love', as an Imagination of the Michael Grail of our time, was revealed *as a real spiritual experience* was one of the most sublime moments of my life. In the seventh chapter I tried not only to describe this Imagination but also to indicate the path whereby every anthroposophist may be helped to come to a similar experience.

In one of his lectures Rudolf Steiner referred to the Grail 'as the holiest thing in the whole of human evolution'. Anyone who has experienced it in the imaginative form of the Foundation Stone will for ever lose all intellectual doubts as to the esoteric significance of the Christmas Conference for our time, and he will be filled with the deepest reverence and gratitude, and with the longing to give all his forces to the sacrificial serving of this holy 'thing' in the world, to a readiness to be 'true' to it 'even unto death' (an expression of Novalis).

In conclusion, mention should also be made of a further circumstance, without which the description of how the book *Rudolf Steiner and the Founding of the New Mysteries* came into being would not be complete. For as regards its content it should be made quite clear that it could not have arisen at all, or at any rate not in the form in which it did, if the author had not roughly a year before beginning work on it been able to become a member of the First Class of the School of Spiritual Science and if *daily* work with the mantrams had not become for him a real life's necessity. Thus wherever mention is made in the book of the esoteric content of the

Christmas Conference, this refers to the content of the First Class, inasmuch as for the author one is spiritually inseparable from the other, like the seeds and the fruit in a single living cycle.

When I wrote my book, there were probably only two or three people in my country for whom the theme of the Christmas Conference had some significance. This situation has subsequently changed considerably, but at the time, at the beginning of the eighties, my mind was inwardly directed while writing the book towards the anthroposophists of Central and Western Europe. For the theme, connected as it was with the spiritual-occult history of the founding of the *General* Anthroposophical Society, guided my inner eye towards the density of the anthroposophical movement *throughout* the world.

I felt connected with all the forces of my soul to this movement and its earthly destiny. The establishing on Earth of a modern Michael community, which is called in our time to become a new brotherhood of knights and guardians of the Holy Grail, is what I conceived to be the principal task of the General Anthroposophical Society on the esoteric plane. This conception of its inner task lives within me to this day, and my book *Rudolf Steiner and the Founding of the New Mysteries* was offered as the contribution of one human being, who was born and grew up in Eastern Europe, to the general task of bringing this high aim to fulfilment.

As confirmed through my subsequent destiny, once I had become fully aware of my inner connection with anthroposophical work not only in Eastern but also in Central and Western Europe, I was then led, despite all the outward hindrances, first to Western Europe and then to Central Europe, which has now become the new field of my anthroposophical activity.

Sergei O. Prokofieff
Dornach, November 1986

THE MYSTERY OF THE PATH
OF RUDOLF STEINER'S LIFE

1. The Years of Apprenticeship

Who was Rudolf Steiner? This is a question that sooner or later, not out of curiosity but full of amazement and reverence, arises in anyone who knows his works in theoretical or practical areas. Extraordinarily stimulating and fruitful impulses spring from these works. If we look for sources to answer this question we find, in the first instance, memoirs of contemporaries who met him and whose lives were so completely transformed through this meeting that, upon looking back, it seemed to them that their life divided into the periods before and after this event. They communicate to us the destiny-shaping effect, always filled and suffused with warmth, that emanated from Rudolf Steiner.

Others, such as his biographers, emphasize the phenomenal extent of his work: 350 printed books—42 written books, and over 300 setting down the spoken word. Also, there are his epoch-making buildings, world-wide Waldorf education, anthroposophical medicine, biodynamic agriculture, curative education, eurythmy, speech-formation, the Mystery Dramas, and, not least, the idea of social renewal—the threefold life of the social organism.

The more we occupy ourselves with this question about his life and his work, the more do we become aware that the wisdom which he brought to our time comes from springs that only through him have begun to flow again. For he shows himself to be a fully-conscious inhabitant, not only of our sense world, but also of the supersensible world that lies at its foundation. In him we recognize an initiate. But do we not lose him in the very moment of that recognition if we do not ask more deeply and more penetratingly the question: *Who was Rudolf Steiner?*

From ancient history and fragmentary tradition we know of the great initiates of the past. The life of such an initiate is different from the course of other lives; every detail of his life is significant and is not subject to coincidence or chance. The wide and comprehensive experiences of many generations of spiritually-seeking human beings, the experiences of a whole cultural epoch, find in the initiate their highest synthesis and are thus lifted to a still higher level. His life becomes an example and archetype for future generations. The images of Zarathustra, Hermes and Moses shine towards us like wonderful stars out of the depths of the past, but we can trace their influence over many centuries—indeed, sometimes even over millennia. They are creators of cultures, founders of religions; they tread new paths. But since the beginning of the Christian era the impressive images and myths of their lives have been fading; they move into the shadows, their influence disappears and instead there emerges a type of new general and more external human culture. The knowledge of true initiates does indeed still penetrate through to us out of the early centuries of the Christian era: knowledge of Manes, Parsifal, or Lohengrin, and also of the saints. Their influence is still felt to a certain extent in the midst of humanity, but they are not always immediately real and tangible.

To be sure, we sense that the great initiates are still at work, unnoticed behind the scenes of outer history. We know of Christian Rosenkreutz and others, but they no longer come out of their concealment to walk among men. Nearer to the present, in the European mystics of the sixteenth to the eighteenth centuries, we find the last echoes of a true knowledge. The figures of Paracelsus, Jacob Boehme, Saint-Martin and Swedenborg come to mind. But they are no longer initiates in the strict sense. And in the nineteenth century? Direct perception of the spiritual world is more and more lost and the figure of the initiate is completely concealed behind a veil of secrecy and silence.

While direct access to a higher world seems almost completely closed off, at the turning-point of two centuries—the nineteenth and twentieth— like the first ray of a new light-epoch in the midst of a humanity sinking more and more into the darkness of lost spirituality, Rudolf Steiner appears as an investigator of the spirit. A hitherto unknown stream of the light of 'new revelations' pours into the world; the deepest secrets of Christian esotericism appear before us and fill every aspect of our lives with new meaning and content, and with this the great initiates of the past become visible again in their radiance of eternity and greatness. The pale figures of ancient tradition now appear as real guides of humanity, as older brothers who accompany Rudolf Steiner unshakably and constantly along his spiritual paths. Moreover, Rudolf Steiner shows himself to be the realizer of the occult Christian-Rosicrucian ideals; for out of inner freedom, with the force of his whole being and fired by the impulse of the Time Spirit Michael who is just entering his time of rulership, he opens to humanity a new path of initiation appropriate to the present time. This path, which would unite humanity again with the lost world of the Gods, is introduced into every aspect of human culture, and thereby this path of initiation is open to every single individual when he endeavours to become aware of the ancient Mystery-words sounding forth to us once again from the spiritual worlds: 'Change your thinking, the Kingdom of Heaven has drawn nigh.'[1]

Who was Rudolf Steiner? Is not his life a mystery, as are the lives of all great initiates, which we can approach only with reverence? And does this life not become the archetype of the modern path of initiation, the path which every individual 'I', fully developed in the consciousness soul, should tread, in the same archetypal gesture? Friedrich Rittelmeyer, a contemporary and pupil of Rudolf Steiner, who understood him deeply, said: 'Without Rudolf Steiner having to speak about it, one got the impression of how such a life was prepared long, long beforehand, how at the right moment the necessary helpers were sent, how everything came together for an undertaking which, knowingly and full of wisdom, reaches into the history of humanity. The outer world has absolutely no inkling of this. The life of a guide of humanity who has a mission of the highest order is a work of art worked on by men and Angels together.'[2]

In considering Rudolf Steiner's life we want to make a cautious attempt to raise the veil slightly from the hidden depths of his life, and from the events of those days of Christmas 1923, when we see not only a culmination but, at the same time, a new beginning.

Starting from the fact that Rudolf Steiner himself trod the path of initiation appropriate to our time from the first to the last step, we want to look for the secret of his life first of all in the things he said, as we find them in his books and lectures. In this we will limit ourselves to those key moments and to relationships which throw light on the deeper foundations of his life and which, at the same time, can reveal the Christmas Conference in a new way as the true *Foundation Stone Mystery* of our time. Then the indissoluble connection between these two Mysteries—the biography and the Christmas Conference—will arise before us in which, from the beginning, both earthly and cosmic powers have worked.

In the first of his *Anthroposophical Leading Thoughts* Rudolf Steiner expresses the essential nature of the anthroposophical path of initiation in the following way: 'Anthroposophy is a path of knowledge that wishes to guide the spiritual in the human being to the spiritual in the universe.'[3]

In reality this means that the one who walks this path is, already here in the earthly sphere, supposed to learn to see more and more consciously through to the cosmic forces and laws which proceed from the divine-spiritual world and rule unconsciously within him. But at the same time the human being has to mould his own life into an expression of inter-relationship with the cosmos, right into the minutest details of his daily actions. Transforming and broadening himself in knowledge, he gradually approaches his origins and therefore also that lofty spiritual Being who, since the Mystery of Golgotha, has united with the Earth-sphere—the Christ. In a real meeting with the Christ, the entire preceding path of training, as it was practised in archetype by Rudolf Steiner, is completed. With this the pupil becomes a teacher. As personal witness and servant of Christ he can now step openly before the whole world, can himself guide souls to those portals whence the Holy Spirit sent by Christ flows for the good of the future of the Earth.

We also find elements of this new anthroposophical path of initiation in older Rosicrucian traditions. The medieval Rosicrucians already knew of the connection of specific levels of the spiritual path with certain ages of life. The first period of life, which they counted up to the age of 21, they called the years of apprenticeship; the second, from 21 to 42, the years of the journeyman; and the third, the period after 42, the time of the master.[4]

Rudolf Steiner has called the first period, from birth to 21 years, the period of life in which 'karmic challenges present themselves'.[5] The period from 21 to 42 is called by him the 'Sun-epoch'. During this time the ordinary human being experiences unconsciously—but the initiate in full consciousness—the 'inner mystery of his "I" '; in a very wide sense this is 'the essence of the Sun-Mystery'. Naturally the first 'I'-experience occurs in the human being long before 21, but to experience the inner being of the 'I' and its cosmic relation to the Sun is only possible for the pupil of the spirit from this age onwards. The third period is a 'time of fulfilment', where the initiate can come before humanity as a teacher, for he is now ripe for his spiritual mission and can begin with its realization. Rudolf Steiner himself said of the beginning of this third period of his own life: 'I had reached the age of 40, an age before which no one in the sense of a master may openly appear as a *teacher of occultism*.* Everywhere where someone teaches earlier than this there is an error.'[6]

Each of these three great periods divides into three smaller ones of seven years. In his lectures and books Rudolf Steiner often describes the cosmic laws which form the spiritual basis of human life and work in it as a seven-year rhythm. Three laws are particularly important for us: the development of the nine members of man's being in relation to the course of the cultural epochs of mankind since Atlantean times, and the influence exercised at any given time by a particular planet on this common development

These relationships are shown in the table on page 27.

After this, the cosmos encompassing our whole solar system works on the human being.

Every human being is subject to these laws of development, the initiate as well, but for him they signify more. For him the ages of life become 'differentiated organs of perception' in the spheres of Inspiration.[7] When he looks in Inspiration at his life between 14 and 21 years of age, first of all the true nature of the human astral body reveals itself to him from the aspect of its cosmic origin; secondly, the essence of the Ancient Persian

* Here and in the following pages all italics are those of the author.

26

Age	Members of Man's Being	Cultural Epochs	Planetary Sphere
1–7	Physical body	Atlantis	Moon
7–14	Etheric body	Ancient Indian	Mercury
14–21	Astral body	Ancient Persian	Venus*
21–28	Sentient soul	Babylonian-Chaldean-Egyptian	⎫
28–35	Intellectual/Mind soul	Graeco-Roman	⎬ Sun
35–42	Consciousness soul	Present epoch	⎭
42–49	Spirit Self	Germano-Slavic	Mars
49–56	Life Spirit	American	Jupiter
56–63	Spirit Man	—	Saturn

culture and its secrets as the culture that above all developed the human astral body; and thirdly, the secrets and beings of the Venus-sphere.

Rudolf Steiner stressed that 'in initiation today one is in a certain sense dependent on one's age'.[8] He described this in very concrete terms on 1 June 1924 in Stuttgart: 'But out of one's own perception one can only see the things [which are happening in the Saturn-sphere]† in relation to themselves when one has passed the age of 63. You will understand why it is only now that I begin to speak about certain things connected with the Saturn-existence.'[9]

With these words, Rudolf Steiner indicates to us the role played by the different periods of his own life in relation to the recognition of specific cosmic secrets. For this reason a close look at the personal development of Rudolf Steiner in connection with the seven-year cycles of his life will surely enable us to gain a deeper understanding of his individuality, his mission and his teaching.

The chief source in considering Rudolf Steiner's life is his autobiography, *The Course of my Life*, written between 1923 and 1925. Despite the very easily understood form of its presentation, the autobiography nevertheless contains many indications concerning the hidden forces of development which were working in Rudolf Steiner's life. For this reason, and with descriptions of certain experiences in mind, we have tried to note every word with the

* The planetary sequence Mercury/Venus is the *esoteric* order of these two planets. On many occasions Rudolf Steiner referred to the fact that the Venus of ordinary astronomy is Mercury in the terminology of occultism and the Mercury of astronomy is Venus according to occultism. See the lecture of 2.9.1910 (GA 123) for the esoteric background to this sequence. It is this sequence that is followed wherever these two planets are mentioned in the text of this book.
† The additions in brackets [] are the author's clarifications.

greatest awareness and pay particular attention to every indication of period or age. Reading in this sensitive way, that deep esoteric element which is the foundation of this life can be sensed in many of the lines.

The description of this period in *The Education of the Child in the Light of Anthroposophy* can be of substantial help for an understanding of the first seven years of Rudolf Steiner's life and of the ages of the human being in general. Rudolf Steiner says there that during the first seven years of life the physical body is built up in the child. During this period the outer impressions and influences mould, as it were from outside, the still very formative bodily organism of the child into an instrument of its will, which then realizes itself in all the periods of later life: 'For such a will must have a support in the fully developed forms of the physical body.'[10]

We see then how all the outer impressions, the whole environment of the child at this age, work unconsciously on his bodily organism so that later on they can be a support and basis for the will-impulses which are founded during this period, but which come to consciousness and are realized only much later. Therefore everything that happens at this age can be regarded as symptomatic of, and founding a basis for, the subsequently developing will-impulses of the human being.

Rudolf Steiner was born on 27 February 1861 in Kraljevec (now in Croatia), a small village in that area lying between Central and Eastern Europe. His parents, however, both came from Lower Austria. 'And so it came about that my place of birth lies far away from that part of the Earth from which my family originates.'[11] In this way Rudolf Steiner speaks about the discrepancy between the influences of his heredity and his place of birth. By heredity he comes from a Central European stream which is the bearer of the fifth post-Atlantean epoch and particularly of the 'I'-impulses. Yet he was born on the border of Eastern Europe where, in the future sixth post-Atlantean epoch, the culture of the Spirit Self, of the higher 'I' of man, is to develop. Thus the physical birth constellation of Rudolf Steiner already suggests his mission of preparing the way from the earthly 'I' of man to his true, higher 'I'. And we may truly think of this fundamental birth constellation as the deepest image of Rudolf Steiner's impulse—as the image that was even imprinted into his bodily organism.

Later, in a lecture to a Russian audience, he spoke of the spiritual significance of his birthplace in the following words: 'This is a metaphorical statement, my dear theosophical friends, but speaking metaphorically, I needed only to let myself be led by what was there as a direct impulse in this present incarnation. Do not misunderstand this. There is another fact. Those who were the outer bearers, for example, of that blood from which I come originally came from the German regions of Austria; *I could not have been born there.* I myself was born in a Slavic region, in an area completely foreign to the whole milieu and character of the place where my ancestors came from. And so—I would like to put this as it were symbolically—at the point of departure of my present incarnation it came strongly and symbolically to me that we in Central Europe have the task of freeing ourselves from the special interests of theosophy.'[12]

In 1863 Rudolf Steiner's parents moved to the little railway station at Pottschach in Lower Austria. In this place at the foot of the Alps with its wonderful surroundings he spends the greater part of the first seven years of his life. The strongest impressions during this time are made on the one hand by the beauty and grandeur of surrounding nature, and on the other hand by the small world of the railway station where his father worked.

So from earliest childhood onwards the antithesis of nature and technology, in the deepest sense of spirit and matter as two so far irreconciled spheres, appears strongly in Rudolf Steiner's life. It imprints itself in the consciousness of the child, but still more in his subconsciousness where, again preparing his further path, it evokes the striving to reconcile these opposites in a higher synthesis.

Following Rudolf Steiner's indications, one can also see in this antithesis of nature and technology the twofold effect of the Moon-forces: on the one hand through the nature-spirits who mostly arose during the Ancient Moon evolution[13] and have the task of bringing those impulses of cosmic wisdom to the Earth that were won on Old Moon, and which are expressed most of all in the beauty of nature penetrated through and through with wisdom; on the other hand these elemental beings have nature-demons as their adversaries, who work above all in the technical inventions developed by man. Rudolf Steiner indicates this, for example, in the lectures on *The Fifth Gospel*, where he describes how, when there is an eclipse of the Sun, the Moon-demons emerge from man's technical inventions.[14] Thus we see that the strongest impressions Rudolf Steiner receives during this period are directly concerned with the hidden Moon-forces working in his surroundings.

An important event in this period of his life should be mentioned, which can be looked upon as a prophetic foreshadowing of his future mission. He first experienced a limit to knowledge—and at the same time the wish to overcome such limits—in connection with the spinning-mill into which he often saw the railway wagons disappear, but into which he, as a child, was not allowed to go.

If one compared Rudolf Steiner's description in his autobiography of the first 14 years of his life with what he later presents in *The Education of the Child*, one can find an astonishing inner accord even in the smaller details. In this book he speaks of how the child is to be educated in accordance with the cosmic laws and forces working objectively in him during this time. In adult life Rudolf Steiner could himself see these forces clairvoyantly which, thanks to the karmically predestined course of the events of his childhood and youth, worked on him completely unhindered. Thus if we read his autobiography, up to the age of 14 we can find in the events described there the seeds of almost all the principles that later arise in anthroposophical education.

The second period in Rudolf Steiner's life begins in 1868 when his parents move to Neudörfl in Burgenland. In this year Rudolf Steiner reaches the age of seven—a decisive point in the development of every child, for now the etheric body is born. After the physical body, the etheric body is the first supersensible member of man's being which, having gradually released itself up to this time from its etheric sheath, now begins to follow an independent life of its own.

For Rudolf Steiner this inner process, the 'birth' of the first supersensible member of his being, is at the same time the beginning of supersensible experience. Soon after the move from Pottschach he has an experience in the station waiting-room, where a relative appears to him who at that moment, far away in another place, had just died. He speaks about this in a lecture in Berlin on 4 February 1913,[15] and relates how this was his first clairvoyant experience. What is characteristic about this is that here Rudolf Steiner had an etheric experience—for in the moment of death and during the first few days following it, the soul of the one who has died is still enveloped in his etheric body, in the spiritual world.

From this moment onwards the whole world of the elemental spirits of nature is also revealed to Rudolf Steiner. Later in the same lecture he says of his life then: 'From that time onwards the boy lived with the spirits of nature—which can be observed quite especially in such an area—with the creative beings behind things, in the same way that he experienced the outer world.'[16] He also speaks of the consequences of these first supersensible experiences in his autobiography where he clearly establishes a connection with the beginning of the second seven-year period: 'I have two ideas which although undefined nevertheless play a major role in my soul life before my eighth year. I distinguished between things and beings you "see" and those you "don't see".'[17]

During the years following the move to Neudörfl, the intensity of his experience of life in the spiritual world increases so that he can soon say of himself: 'But I also have to say this: I liked living in this world, for I would have had to feel the sense world like a spiritual darkness around me if it had not received light from this side.' One can also perceive in these words the changes in his clairvoyance during the following years. They brought a far more intimate and personal experiencing of nature in Neudörfl than there had been in Pottschach. If one compares the descriptions of the two landscapes in the autobiography, one can feel the difference vividly. The character of this intense, spiritually conscious living with nature around Neudörfl was later poured into a poetic form by Rudolf Steiner in the fairy-tale narrated by Felicia Balde in the Mystery Drama *The Soul's Probation* (5th Scene).

In *The Education of the Child*, Rudolf Steiner emphasizes that living with nature as well as with art and religion is of particularly great significance for the development of the child in the second seven-year period. Everything that is omitted in this respect during this time cannot be made up for later but comes to light as this or that irregularity in the development of the etheric body which, in consequence, leads to deficiencies in character or defects in the realm of the emotions, or in general health for the whole of later life. Bearing this in mind, it is particularly impressive how just at this time Rudolf Steiner received the first impulses not only for art but also for religion. For in contrast to his family's way of life, he becomes an acolyte at the Neudörfl church where he experiences the supersensible element of the Catholic Mass exceptionally strongly. On the other hand, through the geometry teacher at his school, he receives his first impulse towards art: 'I owe him a great deal besides. He brought me the artistic element. He played the violin and piano, and he drew a lot. Both attracted me strongly to him . . . He particularly loved drawing, and already at the age of nine he got me to draw with charcoal pencils.'

A little later Rudolf Steiner is introduced by the doctor from Wiener-Neustadt to the great representatives of German literature—Goethe, Schiller and Lessing—and by the clergyman of Neudörfl to the Copernican world-system which, as is known from Rudolf Steiner's lectures, presents the physical-etheric picture of the universe in contrast to the Ptolemaic system which is its astral picture.[18]

We can see that new social relationships are connected with the development of the growing boy at this time when we read how Rudolf Steiner met the villagers of the area while collecting wood, and of how in their conversations they told him of their life experiences, and while doing so often 'did not heed that they had a child in front of them'.[19]

As well as these meetings with people, Rudolf Steiner had a meeting of a quite different kind at this time—he encountered geometry. The child who up to this time was completely alone with his perceptions of the spiritual world and who suffered under the impossibility of finding an objective inner basis for them, now won through by means of geometry to an inner proof of the laws that hold sway in supersensible experiences just as they do in those of the sense-world. 'The reality of the spiritual world was as certain for me as that of the sense-world. But I somehow needed a sort of vindication for this acceptance. I wanted to be able to tell myself that the experience of the spiritual world is as little an illusion as that of the sense-world. In geometry I said to myself, here one may know what the soul alone experiences through its own strength; *in this feeling I found the vindication for speaking in the same way of the spiritual world that I experienced as of the sense-world.*'

Here one should add that geometrical forms harmonize particularly well with certain currents in the etheric body, whose forces are readily enlivened by an inner contemplation of these forms. This is why Rudolf Steiner says: 'The fact that in the soul one can live in the shaping of purely inwardly contemplated forms without impression of the outer senses gave me the greatest satisfaction.' The geometry of the etheric body, which one can contemplate 'without impressions of the outer senses' and which has its correspondence in sense-perceptible geometry, brought him real joy: 'I know that it was in geometry that I first knew happiness.'

But already in the next period of his life concrete tasks were arising out of this experience of geometry, and it is here that an important peculiarity of his future mission has its beginning. 'In my relationship to geometry I have to see the first germination of a particular perception of the world which gradually developed in me. It already lived in me more or less unconsciously during my childhood and took on a definite, fully conscious form around the age of 20.' He says of this perception: 'I had the feeling that one should carry in oneself the knowledge of the spiritual world just as one does that of geometry.'

Around the middle of this period there is another important event: in 1872, instead of going to the *Gymnasium* (Grammar School), he went to the *Realschule* (Secondary Modern School) in Wiener-Neustadt. Seen outwardly this decision came about because his father wished him to become a railway engineer. But seen from within there was a deep karmic meaning in this circumstance, which Rudolf Steiner first pointed to half a century later in the lecture on 19 July 1924 in Arnhem. In this lecture he says that if he had gone to the Wiener-Neustadt *Gymnasium*, which was run by Cistercian monks, he would certainly have become a priest in that Order. Seen in this way this event also had a determining significance for Rudolf Steiner's future path, a path completely in the spirit of the coming new Age of Michael which had to find, not from without but from within, its own deeply inner relationship to Christianity out of full inner freedom and bound to no historical tradition—or in other words, a path which had to wrestle through to the Christ-impulse directly in that sphere where it exists as undeniable spiritual reality.

Important things happen also during the years at the *Realschule*. One we can mention is Rudolf Steiner's first independent attempt to get into the skin of the materialistic dragon in order to get to know it from within, to fulfil out of inner feeling that which seven years later his Teacher indicates to him as being the most important task in his whole spiritual mission. This occurred when he read a treatise by the *Realschule* director, *Gravity regarded as an effect of movement*, and later his book on the same subject. This treatise, arising as it did out of the purely materialistic impulses of the age, and which Rudolf Steiner could not fully understand at that time because it contained higher mathematics, evoked in him a deep longing to understand it: 'I had nothing in me which in any way might induce me to profess this outlook; but I had the feeling that it would be of great significance for me if I could understand the things said here in this way.' Thus the wish awoke right at the beginning of the path of his life to get to know the forces of the age that wish to snatch into their own grasp dominion over mankind in the future.

Another important experience at this time was the meeting with the projective geometry teacher of which Rudolf Steiner later speaks in more detail in the Karma lectures.[20] Here we see how his relationship to geometry comes to life again, this time not on an etheric-pictorial level but more on a thought-filled, conscious level which, as he was acquainting himself at that time with the fundamental principles of mathematics and physics, awoke the most intense wish in him 'to get to grips with nature in order to win through to an orientation towards the spiritual world that stood so self-evidently before my gaze'.[21] And here the transition to the third period is indicated, at the beginning of which we can place the words: 'I told myself that one would only be able rightly to manage the experience of the spiritual world through the soul if one's thinking could be brought to such a configuration as to be able to reach the essence of the phenomena of nature.'

And it is during this time that Rudolf Steiner also began to come to grips successfully with his school subjects. 'Only in the second half of the second class did things go better. Only then did I become a good pupil.' This happened when he was 14, when he slowly began to master German spelling. In the Karma lectures he later relates how extraordinarily significant it had been for his occult development that he had learned to spell so late.[22]

In this second period, coming as it does under the sign of Mercury whose forces particularly configure the etheric body and thereby the later physical *health* of the individual, the foundation may perhaps have been laid for his good physical health through the daily walk from Wiener-Neustadt to Neudörfl during the whole of his *Realschule* time (1872–79). Later he says about these walks, which in winter he had had to make through fields of deep snow almost without a path: 'I think I must say that it is my belief

33

that the particular degree of health which I now have can perhaps be traced to the other exertions which are connected with my going to the *Real-schule*.'[23] Three of the seven years spent at the *Realschule* come under the direct influence of the Mercury forces.

The third period now begins in Rudolf Steiner's life. As described in *The Education of the Child*, it is in this period that the young individual begins with the definitive shaping and making independent of his own thought-life. The inclination to develop the forces of thinking is one of the most decisive characteristics of this phase, for the Venus forces dominate during this period and the astral body, the bearer of the thought-forces in man, is developed. For Rudolf Steiner this period of his life begins with his particularly intensive efforts to come to an understanding of Kant, whose main work, *The Critique of Pure Reason*, comes into his hands when he is 14. Through Kant, fundamental questions confront him related to the nature of thinking, to its role in human development, its capabilities, but also to the problems of overcoming limits to knowledge, where Kant's philosophy stopped and with it the whole of Western European culture: 'During the holidays my readings of Kant were eagerly continued. Indeed, I read many pages more than 20 times at one sitting. I wanted to come to a judgement about how human thinking stands in relation to the creative work of nature.'[24] This thinking is already indicated in these words which Rudolf Steiner later brought to his book *The Philosophy of Freedom (The Philosophy of Spiritual Activity)*, to the experience of the reality of the world that arises out of the union of idea and percept.

'On the other hand I was constantly occupied with the breadth of the human capacity for thinking. I felt that thinking could be developed into a force which really encompassed the objects and processes of the world.' Here we find an expression of how during this time he begins to struggle towards a new thinking which he has to accomplish for all mankind. From now onwards the problem of thinking in all its aspects assumes a central position in all his spiritual investigation: how can one so transform and strengthen thinking that it can become a suitable means for penetrating into the supersensible worlds, and at the same time be a basis that lends supersensible knowledge the same authenticity inherent in mathematical truth? And yet this struggle concerning the nature of thinking leads him inexorably to a way of looking at things where thinking itself begins to point towards its higher source, towards the question of the human 'I' which alone can begin to throw light on the secrets and possibilities of thinking. In this way a significant turning-point is prepared in Rudolf Steiner's development: the transition from the problem of thinking to that of the 'I'—from Kant to Fichte. But precisely at the age of 14 he also begins his 'more than 15 years' experience as a teacher and private tutor'. This gave him the opportunity of coming into direct contact with the developmental processes of the soul forces in the human being which are principally connected with the astral body: '. . . I was obliged at an early age to give my attention to a practical knowledge of the soul. I became acquainted with the difficulties of human emotional development through my pupils.'

Thus Rudolf Steiner gradually approached the year 1879, the beginning of the new Michael Age, an age where from now onwards a new stream of supersensible revelation is to come to humanity from the heights of the Sun-sphere in order to give the impulse for spiritual renewal. Now that Michael, the mighty Archangel of the Sun, had conquered the adversary forces in the spiritual world, mankind too must gradually accomplish the same for the Earth-sphere in accordance with the archetypal picture of the victory of Michael over the Dragon. In order to achieve this victory, the human being today must above all drive the influences of the adversary forces out of his thinking, out of his intellect, which is so deeply submerged in materialism, and attain union with the sphere of Michael through the spiritualization of thinking, so that on the basis of this reuniting with the spirit a truly spiritual culture can be founded. Therefore it will not astound us that this year that is so important for the whole development of mankind on the Earth was also of great significance in the inner development of Rudolf Steiner.

In 1879 his parents moved to Inzersdorf near Vienna. In the summer of this year, with the beginning of his studies in Vienna, he gets to know the works of Fichte and he is confronted with the question: what is the 'I'? This is the fundamental problem of Western philosophical thought, and the search for an answer will prescribe the direction of his further activity.

Rudolf Steiner's mission can be seen as that of founding spiritual science as a science of the higher 'I' or Ego in the human being, and of showing the path towards this. The most important achievement towards the realizing of spiritual science during that time was the new perception of the essence of the 'I': 'My endeavours to formulate natural-scientific concepts finally brought me to see in the activity of the human 'I' *the only possible point of departure for true knowledge.*' But this perception of the central significance of the 'I' in the process of knowledge confronted Rudolf Steiner with yet another task, to find again the path from 'I' to world, to nature, which he formulated at that time as follows: 'Before, I had struggled with trying to find concepts for the phenomena of nature, out of which one might find a concept for the "I". Now, from the other side, I wanted to break through from the "I" into the creative process of *becoming* in nature. Spirit and nature stood out at that time in my mind in their complete antithesis. For me, a world of spiritual beings existed. It was a direct perception that the

"I", which is itself spirit, lives in a world of spirits. Nature, however, did not want to enter into the spirit-world which I experienced.' With these words Rudolf Steiner points clearly to another important side of his future mission on Earth: to unite nature and spirit through the 'I'-impulse and thereby pave the way towards the spiritualizing of human culture. This goal demanded almost superhuman effort, and he was to attain it only at the age of 40, when the time had also arrived for him to come before the world as a Teacher.

It is no coincidence that Rudolf Steiner takes up these two fundamental tasks of his mission for the future in connection with the 'I'-impulse for the first time precisely in 1879, the year which is to see the beginning of the new Michael Age; for the spiritual events which take place at this time behind the physical appearances are so significant that they must also find reflection in the Earth-sphere, in the sphere of humanity. It is also a deeply significant event for the Archangel Michael, as we know from Rudolf Steiner that he once again takes upon himself the guidance of mankind. This is a turning-point in his own evolution, which from now on unites him in a special way with the development of the Earth. Rudolf Steiner describes this spiritual process in a lecture on 17 February 1918 in Munich, in these words: 'Shortly before the middle of the nineteenth century, around the beginning of the forties in the nineteenth century, the Archangel Michael gradually rose from the rank of an Archangel to that of a Time Spirit, and attained a development that enabled him to work into human life not only from the standpoint of the superphysical but directly from the standpoint of the physical-earthly.'[25]

From various different descriptions given by Rudolf Steiner of the three lower Hierarchies, we know that the Angels have developed Spirit Self and have a special relation to the human astral body, as have the Archangels to the etheric body, and the Archai—the Time Spirits—to the physical body, because they have already ascended to the stage of Spirit Man. Michael too must raise himself up to the rank of a Time Spirit in order to work on the whole human being—even into the physical body—or, as Rudolf Steiner says, in order to be able to descend into the Earth-sphere.

But there is also something else connected with this descent of Michael into the Earth-sphere. Rudolf Steiner describes in a lecture of 2 June 1907 how the nature of the Beings of the Hierarchy of the Archai consists of seven parts or members, the lowest of which corresponds to the fourth member of man's being, to the principle of the 'I'.[26] This is connected with the fact that the Archai—who in spiritual-scientific terms can also be called the Spirits of *Personality*—are the first 'I'-beings in our cosmos, who went through their 'human' stage on Old Saturn, and who at that time laid down in the germ of the human physical body formed by the Hierarchy of the

36

Thrones the disposition towards the 'I'-development during the stage of Earth evolution. If we bear in mind that Michael in his capacity as Time Spirit—that is, as a Being whose lowest member is the principle of the 'I'—is entering the sphere of the Earth, namely into that sphere where since the ancient Lemurian age the 'I' of every individual human being is to be found,[27] we can say that this descent which occurred in 1879 also gives Michael in his capacity as Time Spirit the possibility of reaching the human 'I' in its own realm. All questions arising in the human being concerning the secret of the 'I' have been inspired since 1879 by Michael from the sphere immediately bordering upon the Earth. Thus we can say: Rudolf Steiner's experiences in 1879 described above, in connection with the problem of the 'I', and indissolubly bound up with his further mission on Earth, are the result of Inspiration received by him at that time directly from Michael himself.

But this year which is so significant for humanity and which comes about the middle of the third seven-year period in Rudolf Steiner's life—in that period, that is, where the human being predominantly develops and becomes aware of the forces of the astral body—this year not only brings him a central experience of the problem of the 'I' but also extraordinarily significant occult experiences. He says about this simply: 'From now on [in the summer of 1879] I worked more and more consciously to pour the direct *perception* I had of the spiritual world into the form of *thoughts*.'[28] One can already sense in these words the peculiar characteristic of the new clairvoyance of the Michael Age. Rudolf Steiner speaks about the object of his spiritual vision at that time in the *Notes of Barr*: 'At this time [the period of acquaintanceship with Fichte]—and already this belongs to the external occult influences—comes complete clarity concerning the concept of time. This knowledge was in no way connected with my studies, but was directed entirely out of my occult life. It was the realization that alongside forward-moving evolution there also exists an interfering and backward-moving one—the occult-*astral* evolution. This realization is the precondition for spiritual vision.'[29] After he had made such a decisive step on his spiritual path he had fully developed the ability to follow those who had died beyond the gate of death: 'I perceived ... the spiritual world as a reality. The spiritual individuality of every human being revealed itself to me in all its vividness ... I followed human beings who had died further on their way into the spiritual world.'[30]

After he had set himself these life-tasks *out of his own forces* and had attained that maturity in the conscious development of these forces necessary for their realization, the pupil was ready to meet the Master's messenger, for he writes: 'I did not meet the Master straight away, but someone sent by him.'[31]

And we must regard the meeting of the 18-year-old Rudolf Steiner with the herb-gatherer Felix Koguzki (1833–1909) as a particularly important event of 1879. For Rudolf Steiner he was the first person with whom he could speak openly about his inner experiences. At that time this was a significant help, for the spiritual loneliness which had already begun in early childhood had increased considerably during the third seven-year period of his life: 'And that is how it was everywhere for me concerning my perception of the spiritual world. People did not want to hear about it.'[32] With this simple man of the common people 'one could talk about the spiritual world as though with someone who had experience of it ... he opened himself to you as though he as a personality was only the organ of speech for a spiritual content which wished to speak out of hidden worlds. When one was with him one could have deep insights into the secrets of nature. He was fully initiated into the secrets of the properties and effects of all plants and their relation to the cosmos and to the nature of the human being. Acquaintance and converse with the spirits of nature was something completely natural for him, something mentioned without enthusiasm, and yet therefore arousing enthusiasm all the more.'[33]

Outwardly Rudolf Steiner's life was filled at this time on the one hand with his studies at the Institute of Technology where 'official study was geared towards mathematics, chemistry, physics, zoology, botany, mineralogy and geology';[34] on the other hand, in the first year at the Institute he became acquainted with Karl Julius Schröer, who lectured on history and German literature. This meeting had a deep karmic foundation.[35]

In the person of Schröer, Rudolf Steiner met one of the outstanding representatives of nineteenth-century German culture—someone to whom he owed an essential understanding of the realm of aesthetics. 'One was drawn to him with one's *whole being* ... It was as if one were in an idealist oasis in the middle of the dry materialistic desert of German education.'[36] At this time Schröer was completely absorbed in his studies of the works of Goethe. 'All his thoughts and life were devoted to Goethe. He was working on the edition and introduction of the second part of *Faust* and had already published the first part.'[37]

Rudolf Steiner later says the following concerning his intimate conversations with Schröer about Goethe: 'When I was sitting alone with Schröer, I really always had the feeling that a third person was present: Goethe's spirit.' The deep respect and love which Schröer nurtured towards Goethe passed over to Rudolf Steiner and deepened their friendship. He was later appointed on Schröer's recommendation to work on the editing of Goethe's natural-scientific writings and was able to refer to these in his own early writings on a theory of knowledge, when he was developing his spiritual-scientific methods.

Thus the meeting with Schröer was of great significance in both his inner and outer life. And yet despite this he could only go with him up to a certain point: 'Schröer was an Idealist . . . He experienced life in the existence of ideas. For me, the life of the spirit was *behind* the ideas.' There is a fundamental difference here between Schröer and Rudolf Steiner. Here the tragedy of the best minds of the second half of the nineteenth century becomes evident, for they could not yet find their way to the new Michael-spirituality which in 1879 had begun to take effect. Despite the lofty and beautiful world of ideas, they could not penetrate through to real, actual spirit and to its essence. Seen in this light the meeting with Schröer is like a sign set up along the path of Rudolf Steiner's life by the guiding powers of the world—a sign pointing to the meaning and significance of his own mission and signifying that, fundamentally, he would be able to rely only on his own forces.

Thanks to these outer and inner experiences, by the end of his third seven-year period and at the beginning of his Sun period (age 21–42) he was prepared for the meeting with the one whom he later called his 'Teacher'. With this meeting the time of Rudolf Steiner's apprenticeship is completed and before him, in accordance with Rosicrucian tradition, lies the stage of the journeyman.

This meeting already bears the mark of the new principle of initiation, the essence of which is that the student must always make the first step and only then does the answer follow from the spiritual world. This principle is expressed for all future times in the words of Christ, 'Knock, and it shall be opened unto you'. It is also comprised in Parsifal's initiation, when in the Grail Castle he must be the first to ask, out of compassion and love, the question as to the meaning of the things that take place there.

Concerning that significant meeting, which occurred shortly after his twentieth birthday, Rudolf Steiner says: 'In a certain sense my Felix was only the forerunner and herald of another personality who used a particular means in order to stimulate in the soul of the boy, who indeed stood in the spiritual world, the regular, systematic things which one has to know in that world. This personality used . . . in fact, the works of Fichte in order to introduce certain considerations in connection with them—considerations from which certain things arose, where the seeds could be sought for *Occult Science* which the man who grew from the boy later wrote. And a good deal of that from which *Occult Science* arose was discussed at that time in connection with passages from Fichte.'[38] As Schuré tells us, at that time the Teacher also showed Rudolf Steiner the two main opponents against which he would have to measure himself on the spiritual path: the bull of public opinion, and the dragon of materialistic natural science.[39] It is easy to recognize the two spiritual adversaries, Lucifer[40] and Ahriman, in these

39

images. Even from early childhood Rudolf Steiner had felt it to be his mission to 'crawl into the skin of the dragon' in order to conquer it. Now what he had borne within for so many years was raised into the full light of consciousness and strengthened by the Teacher.

Through the meeting with his Teacher, everything that Rudolf Steiner had experienced spiritually up to that point was brought into an ordered system and raised to a new level. From now on the inner experiences take on the rigour and objectivity inherent in the sciences of geometry and mathematics: 'A spiritual vision came before my soul which was not based on a dark, mystical feeling. It took its course rather in a spiritual activity whose transparency was fully comparable with mathematical thinking. I was approaching a frame of mind where I could believe that I might consider the perception of the spiritual world, which I bore within me, as justified also before the formula of natural-scientific thinking. I was 22 when these experiences were passing through my soul.'[41] Thus, through this intense inner development and through the occult experiences he had in his work on Fichte, whom one can call the 'philosopher of the "I"', Rudolf Steiner was prepared for the next period of his life—the Sun-period. During this time all his forces were devoted to the riddle of the being of man, or to the secret of the 'I' in which all the wisdom of man flows together. Before him lay the task 'of reuniting science and religion; of introducing God into science and nature into religion.'[42] But seen spiritually, the mystery of the 'I' cannot be separated from the Sun Mystery, nor equally therefore from the Christ Mystery. For Christ as the World Logos suffuses all nature with His Spirit, fills the spiritual worlds with His Light and works at the same time as Divine Person in the most hidden, most holy inner sanctuary of the human 'I'. Only because Christ through the Mystery of Golgotha has united Himself with the Earth and since that time has been working in every individual human 'I' can He unite the spirit world and nature.

When Rudolf Steiner stood on the threshold of the next great period of his life, there lay before him the task of recognizing the activity of the Logos in nature and in the human 'I', and of bringing the secret of this activity to direct spiritual perception.

2. The Great Sun Period

At the beginning of the next great phase of Rudolf Steiner's life there are also marked outer changes. He eventually moves to Vienna and on Schröer's recommendation he begins working, in 1882, on the edition mentioned earlier of Goethe's natural-scientific writings in Kürschner's series *Deutsche Nationalliteratur*. He had been looking at Goethe's natural-scientific work since 1880,[1] but now he was able to come into contact with literary circles also. He wrote an introduction to Goethe's botany, zoology, geology and colour theory for Kürschner's edition of Goethe's collected works. Goethe's natural-scientific outlook and approach provided Rudolf Steiner at last with the long-sought foundation for a uniting of nature and spirit, making possible the transition from a natural science to a spiritual science or 'modern theosophy' (anthroposophy), the foundation of which was laid by Rudolf Steiner in this work. Later he writes about this: 'Anyone who reads these introductions will already be able to find theosophical ideas in them in the form of a philosophical Idealism.'[2]

Inwardly, Rudolf Steiner is nearing the cosmic Sun Mystery, the Logos Mystery, and about this he says in his autobiography: 'The human soul lives in the "Logos"; how the outer world lives in this Logos is the fundamental question in my book *A Theory of Knowledge Implicit in Goethe's World Conception*. [He worked on this book in the middle of the 1880s.] And it remains so in my books *Truth and Science* and *The Philosophy of Freedom*.'[3] These words clearly show how already at the beginning of his Sun period Rudolf Steiner was confronted with the question of the interrelation between the world and the Logos, and the Logos and the human soul. The struggle for an answer runs like an unbroken thread through the next three seven-year periods of his life, and at the end of this phase finds its crowning and fulfilment.

In the Sun period of the human life, between the ages of 21 to 42, it is from 21 to 28 that the sentient soul develops, from 28 to 35 the intellectual soul (or mind soul), and from 35 to 42 the consciousness soul. Yet during this time it is not only the Sun-forces that are experienced but also the powers opposing them. In his lecture on 22 March 1909 in Berlin,[4] Rudolf Steiner describes how Lucifer works primarily in the sentient soul, Ahriman in the intellectual soul and of how in the future—which is already present to a considerable degree in our times—the Asuras will take hold of the consciousness soul through the temptation of the human 'I'. Thus it is

41

clear that in the time between 21 and 27–28 Lucifer approaches man with a particularly alluring intensity.

At this time Rudolf Steiner had inner experiences of a particular kind through his acquaintance with people who at the end of the nineteenth century still lived completely out of impulses from the past. He had already made the first of these acquaintances in the preceding period of his life: Schröer lived completely in the pure world of Platonic ideas; everything around him breathed the purest Idealism. But a certain one-sidedness of world-outlook was hidden here, which became evident in his relationship to Goethe; for he indeed idolized Goethe, but could not follow him in his endeavours towards a renewal of the faculty for knowledge.

Rudolf Steiner indicated[5] that the task of the fifth post-Atlantean epoch is to develop free imagination and a method of research into nature based on phenomenology. If observation is developed rightly in this twofold way the powers of temptation, Lucifer and Ahriman, will gradually be overcome. One can already find the seeds of these two ways of looking at things in Goethe—the world of free imagination in *Faust*, and the phenomenology of archetypes in his natural-scientific studies. It is only in the balance of these two forces that evolution can take its rightful course and Schröer did not have this balance. 'Schröer himself had no connection with science.'[6]

If we look at Rudolf Steiner's life during his time in Vienna, we find him on the one hand engaged in serious natural-scientific studies—he visits Reitlinger's laboratory[7] amongst others. On the other hand he still sees Schröer, whose life's breath is art. Thirdly, he is acquainted with the pessimistic young poetess, Marie Eugenie delle Grazie. In her circle, to which belonged many theology professors, there reigned a deep respect and reverence for the spirit of the Middle Ages, and a strong dislike of Goethe.

These different and various relationships provide him with the experience of how science, art and religion have become separated from the living source of the spirit and of how, when unable to attain to a real experience of the spirit, they are eventually forced to give themselves over to forces that lead to one-sidedness and final isolation. We may assume that already at that time, out of his conscious life in the spiritual world, the necessity of uniting science, art and religion presented itself to Rudolf Steiner with particular clarity. In particular, too, that more conscious seeking after the spirit which he met in the Vienna theosophists grouped around Marie Lang remained alien to him because of her unclear, mystical frame of mind. This, however, did not affect his warm friendship with Rosa Mayreder in this circle. He was looking for 'a meeting with the spirit by means of ideas illumined by the spirit'.[8] So it is also understandable that Sinnett's *Esoteric Buddhism*, the first theosophical work to come into

Rudolf Steiner's possession through a friend, made a repugnant impression on him.[9] It was only in Friedrich Eckstein that he first met a great scholar of classical occultism and of the Cabbala.

His experience of these diverse spiritual streams of the past, all of which wished to continue to play a leading role, was transformed for him into occult experiences, and he devotes the whole of Chapter XI of his auto-biography to a description of them. He says there: 'Towards the end of the first chapter of my life, I felt an inner need to attain clarity concerning certain orientations of the human soul. One of these orientations was mysticism. I found it difficult to gain any relation to mysticism as it appeared in the various epochs of mankind's spiritual development, in Oriental wisdom [M. Lang], Neo-Platonism [F. Eckstein], the Christianity of the Middle Ages [the circle around delle Grazie] and in the strivings of the Cabbalists.'[10]

If one reads this chapter carefully one can sense quite clearly that Rudolf Steiner only accepted mysticism where it had been able to free itself completely from the forces of Lucifer, which are a constant threat to the mystic; for in mysticism 'one has to surrender completely the relation of the human being to the spirit to "subjective feeling".' But it is in the arbitrary nature of the subjective that Lucifer holds sway. And he continues: 'By looking at this with the eyes of the soul, the forces in me which were in inner opposition to mysticism became stronger and stronger.' One can see in this statement how he was wrestling at that time with the first Tempter of mankind, which he then also describes: 'It was not so very difficult to confront this *inner existential conflict* with that clarity which finally rises above it.' In these simple words Rudolf Steiner confirms his inner victory over the luciferic forces of temptation.

The year 1888, in which he completed the first seven years of his Sun period, was particularly important. He writes: 'At this period of my life—about 1888—I felt on the one hand impelled to strong *spiritual concentration*, while on the other hand I led an extensive social life.'[11] We see how strongly he felt the polarity of the two streams in which he had lived from his early youth, and how the urgent need to unite them and thereby complete the Rosicrucian path of initiation for the future became more and more impelling. He later says of this time: 'Thus I led an inner life that had no connection with the external world, while on the other hand my interests were strongly bound up with that world.'

But this intensification in his inner life increased his search even more for forms of thinking suited to the expression of spiritual experiences and to the transformation of thinking in such a way that it could become capable of grasping the spiritual, as had happened with Goethe.

His work on Goethe's natural-scientific writings helped him in his growing loneliness. But Goethe's perception of the world was something alien for those around Rudolf Steiner: 'I found no one with whom I could speak about this perception.'[12] And further: 'The only release I found from the feeling of living in spiritual isolation was reading and re-reading the conversation that took place between Goethe and Schiller as they went away together from a meeting of the Society for Scientific Research in Jena... In a few strokes Goethe sketched for Schiller his "archetypal plant".' In its sensible–supersensible form this 'archetypal plant' at last signified the direct bridge to the world of pure Imaginations. He could now say: 'Goethe's way of looking at things appeared to me to be one in accordance with the spirit.' Goethe's perception of nature also brought him to recognize that the time had come to start writing about his own spiritual experiences. This is clearly expressed in his autobiography: 'Through the detailed introduction which I had to write for the second volume of Goethe's natural-scientific works which I was editing, I felt an inner need to bring my perception of the spiritual world into the form of a presentation visible to thinking.'[13] He then quotes an extract from this introduction on a number of pages where he characterizes the essential nature of man's new relation to the spiritual world, to which he had managed to come at that time. 'The moment thinking takes hold of an idea it merges with the primordial foundation of existence; what is effective in the world that surrounds man is experienced within the human spirit; man *unites* with objective reality at its source. *Man's true communion is his experience of the idea within reality.* Thinking has the same relationship to ideas as the eye has to light, the ear to sound. *It is the organ of perception.*'[14] These words written by Rudolf Steiner in 1888 can be seen as the sum of the magnificent struggle for the true nature of thinking which he began at the age of 14. They bear witness to the fact that the battle for a new thinking—a thinking not in contradiction to spiritual experience but on the contrary actually opening the door to the spiritual world—*that* battle is won, and won for the whole of mankind! This historical fact was the first blow against the second enemy of humanity, Ahriman. This was the first step in the battle to free human intelligence from his power, the first step of human intelligence on its path into the sphere of Michael.[15] The second seven-year span in the Sun period of Rudolf Steiner's life is dedicated to securing this victory once and for all, and the climax is reached with the appearance of *The Philosophy of Freedom*—the *first Michaelic book* in the fifth post-Atlantean epoch.

Rudolf Steiner also says of the end of this chapter of his life: 'During the time I am now describing I gained through spiritual perception a definite insight into man's repeated Earth lives.'[16] From the explanation given later in Arnhem[17] of what he had said to Professor Neumann in 1888 after giving a lecture, *Goethe as the Founder of a New Science of Aesthetics*, to the Vienna

Goethe Society, we can deduce that at the same time he had achieved a clear insight into his own past incarnations. But it also indicates to what extent at that time he had drawn close to the Sun Mystery of the 'I', for it is only here that the source of knowledge is to be found out of which the core of man's being can be gazed upon as it moves from incarnation to incarnation.

However, despite his deep insights into the spiritual world, Rudolf Steiner was unable at that time to join nature and spirit, the outer and inner world, in a final higher unity. Spiritual perception was perfectly self-evident and natural for him but outer life contained many unanswered questions: 'Thus at the age of 27 I was full of questions and riddles *in regard to man's external life*, while at the same time the nature of the human soul and its relation to the spiritual world stood before my inner perception in an ever more complete and definite form.'[18] This perception finally came to expression in *The Philosophy of Freedom*, in the middle of the following seven-year period.

At the beginning of this new seven-year span there are again important changes in Rudolf Steiner's external life. He moves to Weimar to work in the newly-founded Goethe–Schiller Archive, and so spends the greater part of these seven years in Goethe's town. In this place whose very atmosphere bore the seeds of artistic impulses, Rudolf Steiner completed the work on his own conception of art: 'Thus in Weimar I had a direct experience of artistic striving about which, for the most part, I had views that agreed little with the views held by others.'[19] He becomes acquainted here with a large circle of the most diverse personalities who present him with very differing and even conflicting outlooks on the world, so that out of these separate details he is able to piece together and recognize the true countenance of the age and the active forces battling against each other in it. And yet none of these social meetings can assuage his inner loneliness. Just as in Vienna, so here his friends have no interest in his spiritual struggles: 'I had to come to terms with everything that concerned my spiritual perception entirely alone. I lived in the spiritual world; not one among all the people I knew followed me there . . . Such was my "loneliness" in Weimar where I led such an active social life.'[20]

In the second lecture of the cycle *The Occult Significance of the Bhagavad Gita* Rudolf Steiner describes how loneliness experienced in the right way lifts the pupil to the second stage of cognition, to Inspiration. In the further course of these lectures he relates this experience to the two books *Truth and Science* and *The Philosophy of Freedom*, written by him during his time in Weimar, and we can sense his personal experiences in them. For it was just in this very loneliness, which for him is the fundamental prerequisite of the proper mastering of Inspiration, that he had his deepest spiritual experiences. It is at this age that the intellectual soul (or mind soul) develops in the human being, and through this—unconsciously in the ordinary person, but consciously in the initiate—there come to life the forces of the fourth post-Atlantean epoch with its climax, which is at the same time also the climax of the evolution of mankind: the mystery of the Sun Being—the Mystery of Golgotha.

And simultaneously with this there arise the adversary powers; for the intellectual soul is exactly that member of man's being in which Ahriman (who with reference to Rudolf Steiner's lecture on 11 November 1918[21] can be called a Sun-demon) has evolved his adversary forces since time immemorial. An exalted personal experience was connected with the awareness of this polarity for Rudolf Steiner. In the Karma lectures after the Christmas Conference, he speaks to anthroposophists about the deep cosmic secrets of his life which we are looking at here. In the preceding period of his life he had already seen in complete clarity how in his earlier incarnations he was himself directly connected with the sphere of Michael. But knowledge of earlier Earth-lives extends into a knowledge of life between death and a new birth, and so it was an occult fact for him that as the Mystery of Golgotha took place on Earth he was abiding with Michael in the Sun-sphere. Now, in his first incarnation during the new Michael-epoch, he meets him in the Sun-hour of his life on Earth, and just as he had sojourned with Michael in the Sun-sphere during the Mystery of Golgotha at the Sun-hour of mankind and had gazed upon the Mystery of Golgotha from there, so now he is again at Michael's side in the great Sun-hour of his Earth-life, when Michael 'as it were imitating and experiencing for himself the great event of Christ Jesus'[22] descends to the Earth and leads the battle here against the ahrimanic adversaries—a battle in which Rudolf Steiner, as a true pupil of Michael, also takes part.

In a lecture in Torquay on 12 August 1924, Rudolf Steiner says the following about the experiences of this period of his life: 'In the time immediately after the entry of the Michael influence in the eighties and nineties, when the Michael rulership was beginning to take effect behind the scenes of external happenings, those who were passing through the period of the development of the intellectual or mind soul—that is to say, between the ages of 28 and 35—were really living in a kind of aloofness from the physical world. For when a human being is consciously active and alert in the mind soul he is aloof in a very real sense from the material world ... What does this mean? It means that in the mind soul, aloof from the material world, one was able to live in the very world into which Michael was entering on his way down towards the Earth ... Behind a thin veil, a very thin veil at that time, was a world adjoining our physical world. Peculiar conditions prevailed shortly before the close of Kali Yuga at the end of the nineteenth century ... In very truth something mysterious was at work in the closing decades of the nineteenth century. There were momentous happenings, grouped around the spirit we name Michael. Participating in these happenings were strong and forceful followers of Michael, human souls living at that time in their existence between death and rebirth, not yet incarnate in the physical body. But there were also mighty demonic Powers who, under the sway of ahrimanic influences, set themselves in rebellion against what was thus to come into the world.'[23] And further, 'For this reason I lived with all the forces of the mind soul through what was taking place in this world behind the veil, in this sphere of Michael's activity.'

In this way Rudolf Steiner experienced two dramatic events in the cosmic history of Michael. The first is in the Sun-sphere where he witnesses at the time of the Mystery of Golgotha how the Cosmic Intelligence falls from Michael's grasp and the second, 19 centuries later at the beginning of the new Michael Age, is the hard battle led by Michael in the Earth-sphere against the ahrimanic spirits for the Cosmic Intelligence, which had fallen to Ahriman in the previous centuries, and for the true freedom of the human spirit.

This inner nature of Michael's battle with the Dragon came to expression at the beginning of the new Michael Age in *The Philosophy of Freedom*. It is not possible here to go into close detail of this great work of the human spirit in our time, but suffice it to say that, properly understood, this book will be a great weapon in the future, with the help of which Michael can battle against Ahriman in the souls and spirits of human beings. For Michael is the representative of the principle of freedom in the cosmos: 'Michael is the spirit who in the most eminent sense works with human freedom.'[24] The first part of the book describes for us the path of the human soul, which can free the originally cosmic but now fallen Intelligence from the clutches of Ahriman, and can lead the human being through 'pure thinking' into the sphere of Michael. The second part shows the path to true moral freedom. In this sphere alone can the human being become a true follower and server of Michael. This book is like the first ray of sunlight in a new epoch where man lifts himself out of the physical world, from the earthly 'I' to the higher 'I', that can be developed and transformed as Spirit Self out of the purified astral body into the Divine Sophia.[25] For Michael now addresses himself to the incipient, growing Spirit Self in man.

One sees the quintessence of *The Philosophy of Freedom* in the following words: 'It is Michael's will that man be a *free being* who sees in his *concepts and ideas* also that which is revealed to him from the spiritual world.'[26] Later in the same lecture of 19 July 1924, Rudolf Steiner says: 'Michael fills people with the enthusiasm of Michael himself ... so that one can think and yet be a spiritual human being at the same time; *for this is what is meant by the rulership of Michael.*' And this is also the goal of *The Philosophy of Freedom*, for properly read this book is a true occult exercise in itself. Its thought-forms are like pure crystals, the content is *full of life*, as Rudolf Steiner often remarks. For although it arises entirely out of the fifth post-Atlantean epoch, it is already preparing for the sixth, in which the human being will think not only with the physical brain but also with the etheric. For 'in the last third of the nineteenth century Michael descends from the Sun down to the Earth and wishes to take hold of human intelligence.'[27] In a certain sense *The Philosophy of Freedom* is the first descent of Michael into the earthly intelligence of man. Thus for Rudolf Steiner this book is like a bridge between individual human thinking and the world of objective spirit.

Having crossed this abyss, Rudolf Steiner could turn his activity to formulating pure spiritual ideas: 'My further task could only be an attempt to formulate ideas for the spiritual world itself... My life between the ages of 30 and 40 was filled with intense inner struggle for such ideas.'[28]

But there was another problem to be solved during this period in Weimar. 'I now realized how little I had really participated in the external world up to then..., that really the only world I had been familiar with so far was the spiritual world I inwardly beheld. I found it easy to establish a connection with that world. And I began to realize how very difficult it had been for me during childhood and youth to relate myself to the outer world through the senses...'[29] 'The external world really appeared to me somewhat shadow-like or picture-like. It moved past me like pictures, whereas my relationship with the spiritual always had the character of concrete reality... I felt this more particularly during the early nineties in Weimar. I was then adding the final touches to my *Philosophy of Freedom...* What I had received from the external world was experienced merely as a stimulus.'[30]

But to grasp the external world meant to penetrate through to the spiritual reality lying at its foundation; that is, into that sphere from which Ahriman hopes to lead humanity into error in regard to the outer physical world. Coming to terms with the physical world in this way was an *inner* victory for Rudolf Steiner over Ahriman.

In the struggle against the ahrimanic powers, Rudolf Steiner had already achieved a first victory in the realm of thinking at the beginning of this period, in 1888 (see page 44). As a result of this victory achieved out of his own soul forces, the cosmic archetypal image of Michael's battle with the Dragon in the realm immediately adjoining the Earth appeared before him in his next seven-year period. But the battle itself, now having to be continued in the earthly sphere, became still fiercer, for Ahriman had managed to bring the one-sided world perception of materialism into a position of dominance. To overcome Ahriman in this sphere Rudolf Steiner had to work through to an objective understanding of the spiritual foundations of the physical world. In other words, as his Teacher had indicated to him in his youth, the time had come 'to crawl into the dragon's skin' in order to overcome it, and he achieved this in the second half of his time in Weimar by submerging himself in the ideas of Ernst Haeckel and Friedrich Nietzsche. For it was, so to speak, in the mirror of these ideas that the hidden battle waged by the adversary forces became visible.

In Ernst Haeckel, Rudolf Steiner was confronted with the con-temporary view of nature which, in the nineteenth century—the period of the deepest descent of man into matter—had produced the theory of evolution. This was the most significant achievement of the *free* human spirit, but it was built upon a complete and consistent denial of the spirit. In the way in which Ahriman permeated all natural-scientific thinking with his own forces and used it for his own ends, we have to see a most earnest attempt by him to bring the whole of Earth development into his own power.

On the other hand, in the countenance of Nietzsche the tragedy of the human 'I' becomes apparent to Rudolf Steiner—the 'I' which at the deepest point of evolution and while most enmeshed in matter comes to an experience of itself, but cannot raise itself to a new comprehension of the spirit. Nietzsche was a tragic spirit who in strict honesty with himself had to look on the natural-scientific mode of thinking as the fundamental force of his age and, unable to overcome its ahrimanic character, broke in the battle. His personal destiny became a symbol of the future that Ahriman is preparing for the whole of mankind and which can only be averted if the ahrimanic form of present-day scientific thinking can be mastered and newly spiritualized in such a way as to become the servant to the true goals of mankind. In order to reopen the way to the spirit for mankind, and to transform Haeckel's materialistic scientific image of the world into the spiritual science of *Occult Science*, Rudolf Steiner had to tread the thorny path of completely experiencing and reviving for himself the ideas of these two men. And he did this so intensely that for a long time his enemies used his writings on Haeckel and Nietzsche to propagate rumours that he was a materialistic follower of Haeckel or an anti-Christian follower of Nietzsche. He was neither. He had simply to tread this difficult path of knowledge to its very conclusion, so that in the confrontation with Ahriman he would be able finally to conquer him with his own weapons.

This happened at the end of the Weimar period and brought a deep inner change with it. 'I was 36 years of age at the end of my Weimar period. About a year earlier a profound transformation began to take place

49

in my inner life. When I left Weimar this transformation had become a decisive experience. It had nothing to do with the change in my outer circumstances, great though that was. Knowledge and experience of the spiritual world had always been something self-evident to me, whereas to grasp the sense-world through physical perception caused me the greatest difficulty. It was as if my inner soul-experience of sense-perceptions did not penetrate sufficiently into the sense-organs to unite fully with what takes place in *them*. This changed entirely from the beginning of my thirty-sixth year. I became able to observe physical things and events more accurately and completely than before. This was the case in regard to scientific investigation and also to external life in general.'[31] Ahriman could no longer delude him as to the nature of the physical world, and this opened up to him the spiritual realms lying at the foundation of the sense-perceptible world which are veiled for most people by Ahriman. He recognized the nature of the material world and the fundamental error that modern science makes with regard to matter.

Concerning the nature of his spiritual experience at that time, Rudolf Steiner says the following: 'In observation of the physical world one goes completely out of oneself, but it is precisely through this that one comes again into the spiritual world with an increased ability for spiritual observation.' This penetration into the hidden spiritual essence of the material world is a clear sign that Rudolf Steiner is beginning to enter the world of Intuition. For in modern initiation a conscious experiencing of the spiritual world as forming the foundation of the material world is only possible for an intuitive consciousness.

After he had gained the inner victory over Lucifer and Ahriman, he comes once again—although on a higher level—to the basic question of Rosicrucian initiation: 'Thus at this time I experienced with especial strength the complete contrast between the spiritual and the physical.' The whole of the last seven years of the Sun period in Rudolf Steiner's life is dedicated to the solution of this question. 'The whole world outside man is a riddle; it is the original World Riddle; *and man himself is the solution.*'

Here is the transition to the last and most difficult stage of Rudolf Steiner's initiation. He is on the threshold to the essence of man's being, to his 'I', in which the Christ has been active since the Mystery of Golgotha. The reunion of nature and spirit can only be accomplished today by the force of Christ in the human 'I' through a thinking freed from the shackles of the senses. Thus Rudolf Steiner's path leads him from his Teacher in his youth to the Archangel Michael, and finally from Michael, the 'Countenance of Christ', to Christ Himself!

Rudolf Steiner now enters the third seven-years of the Sun period of his life, into the period of the development of the consciousness soul—into the time, that is, in which the individual human being reaches the stage of the fifth post-Atlantean cultural epoch. It is the inherent characteristic of this epoch that the guiding divine-spiritual Hierarchies withdraw in order that human beings, now forsaken by the Gods, might struggle through for themselves to freedom, and then out of their *own* will regain the difficult path back to the spiritual world, their true home. Rudolf Steiner also experiences this process during this period. He experiences how the spiritual powers that up to that time had guided him and stood behind him, shedding light on his way, now seem to withdraw, and in complete spiritual loneliness he also must himself now find his path solely with the aid of *his own* inner light, and must accomplish out of complete inner freedom what humanity as a whole will attain in the near or distant future: a new union with the spiritual world through the principle of the 'I' and the Christ-force working in it.

'All this that was associated with my inner transformation came about in connection with the result of a self-observation now possible ... I felt a certain aspect of the conceptual element in my inner life receding and being replaced by the element of will ... The will increased proportionally with the decrease in the conceptual element.' Rudolf Steiner says the following concerning the withdrawal of the spiritual powers which up to that time had stood behind him: 'With the transformation that took place in my soul life as described above, I must conclude the second chapter of my life. My destiny now took a completely new direction. In Vienna and Weimar the tasks that came to me through outer circumstances were entirely in harmony with my inner striving.'[32]

One can be reminded here of Parsifal, the early representative of the fifth cultural epoch, and his years of being 'distant from God'. This 'God-for-sakenness' holding sway in the fifth epoch enables the adversary powers to fall upon humanity with particular force and whereas earlier they had worked individually, they now begin to do so collectively, particularly in the *social* realm. Here, to an intensified degree, they try to oppose the Christ-force, and to contend with it for the leadership of the epoch of freedom. Thus this chapter of his life brings Rudolf Steiner, who had earlier overcome Lucifer and Ahriman in his own inner life, to a new confrontation in the social realm into which they had already insinuated their fearful, destructive influences.

He has to experience inwardly what he later represents in the left-hand side motif of the 'group' carving of Lucifer and Ahriman, who until the intervention of the Christ-impulse worked together; he has to pass through the abyss of existence and penetrate beyond it to what is represented in the central theme where the image of the cosmic Representative of Man appears before us. By entering into the social life of modern times Christ

51

destroys the combined efforts of Lucifer and Ahriman working in it. As a consequence of their one-sidedness they will suffer the tragic destiny they have prepared for themselves in the cosmos. Lucifer plunges into the abyss, and Ahriman binds himself in the bonds of condensed sun-rays.

Outwardly this new period in Rudolf Steiner's life begins with his removal to Berlin where he becomes the editor of the periodical *Magazin für Literatur* in 1897. 'I did not want to remain silent, but to say as much as it was possible to say'[33]—that was his reason for acquiring the magazine. In other words: 'It was in the nature of the thing that a circle of readers gradually gathered around the new trend inaugurated by me in *Magazin* . . . I wanted to give this young literary trend a spiritual basis, and I indeed found myself in the liveliest association with the most promising representatives of this trend.'[34] Through the magazine Rudolf Steiner also plunges into the most intense social life of the times. He makes personal contact with a large number of people representing the most diverse spiritual and unspiritual movements. In his magazine he comments on nearly all the important spiritual, cultural, historical, social, political, artistic and scientific aspirations of the time. The title index alone of the articles he wrote at that time is impressive.

At the same time his connection with the working class in Berlin begins. 'I had become a teacher at the Berlin evening school for workers. I taught history and science. The workers soon came to like, and could understand, my thoroughly idealistic history methods and my way of teaching. My audience grew. I was having to give a lecture practically every evening.'[35]

Whilst in his practical life Rudolf Steiner was thus getting to know the driving spiritual forces in the social sphere and the classes and groups representing them, on his occult path he goes through a crisis for, as a constant witness to the spiritual background of all the events of the times, he experiences how in the last years of the 'dark age' of Kali Yuga the battle of the forces of light and darkness increases to an unprecedented intensity. He later says: 'I look upon the things I said between 1897 and 1900 as to something which had to be said at some time in view of the trend of thinking that was prevalent. But I also look back to what was for me an intense spiritual test. I learned to recognize thoroughly where the disintegrating forces of the age appear that urge men away from spirit and destroy culture. This insight gave me much of the strength I needed henceforth to work directly from the spirit.'[36]

As before, the 'destructive and disintegrating' forces of contemporary culture appear before him in double form. The countenance of Lucifer shows through in the figures of the Berlin Bohemians of that time, who passed their lives in poetical reveries and nightly drinking bouts; it emerges too in the strivings of personalities such as the idealist anarchist J.H. Mackay who wished to realize his social ideas 'by spiritual means *alone*',[37] and in Max Stirner in whose face the luciferic will burned with the desire to cast himself down from the heights of his 'social egoism' into the abyss. Rudolf Steiner says concerning these deeply disturbing meetings in the social sphere: 'Through my experience with J.H. Mackay and Stirner, my destiny caused me once more to enter a world of thought where I had to go through a *spiritual test*... But at this time, about 1898, my soul ... was to be dragged down into a kind of abyss... All the forces of my soul were engaged in the powerful inner struggle I experienced at this time.'

But something still more powerful was awaiting Rudolf Steiner. Ahriman, the Prince of Darkness himself, approaches him, now however not only as the deceiver on the individual path of initiation but as a mighty world-force that, in opposition to the spiritual powers working in man towards his rightful evolution, wishes to drag present civilization into the abyss of materialism and spiritual death. The one-sidedness of the knowledge and understanding of man and the world induced by Ahriman in the course of human evolution appears in full clarity before Rudolf Steiner's inner eye. It is the one-sidedness that had penetrated from the realm of knowledge into the social realm as the sum total of all the destructive impulses in it: 'It is a realm where one-sidedness in knowledge causes more than abstract deviations. What is error in the human world becomes there a vivid spiritual relationship with certain beings. Later I pointed in this direction when speaking of ahrimanic beings. For them it is an absolute reality that the world must be a machine. Their realm borders directly upon the sense-world. I never for a moment fell prey to influences from this realm in my world of ideas—not even unconsciously. For I took the greatest care that all my spiritual investigations were carried out in *clear, waking consciousness*. Consequently, all the more conscious was my inner struggle with the demonic powers who strove to develop scientific knowledge not into perception of spirit but into a mechanical, materialistic way of thinking. These realms must be experienced consciously by those who strive to attain knowledge of spirit ... I was obliged at that time to rescue my spiritual world-conception through inner battles. These inner struggles took place behind the scenes of everyday experience.'[38] These words show that Rudolf Steiner's battle with the adversary powers became particularly intense at this time when he had to find his way, not only as usual without any external support but now also without the inner support granted him up to the beginning of his years in Berlin. It was a matter now of completing his individual initiation by one last enormous effort to establish an indestructible bridge between the world of nature and the world of the spirit; between, that is, the world that Ahriman wishes to turn into a machine and the world Lucifer wishes to tear away from the Earth and carry into his own domain, on the wings of fancifulness and obscure mysticism in the life of the feelings.

He was able to fulfil this task and preserve his own clairvoyance in those enormous spiritual storms only by the aid of Him who as the central, all-encompassing principle steps between the two destructive powers that wish to drag humanity into the abyss and, overcoming them, brings them into a balance. 'I could only make progress during this period of testing by contemplating the evolution of Christianity with spiritual perception.'

Thus, in his most intense spiritual battles Rudolf Steiner was approaching the central figure of the evolution of the world, the source of the Light that has shone over all human development since the Mystery of Golgotha. 'I found it necessary to enter into a direct living experience of Christianity—and indeed into the world of spirit itself, after the severe inner struggles during the time of testing.' And also: 'At that time my experience of Christianity underwent a severe test. This lasted from the time of my departure from Weimar, where I had completed my task, to the period when I wrote my book *Christianity as Mystical Fact*. Tests of this nature are obstacles placed in one's path by destiny (karma); they have to be overcome in the course of spiritual development.'

Rudolf Steiner overcame these obstacles! At the end of the great Sun period of his life, as an initiate who had attained spiritual victory and completed the long path of his own initiation, he stood in the presence of the deepest secret of the Sun Mystery, of the cosmic 'I'-Mystery that forms the bridge between the world of spirit and the world of nature. He came into the immediate presence of the Being who encompasses the Sun-sphere and fills it with life, and whose Deed on Golgotha is the greatest event of all Earth evolution.

A direct spiritual meeting had grown from the germ of knowledge and Rudolf Steiner speaks about this in the following way: 'Around the turn of the century this germ of knowledge opened more and more. The inner test described above occurred shortly before the turn of the century. This experience culminated in my *standing in the spiritual presence of the Mystery of Golgotha* in a most profound and solemn festival of knowledge.' We can find an indication to give us a sense of the nature of this meeting in Chapter 5 of *Occult Science* where the new Christian-Rosicrucian path of initiation is described. It reaches its climax in a meeting with the Christ, which takes place in the highest sphere of initiation. 'Through this experience the pupil is initiated into the sublime Mystery that is connected with the name of Christ. Christ shows Himself to him as the great human Prototype and Example, united with the Earth's true evolution ... *Having thus come through Intuition to a knowledge of Christ in the spiritual world, the aspirant will find that he is able also to understand what took place historically on Earth in the fourth post-Atlantean period—the time of the Greek and Roman civilization. How the great Sun Being, the Christ, intervened in Earth evolution, and how He is still working in it now and on into the future, the pupil of the spirit knows henceforth from his own experience.* This then is what he attains through Intuition: the very meaning and significance of Earth evolution are communicated to him.'[39]

We see from these words that the essence of the Mystery of Golgotha and the true meaning of Christianity reveal themselves to the pupil only after he has met the Christ in the sphere of Intuition. And indeed how similar this description is to the end of Chapter XXVI of his autobiography, quoted above. We can say therefore that Rudolf Steiner's meeting with the Christ in 1899[40] was exactly like the one he later describes at the end of Chapter 5 of *Occult Science*. In that moment Rudolf Steiner completed his Christian-Rosicrucian initiation: *he experienced a personal encounter with the Christ in the sphere of Intuition.*

He had thereby attained the third and last level on the Rosicrucian path of initiation, the level of Teacher. He unites in a higher synthesis the outer and inner path, the stream of the Magi and the stream of the Shepherds—two world-impulses which are expressed in the two genealogies described in the Gospels of Luke and Matthew. On the path trodden by Rudolf Steiner, the Christ, who since the Mystery of Golgotha has been united with the Earth, reveals Himself to mankind as the Spirit of the Earth who permeates and ensouls the world of nature around us yet, at the same time, as the Divine Person and the true 'I' of every human being and of all humanity is mysteriously present in the holy of holies in every soul.

We shall have to consider more closely the nature of this fusion of the two streams in the Christian-Rosicrucian path of initiation, and for this we must look to the origin of these two Mystery-streams in very ancient times. In the first place they are connected with the two migratory movements out of ancient Atlantis: with the northern migration, which mainly nurtured the external path, the ascent into the macrocosmos, and the southern migration, which developed more the inner path by contemplation of the depths of the individual soul. The northern path was related to the so-called Sun Mysteries, where the pupil had to wrestle above all with the opposing powers of Ahriman, the Sun-demon, which find their strongest expression in the battle between Zoroaster and Angra Mainyu. On the second path, the path more connected with the Moon Mysteries, the pupil had to do battle with Lucifer, the inner tempter of mankind, who opposes Jahve in the Moon-sphere. We can see Buddha's battle with Mara, before his enlightenment under the Bodhi tree, as an image of this struggle with the tempter.

In his last Easter cycle of lectures in 1924, *The Easter Festival Considered in*

Relation to the Mysteries,[41] Rudolf Steiner describes a particularly important aspect of the esoteric nature of these two Mystery-streams, and also calls them the Autumn and Spring Mysteries. Using the example of the Adonis Mystery, he describes in detail how the essence of the Sun-Autumn Mystery lay in a knowledge of the secret of death and resurrection, and of the after-death ascent of the soul into the sphere of the stars. Because of this there was also knowledge in these Mystery-places of the inherent quality of external nature surrounding man, experienced as the physical reflection of the greater world of the spiritual macrocosm. However, the fundamental goal of all the Mysteries of this kind was the eventual ascent of the neophyte into the Sun-sphere to be united with the great Spirit of the Sun, the Ruler of the Sun-realm, the Christ. In these Mysteries the final goal of the whole process of initiation was considered to be this union with the Cosmic Christ as the one wellspring of eternal macrocosmic life and true immortality.

The spiritual path in the Moon-Spring Mystery was of a completely different nature. Here the neophyte chiefly sank into himself, into the depths of his own soul, and by this path gradually ascended to that immortal part of his being that had never descended from the spiritual world through birth (or conception) into earthly existence. On this path the neophyte came to an experience of his life before birth. And an important aspect of this existence before birth is connected with the Moon-sphere where the soul, under the guidance of the Moon teachers of wisdom, forms its etheric body out of the forces of the whole planetary cosmos before a new incarnation on Earth.

And this gradual arising of the etheric body out of the forces of the whole planetary system was experienced with particular intensity by the pupil in the Moon-Spring Mysteries. But something else was connected with the experience of this spiritual process. By being in the midst of the forces and processes of the Moon-sphere, the pupil was gradually able to unite himself with the very essence of the moonlight (in its spiritual aspect) and surround himself with it, thus receiving, as Rudolf Steiner relates, a sort of 'Moon body' with whose aid he could gaze up from the sphere of the Moon into the Sun-sphere and thereby into the spiritual Sun.

And just as the full Moon becomes the bearer of the sunlight, so similarly the pupil, having reached the final goal of these Mysteries, became the bearer of the spiritual forces of the Sun, the bearer of the forces of the Christ—a Christophorus.

Thus we see that in both the Sun and the Moon Mysteries, either through a knowledge of outer or of inner realities and although by completely different paths, the pupils of the spirit finally arrived at one and the same goal—the union with the Cosmic Christ in the sphere of the Sun.

However, until the Mystery of Golgotha it was not possible anywhere on the Earth to unite these two paths, for it was only through the sacrifice of His descent from the Sun to the Earth that Christ brought the possibility for every human being to receive simultaneously the fruits of *both* Mystery-streams, through their full and final union in the actual awareness and experience of His Being *in the sphere of the Earth.*

Since the union of the Christ with the Earth, it is no longer possible to find him in the sphere of the Sun; this had consequences of great significance for these two Mystery streams. For the final goal of both these Mystery-streams as hitherto conceived had become unattainable, in view of the fact that the ultimate object of their aspirations can be achieved today neither through a trance-like nor an ecstatic ascent into the Sun-sphere, as was the case in olden times, but only through a conscious union with the Christ in the sphere of the Earth. However, where this did not take place and where the two streams continued to develop separately without the new experience of Christ, they soon fell prey to adversary forces. Thus the first stream, which quickly fell into the grip of ahrimanic forces, is cultivated even up to the present day, mainly by certain western brotherhoods. These brotherhoods, in the words of Rudolf Steiner, are developing a type of 'occult materialism' of the most terrible kind, to lead humanity along the fastest path to destruction and of which modern materialistic science is only a faint reflection. The second stream was quickly seized upon by Lucifer and appeared in the most diverse mystical movements finding their expression in all forms of ecstatic and trance-like release from the body, as practised in different occult systems in the East and now also in the West, and which finally causes the one who practises them to lose his individual 'I' and thereby also the possibility of attaining the goal of Earth evolution.

In contrast to these two streams, the most important goal of all truly Christian Mysteries—and particularly of the esoteric schools of the genuine Rosicrucians—was always the union of these two main streams through a direct experience of the Christ in the Earth-sphere. And this goal of the Christian-Rosicrucian path in its renewed form and in accordance with the new epoch of Michael was attained by Rudolf Steiner around 1899, when through his personal encounter with the Christ in the sphere of Intuition he completed the preparation for realizing his great mission amongst mankind. This personal meeting with the Christ is also the spiritual sum total of his inner development during the course of the Sun period of his life.

Now, however, it is necessary to look at the nature of the path of initiation completed by Rudolf Steiner at this time. It has already been mentioned that a clairvoyant who looks back over the different ages of his life can penetrate through them to the spiritual essence of each historical epoch in the development of humanity as a whole, and also to the cosmic secrets connected with them. Thus, when the initiate contemplates in Inspiration his first seven-year period, he is able to experience all the secrets of ancient Atlantis, for it was here that above all the physical body was developed. When he contemplates his second seven-year period, he experiences the secrets of the first post-Atlantean epoch, and so on. It follows therefore that at the end of his sixth seven-year period Rudolf Steiner could survey all the cultural epochs of mankind from ancient Atlantis up to our own fifth post-Atlantean epoch and could renew the wisdom of these past ages through his own experience of the Christ in the spiritual world. Thus we see that in the truest sense Rudolf Steiner himself realized in practice what is described in his lecture in Neuchâtel on 27 September 1911[42] as the initiation of Christian Rosenkreutz. In the thirteenth century Christian Rosenkreutz was inspired by twelve teachers, seven of whom bore within themselves all the wisdom of Atlantis while five bore the wisdom of the five post-Atlantean epochs. And likewise now, but in a different form and in harmony with the epoch of Michael, Rudolf Steiner trod an independent path of initiation. He no longer used the outer techniques rooted in the obsolete traditions of the ancient Mysteries but walked a purely inner meditative path, which he realized in the new Michaelic spirit through the supersensible meeting with the Christ.

It is possible to make a direct comparison of this all-important event in Rudolf Steiner's life, which occurred about 1899, *with the experience of St Paul on the way to Damascus* and which, in an occult sense, was also a personal meeting with the Christ in the spiritual world. This meeting can occur firstly on the level of Imagination—which was the case with St Paul—and can happen in our time as a meeting with the Etheric Christ; it can also occur in the sphere of Inspiration, where Christ appears as the great Sun Spirit and approaches the clairvoyant in the *form* of the Greater Guardian of the Threshold; and thirdly in the sphere of Intuition (described by Rudolf Steiner at the end of Chapter 5 in the *Occult Science*), where this meeting constitutes the true goal of the Christian-Rosicrucian spiritual path. Christian Rosenkreutz's initiation in the thirteenth century was also brought to fulfilment in such a meeting. Light is shed on this by the fact that the twelve accomplished this process of initiation right into the physical body of the thirteenth, which as a result became 'completely translucent'. In *Occult Science* Rudolf Steiner indicates quite definitely that only intuitive knowledge is capable of working right into the human physical body.[43] Thus also in the initiation of Christian Rosenkreutz we have a central experience of the Being of the Christ in the sphere of Intuition.

From all this we can see the advance that is possible for the present-day initiate in comparison with the epoch of St Paul. For Paul's experience of Christ in Imagination was a prophetic anticipation of the future; it was bestowed from above as a 'grace of God' on Paul who, according to Rudolf Steiner, was 'born before his time'.[44] But a personal experience of the Christ like this today, on the consciously-taken path of initiation in the new Michael Age, can already lead to a meeting with Christ's cosmic Being in the sphere of Intuition. Rudolf Steiner says the following concerning the different possibilities of knowledge in the two historical epochs of the development of mankind: 'What was opened to Paul as one definite aspect of the awareness and knowledge of Christ can, if we deepen the occultism of our time, open up wider fields of Christ-knowledge for humanity. For in that Paul's perception is expanded from the Mystery of Golgotha to its three preparatory stages [that is, the three cosmic sacrifices of the Christ through the gradual threefold penetration of the being of the Nathan Soul in preparation for the Mystery of Golgotha (see also Chapter 3 of this book)]—in that it is expanded from Paul's perception of Jesus of Nazareth to the life of Christ Jesus, so the Pauline method is expanded to a certain extent *from a single centre* over the whole greater phenomenon of the Christ Jesus life. And being able in this way through dedicated occult investigation to reach the position of making this Pauline method generally accessible for the knowledge and awareness of Christ, a real advance has been made in the knowledge of the Christ.'[45] We see how the so-called 'Pauline method' originated from a single centre—his personal meeting with the Christ in the spiritual realm of Imagination—and how today this method can be extended to the sphere of Intuition which occurred, though under different conditions, in Christian Rosenkreutz's initiation in the thirteenth century. Thus a further development of the 'Pauline method' is possible in the initiation of the present, as is its application in the ever-widening spheres of knowledge of the Being of the Cosmic Christ.

Having thus established the deeply significant correspondence between the initiation of Christian Rosenkreutz and Rudolf Steiner, we may now suggest that that secret Teacher whom Rudolf Steiner met at the dawn of his youth, before the beginning of the Sun period of his life, was indeed *Christian Rosenkreutz himself*. For apart from Rudolf Steiner's path of initiation described above, there is some other indirect evidence on which to base this assumption. First of all it is significant in this connection that through Fichte (see page 39), the Teacher brought his pupil into contact with that wisdom from which the book *Occult Science* later grew. Rudolf Steiner describes this book as the *fruit of Rosicrucian wisdom*. (See Foreword of the 6th edition.) And later in a lecture in Neuchâtel on 27 September 1911, he says: 'Christian Rosenkreutz is reincarnated today.'[46] In the following lecture, on 28 September, he indicates how Christian Rosenkreutz chooses his pupils.[47] A person prepares to undertake something that could result in his death, but at the last moment in the course of events Christian Rosenkreutz intervenes in a particular way and saves him. This is to awaken the feeling in the pupil that without this occurrence he would have died. Such an incident did occur in Rudolf Steiner's life and is described in detail by Friedrich Rittelmeyer: 'He later told me that he had once been suddenly rescued by a "Master" when he was about to do something that could have "brought him death".'[48] And at the end of a lecture on 18 December 1912, again in Neuchâtel, Rudolf Steiner says: 'And the one who is privileged to be near Christian Rosenkreutz gazes with wonder-filled reverence at how consistently he fulfilled the great mission laid upon him, the Rosicrucian-Christian mission of our time.'[49]

These words are of course to be understood mainly in a purely spiritual sense, but they also indicate the character of the relationship between Rudolf Steiner and his Teacher. Friedrich Rittelmeyer writes that when he asked in this connection whether he still sometimes saw his Teacher, Rudolf Steiner answered, 'I do not need to,' whereupon Rittelmeyer adds, 'Quite certainly he felt himself able at any time to establish a spiritual contact without an outer physical presence.'[50] These words of Rittelmeyer's, which were written on the basis of personal conversations, are in turn in complete agreement with what is said by Rudolf Steiner in a lecture on 14 August 1911: 'When the *present-day* guides of humanity move abroad in the world in their human guise, they are not recognized in the external exoteric world. And though we speak in spiritual science of the Masters of Wisdom and of the Harmony of Sensations and Feelings, people would often be astonished at the simple and straightforward humanity with which these Masters come to all lands. They are present on the physical plane. But they communicate the most important teachings not on the physical plane ... but on the spiritual one. And anyone who wishes to hear them and receive teaching from them must meet them not *only* in the physical body of flesh and blood but in their spirit form.'[51] In this sense the spiritual connection between Rudolf Steiner and Christian Rosenkreutz continued during the following years and took on an ever deeper and more encompassing character in the further stages of Rudolf Steiner's development.[52]

We see then that Rudolf Steiner's personal encounter with the Christ around the turn of the century is comparable in the strictest occult sense to the experience of St Paul on the way to Damascus. In his lectures Rudolf Steiner relates how it is only thanks to this event that Paul was able to express what was to become the fundamental principle and goal of all true Christian initiation from that time onwards: 'Not I, but Christ in me.' These words acquire particular significance in modern initiation, being, as they are, words that arise in our time from the *fully developed human 'I'*, which in free sacrifice receives the Christ-impulse into itself. Rudolf Steiner refers repeatedly to these words as the fundamental principle of the path of initiation in the Age of Michael. For Michael, who has the closest, most intimate relation to the human 'I' (see pages 36–37), is also the very Spirit who wishes to awaken man to a conscious realization of 'Not I, but Christ in me'.

This is also the reason why Rudolf Steiner later returned again and again to this Mystery-formula, pointing to it as though to the true foundation of the modern spiritual path: 'The path that is offered to the human being in order that he may make more and more real the words, "Not I, but Christ in me" . . .'[53] In a lecture in Oslo on 20 May 1923, he says: 'With the aid of that power that has descended from Heaven to Earth through the Mystery of Golgotha, it is open for us since that Mystery of Golgotha to acquire from the spiritual world what we may look on as the words of Christ. We can make real the words of Paul, "Not I, but Christ in me"—indeed, Christ in me as a human being when as human beings we speak of the spiritual worlds.'[54]

In an occult sense this means that whoever realizes these Pauline words in himself sacrifices his earthly 'I' to the Christ. Henceforth it is not his own 'I' that speaks through his physical sheath, but the Christ Himself.* And if we now turn again to Rudolf Steiner's life, we recognize that in that moment at the end of his great Sun period where he underwent consciously the experience of Paul before Damascus and thus realized the words 'Not I, but Christ in me'—in that moment he made a great spiritual sacrifice: as an initiate he sacrificed his earthly 'I' to the Being of Christ. *We have in this deed the first stage of Rudolf Steiner's great path of sacrifice.*

This most significant event in his spiritual development concludes the great Sun period. The most profound mystery of the Sun-Logos now reveals itself to Rudolf Steiner. He perceives directly the Logos in the Being of Christ.

Henceforth the Christ Himself acts through the 'I' of Rudolf Steiner. This is expressed in the fact that the whole of his further life becomes the highest form of service to the Being of Christ; and the fundamental principle of this service is expressed in the profound Mystery-words of Christ, 'I am the Way, the Truth and the Life.'

'I am the Way'—these words indicate that true service to Christ at this

---

* See Afterword, pp. 353–58.

stage is the *imitation* of Him.[55] This is the only way in which His Being can be truly and worthily served. Just as He served humanity on Earth even to death on the Cross, so must the human being, having reached this stage of perception, serve Him.

'I am the Truth'—this service can only result today from a true awareness and knowledge of the full cosmic truth of Christ. It is only possible to serve Christ truly through an active *knowledge* of Him; in other words, in full consciousness and absolute freedom. For it is the knowledge of the full truth in Christ that makes man free. 'Know ye the truth which makes you free,' says Christ.

And lastly, the words 'I am the Life' point to the fact that service of this kind must extend right into the life of the Christian-Rosicrucian initiate; this means that from this time onwards all events in his life become more and more the microcosmic reflection of the great macrocosmic events of the life of Christ Jesus on Earth, the archetypal example for every true Christian initiate's path of life. For the most fundamental and important thing that Christ brought to the Earth was not His teaching but His own Divine Person, His life itself for three years in the three bodily sheaths of Jesus of Nazareth, through which all the fullness of macrocosmic life in our cosmos was carried directly into the sphere of the Earth. Concerning the relation of the cosmic forces to the life of Christ Jesus on the Earth, Rudolf Steiner says: 'The Christ was always under the influence of the whole cosmos ... the whole spirit of the cosmos was active in Christ Jesus ... That Being who walked upon the Earth indeed looked like any other man, but the forces that were active in this Being were cosmic forces stemming from Sun and stars, and they directed the body. And what the Christ did was done in accordance with the entire All-Being of the world with which the Earth is connected. Seen in this light the life of Christ Jesus appears as the earthly expression of a particular relation of the cosmos to the forces in man. The truth is that the whole cosmos speaks out in the Christ.'[56]

But what then is the life of Christ in this light? 'From what did the Earth existence of the Christ originate?' Rudolf Steiner asks (in the third lecture of the cycle *The Fifth Gospel*). And he answers: 'It originated from the deepest suffering, from a suffering that surpasses all human imagination of what suffering can be.'[57] The life on Earth of Christ Jesus is founded on endless suffering, on endless *sacrifice*—the sacrifice of a god who became man for the salvation of mankind, for the fulfilment of the meaning of all Earth evolution, of a god who made the greatest of all imaginable sacrifices from the loftiest and purest principle of *freedom*. Thus we must look on the appearance of Christ as a free deed directed to our humanity.

This principle of sacrifice, made in full consciousness and freedom in the name of everything lofty and true, is the basic principle of Christian initiation. In the form that is in harmony with the Spirit of our time this principle also lies today at the basis of Christian-Rosicrucian initiation, for here in its higher stages real service to Christ is also true imitation of Him.

Just as Christ Jesus sacrificed His cosmic existence for the sake of mankind and became man, so too at a certain stage on his spiritual path must the modern Christian-Rosicrucian initiate sacrifice his isolated Earth existence, the forces of his sheaths, to the great macrocosmic Being, the Being of Christ, the Being of the cosmos.

From now on sacrifice is the guiding principle in the life of the initiate. All the spiritual forces in his bodily sheaths, won by dint of pure individual effort, will be sacrificed to the higher forces in the name of the further development of mankind. Our task now will be to follow Rudolf Steiner on the great path of sacrificial service during the period of his open activity among humanity.

3. The Path of the Teacher of Humanity

At the turn of two centuries, when a deep crisis hangs over the evolution of the Earth, Rudolf Steiner appears for the first time before the world as a Teacher of humanity. He begins to realize his fundamental task of bringing what in 1899, and at the end of the 'dark age' of Kali Yuga, had now to come to the Earth as spiritual revelation, and which alone could give human development the vital forces needed for the new ascent to the spirit. 'It seemed to me that the turn of the century must bring new spiritual light to humanity.'[1] With these words Rudolf Steiner begins the description of the next chapter of his life.

Under the sign of Mars, the sphere of the living word, Rudolf Steiner was to bring new spiritual wisdom to the evolution of the Earth. He had reached the period of the Spirit Self (42–49 years of age), and its forces shine over him from now on like the rays of a spiritual sun, filling his words with a fiery power in which the ripened fruits of Christian-Rosicrucian initiation are revealed before the world.

This period (up to 1910) is often seen as the first phase in the development of Anthroposophy.[2] The year 1902 is considered to be its beginning, when Rudolf Steiner joined the Theosophical Society. At that time, as he later says, it was only there that he was able to find an audience sufficiently prepared by earlier work that occult themes could be openly spoken about before them.[3] But joining the Theosophical Society had also a more profound meaning.

'The Theosophical Society was founded in 1875 in New York by H.P. Blavatsky and H.S. Olcott. This inauguration had a distinctly western character.'[4] But shortly after its founding the Society came under the influence of certain eastern-Tibetan brotherhoods and in consequence gradually took on an openly eastern orientation. In contrast to this, right from the outset Rudolf Steiner presented the principle of a *new* occultism. He accepted the invitation to head the German Section of the Theosophical Society, and in so doing gave this traditional, orientally-tinged occultism the possibility of receiving something new, but in such a way as to preserve the continuity of occult tradition in the modern world. This is extremely significant for the development of the spiritual life of all humanity: 'Genuine initiators had stood by its [the Theosophical Society's] cradle and, even though later events brought a certain imperfection, it was therefore a *preliminary* instrument for contemporary spiritual life.'[5] Thus

Rudolf Steiner hoped that the forces of the new revelation that flowed through him into the Theosophical Society would be able gradually so to transform it as to place it anew at the service of world interests shared by all humanity. The Society had moved away from these interests even during H.P. Blavatsky's time by adopting an eastern and consequently an openly non-Christian colouring. 'At the time I accepted the invitation to enter the Society it was the only institution that could be taken seriously in its search for spiritual life. Had the intention and integrity of the Society remained as it was then, my friends and I need never have withdrawn. An Anthroposophical Society could have been formed officially as a special section of the Theosophical Society.'[6,7]

The most important point here, as mentioned above, is that from the beginning Rudolf Steiner joined the Theosophical Society as an initiate of a completely new kind, as one representing modern western Christian-Rosicrucian occultism, but above all as a herald of Christian esoteric wisdom. 'After the first ice had been broken in this way [by the publishing of eastern occult teachings in the works of H.P. Blavatsky] the time had also come when one could speak of things arising from the founts of western occultism...'[8] whose characteristic was its universal-human orientation. Rudolf Steiner therefore based his work from the outset on completely objective spiritual knowledge, the content of which was of universal human interest and addressed as equally to the eastern soul as to the western. He thereby realized the principle of Christian-Rosicrucian esotericism which in accordance with the spirit of the age is the bearer of the Christ-impulse, and speaks to *all* human beings, just as one Sun shines upon all the regions of the Earth. 'It came to me of itself that we in Central Europe are called upon to free Theosophy from all special interests, to the point where it can truly stand before us in Central Europe as a goddess, as something completely and absolutely freed from all human affairs but which nevertheless has as much to do with the human being living in this part of the Earth as with one living in any other part. And so must it always be.'[9]

Right from the start in the newly-founded German Section of the Theosophical Society Rudolf Steiner gave numerous lectures and lecture-cycles, in which to stunned audiences he opened up the grandeur and profundity of Christian-Rosicrucian esotericism, including also all the most significant truths of eastern wisdom, but now clarified and imbued with new life by the fundamental impulse of all Earth evolution—by the impulse of Christ. From the very beginning Christ is the central point of everything: 'Thus in the anthroposophical world-outlook, in the whole tableau of reincarnation, of the being of man, of the view of the cosmos and so forth, the Being of Christ occupies a central position. And anyone who considers this anthroposophical perception of the world in the right way must say: "I can look at everything, but I can only understand it when for me the whole picture is directed to the great central flame, to the Christ." In many different ways I have depicted the teaching of reincarnation, of the human races, of the evolution of the planets and so on, but I have painted here one aspect of the Being of Christ, and light is thereby shed on everything else. It is a picture with a central figure, and everything else circles around that, and I can understand the significance and expression of the outer figures only when I understand the central one.'[10] And concerning the relationship of western wisdom to eastern wisdom he says: 'There is no wisdom of the East that has not flowed into the occultism of the West; and in the Rosicrucian teachings and research you will find in its entirety everything that the great wise men of the East have ever nurtured. Nothing, absolutely nothing that one can learn from eastern wisdom is lacking in the wisdom of the West. But there is this difference, and only this: that the wisdom of the West must gather together all eastern teaching, all eastern wisdom, all eastern research and, without losing one iota of it, must illumine it with the Light that was lit for all humankind by the Christ-impulse.'[11]

Soon after becoming active in the Theosophical Society, Rudolf Steiner writes his basic spiritual-scientific works. In *Theosophy* (1904) he presents the occult membering of man's being and also the path of human destiny after death. For the first time in the western world he also gives a foundation for the teaching of reincarnation as a part of Christian esotericism. In the book that followed, *Knowledge of the Higher Worlds: How is it Achieved?* (1904–08), he sets down the new, modern western path of initiation. And he then binds together all the immeasurable wealth of spiritual knowledge contained in his books, articles and lectures of that time—representing as it does an all-embracing picture of world evolution—into what can be called an encyclopaedia of new Christian occultism, namely *Occult Science—an Outline* (1909). This was all presented in the most rigorous scientific-intellectual form, so that anyone with an open soul and wishing to heed the voice of world-wisdom that speaks through every line and every word can *understand* it. It was during this period that he laid the foundation for a true *science* of the Spirit.

However, the new spiritual impulse that came through Rudolf Steiner, the unusual objectivity, scrupulous accuracy and the wealth of his spiritual research was in no way suited to the leaders of the Theosophical Society at that time, for more and more from 1906 onwards the Society became merely a tool in the hands of those Eastern-Tibetan occult brotherhoods, about whose intentions Rudolf Steiner spoke with such clarity in the third part of the *Notes of Barr* and in many lectures during 1915. For those intent upon following their own special interests Rudolf Steiner, with his uncompromising deduction to the one universal human truth, gradually became an insuperable obstruction. In consequence of this, in January 1913 he was finally excluded from the Theosophical Society. It is particularly important to note that he did not leave of his own accord but was *expelled*.[12] Herein lies the deep tragedy of the Theosophical Society; for in being unable to accept and take up the new spiritual revelation it turned away from its own future and thereby later fell to forces other than those from which it had originally sprung. In expelling Rudolf Steiner, the Theosophical Society—as the bearer of an old traditional occultism—now deprived itself of the last possibility of uniting with the forces that rightfully guide the evolution of humankind. One can see in this circumstance a real tragedy in the spiritual life of all humanity—and one that has had a far-reaching influence on the consequent fate of Europe.[13]

With this we can dispel the reproaches of those who later said that Rudolf Steiner should not have connected the destiny of the movement founded by him with such a 'doubtful' association as the Theosophical Society later appeared to many to be. He himself said that this had been his karma. He had to bring to the traditional occultism which was already strongly in the grasp of forces perniciously opposed to rightful evolution a last possibility of winning through to the light.

Besides his almost immeasurable energy directed during this time to the introduction and foundation of a new science of the spirit, Rudolf Steiner also devoted much effort from the beginning to purely esoteric work. In many cities in Germany and in neighbouring countries there arise new circles of individuals inwardly engaged with the questions of the new spiritual culture, and who wish to tread the path of a pupil of the spirit. Rudolf Steiner gives the most important lectures of that time to these groups, and around 1905 begins giving in them the so-called 'Esoteric Lessons' which give the advanced pupil the possibility of coming into direct contact with the sources of the new revelation.

A little later another aspect of esoteric work is added to this in the form of symbolic ritual ceremony, mentioned in Chapter 36 of his auto-biography. He imprinted this with the results of his own purely anthroposophical researches, while nevertheless attaching himself to the outer forms of an occult society of Freemason orientation that offered him its certificate of the highest grade, together with the right to conduct independent symbolic-ritual ceremonies. In accepting the certificate Rudolf Steiner had wanted to give another stream of traditional esotericism—this time one of western orientation—the possibility of finding its way to the new spiritual wisdom that was to come to humanity in the last third of the nineteenth century: 'Therefore I was in favour of linking, whenever possible, the new with what existed historically.'[14] Later misunderstandings and attacks on Rudolf Steiner showed, however, the tragic inability of western occultism also to find a healthy relationship to the new spiritual revelation.

Despite these difficulties, in the time up to the First World War the work in the individual groups became more concentrated and gradually constituted a complete, *practical* system for a western Mystery-path, and the pupils who had been brought together by this esoteric work came to form in the course of time an Esoteric School.

This, in broad outline, was the first period of Rudolf Steiner's work as a Teacher of humanity. But what was his own development during this time? In the previous chapter we spoke of his central experience in the sphere of Intuition, which occurred at the turn of the century as the culmination of the whole of his preceding spiritual path.

But there was something else connected with this experience. Rudolf Steiner frequently describes in his lectures how the world of Intuition, whose summits he had attained at this time, reaches only to the cosmic border that separates Upper Devachan from the next world-sphere, the Buddhi plane or 'World of Providence'. In a lecture in Berlin on 25 October 1909, he says: '... between death and rebirth the human being ascends to Upper Devachan, or World of Reason. From there he gazes into higher worlds other than the one in which he finds himself, and sees those Beings higher than himself working in these higher worlds.'[15] And concerning these 'Beings' he says: 'Whereas the human being exists in the worlds from the physical plane to the Devachanic plane, it is usual for a Bodhisattva-being to ascend as far as the Buddhi plane, which we in Europe call the World of Providence, or Foresight.'[16]

From this and many similar indications in different lectures it is clear that in being able to follow the path of those who have died, up to the border of the sphere of Intuition (Upper Devachan), the initiate can therefore also gaze from there into still higher spheres. If we consider again Rudolf Steiner's spiritual path, mentioned above, we may infer that that majestic image described by him in his lecture in Berlin on 25 October 1909—an image of the figure of Christ as a sun shining upon the twelve Bodhisattvas that surround Him in the World of Foresight—first arose before his spiritual vision in the time between 1899 and 1901. Around the turn of the century and up to his encounter with the Christ he ascended into the sphere of Intuition, up to the border between the plane of Upper Devachan and the Buddhi plane. From now on he was able, as an initiate, to achieve what at times is also possible for non-initiates after death, namely, he could penetrate from there to a view of the Buddhi plane. This purely spiritual contemplation opened up to him the deeper essence of the eastern teachings about Buddha and the Bodhisattvas and their relation to Christ Jesus, and this knowledge prompted him in the winter of 1901–02, that is *before* he joined the Theosophical Society, to give a cycle of lectures to the literary society of *Die Kommenden* called *From Buddha to Christ.* He tried in this cycle to show 'what a stupendous step forward is signified in the Mystery of Golgotha as seen against the Buddha-event, and how in striving towards the Christ-event the development of humanity comes to its culmination.'[17] He gives another lecture cycle parallel to this in the Theosophical Library of Count Brockdorff in Berlin, which was later reshaped into his book *Christianity as Mystical Fact* and in which a greater part of the chapter 'Egyptian Mystery Wisdom' is devoted to the relation of Christ and the Buddha.[18]

Here it is necessary briefly to reconsider how Rudolf Steiner characterizes the nature of these lofty beings who in the East are called Bodhisattvas. We will limit ourselves in this question—which is one of the most complex in spiritual science and one touched upon by Rudolf Steiner from the most diverse sides—to that aspect which helps us to understand Rudolf Steiner's inner path of development.

A Bodhisattva is a being of a cosmic order who has already surpassed the boundary of actual human development. He is already approaching an evolution comparable to that of the Angel stage and finds himself in a stream of development in which his consciousness extends into the Buddhi-sphere. In other words, the Bodhisattva has already attained a stage of development that, in the natural course of events, will only be attained by the rest of humanity on Jupiter. This finds expression in the fact that the Bodhisattva, consciously from his 'I' and *together* with a Being of the Hierarchy of the Angeloi, is already working on the transforming of his astral body into Spirit Self.[19] In this work he is *inspired* by a Being of the Hierarchy of the Archangeloi.[20] When this work nears its completion the Bodhisattva descends to Earth for a *complete* human incarnation, that is, he goes through the stage that Rudolf Steiner calls the stage of the 'human Buddha'.[21,22] During this last incarnation the Bodhisattva works together with a Being of the Hierarchy of the Angeloi and finally reaches the stage of Spirit Self (the enlightenment under the Bodhi tree). He thereby completes the following cycle of world evolution and no longer needs to incarnate on Earth. The Being of the Hierarchy of Angeloi now ceases to work on his astral body,[23] which has become the glowing body of the Spirit Self (Nirmanakaya).[24] The further development of the Buddha now takes on a form where, through his Spirit Self as the 'I'-principle, he works together with an Archangelos[25] on his etheric body and gradually transforms this into Life Spirit. In consequence his consciousness extends into the sphere of Nirvana, a development which the rest of humanity will only attain on Venus. In this work he is inspired by still higher Beings than the Archangeloi.

On the basis of these communications, we can approach one of the most significant mysteries of Rudolf Steiner's life. Adolf Arenson first indicated this in a lecture given by him on the fifth anniversary of Rudolf Steiner's death.[26] He spoke there of how, from a definite moment onwards, the being of the new Bodhisattva who had succeeded to the place of the Buddha of the Sakya line on the fulfilment of the Buddha's mission on Earth, gradually began to work through Rudolf Steiner. This is the Bodhisattva who, a hundred years before the beginning of Christianity but preparing the way for it, worked through Jeschu ben Pandira, and who in three thousand years' time will become the new Buddha, the Maitreya Buddha: 'A bringer of Good through the Word, through the Logos ... one who will place everything he has at the service of the Christ-impulse.'[27]

Thus we can say that at the turn of two centuries (two thousand years after the life on Earth of Jeshu ben Pandira) Rudolf Steiner experienced in an all-embracing spiritual perception the complete circle of the Twelve Bodhisattvas in the Buddhi-sphere. This experience gave him a deep understanding of the special nature of the mission of the guiding Bodhisattva of our times, the future Maitreya Buddha through whom, however, the full community of the Twelve always works, forming a living whole in which each individual Bodhisattva represents a vital and irreplaceable part.

As mentioned earlier, the Bodhisattva works first and foremost with the Spirit Self—the transformed and purified astral body. Thus we can assume that *the penetration of Rudolf Steiner's astral body* by the new Bodhisattva began around 1902–03 as he reached his seventh seven-year span, which has a particular relation to the principle of Spirit Self. This is a further confirmation of Rudolf Steiner's words that the Bodhisattva was already incarnated and had been born at the *beginning* of the twentieth century.

If we recognize that Rudolf Steiner's connection with the new Bodhisattva is a real occult fact, this can throw a completely new light on certain parts of his autobiography. At the end of Chapter 32 he writes: 'Certainly at that time I stood, fully conscious, within the spiritual world, but I experienced Imaginations, Inspirations and Intuitions about the year 1902, and in regard to many things also in the following years. These only gradually amalgamated and became the content of my public writings.' And at the beginning of Chapter 33 he returns to this again, as though wishing particularly strongly to focus the reader's attention on these years: 'The years from 1901 to about 1907 or 1908 were for me a time when with all the *powers of soul* I experienced the facts and *beings* that *came towards me* in the world of spirit.' If we bear in mind that the 'powers of soul' are connected primarily with the astral body, and if we take quite literally the words 'the beings that came towards me in the world of the spirit', then the overall picture becomes much clearer for us. Even the question of why the word 'beings' is used in the plural is answered by Rudolf Steiner in his lectures. For it is the twelvefold circle of Bodhisattvas in its entirety that works *through* the one Bodhisattva who from this time on directly inspires Rudolf Steiner. He describes it thus: 'One can speak of an incarnation of a Bodhisattva occurring again and again, but one must realize that the Bodhisattva behind all the individuals into whom he incarnates represents a part of that Being who is the personified All-Wisdom of *our* world.'[28] And a little earlier in the lecture he clarifies what the word 'Being' here means: 'One designates this Being with an eastern expression—as the collective entirety of the Bodhisattvas. The Christian outlook would call it the Holy Spirit.' From this we see that through the one Bodhisattva who inspired Rudolf Steiner there worked in him also the whole collective Lodge of the Twelve Bodhisattvas, who all together form the body of the Holy Spirit. In the sixth lecture in *The Gospel of St Luke* he says: 'And in the idiom of the Near-Eastern languages one would have said of such a being as a Bodhisattva incarnated on Earth that he was filled with the Holy Spirit.' Thus one can say that from this time onward, through the Bodhisattva, Rudolf Steiner was directly inspired by the Holy Spirit, which on the Buddhi plane is manifest as a twelvefold Being.[29]

There is, however, another aspect to this. In the lecture already quoted, of 22 March 1909 in Berlin, and in other lectures also, Rudolf Steiner speaks very decisively of how the most important aim of spiritual science is to awaken an understanding of the greatest event in the development of the Earth, the Mystery of Golgotha. And he adds: 'And those who have comprehended that the progress of humanity is dependent upon an *understanding* of the great events of Golgotha are those who, as the Masters of Wisdom and of the Harmony of Sensations and Feelings, are united in the great guiding Lodge of humanity. And just as tongues of fire once came down and hovered like a living world-symbol over those who were gathered together, so too the Light of what Christ Himself called the Holy Spirit holds sway over the Lodge of the Twelve. The Thirteenth is their leader and guide. The Holy Spirit is the great Teacher of those whom we call the Masters of Wisdom and of the Harmony of Sensations and Feelings. It is through them that his voice and his wisdom flow to humanity on the Earth in one stream or another. The treasures of wisdom that are gathered together in spiritual science so as to understand the world and the spiritual beings within it flow through the Holy Spirit into the Lodge of the Twelve, and this is what will eventually bring mankind to a fully conscious and free understanding of Christ and the events of Golgotha.'[30] And we know from other lectures by Rudolf Steiner[31] that this picture of the Twelve guided by the Thirteenth through the Holy Spirit refers to the Lodge of the Bodhisattvas in the Buddhi-sphere. Thus those whom Rudolf Steiner calls the 'Masters of Wisdom and of the Harmony of Sensations and Feelings', and who are united in the great Lodge that guides humanity, are none other than the community of Bodhisattvas.[32]

Even the name 'Masters of Wisdom and of the Harmony of Sensations and Feelings' expresses this, for a true 'harmony of sensations and feelings'—which is connected first and foremost with the astral body—is only possible when the astral body has been transformed into the Spirit Self, as is the case with the Bodhisattvas (see page 69). An astral body transformed in this way then becomes 'Holy Sophia'[33]—becomes, that is, a vessel for the wisdom of the Holy Spirit who leads the Twelve and has his wellspring in the Thirteenth.

This throws new light on the content of a lecture given in Berlin on 26 December 1909: 'What we do in the anthroposophical movement has not arisen arbitrarily; it has not just arisen from some programme set up by this or that person. In the end, all spiritual life has its origin in those sources that we look for in the individualities whom we call the "Masters of Wisdom and of the Harmony of Sensations and Feelings". And in them, if we look in the right way, we find the impulses for how we are to act from epoch to epoch, from age to age. In recent times a great impulse has come to us from the spiritual world. And may we in our circle today point to this important impulse, to an indication, so to speak, which in the course of the last few years has flowed to us in accordance with a measure *taken by the spiritual world on the astral plane.* And it is in response to this impulse that our anthroposophical movement has developed here in Central Europe. We can clothe this impulse approximately in human words in the following way: "Behold what is happening in the world; the words of the Gospels are misunderstood more and more . . ." '[34] Rudolf Steiner goes on to speak of a new understanding of Christ, of a new understanding of the Mystery of Golgotha in the anthroposophical movement.

And in the notes of the esoteric lesson of 14 November 1906 in Berlin, Rudolf Steiner says expressly: 'The great Masters of Wisdom and of the Harmony of Sensations and Feelings are guiding us in our inner struggle for knowledge'[35]—and we can bear in mind that the 'us' here refers primarily to Rudolf Steiner himself. In addition to this, the words above indicate that through the future Maitreya Buddha the *whole* circle of Bodhisattvas, the great Lodge of the Masters of Wisdom and of the Harmony of Sensations and Feelings, was working through Rudolf Steiner. Because of this he was able in the time that followed to talk of twelve different perceptions of the world, of twelve ways of looking at every phenomenon, and so on.

In connection with what has been said it must be emphasized that, in addition to the definition given here of the 'Masters of Wisdom and of the Harmony of Feelings' as the community of Bodhisattvas in the sphere of Providence, other great Teachers of humanity can also be called 'Masters of Wisdom and of the Harmony of Feelings'. For they too are inspired from this sphere and have a direct connection to it. The following words of Rudolf Steiner make this clear: 'We are speaking of incarnations of Bodhisattvas when we pronounce the names of Scythianos, Zarathustra and the Buddha.'[36]

In this sense it can be said of all these sublime Teachers that they were sent, or overshone, by the Holy Spirit. To their number there also belongs Manes, who in the fourth century AD led the spiritual community in which the three Teachers referred to above participated. In this community it was decided to bring the wisdom from the sphere of the Bodhisattvas to mankind—a decision which was subsequently to come to fulfilment primarily through the Rosicrucian stream. Rudolf Steiner says in this connection: 'At that time the plan was formulated in this community as to how all the wisdom of the Bodhisattvas of the post-Atlantean age can flow ever more strongly into the future of humanity. And this plan for the future cultural evolution of the Earth was preserved and then transmitted to those European Mysteries known as the Mysteries of the Rose Cross. The individualities of Scythianos, Buddha and Zarathustra were continually associated with these Mysteries. They were the Teachers in the schools of the Rose Cross—Teachers who sent their wisdom as gifts to the Earth because it was through this wisdom that the Christ was to be understood in His true essence.' And he goes on: 'Thus the European initiate [and today this means primarily Rudolf Steiner himself] looked constantly towards the Turning-point of Time, contemplating the figures of the great Teachers. He knew that through Zaratas, the Buddha and Scythianos there streamed into the culture of the future that same wisdom that derived from the Bodhisattvas and is to serve as a means of comprehending the worthiest object of all understanding—the Christ . . .' Finally, Christian Rosenkreutz, the founder and leader of the Rosicrucian stream in the world—a stream through which the wisdom of the Bodhisattvas is to flow continually into the whole of European civilization—also belongs to this assembly.[37]

It just remains at the end of this theme to draw attention to the tenth lecture in the cycle *The Gospel of St Matthew*, where in a way that allows no other explanation Rudolf Steiner speaks of how the new Bodhisattva works through him, inspiring him. One has only to replace the 'we' with 'I': 'And if Essene teaching is to be renewed in our days, if we are resolved to shape our lives in accordance with the living spirit of a new Bodhisattva, not with the spirit of a tradition concerning a Bodhisattva of the past, then we must make ourselves receptive to the inspiration of the Bodhisattva who will subsequently become the Maitreya Buddha. And this Bodhisattva will inspire us by drawing attention to the near approach of the time when in a new raimant, in an *etheric* body, Christ will bring life and blessings to those who unfold the new faculties through a new Essene wisdom. We shall speak entirely in the sense of the inspiring Bodhisattva who is to become the Maitreya Buddha ... With the knowledge gained from the inspiration of the Bodhisattva himself we declare what form the future manifestation of Christ will take.'[38]

As mentioned earlier, the forces of the Bodhisattva began to penetrate into the astral body of Rudolf Steiner around 1902–03. This process continued until around the middle of this period of his life, until 1906–07. In 1906 he gives a cycle of lectures in Paris. In his autobiography he says about these: 'I look back to the time that led to the course of lectures in Paris as a period when an inner process reached a certain development... In this course of lectures I spoke of a spiritual aspect of man's being which is *fundamental*. I felt this knowledge had gone through a sufficient process of "maturing" to be imparted.'[39] And he then goes on to describe more exactly what is actually meant by this process of 'maturation' of spiritual knowledge.

During this year Rudolf Steiner told a group of Russians who took part in the Paris cycle of his willingness to travel to Russia. Marie Steiner recalls: 'We agreed on a cycle of lectures in 1906 at a property near Kaluga.'[40] One can see this decision to travel to Russia as symptomatic. In the middle of the period of his life that comes under the sign and rulership of the Spirit Self, Rudolf Steiner wishes to visit the land where in the sixth cultural epoch the principle of the Spirit Self is to be realized for the first time in human development as an historical-social fact.[41]

In the middle of the following year the Theosophical Congress is held in Munich. It is here that the first foundations of anthroposophical art are laid, and here that Rudolf Steiner gives his stupendous lecture cycle *The Theosophy of the Rosicrucian*. He talks about the Paris cycle of 1906 at the end of Chapter 37 of his autobiography, and about the 1907 Munich Congress in the middle of Chapter 38. It follows therefore that it is to the time lying between these two events to which the deeply significant words refer, with which he opens Chapter 38 of his autobiography: 'In what follows it will be difficult to separate this account of my life from the history of the anthroposophical movement.'

Henceforth Rudolf Steiner's own *personal* destiny can no longer be separated from the anthroposophical movement, from his spiritual mission. This means that he sacrificed completely his own personal life and all the fruits of his individual development to that stream of spirituality which

74

flows through him from the lofty being we have called a Bodhisattva.[42] But the personal life is rooted in the astral body, for it is this that is the bearer of all personal impulses. Knowing this, we can begin to sense acutely the sacrifice that lies behind the simple words with which Rudolf Steiner opens the *last* chapter of his autobiography.

As an initiate, Rudolf Steiner sacrificed his earthly astral body by placing it at the service of the lofty spiritual being of the Bodhisattva, and—in a wider sense—of the whole circle of the Master individualities who are connected with the high sphere of the Holy Spirit who, from now onwards, spoke through him. This deed marks the *second* stage of Rudolf Steiner's great path of sacrifice. This occurred between 1906 and 1907, that is, around the middle of his seventh seven-year period, which comes under the sign of the forces of the Spirit Self. And this event brings his autobiography, which translated from German is called *The Course of My Life*, to its logical conclusion, for Rudolf Steiner can no longer apply the word 'my' only to himself as an individual on Earth, but henceforth must apply it also to the cosmic being working through him.[43]

From this time onwards (1907) the being of the Bodhisattva embraces Rudolf Steiner's astral body to an ever greater degree. This process continues for three years, up to the beginning of the next seven-year span. And this is the time when, under the influence of the Bodhisattva-impulse working in him, he gives his particularly profound Christological lecture cycles, *The Gospel of St John* (Hamburg, 12 lectures) and *The Apocalypse* (Nuremberg, 12 lectures). There then follows the lecture in Berlin where he speaks in detail of the 'Masters of Wisdom and of the Harmony of Sensations and Feelings', namely, *The Mystery of Christmas* (22 December 1908); and then *The Deed of Christ and the Opposing Spiritual Powers* (22 March 1909), *The Spiritual Hierarchies and Their Reflection in the Physical World* (Düsseldorf, 10 lectures), *The Gospel of St John and Its Relation to the Other Gospels* (Cassel, 14 lectures); and finally *The Gospel of St Luke* (Basle, 10 lectures), given by him in the year of Christ's coming in etheric form into the sphere of humanity.[44] It was also in this cycle that Rudolf Steiner revealed for the first time the secret of the two Jesus children, and thus also the beginning of the Fifth Gospel.[45]

It becomes quite conceivable that it was the inspiration of the Bodhisattva that led Rudolf Steiner to give his most profound Christological lecture cycles, especially if we remember the following words: 'While present-day humanity cannot turn directly to the Bodhisattvas in order to gaze on the Christ with the spiritual eyes of the Bodhisattvas, it is obliged to go to school again to these Bodhisattvas in order to learn that which can finally make the Christ comprehensible.'[46]

Around 1910 the permeation of Rudolf Steiner's astral body by the Bodhisattva is nearing its completion. In his lecture Adolf Arenson says about this: 'When the Bodhisattva had penetrated a certain human soul *as far as the etheric body*, that human being was then ready to come openly before humanity with his mission.'[47] Arenson is indicating here the fact that the Archangel inspiring the Bodhisattva (see page 69) no longer influences only the human astral body, as was the case in earlier times, but also the etheric body. And Arenson continues: 'And then he (the Bodhisattva) is here ... and anyone who knows something of the mission of the Bodhisattva can recognize him.'

But what is the fundamental mission of this Bodhisattva in our time? 'He, who since then [since, that is, the beginning of his mission as a Bodhisattva in a human soul] has been incarnated more or less once every hundred years, is also incarnated today and will be the actual herald of the Christ in His etheric raiment.'[48]

It is in preparation for this great event of the twentieth century that Anthroposophy exists in the world. 'And thus we come to understand Anthroposophy in a completely different way. We become aware that it is something which places an enormous responsibility on us, for it is a preparation for the absolutely real occurrence of the Second Coming of Christ.'[49]

In February 1910 Rudolf Steiner reaches the age of 49 (seven times seven). He thus enters the span of life that comes under the sign of Life Spirit, the transformed etheric body, and in January of the same year speaks for the first time of the Etheric Christ, the most important spiritual event of the twentieth century. From that moment onwards this theme sounds out like a mighty bell amidst the peoples of Europe, calling for wakefulness and consciousness, and renewing the ancient words of John the Baptist: 'Change your thinking, for the Kingdom of Heaven is at hand.'

The decisiveness and power of this revelation of the new Bodhisattva, which occurs in the main in 1910, is staggering (the lectures from this year concerning the Etheric Christ in themselves fill a whole volume), while inwardly Rudolf Steiner makes the transition from the sphere of influence of the Spirit Self to that of Life Spirit. Because of this we must pay particular attention to the way in which he characterizes the changes that occur in him during this year. In the last lecture of the cycle *The Manifestations of Karma*, given on 28 May 1910, he says: 'Thus we recognize human evolution as the working out of human karma and the karma of higher beings, and we understand here that the whole plan of evolution is connected with individual human karma. Let us assume that if in the year 1910 a superhuman individuality did this or that which was carried out on the physical plane by a human being, a contact has thus been established between them. The person is then interwoven into the karma of higher beings.[50] A correspondence has been set up through which a stream from higher worlds

76

brings something quite new into this human being's life, adding something to his karma which will influence his life in one direction or another. Thus human karma is fructified by the universal karma of the world.'[51]

In this and the following years (from 1909 to 1911), Rudolf Steiner imparts all the most important details concerning the essential nature and significance of the Bodhisattva: in 1909 come cycles 7 (GA 110), 9 (GA 113), 10 (GA 114), 17 (GA 116); in March 1910 a cycle of eleven lectures given in Vienna under the title *Macrocosm and Microcosm* in which he talks in detail of the significance for occult development of the World of Foresight (the Buddhi plane), of the world, that is, from which the Bodhisattva draws his impulses; in September comes cycle 15 (GA 123) where he alludes directly to the Bodhisattva that was inspiring him; in 1911 cycle 18 (GA 129), where he again speaks of the 'Masters of Wisdom and of the Harmony of Sensations and Feelings'; and lastly the cycle *From Jesus to Christ,* one of the most significant of the Christological cycles, in which he unveils for the first time the mystery of the Resurrection, related as it is in its particular way to the secret of the etheric body, and therefore also to the appearance of the Etheric Christ. For Christ who rose again after the Mystery of Golgotha in the physical body arises today in the twentieth century in the etheric body. In this cycle Rudolf Steiner also draws attention to the being of the new Bodhisattva who will become the Maitreya Buddha. And there are also many single lectures on this theme given during this time in different cities throughout Europe. (Those collected in GA 130 are particularly important.)

In 1910 Rudolf Steiner brings this new Mystery of the Etheric Christ to artistic expression in his first Mystery Drama, *The Portal of Initiation* (in Theodora's speech in the first scene). And 1911 sees the publication of his book *The Spiritual Guidance of Man* in which he speaks publicly for the first time of the secret of the two Jesus children and of the new appearance of Christ, a knowledge of which is vital for the further spiritual progress of mankind. It is as though Rudolf Steiner brings together in this book the sum of all the first period of his work as a Teacher of humanity.

In connection with the theme of the Second Coming, Rudolf Steiner's observations in the lecture of 27 September 1911 (GA 130) about the *etheric body* of Christian Rosenkreutz—which works continually from the spiritual world—should be called to mind: 'Everything that is proclaimed as Theosophy [Anthroposophy] is strengthened by the etheric body of Christian Rosenkreutz; and those who proclaim Theosophy [i.e. above all Rudolf Steiner himself] let themselves be overshone by this etheric body, which is able to work on them both when Christian Rosenkreutz is incarnated and also when he is not incarnated.' But what is this being overshone by the etheric body of Christian Rosenkreutz leading to in our time? Rudolf Steiner expresses this in the following words from the same lecture: 'The twentieth century has the task of enabling this etheric body [of Christian Rosenkreutz] to become so powerful that it can also work exoterically. Those who are overshone by it are granted an experience of the event that Paul experienced before Damascus.' If we bear in mind that the appearance of the Etheric Christ finds artistic expression in the first Mystery Play—which was given *through* Rudolf Steiner and is called a 'Rosicrucian' drama, we take a further step towards that spiritual reality which stands behind all these facts. Rudolf Steiner continues: 'The work of the Rosicrucians is what makes it possible for there to be an etheric appearance of Christ.' Thus we gain a sense of that harmony and concord with which the spiritual powers guiding humanity are working together for the good of the whole of earthly evolution.[52] For they must all unite in order together to prepare that greatest of spiritual events, the Second Coming of Christ, when their messenger for twentieth-century humanity, Rudolf Steiner, chosen by the cosmic rulership, made his influence felt.[53]

The eighth seven-year span, coming under the sign of the Life Spirit, is also the period in which the influences of Jupiter, the sphere of cosmic wisdom, are especially powerful. This period is particularly favourable also for clothing this wisdom in an artistic form. During this time a Life Spirit suffused through and through with Sun-forces shone over Rudolf Steiner's etheric body. From these etheric forces[54] he was able to give such powerful and all-embracing impulses in the area of art that his biographers often call this period the second phase in the development of Anthroposophy, or the period in which anthroposophical impulses penetrate into the realm of art.

Beginning in 1910 and continuing up to the middle of this period of his life, Rudolf Steiner writes his four Mystery Dramas (one drama each year), which depict in striking and impressive pictures the path of the modern soul to the spirit through initiation. In the spiritual battles fought by the personalities in the Dramas against the forces that impede evolution, against Lucifer and Ahriman, one can sense an echo of the battles fought by Rudolf Steiner himself against these enemies of human development, in the time that was preparing him for his mission.

The artistic and occult fabric of the Mystery Dramas has many different layers and is unusually complex. Rudolf Steiner said that had these Dramas been fully understood he would not have had to write any more books nor give any more lectures. This kind of work, like many other beginnings at the time, was interrupted by the outbreak of the First World War.

Hand in hand with the productions of the Mystery Dramas and thanks to the work of Marie von Sivers, at that time the basic elements were given of an art of recitation or speech-formation, and in 1912 the first impulse in the realm of eurythmy. And in the cycle *An Occult Physiology* (Prague, 1911) Rudolf Steiner was able, out of the forces of his own etheric body, to give indications for a new art of healing, thereby also laying the foundations for a future anthroposophical medicine.

However, this period opens up still further possibilities, for whereas the first seven years of his work as a Teacher of humanity had connected Rudolf Steiner through the Spirit Self with the Hierarchy of the Angeloi, so this second seven-year span connects him more particularly with the Hierarchy of the Archangeloi. This circumstance allows him to penetrate into the nature of the relation of these lofty Beings, the Folk Spirits, and especially of those who guide the European nations. Thus already in the middle of 1910 (that is, in the first year of his new seven-year period) he gives a cycle of lectures in Oslo, *The Mission of the Individual Folk Souls in Relation to Teutonic Mythology*, where he presents a great and majestic picture of the spiritual configuration of the European peoples, as it can be seen by the initiate in the archangelic sphere.

In this year Rudolf Steiner also gives his lecture cycle *Genesis: Secrets of the Bible Story of Creation*, with an occult commentary on the opening verses of Genesis which were written by Moses out of the forces of the *etheric body* he had inherited from Zarathustra.[55]

In 1912 he creates a circle of meditations, *The Calendar of the Soul*, whereby the pupil may gradually come to an experience of the Etheric Christ by following and experiencing the spiritual processes in nature. Each meditation of this little book has arisen out of the purest etheric forces and its value, in truth, is inestimable.

And finally, in September 1913, the building of the First Goetheanum begins, bringing with it new impulses for nearly all the fine arts: for architecture, sculpture and painting, all of which now received the possibility of harmonious union of their aesthetic and spiritual elements, thus anticipating the art of the future.

This then, in general outline, is Rudolf Steiner's outer activity but inwardly, during this period of his life, another mystery is concealed.

In September 1909 in Basle, Rudolf Steiner gave the lecture cycle *The Gospel of St Luke*,[56] in which he introduced the first facts from the Fifth Gospel and revealed for the first time—as mentioned earlier—the secret of the two Jesus children. But what was really new in this in comparison with what he had published earlier? In the previous cycles *The Gospel of St John* and *The Gospel of St John and Its Relation to the Other Gospels* he had already spoken of the fact that Zarathustra, the founder of the Ancient Persian culture, had later incarnated as Jesus of Nazareth, and had likewise already spoken about the relationship between Christ and Buddha, even if not in such detail as in *The Gospel of St John*. What is *fundamentally* new here is the

79

first reference to that heavenly being whom he calls the Nathan Jesus Soul. And he says of this Soul that it is the *etheric body* of primordial, archetypal Man, the etheric body of Adam in the paradisaical condition, which was held back before the Fall in the times of ancient Lemuria. This event is concealed in the words of the Bible that forbid humanity, which has succumbed to the temptation, to eat of the fruits of the Tree of Life (life being the fundamental quality of the etheric body). This is described in the Basle lecture cycle. 'The luciferic influence appeared [in the Lemurian epoch] and also extended its effect into the astral body of this original couple [Adam and Eve]. The physical body was then given over to reproduce itself through all the generations, but with the *etheric body* it was different; for here a small portion of this etheric body was held back and preserved by the Beings that guide humanity. This is expressed in the saying that man has eaten of the Tree of Knowledge of Good and Evil, that is, of that which came through the luciferic influence. But then it is said: now we must prevent him from eating of the Tree of Life! This means that a certain part of the forces of the etheric body were held back. They did not flow down into the successive generations. The primordial, archetypal forces of the Adam individuality were kept and preserved. These forces existed and were now led as a "provisional 'I' " to where the child was born to Joseph and Mary...'[57]

Thus we have the following spiritual constellation in connection with this cycle:

1   In 1909, the *Etheric* Christ appeared and moved in the spiritual surroundings of the Earth.[58]

2   In the second half of 1909, Rudolf Steiner prepares to enter his eighth seven-year period, the period which is overshone by the Life Spirit, the transformed *etheric* body.

3   On 18 September 1909 (almost exactly four years before the laying of the Foundation Stone of the First Goetheanum), Rudolf Steiner speaks in the above-mentioned cycle for the first time of certain facts in the Fifth Gospel, and also of the Nathan Jesus Soul, who is above all a bearer of the *unfallen* cosmic etheric forces of humanity.

In this way Rudolf Steiner inwardly connects the event of the Etheric Christ, the Fifth Gospel and the mystery of the Nathan Jesus Soul into a single unified whole.

But the above-mentioned constellation can be taken considerably further through what is said by Rudolf Steiner in the fifth lecture of the cycle *The Bhagavad Gita and the Epistles of Paul*: 'What appears to St Paul on the way to Damascus is the Christ, and the light in which Christ clothes Himself is Krishna,'[59] or in other words, is that heavenly Being that had later incarnated in the Nathan Jesus. And he continues: '... Christ had

80

taken Krishna as the vesture for his own soul, and *continued* to work through him...' This points to the profound connection between the 'bodily' resurrection of Christ and the Nathan Soul. But if the active presence of this Soul was of such significance at the 'bodily' Resurrection of the Christ, how could it be possible for it not to participate in the *etheric* Resurrection of Christ in the twentieth century, particularly when it is itself primarily of a heavenly-etheric nature? Is it really possible to accept that this heavenly Being accompanies the Christ on His earthly path even to the Mystery of Golgotha and that it subsequently manifests itself to Paul before Damascus as the Risen One's radiant raiment of light 'through which He continued to work', only to be separated from the one whom it had sacrificially served since Lemurian times at the decisive event of the fifth post-Atlantean epoch?[60]

We can enter into this thought still more deeply. In October 1913, exactly ten days after laying the Foundation Stone of the First Goetheanum, Rudolf Steiner gives his first and, one can say, his truly complete cycle of lectures on the Fifth Gospel (other single lectures on this subject only broaden or develop further what was laid as the basis of this cycle of five lectures, *The Fifth Gospel*). Here we are presented with the all-encompassing picture of the most fundamentally important events in the Gospels as they appear in our time in the Akasha Chronicle before the spiritual vision of the clairvoyant. This is also the *only* cycle in which Rudolf Steiner paints so *completely* a picture of almost *all* the events of Palestine. (In the lecture cycles on the Gospels such a complete picture is not given.) It is in this sense, then, that these five lectures approach most closely what could be called a kind of 'Anthroposophical Gospel'.* Rudolf Steiner emphasizes in these lectures that the most essential point of all the events described by him is the fact that, in the course of 33 years, they took place on the *physical* plane. And yet the various spiritual beings spoken of in *The Fifth Gospel* took part in these events in very different ways. Buddha, for example, participated most intensely during the first twelve years; Zarathustra during the first 30 years;[61] and, lastly, the lofty Being of the Christ in the last three years. But there is one being in this Gospel who goes through the *whole* 33-year period—and that is the Nathan Jesus Soul.

But there is still one question: why is it in connection with the Gospel of St Luke that Rudolf Steiner gives his first communications from the Fifth Gospel? Already in reading the Gospel itself we can see that St Luke knew of the secret of the Nathan Soul, for he lists its genealogy back to *Adam*, to God, and points thereby to its divine origin in Lemurian times and also to

---

* In the third lecture of this cycle, Rudolf Steiner says that the Fifth Gospel is the 'Anthroposophical Gospel'.

its connection with the primordial first father of humanity, with Adam. From where did St Luke receive such deep knowledge? He himself says: 'Even as they delivered these things unto us, who from the beginning were eyewitnesses and servants of the Word.'[62] These words of the evangelist pose a significant question: who were these 'eyewitnesses' of the Logos, of the Word, who served Him from the beginning? To find an answer we must first approach the question from another direction.

In the fourth lecture of the cycle *The Gospel of St Luke*, Rudolf Steiner speaks of St Paul's especially deep knowledge of the secret of the Nathan Soul and therefore also of the connection between the old and the new Adam. In the First Epistle to the Corinthians we read: 'Thus it is written. The first man became a living soul; the last Adam a life-giving spirit. But it is not the spiritual body which is first but the soul, and afterwards the spiritual.'[63]

In these words the secret of the Nathan Soul is revealed, for in contrast to the rest of humanity who had fallen to the forces of death and thus had to go through the processes of incarnation, it is 'the living Soul'; and the Christ, in truth, is the life-giving Spirit. This points on the one hand to the secret of the past in connection with the Nathan Soul ('first was the Soul-body'), and on the other hand to the secret of the future, to the Christ Himself ('and afterwards the Spirit-body'). This is expressed also on the physical plane in the fact that the Nathan Soul in the course of 33 years first had to prepare itself on the Earth to receive the Christ Being. St Paul was able to recognize directly these two secrets connected with the Nathan Soul only because Christ had appeared to him on the way to Damascus in the spiritual aura of Krishna. And St Paul then imparted this knowledge to St Luke: 'Paul knew this already; it lies in what is hidden behind his words. And Luke, who wrote the Gospel and was a pupil of St Paul, knew it also.'[64] It is also known through Church tradition that St Luke wrote his Gospel from the words of St Paul.[65] But this last point would appear to contradict St Luke's statement quoted above; for although he wrote his Gospel under the immediate guidance of the apostle Paul, his words nevertheless cannot be attributed to Paul, for Paul himself could not have belonged to the 'eyewitnesses and servers of the Word' who were there *'from the very beginning'*.

But who then was the true witness and server *from the very beginning*, that is, from that beginning referred to in the genealogy in the Gospel of St Luke? It could only have been the Nathan Soul! And a real acknowledgement of this fact can then shed a clear light on the secret of the origin of the third Gospel. It is the result of the direct influence of the Nathan Soul on St Luke through St Paul, so that Luke could reveal its profound secret in the genealogy.[66]

82

In the overall character of this Gospel it is also possible to have a distinct feeling for the effects of the inspiration of the Nathan Soul, for the whole mood of active love and comfort that this Gospel brings to mankind, the 'principle of love, of compassion, of simplicity and even to a certain degree, of childlikeness'[67] that fills every one of its sentences, and also its particularly strong influence on art—all this is the result of the influence of the Nathan Soul. And this whole picture is completed when we also consider the connection of this Gospel to Buddhism; for we know from Rudolf Steiner that in this Gospel Buddhism is brought to life again in its most pure and renewed form through the fact that the Nirmanakaya, the completely purified astral body of the Buddha, permeated the astral body of the Nathan Jesus-child until his twelfth year.

Thus to summarize we can say: in 1909 the Etheric Christ enters the development of the Earth and with Him the celestial-etheric being of the Nathan Soul. At the same time Rudolf Steiner approaches his eighth seven-year period, the period of the Life Spirit, when the human soul becomes particularly receptive to the etheric element. Therefore it is precisely now that he is able for the first time to reveal facts from the Fifth Gospel, but proceeding from the basis of *The Gospel of St Luke*, that is, from the Gospel written with the active aid of the Nathan Soul. And among the first revelations of the Fifth Gospel is the secret of this Soul's earthly and heavenly destinies. All this is indicative of the very real relation of the Fifth Gospel to the Nathan Soul. And who could better help the initiate to read the events in the Akashic Chronicle than the celestial being who, during the great 33 years of offering and service to the Sun-Being of Christ, itself experienced all the events of this Gospel. Thus we can say quite decisively that just as we on Earth have the four Gospels—the Gospels of John, Luke, Mark and Matthew—so in the Fifth we have the Gospel of that being whom Rudolf Steiner calls the heavenly Nathan Jesus Soul.

It is particularly important here to bear in mind that in a special sense none of the Gospel writers is the actual *author* of his Gospel. Rudolf Steiner often said that they present the events in Palestine as it were from four different sides, in that each described what was opened to him by his own particular mode of clairvoyance. In this sense the Nathan Soul is *not* the author of the Fifth Gospel, but is the being thanks to whom it could come onto the Earth through Rudolf Steiner. And just as after the 'bodily' Resurrection of Christ the Nathan Soul through St Paul inspired St Luke to write his Gospel so, after the 'etheric' Resurrection of Christ in the year 1909, the Nathan Soul inspired Rudolf Steiner to reveal the secrets of the Fifth Gospel which he was able to decipher in the Akashic Chronicle with the aid of this Soul.

In confirmation of this we must turn to an exceptionally important statement by Rudolf Steiner on 14 September 1914, exactly one year after the laying of the Foundation Stone of the First Goetheanum: 'And it was at that time [at the laying of the Foundation Stone] that I was able for the first time to speak the words which I not only consider to know, but rather know with all the certainty with which one can know such a thing, that they were heard from the divine-spiritual heights by *that being who was to become the bearer* of the Christ who brings human souls together in harmony. It was, my dear friends, one of the most sublime moments that it has been my privilege to experience during the course of our movement when for the first time I was permitted to speak these words:[68]

> AUM—Amen!
> The Evils hold sway,
> Witness of "I"-hood freeing itself,
> Selfhood-Guilt through others begotten,
> Experienced in the Daily Bread
> Wherein the Heavens' Will does not hold sway,
> For man turned away from Your Kingdom
> And forgot Your Names,
> Ye Fathers in the Heavens.

But in the whole of the development of the Earth there is only one being who 'was to become the bearer of the Christ': the Nathan Soul. In this way Rudolf Steiner conveys to us—and emphasizes quite particularly in this case his own certainty about it—that these words of the ancient macrocosmic Prayer of humanity, which stand at the opening of the Fifth Gospel, were heard by him out of the divine-spiritual heights directly from the *Nathan Soul itself*! For this reason this Gospel, 'as the most ancient, the macrocosmic Gospel, must now sound out like an echo from the West towards the microcosmic Gospels of the East.' For the four Gospels of the Christ who rose 'in the physical body', the 'Gospels of Proclamation', came from the East. But henceforward the Fifth Gospel comes towards them from the West: the Gospel of the Christ who has risen in 'the etheric body', the 'Gospel of Knowledge'.[69]

And to this new *knowledge* of the Being of Christ that is given us in the Fifth Gospel there also belongs the knowledge that this Gospel—through the genealogy that reaches back to Adam, to God, and therefore also into the deepest past of humanity, even into the Lemurian epoch that is a repetition of the Old Moon—contains not only the impulse of the Gospel of St Luke, but points also to an affinity with the impulse of the Gospel of St John[70] and thereby to the impulse issuing from Christ Himself, from the 'new Adam'. For St John, who as His pupil had been initiated by Christ, was the only one able to stand at the Cross during the Mystery of Golgotha; that is, he was the only one able to follow consciously Christ's path from the Last Supper to the day of Pentecost, while the other apostles went through this period in a state of dulled consciousness.[71] Through the inspiration of the Christ, St John could therefore write the most profound Gospel and could give, at the end of the Apocalypse, a picture of the future Jupiter-existence.[72] Thus we can consider the Gospel of St Luke as being connected more with the Moon, and the Gospel of St John more with Jupiter. These two impulses are then united in the Fifth Gospel, of which Rudolf Steiner says that it is connected 'with the Moon and Jupiter',[73] with the past and the future, which means with that which encompasses time—eternity.[74]

Thus the Fifth Gospel is the eternal revelation of the Christ of His own Being, which has been revealed to all humanity in our time by Rudolf Steiner by means of the Nathan Soul. This Soul continues to serve and offer itself up to the Being of Christ in the spiritual worlds and, having appeared to St Paul on the road to Damascus as the glowing aura of the Risen One, appears now as the cosmic archetype of future humanity permeated through and through with the forces of the Living Christ. This Soul appears to us as though like a divine reflection of the far future, like an image of a humanity that has finally raised itself out of the abyss of the Fall and through complete freedom of self-offering becomes the one body, the one vessel of the Spirit that gives life to the universe, of the divine 'I' of humanity, of the Christ Being. This is the realization of the lofty ideal of a divine mankind, of which Vladimir Soloviev already had a dim presentiment, of a divine mankind which will enable the human being to realize himself as the Tenth Hierarchy.

This character of eternity possessed by the Fifth Gospel also determines the peculiarity of the structure of the five lectures of the main lecture cycle given in Oslo. This cycle is organized in such a way that, after a first introductory lecture, in the second lecture we are led through the events from the day of Pentecost to the Mystery of Golgotha, and are dealing with the inspiration of Christ Himself who comes towards us from the future. This is also the reason why the events in this lecture are described in reverse order, for everything here is moving towards us from the future, from the Jupiter-sphere whose image is the image of Whitsun, when the cosmic Spirit of Love—who on Jupiter will hold sway even in the manifestations of nature—alighted upon the Apostles. In the following three lectures we then have the 'correct' sequence of the events. Thus the first of these lectures describes what happened during the three years from the Baptism in the Jordan to the Mystery of Golgotha. This is the time in which the Christ Being worked through the Nathan Jesus Soul. We have here a balance between future and past—a balance in which the meaning of the Earth is realized. The next lecture deals with the past, that is, with the life of

Jesus from the ages of 12 to 30, to the Baptism in the Jordan, and the fifth lecture is dedicated to the uniting of future and past. It begins by describing a conversation of Jesus with His mother before the Baptism in the Jordan, in which Jesus tells her of all the most important experiences of His life up till then. The lecture then leads us through the scenes of the Baptism and the consequent temptation in the desert where Christ Jesus, for the future of the whole Earth, overcomes the dark forces of the past that pervert the course of evolution. And the conclusion and culmination of this lecture is the transformation through Christ Jesus of the great, ancient macrocosmic prayer into the microcosmic Lord's Prayer, in which we are given the cosmic image of the future that redeems the past, as well as the great picture of the salvation of all the Earth through the forces of the Christ-impulse. At this turning-point of the evolution of the Earth, the Being of Christ and the Nathan Soul work together: the future unites with the past; the New Adam unites with the Old; the impulse of Love with the impulse of Wisdom. It is at this point that the Fifth Gospel, the Gospel of Eternity, arises. Because of this it is also above all the 'Gospel of Knowledge', permeated by the infinite Light of Love and Sacrifice. For all the wisdom of human evolution that was preserved in the greatest purity in the heavenly soul of the Nathan Jesus[75] and strengthened by the 'earthly' wisdom of Zarathustra was absorbed in the mighty Sun-Ego of the Christ and transformed by Him. After the Mystery of Golgotha it streamed into the world as Cosmic Love, as a Love that permeates every word of the Fifth Gospel and comes to full expression in the events on the day of Pentecost, as depicted by Rudolf Steiner in the second lecture of the cycle. And this deepest secret of all Earth evolution is probably best expressed in the following words from *Occult Science*: 'Wisdom is the prerequisite of Love. Love is the fruit of wisdom that is reborn in the "I"'[76]—and this is also the essential nature of the Fifth Gospel.

'One of the most sublime moments that it has been my privilege to experience during the course of our movement,' is how Rudolf Steiner describes the moment at the laying of the Foundation Stone of the First Goetheanum, when for the first time he was able to read 'as the first disclosure from the Fifth Gospel' the words which he himself called 'the macrocosmic voice of the ancient, eternal Prayer, sounding out anew.'[77] This Prayer was given to him directly out of the lofty Sun-sphere by the being of the Nathan Soul. Thus Rudolf Steiner begins the series of lectures entitled *The Fifth Gospel* with this Prayer, with this cosmic 'Our Father' that now, for the first time in the history of humanity, was to be heard on the physical plane.

But why was it from the being of the Nathan Soul that Rudolf Steiner received these sublime words? What is the connection between this Soul and the ancient Prayer of humanity? This is partly answered in the fourth lecture where it is related that, while journeying, Jesus of Nazareth came into contact with a heathen cult and was transported into lofty spiritual spheres in which, from the mysterious voice of the Bath-Kol, he heard the 'macrocosmic Our Father' for the first time.

But this connection between the being of the Nathan Soul and the 'ancient, eternal Prayer' goes still deeper and reveals significant secrets of the whole coming-into-being of humanity. For in this Prayer we have a profound plea for succour and redemption, which since Lemurian times has risen up unceasingly to the Gods from a humanity cast through the Fall into the earthly realm, and falling more and more to the forces of Lucifer and Ahriman. This cry of anguish and despair, this plea for salvation was heard by the divine Sun Being of Christ, who out of Grace and unbounded compassion resolved to come to the aid of mankind and through the Mystery of Golgotha give to it a new impulse to rise up out of the kingdom of death.

A closer examination of the seven principal lines of the macrocosmic Our Father reveals that the text consists of two parts.[78] In the first part ('The Evils hold sway ...') humanity entreats the higher worlds for salvation of the astral, etheric and physical bodies that have become subject to death as a result of the fall of the human 'I'. In the second part ('Wherein the Heavens' Will does not hold sway ...') it calls to Christ Himself and prays to Him for divine redemption, turning in this not directly to Him but to the heavenly Hierarchies that offer themselves up to Him and serve Him ('Ye Fathers in the Heavens'). (It only became possible to turn to Christ directly from the earthly sphere after the Mystery of Golgotha.) This falling humanity turns first to the First Hierarchy that represents the will of the Father; then to the Second Hierarchy, to the realm of the Son; and lastly to the Third Hierarchy, which holds the secret of the Name of the Holy Spirit.

In this way humanity, sinking into the abyss, calls on all nine Hierarchies and prays through them to the Christ for deliverance of the human 'I' that is falling ever deeper to the forces of the Earth and of evil. And the full and final answer of all the Hierarchies of the cosmos to this cry is given on the Earth in the Mystery of Golgotha. This is the truly redeeming deed for the innermost essence of the human 'I', and is preceded by the significant scene of the transformation by Christ Jesus of the macrocosmic Our Father into the microcosmic Prayer.

Along with all that has just been said, if we bear in mind also the description of the three pre-Christian sacrifices of Christ through the Nathan Soul which, as Rudolf Steiner relates, prepared in the preceding epochs for the Mystery of Golgotha in the spiritual worlds,[79] and at the same time were the stages through which the 'Kingdom of Heaven' (in the person of Christ and the Nathan Soul that offered itself up to Him and served Him) gradually drew near to Earth[80] in answer to the cry from a humanity sinking into the abyss—if we bear all this in mind and turn again to the *complete* text of the macrocosmic Our Father, the following picture emerges. (To begin with, we shall consider the four pleas in the first part in reverse order.)

The first plea of humanity—for the deliverance and healing of the physical body (whose sense organs, its oldest part, were created by the First Hierarchy on Old Saturn)—was answered by the Nathan Soul as an Archangel-*like* Being[81] at the end of the Lemurian epoch.[82] (This plea is the fourth in the prayer—see diagram on page 90, right-hand column.) And the Nathan Soul answered it by sacrificing its own etheric forces from the lofty Sun-sphere so that, enrobed in them, the Christ Being could heal the human physical body.

The third plea of the Prayer—for deliverance and healing of the etheric body (which regulates the interaction of the life organs that were first created by the Second Hierarchy on Old Sun)—was answered by the Nathan Soul at the beginning of the Atlantean epoch by offering up its own etheric forces from the planetary sphere, so that through them the Christ Being could bring about the healing of the human etheric body.

The second plea of the Prayer—for the deliverance and healing of the astral body, whose fundamental forces of thinking, feeling and willing were laid down by the Third Hierarchy on Old Moon—was answered by the heavenly Nathan Soul at the end of the Atlantean epoch, from the sphere immediately bordering the Earth, through the sacrifice of its etheric forces, availing itself of the forces of Sun, Moon and Earth, so that the Christ Being, as though enrobed in these forces, could bring about also the healing of the human astral body.

Thus in the three parts of the macrocosmic Our Father we have above all a plea to the Nathan Soul to descend from the spiritual worlds. Thereupon this Soul draws near the Earth in three cosmic stages in order, as answer to the first plea, to incarnate on the physical plane in the person of the Nathan Jesus-child. This Soul thereby offers itself once again to the Being of Christ, and this time for the salvation of the human 'I' itself.

As mentioned above, the second part of the Prayer consists of the imploring entreaty of humanity, directed through the nine Hierarchies to the Christ Being who alone can save the human 'I' from ruin and who alone can thus give the meaning and goal to all Earth evolution. Like the Nathan Soul, Christ too hears the threefold cry of a humanity sinking into the abyss, and descends through three stages to the Earth. Rudolf Steiner often described this descent. In the beginning the Christ Being was in the highest spiritual sphere, above the World-Will that is the primordial creative ground in our universe. This condition is expressed in the Gospel of St John:

88

'No man hath seen God at any time; the only begotten Son, which is in the bosom of the Father, he hath declared him.'[83] This is that sublime aspect of the Christ of which the ancient holy Rishis said: Vishva Karman,[84] he is above our sphere. In the lecture of 25 December 1923, Rudolf Steiner speaks in detail of how the highest sphere to which an initiate could penetrate in the first epoch after the great Atlantean catastrophe was the sphere of the First Hierarchy, the Seraphim, Cherubim and Thrones. In the cycle of 1909,[85] concerning the spiritual Hierarchies, he relates that the sphere of activity of the Seraphim and Cherubim is the zodiac itself. From this we can see that at this level the Christ Being acts from beyond but also *through* the zodiac, from the sphere that is also the sphere of the macrocosmic principle of the World-'I',[86] whence the Jahve-Elohim received the primal impulse for the creation of the individual human 'I'[87] in the epoch of ancient Lemuria. It was from this loftiest macrocosmic 'I'-sphere, above the Seraphim, Cherubim and Thrones, that the Christ Being originally worked.[88] And it is to this sublime aspect of His Being that humanity, sinking into the abyss, first turns and entreats the Christ, by means of the First Hierarchy, to come one stage nearer. And out of boundless compassion for humanity, the Christ descends one level from His unimaginable heights. The Christ Being thereby enters the circle of the zodiac, the sphere of the First Hierarchy, which is also the creative world of the Cosmic Will.

Again the cry of humanity that is sinking into the abyss reaches the Christ, but this time through the Second Hierarchy who together form the great *kingdom* of the Sun. And at this cry Christ descends into their sphere, into the Sun-sphere, where He is manifest as the great Sun Spirit, as Ahura Mazdao, the great astral aura of the Sun[89] which Zarathustra once gazed upon.

And finally the cry for aid and salvation rises up out of the depths for a third time, and this time to the sphere of the Spirit, the Third Hierarchy. And at this cry the Christ descends still one stage nearer to humanity. He descends into the sphere of the Third Hierarchy, into the etheric sur-rounding of the Earth and reveals Himself there to Moses, through his servant Jahve,[90] in the burning bush, in the elements on Mount Sinai, and tells him His secret name: *Ejeh asher Eheh*, 'I am the I AM'.[91]

Thus we see how through the four cries of the first part of the mac-rocosmic Our Father, the lofty Archangel-being of the Nathan Soul des-cends from the Sun-sphere until his appearance in the physical world. At each stage of this cosmic descent he sacrifices his etheric forces to the Being of Christ, thereby saving the human physical, etheric and astral bodies and finally, through his incarnation on Earth, also makes possible the redemption of the human 'I'.

In answer to the three cries in the second part, the Christ Being descends to humanity through all nine Hierarchies and, harkening to the first plea (in the first part), enters at the Baptism in the Jordan into the bodily sheath of the Nathan Jesus that was already prepared for him on the Earth, in order to save the human 'I' and with it the goal of Earth evolution. The first cry (in the first part) for the salvation of the human 'I' is directed simultaneously to the Christ and to the Nathan Soul, for the answer to it can only be their union on the *physical plane*. This occurs at the Baptism in the Jordan where the Christ Being enters the bodily sheaths of Jesus of Nazareth. It is only through this final uniting of the two streams, the macrocosmic (the path of Christ) and the microcosmic (the path of the Nathan Soul) that the 'I' of man can be saved and the impulse of reascent be given to all evolution. This is the profound content of this cosmic Prayer.

We must now note that the sequence of the pleas in the first part of the Prayer for salvation of the individual members of man's being ('I', astral, etheric and physical bodies) is in reverse order in relation to the progression of time in which this salvation took place (the physical body in Lemurian times; etheric and astral bodies in Atlantean times; the 'I' in the fourth post-Atlantean epoch). This change in the sequence of lines in the Prayer is connected—aside from the secret concerning the *content*, which we have already mentioned—with the secret of its *composition*. When we look at the sequence in which the Prayer turns to the different members of man's being and then to the divine World Powers, we find the following arrangement:

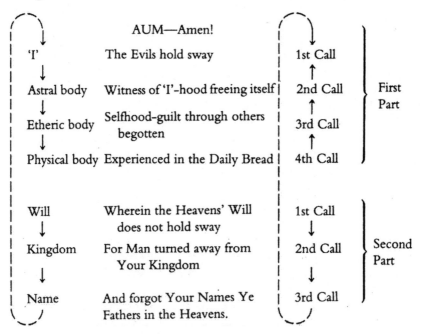

90

Here in the first part we have the complete descent of humanity onto the Earth, into the physical world, from the moment onwards when in ancient Lemuria the Spirits of Form (the Elohim) bestowed upon it the principle of the 'I'. In the second part we have the 'descent', necessitated by this, of the macrocosm through the three threefold Hierarchies that comprise the hierarchical spheres—the sphere of the Father (Will), of the Son (Kingdom) and the Spirit (Name)—and also through the phases of Saturn, Sun and Moon[92] up to the Earth phase, where for the first time for humanity the outer conditions are given for the attainment of the 'I'.

These two downward streams, the microcosmic and the macrocosmic, find expression in the Nathan Soul. This soul, in preparation for the Mystery of Golgotha, descended to Earth as the heavenly archetype of humanity. Stage by stage it prepared for itself in the cosmos the bodily vestures or sheaths with which it was later to incarnate on the Earth as the Nathan Jesus-child.[93] The second stream is the image of the path of Christ who descends to Earth to fulfil the Mystery of Golgotha. Thus in its composition the macrocosmic Our Father is the image of descending evolution in its double aspects—human and cosmic. And the greatest significance of the appearance of Christ on Earth and the Mystery of Golgotha lies in Christ's uniting of Himself with the Earth, so that the great downward evolution of humanity and the cosmos is henceforth transformed into an upward, ascending one.

In the fifth lecture of *The Fifth Gospel* cycle, Rudolf Steiner describes as the decisive turning-point in the development of humanity, and the cosmos, the moment in which Christ Jesus transforms the great macrocosmic Prayer into the microcosmic Our Father: 'And now there came into His mind the voice of the Bath-Kol and He knew that the most ancient formulas and prayers would have to be made anew; He knew that man would now have to seek the path into the spiritual worlds *from below upwards.*'[94]

Already from the name 'microcosmic Our Father', we can sense that what earlier in the 'descent' was brought by the Gods out of the cosmos will, for the ascent, no longer be able to come from without but from the innermost being of man, from the human 'I' that has become free, from the holy of holies in which since the Mystery of Golgotha the Christ lives, and to where He has borne all the fullness of the spiritual forces of the Father.

Herein also lies the reason why Christ changes the plural form into the singular in the first lines of the Prayer. This indicates the great transition of humanity from the epoch of cosmic necessities to the epoch of individual freedom, from the forces of the past to the forces of the future or, in other words, the development is indicated in whose very centre the Mystery of Golgotha stands as a deed of Eternity that embraces the whole evolution of our cosmos. In a renewed form corresponding to the new ascent into the spiritual worlds 'from below upwards' the microcosmic Our Father, whose impulses will work for all future time, was given to humanity.

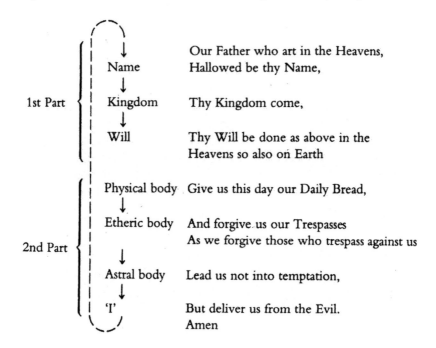

1st Part	Name	Our Father who art in the Heavens, Hallowed be thy Name,
	Kingdom	Thy Kingdom come,
	Will	Thy Will be done as above in the Heavens so also on Earth
2nd Part	Physical body	Give us this day our Daily Bread,
	Etheric body	And forgive us our Trespasses As we forgive those who trespass against us
	Astral body	Lead us not into temptation,
	'I'	But deliver us from the Evil. Amen

Thus in the microcosmic Our Father we have an image of the cosmos and of humanity that ascend again as they permeate themselves with the Christ-forces.

In the first part of the Prayer we see a new ascent of the cosmos through the spheres of the Spirit, the Son and the Father, and at the same time through the Jupiter, Venus and Vulcan conditions. This is made possible through Christ who, having united Himself with the Earth through the Mystery of Golgotha, gradually guides the Earth to an ascending path of evolution on which it is to become a sun—to be transformed from a planet into a star. And in the second part, corresponding to this image of the ascent of a humanity imbued with Christ, we have the simultaneous ascent of the heavenly archetype of humanity, of the Nathan Soul, serving the Christ as His raiment.[95]

But this magnificent prospect of the future incorporated in the microcosmic Our Father by Christ cannot be fully realized in our time without the free and conscious participation of humanity. And humanity will be able to advance into the future in the right way only through a true knowledge of the past—the past that sounds out to us from the macrocosmic Our Father. Thus from the esoteric standpoint these two Prayers are inseparably connected. Herein also lies the reason why the text of the macrocosmic Our Father, which looks to the cosmic past of the Earth and mankind, had to be heard for the first time at the laying of the Foundation Stone of the First Goetheanum—the only building of the new age orientated completely to the future of the world, and built as the first step of human beings in the epoch of human freedom, on the path towards realizing the lofty goals that are presented to all mankind in the microcosmic Our Father.

So having considered the esoteric content and meaning of this Prayer, we must now turn to the event at which the macrocosmic Our Father was read and revealed in its cosmic significance for the first time on the physical plane. This occurred on 20 September 1913 in Dornach, at the laying of the Foundation Stone of the First Goetheanum. And a better understanding of the spiritual significance of this event will help us to penetrate more deeply into the mystery of the path of Rudolf Steiner's life.

Later on, Rudolf Steiner often said that the position of Anthroposophy in the world changed with the founding of the Goetheanum, as though having received its centre on the physical plane Anthroposophy thereby also received a spiritual-social basis. This worked through what spoke to each individual out of the spiritual mystery-forms of the First Goetheanum—the building which appeared as the *visible* Centre of Light that openly rayed out its forces into the world, but because of this also took upon itself the full weight of the opposing forces of darkness. Rudolf Steiner knew from the beginning that with the founding of the Goetheanum the difficulties in the development of Anthroposophy arising from the forces hostile to the rightful evolution of humanity would increase significantly: 'We know what we have to do, and why this Stone [the Foundation Stone of the First Goetheanum] is to betoken knowledge, love and firm strength, and why for numerous opponents this Stone needs must become a Stone of offence and vexation ... Therefore we will need to be properly awake and watchful and to stand courageously at our posts!'[96] In these words one can already sense the tragic gravity of the battle for the further development of Anthroposophy in the world, which Rudolf Steiner consciously took upon himself with the decision to build the Goetheanum. For this reason the Mystery-act of the laying of the Foundation Stone was connected for Rudolf Steiner with an enormous sacrifice—one made for the sake of the founding of the Centre of the New Mysteries, whose central point the Goetheanum was now to become.

But one can only gradually approach the spiritual significance expressed in Rudolf Steiner's act of laying the Foundation Stone in the event that also signified the culmination of his eighth seven-year period and occurred approximately in the middle of it.

However, before we turn to this question we must look in more detail at the Mystery-nature of this act.

Even the place itself of the laying of the Foundation Stone and its surroundings were already connected from ancient times with many spiritual streams which crossed Europe in all directions, gradually forming the particular nature and quality of her spiritual configuration. Already in times of great antiquity there was a Druidic holy place near Dornach. Later, Irish monks settled there and spread Irish Christianity. One of their centres was in the north-west, in Alsace, and Parsifal, too, had decisive experiences in this region while searching for the Holy Grail. In the sixteenth century Paracelsus, who drew his inspiration from Rosicrucian wisdom, was active in Basle. And in 1499 a battle was fought near Dornach which was of decisive significance for the preservation and freedom of Switzerland—that European state in whose founding the purest impulses of the fifth post-Atlantean epoch were at work. Of course all these streams and events left their mark in the spiritual aura of this place that is so richly steeped in the most diverse spiritual and occult traditions.

All this certainly came before Rudolf Steiner's inner gaze when, after the Basle cycle *The Gospel of St Mark* in the autumn of 1912, he interrupted his journey to Edouard Schuré in Alsace by stopping off in Dornach where Marie von Sivers (later Marie Steiner) and some of her close friends had gone for a short rest and holiday.

But something else also appeared before his inner gaze at that time. As Rudolf Grosse remarks in his book, Marie Steiner's memories of that first morning in Dornach are of unusual significance: 'But the next morning Rudolf Steiner awoke as never before. He was haggard, as though crushed; a dark shadow hung over him. There was no apparent reason for this, such things never happened to him—to him who, despite continual activity and hurry, lived in eternal harmony. It passed, but I nevertheless had the feeling, which in the course of time has often recurred, that in that night he foresaw a great deal which he had to forbid himself to think about.'[97]

What came before Rudolf Steiner in that night? Was it the presage of the difficult future, the tragic nature that cannot be expressed in words, of his further path for humanity with the whole series of sacrifices which alone would enable him to fulfil his work on the Earth? We can only guess all this. Only one thing can be said with certainty: the path that Rudolf Steiner had taken since the turn of the century now reaches a still higher stage—one filled with sublime revelations and deep tragedy. 'Basle has a favourable karma'[98]—in these simple words that nevertheless say so much to the heart, Rudolf Steiner expressed to Dr Emil Grosheintz the essence of his decision to build on this place the centre of the anthroposophical movement.

If we try to enter into Rudolf Steiner's words at the laying of the Foundation Stone on the Dornach hill in the autumn evening of 20 September 1913, and if we try to become aware of their cosmic significance, a picture arises before us of a *true Mystery-act* performed at the same moment on both the physical and etheric planes. And the more one endeavours to experience the Mystery-nature of this act of foundation in its spiritual–physical reality, the stronger becomes the feeling that on that evening—not only into the spiritual aura and the soil of the Dornach hill but into the development of all western spiritual life—there was laid the seed of that new striving and aspiration towards the spirit which, having then passed through the full metamorphosis of *birth, growth, death and resurrection*, bore fruit in the Christmas of 1923–24.

These two Mysteries, the Mystery of the founding of the First Goetheanum and the Mystery of the Christmas Conference of 1923–24, come before us as though through a hidden spiritual continuity whose secrets we shall try to touch on later. For the time being it is only possible to say that what was physically placed into the soil of the Dornach Hill was the 'symbol of the human soul' that enters upon the new path of initiation, the path of the New Mysteries whose meaning and content were revealed by Rudolf Steiner only ten years later at the Christmas Conference of 1923–24.

Having thus looked separately at these two most important events in Dornach on 20 September 1913—the laying of the Foundation Stone of the First Goetheanum and the first reading of the macrocosmic Our Father—we must trace their connection from still another side. For their union in *one* Mystery-act is of profound significance. Rudolf Steiner spoke about this in Oslo in the fourth lecture of *The Fifth Gospel*: 'There is such a thing as an occult duty. And it was to fulfil such an occult duty that I then had to pass on what Jesus of Nazareth had perceived at that time through the transformed voice of the Bath-Kol...'[99] With this Rudolf Steiner emphasizes the profound occult significance of the *union* of these two events, and the words spoken directly at the laying of the Foundation Stone shed light on the essential nature of this union: 'If we can hear humanity's cry of longing for the spirit, and if we wish to build the building of Truth from which the message of the spirit is to be proclaimed more and more ... then we understand rightly what it is we are doing this evening.'[100]

The fundamental task of humanity in the fifth post-Atlantean epoch is to win through to full inner freedom. For this reason, from the fifteenth century onwards humanity has been gradually forsaken by the Gods. But this god-forsakenness led in the course of time to the point where the soul today can no longer bear to be in this condition. From the subconscious soul-forces of all humanity there rises up to the higher worlds a new call, a new cry for the spirit. For contemporary humanity stands before a choice: either to find the path to the new Spiritual Light or to fall once and for all to the influence of the processes of wasting and decline. In this sense, Anthroposophy—as the present-day primordial proclamation of the spirit, as a true spiritual impulse leading humanity into the epoch of freedom and to the fulfilment of the great ideals of the microcosmic Our Father—and that building of Truth from which these ideals should ray out into the world, are the real answer to this cry that so racks the soul of modern humanity. The act of the laying of the Foundation Stone is a true continuation on Earth of those cosmic deeds connected with the descent of man of which the macrocosmic Our Father speaks. They led to the greatest events in the development of the Earth—to the Mystery of Golgotha through which the Christ Being united with the Earth. He thus gave meaning to all Earth development and with it also a mighty impulse for a new ascent. This impulse finds its final expression in the microcosmic Our Father. Thus we can recognize the laying of the Foundation Stone as the first act of sacrifice coming from the free human will won on Earth and directed to the new ascent, to a new union with the spirit through receiving into oneself the forces of the Living Christ who is active henceforth in the sphere of the Earth.

Thus at the Foundation Stone ceremony, Rudolf Steiner could rightly say, 'We must have the strength of consciousness to gaze out into *far distant cycles of time* in order to become aware of how the mission, whose distinctive symbol this building is to become, will be included among the *great missions of humanity* on our Earth.'[101] Two days later (on 22 September 1913) Rudolf Steiner reiterates this thought to a larger group of people: 'This laying of the Foundation Stone must be regarded as an act of great responsibility, if only for the reason that we would be right to remember the act of the evening before last as one whereby we have also laid the cornerstone of our consciousness, so that what we carry as our aspiration is included in what we perceive as the mission of the Earth.'[102]

In conclusion, we can follow our theme in chronological order. In the autumn of 1912, after his Basle cycle *The Gospel of St Mark* (ending 24 September 1912), Rudolf Steiner came to his inner decision—exactly one year before the laying of the Foundation Stone—to build the Goetheanum at Dornach. At the following Christmas of 1912–13 he gives his lecture cycle *The Bhagavad Gita and the Epistles of Paul*. Here, in the fifth lecture on 1 January 1913, he speaks about Krishna and of the participation of the Nathan Soul in St Paul's experience before Damascus. In the middle of 1913, in May and June, he gives the cycle *The Occult Significance of the Bhagavad Gita*, in which Krishna is the main subject. In the seventh lecture of this cycle he indicates that he did not speak about the secret of the connection between Krishna and the Nathan Soul in his Basle cycle *The Gospel of St Luke* in 1909, because he did not yet know about it at that time. On 20 September 1913, the first reading of the macrocosmic Our Father at the beginning of the Fifth Gospel takes place at the laying of the Foundation Stone. On 1 October 1913, the cycle *The Fifth Gospel* was given in Oslo, and from then onwards in various cities in Europe there follows one lecture after another on this subject, right up to the beginning of the First World War. At Christmas 1913–14, Rudolf Steiner gives a cycle of lectures in Leipzig entitled *Christ and the Spiritual World and The Search for the Holy Grail*. In three of these lectures lasting almost up to the last day of 1913, he reveals a further secret concerning the Nathan Soul in connection with its three supersensible, heavenly sacrifices that were the cosmic preparation for the Mystery of Golgotha. Following this and up to the summer of 1914, the Fifth Gospel and the three cosmic sacrifices of the Nathan Soul appear as two parallel themes that nevertheless sometimes combine. Thus, at the beginning of the lecture on 5 March 1914 in Stuttgart, Rudolf Steiner straightaway directly links an examination of the three pre-Christian sacrifices of Christ with an examination of the Fifth Gospel. In a Paris lecture on 27 May 1914, these two themes are finally united into a single whole. In this lecture he first gives an all-embracing picture of the three pre-Christian sacrifices of Christ through the Nathan Soul, and then the history of the life of Jesus of Nazareth according to the Fifth Gospel, up to the Mystery of Golgotha. He also reads once more the text of the macrocosmic Our Father.

Thus we have come close to an understanding of the sacrifice that was made by Rudolf Steiner in the building of the First Goetheanum, and which began at the laying of the Foundation Stone at Dornach on 20 September 1913. In his book Rudolf Grosse has already pointed to this profound mystery of Rudolf Steiner's life: 'Already in the first year of building, in July 1914, the secret of life, the relation of the building to the human etheric body, comes to one from Rudolf Steiner's words. The particular etheric aura that had surrounded true ancient Mysteries was present here from the beginning. One had more and more strongly an impression of a deep etheric connection between the building and the builder—one that had as of necessity to be woven about the place in order that it be able to receive and absorb the highest impulses of a new Mystery-centre.'

These words direct us to a sacrifice that was the real foundation of the building, and which lay in the fact that Rudolf Steiner had to give up *forces of his own etheric body* in order to weave a spiritual aura around the Dornach hill, an aura such as always surrounded all true Mystery-centres in antiquity, and which was to serve as a vessel for those lofty spiritual impulses which were to descend at this place so that it could become the real centre of the spiritual life of western humanity.

But the mysterious connection 'between the building and the builder' first became plainly apparent after the fire. Rudolf Grosse says of this: 'The destroying fire, the *death* of this building, *had* therefore to result in a profound effect, to be a terrible blow to the physical and etheric sheaths of the builder. Only those could perceive this who had some idea of the Mystery-secrets of the Dornach hill.'[103] Rudolf Steiner himself, in a letter to Marie Steiner on 15 October 1924, talks of how this terrible blow of the burning of the Goetheanum afflicted his etheric body: '... Some time ago I told you how since January 1923 the connection of the higher members of my being with my physical body was no longer entirely intact: in the life of the spirit I have, in certain respects, lost the immediate connection with my physical organism. Not with the physical world. On the contrary, the healthy judgement of the physical world became stronger and stronger, and also more extensive ...'[104] And again, eleven days later, he writes: 'As you know, since January 1923 I have been greatly estranged from my physical body. *It is because of this* that the necessity has arisen for the ever-increasing medical care.'

Thus we see that at the foundation of the Goetheanum building, the future centre of the new Christian Mysteries that was to come under the guidance of the Time Spirit himself,[105] lies Rudolf Steiner's great sacrifice, for *as an initiate he offered up the forces of his own etheric body* for the building of the centre of the new spiritual life.

This is the *third* stage of Rudolf Steiner's path of sacrifice—one where he offers up to the guiding powers of world development the spiritual forces he had been able to elaborate in his own etheric body on his individual path of development. And he thus relinquishes any personal benefit from these forces, in order that they could be used by the higher powers for the good of all human development.

But this sacrifice, begun by Rudolf Steiner on the day of the laying of the Foundation Stone of the First Goetheanum, was connected also in a very special way with the heavenly being of the Nathan Soul and its task in the evolution of humanity. For what is this task of the Nathan Soul in the cosmos? We can say in answer that it is *the cosmic principle of etheric sacrifice*. It offered up its etheric forces four times to the Sun Being of Christ, three times in the cosmos and once on Earth, actually serving Him as His bodily sheath! And when in the new epoch of human freedom and of the deepest descent of humanity into the abyss of materialism, and when for the founding of the new Mystery-centre and for the sake of the reuniting of humanity with the spirit, Rudolf Steiner decided to make the same sacrifice—even if only in a more microcosmic way, yet nevertheless in essence the same sacrifice that the Nathan Soul had made more macro-cosmically three times in the spiritual worlds and once on Earth—can there be any doubt that the Nathan Soul itself was present, blessing and aiding Rudolf Steiner at the time of his act of offering?

One can clearly observe how in *the autumn of 1912* after the decision to build the Goetheanum in Dornach, the revelations of the Nathan Soul concerning its being and its cosmic destiny become more and more concentrated until finally, at the moment of the act of laying the Foundation Stone, Rudolf Steiner receives the macrocosmic Our Father from this Soul *itself*. This prayer brings to expression the essential nature of this being's relation to the Christ and to humanity and, at the same time, is the beginning of the Fifth Gospel now to be gradually revealed until the outbreak of the First World War. In all this one can see, conveyed through the Nathan Soul, the cosmic answer as it were of the spiritual world and of Christ to the etheric sacrifice and the vow—of which Rudolf Steiner speaks at the laying of the Foundation Stone—to serve the great mission of the Earth—that is, to serve the Christ Being from whom all Earth evolution receives its cosmic mission and goal. And the plea with which Rudolf Steiner turns to all the nine Hierarchies for the blessing of the holy act at the laying of the Foundation Stone is directed also to the Nathan Soul. At that time Rudolf Steiner expressed in the following Mystery-words the reflection in his act of this Soul's cosmic sacrifice: 'Thus be veiled' (*So werde verhüllt*).[106] In these words he also showed *how* the act of sacrifice of that moment had to be related to the acts of sacrifice of those lofty Beings who from the spiritual worlds guide the development of humanity in unceasing service to the Being of Christ.

Right from the beginning of the building work, which began immediately after 20 September, one could sense how everything to do with the construction was alive, permeated with life. As from a seed, the Goetheanum grew steadily from the Foundation Stone that in its esoteric essence was the true 'symbol of the human soul'. It did not follow the laws of the dead mineral world, but rather the laws of change and metamorphosis inherent in the etheric plant-world. This building, unique in the history of European architecture, was in truth a *living* being. It was for this reason that after the fire Rudolf Steiner could say, 'The Goetheanum has died.'[107] Many of those who helped to build the Goetheanum also felt this very particular relation to it. For example, the Russian writer Andrei Belyi worked on the building from 1914–19, and wrote then: '... In the winter, having all clambered up under the cupola, we thronged around our "Mars" and finally finished it. It took all the spring and summer of 1915 to finish the "Jupiter". "Jupiter" and "Mars" are our forms;[108] I loved them as if they were my own little children. But I shall never see them again—for when I do they will offer me a different aspect: I shall see them from below. I shall never climb up to the cupola again. So farewell you forms, into which I hammered a part of my life. Now they are up there, high, oh! so high, and a part of my soul is higher than my self!'[109]

From esoteric as well as from certain external reasons mentioned above, one can suppose that the Goetheanum would have been finished in 1917 or by the beginning of 1918, but the war that broke out in August 1914 made this impossible. The work on the building was slowed down considerably and was not completely finished even in 1922.

In various statements by Rudolf Steiner, one can get the impression that in the time just before the outbreak of the war Europe was faced spiritually with a definite choice of two alternatives. On the one hand the forces of darkness that wish to drag humanity into the abyss were growing stronger and stronger; and on the other hand, since the end of Kali Yuga in 1899, there shone the new revelation of the spirit like a first ray of light in the skies of Europe, overcast with dense cloud and darkened by the materialism of the nineteenth century. Which path would humanity choose? This choice would be decisive for the future destiny of Europe in the twentieth century, in the century in which the greatest happening of the fifth post-Atlantean epoch occurs—the appearance of Christ in the etheric world. The onset of the First World War was a terrible answer to this alternative. Rejecting the new spirit Light, Europe plunged into the abyss. From that moment on many impulses of the past, in which at the beginning of the century one could have placed hopes, lost their strength.[110] The whole of the twentieth century was threatened by catastrophes and the First World War was far from being the worst of these, but it determined the character of the further development of these catastrophes now threatening all humanity with still greater disaster.

For Rudolf Steiner this fateful event was a sign that the first step had been taken towards the 'War of All against All'. But the more decisively Europe moved towards the future catastrophe, the more urgent became the need to create a counterbalance, to counteract the coming calamities with effective social impulses which alone can help humanity, and whose prime source is direct and conscious insight into the spiritual world. All this determined the next, the third stage in the development of Anthroposophy: it had to turn outwards to the surrounding world and give effective social impulses to all areas of human life, above all to the spheres of education, medicine, religion, science and social relations as such.

Before we conclude this description of Rudolf Steiner's eighth seven-year period, it remains to mention that during the war years, besides a great deal of spiritual-scientific research into life between death and a new birth (a theme that was particularly acute in the context of the terrible events of those years, and to which the majority of his lectures were dedicated), Rudolf Steiner also attained to complete clarity in his research into the threefold nature of the human being. It is in these war years that the anthroposophical teaching of the three systems of the human organism takes shape: the head, the rhythmical system and the metabolic system, through which the fundamental etheric-physical archetype that lies at the basis of the forming and appearance of the human body finally becomes fully apparent. What Goethe had attained for the plant kingdom and had striven for in the animal kingdom was now achieved by Rudolf Steiner for the highest kingdom of nature—the human kingdom. In this threefold membering of man's being we have the purest etheric-physical archetypal idea of man. In 1917 this teaching was brought into a form intended for a wider public in the book *Riddles of the Soul*. This work, along with the Prague lecture cycle in 1911 *An Occult Physiology*, provided a firm basis for the anthroposophical medicine developed later (1920). And finally, the full scope of these spiritual-scientific investigations enabled Rudolf Steiner to come to that knowledge which he later set into the first section of each of the three parts of the fundamental anthroposophical *Foundation Stone Meditation*, given by him at the Christmas Conference of 1923–24. On 25 December 1923, after reading the three first sections of each of the three parts of the *Meditation*, Rudolf Steiner summed up his spiritual-scientific research during the war years thus: 'When I today look back, particularly on what it was then possible to bring from the spirit-worlds while the terrible storms of war were shaking the world, it must be epitomized in this triad of verses that your ears have just heard.'[111]

The year 1917 saw the transition of Rudolf Steiner's life to a new seven-year period, and at the beginning and end of that same year he gave two lecture cycles. On 6 February 1917, in the first lecture of *Building Stones for an Understanding of the Mystery of Golgotha*, he speaks again and with a quite particular warmth of the etheric coming of Christ, and of how Christ Himself does not come to mankind only as the Lord but as a brother and loving friend, bringing not only comfort and strength but also will and right action. Every word of this cycle—the fourth lecture of which coincided with Rudolf Steiner's forty-sixth birthday—is as though filled with the warm golden light of the winter Sun, gradually growing in strength. But at the end of the year, like an image of the shadow cast by contemporary events that set themselves against the bright life-bringing rays of the growing Sun, came the two lecture cycles *The Karma of Materialism* and *The Fall of the Spirits of Darkness*. These two polarities, the growing Sun and the shadow that opposes it all the more, anticipate as it were the whole magnitude and the tragic element of this last *complete* seven-year period of Rudolf Steiner's life.[112] For in this period he comes particularly under the influence of the Saturn-sphere and at the same time is permeated by the fiery and glowing forces of Spirit Man—that is, of the goal of the evolution of our cosmos.

At this time Rudolf Steiner also entered into a particular and special relationship with the highest spirits of the Third Hierarchy, with the Archai, or Time Spirits, who are the bearers of the principle of Spirit Man in our cosmos. But he enters mainly into a relationship with the highest of them all, with the Spirit of our age who has the present-day guidance of all western humanity—Michael. This of course does not mean that it is only now that Rudolf Steiner places himself under the direct guidance of Michael. He had been deeply connected in previous incarnations with this lofty guiding Being, but it was in this life that the guidance showed itself with the greatest clarity. It had begun in the first seven years of the Sun period of his life and reached the stage of objective and conscious vision in the second seven-years, through which he could come to an awareness and a realization of his mission as one of sacrificial service to this lofty Spirit.

As Rudolf Steiner began the ninth seven-year span of his life—which comes particularly under the influence of the Saturn forces—he drew near in a certain way to the completion of his earthly-cosmic journeying through the planetary spheres, and thereby approached spiritually also the limits of the solar system. Here the inspirations of the whole divine macrocosmos could be received and only here do the great, all-encompassing secrets of Michael's Sun-sphere, which are the foundation of all human development, appear before Rudolf Steiner in their true archetypal form. '... For if one wants to penetrate to an understanding of what is related to the secrets of Michael, and which works and rays outwards from the spiritual region of the Sun, one must look up from the Earth to the secrets of the universe through the wisdom of *Saturn*. Then one must be able to sense and to live in that twilight in the spiritual world that stems from Oriphiel, the ruler of Saturn, who at the time of the Mystery of Golgotha was the guiding Archangel, and who will again be the guiding Archangel when the Michael Age has run its course.'[113]

But in our time Michael influences earthly events from the Earth-sphere itself, into which he descended in 1879. Thus, his influence works directly in the midst of humanity and primarily in the sphere of social relations, and it is here in the social sphere that the decisive battle takes place for the future fate of humanity. This is the true battle of Michael against the Dragon, in which mankind in this epoch of freedom must also take part, for the outcome of this battle lies above all in the hands of humanity. It is imperative to recognize what it is that makes the situation in our epoch of freedom so critical. With the greatest possible seriousness we must recognize that not only does mankind depend on the Gods, but *the Gods also depend on mankind.*[114] For this reason Anthroposophy, which was sent to the Earth by Michael, should always be there at his side, supporting him where his battle against the adversary forces is particularly hard and where human beings, out of a lack of understanding for the true nature of events, come least to his aid—that is, not only in the realm of thinking, as exemplified by *The Philosophy of Freedom*, but also in the social realm.

Rudolf Steiner's activity was to develop from this time in two main directions. On the one hand the spiritual Michaelic impulses were to be introduced and worked into the different realms of the cultural life and especially into the social sphere, which in our time has been usurped to the greatest extent by the powers opposed to Michael. On the other hand Rudolf Steiner founded the new science of 'occult sociology'. This had to prove itself a force capable of directing the development of right outward activity which, issuing as it did fully from contemporary Christian eso-tericism, had the goal of developing—even if only among a small group of people—a true social-occult understanding of the happenings of that time.

From the second half of 1916 onwards, this occult-social theme gradually became the main theme of Rudolf Steiner's lectures. It demanded an extremely comprehensive investigation of the underlying spiritual causes of our epoch. And although the actual Christological theme does not always come to the fore in these extensive lectures, given mainly in Dornach between 1916 and 1921, one can nevertheless bring all the lectures of that time under one general heading: the activity of Christ as seen from the standpoint of the Michael-sphere. For precisely in our time, when the Etheric Christ moves through all the life of contemporary humanity, His words, 'For where two or three are gathered together in my name, there am I in the midst of them',[115] take on a very particular significance. Thus the Christ-impulse lives in the present day particularly in the social sphere, in that sphere of life that is shared and connected with others. Here it works in the form brought through Michael who is the herald of the Christianity of the future, the Christianity of the epoch of human freedom.

Therefore in this new, particularly Michaelic period of his life, Rudolf Steiner sets as his main task the developing of a truly social-occult understanding of the fundamental events of the epoch, and also the unveiling of the intentions of the spiritual powers at work in it that wish in the present to contend Michael's right to lead humanity. The content of these lectures is such as to *awaken the necessary consciousness* and bring an understanding of the spiritual impulses that will battle against each other up to the end of the twentieth century and indeed even into the twenty-first. And although, as already mentioned, we may not find the name of Christ or of Michael so often in these lectures, one can nevertheless sense how literally through every word there sounds the voice of Michael-Christ (see: *Anthroposophical Leading Thoughts*, Nos 2, 11, 24) urging for wakefulness: 'Why sleep ye? rise and pray, lest ye enter into temptation.'[116] 'Arise and be watchful'—this was the main theme of the lectures of those years. But despite this the vigilance fell short. Of course there was still a great deal that revealed itself to Rudolf Steiner's inner gaze, but he could not speak about it openly. Dornach resembled too strongly a besieged fortress, not only in the physical sense but also in the spiritual. And the spiritual forces of those on whom Rudolf Steiner could rely were still too weak. Nevertheless, from individual remarks to be found in the different lectures of that period, one can form an almost complete picture of the spiritual forces that at that time, in the first quarter of the century, determined and directed events from behind the scenes. And a great many of the ruling spiritual influences that can be observed today in the last quarter of the twentieth century also become clear and evident. For there is a great deal in these lectures that is prophetic, that points to the future, and which only very few anthroposophists at that time could fully understand. To a great extent Rudolf Steiner addressed himself at that time to us, to the anthroposophists of the last quarter of the twentieth century, for this is the time in which those spiritual forces and streams, whose sources we must seek in the last third of the nineteenth century and which it is essential to strive to understand, will come fully into the open.

In this sense these lectures are relevant also in our time—perhaps even more so than half a century ago.

Alongside the social theme of 1916 to 1920 came the cosmological theme. This comprised, as it were, the other side of Michael's revelation, for Michael is above all a cosmic Sun Spirit, a Spirit who in his quality as the reigning Time Spirit of the present, stands at the centre of all the cosmic interrelations of our solar system. Seen like this, the social and the cosmological themes form the basis for right human *action* in the world today, action founded on a true understanding of an individual for his interconnection with other human beings on the one hand, and with the spiritual cosmos on the other.

'Love the Lord thy God, and love thy neighbour'[117]—these two fundamental Christian commandments can be realized in a new way in accordance with the epoch of human freedom, not by people subordinating themselves to a commandment but by *understanding*, by comprehending. The impulse for this comes directly from the Sun-sphere of Michael. This is the beginning of the new Michaelic Christianity, at the foundation of which must lie the complete concord and harmony of Heaven and Earth, for only this can bring about *right* social deeds, deeds that, flowing from human freedom, are in complete harmony with the forces of the cosmos that guide humanity.

But in this Michaelic period of his life the cosmic Mystery of Michael itself was also unveiled to Rudolf Steiner. The statements about this Mystery that begin at this time occur more and more often and become ever broader in scope and grandeur right up to the end of Rudolf Steiner's life. They reach a climax in the final disclosure of the fundamental cosmic secrets of Michael in the Karma lectures, in the Michael Letters, and in the founding of the First Class of the Free School of Spiritual Science which, as a heavenly-earthly institution, stands directly under the leadership of Michael. One can say that this 'Michael Theme', which was present in the anthroposophical movement from the beginning,[118] attains in this period an unprecedented concreteness and significance.

On 17 February 1918 in Munich, Rudolf Steiner gave a lecture with the theme 'Signs of the Times—Michael's Battle and Its Reflection on Earth'. In this he indicates for the first time the existence of the spiritual law of the repetition of events in the historical development of humanity. And in October of the same year he gave a cycle of six lectures in Dornach entitled *Three Streams in the Evolution of Mankind: Connection of the Luciferic-Ahrimanic Impulses with the Christ-Jahve Impulse.* He describes the interaction of these three impulses in the evolution of mankind and in particular the problem of establishing a balance between Lucifer and Ahriman through the Christ-principle. Later, towards the end of 1919 and approximately in the middle of Rudolf Steiner's ninth seven-year period, the Michael theme reaches a particular intensity. On the one hand, during the course of 1919, Rudolf Steiner speaks in many cities of the incarnation on Earth of Ahriman at the turn of the century, and of the effect of this occurrence on the fate of all world culture. On the other hand, in November of the same year he gave the first big lecture cycle dedicated entirely to the Michael theme: *The Mission of Michael, The Revelation of the Secrets of Man's Being* [published in English as *The Mission of the Archangel Michael*]. This cycle was given by him almost exactly one year after the cycle *Three Streams in the Evolution of Mankind*, and seems to a certain extent to be its continuation in so far as the balance between Lucifer and Ahriman through the Christ-principle is again the theme, but seen now as it were from the perspective of the new revelation of Michael—the Spirit who leads individuals to this balance. And the further fate of all Earth development depends now on finding this balance.[119]

'I am with you always, even unto the end of the Earth'—Rudolf Steiner takes these words of Christ as a basis and commenting on them continues: 'But that means: I have not only revealed myself to you in the days when the Gospels were written, but I shall always speak to you through my Spirit of the day, Michael, if you seek the way to me.'[120] In these two lines is revealed to us in essence the whole fundamental character of the new Michael revelation of the present epoch. In the following lecture Rudolf Steiner says of this revelation: 'We are now living in the time of the Michael revelation. It is there before us just as the other revelations are. But it no longer imposes itself on the individual, because the human being has entered upon the development of freedom. We have to approach and meet Michael's revelation. Be careful not to fail to recognize what would be given in this Michael revelation to humanity of the present and the near future if people were to approach it in freedom.' After this Rudolf Steiner turns to such specific questions as what does it mean 'to think in a Michaelic way?', what is 'the Michael-path that has its continuation in the Christ-path?', and what is a 'Michaelic culture' as the true culture of future humanity when 'one will not have abstract matter and abstract spirit, but spirit, soul and body interacting in unity?'

However, the inner climax of this cycle is without doubt the end of the second lecture on 20 November, where Rudolf Steiner describes the secret of the two central missions of Michael—the old and the new from which have arisen two of his most significant revelations. One of them prepared the way for the Mystery of Golgotha and lies in the first verses of the Gospel of St John: 'In ancient times the Word lived in a spiritual form, but the Word became flesh and dwelt among us.' The second was to come into effect only from 1879, the beginning of the new Michael epoch, and proclaims: 'And human flesh must again become permeated by the spirit so that it may become capable of dwelling in the kingdom of the Word in order to behold the divine secrets.' Thus 'the Word become flesh is the first revelation of Michael, and the second revelation of Michael must be the flesh become spirit'.

In essence these words conceal the profoundest Mystery of the human physical body and its future connection with the Michael-Christ impulse. This Mystery first unveiled itself to Rudolf Steiner in all its fullness in this period of his life that stood under the sign of Spirit Man.[121]

From this time onwards Rudolf Steiner's insight into the Michael-sphere, whence he receives ever more new revelation, acquires an especial strength and depth. And precisely this side of his spiritual investigation comes to the fore now, developing further and further and revealing to us yet another aspect of his mission, namely, that of Rudolf Steiner as the herald of the present ruling Time Spirit.

106

Emil Bock once said that Rudolf Steiner had been the Archangel Michael's right hand. This is an occult fact. In his lecture on 28 May 1910, Rudolf Steiner indicates that in principle this is possible. He uses here the example of General Miltiades, and stresses the following: 'Let us look at the example of Miltiades or some other personality who played a role in the great plan of the history of their people. Certain things in their lives were determined by the karma of higher Beings, who allotted them their place. What was to fall to the lot of *all humanity* flowed into the account of their own personal karma. And inasmuch as they carried it out, as they con-tributed their own deeds and efforts to it, it became their own individual karma. Thus we live and weave in the macrocosm with our individual karma, as a world in miniature, as a microcosm.'[122]

In this example we can see how in the great historical events of the world the karma of the single human individuality is linked with that of higher Beings. Thus was Rudolf Steiner's karma connected with the karma of Michael. In other words, in order to work through him, Michael had to take Rudolf Steiner's karma upon himself. For without the work on Earth of this, his greatest pupil and herald, Michael's situation in the twentieth century in relation to the world of men and to the world of certain Gods would be extremely difficult. Thus, in the new epoch of freedom, as though prophetically anticipating his future, the human being is called upon to work consciously with the Gods who, following the example of Christ, wish now to unite their heavenly-supersensible destiny with the destinies of human souls on Earth.

As mentioned already, as well as developing the social-occult theme, which was particularly aimed at enabling anthroposophists to develop a true understanding of the underlying spiritual causes of current events, the other foremost work of Rudolf Steiner during this period was dedicated to the task of giving new impulses to the practical areas of life, and especially to those in which the anti-Michaelic forces were particularly strong. This was above all the case in the social, educational, scientific, medical and religious spheres—that is, in those areas through which in ancient times the fundamental impulses of the Mysteries had come.

This work of Rudolf Steiner now brought a large influx of young members into the Society, who hoped to be able to apply Anthroposophy in more specific areas, for instance in science. And as though in answer to these promptings coming from outside, there began a rapid and energetic development of the anthroposophical daughter-institutions.

At the end of 1918 there begins the development of the threefold social organism, of which Rudolf Steiner said that it was wanted by Michael himself.[123] The idea of a threefold social organism was then developed further in the following year in the book *The Threefold Commonwealth* [published as *Towards Social Renewal.*], and in a series of articles published in 1920 under the title *In Ausführung der Dreigliederung des sozialen Organismus (The Threefold Order of the Body Social)*. From 1919 attempts were made to realize materially the idea of the threefold social organism in the practical life of Europe of that time.

In the middle of 1919 the first impulses for a spiritual-scientific renewal of the art of education are given, from which there gradually arises the system of Waldorf education.

Then at the end of 1919 Rudolf Steiner gives his first lecture cycle on science. This area is deepened and in the following years opens up new perspectives for a spiritual-scientific renewal of science. And 1920 sees the energetic beginnings of the development of anthroposophical medicine, which led to the founding of the Clinical-Therapeutical Institute in Arlesheim by Ita Wegman.

In 1921[124] the renewing impulse of Anthroposophy as the new revelation of Christ in the twentieth century broadens into the realm of religion. The Christian Community is founded in 1921–22, headed by Friedrich Rittelmeyer.

Thus by 1922 anthroposophical impulses had taken deep root in the most diverse spheres of specialized knowledge. However, despite the fact that much in these offshoot endeavours of Anthroposophy soon began to bear fine and much-promising fruit, this wider development of Anthroposophy was also beset with significant difficulties. These arose not only from increasing opposition from without but, first and foremost, from the inner unpreparedness of many anthroposophists who carried anthroposophical impulses with great enthusiasm into important spheres of human life and activity, and yet did not fully understand the vital essence of Anthroposophy itself. They had not understood that right from the beginning Anthroposophy possessed, and possesses, a *profoundly esoteric* nature which it always preserves, also when applied to the practical spheres of life.

Due to this lack of understanding for the true nature of Anthroposophy, a large number of mistakes soon began to be made and their consequences became more and more destructive for the Society. This came to expression in the first place in the increased antagonism of the outside world towards the anthroposophical movement. Rudolf Steiner looks back on this in a lecture in Dornach on 12 April 1924: 'For we did not yet have this antagonism towards us in 1918. We had individual opponents of course, but we were not concerned about them and did not need to be. In fact, this opposition has only arisen since 1918.' And on 16 April 1924 he says: 'And thus it is that roughly from 1919 onwards, since the time during the war years when the directing of the Anthroposophical Society was difficult, all sorts of aspirations have arisen in the Anthroposophical Society—aspirations stemming from various ambitions among the members, which fundamentally have had a harmful effect on what has to do with Anthroposophy. They are harmful in the sense that because of them the antagonism of the outside world has significantly increased.'[125] And he goes on to speak of how at that time he had had to give each individual anthroposophist the possibility of making these mistakes so that afterwards, when they saw the baneful consequences they themselves had brought about, they could recognize this fact in full freedom. New esotericism requires absolute respect for the free will of every human being, but we have to imagine what the cost of this was for Rudolf Steiner! One only has to think of the collapse of the moves towards a threefold social order in 1919. The mistakes and difficulties that arose with the broadening of Anthroposophy's field of activity were, amongst other things, a consequence of the fact that just as this expansion began to make evident the greater need for a purely esoteric relation to Anthroposophy, all esoteric work in the Society had to be suspended at the beginning of the First World War. This weighed heavily on Rudolf Steiner when five years later Anthroposophy entered the areas where the forces warring against Michael were particularly strong. It would have been necessary not only to unite oneself with Anthroposophy as a cultural-spiritual stream but also to take it up into oneself as something of a purely esoteric nature. This, however, did not necessarily occur in every case during this time.

Because of this Rudolf Steiner gradually became aware that his task must be to realize on the spiritual-historical plane, in the reality of the relationship of human beings in the social sphere, that sublime synthesis of outer and inner which on his path of Christian-Rosicrucian initiation he had been able to accomplish in himself by 1899, thereafter coming before humanity as a Teacher. This sublime synthesis, however, could only be realized through a new *esoteric impulse* in the anthroposophical movement.

The purely esoteric work interrupted by the war had to be revived, but now on a completely new level. For only this could establish a harmony between the original, purely spiritual wellsprings of Anthroposophy and its broadening out externally into diverse and more specialized areas of human knowledge. Moreover, the esoteric work in all its facets, and preserving its fundamentally Rosicrucian character, now had to receive an even more definite orientation towards the sphere of Michael; for since 1879 when Michael began working in the Earth-sphere, true esoteric impulses had to be brought to all areas of human social activity and practical life.

It is possible to connect with this new task the mysterious fact that the First Goetheanum, even up to its tragic destruction, was neither officially opened nor *inaugurated*. While giving a course in the School of Spiritual

109

Science at the Goetheanum in September 1920, Rudolf Steiner stressed emphatically that the course must on no account be seen as the opening of the Goetheanum: 'The 26th September [the beginning of the course] is not to be misconstrued as an opening of our Goetheanum ... The opening of the Goetheanum lies far off in the future.'[126]

Rudolf Steiner first spoke about the conditions under which the opening and consecration could have taken place, after the fire. In his article on 18 March 1923, *Das Goetheanum in seinen 10 Jahren* ('The Ten Years of the Goetheanum'), he wrote that the opening of the Goetheanum 'would have taken place only if it had been possible to create an occasion that in every detail would have been in absolute harmony with the original idea behind the building.'[127] But then what was the 'original idea' of the Goetheanum? In essence this idea is Anthroposophy itself, for Rudolf Steiner said more than once that the Goetheanum was visible Anthroposophy on the physical plane, and that the 'original idea' of this building had the same supersensible sources as all spiritual science. Moreover, by the occasion in the Goetheanum spoken of here, one was to understand an occasion in which there pulsated the whole complex and many-sided life of the Society, which in turn is the mediator between Anthroposophy in its ideal-spiritual aspect (which was also expressed in the forms of the Goetheanum) and the rest of the world, into which these anthroposophical impulses were to come, either directly or with the help of books or public lectures or through a renewal of the different scientific, artistic or religious trends of the time. In this way the outer activity that in time was to flow from the Goetheanum was to correspond completely with the deep esoteric impulses that had shaped the outer forms of the building.

From all this we can see what the Goetheanum was to become. Uniting outer and inner in absolute harmony—which is only possible through genuine esoteric work—it was to be inaugurated and opened as the Mystery-centre of our time, as the very centre of a new esotericism of the West, serving Michael-Christ.

Yet despite all Rudolf Steiner's efforts in this respect, the wakefulness and vigilance of the members was not strong enough and their spiritual forces insufficient; they were paralysed by the catastrophic events and difficulties of that time so that the adversary powers proved stronger. And on New Year's Eve of 1922 the tragedy struck. The Goetheanum was consumed in a sea of fire. And thus the synthesis, as the crowning of a long path and of stupendous work, could not be attained through a constant, progressing development.

And yet it had to be brought about, but now as a pure act of sacrifice that grew from a great sorrow bordering almost on despair, and because of this one can say that this synthesis became all the greater, all the more significant. The new Mystery-centre was to be born out of the flames of the fire that consumed the Goetheanum. Its foundation was to be laid through the greatest imaginable sacrifice of which the human being is capable, and was offered up by Rudolf Steiner on the altar of all mankind.

As we approach this chapter in the history of the anthroposophical movement we approach also the question which has often come up among anthroposophists: 'Was it really impossible to avert the tragedy?' 'Did Rudolf Steiner really not know?' Supported by everything that has been said in the previous chapters we must answer quite definitely that, yes, Rudolf Steiner *knew* of the approaching misfortune. He knew this above all because already at the laying of the Foundation Stone the destiny of the Goetheanum was connected in the most intimate fashion with the destiny of his own etheric body. It was impossible that he should not know of this destiny. But why did he remain silent at that time? This then is the second question, but one can also answer it. The most important thing here was that the Goetheanum *could not be protected from outside*. Ever since the outbreak of war the Goetheanum had been guarded day and night. All the external measures one could possibly take to protect the Goetheanum had been taken. But the chief danger was not here. The chief danger lay in the ever-weakening wakefulness of the Society members, whose inner activity had been gradually eroded under the pressure of outer events and the growing difficulties within the Society. They had fallen asleep. Despite all his efforts between 1916 and 1921, Rudolf Steiner was unable by his lecture work to awaken among the members sufficient consciousness or the necessary social understanding—and the fateful consequences now took their toll. In face of the growing power of the adversaries, the Goetheanum and the etheric forces of Rudolf Steiner that were connected with it lost the necessary support from the side of the members. For the Goetheanum had been founded and built according to purely spiritual and occult laws and could not simply be destroyed by forces of external circumstances—had that been so, it would have happened long before 1922. It could only become vulnerable through a weakening of the inner, spiritual defence of the members of the Society. In this situation tragedy could befall it at any moment, for no external means could avert it. And Rudolf Steiner knew this more than anyone.

Yet what could he do? It was not possible to speak out loudly and openly of the coming danger, because the fundamental law of the epoch of freedom—never directly to influence the will of another human being—would be grievously transgressed thereby, and also because it would not have been of any help. For only the *inner* activity of the Society members could save the situation—but this proved itself insufficient.[128]

However, Rudolf Steiner did once speak of the danger that

111

threatened—on 23 January 1921—and he reminded his listeners of this five days after the burning of the Goetheanum, in his first lecture for those who had worked on the building: 'It is difficult to express something of the pain I experience. I know how intimately you share in what has happened, so I do not need to say many words. But I can perhaps take this time to draw attention a little to the fact that already on 23 January 1921, here in this hall, I read something from a pamphlet in which was displayed the statement of an opponent—or one could actually say, of an enemy—for this statement read at that time thus: "There are enough spiritual fire-sparks and lightning that hiss towards that wooden mouse-trap, and it will certainly need a good deal of Steiner's cleverness to work so appeasingly as to prevent a spark of real fire from one day bringing that splendour of Dornach to an ignominious end." '[129]

Assya Turgeniev, who was herself a witness of all these events and was also present when these words were read out, quotes them in her memoirs, and writes further about that evening of 23 January 1921: 'With a vague feeling of powerlessness we did not understand what lay behind those words, and the strength to oppose and ward off the approaching danger was lacking in us—it was an inability to act, just as had been the case in those first days of the war when Rudolf Steiner tried to call us to wakefulness and vigilance in relation to the events taking place.'[130]

In this situation Rudolf Steiner could do only one thing: call again and again for wakefulness and responsibility, and give in his lectures the necessary basis of knowledge that would further this. And precisely in these years he did this with particular intensity. Suffice it in this connection to refer to the extensive lecture cycles given by him in 1922; for example, at the Vienna Congress in June; the 'French Course' *Philosophy, Cosmology and Religion* in September; the pedagogical course *The Younger Generation* in October, as well as many other lectures and cycles in different European cities.

Despite this, Rudolf Steiner's call now, as in the first days of the war, was not heeded sufficiently and the tragedy was not averted. We therefore have to recognize that the members of the Anthroposophical Society could save neither the physical Goetheanum nor the forces of their Teacher's etheric body that were sacrificed into it! Yet despite this it was Rudolf Steiner who had to bear the full force of the terrible blow, which directly afflicted his etheric body (and the forces of darkness knew this)—it was he who, in all the chaos of impotence and despair that followed the fire, would not allow the spiritual work to be broken off for an instant. Everything which had been previously planned for the day that followed the fire was carried out as appointed. For Rudolf Steiner knew better than anyone else that the forces which had destroyed the Goetheanum just a few hours before were also looking for a breaking-point in his anthroposophical work. And we can only have the faintest inkling of what it must have cost him as an initiate and as a man to continue the work without pause, even on the day immediately after the tragedy. And this act surely bears witness to the extraordinary spiritual heights and to the powerful control over himself he had attained at that time.

But although Rudolf Steiner could bear these things, the Society could not. After the fire, therefore, the processes that bore witness to its inner disintegration became significantly stronger. Rudolf Steiner was obliged to confirm this at the beginning of the opening talk of the Christmas Conference in December 1923: 'The first sight you had again of this place as you climbed the Dornach hill was of the mound of debris that has remained of the Goetheanum which was destroyed a year ago. And in the truest sense of the word, this sight that speaks so deeply to our hearts is a symbol of the outer manifestation not only of our work, our endeavours on an anthroposophical footing here and in the world, but this heap of rubble is in many respects symptomatic of affairs in the world in general.'[131]

One can suppose that the split in the German Society and the separating off of the so-called 'Free Anthroposophical Society' (*Freie Anthroposophische Gesellschaft*), in which particularly the younger members drew together, was what led to these words that are so deeply tragic. Faced with this fact during the Stuttgart Conference at the end of February 1923, Rudolf Steiner had been obliged to give his consent. But while in Holland in November 1923, he expressed profound doubts in the presence of Zeylmans van Emmichoven as to whether he would be able to remain connected with the Society,[132] and he stated at the Christmas Conference: 'It was a difficult decision for the reason that, fundamentally, such an expedient contradicted the whole foundation of the Anthroposophical Society ... It was an anomaly. And this was perhaps one of the most significant symptoms that then influenced my decision to say to you here that I can continue to lead the anthroposophical movement in the Anthroposophical Society only if I myself act as chairman of the new anthroposophical society that is to be founded here today.'[133]

But despite these disheartening events Rudolf Steiner directed his activity more strongly than ever towards overcoming the ever-present difficulties and obstacles by means of positive work and especially by further developing Anthroposophy itself. Thus from March to the end of 1923 he developed the theme of the anthroposophical renewal of the basic Christian festivals. The beginning of this was made in *The Cycle of the Year* and *The Four Seasons and the Archangels*. In this way Rudolf Steiner placed the counterweight of all the positivity upon which he could possibly draw from the spiritual wellsprings of Anthroposophy against all the negativity coming from outside. In these lectures he unveiled for those listening the true occult foundations of the central Christian festivals. Learning to live with and into the course of the year was intended to awaken those inner forces that would be able to cope with all that was tragic and hard to bear in the situation that had arisen.

In the elaboration of this subject the occult significance of the autumn festival of Michael has a special place. One can say that this festival now receives its proper meaning and content for the first time in the external history of Christianity. Since then, the festival of Michael that was won anew for all humanity by Rudolf Steiner forms a most vital element of the inner life of every anthroposophist, as do the other renewed festivals of Christmas, Easter, Whitsun and St John's Day. In an Imagination of solemn grandeur Michael himself comes before humanity as the new Time Spirit, imperiously pointing with his flaming sword to the higher 'I' of man, to which he henceforth turns.[134]

At the end of January 1923, Rudolf Steiner begins a series of single lectures which it was hoped would awaken in anthroposophists a deeper understanding of the tasks and the true essence of the anthroposophical movement and the Anthroposophical Society, together with a greater awareness of their relation to one another. In June of the same year, in Dornach, he then gives a whole cycle of eight lectures on this theme, *The Anthroposophic Movement*, in which he gives an overview of the development of Anthroposophy from the first steps in the Theosophical Society up to 1923.

In mid-July of this year the social theme appears again briefly (GA 225), but is then followed by a whole series of powerful cycles and single lectures dealing from many different aspects with the many-sided and intricate connections between the human being and the cosmos. These include *The Evolution of Consciousness, Man as Symphony of the Creative Word* and *Supersensible Man*.

Throughout the whole of this year, Rudolf Steiner also works on preparing and completely remoulding the Society. This showed itself in the founding and organizing in different countries of national societies from which, at the Christmas Conference of 1923–24, the General Anthroposophical Society was to arise with its centre at Dornach.

And finally, this year of extraordinary exertion and intense work culminates in one of Rudolf Steiner's most significant cycles, *Mystery Knowledge and Mystery Centres*, in which for the first time in the history of humanity the inner essence of the main western Mysteries is unveiled and whose content, until the time of their destruction at the beginning of our era, had been most carefully guarded. Only initiates had had access to them in the hidden sanctuaries and temples of antiquity. In these lectures secrets were disclosed that had not become part of external history after the final collapse of European Mystery-life, but had been carried by their last hierophants into that world from which they had once come to the Earth. Here, images of the most important Mystery-centres of antiquity arise before us with astounding clarity—Hibernia, Samothrace, Eleusis, Ephesus—centres that determined the development of western culture right up to the beginning of the Christian era, and which found their continuation in medieval Rosicrucianism.

Only after the Christmas Conference did Rudolf Steiner disclose in the Karma lectures the source of this most profound knowledge of the ancient Mysteries on the Earth; he had brought it directly from the supersensible School of Michael. For what he presented in this cycle was the earthly repetition of what Michael himself in the supersensible world had brought to the assembly of human souls and spiritual powers that are kindred to him.[135] In a lecture on 20 July 1924 in Arnhem, as though with a voice no longer human but vibrant with an almost cosmic tone, Rudolf Steiner spoke of the all-encompassing address Michael had once given in the lofty supersensible School, where he told of the decline of the old Mysteries and the necessity of founding new Mysteries on Earth, turning above all in this to his greatest pupil who was to realize this on Earth—to him, that is, who at Christmas 1923 laid the foundation for the centre of the new Michael Mysteries on Earth:

'For as long as the human race has peopled the Earth in human form there have been Mysteries on the Earth: Sun-Mysteries, Mercury-Mysteries, Venus-Mysteries, Jupiter-Mysteries, Saturn-Mysteries. The Gods sent their secrets down into these Mysteries, and individuals who had been properly prepared and trained were initiated there. So that one could know on Earth what was taking place on Saturn, Jupiter, Mars and so on, and how these things worked into and influenced the development of humanity on Earth. There had always been initiates in the Mysteries who conversed with the Gods. In an instinctive, ancient form of clairvoyance the initiates received the impulses that were sent to them in the Mysteries. And this, except for a few traditions—as Michael related to those kindred to him—has vanished from the Earth; it is simply no longer there. The impulses can no longer flow into the Earth. It is only in the most sub-ordinate realm, in the realm of reproduction, that Gabriel still has the power to direct lunar influences into the development of mankind. The ancient traditions have more or less vanished from the Earth, and with them has vanished the possibility of nurturing the impulses that enter into the subconsciousness and therewith into the different bodily sheaths of the human being. But if we now look back on all that was once brought to people in the Mysteries like a gift of Heaven, if we survey this wonderful

115

tableau and look down onto that cycle of time, we find Mystery-places there and see how heavenly wisdom flowed down into these Mysteries, how individuals were initiated by it, and how Cosmic Intelligence came down among human beings from our holy Sun-sanctuary in such a way that the great Teachers of humanity had ideas, thoughts, concepts, of a purely spiritual order, but which had been inspired into them from the sacred Sun-sanctuary. This has vanished from the Earth. We see this when we look back on ancient epochs. For we see it gradually vanishing from Earth development in the age of Alexander and what followed it. And we see how gradually the now-earthly Intelligence spreads out among humanity. But the vision of this has been left to us: we cast our gaze on the secrets into which initiates of the Mysteries were once initiated. Let us bring them to our consciousness! Let us bring them to the consciousness of those spiritual beings who were never in an earthly body but live in an etheric form. Let us bring it to the consciousness also of those souls who were often on the Earth in earthly bodies, but who are now present and belong to the community of Michael—let us bring it to *the consciousness of these human souls*. Let us outline the great teaching of the initiates that once streamed down to the Earth in the old form through the Mysteries—let us outline this before the souls of those who by Intelligence were connected with Michael.'[136]

And Rudolf Steiner continues: 'And then the whole of the ancient wisdom was gone through—if I can use such an earthly, almost trivial-sounding expression in this context.'

This ancient Mystery-wisdom that still belonged to the epoch of the descent of humanity, to the epoch of the macrocosmic Our Father, was now revealed so that in the great Mystery-act of the Christmas Conference of 1923 it could be transformed into the wisdom of the New Mysteries— the Mysteries that lead to the realization of the ideal of the microcosmic Our Father in the epoch of human freedom.[137]

At the time of the Christmas Conference, Rudolf Steiner was nearly 63. According to the seven-year law of development, the human being crosses the boundary of the Saturn-sphere at this age. He was now open to the influence of the whole cosmos! This was Rudolf Steiner's inner con-stellation when he was faced with the necessity of making the most difficult decision of his life. For as the earthly representative of that spiritual wisdom that came to manifestation in the world as the content of the anthro-posophical movement, he was faced at that time with the impossibility of guiding this anthroposophical stream into humanity. The Society, whose main task it should have been to nurture the fruits of this movement and carry them into the world, proved itself a completely unsuitable instru-ment. Rudolf Steiner himself said that the Anthroposophical Society 'did not show itself in the course of time to be of such a nature as could be connected with a genuine and true nurturing of Anthroposophy'.[138] Thus he found himself faced with the difficult alternative of either dissolving the Society and therewith also giving up the possibility of introducing Anthroposophy to a wide circle of people, or of completely reorganizing it in such a way that as its leader he would also take its earthly affairs into his own hands. However, to dissolve the Society would mean a renunciation right at the beginning of the new epoch of those great social goals that Michael, the Time Spirit himself, had set before humanity. Rudolf Steiner therefore decided upon the second alternative—and in so doing offered himself up for its fulfilment.

It is not possible to come nearer to the inner essence of the mystery of Rudolf Steiner's life without understanding the full significance of this decision and the magnitude of the sacrifice that followed it. For in this decision Rudolf Steiner stood before the Golgotha of his life.

It has often been described in anthroposophical literature what this decision of Rudolf Steiner's signified when up till then only the representative of spiritual wisdom, a teacher and counsellor, he now had to take upon himself, along with the leadership, all the earthly affairs of the Society. And we also know that, in answer to this step, those spiritual powers that had guided and directed the anthroposophical movement through him in the world could have withdrawn. Rudolf Steiner presented this in the following way in a lecture in Arnhem on 18 July 1924: 'One can say that in a certain sense what was undertaken at Christmas had quite an element of risk. For there was a certain possibility that, because the leadership of the Anthroposophical Society was now joined with the representing of the wealth of spiritual wisdom, those spiritual powers that guide the anthroposophical movement in the spiritual world might withdraw this guidance.' These words show clearly that in this decision Rudolf Steiner put his whole mission on Earth at risk. He had to perform an act the consequences of which even he, a great initiate, did not know. And the question naturally arises here: why did Rudolf Steiner not know?

Here we touch upon the most profound essence of the new Christian Mysteries, and together with this the hidden seed of the future evolution of humanity—the secret of humanity as the Tenth Hierarchy. For this reason we must look upon this act by Rudolf Steiner as one strongly pointing towards the future. For what will be the nature of this humanity as the Tenth Hierarchy that is to represent the principle of freedom and love in the cosmos? Rudolf Steiner describes it by saying that the human being of the future will not be able to act in the cosmos from any sort of external stimulus, but only out of the inner core of his own being, permeated through and through with the Christ.

Already in the creation of the world by the Elohim we see this great hierarchic principle: '... And the Elohim said, Let there be Light! And there was Light. And the Elohim saw the Light, that it was good.'[138] Thus a truly hierarchic deed in freedom is one that first of all puts into effect an impulse arising purely from within, which only then is followed by the evaluation and knowledge of that deed. Only under these conditions can a deed or act manifest itself as a deed of love. And this great hierarchic principle of freedom and love was brought to the Earth by the Christ through the Mystery of Golgotha and implanted into human evolution in which, through all future conditions of the Earth—through Jupiter, Venus and Vulcan—it will henceforth develop and grow.

But how was the Christ able to carry this principle into Earth evolution? Only when Christian tradition unites with spiritual science can it provide an answer to this question. Out of divine compassion did the Christ descend from the Sun to Earth, and enter the bodily sheaths of Jesus at the Baptism in the Jordan. The Cosmic Christ Being was three years on the Earth in order that He might share the destiny of humanity right to the end. From a God, Christ became man. Step by step the Son of God became the Son of Man. This process, of such solemn grandeur as was only possible through infinite love and compassion for mankind, reached a certain culmination in that scene of profound drama in the Garden of Gethsemane where Christ is forsaken not only by His disciples but also, due to His finally complete and total union with the bodily sheaths of Jesus, by those macrocosmic Father-forces that He had resolved to renounce for the salvation of mankind.* He is alone. The world of the Gods and the world of man withdraw from Him. In the absolute freedom of this infinite loneliness He resolves to realize the principle of pure cosmic love on Earth. And when this greatest decision of all the development of our cosmos was taken, the Father in whose Divine Person all the Hierarchies are encompassed, raised up the Christ and endowed Him with a still greater fullness of cosmic forces than those He had had to give up through His descent to Earth for the salvation of mankind.†

It was only through the macrocosmic deed of Christ that the seed of that divine force of love which lives in complete freedom could be implanted into human souls. Henceforth it will gradually prepare humanity for its mission in the cosmos as the Tenth Hierarchy, as a Hierarchy that one day will be called upon to create cosmically, solely out of itself. For this reason,

*Rudolf Steiner describes this scene in detail in lecture 9 of the cycle *The Gospel of St Mark*.
† This is the meaning of the words of St Paul, that the Father raised up the Christ after His death (Corinthians I, 15: 15).

118

since the Mystery of Golgotha this lofty hierarchic principle of freedom and love had also been the foundation of every true Christian initiation. We meet a picture of this principle later in Parsifal, where in the Grail Castle he must be the *first* to ask the question, that is, the first to take a step out of complete inner freedom, allowing himself to be guided by the principle of love and compassion alone. If an individual takes this step out of his solitude and freedom in such a way that he contributes towards the fulfilment of cosmic purposes, the spiritual world answers; if this is not the case, it is silent. And in a similar way will mankind work creatively towards fulfilling its own future responsibilities in the cosmos.

Rudolf Steiner describes this in *Knowledge of the Higher Worlds* as the third trial, the so-called 'trial by air', where the pupil of the spirit must act in complete inner freedom, moved only by compassion and love. Only when the pupil has passed this test can he enter into the realm of the spiritual world which is called the 'Temple of Higher Knowledge'.

Rudolf Steiner experienced this trial often at different stages of his path of initiation. The first time was in his early youth just before his meeting with the Master; then at the end of his time in Berlin; and finally at the laying of the Foundation Stone of the First Goetheanum. And each time when the act of offering had been done—and done *in the right way*—the spiritual world answered with particularly significant spiritual revelations. This was now to happen at the highest stage attainable for an incarnated human being. The initiate was to accomplish a deed that was the micro-cosmic image of what the Christ had accomplished macrocosmically in the Mystery of Golgotha. On the historical plane, openly before all and for the first time since the beginning of the epoch of freedom which mankind entered at the beginning of the fifteenth century, Rudolf Steiner accomplished a deed stemming from the purest forces to awaken in a human being since the Mystery of Golgotha, and which rank him among those belonging to the Tenth Hierarchy.

In freedom and love, supported by nothing external, neither by the world of man nor the world of the Gods, but purely from the Christ-impulse in his own heart, Rudolf Steiner resolved to take on the leadership of the Society and therewith to bind his own spiritual destiny with its destiny, both on Earth and in the spiritual worlds. We are touching here upon the most significant and decisive secret of Rudolf Steiner's life, and must ask what is meant in an occult sense for him to take upon himself the earthly affairs of the Society, thereby joining the hitherto separate Anthroposophical Society and anthroposophical movement into a single unity. It meant in the truest sense that from then onwards, before the spiritual world, Rudolf Steiner took upon himself the full occult responsibility for the actions of every member of the Society. Every member is

119

free as before. His connection to the anthroposophical movement and Anthroposophical Society, now welded together into a unity, rests solely on his *understanding* of the inner essence of the Christmas Conference. Nevertheless, the karmic consequences of the wrong actions of every individual, connected now or in the past with the Society, also directly affects the destiny of Rudolf Steiner. This is the meaning and significance of the fact that Rudolf Steiner has taken upon himself the *karma of the Anthroposophical Society*.

In her first publication of the proceedings connected with the Christmas Conference, Marie Steiner writes: 'Primarily, everyone who took part in this Conference was as though lifted beyond himself, was suffused with warmth yet at the same time inwardly deeply shaken. But a destiny hovered over the occasion that would have to be carried out in other spheres of existence. The outcome showed what it meant for Dr Steiner *to take our karma upon himself.* And therein lies the deep esoteric nature of this deed of self-offering.'[140]

But what does it mean in a real occult sense *to take upon oneself* the karma of an individual, a group of people or a whole society? To come to an understanding of this, as we are dealing here with a Christian Mystery-deed, we will have to turn again to the macrocosmic Archetype, to the life of Christ Himself. For what was the inner essence of the death of Christ on the Cross? What happened in that moment when, from the body pierced by the spear, the blood of the Saviour began to flow? In that moment, Christ took upon Himself the karma of the *whole of humanity*. Wounded by the spear of humanity's karma that was heavily laden with sin, with bad karma, His blood, which, according to Rudolf Steiner, is an image of the 'excess, egoistic blood' of mankind, flowed to the Earth as a free offering. In the death on the Cross He atoned cosmically *right into the physical body* (for karma works even into the physical body!) for the consequences of humanity's karma. He gave humanity the possibility of not falling irrevocably to those forces of death which were the consequences of their sins and which were more and more gaining a hold.

By looking at this macrocosmic Event we can understand that any microcosmic happening similar to it is always a reflection of this great Archetype and can only be understood through it. *What Christ did for the whole of mankind in taking upon Himself its karma was done at the Christmas Conference by Rudolf Steiner, as the true pupil of Christ Jesus, for the members of the Anthroposophical Society.* Thus the macrocosm was mirrored in the microcosm. Thus the earthly Teacher followed as pupil in the footsteps of the Cosmic Teacher. It is vital that every member of the Society takes this to heart.

Only from this can we understand aright what Marie Steiner further wrote: 'But our human and Society karma unburdened itself onto him—and this occurred immediately after the Christmas Conference. For on the last day, on 1 January 1924, he fell suddenly and very gravely ill. It was like the blow of a sword that struck at his life ...'[141] This illness that struck him 'like the blow of a sword'—and that is a realistic imaginative picture—was the effect of the heavily-fraught karma of the Anthroposophical Society reaching even into his physical body. And with all the seriousness due to such a conviction we must say that when we really understand what it means, in the profoundest occult sense, to take on the karma of other human beings, then we have to see that Rudolf Steiner *had* to fall ill, for these two things cannot be separated from one another. Just as once Christ on the Cross was pierced by the spear of the fraught karma of all humanity, so was the body of His pupil pierced by the 'sword' of the difficult karma of the Anthroposophical Society.

It follows therefore that the illness that struck him on the last day of the Christmas Conference was no ordinary one, but one of a very special nature. In it Rudolf Steiner lived out, even in his physical body, the karma of *others*.[142] The karmic flaws of the Society, the past mistakes, errors and shortcomings of the individual members and the confusion in their individual karma, all came to outer expression in the bodily sufferings of the Teacher—they became *physically visible*.[143] Only when we understand this—and understand it not only with the head but take it into the deepest impulses of our hearts and souls—only then will we be able to understand just what a sacrifice was made by Rudolf Steiner at the Christmas Conference. *It is the deepest mystery of that Conference that for the building of a centre of the new Michael Mysteries that can lead humanity once again to a union with the spirit and thereby renew its spiritual and cultural life, Rudolf Steiner offered up the forces of his physical body.*

This *fourth* and highest stage of Rudolf Steiner's path of self-offering, that all-encompassing synthesis of outer and inner, of the exoteric and the esoteric, as mentioned above, was accomplished now also on the historical-social plane.[144] Henceforth the Michaelic esotericism could flow directly into all the separate branches of human knowledge and in time would lead to a renewal of western culture in the spirit of Michael. In the working-together of the esoteric *Vorstand*, the leadership group, and the sections of the Goetheanum that were permeated with esotericism and founded during the Christmas Conference, we have the complete and harmonious uniting of two fundamental kinds of spiritual work in one foundation which, at the same time, was also a centre for the New Mysteries.[145]

Out of love for humanity Rudolf Steiner, in deepest solitude, separated from the spiritual powers that had hitherto been guiding him, though permeated through and through by the Christ Spirit, thus performed on

121

that last day of the Christmas Conference his act of self-offering even to the point where the consequences of it reached into his physical body.[146] The spiritual world answered this act with a resounding cosmic affirmation. And it was as though all the gates of Heaven were opened, for then did Michael, the sublime guide of the present epoch, endow anew his greatest servant on Earth with spiritual revelations whose fullness we can barely imagine, and which now flowed down to all humanity through his lips.

Anyone who submerges himself in the deep and many-faceted nature of the new revelations that have flowed through Rudolf Steiner from the Michael-sphere, anyone who tries to bring to life within himself this time of over half a century ago, can even today gain an impression of what really took place at that time. And anyone who had the good fortune at that time to look directly into Rudolf Steiner's eyes could see *through* his physical body, through the physical sheath, which was already no longer *his* sheath, to the spiritual world gathered behind him and speaking through him— and at the head, Michael and those kindred to him. From now on, as Rudolf Grosse writes, 'Rudolf Steiner was accepted and confirmed by the guiding powers of humanity's destiny, was affirmed and bestowed with a new spiritual honour which signified an ascent and the transference to him of plenary powers that are beyond imagination...'[147]

Rudolf Steiner's own words concerning his great inner victory, the most significant event of his life, and the great answer of the spiritual cosmos to his act of sacrifice in the name of humanity, are these:

Paris, 23 May 1924: 'I can look today to the extraordinarily significant fact ... that since the Christmas Conference the spiritual impulse that must come down from the spiritual worlds if the anthroposophical movement is to continue in the right way has increased decidedly, so that since the Christmas Conference our anthroposophical movement has been able to grow more and more esoteric and will continue to do so...'[148]

Dornach, 22 June 1924: 'It can be said today that in the spiritual worlds a decision has been made such that, since the Christmas Conference, the wellsprings of the spiritual world are more open than hitherto.'[149]

Arnhem, 18 July 1924: 'One may say that these spiritual powers come now with a greater grace, with greater good will to meet what flows through the anthroposophical movement.'[150]

Torquay, 12 August 1924: 'One can say that since the founding of the Anthroposophical Society at the Goetheanum, those spiritual powers from whom we have our revelations look down upon us with absolute goodwill, with greater good will than was previously the case.'[151]

London, 24 August 1924: 'But now it can be said that things have turned out in such a way that, since the Christmas Conference, not only has the spiritual world not withheld its revelations but on the contrary has looked down with even greater benevolence on what is happening in the anthroposophical movement in the Anthroposophical Society. And the gifts from that world have become significantly richer since the Christmas Conference, *so that indeed also in connection with esotericism we can look back to the Christmas Conference with full assurance.*'[152]

What Rudolf Steiner was speaking about now was the revelation of those deep secrets of the Michael-sphere that had been open to his inner gaze since the eighties and nineties of the nineteenth century, but which it had been impossible to speak about. But now, because of the sacrifice he had made at the Christmas Conference, the ahrimanic demons opposing Michael could no longer prevent Rudolf Steiner from unveiling to all humanity the full depths of the Mysteries of the Time Spirit Michael, which touched upon the most important secrets of the spiritual-historical coming into being of contemporary mankind. Rudolf Steiner says of this:

'Also in the bosom of the anthroposophical movement a great deal still had to be carried forward that in a certain sense has remained a Michael secret. Belonging to this were above all those truths relating to historical connections. For some months now it has been possible—and has now become possible also for me—to speak of these things without restraint. That is why this now occurs, has occurred, and indeed is meant to occur here ... For this is connected with the unveiling of the Michael secrets, which happened in the way I have described to you ... Indeed, through everything that it has been possible to give to the Anthroposophical Society only since the Christmas Conference, and by the way in which since that time I myself have been allowed to work occultly—for these are not new things, in occult matters one cannot immediately communicate what one discovered only yesterday; these therefore are old things—through this has come the added fact that the demons [the opponents of Michael] must keep silent, whereas before I was prevented by them from speaking out.'[153]

Thus by a great sacrifice the right was won to bring to humanity those revelations without which it could not develop further.

Only after Rudolf Steiner had united his karma at the Christmas Conference with the karma of the anthroposophists was he able, still during the Conference, to reveal to them his own past and in the following lectures their past—their karma. For to speak now of their karma was to speak at the same time of what was inseparably connected with his own destiny. He could now disclose to them the secrets of the Michael-sphere in so far as these concern the spiritual-historical evolution of humanity or the destiny of the anthroposophists as the true followers of Michael. From now on he revealed to them the deepest mysteries of the cosmic being of the guiding Time Spirit, and attained thereby to a still higher stage in realizing his mission and his service.

But what was achieved by Rudolf Steiner during that time? If we look at this lecturing work, which was unparalleled in scope and depth following the Christmas Conference, if we try to imagine clearly what it meant in nine short months to give 338 lectures and 69 talks in almost all branches of knowledge, thereby transforming each separate sphere and suffusing it with powerful impulses towards the future, opening up immense spiritual horizons to the anthroposophists and, through them, to all humanity— then we will understand what was happening here.

Starting immediately after the Christmas Conference, Rudolf Steiner fulfilled with his own life the second cosmic Michael revelation on Earth of which he had spoken four years before in a lecture on 22 November 1919:'The Word become flesh is the first revelation of Michael.'[154] 'And the time must come when flesh becomes Word once again and learns to dwell in the realm of the Spirit'—this is the second Michael revelation. And Rudolf Steiner's life from the Christmas Conference onwards was one where in truth his flesh became Word. For his physical forces ebbed away more each day, his flesh waned, as it were, dissolved away, vanished; but through it the World-Word resounded more and more mightily, for it was the Word of Michael himself who now spoke through Rudolf Steiner, and who through him founded the First Class of the School of Spiritual Science as the true centre of the new Michael Mysteries that henceforth stand under his direct guidance.

Having journeyed through nine seven-year periods and nine planetary-hierarchic spheres, after the Christmas Conference Rudolf Steiner entered into the tenth sphere, into the sphere of the future Spirit Man. It is the secret of this last period of his life that in it he showed people what it means to realize on Earth the second Michael revelation in which the essence of the future lies.

We must now look in more detail at the last months of Rudolf Steiner's life and at the tragic mystery of his death. Why is it that up to the last moment he said nothing of his departing but repeatedly asserted that he would recover, that his work would be continued, that there was still so much to do, that he still had so much to add to what had already been given, in order to develop and enrich it further? All the Society believed up to the last moment that he would recover and he nourished their hope ... Then suddenly he was gone, quite unexpectedly, in the deep tragedy of his complete silence—not a single word, not a single indication or conscious 'No' to the question 'Who ... ?'

The decease of every human being is a mystery, but where the decease is that of a great initiate this event becomes an event of the greatest mystery. However, everything that has been said hitherto can assist us in our attempt to shed some light upon it.

If we bear in mind what has been said concerning the peculiar nature of Rudolf Steiner's illness, we can see that this was not *his own* illness but the spiritual illness of the Society which only became outwardly visible in the physical suffering of the Teacher. This karmic malady of the Society, the malady of unresolved, difficult karma, gradually consumed Rudolf Steiner's physical body. From this it is clear that the healing of Rudolf Steiner's illness no longer depended *on him*. He could not heal himself, for since the Christmas Conference his physical body *no longer belonged to him*. For this reason also no outer medical aid could help him. Certainly he had need of the care of the friends and doctors around him—Ita Wegman, Ludwig Noll and others could assuage his suffering for a time—but despite all their selfless efforts it was beyond their power to cure him completely, for they could not eradicate the cause which was rooted not in him but in the Society.

This also explains why almost immediately after the Christmas Conference it was so important for Rudolf Steiner to reveal to the members of the Society their own past. For the people who were brought together in the Anthroposophical Society came from the most diverse streams—even from streams that in the past had been at enmity with one another. They brought with them karma that was complex, difficult and far from resolved. And it was these impulses of unresolved karma working in the subconscious that gradually led to the point in 1923 where the Society could no longer serve as a fitting instrument for realizing the spiritual impulses of the anthroposophical movement in the world, but instead became more and more an obstacle to them, only hampering and complicating their attempts to find their rightful place amongst mankind.

Ever since he had emerged as a Teacher, Rudolf Steiner had known from his insight into the secrets of the Michael-sphere that only by the union of the representatives of so many spiritual streams and Mysteries of the past could the seed for the future spiritualization of humanity be created. This is why right from the beginning of his anthroposophical work—still while within the fold of the Theosophical Society—he tried to awaken in those around him a stronger consciousness of these questions. In his lectures in 1924 he reminded his listeners a number of times of his attempts in 1902 to give a lecture on 'Practical Exercises in Karma'. These attempts were thwarted at the time by the hostile attitude of some of the leading personalities in the Theosophical Society towards them. Yet despite this initial failure, he nevertheless tried in the following period— and particularly in 1905—to shape his work in such a way as to give the

125

anthroposophists the possibility of balancing out and rectifying old karma, for the dark adversary forces continually exploit karma that has not been balanced out for their own ends. Through the founding of the Michael Mysteries on the physical plane, Rudolf Steiner gradually wanted in the future to approach a *conscious* founding of *new karma* amongst anthroposophists in the spirit of the Michael-impulse. The intensive esoteric work that unfolded under his guidance, first within the Theosophical Society and then in the separate Anthroposophical Society until its tragic disruption at the beginning of the First World War, was his most significant attempt at that time to enable the anthroposophists to work on their karma in this direction.

The next attempt was connected with the building of the Goetheanum, for the combined work on this unique temple for the new spiritual life again offered the opportunity of putting old karma in order and founding new karma.[155] But the Goetheanum was tragically taken away from the anthroposophists on the physical plane...

Having taken upon himself the karma of the anthroposophists at the price of physical suffering, Rudolf Steiner could now tell them of their own karma in the hope that they would thereby be able to work consciously on it. He hoped that such knowledge would give them the strength to overcome the impulses of enmity and disharmony rooted in the depths of antiquity, and that finally, if not actually to redeem their old karma, it would at least partly balance it out, purify and clarify it, and make them work consciously for a new karma that since the Christmas Conference he had revealed to them as a common Michael karma.[156] *And this would have cured Rudolf Steiner*, for the unresolved karma of the Society was the true cause of his illness. To the last moment of his life he hoped that this would be understood. He spoke of his recovery, for he believed that by the understanding of the impulses of the Christmas Conference the Society would strive to realize them and that anthroposophists, following the vital call of Michael, would found a new karma among themselves, thereby *giving him the possibility of regaining his health* and remaining with them a while longer.

But it did not happen. The Society would neither overcome the old karma *to the necessary degree* nor press forward to found the new. The Society did not offer Rudolf Steiner the possibility of remaining on the physical plane, for its love for him was not sufficient. What was necessary here was to develop the will—through a right *understanding* of what had taken place at the Christmas Conference—to overcome everything personal and to bear Rudolf Steiner's cross with him, that is, to become a conscious colleague in the sphere of karma.

And in that moment when the forces of the Society proved insufficient in this respect, Rudolf Steiner had to leave this world and leave it in complete silence, with no word of either approval or reproach. But his silence said: That which you were unable to do while I was with you, you must now achieve without me, in the most profound freedom and loneliness, and without my immediate guidance. You must now accomplish it through what can spring forth from your hearts when they are filled with the impulses of Michael-Christ, which were brought by the spiritual world through me into the Christmas Conference. For in these impulses I continue to be connected with you; through the Christmas Conference my karma is inseparably bound with yours. And if you remain true to these impulses of the Christmas Conference and realize them in sufficient degree, I will be able to complete among you what has been left undone.[157]

In this silent yet extraordinarily significant passing of Rudolf Steiner from the physical plane, every anthroposophist who feels himself connected with Rudolf Steiner, and through him with the spiritual Beings who have guided and continue to guide the anthroposophical movement and with whom Rudolf Steiner remained united also after his death—every such anthroposophist must feel in all the tragic enormity of this event the strongest possible impulse to work further towards realizing the aims of the Christmas Conference, fully aware that in so doing he creates the possibility for Rudolf Steiner to return to us and act among us for the completion of his concern on Earth.

In a lecture on 29 August 1923 at Penmaenmawr, Rudolf Steiner once spoke of the possibility of the future working on Earth of the successor to the old Bodhisattvas: 'Therefore humanity will wait in vain for the coming of one of the successors of the old Bodhisattvas. For whether a Bodhisattva appears for humanity or not depends on whether humanity comes to meet him with *understanding*.'[158] And further: '. . . it is not humanity that has to wait for the Bodhisattva, but the Bodhisattva who has to wait for humanity to come towards him with understanding before he can speak in their language, for humanity has entered the epoch of freedom.' These laws of world guidance permeate all levels of existence.

For this reason the further possibility for Rudolf Steiner to work openly on the Earth at the end of the twentieth century also depends on whether we can approach him, and in particular the central deed of his life for humanity—the Christmas Conference of 1923–24—with sufficient *understanding. Today it is not we who must wait for Rudolf Steiner but Rudolf Steiner who waits for us.* And he *is* waiting.

It is because Rudolf Steiner connected his own karma after the Christmas Conference with the destiny of the Anthroposophical Society on Earth that only the Anthroposophical Society can create today the conditions needed for his further activity within it, for the founding of the

Second and Third Classes of the Esoteric School and for the completion of the mission he began at the Christmas Conference—the founding of a centre of the new Michaelic-Christian Mysteries. This centre has *already* been founded, but *not yet completed.*[159] Whether it is completed or not now depends on the members of the Anthroposophical Society, on their understanding of the fundamental impulses of the Christmas Conference and their willingness to work on in its spirit.[160] For Rudolf Steiner himself spoke constantly about the fact that the working of the Christmas Conference would continue.[161] And this continuing activity of the Christmas Conference right into our time is a sure sign of the spiritual presence of Rudolf Steiner, a sign which has indeed accompanied the Anthroposophical Society all these years through the constant presence in it of souls honestly striving in their anthroposophical work to remain true to this central impulse. *For we must give Rudolf Steiner the possibility of working among us again.*

The destiny at the present time of the whole of Anthroposophy in the world depends on the realization of the impulses of the Christmas Conference. It is therefore not surprising that this *most important event of the twentieth century* on the *physical* plane for the spiritual life of western humanity has led to tragic conflicts within the Anthroposophical Society itself. But those anthroposophists who talk of the 'failure' of the Christmas Conference consciously or unconsciously further the impulses of those powers who seek to prevent Rudolf Steiner from completing his mission. At the same time these powers wish thereby to separate Anthroposophy from the spiritual forces that have guided it since the Christmas Conference, and to rob them of the possibility of realizing the purpose for which they sent Anthroposophy to the Earth, and for which they gave it their *benediction* through the Christmas Conference.[162]

To conclude this outline of Rudolf Steiner's life, we must return once more to the viewpoint from which our deliberations began. We said that the spiritual height attained by an initiate depends on the degree to which his life reveals the great laws that lie at the foundation of our cosmos. During the evolution of humanity these could appear *completely* only once on the physical plane—in those three years when the Christ Being dwelt in the bodily sheaths of Jesus of Nazareth. For this reason, since that Event the greatness of an initiate—especially of a Christian initiate who has trodden the Rosicrucian path—depends on the extent to which he can make his individual life a true microcosmic reflection of the macrocosmic path of Christ Jesus.

Since this was the path taken by Rudolf Steiner, we must look briefly again at the second half of his life, and see how it relates to the macrocosmic

Archetype of the new initiation that in the present epoch of Michael has for the first time become accessible to all mankind.

As said earlier, Christ's great path of sacrifice was such that in answer to the cries of a humanity sinking into the abyss He resolves to descend for its salvation. On His cosmic path to the Earth, while still beyond the zodiac sphere, Christ reveals Himself at first in the macrocosmic forces of the World-'I' as Vishva Karman; then He reveals Himself as Ahura Mazdao in the macrocosmic astral forces, whose sphere reaches from the Sun to the fixed stars; and finally in the sphere of the macrocosmic etheric forces as *Ejeh asher Ejeh*, the 'I am the I AM'. Here He already works down into the elements that are under the influence of the Moon-sphere, which is the closest to the Earth. These are the three cosmic stages through which Christ approached the Earth until, after the Baptism in the Jordan, His great Sun Being sank directly in the course of the three years into the bodily sheaths of a man, gradually identifying Himself with them. God became man.

For the sake of humanity the Divine Being of Christ is prepared to sacrifice the forces that have been His own since the creation of the world, and to give Himself up to unimaginable pain and suffering, as is revealed to us in the Fifth Gospel.

For in order to enter as 'I' into the three bodily sheaths of Jesus of Nazareth at the Baptism in the Jordan, Christ had to leave behind the macrocosmic forces of His 'I'.★ The holy Rishis had once received intimations of these forces from beyond the boundary of their own sphere. As Christ descended into the astral body of Jesus of Nazareth He renounced the forces of His own macrocosmic astral body, which Zarathustra had once beheld as the radiant aura of the spiritual Sun (and this is why Christ appears to the Apostles on the water *at night*). Later, when He entered fully into the etheric body of Jesus, Christ relinquished His macrocosmic etheric body which Moses had seen in the burning bush (this is why Moses appears again in the scene of the Transfiguration). And finally, in uniting completely with the physical body of Jesus of Nazareth in the Garden of Gethsemane, Christ sacrificed His own macrocosmic Being.[163] He renounced the macrocosmic greatness of all the Father-forces that had been His since the beginning of the Earth, and the Son of God became the Son of Man, uniting Himself totally with the physical body of a human being in order to offer it up in Golgotha; for only by knowing death could Christ overcome it and thereby unite Himself with the whole Earth-sphere!

Thus we see that at the basis of Christ's path of sacrifice and redemption

---

★ In many artistic representations of the Baptism scene this fact is expressed by a group of Angels who remain on the far side of the Jordan.

lie *four* macrocosmic sacrifices. Stage by stage, beginning at the Baptism in the Jordan, He relinquished the cosmic forces of His 'I', then His cosmic astral body, and subsequently His etheric body. Lastly, in the Mystery of Golgotha, Christ sacrifices His physical body which, since the night in the Garden of Gethsemane, really is *His body*, for He alone of all the Gods has won full and complete knowledge of the Mystery of incarnation, of death and of resurrection.[164] And so there opens before us the macrocosmic path of Christ during the three years of His life in the bodily sheaths of Jesus of Nazareth, as spiritual science has revealed.

With the greatest reverence we can now perceive the harmony which exists between this path and the path of Rudolf Steiner, who in the *four* great sacrifices of his life revealed himself as a great earthly follower of Christ Jesus. To the powers that guide world evolution, which since the Mystery of Golgotha are led by Christ Himself, Rudolf Steiner offered up the forces of his 'I' (this occurred about 1899), the forces of his astral body (about 1907), those of his etheric body (from 1913 onwards)—and finally, at the Christmas Conference of 1923–24, the forces of his physical body. Thus we can say: the life path of Rudolf Steiner, who lived among us as a human being among other human beings of the twentieth century and whose life we can compare with that of the greatest initiates of the past, initiates who are known to us through legends and traditions but who only acquire concrete shape and vigour through spiritual science, is revealed to us in its true majesty and beauty.

Thus the life path of Rudolf Steiner, who lived among us as a human being on Earth, unveils itself to us as a profound Mystery of the twentieth century and as the archetypal image of the new path of initiation.

And we can say: He who was able to follow in such a sublime way the great three-year path of sacrifice of Christ Jesus on Earth, follows without doubt also the further path of Christ through the spiritual spheres after death. Therefore we can conclude this outline of the *Mystery of the path of Rudolf Steiner's life* with the closing lines of the penultimate chapter of Rudolf Grosse's book *The Christmas Foundation*: 'If in the twentieth century the Etheric Christ moves among humanity, then there also moves with Him the one who placed in the world the Christmas Conference in the spirit of the Christ-Sun as the beginning of a Cosmic Turning-point of Time.'

THE BIRTH OF
THE NEW MYSTERIES

The First Goetheanum, 1922

4. The Earthly and the Supersensible Goetheanum

When today we survey the whole of Rudolf Steiner's earthly work in all its greatness and many-sidedness, we are struck first and foremost by his two most significant acts which also mark the decisive turning-points in the development of the anthroposophical movement and the Anthroposophical Society: the laying of the Foundation Stone followed by the building of the First Goetheanum, and the Christmas Conference of 1923–24.

We have already attempted in the first part of this book to show the deep Mystery-character of these two acts, and the special secret relation that existed between them. Having looked at these events more from the point of view of their relation to the course of Rudolf Steiner's life, we must now go more deeply into the inner nature of the destiny of the Goetheanum itself, and view the secret of its connection with the Christmas Conference from yet another angle, so that these two events may be seen as foundation stones laid at the centre of the new Michael Mysteries. Moreover, we must ask what significance these Mysteries have for the spiritual life of the western world today, and where their place is to be found in it.

However, before we turn directly to these questions we must return once more to Rudolf Steiner's four great life-sacrifices, bearing in mind that each of these was primarily related to one of the four members of the human being. A very specific inner connection can be seen between the first two sacrifices, but even more so between the second two, and an understanding of this will provide us with the point of departure for our further study.

Of the four fundamental members of the human being, only the 'I', as the essential core and centre of our being, is the bearer of our truly individual qualities and attributes. In the 'I' every human being carries with him his own individual microcosm that is unique in the whole universe and irreplaceable. With the astral body it is different. This is the bearer of the feeling-life and emotions within the human being, the bearer of his antipathies, sympathies and also of his life of thought. But in this sphere the human being is not so inwardly enclosed as he is in his 'I', for the feelings and thoughts experienced in the astral body can find an echo, a response in others, even though the life of the human being in his astral body remains within the boundary of his individual-personal existence. In regard to the etheric body, every human being is able to step beyond the boundary of his individual, separate being. By virtue of the etheric body each human being moves from his personal isolation out into a social element, enters into connection with one or other group of people with whom he is karmically connected; with his family, with those around him, and so on. This social function of the etheric body is indicated in the microcosmic Lord's Prayer:[1] 'And forgive us our trespasses as we forgive those who trespass against us.' It is through the etheric body that we enter into relation with other people or whole groups of people.

The human being penetrates yet more deeply into the social sphere by means of his physical body. While through his etheric body he is a member of a definite group of people, in his physical body he is related to humanity as a whole, is a member of all mankind. This is expressed in the microcosmic Lord's Prayer in the words, 'Give us this day our daily bread,' which point to the fact that the need for daily bread to maintain physical life exists for *every* human being, thus uniting all humanity into a single organism, into a living, indivisible whole. The first two members, the 'I' and the astral body, are more connected with the individual-personal principle in man, and the other two, the etheric and physical bodies, more with that which is of general human significance, with that which of necessity finds expression in the social element.

From this it follows that Rudolf Steiner's first two sacrifices, occurring about 1899 and 1907, related primarily to the forces of the 'I' and the astral body, and therefore had a more intimate, individual-personal character— which is not to detract in any way from their wider significance for all humanity as deeds in the service of the spiritual powers that guide it. On the other hand, this is also why the knowledge of these sacrifices became known comparatively late, and then only through indirect indications by Rudolf Steiner himself.[2]

The last two sacrifices (as described in Part I) were connected more strongly for Rudolf Steiner with the etheric and physical bodies. Consequently they are of a completely different nature, being fundamentally distinguished from the first two in that Rudolf Steiner could not effect them alone, but only with the active participation of others.

This most important characteristic of the two last sacrifices, namely, their *occult-social nature*, was of decisive significance not only for the further development on Earth of the anthroposophical movement but also for the Anthroposophical Society itself—which means for the further destiny of Anthroposophy in the world today.[3] Because of this they became a firm foundation upon which the centre of the new Michael Mysteries could come into existence, into whose temple *every* human being who is of good will may enter, who wishes to dedicate himself in freedom to higher development and to sacrificial service for the good of the world.

There is another aspect from which we can get an indication of the secret relation between the laying of the Foundation Stone, the building and further fate of the First Goetheanum, and the Christmas Conference of 1923–24.

If one thinks deeply about the Mystery-words spoken by Rudolf Steiner at the laying of the Foundation Stone of the First Goetheanum, if one reads the memoirs of different individuals concerning that evening in Dornach on 20 September 1913, and if one then tries to live into the sculptural-imaginative forms of the First Goetheanum, one can sense how closely it is related to the anthroposophical *Meditation*, 'Soul of Man...', given by Rudolf Steiner during the Christmas Conference, and to the overall nature of the way in which the Conference was conducted.[4]

In his book *The Foundation Stone*, Zeylmans van Emmichoven summarizes the connection between the First Goetheanum and the *Foundation Stone Meditation* as follows: 'Already in the threefold call to the Soul of Man one can experience the deeply moving fact that Rudolf Steiner had been able to bring down the stupendous Imaginations that lived in the Goetheanum building—Imaginations which had then gone through the consuming forces of fire, only to rise into spiritual heights—and to bring them back in an inspirational form as the Foundation Stone verse.'[5] In these few words, our attention is directly drawn to the purely *esoteric* connection between these two events, the knowledge of which is essential for an understanding of the inner nature of the centre of the New Mysteries founded during the Christmas Conference.

A very particular feeling can arise in someone who sees the architectural forms of the First Goetheanum for the first time, a feeling caused by the immediate impression this building can make on us. Imagine we see it from a distance, perhaps from one of the hills surrounding Dornach, so that we have a clear view over the landscape round about, and in the middle is the double-domed building tiled with silvery slate faintly glimmering in the light of the setting Sun. If we try to imagine this picture as clearly as possible, a spontaneous feeling arises in us that in this unusual building a secret is hidden.

And indeed no other building in the architecture of the world has provoked such contrasting feelings as the Goetheanum. It has excited the full gamut of human reactions from deep, selfless love to fanatical hatred. This unusual relationship to the building poses the question: What is the cause of such a 'division of the spirits'? Does it lie in the building itself, or in the individuals who come into contact with it?

During the ten years in which the Goetheanum was built, Rudolf Steiner spoke often of the meaning and significance of this building—of the building as a whole and of its individual elements and details. And it is among his many and various indications concerning this that we can find the answer to our question. The answer is: *'Und der Bau wird Mensch'*—*And the Building Becomes Man*. In these few words engraved in the rose south window of the Goetheanum, we have an indication of the special relationship that exists between the building and the secret of every individual human being, of every human life. Looking at the Goetheanum in this light gives us an understanding of our deep affinity with it and of the fact that the relation we have to it is fundamentally determined by the relation each of us has to *self-knowledge*; for that hidden inner being of man which we seek on the path of self-knowledge became visible for the first time to the external eye in the architectural forms of the Goetheanum. Hence it becomes clear that the cause of the 'division of the spirits' is not to be found in the building and its unusual forms but in the individual human being, for the relation of people to the First Goetheanum differs only as much as does their relation to self-knowledge. This is also the reason why Rudolf Steiner once said that the most tragic thing about the Goetheanum's destruction was not that it had been taken away from the anthroposophists on the physical plane, but that the whole of western humanity had been deprived of the sight of its forms—a sight in which was revealed the path to true self-knowledge.

From this we see that it is impossible to understand the deeper essence of this building without penetrating into the secret of man, but the numerous indications of spiritual science allow us a glimpse of it. There is a particular aspect of human evolution connected with this which is of great importance for our further study here.

From different descriptions given by Rudolf Steiner, we know that there are two experiences which only a human being can undergo and which distinguish him radically from all the divine beings in the cosmos, even though these stand infinitely higher than man in the ranks of the Hierarchies. Birth and death as experienced by the human being do not exist for the Gods in the spiritual world. These are experiences exclusive to the human being, who seeks incarnation in the physical world. Thus the fundamental secret of human life reveals itself to us only in a knowledge of birth and death. However, we should not imagine these only as portals, allowing the human soul to enter into or leave the Earth-sphere, but rather it should be realized that the forces of birth and death are woven into the whole of human life on Earth and only appear to be a culmination at the beginning and end of it. What then is the deeper nature of these two most important events of human life?

At birth the higher 'I', the cosmic 'I' in which the human being lives until the descent into an earthly body, recedes, but the individual 'I' is thereby born. For the whole of physical life it is bound up with the perceptions of the sense-world, and through the gradual development of this individual 'I' on Earth the human being in time wins through to true inner freedom.

Death, in this sense, is the opposite of birth. Here our lower, earthly 'I' that was fettered to the perceptions of the external senses is extinguished, and the consciousness of the human being for his higher 'I' awakens, enabling him now to partake in a cosmic life.

Out of these two most important human experiences connected with existence on Earth there arose in the course of time two Mystery-streams. Those belonging to the first stream strove through a knowledge of the forces of birth to penetrate into the secret of how the human soul entered from pre-earthly existence into earthly life. Those in the second stream strove through a knowledge of the forces of death to penetrate into the secret of the soul's ascent into the spiritual world.

The dark age of Kali Yuga began in the year 3001 BC. During this dark cosmic epoch, in order to win through to inner freedom, humanity plunged finally into the sphere of matter, and from this time onwards the Mysteries of Birth predominated. These gradually led humanity, through the individualization of consciousness, into the physical-material world in which, for freedom's sake, it renounced its connection with the supersensible worlds. The Mysteries of Death were sacrificed to the Mysteries of Birth.

The emergence of the pyramid form in Egyptian architecture shortly after the beginning of Kali Yuga bears witness to the fundamental tendency of this age towards a sinking into matter. Likewise the Egyptian custom of mummification that arose about the same time speaks clearly of how true knowledge of the Mysteries of Death was slowly fading.[6]

Later, in the flowering of ancient Greece, knowledge of the Mysteries of Death is finally lost entirely. Direct spiritual perception of the life of the soul after death becomes more and more inaccessible. The Mysteries of Birth take the lead, and death becomes something that is feared. The words of the Greek hero, in which is concentrated the whole basic mood of that age towards the world, ring deeply tragic: 'Better to be a beggar on Earth than a king in the realm of the shades.' And yet, even at that time humanity passes through a short but astoundingly harmonious epoch of its development, in which it experiences in itself the equilibrium and balance of all earthly forces. Humanity was already the captive of these forces to a considerable extent, and yet it perceived them in an unusually inspired and spiritual way so that in the Greek temple, with its balance of the forces of weight and levity, of Heaven and Earth, matter was brought into complete harmony with the spirit. And in the figures of the Greek gods we have images of deified man. In Greek art we meet the human being standing fully on the Earth yet experiencing himself in harmony with the spiritual forces that penetrate and form him.

However, the influence of the Mysteries of Birth worked particularly strongly in the people who, to a great extent, were to prepare the subsequent, the fifth post-Atlantean epoch. These were the Romans. In elaborating the beginnings of a jurisprudence in which they set down the principle of *jus civile*, the Romans were the first to talk about the rights of the individual, and they thereby paved the way for the social self-determination of the individual human 'I'. The impulse for this was drawn from knowledge of the Mysteries of Birth and their secrets. The Romans were also the first to find the architectural form that brings to expression the essence of these Mysteries. This was the cupola, the dome, which is perhaps most perfectly achieved in the Roman Pantheon, the temple of all the Gods. Here the cupola form, which is a reflection of our head organism having its archetype in the dome of the human cranium, leads us indeed to the very essence of the Mysteries of Birth. The human head is immobile. It rests majestically above the human body, which is in constant movement. And like the head, the cupola is also completely static, subject in its architectural forms only to the laws of space and of the material world, and thus appearing in this sense as the expression of that intellectualistic principle that was to become predominant among humanity.

From another aspect the cupola, like the human head, is also a reflection of that starry sphere continually circling about earthly man, unchangingly directing him to his life before birth, to that existence among the stars in which he lived until his descent to Earth. However, this spiritual existence appears in the cupola only as a dim memory. For though a likeness of the starry sphere, the cupola at the same time also limited man's range of vision and no longer allowed him to penetrate through this sphere to the world of pure spirit beyond. Thus we experience in the cupola-form an image of the human being who has become separated from his starry spiritual home, which he experiences no longer in himself but views externally in the dead laws of space. In the Pantheon man stands at the centre of the cupola. And although the Gods still surround him, he perceives them more and more in an external and abstract way, for little by little he is freeing himself from his connection to them.

Thus the cupola gradually limits man's range of vision to perceptions accessible to the external bodily senses alone; and in experiencing in himself how cosmic consciousness fades and earthly consciousness awakens, the human being gradually prepares himself to become a purely earthly but at the same time a completely free being. And later, when the cupola-form began to find its way into Christianity, it was even used

138

initially in the building of baptistries, of circular churches that through their form point to the secret of baptism in which one saw the symbolic image of man's birth out of the spirit. And indeed, from the beginning of the epoch of the consciousness soul, the dome of St Peter's cathedral has risen high above the Christian world as a symbol of the final triumph of the Mysteries of Birth, through which man has become a being who seeks the truth exclusively on the physical plane and there sets himself his own aims. In this sense the later onslaught of materialism is none other than the result of the once so powerful and deeply spiritual Mysteries of Birth that had now fallen into decay and decadence. The esoteric principle of these Mysteries was expressed in the words *Ex Deo nascimur*, and their corresponding architectural form was the cupola.

With the Mysteries of Death it was quite different. Humanity had had to lose all knowledge of these Mysteries with the onset of Kali Yuga, when it finally united itself with the material world. Because the knowledge that death can be the awakening to the true higher life slowly vanished, humanity was also no longer able to grasp the spiritual principle of death and finally became almost entirely cut off from its spiritual home, from the higher supersensible worlds, and succumbed more and more to the adversary powers of Ahriman and Lucifer. In other words, humanity at that time was faced with the real possibility that the goal of Earth evolution would never be reached, and that death would finally overpower human souls.[7] One thing alone could save it: there would have to be brought into human evolution a new knowledge of death as the mystery of the transubstantiation of the lower, mortal 'I' into the immortal, higher 'I'; that is, into Spirit Self.[8]

This great deed, giving again to Earth evolution its cosmic meaning, was performed by Christ Jesus who, having overcome the forces of death in the Mystery of Golgotha, showed humanity the true countenance of death to be the Mystery of ascent to the higher life, the resurrection of the individual 'I' to eternal, indestructible existence in the starry worlds.[9]

In architecture these new Mysteries of Death found their most perfect expression in the Romanesque and Gothic cathedrals based on the form of the cross as the symbol of death; the altar, too, was built in the form of a tomb—and both are reminders of the Mystery of Golgotha. One who walks beneath the vaulted arches of a Gothic cathedral can clearly feel how everything in him strives upwards into the heights of the spiritual world. To the immobility of spatial architecture there is added here the element of time, of movement. Time enters into battle with space. It is as though the soul struggles to pull itself free of the darkness of the body, to overcome the body's forces and surmount the laws of space that bind it, with the aid of the impulse of time that is bestowed upon the soul through its connection with Christ.[10] Gothic architecture is dynamic, resembling a flame in the soul that consumes material substance and strives towards the threshold of death—symbolized in the tomb-like altar in the East. The final union with the spirit, with the higher cosmic existence, is possible only beyond this threshold. Thus the Gothic cathedral leads us from the cross, on which the earthly lower human 'I' is crucified, to the resurrection in the life beyond, in the higher cosmic 'I'. In this sense, in the Gothic cathedral the esoteric principle of the new Mystery of Death, *In Christo morimur*, finds its most perfect exoteric expression.

Subsequently the cupola and the cross existed side by side in European architecture as the architectural forms of the two fundamental Mysteries of human life. On the other hand, however, even from early Christian times there arose more and more the urgent necessity of uniting these two Mysteries or, in other words, of realizing artistically the principle of *Per Spiritum Sanctum reviviscimus*, which expresses the new awakening of the soul in the higher worlds. For in this principle the possibility is given—not only after death but *during life on Earth*—of finding a path in consciousness to Spirit Self, to the higher human 'I'. The Spirit Self, in the terminology of esoteric Christianity, is the spark of Divine Sophia or the Holy Ghost in man.[11]

However, a realization of such a synthesis, which could only stem from a living metamorphosis of human consciousness, could not be achieved in an organic way until the end of Kali Yuga. For this reason the attempts that were made in this direction proved in the last analysis to be only a more or less intellectualistic combination of the principle of *Ex Deo nascimur* with *In Christo morimur*, and did not ascend to the new principle of *Per Spiritum Sanctum reviviscimus*. The most significant example of this is the cathedral of Santa Sophia in Constantinople, built in the sixth century. It is an example of the attempt to combine the Greek cross—which from the beginning had been the basis of the Santa Sophia cathedral—with the cupola-form; an attempt which, however, does not achieve an organic synthesis but only an external combination of the two principles, so nothing new could arise. In a deeper sense the reason for this was that at that time the human soul was as yet unable, by a truly inward *awakening* in the spirit, to attain to an immediate experience of the supersensible worlds in clear waking consciousness.

The possibility of attaining this harmonious synthesis through the *Per Spiritum Sanctum reviviscimus* was reached by humanity only after the end of Kali Yuga in 1899. After that year the gates of Heaven are open, and it is now possible for every human soul, even during life in the physical body, to seek a union with the higher, cosmic 'I'.

Today the human 'I' that takes up the new Christ Revelation in the twentieth century can experience a true awakening in the spirit, a fully conscious reuniting with the higher spiritual worlds, which it had once to forsake in order to attain to individual freedom in the world of matter.

This new principle of ascent into the higher worlds through imbuing oneself with the Christ-impulse was given to us in the sculptural-archi-tectural forms of the double-domed Goetheanum, where the cupola-form itself came, as it were, into movement, as expressed in the constant inner onward flow of the forms of the smaller cupola to the larger one and back again.

Thus time here does not enter into a battle with space as it does in the Gothic cathedral but spiritualizes it, thereby giving matter itself the pos-sibility of becoming deified, of entering and becoming part of the kingdom of the eternal spirit. Concerning the human soul, the metamorphosis moulded in the forms of the Goetheanum presents to us an image of a human intellect that is transforming and spiritualizing itself, an image of human thinking that frees itself from the fetters of space, from the imprisonment of rigid thoughts hardened in matter and transforms itself into an inwardly mobile, *living* thinking. And this living thinking seeks its source in the eternally alive and creative spirit that reveals itself in the human being as the overshining Spirit Self. And so we can say: in the Goetheanum the immobile becomes mobile, the dead becomes alive; for the mobility of its dome-form gives us an image of human thoughts becoming enlivened,[12] an image of their redemption from the kingdom of death by their resurrection in the kingdom of the spirit.

We therefore find that a study of the sculptural forms of the Goetheanum opens up a path that leads the human being in full freedom from his earthly to his higher 'I', from earthly to higher consciousness. In regard to this, the smaller dome of the Goetheanum shows us an image of the human 'I' as microcosm and how, by developing from past to future through seven post-Atlantean cultures, this 'I' takes up into itself the Christ, who is portrayed in the 'Group' carving in the East of the building and, correspondingly, in the painting on the smaller dome above it. For only the Christ-impulse gives the human being the possibility of seeking a union with the macrocosm. Its image—the higher, cosmic human 'I'—is carved into the larger cupola, in its seven columns which represent the whole evolution of the world from Old Saturn to the Venus existence and, in the painting of the creation of the Earth, by the Elohim who from the cosmos bestowed upon man his 'I'-consciousness.[13] Taken altogether, in the living metamorphosis of both cupolas there appears before us the essence and goal of all human devel-opment: having fulfilled the task of the Mysteries of Birth by descending completely to the physical plane and finding there the individual 'I', man now in a free act of love takes into himself the Christ-impulse and with its

141

aid seeks to ascend again. He strives, not after death but already *during life*, to find a path to the macrocosm and, by virtue of the Christ-force, to preserve there completely his individual divine 'I'-consciousness.

Today the soul is seeking a true *awakening* in the spirit! It seeks during life to experience death as the Mystery of resurrection of the higher 'I' in man, which alone can lead him into the divine spiritual existence of the starry worlds. And as a great answer of the cosmos to this profound striving of the soul of modern humanity there came to the Earth the architectural forms of the First Goetheanum. In these forms people received for the first time the possibility of perceiving not only *Ex Deo nascimur* and *In Christo morimur* but also a complete and harmonious union in *Per Spiritum Sanctum reviviscimus*, which the individual can find in the free ascent to the higher 'I', to Spirit Self, by passing in full consciousness through the Mystery of Death in Christ.

This is why there was originally no cross-form in the Goetheanum—it was not a part of the ground plan as had been the case in the Gothic cathedrals or in the Santa Sophia cathedral. In the Goetheanum the cross-form arises organically out of the living metamorphosis of the soul, out of its urge to unite itself while still in the body with the higher worlds, with its true divine-spiritual home. Therefore, not due to dogma, but because of a living metamorphosis, the main (East-West) axis of the building is crossed by the transverse axis which arises through the union of the two cupolas, the microcosm and macrocosm and which, in contrast to the main axis that expresses the necessity of world evolution, is the result of free human deeds, namely, the will to ascend from the lower 'I' to the higher by taking up in freedom the Christ-impulse, and realizing in oneself the rulership of the Spirit: *Per Spiritum Sanctum reviviscimus!*

Thus in the forms of the First Goetheanum we have before us the deepest secret of the human being. It is the secret of man who awakens in spirit to a higher life when he is able consciously to unite in himself the Mystery of Birth and the Mystery of Death in their final synthesis. And this synthesis can only be attained in the Mystery of Eternity,[14] the Mystery of the Spirit that is eternally alive. The Goetheanum shows the image of man in his eternal and his divine aspect. And just as the human body, according to the Apostle Paul, is the temple of the Holy Spirit[15] who as Bearer of the Divine Wisdom of all the Cosmos lives in this body—itself the result of the work carried out on it by all nine divine-spiritual Hierarchies since the time of Old Saturn—so, too, is the Goetheanum the true house of 'Anthropos-Sophia', of the wisdom of man that is born of the Holy Spirit. It is in this building that Anthropos-Sophia, the cosmic wisdom, has for the first time become visible on the physical plane to earthly human eyes.

This is why in the Goetheanum the speaker's podium was placed in the centre of the cross. From this place Anthroposophy as the true spiritual revelation of the wisdom of man, as the World of the Spirit itself, was to be proclaimed to modern humanity. The forms of the Goetheanum were to have been the sculptural embodiment of this Word, and speaking, living forms, like a larynx created for the speech of the Gods by the love and will of human beings. Rudolf Steiner spoke of this in a lecture on 31 December 1923, on the anniversary of the tragic destruction of the Goetheanum: 'And if our Goetheanum had been completely finished, then from the entrance in the West one's gaze would have fallen on that statue in which the human being would have been called upon to know himself to be a cosmic being, placed between the luciferic powers and the ahrimanic powers in an inner equilibrium of his being borne by the Gods. And if one looked up to the forms of the columns and architraves, one saw that they spoke a language—a language that seemed to carry further the spiritual content interpreted in the form of ideas from the podium. The words resounded on along the sculptural forms. And above in the cupola those scenes could be seen which were able to bring the evolution of humanity closer to the spiritual gaze.'[16]

Thus the human being, just by looking at the sculptural forms and colours of the First Goetheanum, and immersing himself meditatively in them, was to become gradually capable of *hearing* their language in himself as the language of *the spirit awakening in him*, as the Word of the Gods of the cosmos, which addresses itself to

... thine own I
... For thy free willing   (III, 9–11 [9–10])*

revealing to him the deepest secrets of his own being, and encompassing in itself the past, present and future of world evolution.

The living, etheric Word of the Gods, revealing itself in physical form and wishing in our time to speak to man through his awakening higher 'I'—this was the First Goetheanum. It was the embodiment of Anthroposophy itself, a true House of the Word, in which every human being could experience his own being as though in its heavenly archetype.[17] It was hoped that the Goetheanum would be this for every anthroposophist, and it was this above all for Rudolf Steiner.

Numerous statements by Rudolf Steiner bear eloquent witness to this:

* The lines are from the text of the *Foundation Stone Meditation*, the complete text of which is given on p. 347ff. The Roman numeral refers to the part of the *Meditation*, and the Arabic numeral to the corresponding line. Additional numerals (in square brackets) denote the lines in the German text of the *Meditation* given on pp. 350–52, where these differ from the English translation.

'... for one will see in the forms, which surround us there as artistic, one might say, "impress-forms", a reflection of what in the living word should be done, be said and be carried out in our building. A living word—that is what our building is!' (7 June 1914).[18] 'In its inner forms our building is to speak—and to speak the language of the Gods' (17 June 1914).[19] 'If we listen to the organs of the Gods which they themselves created when, as Elohim, they gave man to the Earth, if we listen to the etheric forms of the plants and reproduce these forms, then, as nature created the larynx in man for speech, so we create the larynges through which the Gods can speak to us' (17 June 1914). 'This will become alive in us and we will experience the following: You sit here and the Spirits of the World speak to you'; for the Goetheanum 'is the house of speech, the speaking house, the house that is alive in all its walls' (17 June 1914). This secret of the etheric word, which spoke in the forms of the Goetheanum and was of a unique nature, came mainly to expression in that the Goetheanum in its innermost essence was connected to the opening words of St John's Gospel, which Rudolf Steiner indicated in a lecture on 2 December 1923 in Dornach, three weeks before the beginning of the Christmas Conference: 'For this Goetheanum was a place in which the intention—and also the practise—was to speak about matters connected with the beginning of St John's Gospel: In the beginning was the Word. And the Word was with God. And a God was the Word.'[20]

But there was another Mystery connected with the Goetheanum which we have already touched on in connection with the description of the third, the etheric offering of Rudolf Steiner. For the deepest secret of the First Goetheanum lay in the fact that it was not only built according to the principle of metamorphosis in the plant kingdom and contained in itself a conformity to the laws of a living being, but *was itself a living being*, that is, a being having both a physical *and an etheric* body. In his book *The Christmas Foundation*, Rudolf Grosse draws attention to this secret which is connected with the laying of the Foundation Stone, with the building and later with the destruction of the First Goetheanum. 'The clear and direct consequence of the sentence "The Goetheanum has died" [i.e. died before its proper opening] cannot be expressed in any other way; it follows therefore that *it had existed until then as a living being.*'[21]

The following words of Rudolf Steiner also speak of the possibility of such a 'living architecture', of a temple that is a living being: 'This is the purpose of our age, to create the beginnings of a temple art that can speak loudly to the people of the future. The temple is man, man who receives the spirit into his soul.'[22] The nature of such an architectural art, which, however, can only be created by one who has penetrated not only into the mysteries of the physical body but also into those of the ether or *life* body, was characterized by Rudolf Steiner particularly clearly in a lecture in

Dornach, on 29 December 1914: 'We learn to know, as it were, the most external part of our being—that which goes on through the activity of the etheric body on the physical body—in a spatial system of lines and forces . . . When we describe here schematically the most external boundaries of our physical body, then we push out the inner laws that are impressed upon the physical body by the etheric body, push them out of ourselves and thereby there arises the art of architecture. All the laws that exist architecturally concerning the joining and articulating of materials are also to be found in full in the human body. The art of building, of architecture, is the projection of the laws of the human body outside into space . . .'[23]

The side-windows of the fourth South window also point to this secret of the interaction between the physical and the etheric principles in the forms and colours of the First Goetheanum. Here, in the colour of peach-blossom—that is, in the colour of the human etheric body—a human countenance is portrayed that has a correspondence to the West entrance of the Goetheanum.[24] In the central motif of this window a picture is given of the human being who experiences the Etheric Christ.

We must now ask: what, in the outer architectural forms of the Goetheanum, was the tangible expression of its hidden essence, was its similarity to the human physical-etheric organism which Christ repeatedly calls in the Gospels 'the temple of the human body'? In what way did this living, essential physical-etheric principle of the Goetheanum appear externally? To find an answer we must bear in mind that the human body as such is primarily based on two different material substances, the solid and the fluid. It is from solid and fluid substances that the human being forms his *visible* physical body. But whereas the solid principle is actually an expression of physical laws, the fluid principle in its constant mobility—the movement of blood and sap—is, in contrast, a visible image of the etheric laws of the human organism, an outer expression of the activity of the etheric body.[25] Rudolf Steiner spoke on many occasions of how it is in the solid element which forms the physical body that the influences of the fixed stars and, above all, of the zodiac come mainly to expression. The human physical form, inasmuch as it consists of solid substance, is founded on the laws of the zodiac, of the spatial cosmos—that is, on a twelvefold principle.[26] In the life-organs of the human organism, which in their movement and constant mobility are connected with the fluid element, there come to expression the forces of the human etheric body in which there work the deeds of the stars, the forces of the constantly moving planets, the laws of the time cosmos—therefore a sevenfoldness.

In numerous lectures Rudolf Steiner describes how the essential nature of the material, immobile-solid form of the human being consists of twelve spatial parts which stem from the twelve signs of the zodiac, and how the fluid, mobile-etheric being of man stands under the influence of seven 'temporal' parts which arise from the seven main planets of our solar system.[27] For the primary laws of the physical body are spatial laws, and those of the etheric body are temporal laws.[28] The etheric body is in constant movement, change, metamorphosis. The physical body, on the other hand, is immobile and invariable as regards the relation and proportion of the twelve fundamental parts to each other. These two types of laws[29] of the human organism are realized to the highest degree in the sculptural forms and colours of the First Goetheanum.[30]

However, we should not look on the movement, the metamorphosis, of the plantlike etheric forms of the Goetheanum as just something formally symbolic or 'only architectural' but as the expression of its own purely etheric laws, similar to the movement of sap in plants or of blood in man. In this it expresses, right into the physical, its spiritual-etheric reality—the reality of the Goetheanum as a living being. One can say that in the Goetheanum there are made externally visible those deeply hidden cosmic laws, according to which the human being daily takes into himself solid and fluid substances and unconsciously builds up the physical body and maintains the etheric body, the bodily-fluid organism. Thus the twelve-foldness as the expression of the physical-solid principle, and the seven-foldness as the expression of the etheric-life principle, play an important part in man. In the smaller cupola the twelvefold principle is more in evidence: twelve thrones below, twelve columns and capitals, and above in the dome twice six initiates[31] representing post-Atlantean evolution. In the larger cupola on the other hand, it is chiefly the principle of seven that is more active, by virtue of which the laws of metamorphosis and movement appear with particular strength: twice seven columns and twice seven capitals of seven different types of wood, representing the whole of the planetary evolution from Old Saturn to the Venus condition. And in the dome are the seven creating Elohim and the depiction of the six days of creation, which are then encompassed by the peripheral circle of the dome as the seventh day, on which the Elohim could look together upon what they had created. Thus in the smaller cupola the laws of the zodiac hold sway, and in the larger cupola those of the planets.

Finally, the carving of the 'Group' was to have stood in the east of the building, and the statue in these surroundings was to depict Christ approaching from the macrocosmic 'I'-sphere,[32] from the sphere beyond the zodiac, and proceeding from east to west through all the planetary spheres and all the epochs of Earth development[33] until, in the twentieth century, He appears in the Etheric Body whose sevenfold laws are depicted in the larger cupola.[34]

Drawing all this together, one can say that the Goetheanum, built in accordance with the cosmic laws of the physical and the etheric principles, was to have been an image of the ideal human being who, consisting of physical and etheric body, was in a condition of divine sleep.[35] The higher members of this being—the astral body and 'I'—had then to be brought down to it by the conscious work of human beings, of people permeated through and through with Anthroposophy and its spiritual knowledge stemming from Imagination, Inspiration and Intuition. Only by this activity could the Goetheanum become in truth the 'House of the Word', '... the building founded on truth from which more and more the voice and knowledge of the spirit should be proclaimed'.[36] This is why Rudolf Steiner always emphasized that under no circumstances should one approach the Goetheanum only with the intellect, that one cannot 'explain' it, for its forms should be perceived in the first place not through thinking but in the spheres of feeling and the will. This building was to awaken one to an experience and realization of the goals of the world. Rudolf Steiner expressed this in the following way in his notes for a lecture on 20 June 1914: 'People need at first only to *will* while moving from column to column. A feeling for life awakens in the right way when they understand the columns. In the cupola: the soul. In the forms: the body...'[37]

Created out of the wisdom of the whole cosmos, the Goetheanum was to lead man to a complete transformation of his feeling and willing, to direct him towards pure love and to sacrificial service for the spiritual powers that guide humanity. Thus the Goetheanum as a totality, with the carved Group in the East as its central point, was in truth a temple for the sleeping New Isis[38] resting in it, for the Divine Sophia who is an image of the higher 'I' in man—his Spirit Self. And this New Isis, the Divine Sophia sunk in a holy temple sleep, was to have been awakened by those individuals who acted out of a feeling and willing that was inwardly transformed by the colours and forms of the Goetheanum, so that in the spirit of the Word of which the opening of St John's Gospel speaks to us, they could then carry into the world a strong will towards right social action, a will permeated and tempered by true love. For the Goetheanum, which was built on the love and offering-will of human beings who were permeated by the cosmic wisdom of Anthroposophy, was to have become the spiritual centre of contemporary humanity, from whom new impulses for social healing could ray out into the world.

Thus we must look on the Goetheanum as a living being, and as such should seek an inner relation to it.[39] And then all the history of its earthly and supersensible destiny stands before us like a complete life-cycle, beginning with the placing of the seed in the Earth and continuing through

147

the stages of birth, development and growth to death, and then to its resurrection in a spiritual form.

The description of the events in Dornach on 20 September 1913, and also Rudolf Steiner's profoundly esoteric words in connection with the laying of the Foundation Stone of the First Goetheanum, point to the fact that from the beginning this was something living. As a real seed out of which the whole building of the Goetheanum later grew, the double dodeca-hedron of the Foundation Stone was lowered into the earth. In its form—like a plant-seed already containing the whole future plant—there was concealed the fundamental principle of the future building. In his address at the laying of the Foundation Stone, Rudolf Steiner said about this: 'We have formed this Stone as a symbol of the human soul which dedicates itself to our great task. It is a symbol for us in its double twelvefoldness, of the striving human soul embedded as microcosm in the macrocosm. For Anthropos, the human being, has his origin in the Beings of the divine-spiritual Hierarchies. So this, our cornerstone, is a symbol of our own soul, which we dedicate to what we have recognized as the true spiritual endeavour for the present time.'[40]

If we look carefully at the document that was placed inside this Foun-dation Stone, we can sense how everything in these texts and drawings is alive, filled with true etheric life. The two letters at the top, IN, already point to this, and Rudolf Grosse deciphers these as 'Jesus of Nazareth'. Thus we can experience them as drawing us to the Nathan Jesus Soul. For this Soul is indeed the ideal cosmic archetype of the human soul, the archetype of all humanity, pointing first to its most distant past when it was preserved from the Fall in the bosom of the Hierarchies, and pointing at the same time to the most distant future, to an image of a humanity completely permeated by Christ. For when Christ appeared to St Paul on the road to Damascus He appeared in the radiant aura of the Nathan Soul. We find this archetype of the human soul depicted in the centre of the document in the form of two dodecahedra. These show us in a cosmic picture how the purest essence of the human soul has remained since Lemurian times in the lap of the divine-spiritual Hierarchies, whose streaming etheric forces lovingly surround and bear it, and form around it something like a divine chalice, a cosmic Grail. But the letters written into this picture of the human soul, which express the three most important Rosicrucian sayings, point strongly to the future in a picture of the human being who is completely and utterly permeated by the Christ-force. Above this, how-ever, the word 'Anthropos' refers to the present where the human being, having become individually free for the first time, completes the transition by virtue of his connection with Christ, from the cosmic past to the cosmic

148

future. The human being, Anthropos, whom the Foundation Stone speaks of here as the one who 'wills to seek himself in the spirit, who wills to feel himself in the World Soul, who has an intimation of himself in the World-"I", accomplishes by the transformation in freedom of his feeling and willing, through wisdom of the spirit, the transition from passively resting in the lap of the Hierarchies to an active creating with them in the future.[41] From this Foundation Stone, from this true symbol of the human soul lowered into the 'solidified kingdom of the elements', there then grew the whole building in a natural physical-etheric metamorphosis, as though from a living seed. It was a building which, as Rudolf Steiner described, 'in all its forms is *an embodiment of the spiritual Being to whom we have dedicated ourselves.*'[42]

It took nine years to build the Goetheanum. It grew in three periods of three years; and every soul that participated in this process could itself inwardly grow with the forms, and could thereby sense in itself a true awakening of the spirit. For participation in the building of the First Goetheanum was in itself a path of initiation. This is expressed by one of the participants, Margarita Voloshina, in a letter to Russia written from Dornach in 1914: 'I looked at the Temple as it was shining before the setting Sun; and I thought that anyone who possibly could, anyone who was capable of seeing and feeling, ought to be here. It tore my heart that the whole world cannot take part in this building on the physical plane. To grow with its growth, to live into all the details, is a path of initiation ... Since the time of Hiram there has been nothing that can compare with it. "It is in truth the embodiment of the Being whom we serve," is what Dr Steiner said in Vienna ... I only regret that I was not here right from the beginning—one should see it growing every day...'[43]

And so, as though in a natural process of growth, the Goetheanum continued to be built and worked on until New Year's Eve 1922–23, when it was tragically taken from the physical plane by the forces of the element of fire. Then, like a living being, having gone through the process of death and disembodiment, it appeared during the Christmas Conference as a purely spiritual reality, as the *Spirit of the Goetheanum*, about which Rudolf Steiner spoke on many occasions at that time with such decisive clarity and directness that quite of itself there arises the impression that from that moment onwards we are dealing with the spiritually resurrected Goetheanum, with the Spirit of the Goetheanum that not only inspired Rudolf Steiner to create the *Foundation Stone Meditation*, but which was also constantly before his inner gaze as an immediate supersensible reality, as though permeating and raying out over the whole of the Christmas Conference. One has only to look at a few of Rudolf Steiner's statements to be able to feel this. For example, already by 27 December 1923, in answer to a remark of the Dutch anthroposophist van Leer, that since the fire the anthroposophists no longer had the Goetheanum, Rudolf Steiner said: 'From our point of view we have not lost the Goetheanum. From our point of view the Goetheanum still exists. We stand here *like a Goetheanum in the soul*, as a soul-Goetheanum ... One really *can* say that the building has remained in soul ... Before our spiritual gaze the Goetheanum is standing here!'[44] Later, on 31 December 1923, on the anniversary of the fire, Rudolf Steiner said in a lecture: 'The Goetheanum could be taken from us. The Spirit of the Goetheanum, if this is what we honestly and sincerely wish, cannot be taken from us.' And finally, at the end of the Christmas Conference, he spoke most expressly about the secret of the 'resurrected' Spirit of the Goetheanum, in answer to the words of thanks spoken at that time by Klaus Werbeck on behalf of all the anthroposophists present at the Christmas Conference. He then said: 'But my dear friends, I know that I have been permitted so say what has been said, for it was said in full responsibility looking up to the Spirit which is here, shall be and will be here—the Spirit of the Goetheanum. In the past few days I have allowed myself to say many things in his name, which I would not have expressed so strongly had it not been while looking up to this Spirit of the Goetheanum, to the benign Spirit of the Goetheanum. And so please allow me to accept then this thanks also in the name of the Spirit of the Goetheanum for whom we wish to work and strive and labour in the world.'[45]

If we bring all these separate statements of Rudolf Steiner's together, we can feel how they present us with a problem of the utmost importance. One can perhaps formulate this in the following way: What is the 'resurrected Goetheanum' now, what does the 'Spirit of the Goetheanum' mean, and what will be its significance for the further development of the anthroposophical movement and the Anthroposophical Society?

To find an answer to these exceptionally important questions we must first look inwardly to the fateful day of 31 December 1922 and ask: What, in a profoundly esoteric sense, happened on that day when the earthly Goetheanum, consumed by the element of fire, vanished from the physical gaze of human beings forever? Here we must turn with particular awareness to the *content* of the lecture that was the last to be heard in the great auditorium of the Goetheanum and which sounded out in particular harmony with the Goetheanum's forms, so that everyone who heard it could experience how within himself, as though in answer to the words resounding from the podium, the living forms themselves of the Goetheanum came to life and began to speak 'a language that was a continuation of the language which, as it were, interprets into ideas the spirituality which came from the podium', and how this language responded to what, in the words of the lecture, directed the inner gaze of the listeners 'to the ascent from earthly realms into starry realms which expresses the will, the wisdom and the light of the spiritual cosmos.' This powerful lecture concludes a cycle of twelve with the title *Man and the World of Stars and The Spiritual Communion of Mankind*, given between November and December 1922 in the Goetheanum. In this cycle, after looking at the inner nature of the seasons from an occult point of view, by which he depicts the physical-etheric processes of our planet in relation to the human physical-etheric organism, Rudolf Steiner then comes to what is in effect the culmination of the whole cycle. He speaks of how the human being, in taking into himself solid substances for the building-up of the physical body, can experience in them the essential being and principle of the starry world, the world of the fixed stars, which is represented above all in the twelvefoldness of the zodiac: 'In the substance of the Earth, which is a part of the activity of the Earth, we take into ourselves the essence and being of the stars, the being of the heavens. But we must be aware that as human beings, in our will, in our will permeated with love, we transform what has become matter back into spirit. We accomplish a true transub-stantiation when we become aware of our place in the world in such a way that the thinking-spiritual life in us becomes alive.'[46]

Rudolf Steiner then goes on to speak of how the human being, in that he takes into himself liquid substances of the Earth (which in their mobility are an expression of the human etheric body) in order to build up the physical body, can experience in these liquid substances the *deeds* of the stars or, in other words, the sevenfoldness of the movements of the planets. Having described the essential nature of this process, he then indicated that by consciously penetrating them with true feeling, man can also transform the liquid substances taken in by him into pure spirit. And he continues: 'Whereas it is in the will that I can see the being and weaving of the stars as they transform themselves into the spiritual content of the future, it is in *feeling* that I see the wisdom-filled transformation of that which is given me here on Earth inasmuch as, through what permeates my liquid-organism, I absorb the reflection of celestial deeds' [i.e. planetary movements]. And when an individual has permeated himself completely with the essence of Imagination, Inspiration and Intuition, which have been opened to him by spiritual science, then, related to the world in this way, he can 'experience himself as a being who wills and feels. Fully given over to the divine working in the cosmic world-existence surrounding him, he can experience *as transubstantiation that which is thus carried out by him in the great temple of the cosmos* in which he stands in a purely spiritual form as the offering being. What would otherwise merely be an abstract knowledge now becomes a relationship to the world that is felt and willed. The world becomes a temple, a house of God. The human being who has true

151

knowledge [that is, who is permeated with Imagination, Inspiration, and Intuition] and who takes strong hold of his feeling and will, becomes an *offering being*. The fundamental relation of a human being to the world ascends from knowing about the world to a world-sacrament, to a cosmic-sacrament.'

At the end of the lecture Rudolf Steiner gives two mantric verses which contain in concentrated form the essence of the spiritual communion of man, which is the actual promised goal of the Earth. For the Earth, as a physical-etheric being belonging to the past, can attain its future—which consists in its transformation into a spiritual existence—only if man accomplishes the cosmic sacrament and thus transforms it into spirit. These two verses are as follows:

In Earth-activity draws near to me,
Given to me in substance-imaged form,
The heavenly Being of the Stars.
In Willing I see them transformed with Love.

In Watery life stream into me,
Forming me through with power of substance-force,
The heavenly Deeds of the Stars.
In Feeling I see them transformed with Wisdom.

                    (Translation of G. & M. Adams)

Es nahet mir im Erdenwirken,
In Stoffes Abbild mir gegeben,
Der Sterne Himmelswesen:
Ich seh' im Wollen sie sich liebend wandeln.

Es dringen in mich im Wasserleben,
In Stoffes Kraftgewalt mich bildend,
Der Sterne Himmelstaten:
Ich seh' im Fühlen sie sich weise wandeln.

If one tries to go more deeply into the significance of this cosmic sacrament, whose essence lies in the transformation of physical-solid and mobile-etheric substances into pure spirit through the feeling and willing of the human being who is permeated through and through with higher knowledge, it becomes possible to sense its deep inner affinity with the tragic events of New Year's Eve 1922–23.

Even while the Goetheanum was still being built, the powerful Imaginations, Inspirations and Intuitions that had earlier given rise to *Occult Science* began now to show themselves in a sculptural-artistic form. But in the Goetheanum they had become a living, speaking, etherically formative

152

Word, a Word of God addressed to man (see pages 143–44). Thus in the Goetheanum we have the *first* great Michael-revelation—a revelation that had become visible to the physical human eye: 'And the Word became flesh.'[47] The Word of the Gods, which had already been proclaimed in *Occult Science*, 'became flesh' in a very real sense in the forms of the Goetheanum, and because of this the Goetheanum could become the true 'House of the Word', '... an embodiment of the spiritual Being to whom we have dedicated ourselves.'[48]

The Goetheanum—which in its basic architectural forms reflected the laws of the fixed stars, and in its mobile metamorphosing forms described the cosmic deeds of the planets—revealed through these two elements the essence of the physical-etheric principle in man. And this Goetheanum in the night of New Year's Eve, by undergoing in the element of fire a solemn act 'of transubstantiation in the great temple of the cosmos', became pure spirit, became the Spirit of the Goetheanum.

This Goetheanum, built in the world as a willed act of love, built by human beings who had taken into their hearts the new revelation of the spirit, passed over henceforth in accordance with world karma into the great temple of the cosmos and, identifying itself with it, became thereby the archetypal image of the *second* great Michael-revelation, according to which all that is 'flesh' must in the future become spirit again and dwell in the kingdom of the spirit.[49] Together with this, the Goetheanum became for modern man the archetype of the true communion, the beginning of a cosmic sacrament appropriate for present-day humanity, which awakens in man a new feeling and a new will. In this way, by the will of world karma, the greatest evil was to be turned into good. What world karma had allowed to happen was given to mankind as a great archetype of how in the future—but already begun in our time—there can take place *in a purely spiritual way* within every individual who strives for spiritual knowledge a true spiritual communion, a transformation of *matter into spirit*. And this is the beginning of the process of spiritualizing the Earth. What was once brought about by human hatred, by a temporary victory of the forces of darkness over the forces of light, is in the future to serve man in a purely spiritual way as the archetype of the most profound love and self-offering. The greatest evil is to be transformed by a 'will permeated with love' into impulses for the greatest good and inner offering; it is to be transformed into the impulse of a Christian living into, and union with the essential central principle of the world, where the act of communion becomes a spiritual uniting with the forces of the Living Christ who since the Mystery of Golgotha works as the new Spirit of the Earth, which man alone through the union with the Christ-forces can spiritualize and save, thereby also enabling the Earth to receive the seeds of the future Jupiter condition.

153

Such an understanding of the nature and significance of the destruction by fire of the Goetheanum for the whole further development of humanity on Earth can throw light not only on the deeper connection between this tragic event and the Christmas Conference of 1923–24 but also on the spiritual causes underlying the mystery of the last months of Rudolf Steiner's life on Earth when, as an initiate and as a human being, he showed us by his great example what it means at the highest level in an individual human life, out of the purest love and free self-offering, to turn into good what had been manifest as a tragic archetype for all humanity on the night of New Year's Eve 1922–23.[50]

But there is something else connected with the events of that night. In a lecture given by Rudolf Steiner in Dornach on 31 December 1923, on the anniversary of the fire, he describes in detail how the essence of what was taught by the medieval teachers of the Rosicrucians was that man consists of a physical-solid body which is created and formed by the activity of the highest Beings of the First Hierarchy, but that in their sphere man has only a mineral existence. They further taught that man carries within him, as an expression of the etheric body, fluid substances in which the lofty Beings of the Second Hierarchy are at work; in their sphere, however, man has only a plantlike existence. Thereafter the pupil was taught that the air substances within him were above all an expression of the astral body, into which the Beings of the Third Hierarchy descend, in whose realm man has as yet only an animal-like existence. And finally the Rosicrucian Master instructed his pupil in such a way that henceforth it was plain to him that he 'lived on the Earth only by virtue of the fact that he bore within him the element of warmth. But the Rosicrucian pupil perceived this warmth, this physical warmth which he bore within himself, as the actual earthly-human element in him. And he learnt more and more to experience how soul-warmth and spirit-warmth are related and akin to this physical warmth. And ... in that moment when this secret of the relationship of the warmth-element with the human-earthly element became clear to the pupil of the Rosicrucian Master—in that moment he knew how *to unite the human in himself with the spiritual.*'[51] Then the pupil could say to his Master: ' "I leave you now with the greatest comfort I could receive on Earth. For because you have shown me that earthly man's true element is warmth, you have thereby given me the possibility of joining my physical nature to the elements of soul and spirit. I do not reach the soul-element in hard bones, in fluid blood, in the air of breath. But I do reach it in the element of warmth." And it was with a great inner peace that those who had been thus instructed in those times left their Masters. And from the peace in their faces, which was a result of this great comfort, from the peace in their facial

154

expression, there gradually developed that gentle gaze out of which the language of Heaven can speak.' Thus a form of instruction was given 'which took hold of the whole human being, a form of instruction that *enabled the human soul to unite its own being* with the spirit in the cosmic sphere'. This, however, was only possible through a knowledge of the hidden nature of *warmth* or *fire*, in which the free human 'I' can be found on Earth. For this reason one can call the instruction given by those medieval Rosicrucian Masters the teaching of the fire or warmth element—the only element in which man can experience himself as an inwardly separate, individual being endowed with an 'I'.[52]

On 31 December 1923, Rudolf Steiner ended this description of the instruction given by the medieval Rosicrucian Masters by recalling his last lecture given exactly one year before: 'The last time that it was my privilege to stand on this podium, which had been constructed in harmony with the whole building, I tried to direct the attention, the inner gaze of the listeners at that time to the ascent out of earthly realms into the starry regions which express the Will, the Wisdom, the Light of the spiritual cosmos. I know that at that time, like guardians, many of the spirits who had instructed their pupils in the Middle Ages were present as I described this to you.'[53]

And in order to have a full picture of that fateful evening, let us also recall that the fire consuming the First Goetheanum was only discovered about an hour after the lecture had ended, when smoke from the flames which had already raged for hours inside the double walls finally filled the space between the cupolas and then poured into the building and billowed from it on all sides. But as Assya Turgeniev reports,[54] as they were preparing for the evening performance, that is, *some hours* before the lecture, the eurythmists had heard 'strange noises'—the sound of the flames burning the wood between the double walls of the Goetheanum.

We now have all the individual elements which can unite before our inner eye into a true picture of the events of that tragic evening. If we try to picture them to ourselves, we see Rudolf Steiner in the centre of the building, standing on the podium. From there he is speaking of the great cosmic communion of man, of how the world becomes a temple and everything in it is transformed into pure spirit. The development of the Earth is hereby given its cosmic future, which can be reached on Earth only through the free, self-offering action of man—of man who, in deeds of love springing from a conscious readiness for self-offering, accomplishes 'the act of transubstantiation in the great temple of the cosmos'. At the same time, in a semicircle around Rudolf Steiner in the spiritual world bordering the Earth, there stand the medieval Rosicrucian Masters who

155

taught that the deepest, most essential nature of their teaching was the great secret of *the element of fire* in which man finds the relation of his own nature to the sphere of the Gods, to the spiritual-cosmic sphere, and thus in his holy of holies experiences himself as an individual, free 'I' permeated by the Christ. Those medieval Masters of the 'teaching of fire' stand here like spiritual guardians at a baptism, which since the Mystery of Golgotha is no longer performed with water but with the spirit and with *fire*.[55] And all around between the double walls of the Goetheanum the fire element is already ablaze and raging, though the people are as yet unaware of it. But it is seen by the one who, with superhuman greatness in this moment, stands at the lectern and reveals to humanity the secret of the cosmic communion with the spirit, the secret of the future promised to the Earth.[56] And it is seen also by the guardians standing spiritually around him, the true Rosicrucian Masters who have appeared at this great baptism by fire from the regions of the stars.

If one tries to picture to oneself all the spiritual-physical reality of this scene, then living into it in this way can serve as a powerful incentive to work towards the realization of that 'deed in the Spirit' of which this scene, inscribed eternally in the Akashic Chronicle, has ever since been the archetype in the cosmos. Today this memory can awaken the impulse in the soul of every anthroposophist towards an inner spiritual communion, enabling the soul 'to unite its own being with the spirit-sphere of the cosmos'. It is the impulse towards a communion with 'the Will, the Wisdom and the Light of the spiritual cosmos'. The first step on the path towards a realization of this lofty goal must be a *pledge of loyalty* to the Spirit of the Goetheanum, which every anthroposophist can make in his own heart—to the spirit whose activity today stems from those cosmic spheres into which the human being is to enter through the 'cosmic sacrament'.[57] For if 'everything that comprises our relation to the world recognizes itself in man as above all a cosmic sacrament, then this is the first beginning of what must happen if Anthroposophy is to fulfil its mission in the world'.[58]

What will ensure that Anthroposophy can fulfil its mission in the present world is the pledge of loyalty to the Spirit of the Goetheanum, of whom Rudolf Steiner spoke so significantly at the end of his evening lecture in Dornach on 31 December 1923: 'We will only be made worthy through what has been laid upon us by virtue of the fact that it was our privilege to build the Goetheanum if today, in remembrance of this, we make a pledge—each one before the divine-best that he carries in his soul—to remain faithful to the *spiritual impulses* that had their external form in the Goetheanum. The Goetheanum could be taken from us, but the Spirit of the Goetheanum, if this is what we honestly and genuinely want, cannot be taken from us. And it can be taken from us least of all when in this solemn and earnest hour which separates us by only a short time from the moment when, a year ago, there were flames blazing from our beloved Goetheanum, when in this hour we not only feel again the pain, but out of this pain we pledge ourselves to remain true to that spirit for whom over ten years it was our privilege to build this place. For, my dear friends, if this inner pledge springs honestly and genuinely from our hearts today, if we can transform the pain, the suffering, into an impulse to act, *then we will also turn this woeful event into a blessing*. It will not lessen the pain, but it rests upon us to find in the pain the spur to action, to deeds *in the spirit*.

'And so, my dear friends, we look back on the terrible flames of the fire that filled us with such inexpressible sadness, but let us feel today, praising the best divine forces in us, the holy flame in our hearts which can enlighten and warm spiritually that which was intended in the Goetheanum, while we carry this will out through the waves of humanity's progress.'

These 'spiritual impulses' that awaken one to 'deeds in the spirit', this Spirit of the Goetheanum that is to light 'the holy flame in our hearts', give us the possibility of working in the right way towards these lofty tasks and goals that were placed before all humanity on the fateful day of New Year's Eve 1922–23 by world karma itself.

We have looked at the fiery destruction of the First Goetheanum from the point of view of its immediate spiritual-physical reality, but we must now approach this event from still another angle. For it is also connected with a profound occult-historical perspective encompassing almost the entire history of the development of western humanity, beginning with the epoch of ancient Greece. And these occult-historical interconnections arose before Rudolf Steiner in all their depth and significance during the fire. In a lecture on 2 December 1923, he says that the following words 'condense the flames of the Goetheanum as though into letters of a script:

Behold the Word
In the consuming Fire.
Find the answer
In Diana's House.

The fire-akasha of New Year's Eve already speaks these words very clearly along with much else besides.'[59]

The first two lines of this four-line verse are connected, as mentioned earlier, with the second Michael-revelation which became manifest in the Goetheanum fire. The next two lines lead us into the profound secret of the historical genesis of mankind inasmuch as this is connected with the cosmic development of Michael. They also set us a very real task:

Find the answer
In Diana's House.

Later, in the lecture of 31 December 1923, Rudolf Steiner speaks more definitely of this secret: 'Already in this Goetheanum, for one who was sensitive to this, there could be seen a reminder of the Temple of Ephesus.'[60] For this reason, in order to solve the problem presented here we must turn to the Ephesian Mysteries.

Rudolf Steiner indicates that a fundamental characteristic of the temple at Ephesus and the Artemis Mysteries is their hidden connection with the beginning of the St John Gospel. He speaks in particular detail about this in the cycle *Mystery Knowledge and Mystery Centres*, given immediately before the Christmas Conference, where the lecture on 2 December was dedicated to a description of the Ephesian Mysteries. He says there: 'And a person who having attained imaginative perception of world history approaches these significant words "In the beginning was the Logos" is directed again and again by an inner path to the ancient Temple of Diana at Ephesus. And for an understanding of that which resounds like a riddle out of the first verses of St John's Gospel, the one who is initiated to a certain degree into the secrets of the world is directed to the Mysteries of the Temple of Artemis, of Diana.'[61] For the essence of the riddle lay in the fact that the Ephesian path of initiation led the pupil from an experience of the Micro-Logos, which reveals itself in the human organs of speech, to a gradual penetrating through to the activity of the Macro-Logos that streams through the whole universe, of which the opening of St John's Gospel speaks.

In the lecture-cycle given by Rudolf Steiner during the Christmas Conference under the title *World History in the Light of Anthroposophy*, the Ephesian Mysteries are presented in still greater detail, this time from the point of view of their historical–geographical interrelationships and their significance for the further development of European spiritual life.

We must select from the different descriptions of the Mysteries of Ephesus given in this cycle a few that are particularly important for our study. In the third lecture of the cycle Rudolf Steiner describes how the pupil, having identified with the temple-image of Diana, could participate in a spiritual-cosmic experience of the processes of nature around him, for 'as one entered with one's feelings into the image of Artemis one received an inner perception of its connection with the etheric realms. One felt at one with the world of the stars and with the processes of that world. One did not feel the physical substantiality inside the human skin, one felt one's cosmic existence. One felt oneself in the etheric element.'[62] And he goes on to indicate how an awareness of this kind of the starry world led the pupil to penetrate through into the secrets of the cosmic past of the Earth.

Later, in the fifth lecture, Rudolf Steiner speaks of how the Ephesian Mysteries were the intermediary between the more ancient Mysteries of the East and those that were at that time truly Greek. They thus served as a link between East and West, being as they were a Mystery-centre in which spiritual wisdom was preserved, even up to a relatively late time, in an absolutely pure form and in complete balance between the Greek Mysteries, which were of a more luciferic nature, and the Mysteries of the East, which had fallen increasingly into decadence and thereby also under the influence of Ahriman. Rudolf Steiner said of this balance 'that in a certain sense, in Greece the wave of civilization came in a luciferic form, whereas over in Asia it was held back in an ahrimanic way: the balance was held in Ephesus.'

By virtue of this distinctive characteristic, the Ephesian Mysteries could on the one hand preserve in a pure form the deepest tradition of the more ancient eastern Mysteries, and on the other hand were also therefore able to prepare the way for modern humanity whose development can progress healthily only in a balance between the forces of Lucifer and Ahriman.

Yet another defining feature of the Ephesian Mysteries was of particular importance for the further development of mankind. This lay in the fact that those secrets of the spiritual cosmos which in the ancient Mysteries were opened only by living into the inner essence of the cycle of the year now became accessible to the pupil of the Mysteries of Ephesus independently of the processes of outer nature, that is, stemming entirely from an inner strengthening of his soul forces. 'The Mystery-pupils there had to rely on their own inner maturity and no longer on the natural course of the year. *Thus traces of individual personality appeared there for the first time.*' These words of Rudolf Steiner indicate that it was particularly in the Ephesian Mysteries that the principle of *Ex Deo nascimur*—from the Divine springs the individual human personality—became a very real experience for the pupil.

Thus we see that as a whole the Mysteries of Ephesus strove on the one hand, through an experiencing of those cosmic truths of which the opening words of St John's Gospel speak, to prepare humanity for the future Mystery of Golgotha, and on the other hand to prepare conditions so that humanity should become completely immersed in the Earth, in order to attain there the impulses for individual freedom.[63] From this becomes clear the unique position these Mysteries were to have in the whole further development of humanity, in order to ensure a proper transition from the epoch of Mystery-knowledge to the epoch of intellectual or philosophical knowledge. Such an understanding of the significance of the Ephesian Mysteries for future human culture can also throw light on the intentions of those adversary forces which lay behind the terrible deed of Herostratus. For the burning of the temple in 356 BC did not only destroy the last pure oasis of the Mystery-life of that time but was also intended to impede altogether the establishing of the foundations for Mysteries in Europe needed to prepare its future 'intellectual mission'; for the 'demonic beings' behind Herostratus' deed 'had planned fundamentally to let nothing spiritual come over into this European civilization'.[64] But at that time also this great tragedy, which world karma had allowed to occur, was in its own unique way turned into good, so that the *rightful* transition from the ancient Mystery-wisdom to the new, more intellectual-philosophical epoch, of development of western humanity could nevertheless take place.

The task of carrying out this world transition, which could not be put into effect by the *direct* action of the Ephesian Mysteries and yet was to determine the whole following spiritual evolution of western humanity, was given by the guiding world powers to Aristotle (384–22 BC). To the one who in his previous incarnation had himself been a pupil of the Ephesian Mysteries[65] and had been able at that time to penetrate deeply into their hidden essence—to him fell the task of giving to humanity the strongest impulse towards further individual development, an impulse which in the epoch of the temporary extinction of the Mystery-wisdom was to prepare humanity for the rightful emergence of the 'I'-principle and the future epoch of freedom.

Aristotle was 28 when the Temple of Ephesus was burnt down, an event in which a world-sign was given that henceforth all Mystery-wisdom would withdraw from the direct guidance of humanity. And deeply moving is that universal, historical conversation which took place between Plato—by then greatly advanced in years—and the young Aristotle. It was a conversation which Rudolf Steiner knew of directly from the Akashic Chronicle. 'Plato says: "Many things which I said to you and the other pupils did not seem quite right to you. But what was said is, in the end, nothing other than the extract of the most ancient, holy Mystery-wisdom. But in the course of development, man will take on a form, a configuration, an inner organization, which indeed will gradually lead to something higher than we have in man today, but which will also make it impossible for man to accept that which we Greeks have as natural science in the way I have described it today."—Thus did Plato explain to Aristotle: "And therefore I shall withdraw for a while and leave you to yourself. Try in the thought world—for which you are particularly gifted, and which is to

160

become in the course of many centuries the thought world of people generally—try to put into the form of clear thought everything you have learnt here in my school.'' And Rudolf Steiner adds: 'Aristotle and Plato remained apart, and Plato carried out thereby a high spiritual task through Aristotle.'[66]

And so thanks to this 'high spiritual task' Aristotle was able to present the Mystery-wisdom of Plato in a language of clearly defined spiritual and yet at the same time earthly concepts, which gradually 'in the course of many centuries' were to become 'the thought world of human beings'. All the Mystery-wisdom of that time was fashioned in this way by Aristotle into strictly logical, intellectual-abstract forms, which in the future were to become the foundation of a purely human faculty of thinking. And because this wisdom now took on a more conceptual character and was spread in the following period over Europe and Asia, there was thus implanted in European humanity the strongest possible impulse to descend into the world of matter. And yet this impulse was implanted with the full consent of the spiritual powers that guide the evolution of the Earth; for it was implanted in such a way that the wisdom of the Mysteries, having ceased to guide man directly, could nevertheless remain with him as though in the form of a fine concentrated extract, to prepare him on the one hand for a proper use of the forces of the intellect, and on the other hand for a true comprehension of the nature of the material world surrounding him—the world in which he was now to undergo the rigorous schooling of the emergence of the 'I'.

One can sense all this when one compares inwardly the philosophies of Plato and Aristotle, and Rudolf Steiner summarizes the results of such a comparison in the following words: 'If a modern human being reads Plato with a truly spiritual, meditative sensitivity, he feels after a certain time as though his head were a little higher than his physical head, as though he were slightly loosened from his physical organism... With Aristotle it is different. With Aristotle one would never have the feeling that through reading his works one was becoming loosened from one's body. But when one reads Aristotle out of a certain inner meditative preparation, one has the feeling that he works directly in the physical human being. It is through Aristotle that the physical human being progresses one step further.'[67]

From these words it is clear that the more imaginative philosophy of Plato, working as it still was entirely in the spirit of the initiation principle of the ancient Mysteries,[68] induced a partial excarnation of the human being. Aristotle's philosophy on the other hand, which in its more human, logical form also preserved a connection with the Mysteries, induced the tendency to incarnate more strongly, to penetrate more intensively into the physical body. An impulse was thereby given to European humanity for

161

new development—the development of which Plato had spoken in the conversation with Aristotle—which was to become of fundamental importance for humanity for many centuries. One can thus say that in his philosophy Aristotle made the first attempt to think not only with the etheric brain but *also* with the physical brain. Plato still drew the impulses for the creation of his teaching from etheric thought-forces. But it was not only from the etheric but also from the earthly forces of the physical brain that Aristotle tried to create a new vessel for the cosmic wisdom of antiquity.[69] For only by the human spirit's penetrating more deeply into the physical body, more deeply into physical matter, could humanity finally be guided to the attainment of complete inner freedom and to the awakening of the individual 'I'.

We must look from still another angle at this extremely important transition carried out by Aristotle. In far more ancient times—in the Egypto-Chaldean cultural epoch, for example—we find a humanity on Earth still completely under the guidance of the spiritual world. This guidance during that epoch was primarily possible because man at that time could to a large extent still awaken in himself clear memories of those Imaginations in which he had lived before birth, and from which he could draw directly the spiritual impulses for his life on Earth. The mythological images of different peoples are the expression of this condition.

In the Greek cultural epoch these memories of pre-earthly Imaginations had already become weaker. In Pythagoras and Heraclitus they are still relatively alive, but by Plato's time the immediate experience of these Imaginations is lost to such an extent that even Plato no longer speaks of the world of Imaginations so much as the world of Ideas.

Despite this, however, the Greeks still clearly sensed that the origin of their ideas, of their forces of thought, was not to be found in this life on Earth but in the life before birth, in the world of living Imaginations. Rudolf Steiner describes this particular nature of Greek thinking as follows: 'The force of thinking which the Greeks developed was such that, as they went through birth the pictures of experiences before birth were to a certain extent lost. But there remained that power of thinking which had been used before birth to give sense and meaning to these pictures. And this is the peculiar nature of Greek thinking, that it is completely different from our so-called normal thinking. For this Greek thinking consisted in that which could be learnt by working on the Imaginations which one had before birth. Very little was remembered of the Imaginations before birth but the most important thing—which then remained—was the mental acuteness which they had to use before birth in order to find their way in the world of which they had made Imaginations.'[70] In this way a living thinking was preserved in Greek culture as a whole in place of the

Imaginations. The Greeks experienced that the source of this thinking was to be found in their pre-earthly existence.

But a few thinkers even in that period still preserved a dim memory of the pre-birth Imaginations. Plato himself belonged, to a certain extent, to the last of these. Thence came his remarkable relationship to ideas as real living beings, for directly behind these there glimmered for him the pictures of the Imaginations, the living thought-beings. This is also the main reason why the teaching of the pre-existence of the soul—which led directly into the teaching of reincarnation—was so close to Plato.[71] For he constantly felt that there, in pre-earthly existence, in the world of Imaginations, were to be found the true sources of the ideas he experienced. One can describe this experience of Plato in the following words: 'My thoughts, my ideas are in essence not created by me, but flow to me like a gift from the divine-spiritual worlds in which I sojourned before my descent to Earth.'

But a living thinking, drawing its forces still entirely and solely from the spiritual world in which the soul abides before birth, could never have brought man to real inner freedom. For a thinking of that kind, in so far as it still drew life from the force of the Imaginations, functioned to a high degree with the necessity of a force of nature. As long as man allowed himself to be stimulated in thought by the force of Imaginations behind this thinking, he himself did not yet really think. But in order to attain his freedom and the full development of individual 'I'-consciousness, he had finally to renounce this direct influence of the Imaginations entirely. In other words, he needed to find a transition from the living thinking that bears reality in itself to a thinking that is only *a reflection, an image* of reality. For 'a reflection after all is nothing but a picture, it does not press the soul, does not compel it.'[72] And 'in an age in which consciousness has the tendency only to reflect, the impulse for freedom can take shape. Anything else would force man to action. But when he lives in mental pictures, which are nothing more than images that only reflect reality but are not reality itself, then no reality can compel him. In such an age he can evolve his impulse for freedom.' The force of thinking that was still permeated by Imaginations had to be extinguished. 'And the most important aspect of the development of the fourth post-Atlantean epoch—which continued into the fifteenth century—was that this force of thinking declined.'[73] And it was indeed Aristotle's task to pave the way for this new development. In order to do this he was obliged above all to eradicate for a time from human evolution the knowledge of the origins of imaginative thinking, that is, to eradicate the teachings on the pre-existence of the soul before birth in the spiritual world which is, in essence, also to deny the teaching of reincarnation.

We find in Plato both the teaching of the pre-existence of the soul and the teaching of reincarnation in their ancient pre-Christian form,[74] but we no longer find them in Aristotle.[75] Rudolf Steiner speaks about this as follows: 'For Aristotle the individual spirit, the individual human personality as such, simply did not exist before the human being came into existence in the physical world: the spirit came as a new creation directly out of the spiritual world when a human being arose on the physical plane. This is something that one can only describe as a "creation by the Godhead", which coming directly from the spiritual world is united with what originates from the father and mother. So the human spirit ... does not exist at all prior to this. God creates it [at birth]* ... And the return of the spirit ... in a bodily incarnation in the physical world was out of the question.'[76,77]

In this sense Aristotle prepared the way for the future Christianity, for 'it was the task of Christianity to withdraw for a while the wave of development which awakens in man a consciousness of repeated lives on Earth'.[78] For the old teaching of reincarnation was compatible neither with true human freedom nor with a really individual 'I'-consciousness. These could develop in humanity only on the basis of the Christ-impulse which was to enter earthly evolution through the Mystery of Golgotha, and for which it was Aristotle's task to prepare the way. Therefore, in its old form, knowledge concerning repeated lives on Earth had for a time to withdraw into the background, so that nineteen centuries after the Mystery of Golgotha, at the end of the dark age of Kali Yuga, it could be given again to humanity, this time in a new, a scientific form, a form appropriate to the fully developed and free 'I'. Rudolf Steiner expressed this thought as follows: '*This scientific basis for reincarnation was established at no time before our own*, so that with respect to a teaching concerning the spirit we are now at a *turning-point*: for, it is only through spiritual science that we can now move beyond Aristotle in a true and genuinely fundamental way.'[79] The loss of a knowledge of reincarnation came about, as we have seen, because until the end of Kali Yuga humanity was to go through the hard school of the emergence of the individual and free 'I' in the earthly world. But for this it had also to learn to value this world as a truly necessary part of its spiritual development. A consciousness of this nature, however, could arise only from a feeling for the absolute value and uniqueness of each individual human life—and Aristotle was to give this impulse. He was to draw the attention of all humanity to the world of the senses, *for it was to this world that the Christ would soon descend*, in order to give to it the new impulse for a

* According to indications given by Rudolf Steiner, Aristotle's view of the origin of the human spirit is such that he must have experienced the spiritual principle of *Ex Deo nascimur* particularly strongly.

subsequent ascent. Thus Rudolf Steiner says of Aristotle that although he assumes only one incarnation of the human being on Earth, nevertheless 'this one life has for the human being its own great significance and importance', for '. . . Aristotle gives great importance to his assumption that there is such a thing as a physical incarnation, and that it is *an aim of the Gods* to guide the human being into an earthly body.' And he continues: 'Aristotle valued the sense world not for its own sake, but as a prerequisite for the ascent into the spiritual world. For the feeling of the Occident always leads, in a certain way, to a recognition of the sense world as imbued with the divine and the spiritual. And though materialism may deny this for a while, it nevertheless lives on in the heart and must always do so as long as the fundamental conditions of the occidental spirit are present. And in Aristotle this lived as the prerequisite of all human evolution.'[80]

And so, in the time before the Mystery of Golgotha and arising from a genuinely Christian impulse, the teaching of reincarnation in its pre-Christian form had to be concealed from European humanity. With the beginning of the twentieth century this teaching was to be given to it again, but now out of the deepest wellsprings of the new revelation of Christ, who from the twentieth century onwards appears as the Lord of Karma,[81] when its laws would form the basis of individual human development through repeated lives on Earth.[82]

This is why Rudolf Steiner defines the most important mission of Anthroposophy as being able to bring to European consciousness the true teaching of reincarnation and karma in their new and henceforth deeply Christian form. Through Anthroposophy this teaching is gradually to permeate the whole of the social life of humanity and become the foundation of the soul-configuration of every modern human being. For this is, at the same time, the first step towards a future spiritual culture.[83]

In continuing our study of the world mission of Aristotle, it is necessary to emphasize particularly that he worked completely in the spirit of that which in his previous incarnation he had learned and mastered during the time of his pupilship at Ephesus: the perfect balance of the luciferic and ahrimanic elements. For he was able on the one hand, through his strict thought-forms, to overcome the luciferic glitter, the illusory semblance peculiar to the whole of ancient culture in general,[84] and on the other hand, by virtue of the fact that through his connection with the being and essence of the Mysteries his observations of nature were still imbued with spirit, he was able to avoid the danger of falling under the influence of Ahriman. Then he was able to weave this balance of the luciferic and ahrimanic impulses like a ferment into the further development of European civilization.[85]

Aristotle's most important task, however, was to create the necessary conditions for the appearance in Earth development of a purely human intelligence, and gradually detach this from the divine Cosmic Intelligence. 'In Aristotelianism lay ... the separation, the crystallizing-out of earthly intelligence from Cosmic Intelligence. In what was later called Aristotelian logic lies the emergence of that framework of thought which in all the following centuries was then to become *human* intelligence.'[86]

In this way Aristotle accomplished for all future centuries the transition from the ancient Mysteries to philosophy.

During the first Christian centuries and throughout the Middle Ages Aristotle's philosophy flows like a subtle and never-ceasing current through all the spiritual life of the West. Many generations of philosophers and thinkers learned through it to develop first a more personal but later a fully individual thinking, yet without breaking the connection with this philosophy's supersensible sources.

Aristotle could only bring about this transition (which was so important from a cosmic standpoint) to the future condition of consciousness of western humanity because he lived in an epoch under the rulership of the Archangel Michael (the last epoch to be ruled by him before our own) who, as guardian and keeper of the Cosmic Intelligence, inspired Aristotle and Alexander from the supersensible world to their deeds of greatness. This happened because 'he sent such signs from the spiritual Sun realm to the Earth as were able to inspire the actions of Alexander on the one hand and the philosophy of Aristotle on the other and were able to bring about, so to speak, the last phase of inspired, spiritual intelligence on the Earth...'[87] This Michaelic Intelligence, inspired from the cosmos, appeared in Aristotle's philosophy as its hidden esoteric core. Here too lies the wonderful nature of Aristotle's philosophy in that although to a great extent it was already human in form, in its deeper, more hidden content it was still completely inspired by the spiritual world. For only a philosophy of this kind could enable humanity to accomplish in the right *spiritual* way the transition to free, individual thinking—to take, that is, the path leading to where, out of complete inner freedom, the impulse of the Mystery of Golgotha could be taken up.

Thus, in an astonishing way, this earthly work of Aristotle survived in Europe in subsequent times completely inspired by Michael, the Countenance of Christ, and through him by the Sun-Being of Christ Himself. And in later generations many thinkers looked on Aristotle as the great philosopher who prepared mankind for the Mystery of Golgotha. The writings of the most important Scholastics bear particular witness to this in the thirteenth century and they saw in Aristotle the *praecursor Christi in naturalibus*, just as in John the Baptist they saw the *praecursor Christi in gratuitis*.[88]

To complete our study of Aristotle's place and significance in the world development, we have still to consider an exceptionally important event which not only stands as a great sign in the destiny of Aristotle, but which also had a particularly profound influence on the destiny of humanity as it developed towards freedom. For in consequence of this event, although the ancient Mysteries were dying out and humanity was gradually becoming distant from the guidance of the spiritual world, Aristotle found a way by means of which the divine wisdom of the secrets of the cosmos remained accessible, even though in abstract form. This event can serve as the key to an understanding of the essence of Aristotle's mission. It can help us understand why the transition from Mystery-knowledge to philosophical knowledge which Aristotle had to bring about was, from the spiritual point of view, accomplished by him in the *right* way—was accomplished, that is, in complete harmony with the spiritual powers that guide humanity.

We find the description of this profoundly significant event in the lecture given by Rudolf Steiner in Dornach on 22 April 1924. He describes there how, through Aristotle's meeting with the Cabiri Mysteries at Samothrace, there arose in him (Aristotle) a *memory* of his past incarnation as a pupil of the Ephesian Mysteries. This caused him to be inspired directly out of the cosmic-etheric sphere with all the wisdom of the Ephesian Mysteries, which as a result of the demonic deed of Herostratus had passed through the fire element into the etheric cosmos surrounding the Earth. And this purely cosmic Inspiration, having passed into the supersensible spheres of the spiritual Ephesus, evoked in Aristotle the impulse to create the 'world alphabet' of his ten *Categories*. These *Categories*, externally accessible and yet at the same time deeply esoteric, accompanied humanity in the time that followed, like the golden thread of Ariadne, on its tortuous and complex paths to an understanding of the surrounding world of nature, and were like a flaming torch for a humanity sinking into matter; for these ten *Categories* of Aristotle '... contained what, through intelligence, is to guide us up into the spiritual world'.[89]

Because the will of Aristotle and of Alexander was permeated with the impulse to serve Michael and his sphere, the wisdom-filled divine guidance was able to transform into good the greatest evil, brought about by the deed of Herostratus, and to use this good for the further development of all mankind.

Such were the consequences of this event for the development of the world. But for our study there is, when we understand the inner essence of this experience, another important aspect by means of which Aristotle was

167

able to create the *Categories*; for such an understanding reveals to us an essential characteristic of Aristotle's spirituality, namely, that the impulse of *memory* was particularly strong in his soul. We have seen that although Aristotle rejected any teaching of the pre-existence of the soul in his philosophy,[90] this philosophy was nevertheless inwardly completely founded on a *force of thinking* peculiar to itself which, in its more inward nature, was a *memory* of pre-earthly existence. Aristotle, it is true, no longer experienced, as did Plato, concrete Imaginations behind ideas from the life before birth, and in this sense the ideas were not for him independent beings (thought-beings). But *the process of thinking itself was a kind of memory for him,* for there were forces at work in his thinking that were a memory of the thought-forces inherent in the soul before its descent to Earth. And to the extent that Aristotle was still possessed of a living thinking, that thinking was still a *memory*, a memory of the life of the soul in the spiritual world. Thus we see also that the most important impulse in connection with the creation of the ten *Categories* was the impulse of the *memory* of his life during his previous incarnation, for this impulse enabled Aristotle to receive the *Categories* through the inspiration of the temple at Ephesus, now working from the expanses of the ether.[91] And finally, the philosophy of Aristotle as a whole bears to a high degree the stamp of the last true *memory* of the ancient Mystery-wisdom. 'And in Aristotle everything appears to us like ancient treasures of wisdom that are—one can only say in this case—abstracted into logical forms, like living worlds brought into the form of concepts. But because Aristotle stands, as it were, at the closing gate of the ancient Mystery-stream, there nevertheless breathes in him still something of what was ancient wisdom.'[92] From these words one can clearly sense how Aristotle was one of the last who still *remembered* inwardly the greatness of the ancient wisdom, and tried to clothe this wisdom in thought-forms of such a nature that in them it could live on through all the subsequent development of mankind. From this it is clear that the fundamental mood of the soul and personality of Aristotle, who lived at the point of transition of two epochs of world development, corresponded to the *memory* through which, also in this incarnation, he was connected with the Mysteries, even though he was neither a pupil of them nor, in the strict sense of the word, an initiate.

Then there took place the Mystery of Golgotha, the turning-point of all Earth evolution. Aristotle and his pupil Alexander, the most faithful followers of the Archangel Michael, experienced this event from Michael's lofty Sun-sphere. There they witnessed Christ's departure from the Sun in order to fulfil the Mystery of Golgotha on Earth. And this deeply moving experience of the Mystery of Golgotha from a cosmic standpoint engendered in the souls of Aristotle and Alexander a powerful impulse that was 'the challenge to set a new beginning—not to continue what was already on the Earth but to begin completely anew. Of course that constitutes also a kind of continuation; the old was not simply removed from the world. But a powerful new impulse to bring Christianity into the civilization of the Earth in a particular way was what now filled Alexander and Aristotle.'[93] 'They did not see Christ arrive on Earth; they saw Him depart from the Sun. But everything they experienced formed itself in them into this impulse: under whatever circumstances they must work towards a situation where the new rulership of Michael—to which Alexander and Aristotle wished to remain true with every fibre of their being—was to bring not only a deeply founded Christianity but also a vigorous one. This was to begin in 1879 and last for three to four centuries.'

But with the departure of Christ from the Sun there occurred another important cosmic event. The World Intelligence, kept and administered in the cosmos from time immemorial by Michael who directed it from his lofty Sun-realm into the heads of men, was now to leave the Sun-sphere of Michael and gradually descend to the Earth. It was eventually to become there the possession of human beings, so that step by step on Earth there could develop a fully individual thinking—a thinking, that is, in which thoughts would then be brought forth by man himself and not inspired into him from the cosmos. This first became possible in the eighth century after the birth of Christ when the Cosmic Intelligence, having left the sphere of Michael after the Mystery of Golgotha, finally arrived fully on Earth. The works of Scotus Erigena bear witness to this, for he was one of the first philosophers to bring forth his thoughts through his own activity.

It was also from the Sun-sphere that Aristotle observed this descent of the Cosmic Intelligence to the Earth. He saw how the time was thereby prepared when with the emergence of the consciousness soul and relying completely on the forces of the Intelligence which had now become its own, humanity would finally turn entirely from the spiritual world, and in order to attain full freedom would expose this Michaelic Intelligence now in its possession to the terrible danger of falling to the power of Ahriman.

In order to prepare in the right way for this future epoch of the consciousness soul, and also for the new, future rulership of Michael—for the epoch, that is, when for the first time since it sank from his sphere the Cosmic Intelligence would have the possibility to return to Michael, and thereby reunite the world of man and the world of the Gods, the world of nature and of spirit which had been separated since the eighth century—in order to prepare for this, Aristotle incarnated again in the thirteenth century as the great Dominican philosopher of the Middle Ages, as the foremost representative of medieval Scholasticism, Thomas Aquinas

169

(1225–74).[94] For now, on the threshold of the epoch of the consciousness soul, Thomas Aquinas was to cast into a completely new form what had arisen in the fourth century BC as the philosophy of Aristotle, and which at that time had been inspired by the Mysteries and by the Cosmic Intelligence. Moreover, he was to accomplish this by using *purely earthly faculties*—for the Cosmic Intelligence was henceforth on the Earth.

Connected with this is the deeply significant fact that there is a repetition of the process in the fourth century BC when, as a consequence of his conversation with Aristotle, Plato had withdrawn more into the background and left the field open to his greatest pupil. This however occurred this time in the supersensible sphere above the Earth, when at the end of the twelfth and the beginning of the thirteenth century the Platonists of the School of Chartres had recently ascended into the supersensible world. In their teaching had lived the last glimmer of the ancient Mysteries, their wisdom having been drawn from the inspiration of the Michaelic Cosmic Intelligence. They now handed over to the future Dominicans, who were descending to Earth with Thomas Aquinas at their head, the leadership of the earthly affairs of humanity. 'It is now your task, at the dawn of the epoch of the consciousness soul, to cultivate the intellect.'[95] This is what they said at that time to the souls on whom it rested to lay the foundation on Earth for humanity to enter into the epoch of freedom in the right way, and at the same time to bring about the first stage of the Christianizing of the now earthly Cosmic Intelligence of Michael.

Thus, at the same time a truly gigantic task stood before Thomas Aquinas: to recreate in the Christian spirit and entirely out of his own individuality the Aristotelian philosophy which had originally been entirely inspired by the Cosmic Intelligence of Michael.

The friend and teacher of Thomas Aquinas, Albertus Magnus, had already begun this work at the beginning of the thirteenth century. It was his task to prepare the way for his great pupil,[96] who was then to continue it and bring it to a supreme culmination. This work demanded of Thomas Aquinas such an intense, individual working over of the entire heritage of Aristotle's thought, that there arose from this the most subtle and penetrating *human* thinking possible. The Cosmic Intelligence of Michael, which had become human intelligence since the thirteenth century, attained here its greatest development and flowering. The reason for this was that 'the Dominicans could not elaborate the personal principle of intelligence in any way other than in the greatest possible faithfulness to the Michael-sphere.'[97] 'All modern intellectual endeavour, where this was not infiltrated by Arabism, originated now in Scholasticism.'[98] Scholasticism in the form evolved by Thomas Aquinas and Albertus Magnus laid the secure foundation for modern intellectual endeavour, which could then develop

170

in the later epoch of the consciousness soul. Without the work of these two personalities this epoch could not have begun in the right way, for neither the teaching of the Platonists of the School of Chartres nor the Aristotelian teaching in its old form could create the necessary foundations for the epoch of freedom, because in one way or another they were both inspired by supersensible wisdom. It was only in the Scholasticism of Thomas Aquinas, founded as it was on completely earthly but nevertheless unusually alive and inwardly mobile human intelligence, that the secure fulcrum could be found for the epoch in which man, estranged from the divine-spiritual world, would be called upon to bring forth creative activity entirely out of himself.

From all this we can see what was the most important attribute of Thomas Aquinas's thinking. For just as in Aristotle a continuous process of *memory* lay at the basis of his life of soul, so at the heart of the soul-life of Thomas Aquinas lay the impulse of unceasing *contemplation (Besinnen)*, a contemplation of such a nature as enabled him in reality to penetrate to the *meaning (Sinn)* of a thing. According to Thomas Aquinas, the human being conjured out the meaning of an external thing from within through the process of *contemplating* it.[99] Only this fundamental attitude of Thomas Aquinas's soul could bring him to that astonishing technique of individual thinking (possessed also by the other representatives of Scholasticism)—a level which, according to Rudolf Steiner, has never again been attained among human beings and in which, in the time that followed, 'all modern intellectual endeavour was rooted.'

This truly stupendous work of Thomas Aquinas in the realm of thought, to prepare for the future of humanity in the fifth post-Atlantean cultural epoch, was accomplished in the midst of a ceaseless and most testing battle with the opposing forces of Lucifer and Ahriman, which sought particularly strongly during this time to pervert the stream of spiritual development in which Thomas Aquinas stood as leader. The result of this was that the balance between these two powers, achieved as though naturally by Aristotle in an earlier time, had here to be attained through persistent and excruciating struggle. The reason for this change lies in the fact that on the threshold of the epoch of freedom the influence of Lucifer and Ahriman increased significantly. For the Cosmic Intelligence, directed during the epoch of Aristotle entirely by supersensible powers, was now at the disposal of human beings on Earth, thus offering the adversary powers the possibility of snatching it for themselves. Hence, 'in the thirteenth century the great, burning question in the souls of the founders of Scholasticism was: What is happening to the leadership of Michael?'[100]

The danger threatened at that time on two fronts. On the one side there arose the old Aristotelianism, influenced by the Arabism of Averroës,

Avicenna and other Arabian philosophers, in whose souls there still secretly worked the powerful impulse that had once flourished in the near-Eastern culture at the court of Harun-al-Rashid in Baghdad. This Aristotelianism, influenced as it was by Arabism and being therefore in its inner nature completely alien to Christianity, came later to Europe via Africa and Spain. An unequivocal luciferic element came to expression in this stream, for the Arabs tried to spread Aristotelianism in the form that had been appropriate only in the epoch before the Mystery of Golgotha, when the Cosmic Intelligence still belonged to Michael and inspired thinking on Earth from the cosmos. But the forces which try in an unjustified way to extend into the future what had been right only in the past are luciferic forces. And it was with these that Thomas Aquinas had in reality to fight while asserting for all humanity the purely Christian teaching of the immortality of the soul, and defending for every individual human being the possibility of retaining his individual principle, his 'I', in the spiritual world after death.

On the other side there arose the opposing forces of Ahriman. This came to expression above all in the stream of Nominalism which wanted to see in the world of ideas and in individual perceptions only names and forms devoid of content. Nominalism, which was to have a dominating posi- tion—and rightfully so—only from the beginning of the epoch of the consciousness soul, tried here to appear almost two centuries too soon so as to rob human beings of the possibility in the future of placing their indi- vidual intelligence at the service of Michael. In this way Ahriman attempted to pervert the proper entering of humanity into the future age of freedom.

These two great battles were fought out at that time by Thomas Aquinas and other Scholastics, and in this way the balance was established once more between Lucifer and Ahriman before the beginning of the epoch of the consciousness soul. This balance, however, was only attained through the fact that Thomas Aquinas was deeply imbued with the Michael-Christ- impulse which he had taken up into himself while still in the spiritual world, as he experienced the two greatest cosmic events in the spiritual evolution of humanity. We have already mentioned the first event—the Mystery of Golgotha—which was experienced by him from the lofty Sun- sphere. The second occurred in the supersensible world immediately bordering the Earth, when in AD 869 the Christ Being united with His Life Spirit.[101] This event was experienced by Aristotle, who together with Alexander was confronting Harun-al-Rashid and his counsellor in the supersensible world. And a real 'spiritual battle'[102] took place there between Aristotle who wished to serve the Michael-Christ-impulse, and the Aristotelianism that was now completely in the service of an Arabism acting against Christianity.[103] At this supersensible council Aristotle and

172

Alexander, filled with the light radiating from the supersensible union of the Christ Being with his Life Spirit, came to an unshakable resolve: to found on the Earth a spiritual stream which would 'lead Aristotelianism and Alexandrianism over into Christianity through the impulse of the leadership of Michael.'[104]

In this way Aristotle, having experienced directly from the supersensible world the two greatest events of world evolution, was able in his following incarnation[105] to bring about 'the entering (*Sichhineinstellen*) into the spiritual development of civilization of what was and is *Christian Aristotelianism*, which was to prepare for the new age of Michael...'[106] According to Rudolf Steiner's indications, the essence of this preparation for the new Michael epoch—which was to begin only in the last third of the nineteenth century—was that Thomas Aquinas, once he had given to his teachings on Aristotelianism the individual-personal form which in a purely Christian sense underlay the experience of the human personality, of the individual ego, was able to ask with all the sharp penetration of his thinking the most important question of the medieval Scholastics—the question on whose answer right up to our time the whole fate of the western world depends, as does also the major problem of the new epoch of the rulership of Michael which began in 1879. From our knowledge of Anthroposophy we can formulate this fundamental question as follows: Can the Cosmic Intelligence which fell to the Earth and became human intelligence, and which since the beginning of the new age has become ever more strongly usurped by ahrimanic forces—can this Intelligence be given again to Michael?

Thomas Aquinas perceived this question in this way: he experienced on the one hand how he himself was deeply permeated with the impulse to serve Michael-Christ, and how there lived in him the will to develop Aristotelianism further in this spirit (so far as this was possible in his time). On the other hand, he felt that the Intelligence in sinking from the Michael-sphere down into the sphere of the Earth had undergone a kind of fall into sin, had succumbed to original sin. Being now completely earthbound, the Intelligence could no longer penetrate through to the sphere of pure spirit, to the sphere of Divine Revelation. It could attain on Earth to the greatest perspicacity and subtlety, but the most essential truths of belief—that is, secrets of a supersensible nature—remained unattainable to it.

This deeply tragic dichotomy of that time was connected with the fact that in the truths of revelations there still lived—albeit in an abstract form—a wisdom stemming from the first four centuries after Christ, but also from more ancient times when Michael still held sway over the Cosmic Intelligence and from his Sun-sphere sent down the revelations to

173

human beings on Earth. In the intellectual cognizance of the world surrounding him the human being at that time already used everywhere *his own intelligence* which, in essence, was the Cosmic Intelligence of Michael that by the thirteenth and fourteenth centuries had descended finally and fully to Earth.

Therefore we cannot speak of such a division until the eighth or ninth century AD, and still less so in earlier epochs. Aristotle, for example, knew nothing comparable to this, for in his times revelation and knowledge were still inseparably united, having one and the same source in the cosmos beyond the Earth. According to what Rudolf Steiner has said, human beings received '... spiritual revelations and ideas together; so that people did not look on ideas as something they had formed and elaborated themselves but as something revealing itself in the spirituality of man'.[107]

However, already in the thirteenth century there stood before Thomas Aquinas, in its full magnitude and significance and urgently requiring a solution, the following problem: how can individual human intelligence which has been won by all humanity, but which has also fallen into sin— how can this intelligence be redeemed; how can it be permeated with the great force of redemption brought to the Earth by Christ Jesus? How can Christ Himself enter into this human intelligence? This was the most vital question of the Scholasticism of the later period.

At the end of his lecture on Thomas Aquinas, Rudolf Steiner puts this question in the following way: 'Fundamentally speaking, there was living in this question of the later Scholasticism the question of Christology. And what could not be answered for the later Scholasticism was the question: How does Christ enter human thinking? How does human thinking become imbued with the Christ? How does Christ guide individual human thinking up into the sphere where it may unite with what is the content of faith?'[108] In other words, how can human thinking find its way again into the spiritual world, so that the Cosmic Intelligence which has descended to Earth can be brought again to Michael, thereby giving all the spiritual life of the West the impulse to raise itself up to the spirit, to unite itself with the divine, supersensible worlds?

In the age of Scholasticism this question could not be answered. Only in the new epoch of Michael, beginning in 1879, did this become possible.

In preparation, however, for this time, the division of the world into a sphere of revelation and a sphere of knowledge, to which the Scholastics subscribed, brought them—and above all Thomas Aquinas—another exceptionally important task; a task which, in addition to everything we have already considered in connection with the work of Thomas Aquinas, was related in a special way to the spiritual constellation of the year AD 1250.[109]

On many occasions in his lectures of the years 1910 to 1913, Rudolf Steiner characterizes from different angles the spiritual significance of the year 1250 as the darkest period in the whole history of Kali Yuga. At that time direct access from the Earth to the higher worlds was closed even for the highest initiates. For a short time an impenetrable spiritual darkness lay over the Earth. Nevertheless, this period in the development of the Earth was necessary, for on the threshold of the world epoch of human freedom, which was to begin in 1413, mankind had to pass through a short period of complete separation from the higher supersensible worlds. It is therefore not surprising that the powers opposing the true path of human development tried particularly intensely to exploit this for their own ends. Thomas Aquinas was 25 in 1250 when he began his stupendous battle with Arab-influenced Aristotelianism[110] as well as with Nominalism. But this battle with the luciferic and ahrimanic forces working in these two streams was connected with another no less difficult battle, in which Thomas Aquinas had to fight more inwardly against these two tempters of humanity, so as to ensure that these powers in using the spiritual vacuum of 1250 and its consequences did not tempt humanity onto a path which would prevent it from entering in the right way into the epoch of freedom, and from the full development of the individual 'I'.

We can get an approximate idea of this second battle which the Dominican Scholastics—and in particular Thomas Aquinas and Albertus Magnus—had to wage almost all their lives, when we bear in mind what was said by Rudolf Steiner in the lecture on 15 August 1922 in Dornach. He describes there in detail how the unavoidable division of the world into the sphere of revelation and the sphere of knowledge, in which humanity found itself at that time, had the consequence later, at the beginning of the epoch of the consciousness soul, that one of these realms was to a significant extent finally seized by Lucifer and led to a one-sided luciferic mysticism. The other sphere, occupied by Ahriman, subsequently came to the fore as modern ahrimanic science. What, however, as an assault by the opposing powers was appropriate and right for the fifth post-Atlantean epoch—in the course of which, according to Rudolf Steiner, the whole of humanity would consciously experience a confrontation with evil[111] and, by resisting it, be able to develop the inner forces of the 'I' for all further evolution— did not in any way fulfil the laws of the previous, fourth post-Atlantean epoch. Had the adversary forces succeeded in the years following the spiritual vacuum of 1250 in forcing a luciferic mysticism on the one hand and an ahrimanic science on the other onto a humanity not yet mature enough for them, the people of the thirteenth century would have been utterly helpless in the face of such forms of evil. For prior to the epoch of the consciousness soul, humanity was not yet ready to meet evil *consciously*.

175

To experience the forces of evil in a consciousness unprepared for them would be to threaten with destruction the delicate shoots, just beginning to stir, of the 'I'-consciousness, which later, in the fifth post-Atlantean epoch, was to become the central characteristic of humanity.

In the face of this, there stood before Thomas Aquinas and Albertus Magnus an exceptionally important task. Although at that time they could not unite the two separated realms—the realm of revelation and the realm of knowledge—they nevertheless still had to hold an inner balance between the two, so as to prevent the adversary forces from gaining power through them before the beginning of the epoch of the consciousness soul.

This balance, so necessary for the further development of humanity, was achieved by Thomas Aquinas and Albertus Magnus in a twofold way. On the one hand they had to permeate the realm of revelation with a network of concepts so subtle and intricate as to be able to protect it from falling to a mysticism dominated by Lucifer. In this, as before, they considered that the fundamental tenets of faith had come into the world through revelation from above, surpassing all human understanding and attainable by no single ordinary *human* faculty. Having, however, been received *post factum* into human consciousness, these tenets can there be substantiated with the help of the most subtle and unusually perfected system of human concepts. On the other hand, in their studies of the natural world Thomas Aquinas and Albertus Magnus strove everywhere to see in nature the reality of the spirit. For Albertus Magnus the world of nature was peopled by nature spirits, and Thomas Aquinas wrote of the spiritual beings, the Intelligences, that work in the outer planets and the stars. In this way the danger of science becoming ahrimanic was averted, and the inner balance between the forces of Lucifer and of Ahriman attained by Thomas Aquinas and Albertus Magnus was likewise woven into the development of humanity (in addition to the outer victories over Arabism and Nominalism) as the most powerful counteraction to the impulse of darkness of 1250.

If one considers from this point of view the history of the Middle Ages before and after the year 1250, one can see clearly that the closer this moment approaches the darker and more threatening become the clouds gradually amassing over the spiritual sky of Europe. The epidemic of ecstatic luciferic mysticism increased and during that time even such significant mystics as, for example, Mechthild of Magdeburg or, in the previous century, St Hildegard, were not entirely free of a certain luciferic influence.[112] In England there was Roger Bacon (1214–94)[113] who, inspired to it by ahrimanic spirits, tried as early as the thirteenth century to plant the first seedlings of what only much later was to arise in humanity as an ahrimanic natural science.

Against these two destructive streams in the thirteenth and fourteenth

176

centuries, the teaching of Thomas Aquinas stood like an unshakable wall of rock. By the second half of the thirteenth century it had already attained such authority and influence in Europe that it was everywhere studied in the monasteries, and acted there as a healing element against the one-sided mysticism, while posing at the same time an insuperable barrier in the path of such personalities as Roger Bacon.

Concerning the preparation for the future epoch of the rulership of Michael, the greatest service of the Scholastics showed itself, as we have seen, in the fundamental question concerning the union of revelation and knowledge, of faith and reason, religion and science. In other words, the question in all its acute penetration and tragedy concerning the redemption of human intelligence was put and inwardly experienced by the Dominican Scholastics especially, and above all by the greatest of these, Thomas Aquinas. 'In 1274, when Thomas Aquinas died, this question was alive in world history. Thomas had only been able to penetrate to the point of formulating the question which stands like a deep need of the heart in the spiritual culture of Europe.'[114] Thus Thomas Aquinas went over into the spiritual world having fulfilled his high spiritual task. At the same time, however, he bore within him the strongest inner impulse to solve this great problem that stood before all mankind, and on whose resolution depended the future destiny of all world culture. He bore within him the greatest longing to resolve this problem as soon as it should become possible to do so.

This task was then fulfilled by Rudolf Steiner. His *Philosophy of Freedom*, published in 1894, already brought an answer to the fundamental question: How can human intelligence enter again into the sphere of Michael—how can it be redeemed and permeated by the Christ-impulse? In other words, How can the transition be found from a thinking bound to the physical brain to an etheric thinking, a thinking suited to bring man close again to the spiritual world, to that world in which ever since the beginning of the twentieth century the Etheric Christ has moved among humanity? In the new epoch of Michael a new way was thus paved to the spirit and there began the new era of the ascent of humanity, of the redemption of mankind through the impulse of Michael-Christ.

What Rudolf Steiner first presented to the world in a more philosophical form in his *Philosophy of Freedom* was later actually accomplished by him as the true world transition from philosophy to the New Mysteries. The climax of this was the Christmas Conference of 1923–24 when, through the founding of the new Michaelic-Christian Mysteries, the first impulse was given for the reascent of humanity into the spiritual worlds in the spirit of Michael.

We therefore have before us the three great, majestic figures who

177

encompass in their work the entire development of western spiritual life: Aristotle, Thomas Aquinas and Rudolf Steiner. All three acted out of the purest impulse of Michael-Christ, an impulse that was established through them in humanity on Earth and which guides that humanity in the spirit of the great world goals of the divine leadership of the cosmos. Without the activity of these three personalities it would in truth have been impossible to attain, in the right way, human freedom and individual 'I'-consciousness within western civilization. There would have been considerable obstacles placed on the path towards realizing the goals of the Earth and the goals of humanity as the Tenth Hierarchy. For in the most difficult moments of the last three millennia, these three personalities have appeared and exerted an influence on the destiny of all subsequent human development. Aristotle was the last to stand at the gates of the ancient Mystery-knowledge—gates which from his time onwards had to be closed to humanity. But a *memory* of what lies behind those gates was to be carried by him like a ferment into all subsequent development. As though prophetically pointing to the future, it was for this reason that he had to bring about the transition from cosmic–etheric–spiritual thinking to physical, earthbound thinking—to logical abstract concepts. From this moment, for the sake of attaining free, individual 'I'-consciousness, there begins the last stage of the descent of humanity into the sphere of matter, the deepest point of which was reached in the year 1250.

And it is at this moment that Thomas Aquinas appears. In the process of *contemplation (Besinnen)* he develops earthly thinking, now completely in the possession of man, in the spirit of the truly Christian impulse of that time—creating thereby the preconditions for the truly Christian person-ality to arise. In this he brings earthly, human thinking to the greatest perfection, laying the foundations for the fifth post-Atlantean culture, for the healthy emergence in humanity of the consciousness soul.[115]

And finally, at the beginning of the new epoch of the rulership of Michael there is Rudolf Steiner, who out of conscious *spirit-vision* raises the Cosmic Intelligence (which through the previous centuries had become completely earthly, human and personal) up into the Sun-sphere of Michael. By this he opens up a new epoch in the evolution of humanity, the epoch of the conscious union of man with the spiritual world. One can also say that to humanity, which in the new era has already passed sufficiently through the school of freedom from the spiritual world and of the emergence of the 'I', Rudolf Steiner gives a new impulse to win for itself a living, etheric thinking. This can unite humanity again with the world of the Gods, with the cosmic sphere of the spirit, for 'Michael's mission is to bring into the etheric bodies of human beings the forces through which their shadowy thoughts can again have *life*: and to these living thoughts the souls and spirits of the supersensible world will then draw near'.[116]

It is particularly important that anthroposophists are aware, with the utmost clarity, of the origin and development of western spiritual life and of the full significance of the astonishing, uninterrupted stream that stretches from Aristotle to Rudolf Steiner and flows onward into the future. Of this spiritual stream, of this astounding continuity that permeates the whole history of western spiritual life, Rudolf Steiner says: 'In the seventies and eighties of the nineteenth century it was possible through new direct spiritual knowledge to link up with the remnants of those events which I have described to you.[117] There is a wonderful connection here, for one sees from it that Aristotelianism and the campaigns of Alexander existed in order to maintain the link with the old spirituality, to give impulses which would last just long enough until the coming of new spiritual revelations.'[118]

Thus the spiritual life of western humanity developed between these two pillars of the human spirit—Aristotle and Rudolf Steiner—of whom the one, in antiquity, was still inspired from the cosmos by Michael, whereas the other, out of inner freedom and a fully developed 'I'-consciousness, placed himself in the new epoch of the rulership of Michael completely in the service of the impulse of Michael-Christ.

When we look at the earthly work as a whole of these three personalities whose fundamental spiritual focus was their service to the lofty sphere of Michael, we see how the Michael Mystery, connected as it is with the heavenly and earthly destiny of the Cosmic Intelligence directed by Michael himself, is reflected in each of their own personal destinies in a very special way. In order, however, to understand the extraordinarily important interrelation here, one must bear in mind the numerous indications by Rudolf Steiner that it is particularly in the element of thinking that each human being finds the true individual experience of the 'I', for such indications reveal the inner relation and affinity of the destiny of the 'I' with the destiny of the Cosmic Intelligence of Michael. They speak of the fact that the Mystery of Michael is directly connected to the Mystery of the 'I',[119] and on this basis we can approach the work of these three personalities from still another side.

It has already been said that Aristotle was a man who, in the last epoch under the rulership of Michael, still conceived his thoughts as coming from the spiritual worlds, directly from the lofty Sun-sphere. In this sense he also experienced the origins of his 'I'-consciousness as being rooted in the divine world. Thus the words of the *Foundation Stone Meditation* (I, 9–11):

Thine own I
Comes to being
Within the I of God,

correspond completely to his inner mood. He, at any rate, most certainly still carried in him a living memory of this kind of experience.

With Thomas Aquinas the situation was quite different. The world did not appear to him in that divine wholeness with which it had appeared to Aristotle. The Michaelic Intelligence, as already mentioned (see page 169), was now on the Earth, and on the basis of this there begin to awaken in humanity the first stirrings of an 'I'-consciousness. The individual human 'I' begins of itself to create thoughts and in this creation to become aware of itself. For Thomas Aquinas the world was separated into two parts: into the realm of revelations that are beyond the comprehension of the intellect—primarily the revelation of the New Testament principle of the 'I am', the World-'I' of Christ—and into the realm of intellectual knowledge where the human being, by understanding the external world surrounding him, passes through the school of the emerging individual 'I'. The problem of reconciling the two, of uniting the human 'I' with the World-'I' was, as we have seen, the major problem of later Scholasticism. It was also Thomas Aquinas's most profound conviction that this problem could not be solved during life on Earth, because of the fall of human intelligence into sin. The human being had therefore to wait until, in the world after death, he could attain a union of his own 'I' with the World-'I' of Christ which, in essence, is expressed in the words (II, 9–11):

Do thine own I
Unite
Unto the I of the World.

And lastly, in Rudolf Steiner we have before us one who, having raised himself up through his completely free 'I' to the highest levels of modern Christian initiation, was able in the most real sense to spiritualize individual human intelligence, and through its permeation with the force of Christ to bear it once again up into the sphere of Michael so as to receive from there the Light of the Being of the World (*Weltenwesens-Licht*), which brings to the free human 'I' in our time a true awareness of the world goals of our cosmos and of the mission of earthly humanity (III, 7–11). We can therefore say that Rudolf Steiner's work is the realization of what may be called the modern Michael-revelation which is accessible to human intelligence, and of which Rudolf Steiner speaks in the following way: 'Michael wishes man to be a free being who, in his concepts and ideas, also understands what is revealed to him from the spiritual world.'[120] This description of the new Michael Mysteries corresponds completely to the words (III, 9–11):

> On thine own I
> Bestow
> For thy free Willing.

We can summarize what has been said above as follows. The study of these three historical personalities leads us directly to the very essence of the evolution of humanity, as far as this comes to expression in the *Foundation Stone Meditation*. The connection that we have seen here can, however, be significantly deepened when we call to mind the relation of Aristotle, Thomas Aquinas and Rudolf Steiner with Spirit-recollection, Spirit-mindfulness and Spirit-vision. We will turn again to this question, but now directly in connection with the *Foundation Stone Meditation*.

What is the 'Spirit-recollection' of Aristotle? It rests, as we have already seen, on the fact that in him the thinking process itself, the powerful forces of his thought, were a living memory of the spiritual faculties possessed by the soul before its incarnation into the body. Aristotle always had the feeling that his thinking was continually being born out of the divine, and this impression was in a very deep sense like an inner and largely sub-conscious memory of pre-earthly existence. Hence the experience of *Ex Deo nascimur* in regard to the origin of his thoughts was particularly close to Aristotle.

What does 'Spirit-mindfulness' mean in Thomas Aquinas? We have seen that, in a tragic way, the whole world was for him divided into the realm of revelation and the realm of reason, and in such a way that for the human being incarnated in the body their union was only possible after physical death. But even here this could occur *only* if the human being had taken up the Christ-impulse during life on Earth. Thus 'Spirit-mindfulness' (or 'Spirit-contemplation'), practised in the right way and in the sense understood by Thomas Aquinas, was to bring the human being to an actual experience of *In Christo morimur*, to the highest goal of the true Christian life.

And the 'Spirit-vision' which Rudolf Steiner served is a direct, fully conscious penetrating by the human being, while still in the physical body, into the supersensible worlds, through the true redemption of thinking—a redemption leading the human being to resurrection in Spirit Self, in his higher 'I'. We can only express the true inner essence of what in the case of Rudolf Steiner we must call 'Spirit-vision', in the words *Per Spiritum Sanctum reviviscimus*.

We therefore find a striking correspondence between the fundamental spiritual striving of these three historical personalities and the *Foundation Stone Meditation*. If we now bear in mind that the *Meditation* itself brings to expression the whole of human development from the past to the present and on into the future, we indeed draw very near to an awareness of the true significance of these three personalities and of their place in the evolution of humanity. And this awareness can help us to realize fully the uniqueness of that *human* individuality which, in proceeding step by step through an individual and yet universal-human development, appeared in the world in turn as the greatest philosopher, the greatest Christian thinker, and the greatest initiate of our present age.

From this we see that only the long spiritual path taken by him—which in many respects was a tragic one, leading as it did through the most difficult stage of the coming into being and development of all humanity—this path alone enabled him, in the new epoch of Michael, to not only pass in his inner development through the seven stages of modern Christian-Rosicrucian initiation but also, after the Christmas Conference, to enter fully into the lofty circle of the Masters of Wisdom and of the Harmony of Sensations and Feelings.

Since the Christmas Conference Rudolf Steiner has been a member of this great Council. (Bearing witness to this, among many other indications, is the Imagination given by him after the Conference in response to a question concerning his relationship to Christian Rosenkreutz.)[121] He entered at that time into the circle of Teachers that includes the greatest Adepts of humanity: Christian Rosenkreutz, Manes, Zarathustra, Buddha, Scythianos . . . However, when one speaks of Rudolf Steiner as an initiate of the circle of the Masters of Wisdom and of the Harmony of Sensations and Feelings, it is necessary, in regard to him, to be aware of a specific difference.

If we look at the particular nature of the initiation of the other individualities of this circle, we see that it is such that even in ancient times they had already stepped out of the general stream of human evolution to tread a path of initiation that surpassed by far what an individual human being under normal conditions could reach; each of them had to undergo something during his initiation that was completely unattainable for the rest of humanity.

In the case of Rudolf Steiner, however, we have before us an individuality who in no previous incarnation had been through a particular initiation *outside* the general stream of humanity, but who had faithfully gone *with* this stream and in his own destiny experienced with it all the important stages of humanity's development.

At the dawn of the Babylonian–Chaldean–Egyptian epoch, but before the onset of Kali Yuga, *this* individuality was still possessed of an elemental, ancient clairvoyance. At the time of Heraclitus, when proportionally with the approach of the middle of Kali Yuga the elemental clairvoyance in humanity begins to wane and access to higher knowledge is only through the activity of the Mysteries, this individuality becomes a pupil at Ephesus, just like the hundreds of ancient Greeks who were at that time pupils in the different Mysteries.

Later, shortly after the middle of Kali Yuga, having reincarnated in the personality of Aristotle, this individuality, together with the greater part of humanity at that time, loses completely the last remnants of the old clairvoyance. In the darkest period of Kali Yuga, as Thomas Aquinas, and now without any direct perception of the spiritual worlds, he lays the foundation for the purely human earthly reasoning-power, for the individual faculty of thinking.

We have before us here the astounding fact that the greatest Christian initiate of the twentieth century—Rudolf Steiner—in his previous incarnations that were so vital for the development of contemporary humanity, was not an initiate in the traditional meaning of the word and, as was also the case with the majority of people in those times, neither was he clairvoyant.

Thus we see that the most characteristic aspect of all Rudolf Steiner's incarnations is the fact that he unfailingly treads the evolutionary path of *all* humanity. This special quality of Rudolf Steiner's spiritual path leads us to perhaps the deepest secret of his individuality, a secret that one can try to define in the following way. When the spiritual Hierarchies guiding the evolution of humanity allowed the dark age of Kali Yuga to break over the Earth, for the sake of the realization of human freedom and for the full development of the principle of the 'I'-consciousness, they had before them as their goal the essential idea of human development in this period— the gradual descent of humanity from the spiritual worlds, its development to freedom and 'I'-consciousness through the experience of individual thinking, and finally its *conscious and free* ascent back to the spiritual worlds.

To what extent the path taken by humanity during the last five millennia has strayed from the goals of the higher Hierarchies—that is, to what extent the realizing of their aims has been impeded by man succumbing too strongly to the adversary forces—is something every anthroposophist today, by looking at the historical development of humanity in this period, can judge for himself. What this development would have been in an ideal situation, however, what humanity would have become if this lofty Idea of the Hierarchies had been realized in the earthly world in its entirety—this we find reflected in the *successive incarnations* of Rudolf Steiner. In other words, in the sequence of Rudolf Steiner's incarnations the divine primal

Idea of the Hierarchies concerning the development of man found its most complete embodiment. But we can only say such a thing when we look at the results and fruits of his life on Earth as Rudolf Steiner. For when on 27 February 1861 he incarnated in Central Europe, his later spiritual path was not absolutely predetermined. He did of course come into the world with outstanding spiritual abilities; nevertheless, the question as to whether they would be fully realized or not was completely open. And yet so very much was connected with the fulfilment of his life's mission! For Rudolf Steiner it meant this: in the epoch of freedom, would he be able, by his own forces, to attain *completely* his own initiation and thereafter prepare the way for all humanity towards the attainment of those goals placed before it by the spiritual Hierarchies before Kali Yuga?

For the lofty Council of the Masters of Wisdom and the Harmony of Sensations and Feelings the problem was: would it be possible for *even only one human being*, having followed solely the path of development shared by all humanity, to ascend *from the midst of that humanity* to their circle—to the circle, that is, of individualities who for long ages past have taken a path of superhuman development? For Rudolf Steiner, having fulfilled his task, was to enter their circle, not in the way that in the past other highly developed individualities had done, but was to come to them by the path on which in the future *all humanity is to enter their circle*. And he was the first to open this path for mankind! Thus every anthroposophist who today works in the spirit of esoteric anthroposophical practice is already on the path that gradually leads him to a union with this lofty Council of Teacher Adepts, the guides of present-day humanity.

And finally, there stood before the divine-spiritual Hierarchies the question whether humanity would be able to accomplish at all the development which, in the dark age of Kali Yuga, they had allowed to come upon the world. For even if only *one* human being *from the midst of humanity* realized this development; if only one individual fulfilled the 'eternal aims of Gods' (III, 7), which the Gods today 'On thine own I/ bestow/For thy free willing' (III, 9–11), this would be a great token for the Gods, for the realization of their sublime Idea for the evolution of humanity on Earth. The fact that Rudolf Steiner, as the representative of humanity, out of his individual freedom and his fully developed 'I'-consciousness, realized this lofty Idea of the Hierarchies in his own inner development was of the greatest comfort to the spiritual worlds, for it showed that in the present situation of humanity on Earth it is *possible* to ascend again in a free and conscious way into the higher worlds, and that this path could be taken by humanity.

From this we see what the succession of Rudolf Steiner's incarnations means for humanity, and what it will mean in ever greater measure in the

184

future. For as he went through the different epochs of history he represented the ideal archetype of humanity's course of development, in that he brought to expression in the most complete way the fundamental Idea of human evolution,[122] leading from the past to the present and on into the future. He reached the summit of this Idea (for the present cycle of development) in this, his life on Earth as Rudolf Steiner, by virtue of the fact that he has been, and for long ages to come will be, the true archetype for the further development of present-day humanity, as well as for every individual who out of a deep need of soul strives for genuine spiritual knowledge. Herein also lies the reason why Rudolf Steiner, in all the sublimity of his own development, can nevertheless be so wondrously close to every anthroposophist. He is in truth one of us, and yet so infinitely high above us!

We can therefore sense, as something completely natural and even necessary, the profound inner harmony between the last three incarnations of Rudolf Steiner—expressing as they do the fundamental Idea of all the development of humanity on Earth—and the *Foundation Stone Meditation*, in which this Idea is revealed to us in its most perfect form. But a realization of this interrelatedness can lead us still further when we remember that the Idea of human evolution was incorporated artistically into the architecture of the First Goetheanum. We can therefore speak of a connection between the incarnations of Rudolf Steiner and of the very forms of the First Goetheanum.

But in order to recognize this connection, we must remember again the nature of the transition from Plato to Aristotle. We mentioned earlier that Plato still received the last echoes of Imaginations which flowed to him from the existence before birth, whose outer expression is the world of the fixed stars and the planets. It was there, in the planets, that Plato sought the wellsprings of his ideas. Aristotle, in contrast, drawing together all the Mystery-wisdom of his time, transformed the celestial ideas of Plato into earthly, human thoughts. From all the wisdom of his time he raised up a gigantic 'thought-cupola' in which, it is true, man could no longer perceive the direct descent of living ideas from distant worlds but on the other hand could, as it were, perceive mirror-images appearing as reflections on the inner surface of the cupola. Thus this 'thought-cupola' showed man the reflected images of living thought-beings, but at the same time also *separated* him from a direct experience of them. It is not direct perception that Aristotle's philosophy opens up to us, but only a *memory* of pre-earthly thoughts, of the pre-earthly force of thinking and of its origin in the divine-spiritual world. It is a spiritual cupola, raised over humanity on the foundation of the memory of *Ex Deo nascimur*.

Thomas Aquinas lived in the undying hope that the two spheres, the spheres of divine revelation and of human reason, would be united. It was his firm conviction, however, that such a union was not possible until after death, and even then only under the unalterable condition that the human soul take up the Christ-impulse now while on Earth. In this sense, Thomas Aquinas's whole life was a constant *contemplation* (mindfulness) of *In Christo morimur*. Thus, in its spiritual foundation his philosophy was permeated by that primal idea which, in the realm of architecture, found its most perfect realization in the forms, ever-streaming heavenward, of the Gothic cathedral (see page 139). In this connection, therefore, it is profoundly significant that in 1248 both Thomas Aquinas and Albertus Magnus personally took part in the ceremony to lay the foundation stone of the cathedral at Cologne—a cathedral that was to become the greatest work of Gothic architecture in Central Europe.[123]

And finally we have the First Goetheanum. Here, in the double-domed cruciform construction, there was brought about a higher synthesis of the cupola and the cross, a synthesis of the principle of *Ex Deo nascimur* with that of *In Christo morimur*. For behind the sculptural architectural forms lay the highest principle of spiritual renewal of *Per Spiritum Sanctum reviviscimus*. This was fulfilled by Rudolf Steiner, for the first time in human history, through free and conscious *Spirit-vision*. A true temple of the new spiritual life, built on the foundation of new spiritual revelation and bearing into the world a real knowledge of man and the cosmos, as well as a knowledge of the central impulse of all Earth development which unites them—the Christ-impulse—this is what the Goetheanum was to be for present-day humanity! It was, in reality, to be a path for modern man towards a rebirth in the spirit, a path leading every human being to a conscious and free union with his eternal, heavenly home, with the divine-spiritual cosmos.

But world karma is at work in everything. And just as there was a flaming symbol at the gates through which humanity passed out of the old epoch of the spirit in order to be able to meet the Mystery of Golgotha in freedom and full 'I'-consciousness later on, so here, too, there was a fiery sign at the gates through which, by virtue of a right *understanding* of the Mystery of Golgotha as given to us today through spiritual science, it was to enter again into the spiritual world and experience there the meeting with the Etheric Christ.

Like a symbol of great cosmic evolution, there stand above the two fiery sacrifices the World-words: 'The Envy of the Gods'. These words, as we know from Rudolf Steiner, could be read in the flames of the temple at Ephesus, for this temple was burnt down in the epoch of the macrocosmic Our Father, when the powers that oppose the rightful course of man's evolution approached him from without. 'The Envy of Man' are the words that could be spiritually read in the flames of the Goetheanum,[124] for in the epoch of the microcosmic Our Father, in the epoch of freedom, demonic forces of temptation approach man from within.

But just as in antiquity the wisdom of World Guidance was such that, through cosmic inspiration from the rightful forces of world development and through Aristotle and Alexander who placed themselves completely in the service of world goals, evil could be transformed into good, so, too, in the world epoch of human freedom, through the conscious action of *man himself* out of his own will, even the greatest evil, the greatest tragedy, can serve the further development of all mankind. Inspired by the spiritual Ephesus, by the spirit of the temple that through the fire had now ascended into etheric heights, Aristotle, guided by higher powers, gave humanity the powerful impulse to descend into the sphere of freedom and the 'I'. Inspired by the Spirit of the Goetheanum, which since the fire is still active in a very real sense, Rudolf Steiner in all the greatness of his free act of self-offering gives to humanity during the Christmas Conference of 1923–24 the most powerful impulse for a new ascent to the spirit, to a new spiritual culture in which humanity, having attained to the free 'I', is able to serve in the right way the world aims of the cosmos.

Thus the riddle of the Goetheanum fire finds its answer in the House of Diana. Thus does world karma reign wisely over everything and: 'in the way that the fire at Ephesus was used by Aristotle and Alexander when it burned anew in their hearts, but burned above all outside in the ether, and brought to them from there in a renewed form the secrets which could then be expressed in the most simple concepts—in the same way that the fire at Ephesus could be so used, it will be our task (and we shall be capable of doing this) to use what we must say in all humility was carried out into the ether in the flames of the Goetheanum, namely all that has been willed and intended by Anthroposophy and will continue to be so willed.'[125]

We have at last come close to uncovering the secret connection with the destruction by fire of the Goetheanum, the secret of what Rudolf Steiner during the Christmas Conference called the 'Spirit of the Goetheanum'— that Spirit in whose name, as he said at that time, he could relate much that otherwise could only have been said in a much weaker form. Here we must bear in mind particularly what Rudolf Steiner presented in his lecture in Dornach on 13 January 1924, in which he spoke in detail of the relation of the initiates in different historical periods to the inner nature of the astral light. He relates there how, at the time of the Ancient Persian culture the initiates, in using first and foremost the solid element of earth, inscribed their supersensible knowledge into the astral light. Everything, however, that was thus inscribed by them into the astral light then ascended as far as

187

the boundary of the Moon-sphere. There it was received by the Gods and then returned in a transformed state, remaining thereafter in the sphere of the Earth. But what was rayed back in this way was not a repetition of what had risen but was a kind of answer from the Gods, a reshaping and elaboration by the spiritual world of what had been inscribed into the astral light by the initiates. In the Egypto-Chaldean epoch it was the water element that was used by the initiates to inscribe in the astral light, and the Saturn-sphere that reflected it back. In the Graeco-Roman epoch this inscribing took place by means of the air element, and was radiated back from the fixed stars. In the fifth post-Atlantean epoch the inscriptions were made through the element of warmth, but everything that passed in this way over into the astral light was carried *beyond* the fixed stars and did not return. And so there arose for Christian Rosenkreutz this most important question: How can all that has been written by the initiates—written by them through the warmth element into the astral light—be received again from the Gods? Rudolf Steiner speaks further of this in the lecture mentioned above: 'And it came about that Christian Rosenkreutz, through the inspiration of a higher spirit,[126] did find the way to perceive the rays streaming back, despite the fact that it was a matter of rays returning through the warmth-ether. This happened because other dull, sub-conscious, sleeplike conditions of consciousness were used to aid it, conditions also in which the human being is normally out of the body.'[127] From the fourteenth century onwards, the medieval Rosicrucians had won the possibility of perceiving, in the raying back of the astral light from the sphere *beyond* the fixed stars and in the configuration into which the Gods had transformed it, all the knowledge of our fifth post-Atlantean epoch that had been inscribed through the warmth-ether into the astral light.

But what Christian Rosenkreutz had to accomplish in a subdued condition of consciousness can now, since the beginning of the new Michael-epoch, be brought about in full waking consciousness. And this is what Rudolf Steiner did. At the transition from the nineteenth to the twentieth century, having taken up the latest achievements of science—chiefly Haeckel's all-encompassing theory of evolution—he inscribed all this, with the help of the methods he later presented in his book *Knowledge of the Higher Worlds*, into the astral light through the warmth-ether. He then received *in full consciousness* its reverberation out of the sphere beyond the zodiac.

In the above-mentioned lecture of 13 January 1924, Rudolf Steiner describes this process in detail, explaining it first of all in the example of what had been achieved by the medieval Rosicrucians, and then moving on to a description of his own experience. In particular he says: 'In the Rosicrucian schools, for example, the Copernican cosmology was taught;

but in special states of consciousness the ideas of this came back in the way that I have explained to you here in the last few days. So that, in reality, the Rosicrucians saw that what one received in the first place through modern knowledge had then in a certain sense to be presented, to be offered up to the Gods, in order that they translate it into their language and then return it again to human beings.

'This possibility has remained up to the present time. It is so indeed, my dear friends. If you are touched by the Rosicrucian principle of initiation as understood among us here, study the system of Haeckel, with all its materialism; study it, and at the same time permeate yourselves with the methods of cognition indicated in *Knowledge of the Higher Worlds*. Take what you learn in Haeckel's *Anthropogenesis*. In that form it may very likely repel you. Master it nevertheless; learn all that can be learned about it through studying the natural science of today, and then carry it towards the Gods. And you will get what is related about evolution in my *Occult Science*.'

And he continues: 'That, then, is how it was with the Rosicrucian movement. In a time of transition it had to content itself with entering into certain dreamlike conditions and, as it were, dreaming the higher truth of that which science discovers here in a dry, matter-of-fact way out of the nature that is all around us. But since the beginning of the Michael-epoch, since the end of the 1870s, the situation has been different. The same thing that was attained in the time of the old Rosicrucians in the way above-described can now be attained in a conscious way. Today, therefore, we can say: We no longer need that other condition which was half-conscious; what we need is a state of enhanced consciousness. Then, with the knowledge of nature that we acquire, we can immerse ourselves in the higher world; and the knowledge we have acquired will come to meet us from that higher world. We can read again what has been written in the astral light and, as we do so, it comes to meet us in spiritual reality.'

In this way it was possible to transform the *Anthropogenesis* of Haeckel into the 'spiritual reality' contained in *Occult Science*, as the revelation of the cosmic speech of the Gods themselves.[128]

There is, however, a further secret of our time connected with this truly *heavenly* alchemy, this process of transformation brought about by Rudolf Steiner. He reveals this to us, again in the lecture of 13 January 1924. It lies in the fact that in carrying earthly knowledge into the cosmic sphere as described above, the initiate *meets Michael himself in the spiritual world*. A precondition for this, however, is that the initiate must proceed in the right occult way and absolutely consciously, which has only become possible since the last third of the nineteenth century. Rudolf Steiner presents this in the following words: 'We carry out into a spiritual world the knowledge

189

of nature attained here, or we carry up thither the creations of naturalistic art, or again the feelings we develop out of a religion that works naturalistically in the soul—for even religion has become naturalistic nowadays. And as we carry all this up into the spiritual, then provided we develop the necessary faculties we do indeed encounter Michael.

'So we may say: the old Rosicrucian movement is characterized by the fact that its most illumined spirits had an intense longing to meet Michael, but they could only do so, as it were, in dream. Since the end of the last third of the nineteenth century men can meet Michael in the Spirit, in a *fully conscious* way.

'Michael, however, is a Being with this peculiar characteristic: he reveals nothing if we ourselves do not bring him something from our diligent spiritual work on Earth. Michael is a silent Spirit—silent and reserved. The other ruling Archangels are Spirits who talk a great deal—in a spiritual sense, of course; Michael is taciturn. He is a Spirit who says very little. At most he will now and then give brief directions. What we learn from Michael is not really the word but, if I may so express it, the *look*; it is the power, the direction, of his gaze. *And this is because Michael concerns himself most of all with that which men create out of the spiritual. He lives with the consequences of what men have created.* The other Spirits live more with the causes; Michael lives with the consequences. The other Spirits kindle in man the impulses for what he ought to do. Michael wants to be the spiritual hero of freedom; *he lets men do, and then takes what becomes of human deeds, receives it and carries it on and out into the cosmos, to continue in the cosmos what men themselves cannot yet do with it.*'

In these deeply significant words the secret is revealed to us of how *Michael himself takes part* in the spiritual process undergone by the modern initiate when he carries into the cosmos the knowledge acquired by him on Earth, and how this process is only possible in our time through the conscious meeting of the initiate with Michael in his lofty sphere of the Sun.

Thus, seen as a whole, we have the following occult-cosmic process. At the turning point of two centuries, Rudolf Steiner immerses himself with all intensity in the findings of contemporary science. As an initiate he then bears these to the Gods in the Cosmos and receives this modern scientific knowledge back from them, but translated into the language of the Gods, in the form of the world Wisdom which lies at the basis of the powerful picture of evolution in *Occult Science*. He then incorporates this Wisdom of the Gods into the imaginative forms of the Goetheanum, in which it becomes physically visible. Later, during the fire, these forms pass over again through the substance of the warmth-ether into the astral light and travel into the far expanses of the cosmos—as far as the macrocosmic 'I'-sphere. From there Rudolf Steiner receives them again, but now as the

190

sublime Word of the Gods, as the living Spirit of the transformed Goetheanum returning from the depths of the cosmos.[129]

And so this process was completed once again, but this time at a higher level. For it is not an earthly knowledge but now a spiritual knowledge which ascends once more, through the burning of the Goetheanum, to the expanses of the cosmos, and returns again as the *living Spirit of the Goetheanum!* And for a second time Michael takes part in this cosmic process—this time, however, more directly.

One can sense this in an astonishing way in what was said by Rudolf Steiner during the same lecture of 13 January 1924: 'But when a human being has once done something out of his own inner freedom consciously or unconsciously prompted by reading the astral light, *Michael bears this human Earth-deed out into the cosmos, so that it may become cosmic deed. Michael takes care of the consequences, whereas the other Spirits are more concerned with causes.'*[130] We have already seen above that the Goetheanum incorporated in its sculptural, architectural forms the wisdom of *Occult Science* which had once flowed from the astral light. For this reason, the people working on the Goetheanum accomplished out of their own inner freedom a deed which, in the deepest sense, was kindled by what was read by Rudolf Steiner in the astral light.

In other words: Michael bore the consequences of their activity into the cosmos in order that it could become *cosmic deed.* That this actually happened, that the deed of the Goetheanum was in reality borne by Michael after the fire out into the realms of the cosmos so as to return again to human beings as *cosmic deed,* as the *living Spirit of the Goetheanum* resurrected from the Michael-sphere—of all this Rudolf Steiner speaks at the close of his last Easter cycle, on 22 April 1924: 'What before had been more or less just a matter for the Earth, had been worked on and founded as a concern of the Earth, was carried out in the flames into the expanses of the cosmos. And we—for the very reason that this tragedy has struck us—in recognizing its consequences, may say: Now we understand that it is our privilege to represent something that concerns not only the Earth, but is the concern of the wide etheric world in which the spirit lives. For everything concerning the Goetheanum is also the concern of the etheric realms in which there lives the spirit-filled Wisdom of the World. *It has been carried out into the cosmos, and we are now permitted to permeate ourselves with the Goetheanum impulses returning from the cosmos...'*[131]

'It has been carried out into the cosmos...' These words, together with those quoted above—'... thus Michael bears what is human, earthly deed out into the cosmos so that it may become Cosmic Deed...'—place before us all the deeply moving reality of the events that are connected with the earthly and supersensible destiny of the Goetheanum.

191

And so we can now ask: What is this living Spirit of the Goetheanum that was carried into the cosmos by Michael and returned again from there? Rudolf Steiner speaks of this in the last lecture of the Easter cycle given at Dornach shortly after the Christmas Conference. He says there, after the passage quoted above (see page 187), that what was carried out into cosmic realms through the Goetheanum fire can be used today by anthroposophists: 'There arises from this the fact that in a remembrance festival for the Christmas–New Year time, which is the time when our tragedy befell, we were able to open ourselves to a new impulse proceeding from the Goetheanum. Why? Because we were able to feel that what before had been more or less just a matter of the Earth, had been worked on and founded as a concern of the Earth, was carried out in the flames into the expanses of the cosmos. And we—for the very reason that this tragedy has struck us—in recognizing its consequences, may say: Now we understand that it is our privilege to represent something that concerns not only the Earth but is the concern of the wide etheric world in which the spirit lives. For everything concerning the Goetheanum is also the concern of the etheric realms in which there lives the spirit-filled Wisdom of the World. It has been carried out into the cosmos, and we are now permitted to permeate ourselves with the Goetheanum impulses returning from the cosmos. We can take this as we like—we can take it as a picture. This picture, however, holds a profound truth. And this profound truth is expressed simply when one says: Since the Christmas-impulse anthroposophical activity is to be permeated with an esoteric character. *This esoteric character is there because—through what was also at work in the physical fire as astral light, which radiates out into cosmic space—that which was of the Earth* [i.e. the Goetheanum] *and was borne into the cosmos by the astral light, now works back from there into the impulses of the anthroposophical movement, if we are but able to receive it.* If we can do this, we sense an important element in everything that lives in Anthroposophy. And this important element is the anthroposophical Easter mood which can never be convinced that the spirit dies, but rather that *when it dies through the world it always arises again.* Anthroposophy must hold to the spirit that ever rises again out of eternal foundations.'[132] But this spirit that 'dies through the world' yet 'ever rises again', and to which anthroposophists must henceforth hold fast, this is the Spirit of the Goetheanum resurrected out of the cosmos—the Spirit which since the Christmas Conference works in the Anthroposophical Society as *the principle of the new Michaelic esotericism.*

The resurrected Spirit of the Goetheanum appears to us anew from the Michael-sphere and supersensibly overshines this Christmas Conference. It works from that time onwards in the heart of every anthroposophist who genuinely wishes to place himself at the service of that to which the earthly

Goetheanum was already dedicated, as 'the true symbol of the spiritual life of the new age'[133]—what Rudolf Steiner calls 'the great mission of humanity on our Earth planet', of humanity on whom it rests to become in the future the true humanity of Christ, a divine mankind embodying the great principles of freedom and love in the cosmos.

Just as the earthly Goetheanum was erected, proceeding as it did out of the purest forces of the love and self-sacrifice of people united together in a consciousness of sublime service towards common spiritual aims—just as the Goetheanum was the embodiment in our world of the spiritual impulse *working in the social sphere*—so, too, the Spirit of the Goetheanum that works down from the cosmos is the Spirit of the new *social esotericism*, an esotericism which, in very essence, is the true esotericism of Michael! The Goetheanum passed through death in the physical world and arose again in the spiritual world. Henceforth it can work in humanity as the new esoteric principle and, at the same time, can be found as *the supersensible temple of the New Mysteries* in the soul of every anthroposophist who, being of good will, wishes to work further in the direction of those impulses from the spiritual world which were given to us at the Christmas Conference of 1923–24, given '... with regard to the Spirit that is here, and should be and will be the Spirit of the Goetheanum ... in reverence for the good Spirit of the Goetheanum ... for whom we wish to act, strive and work in the world.'[134]

Only by working in this way can we follow the path to the supersensible Mystery Temple, which henceforth is to be found on the Earth.

The *Schreinerei* (woodwork-shop) hall and stage
at the time of the Christmas Conference, 1923

5. The Christmas Conference of 1923–24

'Thus as far as Anthroposophy is concerned, this Christmas Conference is either everything or nothing.'

Rudolf Steiner, 6 February 1924

On 24 December 1923, the Christmas Conference was ceremoniously opened in Dornach 'for the founding of the Anthroposophical Society in a new form'.[1] This event was to be of fundamental significance for all the further development of Anthroposophy.

On the following day, 25 December, a Tuesday, at 10 o'clock in the morning, the Foundation Stone of the General Anthroposophical Society was laid, with its centre at Dornach.

Rudolf Steiner began the ceremony with a meditative text which is a call of the spiritual world to the human soul in our time: 'Soul of Man...' Before this text was read for the first time, Rudolf Steiner said: 'But first of all may our ears hear these words in order that, in accordance with our aims, we renew out of the signs of the present time the ancient Mystery-words: "Know Thyself!"' These profoundly significant introductory words not only speak of the continuity of Mystery-life but also lead us straightaway to the very essence of the fundamental Mystery of our age, when for the first time among humanity, at the beginning of the epoch of human freedom, there was carried out publicly on the physical plane a Mystery-act that was to renew 'out of the signs of the present time' the whole being of the ancient Mysteries—under the sign, that is, of the reigning Time Spirit of the present—of Michael himself.[2]

In his book *The Foundation Stone*, Zeylmans van Emmichoven describes his memory of this as follows: 'Already from the first speech, from the way in which Rudolf Steiner spoke and began with a particular sign, it was immediately evident that a deed was then being done which led the whole history of the Mysteries of humanity into a new phase.'[3]

Living into the powerful words, filled as they are with cosmic forces, which sounded out at that time into the Earth's aura as the *Foundation Stone Meditation*, we can inwardly experience today, over 60 years after the event, that in reality this happening is imperishable, that a true act of initiation was carried out in seven rhythms before the 700–800 members of the Anthroposophical Society who were present—an act which can now be spiritually re-enacted in the soul of every individual who tries to come to an inner awareness and experience of the sensible-supersensible events of those days on the Dornach hill. For what happened there is a genuine *mystical fact*, the fact that since then there exists a modern path of initiation for human beings that leads directly to the temple of the new Christian Mysteries.

But what occurred during those holy Christmas days on the physical plane within the modest walls of the *Schreinerei*, and on a soul level in the hearts and souls of those present, occurred also spiritually in the supersensible world immediately bordering the Earth, where today the decisive battle is being fought between the forces of Light and Darkness for the leadership of humanity—a battle that is expressed in the great Imagination of the struggle of Michael and the Dragon. Thus, what occurred during the Christmas Conference on all three planes—the physical, soul and spiritual planes—and yet at the same time forms an indissoluble unity was in reality something completely new. It was indeed a beginning, a first attempt from the midst of humanity to participate consciously on the side of the Powers of Light in this difficult battle that is fought today behind the scenes of earthly events.

In his last lecture on the evening of 1 January 1924, Rudolf Steiner characterized the secret of the supersensible nature of that Christmas Conference as 'the beginning of a cosmic Turning-point of Time, to which we want to dedicate ourselves in cultivation of the life of spirit'.[4] In these words, which were followed immediately by the reading of the full text of the *Foundation Stone Meditation*, we have also a direct indication of the spiritual bridge which had been spanned during those days between the events of this Christmas Conference of 1923 and the first Christmas at the Turning-point of Time.

From the lofty '*WORLD* [cosmic]-Creator-Being', which in our cosmos is represented by the First Hierarchy (Part I); from the forces of the Second, the Sun Hierarchy, which creates the 'rhythms of *TIME*' out of 'cosmic rhythms' in unceasing service of the cosmic 'Christ-Will' (Part II); and out of the latter's full manifestation at the 'TURNING-POINT of Time' (Part IV), which signifies the *BEGINNING* of the new era of the spirit proclaimed by the Spirits of the Third Hierarchy to the 'own I' of men for their 'free willing' (Part III)—from this great cosmic whole there flows the *spiritual reality* that stands behind these four words, which contain the essential nature, or—we could say—the quintessence, of what follows in the complete text of the *Foundation Stone Meditation*. It is the aim of the following chapters to show that the *Foundation Stone Meditation* was given as a gateway to this reality with which the impulse and nature of the Christmas Conference are inseparably connected.[5]

With the following words Rudolf Steiner points to a specially important aspect of the Christmas Foundation Meeting, which we shall use as the point of departure for our further considerations: 'In that I had to decide to become the Chairman of the Anthroposophical Society, something which I had always emphasized has, so to speak, been completely turned upside down. For I have always emphasized that, on the one side, there was the anthroposophical movement. This anthroposophical movement was to be understood as the outer configuration of what arose from the content of the spiritual perception which was able to come about in the way that you are familiar with. That was the anthroposophical movement.[6] On the other side, there was also the Anthroposophical Society. This was founded in order to realize, as it were, in its own way, that which comes from Anthroposophy. One had to distinguish between the anthroposophical movement and the Anthroposophical Society. This is no longer the case since the Christmas Conference. Since then, the anthroposophical movement and the Anthroposophical Society have become one and the same thing, have become totally identical, so that it must now be said: Formerly there existed the anthroposophical teaching as cultivated by the anthroposophical movement. Since the Christmas Conference, simply by virtue of what it became there, the Anthroposophical Society itself is now something that is anthroposophical, indeed even esoteric. From the Christmas Conference onwards we have to understand the Anthroposophical Society as something in which Anthroposophy is not only taught, but in which everything that is done *is* Anthroposophy. Anthroposophical activity (*Tun*) is something which, since the Christmas Conference, can no longer be separated from the Anthroposophical Society.'[7] By uniting the anthroposophical movement and the Anthroposophical Society into a single whole, in that Rudolf Steiner took upon himself the chairmanship of the Society—took on, that is, all the burden and responsibility for its earthly affairs—by this genuine Mystery-act there was created something completely new. For the first time in the entire spiritual history of mankind a purely spiritual esoteric stream was joined to the earthly exoteric forms common to every free association of individuals. The result of this was that the esoteric principle could now flow directly into the social sphere of humanity on the physical plane, for a Society had arisen in its midst which was completely open, and yet at the same time was also permeated by a deeply esoteric stream. 'For this reason, at the Christmas Conference the Society had to become completely open and public. [But] ... this will in no way contradict the fact that, on the other hand, it is becoming all the more esoteric.'[8]

We do not find such a joining together of absolute openness and true esotericism anywhere else in the history of the occult-spiritual movements of humanity. In this act there was given to all future development the possibility of introducing the esoteric principle, without exception, into all

197

the separate realms of human knowledge and activity, whereby there were created also the right preconditions for the transformation in the Michaelic spirit of all contemporary culture and spiritual life. For it is out of the Michael-sphere that the impulse comes today to permeate not only the spiritual life but also the social life with appropriate and healthy esotericism. And this is the most important difference between the Christmas Conference and those forms of esoteric work that existed in the Anthroposophical Society before the First World War.

Of course there is no question here of 'two kinds' of esotericism. It was still one and the same fundamental stream of western spiritual life, connected as it was with the profound Christian-Rosicrucian traditions, as well as with the new epoch of Michael. During the Christmas Conference Rudolf Steiner himself pointed to this while dealing with paragraph 5 of the Statutes of the Anthroposophical Society, referring to the Free School of Spiritual Science at the Goetheanum which in the future was to have consisted of three classes: 'Please do not be afraid of these three classes, my dear friends. Originally these three classes already existed in the Anthroposophical Society until 1914.'[9] Thus this esotericism in its inner essence was one and the same esotericism, but it appeared at the Christmas Conference—as is clear from Rudolf Steiner's words—in an essentially different form from that of the pre-war period. And it is the significance of this difference that we must now consider more closely.

If we look at the forms of the esoteric work which Rudolf Steiner had begun—while still within the Theosophical Society—at the beginning of this century, we can sense how at first it proceeds fully within the framework of western Rosicrucian traditions. The work was done in small groups which on the one hand had a fairly exclusive character, and yet on the other hand were accessible—as the spirit of the new age demanded—to anyone in the Theosophical Society at that time who sought in the Rosicrucian spirit to go more deeply into the secrets of the world.

Thus, as far as content and principles are concerned, in the path of initiation given at that time to a few very small groups of people, we are already dealing with the purest Anthroposophy—dealing that is, with spiritual science in the form in which it could first arise after 1879, at the beginning of the new epoch of Michael. Nevertheless, in these small groups which were scattered over many different cities and countries of Europe, everything had a private and personal character. Rudolf Steiner acted in them as a free and independent teacher of occultism, not so much developing his own initiatives as meeting the pressing needs of his pupils in the capacity of a representative of supersensible wisdom, and for those wishing to go more deeply into these things there soon arose the so-called 'esoteric lessons'. Later, a ritual ceremony was added to these which, although again purely anthroposophical in content, followed on in *form* from one of the masonically-orientated occult streams existing in Europe at that time.

The most important forms of all these purely esoteric beginnings had their origins in early medieval Rosicrucian traditions when, in small groups all over Europe, pupils gathered around a Teacher. Because the more external Christianity of the Church was no longer enough, they sought in place of this a true Christian *knowledge* of the world and of man. In this way, deeply hidden from outer view, the esoteric life of the West had indeed developed over many centuries. And Rudolf Steiner entered and followed this tradition, remaining in it until 1914.

What was founded at the Christmas Conference was, in comparison to this, something completely new. Here, esotericism entered into the *social life*; it ceased to be the property of a relatively small circle of people striving for union with the supersensible world. Henceforth it is no longer just a personal affair of the individual responsible only for his *own* development, but each individual who now connects with it takes upon himself also a *social* responsibility for the realization of the supersensible impulse of Michael, which since the Christmas Conference works *directly* through the Anthroposophical Society. Thus Rudolf Steiner spoke particularly clearly about this on 25 September 1923: 'And the right ground into which we must lay the Foundation Stone of today is our hearts, in their harmonious *working together*, in their good will, permeated through and through with love, to carry *together* through the world the anthroposophical will.'[10]

By what was accomplished at the Christmas Conference the Anthroposophical Society, with the Free School of Spiritual Science as its centre, became a sensible-supersensible organism in which every individuality is completely free, yet at the same time bears full responsibility for everything connected with the realization of the aims of Michael in our world, as these are revealed to us by modern spiritual science. The ground was thereby prepared for a sensible-supersensible society of human beings who are active in the social sphere and at the same time, by virtue of the participation of each of them in the work of the First Class of the Free School of Spiritual Science, are linked by an invisible bond in the spiritual worlds. In that this is a continuation of the esoteric impulse of the Christmas Conference, the Anthroposophical Society—forming a single entity with the anthroposophical movement—unites since that time, on a purely spiritual basis, the souls of those anthroposophists on the Earth at present, as well as those who are in the spiritual world. In that human beings are freely prepared to offer themselves, the ground is made ready which allows the two worlds, the physical and the spiritual, to work together in the earthly sphere for the good of all future development.

This conscious and free work of human beings towards creating new karma as the foundation for a working-together of the world of man and the soul world first became possible with the dawning of the new Michael-epoch, and at the Christmas Conference was presented as a particularly important and necessary task before all anthroposophists. Thus the most significant result of the Christmas Conference is that the spiritual world can work directly amongst mankind through every anthroposophist who is permeated with the spirit of the Christmas Conference. In the world epoch of human freedom, at the beginning of the new age of light, it rests on us—in all humility and self-dedication—to learn to work together with the Gods, and likewise with the souls of those who are in the spiritual world.

But aside from the totally exceptional position of the Christmas Conference in its significance for the spiritual life of modern humanity, and aside from its fundamentally different nature in comparison to the Mystery traditions of the past, there is still in world history an event which in a certain sense can be looked on as the archetype of the Christmas Conference.

We find a detailed description of this event in Rudolf Steiner's book *Christianity as Mystical Fact*, and also in the Hamburg cycle *The Gospel of St John*. In both these works we are first given a detailed description of the training for ancient pre-Christian initiation in which, after a long period of trials, the pupil was put into a three-day deathlike sleep by the priest hierophant. This experience completed the long process of initiation and was exceptionally dangerous, requiring as it did the almost total withdrawal of the etheric body from the physical. In the fourth lecture of the cycle mentioned above, Rudolf Steiner says the following concerning this: 'This was a process which often took place in the Mysteries. The one who was to be initiated was put into a deathlike sleep by the priest-initiator, and was thereupon guided through the higher worlds. He was then called back again by the priest-initiator into his physical body, and from then on was a witness of the spiritual worlds through his own experience.'[11] But these times of the old initiation had to come to an end. Instead of going through the dangerous, deathlike temple sleep which was accessible only to a chosen few, it was to become possible for *every* individual human being to attain initiation. And this happened through Christ Jesus. Through the Mystery of Golgotha and by uniting with the impulse of Christ, the right access on a purely inner path can be found to the higher worlds.[12] This is the greatest turning-point in all the spiritual life of earthly humanity.

However, every great accomplishment in world development is preceded by a transitional stage, for the old should not simply be cancelled out by the new but should undergo a metamorphosis into something higher. Therefore between the ancient pre-Christian and new Christian initiations there had to be created a crossing-point at which the past and the future could meet in a harmonious unity. In other words, what in antiquity in the hidden depths of the Mystery temple was accessible only to a chosen few was now, at the world 'Turning-point of Time' (IV, 1), to become attainable for all humanity—was to take place, that is, openly in its midst as a social-occult act. Thus the initiation of Lazarus—which was carried out in the old form before all humanity, and yet at the same time was already a purely Christian initiation—this initiation of Lazarus stands before us like the first shaft of light of the new epoch. For Lazarus was the first initiate in Earth development who, having gone through the three-day deathlike temple sleep, was then initiated by Christ Jesus Himself *while He was still on the Earth*. And just as Christ Jesus once carried out on Lazarus that which otherwise occurred only in the hidden Holy of Holies of the temple, and thereby revealed to humanity the inner essence of the three-day temple sleep as the fundamental secret of the old initiation, so too it is in the initiation of Lazarus that we must seek the cosmic archetype of what Rudolf Steiner fulfilled at the Christmas Conference of 1923–24.

But what did Rudolf Steiner fulfil? To understand this we must first turn our attention to the beginning of his public activity as a Teacher of mankind, when for the first time he began to speak of the new Christian-Rosicrucian path of initiation, to which his book *Knowledge of the Higher Worlds* and the fifth chapter of *Occult Science* are primarily dedicated. Since that time, any individual who practises in his own soul life the indications given in the above books can follow this path. Thus, in a form corresponding to our present time, we have the realization of the possibility that exists in human development inasmuch as, since the Mystery of Golgotha, every human being in his own completely individual way and through his connection with the Christ-impulse, can find his way to the Christian path of initiation. But what happened over and above this at the Christmas Conference? During that event Rudolf Steiner revealed to those present the experiences lived through by the soul as it treads the path of initiation. At the same time he led them through these actual experiences, as will be shown later. It can be said that Rudolf Steiner guided these souls on the universal-historical plane through the processes which otherwise take place in the most intimate depths of the temple of the individual soul. Henceforth, not only the indications for the new path of the spirit were given but the *initiation* itself, as such, was for the first time substantially realized in the midst of mankind, as the foundation for the later introduction of the initiation principle into all areas of human life and practical human activities, so as to become in them an actively social factor. For today the principle of initiation in the spirit of the new Michael-epoch should again become an integral part of all human civilization.[13] What Rudolf Steiner had repeatedly described in his books and lectures was brought about there as a *genuine mystical act*, as the complete self-contained process of the new initiation.

Of what did this process of initiation consist? If we turn again to the ancient Mysteries we can describe their culmination—the neophyte's experience of the three-day, deathlike temple sleep—as follows. At this time the pupil found direct access to the spiritual world and experienced there what, without initiation and in the normal course of events, he would otherwise have undergone only after physical death. Thus, during the three-day temple sleep, the pupil passed through the world of life after death. A deathlike sleep of this nature (i.e. a sleep in which not only the astral body and the 'I' but also the etheric body withdrew from the physical body) was no longer necessary after the Mystery of Golgotha. For this reason, for example, the Scandinavian initiate Olaf Åsteson,[14] through his connection with the Christ-impulse in the epoch after the Mystery of Golgotha, was able to experience the path through the after-death worlds trodden by the neophyte in the ancient Mysteries during the three days. Olaf Åsteson, however, was able to experience this *without* the dangerous separation of the etheric body from the physical, albeit with a partly dulled consciousness, which is expressed in the fact that he had these experiences during a sleep of twelve days at Christmastide. For at that time, before the end of the Kali Yuga and the beginning of the new Michael-epoch, it was not yet possible to experience all this in clear, waking consciousness.[15]

Since 1879, however, this has now become possible. For this reason it was necessary for Rudolf Steiner to renew the ancient Mystery-wisdom out of the signs of the present. For the human being of today was to be guided in clear, waking consciousness through that which the neophyte had undergone in a condition of deathlike sleep in the ancient Mysteries, and which Olaf Åsteson experienced in a state of dulled semi-consciousness also while sleeping. This is what Rudolf Steiner did during the Christmas Conference of 1923–24, and herein lies the reason why the fundamental theme of the Conference was the constant call of Rudolf Steiner to wakefulness, to a strengthening and activating of consciousness.

Rudolf Steiner speaks expressly about this on 29 December 1923, a Saturday—the day of Saturn—in his evening lecture, in which he speaks with particular feeling about the connection between the old and the new revelation: 'I have related to you on many occasions how the new life of the spirit was able to begin at the end of the seventies, and how from the turn of the century onwards it has been able to grow more and more. It is our task to receive in all its fullness the stream of spiritual life that is poured down to us from the heights. And so today we find ourselves in a period

202

that marks a genuine transition in the spiritual unfolding of man. And if we are not conscious of these wonderful connections [of the effects of the Aristotelian philosophy right up to the year 1879] and of how deeply the present is linked with the past, then we are in very truth asleep to important events that are taking place in the spiritual life of our time. And numbers of people are fast asleep today in regard to the most important events of all. But Anthroposophy is there for that very purpose—to awaken man from sleep. And I believe that for all those who are now gathered together here at this Christmas Conference, there is an impulse for a possible awakening.'[16] These words, which are spoken in a form corresponding to the world epoch of human freedom, remind us of words spoken in another age and under different circumstances, but which since that time have worked among mankind as the new principle of initiation: 'Our friend Lazarus sleepeth; but I go that I may awake him out of sleep' (John 11: 11). Thus an understanding of the Christmas Meeting should so awaken people that, in waking consciousness in the light-epoch that has dawned, they experience a new meeting with the spiritual worlds and can pass *consciously* through that which in previous centuries was not yet attainable for the full day-consciousness of man.[17]

Rudolf Steiner spoke of the initiation Mystery of the Christmas Conference in his closing lecture on 1 January 1924, in which he presented the experience of the 'threshold', that is, the entering in a way appropriate to our time into the spiritual world, as the meaning of the whole Christmas Conference. He points here for the first time to the significant secret of our age, connected with the fact that today all humanity is experiencing a meeting with the Guardian of the Threshold. To the extent, however, to which people do not have the inner forces to confront the Guardian consciously, they are obliged to undergo this meeting in the state of deep sleep. But then, because their soul life has remained too estranged from everything truly spiritual, the Guardian of the Threshold cannot allow them entry into the higher spiritual worlds. The initiate in our time has the following oppressive, dispiriting picture constantly before him: a scene of sleeping materialistically orientated souls around the stern Guardian who bars the way into the spiritual world which they are unconsciously seeking. And the description of this deeply tragic scene concludes as follows: 'If, during this Meeting, one has earnestly held this before one's own soul, then this Meeting will send into the soul a powerful impulse which can then lead it into vigorous action in the way that humanity needs today, so that in their next incarnation human beings will be able truly to face the Guardian of the Threshold. This means that civilization should become of such a nature that it can stand before the Guardian of the Threshold and be accepted.'[18]

We have in these words a direct indication of the social mission of the initiation path of the Christmas Conference, namely, to prepare human civilization through the right action of anthroposophists in the world to be able to stand consciously face to face with the Guardian of the Threshold. And this work for the good of all humanity in resolute service towards the impulses of the Christmas Conference will find its expression spiritually in that the Guardian of the Threshold will turn to the sleeping, materialistically-minded souls of the present and say, 'Stay outside the Spirit-land...'; and to anthroposophists will say, 'To *perceive the voice from the Spirit-land* you must unfold the strong courage to acknowledge this voice, for you have begun to awaken. Your courage will keep you awake—only lack of courage could let you fall asleep.'

And this voice from the spirit land sounds out at the Christmas Conference above all in the seven rhythms of the *Foundation Stone Meditation*. On 26 December, Rudolf Steiner said of these rhythms: 'So I would like again today to repeat a part at least of the words spoken for you yesterday *at the behest of the spiritual world.*' The courage, however, which every anthroposophist must have openly to acknowledge this 'voice', is the courage to serve the impulses of the Christmas Conference which has itself come into the world directly from those spheres on whose threshold the stern Guardian stands. For what occurred at the Christmas Conference is, like everything else stemming from the realms beyond the threshold, not subject to time. Rudolf Steiner indicates this as follows: 'When you think back on this Christmas Meeting, you will have to say to yourselves that there was something present here that had descended from the spiritual world itself...'[19]

We must look at two of Rudolf Steiner's statements. The first was on 29 December 1923 during the evening lecture: 'I believe that for all those who are now gathered together here at this Christmas Conference there exists an impulse for a possible awakening.' The second was in a lecture on 1 January 1924, in which he speaks of those words with which the Guardian of the Threshold turns today to every anthroposophist who approaches him during sleep: 'To perceive the voice from the Spirit-land you must unfold strong courage to acknowledge this voice, *for you have begun to awaken.*' Taken together, these words express clearly whence the impulse of the Christmas Conference comes which calls for wakefulness, for awakening! We have only to listen with great attentiveness to *every* word of Rudolf Steiner's to feel how it is from the realm of the threshold that this impulse comes, how *it proceeds from the Guardian of the Threshold himself*, who brought the Christmas Conference to the world in our time so that, by 'acknowledging' it, the human being would begin to 'awaken'. For this reason the impulses of the Christmas Conference are just as effective today as they were more than half a century ago, if it is really the individual's *will* to awaken. For this awakening shall lead us into the spiritual world where the Christmas Conference has its origin, and about which the stern Guardian speaks to every individual who consciously draws near his threshold: 'Thus today I stand visible before you just as, invisible, I have always stood beside you at the hour of death. When you will have crossed my threshold you will enter the realm which otherwise you enter only after physical death. You enter it with full knowledge and, henceforth, while you walk outwardly visible on the Earth you will at the same time walk in the realm of death but, in reality, in the realm of eternal life.'[20]

Thus the Christmas Conference, stemming as it does from the 'realm of eternal life', reveals itself as the most powerful impulse preparing not only the individual human being but also, on behalf of all humanity, the community of those gathered there to cross collectively and consciously the threshold into the spiritual world—to realize, that is, that for which Rudolf Steiner laid the foundations in the seven principal rhythms during the seven days of the Christmas Conference. But because the Christmas Conference is in essence eternal, it must therefore also contain that knowledge which is accessible to the soul that lives consciously in the spiritual worlds. In our present cycle of development, however, such knowledge is possible—as follows from the words of the Guardian of the Threshold—only in two cases: either in the natural course of events through the ascent into these worlds after death, or through a proper process of spiritual training.

And thus these two aspects, of what in essence is one and the same process, must form the central point of the esoteric content of the Christmas Conference, from which Rudolf Steiner in those Christmas days guided the members who were present—and with them all those souls who are connected with the anthroposophical stream—through the seven most important stages of human life after death between two incarnations, and through all seven principal stages of the new Christian-Rosicrucian path of initiation. These, however, are the experiences that were undergone by the initiate in ancient times during the three-day temple sleep. And in this sense the ancient Mystery-formula 'Know Thyself!' was indeed renewed.

Taking as our basis the description given in Chapter 3 of *Occult Science* of the life of the soul after death, and enlarging upon this with certain statements by Rudolf Steiner on this subject in his lectures, we find the following overall picture. The first stage of after-death existence, at the moment of dying, consists of the crossing of the threshold into the spiritual world and the subsequent three-day experience of a whole panorama of the past life, as the etheric body gradually dissolves into the wide expanses of the cosmos. In the second stage there begins the actual ascent into the macrocosm, when the soul awakens at first on the astral plane, or the world of Imaginations, where it again experiences the past life but in reverse order, and undergoes at the same time a process of true self-knowledge. Illusions of any kind concerning the soul itself are now impossible. The soul recognizes the true value of its past life as seen from the viewpoint of the cosmos, and in profoundly majestic Imaginations receives a judgment on the past life from the Third Hierarchy, from the Spirits of Soul. This experience awakens in the soul the strongest desire to work to rectify its shortcomings, and this feeling prepares it gradually for life in the higher spheres. In the Moon-sphere—and also in the Mercury-and Venus-spheres—the soul undergoes further similar trials. These are all connected with the slow dissolution of the lower parts of the astral body. In the third stage the soul ascends through the cosmic gates of the Sun, from the world of soul into the Spirit-land, and enters thereby Lower Devachan, or the Sun-sphere proper.[21] Here in the world of Inspiration it works with the Beings of the Second Hierarchy, the Spirits of Light, on transforming the experiences gathered in the past life on Earth into future capacities, passing all the while, in the world rhythms of the cosmic Music of the Spheres, through the four realms of Lower Devachan. In the fourth stage the soul ascends still further in the cosmos, and enters Upper Devachan, into the realm of cosmic Intuition. Here, freed from its lower sheaths, the soul experiences itself as a pure 'I'-being. Now, the Music of the Spheres is transformed for the soul into the World Word, in whose cosmic forces the Beings of the First Hierarchy, the Spirits of Strength, working throughout the spheres of Upper Devachan as far as the fixed stars, reveal themselves to the soul. With these Beings the soul takes part in the further shaping of its future life and gradually draws closer to the final destination of all its journeying—Cosmic Midnight, the great Midnight-hour of Existence. Here, having ascended to the border of Upper Devachan and the Buddhi-world, in the sublime deeds of the First Hierarchy the soul gazes on its future karma in connection with world karma, the karma of the whole macrocosm. This sublime sphere is the culmination of the soul's path after death and here it gathers the first impulses for the following descent, which at this moment now begins. First of all the soul descends again into the Sun-sphere, and this second sojourn in this sphere constitutes the fifth stage of the journeying after death. Here, out of the astral forces of the spiritual Sun, the soul must form for itself a new astral body and is aided in this by higher Spirits, as well as by the souls of others who have died. The possibility of working *consciously* on this is dependent on the degree to which, in the previous life, the soul had elaborated the principle of Spirit Self. In the sixth stage the soul passes through the Moon-sphere, where a new etheric body must be formed. The conscious formation of this, however, depends on a definite degree of development of Life Spirit, over which only that individual is master who, in his past life, has taken the path of spiritual training. Thus, higher beings complete this work for man—beings called, in spiritual science, the Moon Teachers (the Maharajahs of Eastern terminology). Finally, at the seventh stage, the soul wrapped in deep unconsciousness descends directly into the Earth-sphere where it unites with the embryo of its future physical body. Because only one who has developed Spirit Man to a particular degree can pass through this stage and maintain consciousness, the work here is carried out by still higher beings—the so-called Lords of Karma (the Lipikas of Eastern terminology)—and with whose aid the human being now enters a new life on Earth. His journey through the stars is over.

These, in outline, are the seven stages of the soul's existence after death, between two incarnations. Let us now consider also the second possibility of conscious life for the human being in the spiritual world. This possibility is attained through the modern Christian-Rosicrucian path of initiation, which also leads through seven stages. We find an exact description of this path in Chapter 5 of *Occult Science*. The seven stages are set out as follows:[22]

1. Study of spiritual science in which, at first, one uses the judgement gained in the physical world of the senses.
2. Attainment of imaginative knowledge.
3. Attainment of inspirative knowledge (reading the hidden Script).
4. Attainment of intuitive knowledge (work on the Stone of the Wise).
5. Knowledge of the relation of the macrocosm and the microcosm.
6. Becoming one with the macrocosm.
7. Blissfulness in God.

In this sevenfold path an initiation is given which in its totality embraces the *whole* human being. In accordance with this, the pupil at the first stage, proceeding from his usual waking 'I'-consciousness and his own faculty of judgement, must immerse himself in the teachings of spiritual science. At the second stage, through the appropriate spiritual exercises, the pupil must begin the development of his supersensible organs of perception (the lotus flowers) in the astral body, so that having attained a particular stage of development he can enter the imaginative world, or astral plane. The following, third stage is connected with the development of the spiritual organs in the etheric body. During the work at this stage the experiences of the astral body are first impressed into the etheric body, leading later to the formation of an etheric centre in the etheric body itself; this occurs first of all in the region of the head, and thereafter moves into the region of the heart where it becomes a new centre for the currents of the etheric body.

207

The etheric body thus gradually attains its own independent mobility over the physical body, whereby there awakens in the pupil a consciousness which leads him into the world of Inspiration, or Lower Devachan, the sphere of the planets and fixed stars, where he learns to read the stellar script. Finally, at the fourth stage the pupil begins that which, in Eastern esoteric tradition, has always been called 'work on the Stone of the Wise'—that is, work on the *physical body*. A partial release of the etheric body from the physical is then brought about which, in consequence, henceforth enables the pupil of the spirit to enter with his consciousness into the world of Intuition, or Upper Devachan, where for the first time he is considered worthy to experience his 'true "I"', which can be fully recognized only in this sphere. For in the preceding spheres the pupil could perceive this 'true "I"' only through the etheric and astral sheaths surrounding it.[23]

Here in this lofty cosmic sphere, the human being experiences a meeting with the Christ, who comes before him now as the archetype of his 'true "I"'; and thanks to this supersensible meeting he can, in the present cycle of time, begin to transform *in very essence* the three lower members of his being into the three higher ones. In this sense the three subsequent stages of the Christian-Rosicrucian path of initiation relate to the higher members of man's being—to Spirit Self, Life Spirit and Spirit Man. If, therefore, in the first four stages we are dealing primarily with *knowledge* (which of course also has, to a certain extent, the goal of elaborating the higher threefoldness in man), then the further progress of the pupil can be brought about only through the transformation of the *very essence* of his lower sheaths into the higher. For the attainment of the fifth stage presupposes, to a certain degree, the transformation of the astral body into the Spirit Self; the sixth stage, the transformation of the etheric body into Life Spirit; and the seventh stage, the transformation of the physical body into Spirit Man.

The connection between the last three stages of initiation and the three higher members of man's being, according to indications from Rudolf Steiner, is particularly elucidated by the fact that these members are the microcosmic reflection in man of the macrocosmic principles of Spirit, Son and Father. The *principle of the Spirit*, in so far as this is manifest in Spirit Self, bestows on man all the fullness of Cosmic Wisdom (Sophia), but above all knowledge of the relation of microcosm and macrocosm. The *principle of the Son*, which had once incarnated completely on Earth in the person of Christ Jesus and which works particularly through the Life Spirit in man, gives the human being the possibility of truly uniting himself with the macrocosm, with the great world from which, through the Fall, he was once separated. And finally, *the Father-principle*, having its reflection in Spirit

208

Man, leads the human being to the most sublime state of all—to 'bliss-fulness in God'.[24]

From this we see that the ascent to the three highest stages of spiritual development reveals itself as the most significant attainment for the incarnated human being. As we will see later, to ascend thus *in full consciousness*—that is, in the way this occurs in the Christian-Rosicrucian path of initiation—was made possible only through the Mystery of Golgotha. For it was only through the entry of the Christ-impulse into Earth development that the last three stages could be added to the first four and therefore made accessible for all humanity. Before the Mystery of Golgotha only those beings who in themselves had actually grown beyond Earth evolution and had already entered upon a path of cosmic development were able to attain to a conscious and 'natural' experience of these three stages. We have already spoken in detail about these beings (in Chapter 3) and, above all, of those bearing the rank of Bodhisattva, who for the development of their Spirit Self draw their forces from the direct beholding of Christ in the Buddhi-sphere. This beholding reveals to them in the deepest sense the knowledge of the relation of the macrocosm and microcosm: the macrocosmic Being of Christ and the microcosmic being of the Bodhisattvas. At a still higher level there is the Buddha, who already works on the development of his Life Spirit and experiences in this, by virtue of his ascent into the sphere of Nirvana, a union in the most all-embracing sense with all Existence, with the macrocosm. Higher still are the Dhyani Buddhas,[25] who during their work on Spirit Man are in a state that can be characterized in human language only in the words 'blissfulness in God'.

On the basis of these observations it is now necessary to establish how far the soul's existence after death, encompassing seven stages, and the Rosicrucian path of initiation, also in seven stages, are related to one another. The interrelation of the first four stages of both forms of spiritual existence—inasmuch as a process of ascent occurs in both—is evident from what has already been mentioned above. As far as the three subsequent stages are concerned there would appear at first sight to be a certain divergence, as the souls of the dead are connected with a gradual descent to the Earth, whereas for the initiate they are connected with a further ascent into the macrocosm. If, however, we bear in mind that in the last three stages of its after-death existence the soul passes respectively through the gradual shaping of its astral, etheric and physical bodies out of the cosmos—sinking all the while into ever deeper unconsciousness, since conscious participation in this process requires the real elaboration, in the highest degree, of the higher threefoldness of the human being—if we bear this in mind, it becomes clear that here also the two forms of spiritual existence

209

correspond. Thus the initiate at these highest stages develops in himself, freely and consciously, those forces from which, in its descent to the Earth and under the guidance of higher Beings, the soul unconsciously creates the bodily sheaths for a new incarnation—for the initiate the conscious experience of descent becomes a process of further ascent. For as we will see later, the descent of the soul is simultaneously a microcosmic image of the macrocosmic drawing-near of the Christ Being to Earth, through which was given to all mankind the possibility of the greatest spiritual ascent.

We can now move closer to the essence of the Christmas Conference, to its esoteric-mystery nature which comes to expression in the fact that, in the seven principal rhythms given in the course of seven days during Christmas, we can follow on the one hand the seven stages of the spiritual existence of the soul in the period between two incarnations, and on the other hand the seven stages of the new Christian-Rosicrucian path of initiation. This path was openly and publicly brought into being at that time on the physical plane by a deed which founded a new Mystery-centre on the Earth, under the sign of Michael-Christ.

'The laying of the Foundation Stone of the international Anthroposophical Society *through* Rudolf Steiner'—in the programme this was the description of that which 'in accordance with the will of the spiritual world' was brought about through Rudolf Steiner on Tuesday 25 December 1923, on a day under the sign of the cosmic forces of Mars. From what has been given through spiritual science we know that the first half of the Earth's evolution, up to the Mystery of Golgotha, was connected with Mars forces. This day therefore was particularly propitious for the bringing together of all the Mystery-wisdom of the past—the wisdom of the first, the descending half of the Earth's development, which is expressed in the ancient Mystery-words 'Know thyself'—in order to renew it in the seven stages of the initiation of the New Mysteries 'out of the signs of the present'.

From the most ancient times, wisdom had flowed to humanity in the places of initiation from the wide expanses of the cosmos. Now, 19 centuries after the Mystery of Golgotha, the human being who has taken up the Christ-impulse in full consciousness and freedom in himself is, in the New Mysteries, to give this wisdom back to the cosmos—a wisdom which in his 'I' has now become love, and which henceforth radiates back into the expanses of the cosmos from the human heart that wishes to dedicate itself to 'the progress of the human soul, to the progress of the world',[26] and to the realization of the great goals of all Earth evolution. During those days, as the 'dodecahedral, imaginative image of Love', there was to be laid into the hearts and souls of those present 'the dodecahedral Foundation Stone of Love, formed in the image of the cosmos and borne into the sphere of humanity'. This act was to lay the foundation for the new 'I'-Mysteries; for love is 'the fruit of wisdom reborn in the "I"'.[27] In this way all the world-wisdom of the past, which from Old Saturn onwards was woven into world-evolution, is today to be born again in the free human 'I' that is permeated through and through with the Christ-impulse. It is about this that those words of the *Foundation Stone Meditation* speak, which are directed to the World Christmas of the Turning-point of Time in order to form in the depths of the human being that Stone of Love which, through the New Mysteries, is to become the foundation stone of all the future evolution of the Earth until Vulcan, when the wisdom of the past, reborn in the human 'I' that is permeated by the Christ, is gradually to form, as love, the fundamental creative principle in the cosmos.

As the Foundation Stone 'which has its substance from cosmic-human love, has its form (*Bildhaftigkeit*) from cosmic-human imagination, and its radiance of light from cosmic-human thoughts'[28]—thus did Rudolf Steiner define the essence of this 'imaginative image of love', laid during those days into the souls of those present. From this definition we see that as a unified whole the Foundation Stone—particularly in three of its parts—presents a harmonious union of macrocosm and microcosm in the human soul.

In the chapter in his book devoted to the deeper nature of the Foundation Stone, Zeylmans van Emmichoven reveals the connection of the three macrocosmic parts of the Foundation Stone with the nine cosmic Hierarchies—the Spirits of Strength, the Spirits of Light and the Spirits of Soul. The creative activity of these hierarchic Beings—in the form of cosmic Love, cosmic Imagination and cosmic Thoughts—must be recognized in our time by man, so that he can comprehend in himself 'the threefoldness of all Being; cosmic Love reigning in human love, cosmic Imagination reigning in the organization of the human form, and cosmic Thoughts reigning secretly below the surface of the thoughts of humanity'.[29] For only this knowledge can spur the human being freely, out of the forces of his heart's self-offering, to accept the dodecahedral Foundation Stone of Love of the New Mysteries into his soul—that is, to bring about what finds its expression in the fact that he brings his human love, human imagination and human thoughts towards the hierarchic powers which overshine him, that as a true microcosm in the greater world in the macrocosm the human being is part of the great Whole of the Hierarchies; it is expressed also when the human being recognizes himself '*as an individual free being* in the reigning working of the Gods in the cosmos', when he recognizes himself 'as Cosmic Man—as individual man within Cosmic Man—working as such for the cosmic future', and brings to the hierarchic powers which overshine him his human love, his human imagination and his human thoughts.

If now we wish to have a more exact picture of what is to be understood here by 'Cosmic Man', we can take, for example, the description given by Rudolf Steiner in his lecture in Paris on 25 May 1924 (GA 239), in which he speaks of how in the Sun-sphere after death the human being, working together with all the Hierarchies of the cosmos, creates the archetype of his physical body for the future incarnation, but creates it out of macrocosmic man, out of Adam Kadmon, experiencing himself in him in such a way that the inner planets—Moon, Mercury and Venus—through whose sphere the Spirits of Soul work, become his limbs. The Sun, together with the Spirits of Light working in its sphere, becomes his heart and lung system. And the outer planets from the Sun-sphere—Mars, Jupiter and Saturn—which are the doors for the activity of the highest Hierarchies, the Spirits of Strength, become his organs of understanding.

But this sublime experience of macrocosmic man, which for the ordinary human being has always been attainable only after death, and in the Mysteries of antiquity could only be experienced during the temple sleep of three days—this experience occurred in both cases outside the body, far from all earthly things, through the union of the soul with the sublime Sun-sphere. But through the appearance of the Christ, of the great 'Sun Man', and through the Mystery of Golgotha, the great fullness of cosmic life was brought into the realm of Earth. In the words of Rudolf Steiner: 'Thus it is also possible that the figure who went through the Mystery of Golgotha can come before the human soul when one first has the opportunity of looking at cosmic man through human organology. For it was as Cosmic Man that Christ came from the Sun. Until then He had not yet been earthly man. He came as Cosmic Man.'[30] Only now could the impulse be given to all human beings on Earth for the reascent into the macrocosm.[31]

But world evolution runs its course slowly and although, after the Mystery of Golgotha, the possibility for this ascent was indeed given to the whole subsequent development of humanity, nevertheless at that time it could not yet be brought about out of full individual freedom, for this had still to be won by humanity. For this reason a further 19 centuries were necessary before human beings, having gone through the intensive process of individualization within the culture of materialism, could now, in the new age, achieve for themselves to the highest degree the impulse for inner freedom, and finally, in the new epoch of the rulership of the Sun Archangel, Michael, become mature enough for each individual on Earth, *out of a completely free will*, to find himself through the *conscious* union with the

212

Christ-impulse 'as an *individually free human being* in the direct working of the Gods in the cosmos, as individual man in Cosmic Man, working in Cosmic Man for the future of the cosmos.'

This is also why today, at the end of the dark age of Kali Yuga, the Gods turn again from the cosmos towards man, and their voices sound out in the *Foundation Stone Meditation* to earthly man, revealing to him 'what the world has to say to the human being, to human life and to human activity'.[32] Thus in the *Meditation* there rings forth to us from the heights the great cosmic Word of the Father through the Spirits of Strength; there resounds from East to West the Word of the Son through the Spirits of Light; and from the depths of the World, the Word of the Spirit through the Spirits of Soul! And this threefold call of the cosmos, sounding out as it does in the New Mysteries to the human soul—to this call the soul today must give answer. It must give answer through the will to self-offering, to acting out of the spirit, where the soul—out of the cosmic substance 'in which the spirit that flows from the heights and reveals itself in the human head, works and has its being';[33] out of 'the Christ-force, which is at work everywhere in the surroundings, weaving with the airs that encircle the Earth, and which lives and is active in our respiratory system'; and finally, out of the forces of the depths, 'which rise up from the core of the Earth', and 'which are at work in our limb system'—out of all these the soul forms in itself the dodecahedral Foundation Stone which in 'soul-comprehension' it can then 'place as the dodecahedron of man beside the dodecahedron of the cosmos'. It is important to note here that in the answer of the human soul, in the forming of the human dodecahedron the three cosmic forces appear in the reverse order of those in the cosmic dodecahedron, and only the Christ-force, encompassing as it does macrocosm and microcosm, works in the same way in both.

Therefore, to summarize, we have on the one hand in the *Foundation Stone Meditation* the call of the cosmos sounding out to the human soul. In this the Father forces act from the heights, the Son forces from the space around us, and the Spirit forces from the depths of the world. On the other hand, the soul answers the cosmos—an answer in which the soul creates in itself, as a solemn pledge of self-offering towards the active cosmic dodecahedron, the dodecahedron of man, formed 'from the Spirit of the heights, from the Christ-force in the surrounding expanses of the cosmos, from the creative Father power ... streaming from the depths'. Man creates this human dodecahedron in answer to the call of world forces in him when he stands in the world in such a way that in his head, in his thoughts, the Spirit of the heights is revealed, when in his heart the Christ holds sway, and when in his deeds there works the Father force streaming from the depths of the world. This is what the answer of man must be. Where this becomes a reality, we have the beginning of a new era of world development, the beginning of the spiritual ascent of humanity. And this appears before us in the principal rhythm with which, on the first day, Rudolf Steiner gives the *Foundation Stone Meditation*—the rhythm indicating to us the preconditions for entering upon the path of the New Mysteries. It is at this, then, that we must now look in greater detail.

On 25 December 1923, the first day of the Christmas Conference, Rudolf Steiner begins with the reading of the first sections of Parts I–III of the *Meditation*. Here—as Rudolf Grosse has already indicated in his book *The Christmas Foundation*—after the direct threefold call to the human soul, we have in twelve lines (2–13) the gradual process of the soul's incarnation in the physical body, whereby taking possession of this, step by step the soul unites itself first with the limbs (I, 2), then with the heart and lungs (II, 2), the finally with the head (III, 2).[34] Having thus entered the Earth-sphere, the soul continues to live in the physical world and, should it pass through the experiences of earthly life in the right way, that life then leads it step by step through the worlds of space (I, 3) and time (II, 3) to eternity (III, 3), preparing one in a hidden way to experience truly the ocean-being of the Spirit (I, 4), to sense one's own soul-being (II, 4), and to open oneself to the Thoughts of Worlds (III, 4).

The full spiritual reality expressed in these three lines will be experienced only after death by the soul that does not take the path of initiation. But the soul *can* take this path. It can begin to work consciously on itself, to practise Spirit-recollection, Spirit-mindfulness, and finally Spirit-vision (I, II, III, 5–6). If the soul does make the decision to step towards the supersensible world, then there is gradually revealed to it the mystery of the ascent to the higher 'I' of man through the past, the present and the future (I, II, III, 7–11). And thus there is revealed to the soul the secret of the genesis of the 'I' in the course of world-time. This knowledge gives it the strength to begin consciously with the work that can lead to a liberation, a freeing from the effect of the Fall, where gradually the soul wins for itself the ability 'truly to live', 'truly to feel' and 'truly to think' (I, II, III, 13 [12]). This, however, is already the result of the transformation of the human astral body into Spirit Self—into the Virgin Sophia of Christian terminology. The human being then becomes in truth a temple of God, a vessel of the Holy Spirit, and understands himself—in the eternal aspect of his cosmic being, his activity of soul, his spiritual foundations—as a being completely interwoven through body, soul and spirit with the higher supersensible worlds.

Such a conscious ascent of man into the higher worlds would, however, be impossible if the strength for this had to come from human aspirations alone. A genuine initiation can take place only when the spiritual world itself comes to meet the upward-striving human soul. We have already seen that in pre-Christian antiquity this could occur only in the state of a deep, deathlike temple sleep of three days, in which the soul having undergone all the necessary stages of preparation was put into a condition by the priest-hierophant in order that the spiritual world could approach it directly. However, since the Mystery of Golgotha, because the macro-cosmic Being of Christ has been present in the Earth-sphere and since 1899 the new epoch of light has begun, it is now possible to perceive *consciously* the voice of the macrocosm and to enter *in full freedom* into the super-sensible worlds—to experience how in our time the spiritual world itself comes directly to meet all mankind. For it is solely through the deed of Christ on Golgotha that the soul today, in the world epoch of human freedom, can find the way to 'reconciliation' with God—the way to a conscious and free union with the higher worlds. And it is about the fact that this is indeed possible from our time onwards that above all the fourth part of the *Foundation Stone Meditation* speaks.

In earlier times, the Gods drew near to humanity only through a dull, dreamlike consciousness. Now, however, to the human being who allows his heart to be warmed and his head enlightened by the Christ-Sun, the full being and essence of the Cosmic Word of the Gods can be revealed—a Word which addresses itself to the fully conscious human being in the second section of Parts I–III of the *Meditation* in which, in seven con-secutive lines (14–20), the process is described of how, stage by stage, the macrocosm descends to man—which is the indispensable precondition of every genuine path of initiation.

The macrocosm comes to meet the human soul that strives for higher knowledge in three stages. It reveals itself firstly in its highest aspect beyond the Hierarchies: as the sphere of the Father, the Son and the Spirit; as the divine Trinity (I, II, III, 14–15); it then reveals itself as the divine-creative world of the nine Hierarchies (I, II, III, 16–18); and thirdly as the voice of the Hierarchies, as the Cosmic Word calling to man to awaken, and revealing before him his earthly and heavenly destiny—his origin in the Divine, his victory in Christ over death on the Earth and his awakening to new consciousness by uniting with the Spirit, 'From God (the Divine), Mankind has Being—In Christ, Death becomes Life—In the Spirit's Universal Thoughts, the Soul awakens' (I, II, III, 19–20).

Thus, what is experienced by the soul on the path of initiation, and is described in the first section of Parts I–III of the *Meditation*, is only possible in that the entire macrocosm takes part in it, descending to man in the second sections of the same parts which, for this reason, begin each time with the word 'For' (*Denn*). However, an *inner* union of the two sections of

215

each of the three parts is possible for full human consciousness only through the content of the fourth part. Rudolf Steiner places this before us on the first day of the Christmas Conference, as the all-encompassing picture of the new initiation, unveiling this path in its entirety in its seven mighty rhythms. In this way, in the first sections of Parts I–III, he draws our attention first to the microcosmic path to the spiritual worlds—the path from below upwards—and then brings before our mind's eye the Mystery of Christ in humanity, the Mystery through which the connection of the human soul with the world of the Gods—a connection that had been destroyed through the Fall—was re-established (Part IV, Section 1). And finally, for the soul which by living into the second section of Part IV of the *Meditation* has become permeated through and through by the Christ-impulse, there appears the complete picture of the initiation path, the final union of the human soul with the divine-spiritual worlds, the microcosm with the macrocosm, as comes to expression when the first, second and third parts of the *Meditation* are read *in their entirety*.[35]

Looking at the rhythms of the first day as a whole, we see that their principal aim is to establish the connection with the Christ of the human being who is preparing to enter upon the path of the New Mysteries, through an understanding of His all-embracing role in world development. For He it was who brought the possibility of uniting macrocosm and microcosm, the world of the Gods and the world of man: In Him 'the Word became Flesh'. To become fully aware of the infinite significance of this fact for the new initiation is the task of the rhythms of this day.

In the reference added at the end of each of the first three parts of the *Meditation* to the elemental spirits of the four points of the compass, Rudolf Steiner calls directly to these beings through whose sphere the pupil must pass at the beginning of his spiritual path. These spirits of the four elements who received the Christ-impulse at the time of the Mystery of Golgotha, at the time of Christ's union with the Earth, can now show human beings the true path leading to Him.

The call in these three lines, however, holds yet another secret—the secret of the new experience of nature which today, in every stone, in every plant wishes to speak to man of the great Sun Redeemer of the world. For this reason it is most especially the task of modern spiritual science to develop a new way of looking at nature. Rudolf Steiner indicates this, among other things, in his lecture in Christiania (Oslo) on 17 May 1923 (GA 226): 'Through spiritual science we must learn again to see the spiritual in every physical being, to see spirits behind stones, the spiritual behind plants, behind animals and behind man; the spiritual in clouds, the spiritual behind the Sun. If we find the spirit again in all its

216

reality, behind matter, then we also open our souls to the voice of Christ, who wishes to speak to us if only we wish to hear Him.' And on 21 May, in the sixth lecture of this cycle, he speaks as follows: 'Before the Mystery of Golgotha, humanity beheld nature, ensouled and permeated with spirit. Since the Mystery of Golgotha humanity must strive so that nature, ensouled and suffused with spirit, will form the retinue of Christ, so that the spirits of nature are all seen as in the service of Christ, for without Him they could not be seen.' But this new relation to the world of nature about us, which is permeated through and through by the forces of the Christ who shows Himself in it as the true Spirit of the Earth and reveals to us her secrets—this is the new knowledge which Rudolf Steiner calls 'reading in the Book of Nature'. This knowledge, according to his statements, lived in a different pre-Christian form in Aristotle; while in the following epoch, which reached its most complete manifestation in medieval Europe, it was succeeded by the 'Book of Revelation'. But in our time, after the end of Kali Yuga and with the beginning of the new rulership of Michael, it is to emerge—in a more sublime, more all-embracing form than in Aristotle—in the anthroposophically-orientated spiritual science of the present.

In a lecture in Dornach on 1 August 1924, Rudolf Steiner speaks of how essential it is that we again learn to read in the 'Book of Nature', and how this is one of the most important impulses of our epoch—an impulse issuing from the guiding Time Spirit, from Michael himself. For at the present time this book is in the very deepest sense a Christian book: 'And this is the impulse of Michael, namely, to bring human beings, now that the Cosmic Intelligence directed by Michael has come down among them, to open once again the "Book of Nature", and to read therein.' (GA 237). And then addressing himself directly to anthroposophists, Rudolf Steiner continues: 'In fact, everyone who is in the anthroposophical movement should feel that he can understand his karma only when he knows that *he personally* is called upon spiritually to read again in the "Book of Nature", to find the *underlying spiritual causes of nature*, seeing that God has given His Revelation for the intervening time.' This means: since the Mystery of Golgotha the Christ Being, having united Himself with the Earth, has worked in the sphere of its elemental spirits:

The Spirits hear it
In East and West and North and South.

And as a call truly to recognize this, as a call for a new reading in the great and now deeply Christian 'Book of Nature', there sounds out to us three times from the *Foundation Stone Meditation*:

May human beings hear it!³⁶

As a result of the rhythms of this day and having recognized the conditions of its initiation, the soul can enter directly upon that path. There are seven great Mystery-stages to be experienced in the following seven initiation rhythms in the course of seven days of Christmastide.

Rudolf Steiner begins the initiation process itself on 26 December, a Wednesday. This day stands under the influence of Mercury, whose forces carry and permeate that half of Earth development which follows the Mystery of Golgotha, or in other words, the epoch of the realization of the Christ-impulse in the Earth-sphere and in humanity. This day, therefore, is particularly favourable for setting out on the first stage along the new path of initiation. On this day Rudolf Steiner reads the first sections of Parts I–III, and then gives the following rhythm. He first of all points to the three aspects of the soul's activity that it realizes on its path into the higher worlds. These are (I, II, III, 5)

Spirit-recollection   Spirit-mindfulness   Spirit-vision

He then adds to each of these the following corresponding words (I, II, III, 9–11):

Thine own I	Do thine own I	On thine own I
Comes to being	Unite	Bestow
Within the I of God	Unto the I of the World	For thy free Willing

The soul begins its passage through the first stage of the spiritual path by deepening its consciousness of self, a process which is inaugurated by the three distinct soul activities referred to above, each of which furthers the gradual ascent of the soul into the supersensible worlds, in accordance with that part of the *Meditation* in which it is mentioned. Modern spiritual science speaks of three stages of higher knowledge that can be reached on the modern spiritual path. It calls these imaginative, inspirational and intuitive knowledge. Immersion in each of the three aspects of human soul activity now leads the pupil in turn through these three stages, thereby revealing to him one of the three major aspects of Divine Existence.

The first aspect of soul activity, 'Spirit-recollection', as described in the first part of the *Meditation*, results—through the daily reviewing, in reverse order, of the events of the past day—in the pupil becoming immersed in the depths of his own soul (I, 6). Step by step this picture should first bring the pupil to an experience in Imagination of an etheric-panoramic view of his whole life; later, to an experience in Inspiration of life before birth 'in the wielding World–Creator–Life' (I, 7–8); and thirdly, in Intuition, to an experience of the evolution of the cosmos and of humanity extending back to Old Saturn, when the human 'I' still resided fully in the Divine 'I' of the Creator of all Being (I, 9–11). By contemplating the first aspect of the soul's activity, we are brought to a recognition of the Father-sphere in which the secrets of all the cosmic past are preserved.

In Part II the second aspect of soul activity, 'Spirit-mindfulness', reveals to us the secrets of the Son-sphere, and particularly the secrets of His present working in the aura surrounding the Earth. Moreover, just as the backward review of the events of the day was necessary as a preparation for a deepening of the first aspect of human soul activity in the previous exercise, so here it is the study of what is given by spiritual science, from which the pupil can draw new knowledge of the Being of Christ. For this knowledge is the most important requirement of our time. It is through such meditative 'contemplation' or 'mindfulness' of the Christ Being (II, 5) that, with time, the pupil wins for himself a true balance of soul (II, 6). This means, however, that by experiencing the real presence of Christ in the soul, the forces of Lucifer and Ahriman can be brought into equilibrium (as was depicted in Rudolf Steiner's carving of the 'Group'). Thus a contemplation of the Christ from a background of spiritual science gradually leads to a genuine experience of His Being in the supersensible world. Here the Christ first appears to the present-day pupil in His etheric form—in Imagination. At the next stage, in Inspiration, He is revealed in His astral form as the great Sun spirit (the Guardian of the Threshold) who from the lofty Sun-sphere directs 'the surging/Deeds of the World's becoming' (II, 7–8) and helps souls in the life after death to find their way from the Soul-world into the Spirit-world, from the Moon-sphere into the Sun-sphere. And finally, in Intuition, He appears to the pupil of the spirit as the all-embracing 'I' of the world, as the highest representative of the fourth macrocosmic principle in the universe,[37] in the contemplation of which are immersed the twelve Bodhisattvas in the sphere of fore-knowledge, drawing from it their impulses for the guidance of all human evolution. This most sublime gazing upon the Christ in Intuition also reveals to the pupil the cosmic significance of the Mystery of Golgotha, through which the World-'I' of Christ has united with the individual 'I' of each human being (II, 9–11), thereby giving him the possibility of ascending to the highest spheres of the macrocosm.

The third aspect of soul activity, 'Spirit-vision', related to Part III of the *Meditation*, reveals to the pupil that region of the Spirit, that sphere of the future in which the goals of world evolution are to be reached. In its preparatory stage this soul aspect straightaway leads the pupil to the inner nature of meditation, which can be practised only in complete 'quietness of thought' (III, 5). Meditating in this way brings the pupil to a state of thinking with the etheric brain, to an imaginative perception of the 'World Being's Light' (III, 8) and later to the experience of 'empty consciousness'. This experience is the gateway to Inspiration, in which Michael, the guiding Spirit of our time, then comes to meet the pupil, revealing to him 'The eternal aims of Gods' (III, 7), which point to the most distant future of humanity when out of free will the individual human 'I' will realize these divine aims consciously in the universe (III, 9–11). This far-distant epoch of world development is revealed to the pupil in Intuition as the future planetary condition of the Earth.

This is a picture in broad outline of the spiritual path that is opened up through a deepening of these three aspects of human soul activity. However, their connection with the stages of initiation referred to also makes it clear that, if the pupil immerses himself consciously in them, they can eventually lead to a complete transformation of his thinking, feeling and willing (III, II, I, 13), which subsequently reveal to him 'the ground of the Spirit', 'the weaving of the Soul', and 'the All-World-Being' of man (III, II, I, 12 [13]). Thus the ancient Mystery-formula 'Know thyself as spirit, soul and body' becomes for the pupil, in a form renewed out of the signs of the present, something that is known from personal experience.

But just as the thinking, feeling and willing in man can be brought into harmonious co-operation only under the influence of his 'I'-consciousness, so too is it right to talk of the interaction of these three soul activities as a unified whole. And a study of this kind reveals a highly important feature of the rhythm of this day. For seen as a whole, these three aspects of the soul's activity lead the human being to true self-knowledge, opening before him the profound Mystery of the human 'I': its past existence in the bosom of the divine worlds; its subsequent fall from there only to find the connection anew later when, through the working of the Christ-impulse in the Earth-sphere, it became possible once again for the human 'I' to unite with the 'I' of the World; and finally, the indication of the distant future of the 'I', when out of free will it will be able to create in the cosmos with the Gods (I, II, III, 9–11). In this sense the 'I'-Mystery is revealed to the pupil here in its theological, its Christological and its eschatological aspects.

This knowledge of the cosmic and earthly destiny of the human 'I' has a further significance for the pupil. In seeing into this Mystery of the genesis of the 'I' in its gradual development from its lowest to its highest stage, there is also revealed to the pupil the fundamental secret of earthly existence—the secret of death. For an initiation, and while still in the physical body, the pupil experiences that which the ordinary human being

220

experiences only after death, namely, the death of the lower 'I' for the sake of resurrection in the higher. Herein lies the meaning of the Mystery-saying: 'Whoever dies not before he dies will perish indeed when he dies.'[38] But in the deed of Christ on Golgotha the possibility was given to all mankind, through a union with the Christ-impulse, to be reborn out of the kingdom of death in which we are immersed with our lower 'I'—to rise again while still in the physical body, in the higher 'I', in the Spirit Self, for life in the spiritual world. The profound secret of death in relation to what was fulfilled by Christ Jesus in the Mystery of Golgotha is what is revealed here to the pupil of the spirit.

Death is the birth of the higher 'I' in man,[39] just as the death on the cross at Golgotha was the birth of the higher 'I' of all mankind.[40] Only the knowledge of this Mystery can give the pupil the strength not to lose his individual 'I' as he enters into the spiritual world, as is otherwise always the case in crossing over the threshold of death. 'Strengthen yourself to die in Christ' (*In Christo morimur*)—carrying out these words is for us the first step of the new path of initiation.

From this we can also begin to understand why in his *Occult Science* Rudolf Steiner calls this new path of initiation 'the knowledge of the Grail', for the image of the Grail points to the Mystery of the development of the higher 'I' in man in relation to the Christ-impulse. In *Occult Science* Rudolf Steiner writes the following concerning this: 'We read of the Holy Grail in old narratives and legends, and as we learn to understand its deeper meaning we discover that it most significantly pictures the heart and essence of the new initiation knowledge, centring in the Mystery of Christ. The initiates of the new age may therefore be described as the "initiates of the Grail". The pathway into spiritual worlds, the first stages of which were set forth in the preceding chapter, culminates in the "science of the Grail".'[41]

In the lecture-cycle *The Gospel of St John*, Rudolf Steiner says the following: 'In the beginning there was the Mystery of the higher human "I"; it was preserved in the Grail and remained connected with it. And in the Grail there lives the "I" that is connected with the eternal and the immortal just as the lower "I" is connected with the transient and the mortal. And whoever knows the secret of the Holy Grail knows that from the wood of the cross there comes forth quickened, burgeoning life, the immortal "I" that is symbolized by the roses on the black wood of the cross.'[42] From this we see that the Grail Mystery, into which we enter in the rhythm of this 'first' day, leads us to a true knowledge of the 'I'-Mystery. It is also the basis of the further path of initiation, revealing itself as the Mystery of Death and Resurrection, as the transition from the lower mortal 'I' of man to the higher immortal 'I'—a transition in which, thanks to the Christ-force, there are preserved in the higher 'I' all the fruits of the lower. This stage, therefore, also contains the fundamental experience of the threshold, by which the pupil—having reached that degree of maturity necessary for initiation, by uniting himself with his higher, divine 'I'—can enter consciously into the spiritual world.

Thus, that which for the ordinary human being is the tragic event of death becomes for the pupil of the spirit a conscious crossing over of the threshold; the entering, while still alive on the Earth, into the higher worlds in which are opened to him his first experiences of a purely spiritual nature. It is with these first experiences beyond the threshold (which are also the first experiences of the soul after death) that the rhythm of this day acquaints us. One can note here that Rudolf Steiner indicates the profound connection of these first after-death experiences of the soul with the above-mentioned 'I'-Mystery in many lectures when he speaks, for example, of how the possibility of experiencing the individual 'I' in the human being is most closely connected with the continuity of the stream of memory; for where this is disrupted the individual 'I' can no longer be properly perceived. Rudolf Steiner looks at this question in particular detail in the last lecture of the cycle *Anthroposophy—An Introduction* (GA 234), in which he speaks of human memory in relation to the 'I' as passing through three phases.

The first of these phases is connected with the ordinary earthly memory of the human being. It is an essential prerequisite for the experiencing of our natural earthly 'I'-consciousness that the continuity of memory remains unbroken. And this process of remembering past events in the right way comes to expression in the reference to the first type of soul-activity, connected with 'Spirit-recollection'. Next, in the first three days after death we experience a picture-tableau of the sum-total of our memories—being the content of our earthly 'I'—as a unified spatial picture in which the past becomes the present. This is indicated in the *Foundation Stone Meditation* by the next type of soul-activity, connected with 'Spirit-mindfulness'. In this way the rhythm of this day leads us to our first genuine supersensible experience beyond the threshold.

In the further course of this process, however, we experience how this etheric panorama of our past life—and with it our earthly 'I'—gradually moves away from us into the wide expanses of the cosmos. In this second phase we experience in a very real way how 'that which, with the help of our memories, we regarded as our self during life on Earth, how that disperses into the expanses of the universe; how, in a certain sense, it has proved to us and for us its own nullity. And were we only that which could be preserved in our memories between birth and death we would, in just a few days after our death, be nothing.'[43]

222

And yet this experience of one's self as 'nothing', this experience of the death of our lower 'I' and its dissolution into the expanses of the cosmos, can only be withstood in the right way through an inner connection with the Christ-impulse that we have already won on Earth. For that which as our lower 'I' is taken from us in the second phase returns to us again in the third phase from the whole cosmos, but now as our higher 'I'. In the same lecture Rudolf Steiner says: 'There is hardly a stronger proof of man's connectedness with the cosmos than that which emerges after death when, with regard to our subjective inner life, we are deprived of our self, only to have it returned again objectively out of the cosmos.'

It is to this new discovery of the 'I' from the forces of the universe, of our higher 'I', that the third aspect of human soul-activity leads us: 'Spirit-vision'; practise the beholding of the higher 'I'. Experiencing this brings us directly into the spiritual world itself, into the world of Imaginations, and acquaints us with the so-called astral plane or Soul-world whose secrets, however, appear before us only in the rhythm of the following day.

Still on this day, however, Rudolf Steiner draws particular attention to how a *moral sense* arises in the human soul when it experiences that which 'progresses upwards from coming-into-being, to uniting, to bestowing'. We can feel this moral sense when we consider the essence contained in these words of the Mystery of the genesis of the 'I'—the 'I' which ascends step by step to full moral independence, ascends, that is, from the sentient soul, in which it still dwelt in the forces of the Divine 'I' (I, 9–11), to the intellectual or mind soul, in which there flashes up for the first time the possibility of a conscious union with the higher World-'I' (II, 9–11), up to the consciousness soul in which it can attain its final independence, opening itself in full freedom to be overshone by the Spirit Self which bestows upon it the 'eternal aims of Gods' (III, 9–11), the reflection of which we can experience on Earth as the impulses of our moral fantasy. We are thus dealing here with the moral development of the human 'I', which in the cosmic sphere of freedom arises consciously by experiencing that which ascends from 'coming into being' to 'uniting' and 'bestowing'.[44]

On the following day, a Thursday, 27 December, the pupil who in the preceding stage has passed through the experience of the threshold is now led directly into the spiritual world. On this day Rudolf Steiner begins by reading again the first sections of Parts I–III, and then singles out from these the following rhythm: first of all the nine lines which reveal to the human soul the Mystery of the 'I' (I, II, III, 9–11):

Thine own I	Do thine own I	On thine own I
Comes to being	Unite	Bestow
Within the I of God.	Unto the I of the World.	For thy free willing.

To each of these lines respectively is then added (I, II, III, 12–13):

Then in the All–World–Being of Man
Thou wilt truly *live*.

Then 'mid the weaving of the Soul of Man
Thou wilt truly *feel*.

Then from the ground of the Spirit in Man
Thou wilt truly *think*.

Through this rhythm the pupil enters that region of after-death existence in which, after the dispersal of the etheric body into the expanses of
the cosmos, the soul awakens. This is the Soul-world or the astral plane.
The soul dwells here for about a third of the time of the past life, reliving all
the experiences of that life in reverse order but now in their full truth, free
from all illusion and as though 'from within'. This is an essential and
profound process on the path to real spiritual self-knowledge. All the deeds
of the human being, all feelings and thoughts, stand during this time before
the soul in their true, undisguised aspect, in their full significance for the
whole cosmos. Here is revealed to the soul's own gaze the world-secret of
its past life. In his explanations of the rhythms of this day Rudolf Steiner
describes these experiences as follows: 'These utterances (*Aussprüche*) are
like the words of world-secrets inasmuch as these world-secrets rise again in
the human soul as self-knowledge.'[45] Thus the true worth of his past life is
revealed to the human being in the Soul-world after death, for he sees
there the judgment on it of the whole cosmos and experiences this
judgment as a decisive act on the path towards knowledge of his own
being.

But the rhythms of this day lead us still deeper into the after-death
experiences of the soul. This becomes clearer from what is said in the
lectures of 1923, in which Rudolf Steiner depicts how the human being in
his passage through the Soul-world during the first period of life after death
comes into contact with the Beings of the Third Hierarchy, the Spirits of
Soul.[46] These lofty Beings bring before him in mighty pictures the consequences of everything he did, felt and thought in his past life. This is the
great cosmic trial of man, where the higher Hierarchies reveal to him the
extent to which in his deeds, feelings and thoughts he has failed to attain
the ideal of perfection closest to him, the ideal of the higher 'I' of Spirit
Self. Thus, first of all Angels come before him and show him to what
extent during life he had still been unable 'truly [to] *think* in the ground of
the Spirit in Man' (III, 12–13). Thereafter Archangels appear and show him
to what extent he had been unable 'truly [to] *feel* 'mid the weaving of the

Soul of Man' (II, 12–13). And finally the Archai approach; they bring before the human being a true picture of all his life's deeds, and he sees from this how far he still is from being able 'truly [to] *live* in the All-World-Being of Man' (I, 12–13). Also, all our failings and transgressions towards our neighbours, our nation, and all humanity are recognized in their true form by the soul in these Imaginations that are created before it by the Beings of the Third Hierarchy. Such a perception of one's mistakes and shortcomings, as well as the awareness of the harm inflicted by them on the whole cosmos, arouses in the human soul the strongest desire to make good, to rectify this, thus awakening in the soul an impulse towards further perfection.

This is the inner nature of the human being's experiences while passing through the Soul-world of Kamaloka, and it is of these that the rhythms of this day speak.

For the pupil of the spirit on the path of initiation who experiences these spiritual processes in full consciousness, this stage corresponds to that of imaginative knowledge, where—proceeding from the knowledge of the 'I'-Mystery acquired at the previous stage—he must now begin work on the transformation of the astral body into Spirit Self. The secret of the inner nature of the astral body is thereby unveiled to him as he passes through the Soul-world. For that condition of our planet preceding this Earth-phase, namely, the Moon-condition, in which the astral body was given to man as an outpouring from the Spirits of Movement, begins here to become visible. This work of the pupil on the astral body leads gradually—by means of true thinking, true feeling and true soul-life, expressed in right deeds (III, II, I, 12 [12])—to its purification.

In this process are also working the forces of Jupiter, which are particularly strong on this day of the week (Thursday). These on the one hand help the pupil in his work on the realizing of Spirit Self, and on the other hand acquaint him with the nature of the next incarnation of our Earth, with the Jupiter-condition, which is already being prepared on the astral plane.[47]

The rhythm given on the following day, Friday, 28 December, leads us into a still higher sphere. On this day Rudolf Steiner again reads the first sections of Parts I–III, but this time adds to each the first two lines of the second section of each part, indicating that whereas at the previous stage of imaginative knowledge the experiences tend to have a more or less subjective character, at this moment the pupil enters the realm of the objective, where for the first time the secrets of the macrocosm begin to reveal themselves to him.

Rudolf Steiner gave on this day the following rhythm. Again, first the

225

three basic exercises of Anthroposophy:[48] 'Practise Spirit-recollection'; 'Practise Spirit-mindfulness' (contemplation); 'Practise Spirit-vision' (perception, beholding) (I, II, III, 5), to which the following lines are added respectively (I, II, III, 14–15):

For the Father-Spirit of the Heights holds sway
In the Depths of Worlds, begetting Life.

For the Christ-Will in the encircling Round holds sway
In the Rhythms of Worlds, blessing the Soul.

For the Spirit's Universal Thoughts hold sway
In the Being of all Worlds, beseeching Light.

The inner essence of these new rhythms can best be understood by following the further life of the soul after death. For having completed its purification in the Soul-world during the previous stage, the soul now enters into the Spirit-land, into Lower Devachan.

In his book *Occult Science* and in lectures, Rudolf Steiner describes how Lower Devachan consists of four regions through which, one after the other, the soul passes during this time. The first region forms the so-called 'terra firma' or 'mainland' of the spiritual world, and in it are to be found the archetypes of all that is solid, mineral or crystalline—in other words, everything that we on Earth associate with the concept of space, body, with everything that has weight and form. If, going from the above description of this region, we now look at the human body—which as microcosm mirrors in itself all the kingdoms of nature—and ask what archetypes of the different parts of the body are to be sought here, it becomes evident that above all in this first region of Lower Devachan we find the archetypes of our limb system; that is, the archetypes that are addressed at the beginning of the first part of the *Meditation* (I, 2). It is in this region that the forces which create space attain to their highest and most perfect expression, for they reveal themselves here in particular in that balance—existing only in the human kingdom—of gravity and levity which is concentrated in the limb system, and whose most important consequence is the upright posture and the ability to orientate oneself in space.

Having thus established the connection between the 'terra firma' of the Spirit-land and the first part of the *Meditation*, we can go further in this direction. For we can see from this first part that it is not only the forces of the 'first' region of Lower Devachan that are involved in the shaping of our limb system, but that spiritual impulses are implanted in it which extend up to the cosmic sphere of the Father. And thus, through this broadening of

226

our understanding, we come to the following composite picture. From the highest sphere of the Father, who holds sway in the heights (I, 14), spiritual streams constantly flow—as 'embryonic seeds', as essential-divine archetypal forces—into the 'terra firma' of Lower Devachan in order to form there the archetypes of that which on Earth, in the depths of the world, becomes the foundation of being (I, 15) of our limb system and of everything in the four kingdoms of nature which has body, form and weight. And as their name implies, it is the Spirits of Form who play a particularly important part in this great sublime work.

On its after-death path of ascent, the soul then rises into the second region of Lower Devachan, called by Rudolf Steiner the region of 'seas and rivers'. This region contains the archetypes of everything on Earth which has life, that is, which has an etheric body. For this reason he also states in *Occult Science* that a comparison with the blood circulation in the human body—the organic expression of the etheric body—is even better than the one with the myriad forms of the Earth's seas and rivers.[49] This fact points directly to the system of the human body corresponding to this region and which, as the physical manifestation of the etheric forces in man, has its centre in the heart. It is of this that the second part of the *Meditation* speaks: 'Soul of Man/Thou livest in the beat of Heart . . .' II, 2). And also, just as in the previous case, this part too leads us further, to the lofty sphere of the Son, to the spiritual wellspring of the etheric forces that are the foundation of the activity of the heart and the circulation of the blood.

Thus we have the following pictures. From the lofty cosmic sphere of Christ there flows into the surroundings of the Earth an unceasing stream of spiritual will (II, 14). On its way through the second region of Lower Devachan this forms the archetypes of all that which on Earth becomes the etheric foundations of the human heart and circulatory system, and forms also those forces at the basis of the life-processes in the nature kingdoms of plant, animal and man. And in all these living, rhythmical, constantly changing processes (II, 15), the Spirits of Movement are particularly active.

The soul then rises still higher on its journey after death. It comes now into the third region of Lower Devachan, which Rudolf Steiner calls the 'atmosphere' or the 'air circulation' (*Luftkreis*) of the spiritual world. Here are the archetypes of everything on Earth which has the inner capacity to feel and sense. The system in man corresponding to this is all that which is connected with the breathing process, in which the activity of the astral body is revealed in the physical body. The physical centre of respiration, however, is the lung, and thus in the second part of the *Foundation Stone Meditation* we find 'Soul of Man/Thou livest in the beat of . . . Lung' (II, 2).[50]

Going more deeply still into this second part of the *Meditation*, there arises a sublime picture of how, through the working of the Christ Will in the 'encircling Round', cosmic streams flow down from the Son-sphere (II, 14) in order to form in this third region of Lower Devachan the archetypes of the human respiratory system and lungs in their astral nature, as well as the archetypes of all the soul-experiences connected with the animal and human kingdoms. Just as previously with the forming of the heart, so here too, with the forming of the lungs, the Spirits of Form play a particularly central part.

We find unusually fine details in the following rhythm of this day, namely, '. . . in the *Rhythms of Worlds*, blessing the Soul' (II, 15). The word 'rhythm' relates here primarily to the 'region of seas and rivers', of which in *Occult Science* Rudolf Steiner says that the 'streaming life' of this region is perceived as spiritual sound,[51] as music—that is, as rhythm. The words 'blessing the Soul' relate on the other hand more to the 'atmosphere' of the spiritual world, the region of the archetypes of all soul-life, which once having become enlightened and purified can receive the blessing of Christ Himself.

And finally the soul ascends into the highest region of Lower Devachan. Here the archetypes are to be found of everything that man himself creates on Earth—creates first and foremost from the forces of the head (III, 2) inasmuch as this is the bearer of his creative thoughts which, in turn, are the last stage of the descent to Earth of the World Thoughts, the Cosmic Intelligence of Michael (III, 14).[52] Here, in this last region of Lower Devachan, the Spirit's Universal Thoughts, which are to become the archetypes of the earthly thoughts of human beings, raise up an entreaty to the powers of Light (III, 15) which already are the powers of Upper Devachan in whose sphere, as Rudolf Steiner relates in *Occult Science*, reigns the purest divine light of wisdom.★[53]

It is also in this sphere that the soul after death receives the first impulses from the sphere of the fixed stars beyond the Saturn-sphere, from the sphere of eternity whose physical reflection is the human head and brain, as is physiologically expressed in their independence of the earthly forces of gravity (III, 2).

Thus, through the third part of the *Meditation* there arises the following sublime picture. The World Thoughts descend from the cosmic sphere of the spirit into this fourth region of Lower Devachan in order to become there the archetypes of the creative thoughts of human beings, thoughts which arise on Earth by means of the wonderful structure of the head, which itself is a reflection of our whole cosmos. And, as earlier in the three preceding spiritual regions, so here too do hierarchical Beings participate in this cosmic activity—in this case, most particularly, the Spirits of Wisdom.

★ The significance of these two particularly important lines of the *Foundation Stone Meditation* (III, 14–15) will be looked at more closely in the next chapter.

In this way the rhythm of this day reveals to us the inner nature of the four world streams which, particularly by virtue of the co-working of the Second Hierarchy, flow down from the sphere of the Father, the Son and the Spirit into the four regions of Lower Devachan, calling into being the four kingdoms of nature and giving them the possibility of existence and development on Earth. The soul, however, experiences in these regions of Lower Devachan all the fruits of the past life which it has gathered in its bodily sheaths and which it now gradually transforms into abilities for the future life on Earth.

When in the course of his initiation in the rhythm of this day the pupil of the spirit enters consciously into the four regions of Lower Devachan, he comes into the realm of Inspiration, the realm of Divine rhythm, where he can experience the four cosmic streams as sounding out in living tone. These are then transformed for him into the mighty symphony of the Music of the Spheres, whose rhythms can be compared with the rhythmic-musical element on Earth in the first two regions, and with the rhythmic-speech element in the other two. Thus Rudolf Steiner says of the rhythm of this day: '... it is as though from the *world rhythm* that these words sound forth.'[54]

Attainment of this new stage of initiation enables the pupil henceforth to work consciously on the transformation of his etheric body into Life Spirit. This is aided in considerable measure by the Venus-forces, which on this day—a Friday—work particularly strongly, and which reveal to the pupil the secrets of a still more distant incarnation of the Earth, namely the Venus condition, which even now is being prepared in Lower Devachan.[55]

The mention in this rhythm, however, of the *name* of Christ (II, 14) directs us to His working during the ancient Sun-period, then to His relation to the principle of Life Spirit, and finally to the possibility of meeting Him directly in the form of the Greater Guardian of the Threshold. The pupil on his path of initiation—like the soul which on its journeying after death ascends into this sphere—has to experience this meeting, for only the Christ can bring about an entrance into the sphere of the Sun in the right way.[56]

The rhythm given by Rudolf Steiner on Saturday, 29 December, leads us now completely into the sphere of macrocosmic existence. On this day Rudolf Steiner reads all three parts of the *Foundation Stone Meditation*, leaving out only the last three lines of each, those referring to the elemental beings (I, II, III, 21–23), which in their entirety present a picture of the human being as a microcosm completely united with the greater world of the macrocosm. In the rhythm of this day we again have the threefoldness of the fundamental spiritual exercises (I, II, III, 5), but combined now with a reference to all nine divine-spiritual Hierarchies present and working at this level. They are all named here in accordance with the names of Christian-esoteric tradition, but each is also characterized by the nature of its work in the cosmos. Thus the First Hierarchy—the Seraphim, Cherubim and Thrones—are characterized by the words: 'Let there ring out from the Heights/What in the Depths is echoed' (I, 16–18). Related to the next Hierarchy—to the Kyriotetes, Dynamis and Exusiai—are the words: 'Let there be fired from the East/What through the West is formed' (II, 16–18). And lastly the nature of the work of the Third Hierarchy—the Archai, Archangeloi and Angeloi—is expressed in the words: 'Let there be prayed in the Depths/What from the Heights is answered' (III, 16–18).

In his explanations of this rhythm, Rudolf Steiner emphasized particularly that each of the three kinds of hierarchical cosmic activity also gives a picture of how each individual Hierarchy weaves its voice into the great sounding World-Word, which encompasses, forms and gives life to the whole created universe.

In this rhythm there comes before us the sublime image of the great all-embracing working of the Christ as Macro-Logos, in which the cosmic creativity of all nine Hierarchies finds a full harmonious union and completion, merging as they do into the all-one World-Word of the cosmos, whose vital centre is the macrocosmic revelation of the Logos, of Christ.

If in this way we picture the activity of the First Hierarchy as being directed downwards, that of the Second as directed into the surroundings from East to West, and that of the Third from below upwards, we get an image of the cosmic World Cross and sense ourselves at its mid-point, at its centre, while at the same time experiencing ourselves in the middle of the sevenfold path of initiation and in the centre of world evolution from Saturn to Vulcan, as we shall see later. Thus the Cosmic Cross of the three hierarchical streams issuing from the sphere of the Father, the Son and the Spirit, the Cross that is encircled by the seven rhythms of initiation and the seven stages of world evolution, can appear before us as a great Rosicrucian sign—as a cosmic cross with seven roses.

Turning again now to our study of the rhythms in connection with the life of the soul after death, we can characterize this new stage of its ascent, which is contained in the rhythm of this day, as the crossing-over from Lower to Upper Devachan, from the region of the harmony of the spheres to the region of the sounding World-Word. In this region the soul now finds the peace of soul existence, while gradually approaching what Rudolf Steiner calls 'the great hour of Cosmic Midnight'. During this time the soul also reaches its greatest distance from the Earth, ascending amid the mighty sounding of the World-Word to the border between Upper Devachan and still higher worlds, in order to experience something truly extraordinary in this, the highest sphere that the human soul can reach before beginning its descent to a new incarnation on the Earth. Rudolf Steiner describes this in the following deeply impressive words: 'And this life then continues; and as it draws near to the midway point between death and a new birth there occurs something of a very special nature. Just as it is when we stand here on the Earth—particularly in those moments when we look up into the universe as the stars shine down upon us—and have a sense of the grandeur of the heavenly cosmic realms above us, so do we experience something much greater when we are in the spirit realm looking down. For we see how, in a remarkable way, the Beings of the First Hierarchy—the Seraphim, Cherubim and Thrones—perform deeds there in mutual co-operation. Extremely powerful pictures of spiritual occurrences are now revealed if we look at the heavens which lie below us. In the same way that on Earth we now see the script of the stars as we look upward, so [in the spirit world] we see, as we look down, the deeds of the Seraphim, Cherubim and Thrones. And that which takes place between them, which shows itself in sublime and magnificent pictures—we feel about these, in this spiritual existence, that they have something to do with what we ourselves are and what we shall become. For we have the feeling now that what is happening there among the Seraphim, Cherubim and Thrones is showing us what consequences the deeds of our previous life on Earth will have in the next.'[57]

Thus, in this lofty sphere at the Midnight-hour of life after death, there is revealed to the soul the deepest foundations of its karma on Earth. This unfolds by virtue of the soul's perception of the activity of the Beings of the First Hierarchy who, representing the world sphere of the Father in the cosmos, join with the other two Hierarchies in their work on the con-figuration of the future life of each human being[58] and together in this ninefold choir, encompassing the whole of the created universe, are incorporated[59] into the great fullness of the eternal, primordial Cosmic Word. For from this time onwards the soul itself participates in this sublime work of all the divine-spiritual Hierarchies. This proceeds under the lea-dership of the Seraphim, Cherubim and Thrones who, through the sphere of the upper planets, work on forming the spiritual archetype of the future physical body from forces of the macrocosm. During this time the Third Hierarchy creates the system of sense organs, the Second Hierarchy the nervous and circulatory systems, and the First Hierarchy the system of muscles and bones.[60]

Having reached the fourth stage of his path of initiation, which is contained in the rhythm of this day, the pupil now enters the world of Intuition. This enables him to approach the hierarchical Beings that come to meet him here in a purely inward way. In his books and lectures Rudolf

231

Steiner describes on many occasions how, in Imagination, it is only the outer form of these lofty Beings that appears; how, in Inspiration, it is their deeds in the midst of the cosmos; and how it is only in Intuition that their hidden inner being is revealed[61] to the pupil, whereby it is granted him at this stage to behold them 'face to face', as it were.[62] For this reason, and as an indication of just this possibility in the rhythm of this day, they are all named by their esoteric names.[63]

Finally, in this all-encompassing sphere of the Cosmic Word and having completed the first half of his initiation, the pupil will now meet Christ Himself, will experience the Christ Being in Intuition as the great Cosmic Bearer of the World-Word. But this fourth stage of the sevenfold Christian-Rosicrucian path of initiation is connected primarily with the human 'I'. For this reason, through the meeting with the Christ in the sphere of Intuition, the great Mystery-words of the new Christian initiation, 'Not I, but Christ in me', become an inner reality for the pupil. Henceforth the Christ Being is the archetype and goal of all his striving, and his further spiritual development will unfold in the imitation of the great macrocosmic path of Christ Jesus, while the deepest secrets of the cosmic-earthly destiny of Christ begin gradually to be revealed before him.

The Christ who appeared on Earth reveals Himself to the pupil of the spirit as 'the great example for man on Earth',[64] as the image of the future human being of Vulcan. Thus the final goal of all Earth evolution becomes consciously experienced knowledge: the transformation of the physical body into Spirit Man through the activity of the human 'I' imbued through and through with Christ, and the transformation of the Earth-existence into the Venus-condition, which even now is being prepared by spiritual powers under the leadership of Christ in the sphere of Upper Devachan.

But in addition to this momentous view into the distant future, the vision of the pupil, here in this lofty region of Intuition, broadens out on the one hand over all his past lives, over his whole personal past, and on the other hand over all the past of the world, reaching back to the first incarnation of our planet. Rudolf Steiner says of this: 'When Intuition arises, the human being looks back into his past lives on Earth. At the same time, however, with these past lives there arises before one's gaze the whole of the past life of the world.'[65] Thus there arises before the pupil here the world past of our cosmos, reaching back to its most ancient, primordial origins when on Ancient Saturn the highest Hierarchy—the Seraphim, Cherubim and Thrones—laid down the first seed for the physical body of future man.

The pupil's gaze thus embraces at this level the whole cosmic evolution of our Earth from Saturn to Vulcan.[66] It is particularly supported in this by those forces which flow most intensely to the human being on this day—a

Saturday—from Saturn, which as the outermost planet encompasses within the boundary of its orbit all the past and future of our solar system.

It is also to these Saturn forces, which work particularly intensely at the Cosmic Midnight, that in the fourth Mystery Drama the Guardian of the Threshold directs the pupil who is able to experience this sublime moment consciously. The Guardian says:[67]

Perceive and know your cosmic midnight hour!
I hold you in the spell of ripened light,
which Saturn shines on you until through power
of this light your sheaths, illumining yourselves,
can live in stronger wakefulness their colours

(transl. by Hans Pusch)

To this profound Mystery of all world development, stretching from the human physical body (laid down in seed-form on Ancient Saturn), through the 'I' (this is won by human beings on Earth) to Spirit Man (on Vulcan), to this great development from the sphere of the Father (in the past), through the sphere of the Son (in the present), to the sphere of the spirit (in the future) where humanity will be realized as the Tenth Hierarchy—it is to this that the threefoldness of the exercises of remembrance, contemplation and vision of the spirit leads us, and it is of this that the rhythm of this day speaks, revealing to us thereby the immense horizons of world development.[68]

Returning again, in connection with the rhythm of this day, to our study of the soul's after-death existence at the Midnight Hour of the cosmos, we must mention another exceptionally important experience that is undergone by the soul here. Rudolf Steiner describes this in detail in his lecture cycle *The Inner Nature of Man and the Life Between Death and a New Birth*, where he speaks of how in the present cycle of evolution it is only the connection with the Christ which the human being has established while on Earth and then carried across the portal of death into the spiritual world that enables him to preserve his 'I'-consciousness right up to the Cosmic Midnight. If the soul does indeed become imbued on Earth with a true understanding of the Christ-impulse and its significance for the whole of Earth evolution (as was shown in relation to the rhythm of 25 December), in the rhythm of the following day, the 26th, and through a knowledge of the Mystery of the ascent to the higher 'I', it can pass over the threshold of death in the right way, either after normal human death or by entering the spiritual world at the beginning of the path of initiation. But in either case, in order to maintain in the spiritual world its experience of the individual 'I', the soul has need of the Christ. A relation to the Christ, however, can only be established on the Earth, and in full freedom. In other words, in crossing the threshold of death or, which is the same thing, the threshold into the spiritual world in initiation, the human being must 'die in Christ' (*In Christo morimur*).

In the lecture in Vienna on 12 April 1914, Rudolf Steiner presents this as follows: 'We equip ourselves in the right way with the impulses that we need when we pass through the portal of death [that is, in the rhythm of 26 December] if we find a right relation to Christ [rhythm of 25th]. At that moment when it is a matter of leaving the physical body—either because we enter upon spiritual-scientific development or because we truly pass through the portal of death—at that moment everything depends on whether, in the present cycle of time, we stand in relation in the right way to that Being who came into the world in order that we might find a connection to Him.' In the following lecture, on 13 April, Rudolf Steiner takes this further: 'It is this state of being permeated through and through with the substance of Christ that at present gives us the possibility of preserving, at the passing from the physical life into death, the memory of our "I" up to the Cosmic Midnight . . .' And on the next day, he returns to this again: 'To keep this memory [of the "I"] we must die into Christ. Thus the Christ-impulse is essential here: it holds for us the possibility of remembering our "I" right up to the Midnight Hour of Existence.'

But what happens when the human soul, having consciously imbued itself with the Christ-impulse while on Earth, is then able in passing through the portal of death 'to die in Christ' and thereby carry its individual 'I' to the Midnight Hour? According to Rudolf Steiner the following occurs: 'Then, at the Midnight Hour of Existence, the Spirit approaches us. Now we have preserved the memory of our "I". And if we carry this memory up to the Midnight Hour of Existence, to that moment when the Holy Spirit comes to us ... if we have maintained this connection [with the "I"], the Spirit can guide us henceforth to our new incarnation, which we bring about by virtue of forming our archetype in the spiritual world.'

If now we remember that, according to indications from Rudolf Steiner, the Holy Spirit brings to the human being an inner knowledge of the Being of Christ—a knowledge which in the body-free stage after death can only be manifest as a real *co-experiencing* of His great path—we then come closer to an understanding of the great Mystery lying at the foundation of the second half of existence after death, and which can be described approximately as follows. When, through its connection with the Christ, the soul gives the Holy Spirit the possibility of approaching it in the 'right' way at the Cosmic Midnight, then the Holy Spirit carries it to a new incarnation in such a way that *the subsequent stages of descent to the Earth become like a microcosmic reflection of the great macrocosmic descent into the Earth-sphere of Christ, to His incarnation in the body of Jesus of Nazareth.*

In the further course of our study we shall see how the understanding of this Mystery can throw a bright light on the inner nature of the following rhythms of the Christmas Conference.[69] Before moving on to these, however, and proceeding from the facts mentioned in connection with the life of the soul after death at the Midnight Hour of Existence, we must first consider how, on the path of the spirit-pupil, these facts stand in relation to the corresponding stage of initiation.

What then is revealed to the pupil who on the path of inner development has experienced a meeting with the Christ in the sphere of Intuition and has thereby attained to the level of 'Master', when in following the journey of the soul after death he now perceives how the Holy Spirit descends to the soul at the Midnight Hour of the cosmos? There is revealed to him the sublime secret of the source of the Holy Spirit, which descends from a still higher sphere into the region of Upper Devachan. And this highest sphere, into which the soul after death is usually still unable to gaze, is revealed to the initiate at this stage as the cosmic sphere of the Bodhisattvas. Here he gazes upon the majestic, awe-inspiring community of the twelve sublime Beings who are immersed in the contemplation of the Thirteenth. This Thirteenth, however, in whom the initiate recognizes the Christ, appears to him here in the Buddhi-sphere as the great macrocosmic 'I' of the whole cosmos. From this radiant wellspring, from this spiritual Christ-Sun (IV, 15) which stands at the very centre of the cosmos, there streams forth the great Comforter, the Holy Spirit, who overshines the community of the Twelve and through them pours itself out to the spheres below, 'blessing the soul' (II, 14–15). For 'that which Christ Himself called the Holy Spirit reigns as Light over the lodge of the Twelve. The Thirteenth is the leader of these.'[70]

Thus is revealed to the initiate the great Mystery of the Holy Spirit which descends from the cosmic 'I' of Christ into the Buddhi-sphere, the sphere of Fore-knowledge and thence, through the community of the Twelve, flows down into the sphere of Upper Devachan to those souls who experience in it the Cosmic Midnight and, overshining them, accompanies them further on their downward path to a new incarnation.

But the Holy Spirit is now revealed to the initiate as the universal Spirit of Cosmic Knowledge—knowledge in particular of the Christ Being Himself, as well as of everything that was accomplished by Him in the beginning, then by His descent to Earth, by His three years on Earth until the Mystery of Golgotha, and thereafter in all the subsequent development of humanity. Rudolf Steiner says of this in the same lecture: 'This Holy Spirit is none other than that through which it is possible to understand what in reality the Christ did.'

One can say that the initiate at this stage undergoes a great cosmic baptism through the Spirit, for the Holy Spirit descends upon him and the knowledge of what once took place as a mystical fact at the Baptism in the Jordan, when the Christ Being entered into the three bodily sheaths of Jesus of Nazareth and thereby renounced the forces of His macrocosmic 'I',[71] now becomes for the initiate a knowledge from personal experience. And he reaches here also what was beheld by the holy Rishis, when many millennia before the Mystery of Golgotha they turned their spiritual gaze to the distance of the cosmos and said: Vishva Karman, the great macrocosmic 'I' of Christ, is still beyond the boundaries of our sphere.

From here onwards it can be said of the initiate who has attained to this stage that he is 'overshone' by the Holy Spirit, is 'filled' by it.[72] The Holy Spirit now speaks through him and gradually reveals to him—and through him to all humanity—all the further secrets of the heavenly and earthly deeds of Christ. Henceforth the initiate can draw wisdom directly from the sphere of the Holy Spirit, through the community of the Bodhisattvas who inspire him, but particularly through the Bodhisattva who in our cycle of development stands as their leader. A result of this is the new and all-embracing knowledge of Christ which gradually opens to us in the following days of the Christmas Conference.

To round off our study of this fourth rhythm, we must just add that the first contact with the Grail Mystery, which the pupil had in connection with the rhythm given on Wednesday, 26 December (concerning the nature of the 'I'-Mystery (see page 220), transforms itself now into a profound comprehension of this Mystery, so that the pupil is able to recognize at this level the secret of his own true higher 'I'. Thus there appears to him here, in archetype, the sublime Imagination of the Grail— the chalice filled with the divine 'I'-substance and overshone by the Holy Spirit in the form of a dove. This archetype reveals itself now in its two aspects: the macrocosmic aspect connected with the Earth, and the microcosmic aspect connected with the cosmos.

The macrocosmic aspect appears to the pupil through his true understanding of the inner nature of the Baptism in the Jordan, where under the working also of the Holy Spirit the great macrocosmic Christ Being, as the principle of the higher 'I' of each individual human being and of humanity as a whole, entered into the bodily sheaths of Jesus of Nazareth. These three sheaths of Jesus thereby became the chalice into which the macrocosmic 'I' of Christ poured itself, uniting with the flow of Jesus's blood in a way similar to that in which, at incarnation, every human being finds in the blood the physical basis for his 'I'. And this whole event is overshone by the Holy Spirit, the cosmic archetype of Spirit Self in whose form, as Rudolf Steiner has described, the Christ descends to the sphere of the Earth.[73]

And as though like a heavenly reflection of this great macrocosmic event that occurred only once on the Earth, in the far distances of the cosmos there appears its continuous microcosmic re-enactment. For upon the soul of each human being who, in the purified chalice of his 'I' is able to carry the 'state of being permeated through and through with the Christ-substance' right to the higher border of Upper Devachan (is able, that is, to preserve a spark of the divine 'I'-substance of Christ), upon this soul the Holy Spirit, at the Midnight Hour of Existence, descends in the form of a dove so as to guide it then to a new incarnation.

The initiate who also experiences this process can attain in himself to a vision of the Grail, and feel how his 'I' is permeated by the Christ (that is, the chalice of his 'I' by the 'I'-substance of the Christ) while experiencing the overshining by the Holy Spirit.[74] For the baptism with the Spirit which he undergoes at this level can only be brought about through a true communion with the Grail.

The rhythm given by Rudolf Steiner on Sunday, 30 December, leads us directly to the very centre of the Sun Mystery. Having experienced the Christ in the sphere of the highest Hierarchy—that of the Spirits of Strength, who represent in the cosmos the world-force of the Father and who, during the time of the Cosmic Midnight, are the first to appear in the sounding of the Cosmic Word—the initiate now approaches the experience of Christ in His own sphere of the Sun, in the Son-sphere, where he works through the Second Hierarchy, the Spirits of Light.

On this day Rudolf Steiner reads again the first sections of Parts I–III, and for the rhythm gives the three exercises (I, II, III, 5) to which, for the first time since the opening of the Christmas Conference, he adds the whole of the fourth part, 'At the Turning-point of Time', and then repeats the last lines (IV, 20–23 [20–24]):

That good may become
What from our Hearts we would found
And from our Heads *direct*
With single purpose.

The whole of this day, a Sunday, is as though permeated by the radiance of the Spirit Sun (IV, 14–15), the Spirit Light of the World, and is also aided in this by solar forces whose influence is particularly strong on the Sun-day of the week. Thus the rhythm of this day, beginning as it does with a complete reading of the fourth part, unveils before us the profound secret connected with the descent to Earth of the great Sun God, Christ (IV, 1–13).

In the Karma lectures Rudolf Steiner describes in detail the experiences of those human souls who ended their earthly mission that was inspired by Michael in the epoch of Aristotle and Alexander, and who during the Mystery of Golgotha gathered in the lofty Sun-sphere around Michael. There, together with many other spiritual Beings belonging to Michael, they were able to witness the sublime scene of Christ's departure from the Sun. 'He is leaving'—this, as Rudolf Steiner has said, was their great experience.[75]

And it is to this departure of Christ from the Sun, to His macrocosmic path down to the Earth and His entry into its dark sphere, that the Sun-rhythm of this day directs us.[76] In this rhythm our awareness is first guided to the process of the World Spirit's entry at the Turning-point of Time into the stream of Earthly Being (IV, 1–3). It is then indicated how He overcame the deep darkness of night (IV, 4–5) that had held sway in the Earth-sphere through the working of ahrimanic forces, and how at the same time He transformed the deceptive nocturnal light of Lucifer in the human soul into 'Day-radiant Light' (IV, 6–7). Then our attention is drawn particularly to the two principal streams of the ancient pre-Christian initiation—to the stream of Love represented by the shepherds, the 'simple Shepherds' Hearts' (IV, 8–10), and to the stream of wisdom represented by the Magi, 'the wise Heads of Kings' (IV, 11–13)—which now unite into the one Mystery of the Christ Sun. It was in these two principal streams that the initiates of antiquity were also engaged, in the great battle against the forces of Ahriman and Lucifer.

This battle must be continued in our time. Thus Rudolf Steiner says: 'If, in the second half of [Earth] evolution [i.e. after the Mystery of Golgotha] we are to participate in overcoming Lucifer and Ahriman again, we must permeate ourselves with Wisdom and Love.'[77] But this Wisdom and Love can be granted us only by the Christ, who dwells since the Mystery of Golgotha in the sphere of the Earth. From Him do we receive the possibility of bringing the two adversary forces into the right balance, and this is the essential prerequisite for all further development of humanity. For this reason, we turn in the rhythm of this day to Christ Himself and pray to Him to send us love and wisdom 'That good may become'—that is, free from the tempter-forces of Ahriman and Lucifer—'What from our Hearts we would found and from our Heads direct with single purpose.' (IV, 21–23 [20–24]).

But these two principal Mystery-streams of antiquity stand in special relation to the two genealogies of the St Luke and St Matthew Gospels, which on the one hand point to the birth of those two beings who were the bearers of the whole fullness of love and wisdom in the Earth-sphere— to the birth of the Nathan Soul and the birth of Zarathustra—and on the

238

other hand contain the secret of how the four bodily sheaths, into which the macrocosmic Christ Being was later to incarnate, were prepared on Earth. It is St Matthew's Gospel that recounts the preparation of the genealogy of the physical and etheric bodies, that is, of those members of the human being which are particularly strongly connected with the stream of heredity. This genealogy, which extends back as far as Abraham, also encompasses the entire history of the Hebrew people in so far as it was their task to prepare the bodily sheaths of the future Messiah. The genealogy of St Luke's Gospel is connected more with the preparation of the cosmic forces of that astral body and 'I'[78] which would later be capable of receiving directly into themselves the Sun-forces of Christ. This genealogy extends back to Adam, and from him ultimately to God Himself, thus encompassing the entire history of earthly man, from the time of his appearance on Earth out of the divine forces of all the cosmos, right to the events of Palestine.

And so the rhythm of this day places before us a great cosmic picture of the Christ who, abiding in the lofty Sun-sphere, looks down and follows how on Earth, through the deeds of the heart (IV, 21 [22]) and the head (IV, 22 [23]) there are gradually prepared the two bodily sheaths (IV, 8–13) which are later to serve the great goal of His future incarnation on Earth. During this preparation, Christ's gaze embraces the whole evolution of humanity which He guides from the Sun through the Holy Spirit, sent by Him to work through all the succession of generations.[79] In great anticipation[80] the Christ awaits the moment when, below on Earth, the conditions will be created which enable Him to descend and give to all Earth evolution its true meaning and its true goal. For: 'Before the Mystery of Golgotha, the meaning of the Earth lay in the Sun. Since the Mystery of Golgotha the meaning of the Earth is united with the Earth itself. This is what Anthroposophy would like to bring to humanity.'[81]

On its journey after death the soul, having reached at the Cosmic Midnight the culmination of its spiritual existence, now begins its gradual descent back to the Earth. This descent is guided by the Holy Spirit, through whose inspiration the path to a new incarnation becomes a microcosmic re-enactment of the macrocosmic path of the Christ Being towards incarnation in a human body on Earth. Thus, entering again into the Sun-sphere at the first stage of its return journey, the soul is here able to experience microcosmically that which, in connection with the rhythm of this day, we already described as Christ's sublime panorama from the Sun of all human evolution as the gradual process of preparation of the bodily sheaths for His descent to Earth. Something similar is also now experienced by the soul after death. As Rudolf Steiner attests, it is during the second passage through the Sun-sphere that the soul for the first time can look

239

down from there, some centuries before its actual incarnation, in order to unite itself with that etheric-physical stream of heredity on Earth[82] in which eventually its own corporeality will at a later time arise. Rudolf Steiner says of this: 'It is early on that the human being determines into which succession of generations he will enter, if he passes through the Sun-sphere in the manner I have described.'[83]

Furthermore, this immediately precedes the time in which, together with the Beings of the Second Hierarchy in the lower regions of the Sun-sphere, the soul begins to form the first rudiments of its future astral body. During this time the soul gazes simultaneously on the flowing etheric-physical stream of its forefathers below, and on the gradual formation of its new astral body from the cosmic forces of the Sun. It also experiences at this stage the further development of its 'I', which now becomes endowed with the ability to imprint all the experiences lived through in the spiritual world (gathered as they are on the foundation of the previous life)—to imprint these as future faculties and capacities into its newly forming astral body, and later into the other sheaths as well.

Returning now to the initiate, from our preceding study of the rhythm of this day we see that he penetrates at this stage into the inner essence of the Sun-Mystery of Christ. He recognizes the Christ as the great Sun Spirit in the full brilliance of the forces of His cosmic astral body, which Zar-athustra once beheld in its ancient form as the great astral Aura of the Sun, as Ahura Mazdao.[84]

The Christ reveals Himself to the initiate at this stage as the Greater Guardian of the Threshold who, like the 'Cherubim with a flaming sword' at the gates of Paradise, stands at the gates of the lofty Sun-sphere, helping the souls that have undergone purification in the Moon-sphere to accomplish the crossing over from the Soul-world into the Sun-land of the Spirits.[85]

The more the initiate now lives into this region, the more do new aspects of the Sun-Mystery arise before him, and the Christ is revealed to him as entering into the Sun-sphere from above, through the gates of the lofty Sun Spirit of Wisdom,[86] but is revealed also as the 'Inspirer' of the six Elohim, of the Pleroma,[87] through whose gates Christ then descends when leaving the Sun, into worlds below the Sun-sphere on His downward path to the Earth.

The inner nature of the cosmic relation between the Son and the Father, coming to expression in the spiritual connection between the Sun and the cosmos surrounding it; the abiding of the Son in the bosom of the Father; His sacrificial descent to the Earth for the redemption of mankind; the sacrifice fulfilled by the Father before the whole Spirit World in giving over His only-begotten Son to suffering and death; and also the sacrifice of Christ

Jesus on Earth when, entering into the astral body of Jesus of Nazareth, He relinquished the macrocosmic Sun-forces of His own astral body—all this comes before the initiate now as inner experience. Also the inner nature of the ancient Sun-Mystery with its eternal striving for the Christ-sphere, with its aspirations and hopes, and then the fulfilment of those hopes in the central Mystery of the Earth's evolution—the birth, the life, and the death and resurrection of Christ Jesus—all this too is opened to the initiate at this level. All of world history stands before him like a single Cosmic Year, and the birth of Christ on Earth like a great cosmic Christmas.[88]

And finally, the fact that the initiate recognizes the nature of the astral sacrifice of Christ, and that at this stage he can also experience how the soul after death forms its astral body from the astral forces of the Sun-sphere, enables him now to begin with the *inner transformation of his own astral body into Spirit Self*. Thus this work, which at the level of imaginative knowledge still has only a preparatory character, now becomes a process of the conscious transformation of spiritual substances, becomes a true celestial alchemy.

As a conclusion to this fifth rhythm of the Christmas Conference, we have still to mention that the process with which it began, of gradual descent into the Earth-sphere—whose archetype, as we have seen, is the cosmic path of Christ Himself—is at the same time also a picture of how Anthroposophy, as the new proclamation of the wisdom of Michael-Christ, gradually descends from the Sun to the Earth. For this reason, every anthroposophist who immerses himself inwardly in the rhythm of this day can experience in it the first stage of the supersensible preparation of Anthroposophy, can experience the lofty inspirational School of Michael in the sublime sphere of the Sun—and a memory of one's participation in this School can be awakened by the work on this rhythm.[89]

The following rhythm, given by Rudolf Steiner on 31 December, a Monday—the day of the week that comes under the sign of the Moon— brings us directly into the etheric-elemental surroundings of the Earth, into the Moon-sphere. On this day Rudolf Steiner reads again the first sections of the first three parts and, as before, the whole of Part IV. He then gives the following rhythm. First of all, there sounds out the direct call to Christ (IV, 14–15):

O Light Divine,
O Sun of Christ!

and then, for the first time since the inception of the rhythms of the Christmas Conference [these words having up till then been spoken only

241

once, in the rhythm of 25 December] there are added the final words of the first three parts (I, II, III, 21–23):

The Elemental Spirits hear it
In East and West and North and South:
May human beings hear it!

Above all, in this rhythm we have a direct call to the Etheric Christ who works, in our time, in the surrounding supersensible sphere closest to the Earth, and is gradually transforming the elemental world which lies at the basis of our world of nature. We can also associate this working of Christ with the fact that, as Rudolf Steiner has said, since 1899, since the end of the dark age of Kali Yuga, a whole world of new elemental spirits has arisen in the surrounding sphere of the Earth. Thus, for the modern clairvoyant— but also for people with a finely sensitive feeling for nature—this sphere, since the beginning of the twentieth century, looks inwardly completely different from how it looked, for example, in the nineteenth century. For it is now filled with new elemental spirits who 'hear and praise' the Sun-Christ in the etheric sphere of the Earth.[90]

The union of the Christ-Sun with the elemental spirits in one single rhythm reveals to us also the next stage of the descent to Earth of the Christ Being to incarnation in the body of Jesus of Nazareth, to the stage of His entry into the Moon-sphere, into the immediate spiritual surroundings of the Earth where He works through the Third Hierarchy, the Spirits of Soul, who represent in the cosmos the sphere of the Holy Spirit.

This supersensible region bordering on the Earth is gradually being permeated today by the forces of Christ, by those etheric forces which, as the macrocosmic forces of Christ's etheric body, once appeared to Moses in the fire and lightning on Sinai as *Ejeh asher ejeh*, 'I am the I AM'. At that time, however, it was not possible for the initiate, nor even for Moses, to perceive the Christ directly. Moses only saw Him reflected in the Moon-Elohim Jahve who, although belonging to the Second Hierarchy, had sacrificed himself and entered into the sphere of the Third Hierarchy, giving rise thereby to his particular relationship to the Holy Spirit.[91]

In the life after death, the experiences of the soul at this stage in the Moon-sphere, by virtue of the fact that since the Cosmic Midnight it is now accompanied by the Holy Spirit, take the form of a microcosmic reflection of the path of Christ to Earth.

The soul enters during this time into the realm of the Third Hierarchy and, because it is in the Moon-sphere that the new etheric body is formed, the process now begins of preparing for immediate incarnation on the Earth. However, because the conscious participation in this process presupposes that the Life Spirit has already been elaborated to a certain degree—which can only be achieved through an intensive occult development in the previous life—it is therefore carried out, as a general rule, without the soul having any consciousness of it. In the present epoch of world development the souls that are sunk in sleep at this stage are helped by lofty spiritual beings, whom Rudolf Steiner calls the Moon Teachers (the Maharajahs of Eastern terminology).[92] These lofty Teachers of wisdom lived on the Earth long ago and were at that time the great leaders of developing humanity. Later, after the separating of the Moon from the Earth, they followed it and founded a colony in the Moon-sphere, from where today they help the souls passing through the Moon-region who are not yet sufficiently mature to participate consciously in this work to form their new etheric body. Rudolf Steiner describes this process in detail in a lecture in Dornach on 21 April 1924. He describes there how, in creating the new etheric body, these Moon Teachers from their sphere perceive in succession all the planets of the solar system—astonishingly, this succession coincides with the sequence of days of the Christmas Conference—and of how from this perception of the planetary spheres they acquire the forces necessary to weave into the newly forming human etheric body the faculties of speech, movement, wisdom, love and so on.[93]

Thus, at this stage of its after-death journey, sunk in unconsciousness and guided by the Moon Teachers of Wisdom, the soul forms its new etheric body out of the forces of the whole planetary system, that is, out of the macrocosm.

The initiate reaching this stage experiences in the rhythms of this day the immediate working of Christ in the elemental etheric forces of the Earth. Through this working, the four categories of elemental beings of the four corners of the Earth—who according to indications from Rudolf Steiner had remained behind in their development on Old Moon and had thus embodied on Earth the entire wisdom of the Ancient Moon-epoch—are redeemed by Christ and led back to the path of further evolution from which they had been torn by their retardation (see GA 102). This creates for the Earth—and also in relation to nature—the real possibility of reaching its ultimate goal: to become, out of a planet of Wisdom, the planet of Love. For in uniting Himself with the nearest supersensible sphere to the Earth, Christ also draws the elemental spirits to the great impulse of Cosmic Love that was brought by Him into all earthly development. This is expressed in the *Foundation Stone Meditation* in the following words (I, II, III, 21–23):

> The [Elemental] Spirits hear it
> in East and West and North and South

They *hear* the Sun-Christ (IV, 15) in the surroundings of the Earth.

Thus there is here revealed to the initiate the great secret of how the Earth, through Christ's union with it, gradually becomes a new Sun. The rhythm of this day also points to this Mystery by connecting the activity of the spirits of nature—who are under the influence of the Moon—with the forces of the Christ-Sun; and the very mere linking together of the name of Christ—who since the Mystery of Golgotha works as the Spirit of the Earth—with that of the Sun directs us powerfully to the great cosmic future of our planet.

But there is still another Mystery connected with the rhythm of this day. It is the Mystery of the Moon-sphere, the Moon Logos which, as the reflected radiance of the great Sun Logos, inspired all the pre-Christian wisdom of humanity. Today, however, when through the Mystery of Golgotha the Sun Logos Himself has entered into the development of the Earth, it is necessary, with His help, to take up the wisdom of the Moon Logos—which also bears within it all the ancient wisdom of humanity— and transform it. Spiritual science is called upon to lay the foundations for this process. In a lecture in Penmaenmawr on 29 August 1923, Rudolf Steiner says of this: 'But what once existed continues; so it is not that the Ancient Moon Wisdom, the ancient Moon Logos, can cease to be, but that it must continue. It will, however, have to be taken up by the Sun Word which now also, after the disappearance of the last heritage of gnosticism, must again be found.'[94]

But in order today to find the Sun Word anew and to reveal its secrets to human beings, one has to reach that stage in initiation which on the ancient, pre-Christian path was called the stage of the 'Christophorus'. Rudolf Steiner depicts this stage of initiation in a lecture given at Dornach on 21 April 1924.[95] He describes there the so-called 'Moon-Sun Mysteries' of the pre-Christian era, in which the pupil penetrated into the secret of the relation of the forces of Sun and Moon, and at the same time perceived how the human etheric body is formed from the planetary forces of the Moon-sphere. 'And it was at this level of initiation that the human being became a Christ-bearer—that is, a bearer of the Sun Being—not one who *receives* the Sun Being into himself but one who bears it. Just as the Moon itself when full is a bearer of the sunlight, so did the human being become a bearer of Christ, a Christophorus.'

Today, however—after the Mystery of Golgotha—the initiate can become not only a 'Christ-bearer', but also 'one who receives into himself the Christ [*Christusempfänger*], which for the mystic of antiquity was not yet possible, for Christ had not yet united Himself with the Earth. Now, however, when this union has indeed taken place, Christ no longer approaches the human being from without, from the heights of the Sun, but from within the soul, from the holy of holies. For He is present, since the Mystery of Golgotha, in the higher 'I' of every human being, so that the initiate who rises to an awareness of this becomes in reality 'one who receives into himself the Christ'.[96]

Moving on in our study of the experiences of the initiate in connection with the rhythm of this day, it emerges that this level of initiation, connected as it is with the understanding of the activity of the Christ Being in the etheric forces of the Earth, likewise reveals to the initiate the essential inner nature of the Transfiguration of Christ on Mount Tabor, when in order to unite himself completely with the etheric body of Jesus of Nazareth the Christ Being sacrificed the macrocosmic etheric forces once perceived by Moses on Mount Sinai. And the experience for the initiate at this stage of this etheric sacrifice of Christ, and of how the soul after death under the guidance of the Moon Teachers of Wisdom forms its new etheric body, gives him the strength to begin transforming the *very essence* of his etheric body into Life Spirit (where, at the stage of Inspiration, this work had had a more preparatory character).

The sixth rhythm, revealing the Mystery of the third sacrifice, the *etheric* sacrifice of Christ, was given by Rudolf Steiner on 31 December—the last day of the year 1923. And one sees with astonishment how this rhythm connects with that which occurred exactly one year before, on 31 December 1922, namely, the fire at the Goetheanum, in whose flames the etheric forces that had been sacrificed by Rudolf Steiner passed over into the distances of the Cosmic Ether.

This rhythm, however, reminds us not only of the destruction of the Goetheanum, but also of its founding (on 20 September 1913) when Rudolf Steiner began the laying of the Foundation Stone by addressing the elemental spirits of the four points of the compass—who are already permeated by Christ—and calling on them to take part in this event.[97] At the beginning of the Christmas Conference, on 25 December—the day on which the *Foundation Stone Meditation* was read for the first time—he again turned to the elemental spirits and called on them once more to take part in that event. And he turns to them still again on the seventh day, the Moon-day, in order to finally reveal the fundamental secret of their transformation—their union with the Being of Christ.

The connection mentioned earlier, with the principle of etheric sacrifice, can, however, bring us closer to the spiritual reality behind the rhythm of this day only if we bear in mind the following. In Chapter 3 (see page 98) we saw that the principle of etheric sacrifice in the cosmos is deeply bound up with the being and working of the Nathan Soul. Up to the Mystery of Golgotha this Soul was for all the initiates of antiquity the cosmic archetype of the Christophorus and became, after the Mystery of Golgotha, the cosmic archetype of the corresponding stage in the new initiation. For ever since that time the Nathan Soul has been the true archetype of 'the one who receives the Christ', as was perceived by the Apostle Paul on the road to Damascus when he beheld the Nathan Soul as the radiant aura of the Risen One.[98] Through the two following lines, which were spoken as one, the rhythm of this day points directly to the secret of this new relation of the Nathan Soul to the Christ Being after the Mystery of Golgotha (IV, 14–15):

O Light Divine,
O Sun of Christ!

Zeylmans van Emmichoven indicates in his book that out of the five references to the word 'light' in the fourth part of the *Foundation Stone Meditation*, the words 'Light Divine' relate to the Nathan Soul.[99]

Thus, in the sixth rhythm of the Christmas Conference, this Soul is present as a purely etheric being, and the Monday—the Moon-day—on which this rhythm was given, reminds us of the past incarnation of our planet and its repetition in the Lemurian epoch, when the etheric forces of the Nathan Soul were held back by the cosmic forces of Good from further descent into the sphere of the Earth. The immediate presence on this day of the Nathan Soul is also evident in that, in reading the fourth part of the *Meditation*, Rudolf Steiner once substituted for 'with single purpose' (*zielvoll*) the words 'with light' (*lichtvoll*) (IV, 23 [24]). In this way is expressed the true nature of the working of the Nathan Soul after the Mystery of Golgotha as the radiant, light-filled aura of the Risen Christ. (See the words of Rudolf Steiner quoted on page 80.)

This Soul appears to us in these lines as the supersensible archetype of the human being who is fully permeated by the Christ, and moves us to do what has already been accomplished in the world of the elemental spirits who 'heard' and took into their realm the Sun-forces of Christ, which they can now infuse into the whole of earthly nature.[100] Today, out of his free will, man is also to do this. For in our time the human being is called upon to experience nature as permeated through and through with the Christ, in order to find through this awareness the strength and help needed to awaken the Christ in his own soul. It is to this that the rhythm of this day calls us (I, II, III, 23):

May human beings hear it![101]

To finish our description of this rhythm, we must note again that the continuing process of descent contained in it, which the soul undergoes on its path towards a new birth and which re-enacts microcosmically the macrocosmic path of the Christ Being towards incarnation in the body of Jesus of Nazareth—this process of gradually drawing closer to the Earth is a picture of the further descent to Earth of Anthroposophy. For this reason, every anthroposophist who occupies himself meditatively with the rhythm of this day can experience in it the second stage of the supersensible preparation of Anthroposophy, namely, that sublime imaginative cultus that took place at the turning-point of the eighteenth and nineteenth centuries in the supersensible sphere bordering on the Earth, when Anthroposophy as the new cosmic Wisdom of Michael-Christ was being prepared for its subsequent incarnation into the midst of humanity.[102]

The seventh and last rhythm, which was given by Rudolf Steiner on 1 January 1924, on a Tuesday—the day of Mars—leads us into the Mystery of the incarnation of the human being on Earth.

Rudolf Steiner read on this day the whole of each of the first three parts of the *Foundation Stone Meditation*, but omitted the call to the elemental spirits. He then added the following words, referring to them as 'a simple rhythm':

Thou livest in the Limbs,	(I, 2)
For the Father-Spirit of the Heights holds sway	
In the Depths of Worlds, begetting Life.	(I, 14–15)
Thou livest in the beat of Heart and Lung,	(II, 2)
For the Christ-Will in the encircling Round holds sway	
In the Rhythms of Worlds, blessing the Soul.	(II, 14–15)
Thou livest in the resting Head,	(III, 2)
For the Spirit's Universal Thoughts hold sway	
In the Being of all Worlds, beseeching Light.	(III, 14–15)

Thus does this rhythm indicate for us how the great macrocosmic archetype of man—which at the time of the Cosmic Midnight is created in the spiritual world by all nine Hierarchies out of the divine forces of the Father, the Son and the Holy Spirit (see page 230)—how this archetype, as though fading away, is transformed at incarnation into the foundation of our earthly physical body, consisting as it does of the metabolic-limb system, the rhythmic system of heart and lung, and the head-nerves system.

This outcome of the infinitely sublime world of the whole cosmos—this archetype of the human physical body—resides in the cosmos in a hidden way and will bring its development to complete manifestation only in the future conditions of Jupiter, Venus and Vulcan. It did, however, once appear in all its fullness and perfection, in the three years when the Being of Christ dwelt in the body of Jesus of Nazareth; for here, for the first time on Earth, there had arisen a body in the three systems of which the macro-cosmic forces of the Father, the Son and the Spirit were fully manifest. Thus there is given us in the appearance of Christ on the Earth the archetype of the goal and fulfilment of all Earth evolution.

For this reason, the life of Christ Jesus on Earth stands before us as the purest expression of the laws of the cosmos: 'That Being who walked upon the Earth did, to be sure, look just like any other human being. But the forces at work in Him were cosmic forces stemming from the Sun and the stars; *they directed His Body*. And everything Christ Jesus did was done in accordance with the entire Being of the cosmos, with which the Earth is connected. For this reason the constellation of the stars is often hinted at in the Gospels in connection with the deeds of Christ Jesus.'[103] Rudolf Steiner also indicates this influence of the stars when he concludes the description of the rhythm of this day. He says here: 'If I wrote for you in this way the rhythms in their harmony, it is because there really lies within them a replica of the starry constellations. One says, Saturn[104] is in Leo, Saturn is in Scorpio. On this depend rhythms which permeate the world. A primal picture of the spirit lies in such rhythms, as I have written them out for you in the course of these days from our verses, which are inwardly organized throughout in a soul-spiritual way.'[105]

These words of Rudolf Steiner direct us with particular clarity to what took place on Earth during the three years of Christ's existence in the bodily sheaths of Jesus of Nazareth, when these sheaths were so trans-formed by the Christ Being that later, through the Resurrection after the Mystery of Golgotha, there could really come about 'the birth of a new element of human nature: the body incorruptible.'[106] In other words, the fact that Christ inhabited the physical body of a human being had the effect that 'this physical body redeemed the true archetypal form of the physical body for the good of all mankind.'[107] It was thus freed completely from the luciferic and ahrimanic forces of temptation and restored to its 'true archetypal form' or its 'original, primal spiritual form', which is also spoken of in the rhythm of this day.

Taken as a whole, we are directed by this rhythm to the following: to the three-year life of the Sun Being Christ on Earth which was con-summated when, in the Garden of Gethsemane, the gradual union of Christ with the physical body of Jesus of Nazareth became complete and total; and then to the Mystery of Golgotha following this, through which the Christ permeated the sphere of the Earth with His Being by under-going what Rudolf Steiner called the process of His *birth* in the Earth-sphere;[108] and finally in this rhythm we are directed to His Resurrection in an 'incorruptible body' which, in its three systems, is the purest manifes-tation of the forces of the divine Trinity of the Father, the Son and the Spirit.

For the soul which is guided by the Holy Spirit repeats microcosmically at this stage of its after-death journey the macrocosmic process of Christ's union with the physical body of Jesus of Nazareth and His subsequent birth, after the Mystery of Golgotha, in the sphere of the Earth—for the soul this is the period of gradually uniting itself with the embryo of its physical body in the womb of the mother. This period is then completed by finally entering into the world of the Earth at birth. During this time the soul lives through these experiences in an even dimmer consciousness than at the previous stage (of the formation of the etheric body). For the conscious forming of the physical body, as well as the choosing of parents prior to this, already presupposes a certain degree of elaboration of Spirit Man. Since, as a general rule, this is not the case in the usual human being the soul, sunk in a deep sleep, is guided here by still higher beings than the Moon Teachers of Wisdom—beings whom Rudolf Steiner calls the Lords of Karma (the Lipikas of Eastern literature). These help the soul to accomplish in the right way the transition from the supersensible world back into the world of the senses.

The initiate, however, at this stage of initiation, recognizes the fourth and greatest sacrifice of Christ. This occurred after the night in the Garden of Gethsemane, when Christ was abandoned by the macrocosmic forces of the Father which had accompanied Him up till then,[109] and which He now relinquished in order to unite totally with the body of Jesus of Nazareth and to complete thereby the great path of God's becoming man. Also at this stage there is revealed to the initiate the true, the most profound nature of the Mystery of Golgotha and of the Resurrection which followed it.

On the other hand, the initiate can now experience consciously how the soul after death forms its new physical body under the guidance of the lofty Lords of Karma, and the supersensible knowledge of these two processes—the macrocosmic birth of Christ in the sphere of the Earth, and the microcosmic birth of the human being—allows him now to begin trans-forming *the very essence of the physical body* into Spirit Man. By virtue of this work, the initiate gradually frees himself from the guidance of the Lords of Karma, just as at the previous stage in his work on the Life Spirit he freed himself from the direct guidance of the Moon Teachers of Wisdom. According to what Rudolf Steiner has said, he is now able to raise himself above karma.[110] And just as Christ through the Mystery of Golgotha took upon Himself the karma of all mankind, so too can the initiate who reaches this stage take upon himself the karma of other human beings—and, above all, that of his pupils.

The great macrocosmic image of the Cross which is perceived during the Cosmic Midnight—the Cross that is formed of the spiritual streams from the spheres of the Father, the Son and the Spirit, and encircled by the seven roses of the path of initiation—must, to a certain degree, be realized at this level. This realization means drawing closer to what can be called 'bliss(fulness) in God'.

For our further study of the rhythm of this day we must bear still another aspect of it in mind which can shed light on what, on this last day of the Christmas Conference, was carried out by Rudolf Steiner, as well as on the whole fundamental nature of the Conference. For there is contained in this rhythm not only an indication of the 'incorruptible body', which was born through the Mystery of Golgotha and is the goal of all earthly evolution, whose significance for all humanity is expressed in the sublime Christian idea of the universal resurrection of the dead, but also indicated in this rhythm is the path itself to the attainment of this lofty goal.

Rudolf Steiner calls this path the search for the New Isis, the Divine Sophia.[111] The lecture given by him on 6 January 1918 (GA 180) can serve as a key to an understanding of this. In this lecture he speaks about the particular secret of the carving of the 'Group', behind which lies the hidden image of the New Isis sunk in sleep[112] and which is the esoteric image of man who, through initiation, raises himself to his higher 'I' and becomes thereby the twice-born, or 'the one who is born of the spirit'. This process comes about in the way that is portrayed in the carving of the 'Group', that is by a union with the Christ-impulse and by overcoming through this the illicit forces of Lucifer and Ahriman from above and below. We see more specifically how this occurs when we consider more exactly how these two adversary forces work in the three fundamental systems of the human body, which are spoken of in the first half of the rhythm of this day. For as a consequence of man's Fall these adversary powers have caused distortion to arise in the cosmic archetype that was once created out of the macrocosm by all nine Hierarchies. In other words, it is they above all who hinder the three systems of the human body from becoming the purest reflection of the macrocosmic forces of the Father, the Son and the Spirit.

If we take as our basis the representation of the working of Lucifer and Ahriman in the human being, as is given us in the central theme of the carving, then we must say that in it there is revealed to us on the one hand Lucifer, attempting in an illicit way to enliven our head which, in accordance with the 'rightful' guiding powers of the world, must be constantly in a state of dying so as to be able to provide the foundation for our free, self-aware 'I'; and on the other hand there is Ahriman, who likewise seeks in an illicit way to bring the element of death into our limb and metabolic system where, in accordance with the rightful guiding powers, only life should reign.[113] Lucifer works here more through the usual head consciousness, whereas Ahriman works in the subconscious forces of inspiration that permeate the will which is the basis of the metabolic limb system. Thus does the first strive primarily to entice us into the starry expanses of the cosmos and draw us entirely away from the Earth, whereas the second seeks to chain us down to the Earth and not allow us to rise to anything higher. Only the middle, the rhythmic system of heart and lungs, and the imaginative consciousness connected with it, is still free. But it is just this sphere that both Lucifer and Ahriman are eager to get into their power, so as to subjugate human beings once and for all—Lucifer from above and Ahriman from below—in order to bring about what is portrayed in the theme on the left-hand side of the 'Group' carving.

Rudolf Steiner describes this as follows: 'The human being is organized at the present time in such a way that in his head he is held captive by Lucifer, and in the wisdom of his metabolism, in the wisdom of his limbs, he is held by Ahriman.'[114] And he continues: 'What we have described as the middle, the imaginative condition of consciousness is likewise dependent on our heart organization, with its human rhythm.' But what does this middle region of the human being need in order to fill itself with such an inner wisdom as to enable human beings to overcome in the right way the distorting influences of Lucifer and Ahriman working from above and below? Rudolf Steiner says of this: 'By what means does inner logic, inner wisdom, the capacity for inner orientation, come into this middle sphere of our being? By the Christ-impulse—through that which came into the culture of the Earth through the Mystery of Golgotha… Becoming imbued with the Christ-impulse is something which is an integral part of being human.'

Thus the rhythm of this day reveals for us that spiritual path which Rudolf Steiner calls the path of seeking for the New Isis, the Divine Sophia. On this path we can attain to the imaginative consciousness that we are to permeate with the forces of the Etheric Christ who today stands ready to meet us and who, from the middle rhythmical realm of the heart and the lungs, establishes in us the balance between the forces of Lucifer working from above and those of Ahriman working from below. These are the first preconditions necessary for overcoming the forces of temptation in the three systems of our organism, that is, for the gradual transformation of the physical body into the incorruptible body of the Resurrection, in whose three systems the cosmic forces of the Father, the Son and the Spirit, which lie at the basis of it, will come more and more to the fore by virtue of the working in them of the Living Christ.

We are directed to this spiritual process of transformation, extending as it does right down into the human physical body, by the new legend of Isis who through a clairvoyant (imaginative) understanding of the opening of St John's Gospel, in which is contained the teaching concerning the cosmic Logos, the Christ, experiences the transformation of her physical form.[115] For this reason the carving of the 'Group', showing as it does the Representative of Humanity between Lucifer above and Ahriman below is, in truth, an expression of the spiritual words which the clairvoyant of today can read over the sleeping Isis:[116]

I am man.
I am the past, the present, and the future.
Every mortal should lift my veil.

These three lines can help us to get closer to the secret that is connected with the seventh rhythm, and also with the whole way in which the Christmas Conference was conducted. For if we compare them with the rhythm under consideration, the following astonishing picture arises.

'I am man'—these words draw our attention to the image of man who, as microcosm, consists of the three systems of the limbs, the heart and lungs, and the head. Corresponding to these in this rhythm are the words:

Thou livest in the Limbs
Thou livest in the beat of Heart and Lung
Thou livest in the resting Head

and, in the text of the *Meditation* as a whole, to the first sections of Parts I–III.

'I am the past, the present, and the future'—these words, which are made clearer through what was said by Rudolf Steiner in a lecture in Dornach on 4 July 1924, and which can be connected with the first three parts of the *Foundation Stone Meditation*, reveal to us those macrocosmic forces lying at the basis of the three systems of man as microcosm. Thus from the past and through the First Hierarchy there work in the human being the divine forces of the Father. They form the world of space in which man, also in the future, must undergo his evolution. The forces of the Son, who guides this evolution through the Second Hierarchy, work in the present. The Son Himself then descends from the Sun to the Earth and by overcoming the forces of space brings to humanity from the cosmic sphere of time the impulse for a new ascent. He thereby opens for humanity the door to the sphere of the future, the sphere of the Eternal Spirit who works within beings through the Third Hierarchy. Corresponding to this in the rhythm of this day are the words:

For the Father-Spirit of the Heights holds sway
In Depths of Worlds begetting Life

For the Christ-Will in the encircling Round holds sway
In the Rhythms of Worlds, blessing the Soul

For the Spirit's Universal Thoughts hold sway
In the Being of all Worlds, beseeching Light.

and the second sections of Parts I–III.[117]

In the human being of the present, however, the first two lines of this utterance of the New Isis have not yet been brought into a proper relation, for the modern human individual does not yet unite completely in his three systems the past, the present and the future;[118] in other words, he is not yet manifest in them in his *eternal* aspect—the aspect consisting of the purest forces of the Father, the Son and the Spirit, which encompasses all time and is not subject to death. Thus the uniting of these stands before us as the most important task of our time—a task to which the third utterance of the New Isis refers: 'Every mortal should lift my veil.' The way towards accomplishing this task is opened to us only by taking up the Christ-impulse which brought to the Earth the new possibility of uniting the microcosm with the macrocosm. The fourth part of the *Foundation Stone Meditation* speaks of this 'At the Turning-point of Time', and directs us to the fact that the soul must establish in its 'I' a connection to the Christ (IV, 14–19), for according to what Rudolf Steiner has said, it is only this connection that can enable earthly man 'to bring into his otherwise degenerating physical body the "phantom" which has arisen from the grave of Golgotha'[119]—in other words, that 'incorruptible body' which in its three systems consists of the purest forces of the Father, the Son and the Spirit, which have worked on it in the course of the aeons of Saturn, Sun, Moon and Earth, and are to serve as the foundation for all further evolution through the aeons of Jupiter, Venus and Vulcan.

Thus, altogether we have the following picture. In the first line of the words above the sleeping Isis our attention is drawn to man as microcosm, and in the second line to the forces of the cosmos that are the foundation of this and which, since the Fall, have not been able to come to full manifestation in him; in the third line we are told to lift the veil, that is, to allow the macrocosm to appear again in the microcosm in its entirety. This last point, however, is possible only through a connection with the Christ-impulse (which is spoken of in the fourth part of the *Meditation*). For only when we have inwardly united ourselves with the content of this part can we lift the veil of Isis or, which is the same thing, *awaken* her. And what we then perceive *behind* this veil is the complete and harmonious *union* within the human being of the microcosm (Limbs—Heart—Head) (I, II, III, 2) with the macrocosm (Father—Son—Spirit) (I, II, III, 14–15). And it is of this that the concluding seventh rhythm of the Christmas Conference speaks.

Thus does the task, placed before us on 25 December—the day of the first reading of the *Foundation Stone Meditation*—find its fulfilment at this final stage after proceeding through to the end of the sevenfold path of initiation, and we see that the path which is completed by the seventh rhythm can also be called '*the lifting of the veil of the New Isis, the Divine Sophia*'.

If we bring together what we have seen in this last rhythm of the Christmas Conference, we can say that through this 'simple' rhythm there is revealed to us the inner nature of the *whole of the Christmas Conference* as a gradual drawing away of the veil of the New Isis. This was accomplished here for the first time for humanity as an occult-social act and, at the same time, as a genuine Mystery-act by which was opened the door to the temple of the New Mysteries; for today '*every* mortal' is called upon to 'lift' the veil of this temple:[120]

O Man, know thyself!

Like the two preceding rhythms, this one also intimates the descent of Anthroposophy from the cosmos. At the end of a long preparatory period in supersensible regions, she, Anthropos-Sophia, is now to descend to Earth and enter into human souls. The seventh rhythm of the Christmas Conference points to this, speaking to us of the incarnation of Anthropos-Sophia among men which began in 1902 with the founding of the German Section of the Theosophical Society, and of her further earthly development in the course of the following three seven-year periods. Looking at this we can see that from 1902 to 1909 Anthropos-Sophia entered first and foremost into the thought-life of men in order to penetrate it with true Spirit Light, while from 1910 to 1916 she enlivened the human sphere of feeling through the principle of the Son (Christ's appearance in the etheric is first mentioned in the early years of this period). And from 1917 to 1923 Anthropos-Sophia began to permeate man's will with the forces of the Father, so that they may work in and shape all realms of our earthly existence. If, in addition to this, we consider the three systems of the human organism which form the physical basis of our thinking, feeling and willing, the connection between the development of Anthroposophy on Earth and the three named rhythms will be evident. During these three seven-year periods the activity of Rudolf Steiner had clearly one aim: it was at the behest of the spiritual world to reveal to mankind, in a form appropriate to modern consciousness, the divine Wisdom of man encompassing the past, the present and the future—Anthropos-Sophia— the Wisdom which up to that time had been the guarded secret of the Mystery-centres;[121] and this is, in essence, nothing other than the lifting of the veil of the New Isis, the Divine Sophia, over whom stand the words: 'I am Anthropos.'[122]

Rudolf Steiner returned to the *Foundation Stone Meditation* for the last time on the evening of 1 January 1924. He read the whole of it, ending in this way the last lecture of the cycle that he had given during the Christmas Conference under the title *World History in the Light of Anthroposophy*. By doing this he drew this evening into the stream of cosmic rhythms, which are connected with the basis of the anthroposophical *Meditation* and which had flowed throughout the Conference. This is the reason why this evening too has a special significance for us, which becomes apparent when we bear in mind that the three foregoing rhythms were also concerned with the cosmic-human genesis and the further development of Anthroposophy. Thus the rhythm of the Sunday (the Sun-day) pointed towards the preparation of Anthroposophy in the realm of the Sun; the rhythm of the Monday (the Moon-day), its further development in the supersensible sphere immediately bordering the Earth (i.e. the Moon-sphere); and finally the last rhythm, on Tuesday (the day of Mars), its gradual incarnation on Earth and its growth and development amongst human beings in the course of 21 years (1902–23).

If we now bear in mind the whole supersensible-earthly development of Anthroposophy, this can also shed light on the secret of the last gathering at the Christmas Conference on the evening of 1 January 1924. For now, after the seven rhythms, there was given an eighth, which, fulfilling the law of the octave, was to embrace and raise to a higher level the content of all the sevenfold development that preceded it, just as the Christmas Conference itself was to encompass and raise to a higher level the development of the anthroposophical movement of the past years.[123] For this reason Rudolf Steiner emphasized particularly firmly on that evening of 1 January 1924 that the Christmas Conference was a real *beginning*, that it was to be 'a festival of consecration [*Weihefest*] not only of a year's beginning but of the beginning of a turning-point in the cosmos, to which we will give ourselves in dedicated nurturing of the spiritual life.'[124] We can therefore say that the eighth rhythm *is the rhythm of the Christmas Conference itself*—is the rhythm in which the text of the *Meditation* was given in its entirety in the sequence with which it had then to go out into the world in order to become for humanity the gateway that opens the path to the Temple of the New Mysteries. This is also why it was in this lecture—the last gathering—that Rudolf Steiner revealed the real secret of the Christmas Conference; how by its nature it stemmed from the realm beyond the threshold, and how the call to take up its impulse (spoken of in detail at the beginning of this chapter) is the call of the Guardian of the Threshold Himself, before whom all humanity is standing at the present time.

But it is to a conscious experiencing of the threshold to the spiritual world that a union with the impulse of the Christmas Conference is to lead us and, in the spiritual world itself, is to lead to a conscious meeting with that Being under whose sign the Christmas Conference was conducted, and to whom Rudolf Steiner turned at the end of the last rhythm (IV, 14–19):

O Light Divine,
O Sun of Christ!
Warm Thou
Our Hearts,
Enlighten Thou
Our Heads!

Having surveyed the seven rhythms and nine gatherings of the Christmas Conference,[125] we can now look in more detail at the fact that the Christmas Conference began and ended on a Tuesday—the day of Mars—the day on which the influences of that planet of our solar system have a particularly strong effect on the events on the Earth. In this connection we must take into consideration *three* different aspects that were given by Rudolf Steiner when describing the effects of the Mars forces, for each aspect has its own particular relation to the way in which the Christmas Conference was carried out.

The first is the fact that the planet Mars is the representative of the Cosmic Word in our universe, and the beings inhabiting it can be called 'the Keepers of Cosmic Speech'. Rudolf Steiner says the following concerning these: 'But, of the inhabitants of Mars, the beings that are the most important for man are those who in their whole nature actually consist of the sounding Cosmic Word. They are the Keepers of what is Cosmic Speech.'[126] The active, co-operative presence of these beings during the Christmas Conference was therefore of the utmost importance, but particularly on the first and last days when the *whole* text of the *Foundation Stone Meditation* was read. For this *Meditation*, clothed in earthly words, is the celestial speech of the Gods who are turning to human beings today. It is, in truth, an expression of the Cosmic Word itself!

The second reason for the particular significance of Mars during the Christmas Conference is to be found in the special relation of this planet to our fifth post-Atlantean epoch. In his lecture in the Hague on 17 November 1923,[127] Rudolf Steiner speaks in detail of how in the Ancient Indian epoch it was the Moon-forces that had a decisive influence on all earthly events; in the Ancient Persian epoch it was the forces of Mercury; in the Egypto-Chaldean, the Venus forces; in the Graeco-Roman, the Sun forces; and in the fifth post-Atlantean it is the forces of Mars. For this reason it was so necessary to give the forces of this planet Mars the possibility of coming to the fore *twice* during the course of the Christmas Conference which is so deeply bound up with the destiny of our fifth post-Atlantean culture.

And the third reason lies in the fact that Mars is the bearer in our cosmos of the element of iron. Originally there was no iron on Earth, but during the [earlier] time of ancient Lemuria when the Earth still consisted of fire, Mars 'passed through' the Earth and was thus able to endow it with its iron.[128] Since that time iron has been able to enter into the blood of man so as to become there the physical basis for the development towards the free, individual 'I'.

In addition, it is known from numerous lectures by Rudolf Steiner that the ruler of these forces working in the element of iron in both the cosmos and in human blood is Michael himself—the guiding Spirit of our times. With the help of this iron Michael does battle with the ahrimanic forces, both in the cosmos surrounding the Earth and—with the indispensable co-operation of man—also in the human blood.

By placing the Christmas Conference in the framework of the cosmic influences of Mars, Rudolf Steiner thus placed it *under the direct guidance of Michael* whom he described in a lecture two months before the beginning of the Christmas Conference, in an imaginative-cosmic picture, as follows: 'But he appears, directing our attention with his sword to the higher aspect of human nature. He appears pointing with his sword, and we imagine Michael in the right way when we see, in his sword, iron that has been smelted and forged in the cosmos.'[129]

With this gesture of the sword that has been forged from the iron of Mars and which points to the higher 'I' in man, to the awakening of which the Christmas Conference leads us—in this picture we can also imagine Michael himself supersensibly overshining the Christmas Conference and spurring each of those present (but also anyone who tries today to relive the

Conference and experience it for himself) to fulfil its aims. First and foremost, however, he also urges them to *faithfulness and courage* with regard to the impulse of the Conference, for these—faithfulness and courage—are the two fundamental Michaelic virtues of our time. And it is of these virtues that Rudolf Steiner speaks in his last two evening lectures, on 31 December and 1 January. He speaks in the first of these of faithfulness towards the Spirit of the Goetheanum, who had descended to the world from the lofty sphere of Michael and in whose spiritual presence—which he perceived—he was able to conduct the Christmas Conference. In the second lecture he speaks of the courage needed to acknowledge and carry out into the world 'the Voice from the land of Spirits', the Voice of the Gods, whose desire it is to speak to human beings today through the impulses of the Christmas Conference, through the *Foundation Stone Meditation*, and through the School of Spiritual Science.

We already saw at the beginning of this chapter that the most important characteristic of the Christmas Conference is the fact that we can trace in it the complete sevenfold Christian-Rosicrucian path of initiation, which for the first time ever on the physical plane was realized by Rudolf Steiner during those days, openly in the midst of humanity, as an *occult-social act*. Thus, in summing up the description of the significance of the Christmas Conference for the life of the Mysteries and the path of initiation, we must bring to mind once more, in one complete picture, all the seven rhythms described above,[130] so as to see more clearly how in them this sevenfold path of the new western initiation takes shape.

Before we can do this, however, we must first look once more at the last three days of the Conference and briefly consider its rhythms from still one more angle, singling out for this an aspect which is common to all of them: the aspect of *sacrifice*.

Earlier, in the description of the rhythms, we saw that each of these brings to expression one of the stages of the Christ Being's great cosmic-earthly path of sacrifice to the Mystery of Golgotha. Thus the rhythm of Sunday gives us the principle of the astral sacrifice of Christ in both its cosmic and earthly aspects; in the cosmic aspect of Christ's sacrificial descent from the bosom of the Father into the sphere of the Sun, where He was revealed to Zarathustra as its astral aura; and in the earthly aspect of Christ's gradual taking hold of and permeating the astral body of Jesus of Nazareth. The rhythm of the Monday opens to us the nature of the second sacrifice, the *etheric* sacrifice of Christ. We know through this rhythm how Christ descended from the Sun into the etheric surroundings of the Earth, and also how He subsequently united Himself with the etheric body of Jesus of Nazareth. And finally, the rhythm of Tuesday brings before us all

258

the profundity of the Mystery of the physical sacrifice of Christ—His terrible loneliness in the Garden of Gethsemane, the final relinquishing of His macrocosmic forces and His total identification with the physical body of Jesus of Nazareth.[131] The Mystery of Golgotha following this, and the Resurrection, which was the salvation of the 'phantom' of the human physical body, are likewise expressed in the rhythm of this day.

Holding before us now this picture of the three great sacrifices of Christ—the astral, the etheric and the physical, each one appearing in both its cosmic and earthly aspect—we can now ask: What is the significance of these three sacrifices for the further development of humanity?

From various descriptions given by Rudolf Steiner, we know that through the Mystery of Golgotha Christ has united Himself with all future development of the Earth and of humanity right up to the end of Earth evolution—that is, until the Vulcan condition—so that the Individual 'I'-consciousness of every human being, which is won at first on the Earth, can be preserved fully intact in all the future conditions of Jupiter, Venus and Vulcan.

Thus does Christ bestow upon the human 'I' true immortality. And to whatever heights of cosmic existence it may raise itself in the future it will, through its connection with the Christ-impulse, be able everywhere to preserve its individuality, its individual existence.

We spoke in Chapter 3 of those sublime beings who anticipate in our post-Atlantean time the future stages of humanity's development. We spoke of the Bodhisattva-beings who in working together with a Being of the Angeloi are in the process of transforming their astral bodies into Spirit Self, thus anticipating in their individual development the future condition of Jupiter, and by virtue of which their consciousness is able to rise into the Buddhi-sphere, the sphere of Fore-knowledge. We spoke thereafter of the Buddha, who together with a Being of the Archangeloi is working to transform his etheric body into Life Spirit, thus anticipating already today the condition of Venus, and being able to rise in consciousness as far as the plane of Nirvana.[132] And there are still higher Beings who in the terminology of the East are called the Dhyani-Buddhas and who together with a Being of the Hierarchy of Archai[133] are engaged in the transformation of their physical bodies into Spirit Man, anticipating thereby the Vulcan condition, and ascending in consciousness into a sphere above and beyond Nirvana.

But what in antiquity could be achieved only by those beings who had long since surpassed the actual human stage of their evolution and had already entered upon a path of cosmic evolution has become, since the Mystery of Golgotha, accessible to *every* human being through a conscious union with the impulse of Christ. For this possibility of endowing the human 'I' with eternal life—which means, above all, the preserving of individual consciousness on *all* planes of existence—this possibility was won for all humanity by the Christ Being, and could be won only through His great cosmic-earthly path of sacrifice. By virtue of Christ's astral sacrifice man was given the possibility, during the Jupiter condition, of preserving his individual consciousness and of developing it as far as the Buddhi-sphere, in order to recognize from there the great Mystery of the relation of the macrocosm and microcosm: the spiritual Christ-Sun at the very centre, representing the whole macrocosm and, deeply immersed in meditative contemplation of Him, the twelve Bodhisattvas who represent the microcosmic principle. In the future Jupiter existence this will find external expression in that Jupiter will once more separate off from the Sun and a microcosm will again be found to be standing over against the macrocosm. But the true secret of the relation between macrocosm and microcosm will be accessible then to the human being who will have received into himself the impulse of Christ with whose help he will transform his astral body into Spirit Self.

The second, the etheric sacrifice of Christ, gives man the possibility of preserving his individual consciousness also during the Venus-existence and of developing it as far as the sphere of Nirvana, in which there is no longer any separation of microcosm from macrocosm, but rather an absolute and entire union of both. However, also in this final union with the macrocosm—which will be expressed in the Venus incarnation of Earth by the fact that Venus will not pass through a condition of separation from the Sun—because of the etheric sacrifice of Christ, there is still the possibility for man of preserving in its entirety his individual 'I'-consciousness won by him on Earth if, working from the Christ-impulse, he realizes the process of transforming his etheric body into Life Spirit.

And the last and most significant sacrifice of Christ—His complete union with the physical sheath of Jesus in which He, the Son of God, became the Son of Man, followed by His death on Golgotha and His Resurrection in the pure 'phantom' of the physical body—this sacrifice gives every human being the possibility of preserving also in the Vulcan-existence his own consciousness which will be able then to ascend to the sphere above Nirvana and also, because of the part taken by Christ in the process of transforming the physical body into Spirit Man, to preserve the character of the individual 'I'. Thus, since the time of the Mystery of Golgotha, Christ encompasses and accompanies all the cosmic future of Earth evolution.

But this possibility for the human 'I' of individual immortality in all future cycles of development and at all levels of existence, which can now be opened to it through its connection with the Christ Being—this possibility directs us not only to the most distant future of humanity and the world, but also to the immediate present. We already referred to this aspect of the three Christ sacrifices, which is so important for our present time, when we said that what in ancient times was open only to those beings who had already entered upon a cosmic path of development—that is, for the Bodhisattvas, Buddhas, and Dhyani-Buddhas[134]—has now, through Christ's deeds of sacrifice, become accessible to *every* human being who out of his own free will wishes to enter upon the path of initiation that is open today to all humanity through Anthroposophy, and which leads first of all to a direct union with Christ and then, together with Him, to an ascent to ever higher planes of world existence. In other words, a conscious union with Christ in the modern Christian-Rosicrucian initiation can prepare the way, even now in our present cycle of existence, for man to begin to work on the intrinsic transforming of his three lower members into the three higher ones of Spirit Self, Life Spirit and Spirit Man.[135] For it was through the three cosmic-earthly sacrifices of Christ that the possibility was created of uniting these three highest levels of individual spiritual development— knowledge of the relation of macrocosm and microcosm, becoming one with the macrocosm, and blissfulness in God—with the four preceding levels of study, Imagination, Inspiration and Intuition which, *in this form*, are also attainable for the modern human being only through the Mystery of Golgotha, and, for this reason, their fundamental goal is the experien- cing, at the fourth level, of the Christ in Intuition—of uniting, that is, the four levels of knowledge with the three levels of transformation of being.[136] At the basis of this lies the profound principle of sacrifice, whose realization leads to a true imitation of the great sacrificial path of Christ Jesus, as we saw earlier in the description of the mystery of the path of Rudolf Steiner's life.

Therefore, this great cosmic-earthly path of Christ's sacrifice is the foundation which, at the dawn of the new spiritual epoch amongst a humanity with a fully developed 'I'-consciousness, has made it possible to establish the beginning of the new Christian-Rosicrucian path of initiation, the path that was set down in its entirety and completely openly by Rudolf Steiner in the fifth chapter of *Occult Science*, and which was brought into being at the Christmas Conference as a social-occult act, thereby laying in the midst of humanity the Foundation Stone of the New Mysteries.

Turning once again to the question asked at the beginning of these concluding considerations, we can characterize the *seven initiation rhythms of the Christmas Conference* in the following way, as the seven stages of the new Christian-Rosicrucian path of initiation:

1 The study of spiritual science in which the pupil, proceeding from his usual waking 'I'-consciousness, to begin with makes use of the capacity of judgment gained by him in the physical world of the senses—this corresponds to the first rhythm of the Christmas Conference. In this rhythm the knowledge of the 'I'-Mystery and the experiencing of *In Christo morimur* are prepared for by developing a new *understanding* of the Christ-impulse—which is possible today through a study of the content of spiritual science.

2 The attainment of imaginative consciousness corresponds to the second rhythm, in which the pupil enters into the Soul-world or astral plane, and undergoes there a true process of self-knowledge.

3 The reading of the hidden script—that is, Inspiration—corresponds to the third rhythm where, in the sphere of the Sun, through an experiencing of the four spheres of Lower Devachan, the pupil perceives the cosmic archetypes of the four kingdoms of nature, revealed to him here as the unified world alphabet that sounds out in the cosmic rhythms of the Music of the Spheres, and which he is now able to read.

4 The work on the Stone of the Wise—that is, Intuition—corresponds to the fourth rhythm, where the pupil recognizes the inner nature of the physical body in its cosmic origin. On the basis of this knowledge, he is now able to begin working consciously in spiritualizing his physical body.[137] 'For all Intuition works directly on those forces of the supersensible world which work down into the physical.'[138] Also at this stage the Music of the Spheres is transformed for the pupil into the sounding of the Cosmic Word in which, in the sphere of Upper Devachan at the time of the Cosmic Midnight, there are revealed to the pupil in their cosmic deeds, all the nine divine Hierarchies.

5 The knowledge of the relation of macrocosm and microcosm corresponds to the fifth rhythm. This stage of initiation has become accessible to the pupil of the spirit today through the cosmic-earthly astral sacrifice of Christ. And it is expressed in a knowledge of the cosmic relation of Sun and Earth and of the change that occurred in this relation as a result of the Mystery of Golgotha. We are directed to this level, in the rhythm in question, by the fact that, firstly, the exercises mentioned in it themselves express the intrinsic nature of the path of initiation undergone by the pupil as microcosm, and secondly, that the whole of the fourth part of the *Meditation* is read, in which is recounted the macrocosmic path of Christ from the Sun to the Earth, as the cosmic archetype of every true initiation on Earth.

6 'Becoming one with the macrocosm' is expressed in the sixth rhythm. This stage of initiation is possible for the pupil only by virtue of the etheric sacrifice of Christ. Describing this stage, Rudolf Steiner has said that the pupil begins 'to feel himself as though he had grown together with the

whole vast structure of the universe, retaining however at the same time the consciousness of himself as a fully independent being. A feeling nevertheless comes over him as if he were being merged into the whole vast universe, becoming one with it—yet *without* losing his identity.'[139] And Rudolf Steiner emphasizes further in this connection that 'it is essential not to think of this becoming one [with the macrocosm] as though implying that *separate* consciousness should cease and the human individuality be poured out into the All.'[140] In the rhythm of the sixth day the description of the uniting of the 'Christ Sun' with the elements of the Earth points particularly clearly to this stage, for this is the true archetype of the macrocosm's becoming one with the microcosm.[141]

7 'Blissfulness in God'[142] corresponds to the seventh rhythm. This stage relates to man's conscious experience in the transformed physical body, which is now the purest expression of the forces of Father, Son and Spirit. As we have already seen in the more detailed description of this rhythm, the cosmic 'Rose Cross' experienced by the pupil during the Cosmic Midnight in the fourth rhythm must to a certain degree now be realized, for in it is expressed the goal of all Earth evolution. And it is to this, when realized in the seven stages of the new path of initiation, that the forces of the Father, the Son and the Spirit lead, which work and weave in the cosmos in the form of a cross.

Thus the Christmas Conference comes before us as the true path of the Christian-Rosicrucian initiation of our time, directed as it is towards the birth in us of a new human being who is permeated through and through with the Christ and, at the same time, towards the renewal of the life of the ancient Mysteries 'out of the signs of the times'.[143]

If now we compare the content of this chapter with what was presented in the first part of this book as the *Mystery of the path of Rudolf Steiner's life*, it is not difficult to recognize a connection between the *seven initiation rhythms* of the Christmas Conference and the most important stages of this great human life which, as the true archetype of the new path of initiation in our time, must find itself in complete accord with what was realized at the Christmas Conference as a social-occult act of initiation.

It is therefore possible to see a connection between the first rhythm of the Christmas Conference and Rudolf Steiner's third seven-year period. This seven-year span begins with his becoming acquainted with the works of Kant, in whose philosophy he meets the basic problem of the relation of thinking and knowledge. Later, in the middle of this period, through the philosophy of Fichte Rudolf Steiner comes to the most fundamental problem of all western development—the problem of the 'I'. And at the end of this period the meeting takes place of Rudolf Steiner with his

Teacher. From that moment onwards, Rudolf Steiner's spiritual development takes on a strictly ordered character, thus becoming in a true sense a path of initiation. What earlier had developed as it were naturally is now transformed into a consciously trodden path of the new Christian-Rosicrucian initiation.

Going further, one can see a connection between the first seven-year Sun period of Rudolf Steiner's life and the second rhythm of the Christmas Conference. It is during this period that the sentient soul is developed which, as a partial transformation of the astral body, is placed as it were midway between the astral body and the principle of Spirit Self. This time in the life of every human being is particularly favourable for immersing oneself in the world of Imaginations. Therefore during almost all this time Rudolf Steiner occupied himself in the most intensive way with the natural-scientific and literary works of Goethe, some of which—his teaching of the archetypal plant (the *Urpflanze*), for example, but also the images of Goethe's 'Fairy Tale'—already lead directly into the imaginative world. Rudolf Steiner concludes the description of this period of his life with the following words: 'Thus, at the age of 27 I was full of questions and riddles in regard to man's external life, while at the same time the nature of the human soul and its relation to the spiritual world stood before my inner perception in an ever more complete and definite form.'[144] It is known from other descriptions by Rudolf Steiner that such a mode of perceiving the relation of the soul to the spiritual world can be reached particularly by imaginative consciousness, whereas the answers to the 'questions' and 'riddles' concerning the external life of humanity already require the higher knowledge of Inspiration which, among other things, enables the clairvoyant to see behind the scenes of the historical genesis of humanity.

The second seven-year Sun period of Rudolf Steiner's life—the period in which the human being goes through the development of the intellectual or mind soul which, as a partial transformation of the etheric body is situated between the etheric body and the high principle of Life Spirit—is connected with the third rhythm of the Christmas Conference. During this time Rudolf Steiner penetrated more and more deeply into the world of Inspiration, which in turn produced in him a still clearer and more encompassing knowledge of the imaginative world. By virtue of this he was able to make the transition from his work in connection with Goethe's world-view to formulating his own ideas, to giving shape to a new theory of knowledge which already brings man to direct experiences of a purely spiritual nature. This occurred in the books *Truth and Knowledge* and *The Philosophy of Freedom*.[145] On the other hand, it is also during this period that Rudolf Steiner is presented with direct supersensible experiences of the spiritual background of humanity's historical development during the last third of the nineteenth century. The spiritual sphere bordering directly on the earthly world was opened to him, and he perceived there the Archangel Michael who has been working in that sphere since the end of the 1870s. From Rudolf Steiner's descriptions of his experiences during this period in connection with the Moon-sphere (see the quotation in Chapter 2, page 56), we can sense how the imaginative perception here is completely permeated with Inspirations, and in his books and lectures he frequently relates that, whereas Imagination gives only an external image of a being, it is in Inspiration that beings appear to the clairvoyant directly through what they *do*, through their actions.[146]

Still more distinct is the connection between the third seven-year Sun period of Rudolf Steiner's life and the fourth rhythm of the Christmas Conference. It is during this period that the consciousness soul develops, arising as a partial transformation of the physical body and, in a certain way, pointing to the Spirit Man of the distant future. Thus during this period Rudolf Steiner begins to live in a most intensive way into the world of Intuitions and we see that from this time onwards, as he himself relates, he was able to experience the spiritual in the physical world of his immediate surroundings; that is, there begins to be revealed to him from that time the hidden essence of the world of the senses. He writes of this in detail in Chapter 22 of his autobiography. From many other descriptions, we know from Rudolf Steiner that the clairvoyant can comprehend the spiritual essence of the sense-world only in Intuition which works, also in a hidden way, in the human will. Rudolf Steiner now ascends to this sphere in his own inner development. He expresses this most clearly with reference to the beginning of his twenty-seventh year: 'I felt how the ideal [mental] element of my life prior to this time now receded in a certain sense, and the element of will took its place ... The will increased proportionally as this ideal element decreased.'[147] This gradual penetration into the sphere of Intuition led him finally to a direct experience of the Christ Being. He refers to this at the end of Chapter 26 of his autobiography, and it signifies here the completion of his path of 'apprenticeship'.[148]

Therefore the three Sun periods of Rudolf Steiner's life are like an uninterrupted ascent from the experience of the Rosicrucian wisdom, to the sphere of the Archangel Michael, to a meeting with the Christ. And we see in this ascent Rudolf Steiner's three great Teachers: Christian Rosenkreutz, the leading Teacher of western esotericism; the Archangel Michael, the guiding Spirit of our epoch; and lastly Christ Himself, the great Guide of all Earth evolution, the incarnation of the Cosmic Word, the Logos, who gives life to and embraces the whole of our cosmos.

As far as the three remaining rhythms of the Christmas Conference are concerned—expressing as they do the macrocosmic nature of the three supersensible-earthly sacrifices of Christ Jesus—their connection with the three subsequent seven-year periods of Rudolf Steiner's life and the three further sacrifices made by him around 1907, 1913 and finally at Christmas 1923–24 is evident in a natural way from all that has already been said, and nothing need therefore be added.

Thus the mystery of the life of the greatest initiate of our time reveals itself to us as the archetype of the new path of initiation, and this path stands in full harmony with the esoteric essence of the Christmas Conference.

To complete our description of the Christmas Conference as the fundamental Mystery of our time, we can sum up our observations in the following words. In the spirit of the reversed cultus the Christmas Conference stands before us today as a pure Mystery-act. In its sensible-supersensible reality it belongs to the sphere of the everlasting and so is for us, in the deepest sense of the word, a 'mystical fact' that has taken place in the midst of humanity. And to find the way to, and understand, this mystical fact is now the paramount task of every anthroposophist who truly wishes to work in the spirit of Rudolf Steiner's purpose and of those spiritual forces standing behind him and by whose will it was that the Christmas Conference came into our world. And whoever says today that the Christmas Conference has 'failed' does not see that, strictly speaking, he is trying to approach a deeply esoteric event with completely everyday, exoteric concepts; for when something exists in the world as an occult fact, one cannot approach it only with an earthbound way of seeing things. For this reason we must realize clearly that the Christmas Conference, willed as it was by the spiritual world itself, cannot be dismissed by any person who has this or that opinion about it. It is possible to speak of a 'failure' of the Christmas Conference in one sense only, and that is its failure in the souls of individual human beings who have been unable to find access to it.

If, however, we do feel that the impulses of the Christmas Conference are not yet realized in our world to a sufficient extent, then this should strengthen our determination to work more intensively to bring this about. And whoever, with an open heart and a genuine desire to offer himself in service, takes up these impulses and lays them as the Foundation Stone in his own soul can experience: the Christmas Conference is alive! It is here! It is among us and works on... A significant proof of its presence in the world has been the existence of the Anthroposophical Society itself through all the past years. For anyone who acquaints himself today on a spiritual-scientific basis with the working of those forces acting against the rightful course of development in the modern world knows that a foundation such as the Anthroposophical Society could not endure without the

266

help of the spiritual world. This help and also the real presence in the Anthroposophical Society of *actual spiritual forces* is due, first and foremost, to the Christmas Conference through which the Society as a living, unified organism was directly united with the wellsprings of the new spiritual life. It was from these wellsprings that, as a direct consequence of the Christmas Conference, the Free School of Spiritual Science could arise in our world, with its culmination in the First Class whose content is likewise the content of the impulse of the Christmas Conference—it is not possible in an esoteric sense to separate the one from the other. Therefore we should never forget that since the Christmas Conference *every* anthroposophist who has taken its impulse—the *central* impulse of Anthroposophy—sincerely into his heart and who carries this into all the areas of specialized human activity (into education, medicine, science, art, the social movement and so on)—every anthroposophist who does this with full consciousness *already* works esoterically in the world, and thus in a most direct way unites himself with the stream of the New Mysteries of the present, for these are already here on the Earth.

In this sense, a true understanding of the Christmas Conference—to which end this book wishes to contribute—teaches us to overcome the materialistic habits of thinking that are in us due to the distorted nature of modern civilization. The Christmas Conference calls on us to perceive and experience the surrounding world in a purely spiritual and occult way, for it is not itself something that occurred just once on the physical plane, but is a *living impulse of initiation* whose fruits we can carry into all spheres of human activity and human life as the first seeds of a future Michaelic culture.

Like a never-fading Christmas star, a star of the new initiation, the Christmas Conference comes before us today with the same brightness as it did over half a century ago. And today, just as then, to anyone who wishes to lay into his heart the Foundation of the New Mysteries, its voice speaks, saying: Prove yourself worthy of the trust of the Gods. Follow this Christmas star, and it will lead you to the Temple of the New Mysteries, to the Sun Temple of the New Mysteries of Michael-Christ.

Let the words of Rudolf Steiner, which he addressed to the hearts and souls of all true anthroposophists of the past, the present and the future therefore stand at the end of this chapter:[149] 'And so, my dear friends, carry out into the world your warm hearts in which you have laid the Foundation Stone for the Anthroposophical Society, carry out into the world these warm hearts which promote strong, health-giving activity in the world. And help will be vouchsafed to you, enlightening your heads in what you would direct in conscious willing. We will set about this today with all possible strength. We shall indeed see, if we prove worthy of this aim, that a good star will hold sway over what is willed from here. Follow this good star, my dear friends! We shall see whither the Gods will lead us by the light of this star.

O Light Divine,
O Sun of Christ!
Warm Thou
Our Hearts,
Enlighten Thou
Our Heads!

6. The Foundation Stone Meditation

At the heart of the Christmas Conference lies the *Foundation Stone Meditation* which, in seven initiation rhythms that bring to expression the secret of the modern path of initiation, was laid in the souls of those members of the Society who were present during the Christmastide days of 1923–24: 'But the ground into which it was placed as a dodecahedral Stone of Love was the hearts of the anthroposophists ... in their harmonious working together, in their love-imbued good will to carry the anthroposophical will through the world *together* with one another.'[1] And this Mystery-act is not only a part of what is temporal but also of what is everlasting, and everything, therefore, which occurred during those days is still of significance today. Even today we cannot 'carry the anthroposophical will through the world' in the right way—cannot carry it into the world in that spirit which, at the will of the spiritual world and through Rudolf Steiner, was born anew in the surrounding of the Earth during those Christmas days—if we do not lay this dodecahedral Foundation Stone with all earnestness, with all devotion and self-offering into the ground of our souls, if we do not let it sink into the depths of our hearts

> That good may become
> What from our Hearts we would found
> And from our Heads direct
> With single purpose.

What took place in Dornach during the Christmas of 1923–24 was in reality a 'second birth' for the Anthroposophical Society. Through this birth it was united as a unified organism with the sources of the anthroposophical movement—was united, that is, with that spiritual sphere from which, since 1879, the new stream of revelation has flowed more and more strongly to the Earth through the guiding spiritual powers of our cosmos. If, therefore, we truly will that Anthroposophy should fulfil its task within humanity, we have no other way than to place ourselves consciously at the service of those powers who brought the Christmas Conference, the most fundamental Mystery of our time, into our world through Rudolf Steiner.

Thus, for us the Christmas Conference is not just an event which took place at a particular moment in the development of the world, but is the starting-point of a genuine spiritual path that leads all of us, who through our karma have been brought to modern spiritual science, to those goals set by the spiritual Powers who are behind Anthroposophy and inspire it from the spiritual world.

The Christmas Conference is like a 'new covenant' between the Anthroposophical Society and the supersensible powers who guide it, to whom human beings should inwardly pledge themselves. Of this pledge to the Spirit of the First Goetheanum—who as the principle of the new esotericism, as the foundation of the new union between the Gods and man, supersensibly overshone the Christmas Conference—Rudolf Steiner said the following in the last lecture of the Christmas cycle, on 1 January 1924, and similarly in Arnhem on 18 July: 'There is here, in a certain sense, also a promise to the spiritual world. This promise will be faithfully fulfilled.'[2] And the founding of the School of Spiritual Science is a result of this pledge; it is the answer of the spiritual world to the pledge of those who laid the dodecahedral Foundation Stone in their hearts. For the possibility of holding such a Christmas Conference in our time arises from the fact that today the Gods are turning again to humanity and calling upon it to become a conscious co-worker. And today everything depends on human beings. For after 'that which the world has to say to human existence and human life and human activity'[3] has sounded out at the Christmas Conference, man himself must give answer to it!

But what rang out for the first time in mighty cosmic words over 60 years ago still sounds forth for us ever since that time with undiminished force from the spiritual environment of the Earth, calling us to give conscious answer. And there is only one form in which this can happen: in the form that was opened to us by the spiritual world itself at the Christmas Conference. This means giving a pledge to the spiritual powers who guide our epoch, and in sacrificial devotion placing the mighty rhythms of the founding anthroposophical *Meditation* 'Soul of man . . .'—this dodecahedral Stone of Love—into our hearts and souls.

If we are truly prepared to give this answer, if we are prepared to make a pledge of faithfulness and service, if in the light of the best forces in our souls we lay this Foundation Stone of the Christmas Conference in our hearts, we will experience in reality a 'second birth', and like many of those who were personally present at the Christmas Conference will be able to say that in truth there henceforth begins for us a new life.

The threefold call of the *Foundation Stone Meditation*, 'Soul of Man', is a threefold address of the spiritual powers guiding Earth evolution to the human soul of the present. And this threefold call of the spiritual cosmos to the human soul is formulated in such a way as also to contain in the deepest sense the path to the knowledge of this cosmos and of the spiritual forces working and ruling within it. For this reason we must look on the *Foun-*

dation Stone Meditation as the actual path leading us to a direct union with these forces.

But who are these forces? We recognize them in the first place as those Beings who ordained that Anthroposophy should appear on the Earth and who guided its arising among humanity, realizing this through their greatest emissary on Earth, Rudolf Steiner. Thus they were also the Beings working in Rudolf Steiner's life itself, preparing him for his great mission.

We have already spoken in detail in the first two chapters of this book of the Beings who played a part in Rudolf Steiner's initiation. We saw how his individual development followed a steady ascent—from his meeting with Christian Rosenkreutz immediately before the Sun period of his life to the sphere of the Archangel Michael at the end of this period, and to a meeting with the Christ in the sphere of Intuition.

One can call the three seven-year periods from 1902 to 1923—the time of Rudolf Steiner's activity as a Teacher of humanity—the period of fulfilment. At the beginning of this time the Rosicrucian impulse was particularly strong and attained a kind of culmination in *Occult Science* (1909). For this book—the foundation of a modern science of the spirit—contains as it were the quintessence of Rosicrucian wisdom in its three fundamental aspects: the formation of man and the cosmos; the evolution of the world; and the path of knowledge. From 1910 it is the proclamation of the Etheric Christ which comes to the forefront, and this reaches its culmination in 1914 in the lectures on *The Fifth Gospel*. At the end of 1914 the emphasis moves gradually to an occult-social theme where the name of Christ is perhaps not mentioned as often as before, but where the lectures and cycles can be brought together under a common heading of 'Christ and the twentieth century'. Indeed, all the lectures of this period are directed towards developing an understanding of how the Christ-impulse is at work in the modern world. Around 1917, coinciding with the founding of the anthroposophical 'daughter-movements', there is a move to the theme of Michael, which developed further until the end of Rudolf Steiner's life and attained its culmination in the First Class of the Esoteric School.

Thus we see what spiritual forces are involved with the arising of Anthroposophy in the world. And these forces turn now through the *Foundation Stone Meditation* to the humanity of the present, so that any work on this *Meditation* in the spirit of the Christmas Conference is the answer of man to their call, is the expression of his willingness to enter upon a path of sacrificial service to them. In this, Rosicrucianism and the Michael-impulse are only two particular manifestations of the central Christ-force that embraces all evolution: Rosicrucianism manifesting this more in the form of the new initiation and the Michael-impulse in the form of the new revelation (Michael—the Countenance of Christ).

271

Two things point to this central force of our cosmos, to this spiritual foundation of the Christmas Conference which works as an impulse in the world. On the one hand is the fact that the Conference took place during the holy days of Christmas, and on the other is the Conference's connection with the cosmic Christmas that had taken place almost two thousand years before. Rudolf Steiner spoke of this on 25 December 1923, as follows: 'And we can best make strong that warmth of soul and light of soul which we need, if we quicken them with that warmth and that light which, at the Turning-point of Time, rayed forth into the darkness of the world as the Light of Christ. Let us now bring this original Christmas—the primal night of initiation which took place 2,000 years ago—to life *in our own heart, in our mind, in our will,* so that this may help us when we want to carry out into the world that which radiates towards us through the light of thought from the dodecahedral Foundation Stone of Love, formed as it is in the image of the world and placed into the realm of humanity.'[4]

What speaks to us above all of this cosmic Christmas through which the Christ Light shone as 'Day-radiant Light' (IV, 6–7) is the fourth part of the *Foundation Stone Meditation*. And if today, in the spirit of the fundamental impulse of the Christmas Conference, we try to bring to life in ourselves this 'Day-radiant Light' that was enkindled in the Earth-night by the cosmic Christmas, it will be able to flow, transforming and quickening, into our will, into our feeling and our thinking. And then, in the threefold call to the human soul, we shall experience in it a threefold address of Christ Himself. He gives in this *Meditation* an all-embracing knowledge of His Being and awakens a will in the soul to transform completely *its* willing, feeling and thinking in the name of the birth of the new man within.

Thus in the first three parts of the *Foundation Stone Meditation*, the Christ calls for a threefold transformation of our being on the foundation of the threefold knowledge of His Being. In the first part He reveals Himself from the cosmic sphere of the Father[5] and gives us that strength which we find in the new Rosicrucian initiation as the modern initiation of the will. In the second part the Christ comes before us from the sphere of the Son from whence, through the initiation of feeling, He bestows upon human beings His Cosmic Love. And in the third part He approaches us from the sphere of the Spirit, working as it does through Michael, the Spirit of our Age, who is the guardian of the Cosmic Intelligence and who, through the initiation of thinking, bestows upon us the fullness of Cosmic Wisdom. Thus, in the combined working of these three forces there is revealed to us the all-embracing path of the new Christian initiation.[6]

We can now look more closely at the nature of these three forces. In order to do this we can arrange the text of the *Meditation* in a particular way, as follows: the first three parts together in a row, and the fourth part directly below the second. In connecting the second and fourth parts in this way, we are led by the fact that in each of these the Christ-impulse, through the mentioning of Christ's name, is brought to direct expression.★ It is also important to note that Christ is revealed here in two different aspects—in the aspects which *in our time* are both open and accessible to humanity, but along different paths. Thus the second part speaks of that aspect of Christ which is opened to the modern initiate only in the sphere of cosmic *will*. For the very use of the word 'will' (II, 14) here points to the highest realm of Intuition[7] where a personal meeting with the Christ is possible only after a long and difficult spiritual path. Here in these spiritual heights Christ reveals Himself in the aspect of the threefoldness of Father, Son and Spirit, as the all-encompassing World Logos in the radiance of macrocosmic forces that are His from eternity. The fourth part, on the other hand, speaks of how Christ entered directly into the development of the Earth through the Mystery of Golgotha, and of how since then He lives in the spiritual sphere of the Earth—a fact which manifests itself in our time as His resurrection in the etheric sphere. Whereas in Section 1 of Part IV we are directed more to the Mystery of Golgotha, which took place on the physical plane, in the second section the human soul turns directly to Christ in that form in which *in our age* He works in humanity—that is, to the Etheric Christ who suffered the Etheric Golgotha.[8]

Seen in this way, the *Meditation* consisting of four parts becomes threefold (see opposite page).

We can characterize these three Elements again as follows. In Element 1 (Part I) Christ turns to us from the past through the renewal of Rosicrucianism. In Element 2 (Parts II and IV) He works directly in the present, encompassing the whole of our cosmos from the highest sphere of Intuition to the etheric sphere bordering on the Earth, where today—as once by St Paul—He can be experienced by every human being.[9] And in Element 3 (Part III) Christ comes to meet us from the future, revealing Himself through His Messenger, the Sun Spirit of our Age, Michael. Thus the *Meditation* is a threefold revealing of Christ to the human soul.

In order now to go more deeply into this truly inexhaustible wealth of wisdom contained in the fundamental anthroposophical *Meditation*, we must look at each of the three elements separately and in more detail. We will then see how the threefold form of the World Guidance, mentioned above, is there revealed in the minutest detail and yet also as a harmonious unity.

★ As mentioned earlier, the Christ-impulse appears in the first part *in the form* of Rosicrucianism, and in the third part *in the form* of the new Michael revelation.

Element 1	Element 2	Element 3
Part I	*Part II*	*Part III*
Section 1	*Section 1*	*Section 1*
Soul of Man! Thou livest in the Limbs ...	Soul of Man! Thou livest in the ... Heart ...	Soul of Man! Thou livest in the resting Head ...
Section 2	*Section 2*	*Section 2*
For the Father-Spirit of the Heights holds sway ...	For the Christ-Will in the encircling Round holds sway ...	For the Spirit's Universal Thoughts hold sway ...
	Part IV	
	Section 1	
	At the Turning-point of Time ...	
	Section 2	
	O Light Divine, O Sun of Christ ...	

The Rosicrucian wisdom (Element 1, Part I)—which originates from the Father-sphere—had to be renewed after the Mystery of Golgotha by being permeated by the Christ-impulse. This occurred—being likewise the beginning of the Rosicrucian stream in the world—with the *initiation of Christian Rosenkreutz* in the middle of the thirteenth century, as has been described in detail by Rudolf Steiner in a lecture in Neuchâtel on 27 September 1911. At that time the initiation of Christian Rosenkreutz was carried out in such a way that, at a Mystery-place in Europe, twelve outstanding spiritual individualities came together, of whom seven bore within them the wisdom of ancient Atlantis, four others the wisdom of the four post-Atlantean cultural epochs, and the twelfth the more intellectual knowledge of our recent times.

Thus of these twelve, eleven embodied all the pre-Christian wisdom of humanity and the last, in contrast, the new scientific knowledge. As Rudolf Steiner particularly emphasized, because the whole of mankind was in a period of transition during which direct access to the spiritual world was closed, even to initiates, each of that company of twelve drew his knowledge from the *memory* (I, 5) of his previous incarnations when the higher worlds were still open to him. Therefore, in the thirteenth century all the wisdom of cosmic evolution preserved in the memory of the twelve was transmitted to the thirteenth who, absorbing it right into his physical body, was then brought to St Paul's experience before Damascus. This immediate, personal meeting with the Christ enabled him now to transform all this absorbed wisdom in the spirit of the Christ-impulse as it has worked since the Mystery of Golgotha in the spiritual sphere of the Earth. Thereupon the thirteenth gave this most ancient wisdom of humanity, permeated now with the Christ-forces, back to the twelve. This then was the beginning of the Rosicrucian stream, at the basis of which lies the new revelation of Christ from the cosmic sphere of the Father, which in its new form we will have to consider later, in the first part of the *Foundation Stone Meditation*.

The further development of Rosicrucianism then proceeded in such a way that Christian Rosenkreutz incarnated again in the fourteenth century. During this incarnation, after living again through the experience of St Paul—this time at Damascus itself—and having journeyed for seven years to all the occult centres of that time, he founded the Rosicrucian stream proper as the Christian path of western initiation in Europe.

Also during this incarnation, Christian Rosenkreutz laid the foundation for that medieval spiritual path known as *alchemy*, and which Rudolf Steiner describes in detail in his lecture in Neuchâtel on 28 September 1911. This path consisted of three stages. To begin with the alchemist observed the process of salt formation, the meditative contemplation of which helped him gradually to overcome the lower passions of his astral body by directing all the forces of his soul to higher, spiritual thought. This led him finally, after a long period of practice, to an experience of cosmic thoughts, to the thoughts of the Gods. 'I worship the thoughts of the Gods, of the divine-spiritual Beings behind the maya of nature'[10]—thus spoke the medieval Rosicrucian at the first stage. At the second stage he turned his attention particularly to the process concerned with dissolution, which the Rosicrucian called the quicksilver or Mercury process. By immersing himself in this process, which also served to purify the etheric body, the Rosicrucian was able to experience ever higher, more spiritualized levels of love. 'The love of God has worked for thousands of years in the outer world in the same way as it works in my inner being'—thus spoke the Rosicrucian at the second stage. And finally at the third stage, the crowning of the path of initiation, the medieval Rosicrucian had to experience the process of combustion, the sulphur process, which filled him with the will for self-offering, for sacrificial service to the higher forces, and enabled him to work on the purification of the physical body, on its transformation into the body of the future, into the body of the Resurrection. This transformation of the physical body through the highest forces of self-sacrifice can be called working on 'the Stone of the Wise', which was the archetype and goal of all medieval Rosicrucian endeavour. 'That is why the alchemists always emphasized that, in truth, the human body consists of the same substance as the completely transparent, crystal-clear Stone of the Wise.'[11]

In this way these three stages gradually brought the medieval pupil of the spirit to reproduce microcosmically in his inner being the great macrocosmic processes that come to expression in the cosmos in the thoughts, the love and the sacrificial service of the Gods.

It is not difficult to recognize this path in its renewed form in the *Foundation Stone Meditation* where, however, in contrast to the initiation path of the medieval alchemists, it proceeds now in a purely *inward*, meditative way, without recourse to the observations of external experiments. Thus the third part of the *Meditation* leads us to an experience of the cosmic thoughts of the Gods by reproducing them in the thoughts of man: 'Then from the ground of the spirit in Man/Thou wilt truly *think*' (III, 12–13). At the same time, the twofold nature of this part (in Sections 1 and 2) enables us to approach the first stage of a knowledge of the relation of the microcosm and macrocosm. The second part of the *Meditation* leads us to the cosmic love of the Gods, which to begin with must be relived microcosmically by each individual in a spiritualized experience of love. 'Then 'mid the weaving of the Soul of Man/Thou wilt truly *feel*' (II, 11–13). Here the interrelation of microcosm and macrocosm is already deeper. Finally, the first part of the *Meditation* guides us to the direct offering-up of ourselves to the highest Gods. The principle of sacrificial service—which ascends here in cosmic *memory* (I, 5) right to the primal sacrifice of the Thrones on Ancient Saturn, who poured out the substance of warmth or fire which the medieval Rosicrucian observed in the sulphurous processes of combustion, and which served as the material basis of the human physical body ('From God, Mankind has Being' (I, 20)—this principle of sacrifice comes directly before us here and must find a response in our individual service, in our individual self-offering on the altar of the world. This sacrifice will bring us closer to the purely inner process—in accordance with our time—of transforming the physical body into the 'Stone of the Wise'. As described in the sixth lecture of the cycle *From Jesus to Christ*, this is an image of the 'phantom' of the human physical body which was redeemed for all mankind in the Mystery of Golgotha.

Thus the first part of the *Foundation Stone Meditation* contains the most secret ideal of all Rosicrucian striving, as well as the actual goal of its path of initiation, as described for example in the book *The Chemical Wedding of Christian Rosenkreutz* in which the transformation of the human physical body into the body of the Resurrection, through the taking up and

276

absorbing of the Christ-impulse, is the goal and completion of the whole initiation path.

If now we bear in mind that this body of the Resurrection, or 'phantom', is in its very nature and substance the result of the activity of all the higher Hierarchies—reaching as it does from our Earth epoch right back to the beginning of Ancient Saturn, when in order to form the first germ of the human physical body the highest Spirits of the First Hierarchy (I, 16) had to create a whole cosmos out of the 'ocean-being of the Spirit' (I, 4)— if we become conscious of this we will begin to understand the words of the *Foundation Stone Meditation* which speak in this part of the working of the Father-God in the Heights who in the Depths of Worlds (I, 15) brought forth through the First Hierarchy the space-existence (I, 3) of Saturn as the foundation for the genesis of humanity. 'From God, mankind has Being' (*Ex Deo nascimur*) (I, 20)—this Rosicrucian saying directs us to that most ancient condition of our cosmos, when the primal germ of the human physical body was created. At that time this germ belonged to all humanity as a single whole, as a great primordial Adam who was then to evolve further through the aeons of Sun, Moon and Earth. For the creation of the phantom of the physical body goes back directly to the working of the Father-forces on Ancient Saturn. The redemption of this body through Christ Jesus at the Mystery of Golgotha has made it possible for every human being, proceeding from the 'I' that is imbued with the Christ, to work on his bodily sheaths even into the physical body and, in accordance with the highest ideal and fundamental goal of Rosicrucianism, to transform this into the new body of the Resurrection.

In the last chapter of his book *The Christmas Foundation*, Rudolf Grosse also points to the fact that, in a hidden way, there is contained in the first part of the *Foundation Stone Meditation* that path which, through the constant work of the 'I' on the ascending sequence of the bodily sheaths, leads to the complete transformation of the physical body. He writes in detail of the connection between the last lines of Part I of the *Meditation* ('And in the All-World-Being of Man/Thou wilt truly *live*', I, 12–13) and the redemption of the 'phantom' of the physical body at the Mystery of Golgotha. At that event, by virtue of the deed of Christ Jesus, the possibility was given to every human being to *live truly* with his 'I' in the physical body, in the body which henceforth can be redeemed by this 'I'—through its connection with the Christ-impulse—from the kingdom of death into which it was cast by the temptation of Lucifer. For the basis of this 'phantom' was laid on Old Saturn by the Thrones and was subsequently worked on by the Spirits of Wisdom on Old Sun, by the Spirits of Movement on Old Moon, and by the Spirits of Form on the Earth. And this 'phantom', this combined creation of the highest Hierarchies in which,

277

up to the Mystery of Golgotha, the human 'I' could not live because of the forces of death in it evoked by Lucifer—this 'phantom' was restored by Christ in its original essential being as the true, incorruptible human body, the seed of which can be received by every human being who permeates his 'I' with the Christ-force that leads to Resurrection.

In this way a knowledge of the true body of man, as the purest image of the creative activity of the highest Hierarchies from whose realm ('The All-World-Being of Man') it has arisen, leads us also to a knowledge of the relation of the macrocosm and microcosm in the evolution of humanity—the genesis of humanity from the cosmic Father-forces, its Fall from the Father-forces through the luciferic temptation and its reunion with them through the sacrifice of Christ on Golgotha. There is given to each individual human being through this deed the possibility, by transforming the physical body, of gradually partaking of the fullness of cosmic life (I, 12–13). And when this sublime condition is reached, it is the first anticipation on Earth of the future Vulcan condition, when, in the words of the *Meditation*: 'Thine own I/Comes to being/Within the I of God' (I, 9–11). This corresponds to the seventh and final stage of the Christian-Rosicrucian path of initiation, the stage which Rudolf Steiner calls 'blissfulness in God'. With these words, he characterizes also the future Vulcan condition in which the human being will live in a physical body transformed into Spirit Man.

Thus does the first part of the *Foundation Stone Meditation* direct us, in a form renewed 'under the sign of the times', to the transformation of the physical body in which the human 'I' experiences itself in 'the All-World-Being of Man', and in which it can 'truly live' a macrocosmic life. This, however, is the ultimate goal of all Earth evolution, and was the highest initiation ideal of medieval Rosicrucianism.

To what has been said above one should add that this Rosicrucian work on the transformation of the physical body—of the body which finds its greatest spatial expression in the limb system (I, 2)—corresponds in the threefold social organism to the sphere of the free spiritual life.[12] This is why Rudolf Steiner strove to renew almost all areas of contemporary spiritual life under the sign of Rosicrucianism, achieving this above all through the harmonious union and development of the three fundamental spheres of human activity: science, art and religion.[13]

Let us turn now to the second elements of the *Meditation*, in which we consider Parts II and IV. Looking at these together can help us to uncover a deeper aspect of their nature. As a whole, Element 2 of the *Meditation* leads us directly to the cosmic-earthly Mystery itself of Christ Jesus. Here we move from the world of space—that arose along with the first seeds of the human physical body as the result of the acts of sacrificial offering carried

278

out by the First Hierarchy on Old Saturn out of the forces of the Father—
into the world of Time (II, 3), into the world of Rhythm, into the Sun-
realm of the Son (II, 15; 17–18). From this sphere there was incorporated
into the human being during the Old Saturn condition the rhythmical
system of the heart and lungs, whose microcosmic rhythms reproduce the
macrocosmic beat of the pulse and breath of the whole cosmos.[14]

In a lecture at Dornach on 4 June 1924, Rudolf Steiner describes the
great Sun-realm of Christ as the cosmic sphere of World-time. By descending from the Sun to the Earth, Christ descends likewise from the realm
of time into the realm of space in order to bring to humanity the possibility
of uniting itself in a true way with the stream of cosmic time. 'And inasmuch as the human heart, the human soul and the human spirit unite
themselves with the Christ, they find again the stream of time that flows
from eternity to eternity.'[15]

But just as the first part of the *Meditation* places before us the task of
practising *Spirit-recollection*—by virtue of which we can draw closer to the
secrets of the inner nature of the physical body which is connected with the
redemption of its 'phantom' by Christ—so here it is the practice of *Spirit-
mindfulness*. Through this pure time process we can gradually take into our
hearts the new knowledge of Christ which He opens to us today through
modern spiritual science and which stands before us as the fundamental task
of our time.

The most important characteristic of this new knowledge, as is stressed
in the second part of the *Meditation*, is that it can be attained *only* through
inner 'balance of soul' (II, 6). The essence of this balance—the knowledge
of which is one of the most important revelations of the Christ in the
twentieth century—was expressed by Rudolf Steiner in an artistic form in
his sculpture of the 'Group', in which there comes before us an image of
the Representative of Man, Christ Jesus, holding in inner balance the
adversary forces of Lucifer and Ahriman.

To attain within oneself, in the spirit of the second part of the *Foundation
Stone Meditation*, this 'balance of soul' means above all to fight in the right
way against the forces of Ahriman and Lucifer in one's own soul. In other
words, we must fight on the one hand against the susceptibility of the heart,
of the blood circulation (II, 2), through the excitement of which Lucifer
tries as it were to extricate, to 'free' us from ourselves, to tear us away from
all matter; and this expresses itself physiologically in Lucifer's seeking to
push the enlivening forces of the blood up into the brain, so as to counteract in this way the continual processes of death in the head which are the
basis of our waking 'I'-consciousness. Working from this point, he thus
tries wrongfully to draw us away from the forces of the Earth. On the other
hand we must fight against the ahrimanic tendency to bring death into the

279

lungs (II, 2) through an increased production of carbon dioxide. For Ahriman strives constantly to bring death into the whole of our organism, thereby to hinder the spiritualization of the physical body, thus binding us eternally to the sphere of the Earth.

This principle of balance lying at the basis of the Christian-Rosicrucian path of initiation can only be realized by virtue of the fact that Christ, in addition to all the substance of infinite significance brought by Him to human development through the Mystery of Golgotha, also united in harmony—in the deepest sense—the two principal Mystery-streams of antiquity in which the initiates had striven constantly to overcome both the forces of Lucifer and Ahriman which were deflecting the rightful course of human development. They could achieve this, however, only in a limited, one-sided way, for a true balancing of these powers in the time before Christ was not possible. The union of these two principal Mystery-streams of antiquity, making it possible for the first time to establish this true balance of the forces of Lucifer and Ahriman at initiation, was described earlier (at the end of Chapter 2) in connection with Rudolf Steiner's path of initiation, and in connection with the fifth rhythm of the Christmas Conference. We will try now to recapitulate briefly what was said above, but bringing it this time into direct relation with the fourth part of the *Meditation*. Here the shepherds and the Magi of the East—the people of the heart and the people of the lungs (head)[16]—are mentioned *together*, for they have found their union in the single impulse of Christ. In this union the shepherds represent the path of initiation through the meditative con- templation of the inner being (the heart is the archetype of this inward nature), whereas the Magi represent the path outwards into the macrocosm (the lungs, by virtue of the breathing can, like the head by virtue of the sense organs, be seen as an archetypal image of this turning outward). These two ways of initiation are, however, also an echo of the two migratory streams from ancient Atlantis, the Southern and the Northern stream, which can also be termed the stream of love and the stream of wisdom.[17]★

These two streams were represented most completely in pre-Christian times by the two world religions, Buddhism and Zoroastrianism (Zara- thustrianism). Herein lies the reason why the founders of these religions

★ One must note here that the dangers that threatened the pupil on these two paths were also different. In the Northern stream they arose more from Ahriman, the prince of lies, the distorter of wisdom, whereas in the Southern stream they arose more from Lucifer, the prince of egotism, the destroyer of true love. For this reason the union of these two paths in the new Christian-Rosicrucian initiation presupposes, as an absolutely essential condition, the establishing of a balance between these two forces—which is possible only by receiving into oneself the Christ-impulse, as is portrayed in the sculpture of the 'Group'. The dis- tortion which arises in our time by proceeding one-sidedly has already been mentioned at the end of Chapter 2.

both participated in the preparation for the convergence of these two streams in the events of Palestine and why, in the first and third Gospels, we find references to their work. In the Gospel of St Luke the shepherds in the fields experience the appearance of the Nirmanakaya of the Buddha. In the Gospel of St Matthew the three Magi from the East, the esoteric pupils of Zarathustra, journey to give reverence to their Teacher in this new incarnation. All these events show a definite connection with the fourth part of the *Foundation Stone Meditation*. And in a surprising way they are connected also with the second part.

In the development of the world, however, there are many complex forces at work, and although the principal impulse for the union of these two streams entered into Earth existence with the events of Palestine, their actual union did not take place until some time later, and in this way there was reflected on Earth the relation of certain cosmic facts. Thus we find these two streams again in the Christian era—albeit in a renewed form— not as a polarity of North and South, but of West and East: in the West, in the stream of King Arthur's knights of the Round Table, representing the last reflection of the Magi initiation in which knowledge was sought through a union with the macrocosm; and in the East, in the Grail stream, representing the initiation of the shepherds—transformed now by the Christ-impulse—that seeks knowledge through an inner path. Both streams had taken up the Christ-impulse in their different ways, but nevertheless had still to develop separately for nearly eight centuries. We shall now try to look at the occult reasons for this.

In a lecture in Torquay on 21 August 1924, Rudolf Steiner spoke in detail of these two streams in connection with the descent of Christ to the Earth. In the course of this descent, Christ left His Life Spirit in the sur- roundings of the Earth and then incarnated with His Spirit Self into the three bodily sheaths of Jesus of Nazareth, in the East. From the experience of these elements of the Christ-impulse there then arose two new Mystery- streams. From the West worked the knights of King Arthur who perceived in the spiritual surroundings of the Earth the Life Spirit of Christ, and with the help of the impulses they received from this the knights tamed the wild astrality of the European peoples of that time. From the East, on the other hand, the Spirit Self of Christ moved through the hearts and souls of the people and found its esoteric expression in the stream of the Grail. In the same lecture Rudolf Steiner relates how, in the year 869, when the 8th Ecumenical Council took place on the Earth at which 'the spirit was abolished', the Spirit Self of Christ in the supersensible world, coming from the East, united itself with His Life Spirit in the West, whereby this Life Spirit took on the configuration (*Gestaltung*) that was the essential spiritual foundation for the most important supersensible event of the twentieth century—the appearance of Christ in the etheric.[18] This union of the Spirit Self and the Life Spirit of Christ was mirrored on the physical plane by the coming together of the stream of Arthur and the stream of the Grail in the initiation of Parsifal.

In the twentieth century we find the continuation of this event in the laying of the Foundation Stone of the First Goetheanum in Dornach on 20 September 1913. Here, in answer to the four Gospels of the Redemption ringing out from the East, there sounded forth in the new epoch of the consciousness soul the Fifth Gospel—the Gospel of Knowledge—from the West.

All these events, connected as they are with the gradual emergence of the Christ-impulse amongst humanity in the light of East and West, are brought to expression in the *Foundation Stone Meditation* in the words: 'Let there be fired from the East/What through the West is formed' (II, 17–18).

There is a relation here, too, with the deepest content of the Sun Mysteries, or the Mysteries of 'Death and Resurrection', whose inner essence is expressed in the Rosicrucian saying: 'In Christ, Death becomes Life' (*In Christo morimur*). But the Guardians of the secrets of these Mysteries within the cosmos are the Spirits of Light (II, 16) of the Second Hierarchy who, as described by Rudolf Steiner, work in earthly development into the rhythmical phenomena of nature. This is expressed externally above all in the movement of the Sun from East to West (II, 17–18).

From what has been said above, we can see how closely in accord are the second and fourth parts of the *Meditation*. Their deepest relation, however, is that they reveal the two most important aspects of the inner nature of the Christ Being. We must now examine this in more detail, for looking at it in this way can bring us closer to a further aspect of our *Meditation*.

We can begin again with the second section of Part II, 'For the Christ-Will in the encircling Round holds sway.' We have seen that the word 'Will' here points to the lofty sphere of Intuition. In his comments concerning this place in the *Meditation* Rudolf Steiner draws a connection between the working of 'The Christ-Will in the encircling Round' and human breathing.[19] The conscious experience of the breath and, likewise, breathing exercises, belong in the spiritual development of the pupil to the stage of Intuition, as is made clear in *Occult Science*. However, the joining of the word 'Will' with the name of Christ directs us further to that meeting with Christ in the spiritual world which is described at the end of Chapter 5 of *Occult Science* as the highest goal of the Christian Rosicrucian path of initiation.

In the initiation of Rudolf Steiner we were able to note this event around the year 1899 and saw how this personal meeting with the Christ in the sphere of Intuition (that is, on the border of Upper Devachan and the Buddhi plane, the World of Fore-knowledge), also opened up to him an intuitive perception into the nature of the relation between the Christ Being and the being of the Bodhisattvas. The sublime picture of the twelve gazing upon the thirteenth came before Rudolf Steiner around the turn of the century. We can see from this that the experience of Christ in Intuition reveals to the initiate a true knowledge of how the 'Christ-Will' holds sway in 'the encircling Round' of the twelve Bodhisattvas.

'The encircling Round' here means also 'the encircling Round' of the Earth. For it is in the surroundings of the Earth that the Christ-Will finds its fulfilment *through* the realization of the mission of the twelve Bodhi-sattvas. In connection with this it is perhaps appropriate to remember that during its time after death, at the Midnight Hour of Existence on the border of Upper Devachan and the Buddhi plane, the soul unites itself with the forces of the First Hierarchy, with the Hierarchy representing above all in the cosmos the impulse of World-Will (see page 87). At the same time, however, the soul descends in a supersensible way into the sphere of the Earth, and here in the Earth's surroundings participates in all the processes that are involved in the genesis and existence of the material, earthly world around us. From indications given by Rudolf Steiner in a lecture in the Hague on 14 November 1923 (GA 231), it becomes clear that one should not imagine this lofty (Buddhi) sphere as being 'spatially' far from the Earth, but rather as completely permeating the Earth-sphere, the Earth surroundings, with supersensible forces that are physically imperceptible.

To deepen our survey of the *Meditations* still further, we can look for help to the following lines of the second part, which we can add to the words considered above:

For the Christ-Will in the encircling Round holds sway,
In the Rhythms of Worlds, blessing the Soul.

We are given here an exact occult definition of the nature of Christ's activity from the lofty Bodhisattva sphere—from where, through the community of the twelve, He blesses 'in the Rhythms of Worlds' the souls of human beings.

Rudolf Steiner spoke on a number of occasions of how it is the mission of each of the Bodhisattvas in succession to guide whole epochs of world development, in the course of which they show themselves to be in the deepest sense the fulfillers of the Christ-Will in the Earth-sphere, this process signifying for them the preparation for the rank of Buddha. Altogether, however, the mission of all the twelve Bodhisattvas encompasses the whole evolution of our Earth.[20] Thus one could not better define the inner nature of their activity than to say that it has its origins in the pure cosmic laws that govern this evolution: that is, in the 'Rhythms of Worlds'. On the other hand the expression 'blessing the soul' is an exact description of the activity in the world of the Holy Spirit, who descends from this sublime sphere through the Cosmic Lodge of the twelve, and benignly overshines the souls of human beings on Earth.

If we turn again now to the fourth part of the *Meditation* and recall that we are concerned here with a direct address to Christ *in our time*—that is, to the Etheric Christ—then through looking at Parts II and IV together there arises a truly all-embracing picture of the working of the Christ Being. For Christ permeates all the spiritual spheres from the World of Fore-knowledge, or Buddhi-plane (Part II), right to the supersensible world closest to us. Through this world in the twentieth century He moves in His transformed etheric body (Part IV) which is by nature akin to the human Life Spirit of Buddhi.[21]

This sublime spiritual panorama arising from the consideration of Parts II and IV together can be developed still further by certain spiritual-scientific facts contained in the lecture-cycle by Rudolf Steiner, *Macrocosm and Microcosm*. He speaks there in detail of how the separate macrocosmic spheres work into the different organs of man. Thus our sense organs could arise during the development of the Earth only because the spiritual stream from the supersensible, elemental world (the astral world) that flows unceasingly through us was held back and arrested by our spiritual-bodily organization. In the same way our nervous system was created by checking the stream from the spiritual world (Lower Devachan), and our human brain, the bearer of our thoughts and 'I'-consciousness, was likewise formed with the stream from the World of Reason, or Upper Devachan.

However, in the present cycle of world development the human being does not have to be restricted to the level of the normal object-consciousness that is connected with the activity of the brain. He can enter upon a path of spiritual training and thus develop organs of consciousness higher than the brain. He can lift himself up from his everyday, waking 'I'-consciousness to imaginative consciousness. To form the supersensible organs of perception necessary for this he has, by means of the appropriate occult exercises, to hold back within himself the stream that permeates him from a still higher world than the World of Reason. In relation to this highest world, the human being must himself do what at lower levels nature has done for him. In the same cycle, Rudolf Steiner calls this highest world the World of Archetypes (it is also the World of Fore-knowledge, or

Buddhi-plane). Here are preserved the archetypes of all world existence, and only from here can the forces flow that are capable of forming in the pupil of the spirit the organs of imaginative knowledge. In the sixth lecture of the above-mentioned cycle, Rudolf Steiner says the following about this world: '... so that at the same time as we are able to indicate that there is such a thing in the world as clairvoyant consciousness, we have also to say that there must, therefore, be a world from which the forces for the organs of clairvoyance flow—and in spiritual science one calls this world the World of Archetypes. That which can come before us as *Imagination* is ... a reflection of the World of Archetypes.'[22] At the end of the seventh lecture, he adds: 'We shall have to show what sort of organs are needed by the human being in order to gaze into the *imaginative* world; we shall have to show how forces flow from the world of the eternal Archetypes of all things, forming the organs for the imaginative world just as, from the World of Reason, there come the forces that make man ... a being capable of spiritual judgement.' He then describes in the eighth lecture how the pupil of the spirit on the path of modern Christian-Rosicrucian initiation 'must do something to stem the flow of a higher world, to receive forces from a higher world that otherwise simply pass straight through him. For the forces of the World of Archetypes, *do* simply pass right through him. He himself must create a device within him that will reflect them (*Spieglungsapparat*). In the sense in which the human being of today can and ought to do this, it is the methods of spiritual science that create such an inner mirror (*Spieglungsapparat*)—methods which, in working on the soul for the attainment of knowledge of the higher worlds, proceed from so-called imaginative knowledge.'

If we now recall that the new appearance of Christ in the etheric—which is spoken of in the fourth part of the *Meditation* (IV, 14–23 [14–24])—is connected with the first stirrings of a *natural* awakening in man of new, germinal clairvoyant faculties, which according to Rudolf Steiner are *imaginative* faculties, then the *Meditation* reveals to us the secret of their emergence. For Christ who encompasses all our cosmos from the Buddhi-world to the etheric sphere bordering the Earth,[23] through His Etheric 'Golgotha' and His etheric Resurrection, is winning today the forces of the new imaginative clairvoyance for all humanity. Today He bestows on all mankind the possibility of arresting in itself, as it were naturally, the supersensible stream that flows through it from the Buddhi-world, from the World of Archetypes,[24] so that in time every human being, through a natural development of his spiritual organs, will be able to raise himself to a perception of the imaginative world.[25] And this is the great deed of the Etheric Christ in the twentieth century, out of the forces He possesses as a Being who belongs by very nature also to the Buddhi-sphere—which is revealed to us from our survey of Parts II and IV of the *Foundation Stone Meditation*.

From our time onwards this new impulse will work ever more strongly in humanity up to that far-distant epoch when after 2,500 years, and in order to accomplish his mission of fulfilling the portion of the Christ-Will laid upon him in the World of Fore-knowledge, the present Bodhisattva will come and, as the Maitreya Buddha, proclaim to humanity in the language of Imagination the highest teaching concerning Christ.[26]

Thus, until that far-distant epoch, the words of the fundamental anthroposophical *Meditation*, which came into the world through the Christmas Conference, will work amongst mankind, so that human beings who work with it will be able gradually to become conscious helpers in this mighty stream of world evolution that is borne henceforth by the Christ-Will.

This is why the *Meditation* finishes with words addressed directly to Christ:

O Light Divine,
O Sun of Christ!

And when we say them we must be aware that they can be spoken to the Christ Being only out of the depths of a soul that has laid the dodecahedral Foundation Stone of the Christmas Conference in the ground of its heart—the Stone which, being at the same time also the Stone of Love, can serve as the basis for the realization of the words:

Then 'mid the weaving of the Soul of Man
Thou wilt truly *feel*.

This in turn, however, means experiencing directly the Christ Being who, since the Mystery of Golgotha, has been and is present in the innermost soul activity of every human being.

Out of this new relation to the Christ that we have gained through the *Foundation Stone Meditation*, we turn to Him and ask His blessing for that which we carry out from our hearts and from our heads in the service of world development; we ask Christ's blessing 'that good may become what we would direct in *full consciousness of these aims*' (*zielvoll führen wollen*).

But these aims with which we wish consciously to imbue our actions are the aims of the spiritual world, are the aims of Christ Himself. It is of these that the whole of Anthroposophy speaks and which are contained, as the quintessence of all Anthroposophy, in the *Meditation*. We should bring to these aims today that pledge of faithfulness and service which alone gives us the right to say, 'O Light Divine/O Sun of Christ!/Warm Thou our Hearts/Enlighten Thou our heads...'

If now we bear in mind that the words 'Light Divine' relate to the Nathan Soul, then we recognize in the four parts of the *Meditation* a fourfold revelation of Christ for humanity, through four different beings:

Part I	*Part II*	*Part III*
through Rosicrucianism	through the community of the Bodhisattvas	through the Spirit of our time, Michael

Part IV

through the Nathan Soul

Thus all the fundamental spiritual streams and forces that we recognized in the first part of this book as participating directly in the development of Anthroposophy in the world are present also in the *Meditation*.

To conclude this survey of Parts II and IV (i.e. Element 2), we must just note that Part II, relating as it does to the human rhythmic system—the expression of the soul life—corresponds in the threefold social order to the sphere of rights based on equality. In an esoteric respect, however, the problem of the equality of all human beings before the Will of Christ that holds sway in the 'encircling Round' is only presented in the second part. In the fourth part it finds its complete solution in that, after His Resurrection in the etheric, the Christ gradually becomes the Lord of Karma. In the words of Rudolf Steiner: 'We have indicated that the Christ appears on the Earth as Judge; he appears—in contrast as it were to the suffering Christ of Golgotha—as Christ Triumphant, as the Lord of Karma, of whom those who painted the Christ of the Last Judgment already had a presentiment... In truth this is something that begins in the twentieth century and will continue until the end of the Earth. This Judgment (*das Gericht*) begins from our twentieth century onwards and means *the ordering of karma*.'[27] And it is to this that our work together on the *Foundation Stone Meditation* should encourage us. For only someone who has the will to strive selflessly and reverently towards the ordering of the karma of the Anthroposophical Society, and who is prepared to live the *equality* of all anthroposophists in the sight of the new revelation of Christ in the twentieth century as the Lord of Karma[28]—only to such a person does the real possibility open up of turning to Christ with the concluding words of the fourth part of the *Meditation*.

Element 3 of the *Meditation* (Part III) reveals to us the Christ Being from the sphere of the Holy Spirit, which is also the sphere of Eternity and contains in itself all the fruits of the world's future. Christ appears here in our time through His servant, the Sun Spirit Michael, the guiding Spirit of our time. And our work on this part of the *Meditation* leads us to direct 'Spirit-vision' of Michael as he does battle today in the lower regions of the astral world with the ahrimanic dragon, and leads also to a conscious participation in this battle in the name of 'the eternal aims of Gods'. Thus this part contains the deepest secrets concerning the Michael-sphere, and it is to penetrate through to these secrets that is the most important task of the anthroposophical pupil of the spirit.

According to Rudolf Steiner, the resting head—of which we spoke at the beginning of this part—is, in the construction of the human brain, a reflection of the world of the fixed stars encircling our planetary system and which, in its entirety, forms a great cosmic image of Eternity. When by means of this exercise the pupil penetrates through to the spiritual foundation of the head, it then reveals itself to him as the bearer of 'the Thoughts of Worlds', which are at the same time the cosmic thoughts of Michael.

'In quietness of Thought'—that is, in the ascent to 'pure thinking' in the spirit of *The Philosophy of Freedom*, when our normal earthly thinking is brought to complete stillness in meditation—it is possible today to be granted perception of the new revelation of Michael-Christ that has flowed to all mankind since 1879:

Where the eternal aims of Gods
World-Being's Light
On thine own I
Bestow
For thy free Willing.

We have in these words the inner essence of this revelation. For 'the eternal aims of Gods' in the 'World-Being's Light' (III, 7–8) appear in the present Michael-epoch—for the first time in the history of Earth development—to the person who, having spiritualized his thinking, can thereby raise himself consciously into the realm of world freedom.

Significant secrets of the Michael-sphere lie behind these two lines. And in order to draw closer to them, we must look in detail at each line separately.

To what is the first line pointing, where 'the eternal aims of Gods' are spoken of? What is meant by these 'eternal aims'? In a lecture in Vienna on 10 April 1914, Rudolf Steiner described them as follows: 'Before the Gods there hovered as the *goal of their creation* the ideal of man—an ideal that did not exist or express itself as physical man is today, but in such a way that the very highest life of the human soul and spirit could exist and express itself in the perfectly and fully developed endowments of this physical human being. Thus this image of man hovered before the Gods as goal, as ideal, as a religion of the Gods. And as though on the farther shore of the Gods' existence there hovered before them the Temple, which as the highest artistic achievement of the Gods represents the reflection of divine existence in the human form.'[29]

From time immemorial, every human being has perceived these 'aims of Gods' during life between death and a new birth, so as to receive from this perception in the spiritual world the impulses to rightly shape his life on Earth: 'The more we live into the second half of our time between death and a new birth, the clearer does there come before us—so that we cannot overlook it, so that it is always before our spiritual gaze—the most sublime ideal of man, the world aim of the Gods! ... It is impossible there [in the Spirit-land] for a human being not to see this goal of the Gods; for it is placed before his eyes quite unavoidably.' And this final aim of the Gods, this most sublime ideal of man is, in respect of what Rudolf Steiner has said, none other than the image of man who has developed fully his three higher spiritual members of Spirit Self, Life Spirit and Spirit Man—is the image of man who has fulfilled world evolution and, appearing in the cosmos as the Tenth Hierarchy, consciously joins the other nine Hierarchies in the great sounding of the Cosmic Word.

The direct experience of these 'aims of Gods'—which in past epochs was accessible only to the Mystery pupil (and then only in a dulled state of consciousness) and to the soul on its journey after death through the spiritual world—can now, in the new epoch of Michael, begin to reveal itself to the free will (III, 11 [10]) of every human being in the clear light of his waking 'I'-consciousness (III, 9).[30] In this sense, these 'aims of Gods' are nothing other than the first awakening of the higher members in man (and primarily of Spirit Self as the closest spiritual member) who has attained to freedom in the consciousness soul.

But these first rays of the Spirit Self, or the higher 'I', arising in the consciousness soul are the beginning of what, when fully developed, will be the realized goal of the Gods on Earth, where 'in the perfectly and fully developed endowments of the human physical body, the very highest life of the human soul and spirit will be able to exist and express itself.' To begin with, this will be the life of Manas or Spirit Self, and later of the still higher members. The first signs of this new development that is just beginning today, the first harbingers of the fact that human beings can already today receive and take up in their clear consciousness and in their free will the first rays of the radiant 'eternal aims of Gods'—these first harbingers are the impulses of *moral imagination* in the sense of *The Philosophy of Freedom*. These impulses arising out of individual freedom are the result of the fact that today, through the new Revelation of Michael, the human being can take into his consciousness

the eternal aims of Gods
[and the]
World-Being's Light.

Having looked at the first of these two lines, we can now turn to the second and ask: what is meant by the words 'World-Being's Light'? In the above-quoted lecture given in Dornach on 13 January 1924, certain spiritual-scientific facts are brought to light which enable us to find an answer to this question, as follows. The 'World-Being's Light', which is spoken of in the second part of the *Meditation*, is the astral light that streams through all the created universe and which contains in itself, in substance, the cosmic wisdom of the Gods. It is the great mediator between the sphere of the Gods and the consciousness of human beings.

But in the new Michael-epoch our relation to this astral light has also changed; for from our time onwards human beings must learn consciously to read in the astral light 'the aims of Gods' and to act out of free will in accordance with them. Then Michael himself will come to meet man, will carry his deeds into the cosmos, and will incorporate them into the hierarchic structure of the world. Rudolf Steiner describes this process as follows: 'With other Beings of the archangelic Hierarchy one has the feeling that, to a greater or lesser extent, impulses come from them to do one thing or another. Michael, on the other hand, is the Spirit from whom at first no impulses come, because the truly representative period of his rule is the one that is coming now, in which everything comes from human freedom. But when moved by his reading of the astral light the human being 'out of his inner freedom, consciously or unconsciously, does one thing or another, then Michael carries this human Earth-deed out into the cosmos so that it may become cosmic deed. He is concerned with consequences, whereas other spirits are concerned more with causes.'[31]

The perception of the 'eternal aims of Gods', which in the streaming of the astral light are bestowed today from the spiritual world 'on thine own I/ ... For thy free Willing', is the activity that Michael is waiting for from humanity in our epoch. 'For this is what one will learn more and more to strive for: in a certain sense meditatively to *think*, so as to break through to the astral light, to gaze on the secrets of existence and then to come before Michael and to receive from him the assenting look which says: That is right, that is justified before the guiding powers of the cosmos.'

And this is the fulfilment of the words:

Then from the ground of the Spirit in Man
Thou wilt truly *think*.

Immense perspectives are, in truth, opened up in these few words of the *Meditation*. And yet the subsequent lines take us still further, so that we gradually draw near the very centre of the most important cosmic–earthly Michael Mystery, which was presented by Rudolf Steiner in numerous lectures and writings during the last period of his activity after the Christmas Conference. The essence of this Mystery, according to his indications, is the following. In the ascending order of the divine-spiritual Hierarchies, directly involved in the guidance of earthly humanity, Michael, as the most outstanding Sun Archangel, has from most ancient times occupied a special position in that he was entrusted with the guardianship of the Cosmic Intelligence, of the totality of the cosmic thoughts of the Hierarchies, inasmuch as these are connected with the genesis and evolution of humanity. From very ancient times Michael was the mediator, so to speak, between the highest spiritual Hierarchies and developing humanity in that he sent down the 'Universal Thoughts' (III, 14) of the Gods into the heads of human beings. But his place in the cosmos was changed utterly in consequence of the Mystery of Golgotha. For after the Christ Being had left the Sun in order to unite with the Earth, the Cosmic Intelligence—or in other words, the Gods' 'Universal Thoughts', whose regent in the cosmos was Michael—had also to follow along the same path. Thus, from that moment onwards, we see how the Cosmic Intelligence also gradually descends from the Sun-sphere of Michael to the Earth, and finally sinks into the heads of human beings. For human beings had to develop the capacity of thinking their own independent thoughts. This process, which began after the Mystery of Golgotha, continued up to the ninth century when the first independent thinkers appeared on the Earth. From that time onwards the Michaelic Intelligence was on the Earth where it could be prepared by the individual work of different people (reaching a peak in the activity of Thomas Aquinas and Albertus Magnus) to provide the basis upon which, with the onset of the epoch of the consciousness soul, each human being could find his own individual freedom.

However, a great danger was connected with this fall of the Cosmic Intelligence from Michael, and with its descent into the Earth-sphere. For as it entered the heads of individual people it came also into direct contact with earthly matters, thus becoming vulnerable to a gradual usurpation by ahrimanic forces. The influences of these forces grew stronger and stronger as the age of the consciousness soul drew near. 'The Cosmic Intelligence is no longer in the power of Michael but is here on the Earth; may we never allow him to come to rulership over it again'[32]—this is the view of the general cosmic situation as seen from the subterranean sphere of Ahriman. To this end, to the fulfilment of these intentions, the ahrimanic forces have waged battle with ever increasing persistence since the thirteenth century—the age of Nominalism. This battle became particularly intense during the nineteenth century, just before the new Michael-epoch, and has reached its culmination in our time.

In this sense, the battle for the Cosmic Intelligence on the Earth stands as a supersensible fact at the very heart of the historical events of the present. This circumstance also defines the mission of Anthroposophy in the world today which is called upon to spiritualize anew the Cosmic Intelligence— the Intelligence that has become human intelligence and which is sinking ever deeper into ahrimanic materialism—and to return it to Michael. For, as a spiritual Being, Michael cannot enter directly into the Earth-sphere but must wait during the present epoch of his rulership until human beings, out of freedom, themselves spiritualize their intelligence and thereby bring it to where Michael can again guide it. Then he will guide all humanity to fulfil in the right way the 'eternal aims of Gods' the great goals of the divine-spiritual Hierarchies. This, one can say, is the cosmic mission of the anthroposophical movement in our time. And it is expressed in the following words of the *Foundation Stone Meditation*:

> Then from the ground of the Spirit of Man
> Thou wilt truly *think*.

But this thinking in the ground of the spirit of man is the spiritualization of human intelligence, giving it the possibility of uniting itself again with the Michael-sphere.

Having thus looked at the Michael Mystery, we can move now to the lines of the third part of the *Meditation* which express most directly the heart of this Mystery:

> For the Spirit's Universal Thoughts hold sway
> In the Being of all Worlds, beseeching Light.

The inner essence of the Michael Mystery unfolds before us in these lines like a great cosmic Imagination. 'The Spirit's Universal Thoughts' that once held sway under the guidance of Michael in the lofty Sun-sphere have now sunk into the World Being. This above all means the human head (III, 2) which holds within it the quintessence, as it were, of all the previous worlds of Saturn, Sun and Moon. In the head the 'World

Thoughts' of the Gods, cut off from the fount of their origins and by the materialistic nature of contemporary civilization and forced ever deeper into an ahrimanic abyss, 'beseech Light',[33] for a new union with the cosmic sphere of Light, with the Sun-sphere of Michael. This reunion, however, can only be brought about by individuals who work in freedom to spiritualize their own world of thoughts.

Participating in this great mission of modern humanity are also the spirits of the Third Hierarchy, the Spirits of Soul:

> Archai, Archangeloi, Angeloi,
> Let there be prayed in the Depths
> What from the Heights is answered.

The Spirits of this Hierarchy assist in the process of spiritualization, so that the 'World Thoughts' of the Gods—the thoughts that are 'beseeched from the Depths' and rise from the 'ground of the Spirit' in human heads—can be received again in the heights and can enter, in the right way, into the Sun-sphere of Michael. Where this occurs, the human soul as though on the wings of these spiritualized thoughts can enter this lofty sphere and find there a new cosmic consciousness which says: 'In the Spirit's Universal Thoughts, the Soul awakens' (*Per Spiritum Sanctum reviviscimus*).[34]

Like the preceding two Elements of the *Meditation*, Element 3 (Part III) also stands in particular relationship with the threefold social order, corresponding here to the economic sphere that is based on brotherhood. This, however, is the very area of human activity in which, in consequence of the economic theories of the nineteenth century and their social effects, ahrimanic forces are at work today with particular success. And it is into this most strongly ahrimanic sphere that the Michael-Christ impulse should penetrate today—right into every one of its ramifications, including for example, the banking system, stock exchange, and so on.

In a purely spiritual sense, work on this part of the *Meditation* can strengthen the *brotherly* union in the Anthroposophical Society of spiritually striving individuals who once belonged to the most diverse—indeed sometimes even mutually hostile—Mystery-streams. For a true knowledge of the Michael Mystery that is spoken of in this part can help to overcome those distorting impulses of the past that have not yet been lived out to the full. A clear awareness of the spiritual home of *all* anthroposophists, of their belonging to the realm of Michael and to his lofty supersensible School, whose reflection on Earth is the First Class of the School of Spiritual Science, and a consciousness of having taken part together in a great imaginative cultus at the turning-point of the eighteenth and the nineteenth centuries—all this can become the basis for the brotherhood of all true anthroposophists on the Earth, and can awaken in them the feeling: 'Yes, we know one another already; we were together in spiritual worlds and experienced together a supersensible cultus of mighty cosmic Imaginations!'[35] These Imaginations then incarnated on Earth as Anthroposophy. And just as at that time we participated as one united brotherhood in the preparation of these Imaginations in the supersensible world, so it rests upon us today to continue this supersensible act on the Earth in the brotherly union of all anthroposophists, and to work together to bring about the great anthroposophical goals that have been placed before us.

To conclude this description of the three Elements of the *Foundation Stone Meditation*, we must note the three calls to the elemental spirits. What is expressed here is that these calls have already been heard by the elemental spirits of the East, West, North and South. Now, however, man must hear them:[36]

May human beings hear it!

Having looked in detail at the threefold call of Christ in our time to the seeking human soul—a call which finds its fullest expression in the fundamental anthroposophical *Meditation*—we can now touch upon yet another aspect, for we should never grow tired of approaching this *Meditation* from ever new angles. After considering its four parts separately, this aspect can help us to experience it now as a whole unified living organism. In order to do this we must recall that Christ descended to Earth not only as the true spiritual 'I' of each individual human being but also as the 'I' of all humanity. 'Just as the higher "I" is born in each individual human being, so there is born in Palestine the higher, divine "I" of all mankind.'[37]

At that moment the epoch of the relationship of blood and of separate peoples—the time of separateness by reason of descent—was at an end, for Christ addresses only the innermost being of man, his eternal and immortal core, which unites each individual human being with all the rest of humanity. Christ turns to the social community of the future, which is a true anticipation of the Jupiter existence, in which 'no human being can be happy when beside him another human being is unhappy.' To create this new community, the 'new Earth', is the prime mission of a humanity that has taken up the Christ as its higher 'I' and has transformed itself into a unified living organism that is permeated and ensouled by Christ.

In his lectures from 8 to 30 May 1914, Rudolf Steiner spoke with particular feeling of the spiritual-scientific reality of the transformation through the Christ-force of all humanity into a unified cosmic Being—into a Being which would also be the realization of the most cherished

294

aspirations of the Russian philosopher Vladimir Soloviev, concerning divine mankind. Rudolf Steiner describes in detail here how Christ is gradually forming His bodily sheaths in modern humanity: His physical body from all the impulses of human conscience, His etheric body from all the feelings of compassion and love that live amongst people, and His astral body from feelings of wonder, the ability to feel awe, and from true faith (which, according to the Apostle Paul, is the same as the complete certainty of knowledge) for 'faith, wonder and awe are the three forces of soul which carry us beyond the ordinary world.'[38]

Thus, by revealing this profound Mystery of the gradual arising of the Christ-impulse amongst mankind, Rudolf Steiner brings before us the most sublime perspectives of all the future of the Earth and of humanity, which at the same time gives us the real possibility of participating *consciously* and freely in this development. For Anthroposophy is not only a world-view that wishes simultaneously to be a 'spirit-view', but is a real *spiritual force* that awakens our conscience, deepens and spiritualizes our love, and strengthens our wonder and faith in the divine wisdom of the world. For that reason we have in Anthroposophy the first rays of that far-distant future. And we are given in the *Foundation Stone Meditation* the possibility of working to bring this about, for it is in the individual parts of the *Meditation* that we must look for the strongest impulses for this work.

And so from this point of view we can relate the forming of *conscience* to the first part of the *Meditation*, which speaks of the physical body and in particular of its limbs. In various lectures Rudolf Steiner points to the fact that the appearance of conscience—around the fourth century BC—was intimately connected with the particular configuration of the physical body of that time. In an article 'Memory and Conscience', published on 22 March 1925 in the magazine *Das Goetheanum*, Rudolf Steiner writes in connection with this question: 'The forming of the conscience occurs as a purely spiritual process, but in the *metabolic-limb system*.'[39]

Similarly we can connect the feelings of *compassion* and *love* with the second part of the *Meditation*, which speaks of a knowledge of the many-sided nature of the soul life, of the 'Soul-being' (II, 4), and of true feeling ''mid the weaving of the Soul of Man' (II, 12[13]). But the soul—as Rudolf Steiner says in the penultimate lecture of the cycle *Manifestations of Karma*—is, in essence, refined love.

The feeling of reverence and wonder with regard to knowledge—which means above all with regard to 'the Spirit's Universal Thoughts' (III, 14) in which are revealed the 'eternal aims of Gods'—and true 'faith', which awakens when the human being works inwardly in purifying his astral body[40]—all this points clearly to the third part of the *Meditation*.

Thus we see how the first three parts of the *Meditation* give us the possibility of working in a purely inward way on the creation on Earth of the sheaths of the Christ Being here among humanity. The first part contributes to the building of the physical sheath, the second to that of the etheric sheath, and the third to the astral sheath. When these sheaths are formed, then Christ Himself, as the higher 'I' of mankind, enters into them—and it is of this that the fourth and last part of the *Meditation* speaks: 'At the Turning-point of Time . . .'

In this sense, work on the *Meditation* is a *conscious* creating of that great *Immortal Individual* which once dimly hovered before the spiritual gaze of Goethe, and which is the image of *all* humanity—a humanity which permeated and ensouled by the Christ-impulse stands in the cosmos as a unified Being whose physical body is formed from all the deeds of human conscience, whose etheric body is formed from the feelings of compassion and love, whose astral body is formed from reverence wonder and faith, but whose 'I' is Christ Himself, the 'Representative of Man', who at the same time is at work in the holy of holies in every individual human soul. For 'the Christ-impulse can be the same for all humanity, and yet it is also a personal matter for every individual.'[41]

The synthesis of the universal and the individual is thus realized here in its fullest and highest degree. Here in free creativity the soul can give back to the cosmos that which it once received from it at the origin of its existence. The festival of Whitsun is a presage, an anticipation of this, in that the Apostles began to speak in many different tongues and yet were understood by all people.

However, this process of the gradual spiritualization of humanity is by nature a long and complex one, for the Christ-impulse has, at first, no sheath among humanity. 'He must therefore first receive a sheath through the further development of the Earth. And when the Earth comes to its end, then the fully developed Christ will be Last Man, just as Adam was First Man around whom humanity in its diversity has grouped itself.'[42] 'Thus the future evolution of humanity will take place through a co-operation of the moral impulses of human beings with the Christ-impulse. We see before us humanity in the perspective of a great integrated organism. Inasmuch as human beings come to learn how to weave their actions into this great organism, learn how to form their impulses through their own deeds like sheaths around it, will humanity in the course of Earth evolution create the basis for a great community which can be permeated through and through by the Christ-impulse and by Christ Himself.' Thus 'a thought which can fire one to good deeds, even to intense moral impulses, is the thought: You are working to create this immortal Individual, you are making yourself a part of it.' For '. . . what you do to build up this great immortal Individual, in the way described above, is something you do for the further development, for the continued life of the World-organism.'

Thus the *Foundation Stone Meditation* gradually leads us, in union with all humanity, into the divine-spiritual macrocosm where alone it can find its real immortality and true existence. The complete *Meditation* in its four parts places before us and shows us the way to the sublime image of mankind as divine mankind, permeated by Christ and led by Him towards the creation of the Tenth Hierarchy.

But this great cosmic future of mankind, as we have seen, can be realized only through the harmony of the free impulses of individual human beings: from the impulses of their conscience, compassion, love and wonder, and above all from the genuine wish in each individual human being to open his heart to the Christ-impulse, to sacrifice for Christ the separateness of his 'I' in the sense of the words of the Apostle Paul: 'Not I, but Christ in me'. For as we have seen in the example of the course of Rudolf Steiner's life— as the archetype of the new Christian-Rosicrucian initiation—this act of sacrifice lies at the very heart of the modern path of initiation when rightly followed, and is at the same time its goal. Thus it is also equally justified to see in the *Meditation* the path of the *individual* human being who in taking the Christ-impulse freely into himself thereby receives the strength to realize his own cosmic future. And for this the *Meditation* brings a picture before us that is incomparable.[43]

For if we bear in mind that each of the first three parts consists of two sections (a microcosmic and a macrocosmic section), and if we add to these six sections the whole of the fourth part, we have before us a text consisting of seven parts. And from what has already been said it is not difficult to recognize that the first sections of Parts I–III—in which Space (I, 3), Time (II, 3) and Eternity (III, 3) are spoken of—relate respectively to the creation and inner essence of the human physical, etheric and astral bodies. For the fundamental peculiarity of the physical body is its extension in space as well as its vertical orientation (I, 2) which is determined by the structure of the limbs. In earliest infancy the child masters this upright posture which is the distinguishing feature of the human kingdom. The etheric body on the other hand, as bearer of memory, lives completely in the flow of time. For this reason Rudolf Steiner also sometimes calls it the 'time-body' (*Zeitleib*).[44] And the astral body which, as bearer of thinking, is connected with the head-nervous system, belongs in substance to the great astral realm of the cosmos, to the sphere of World Thoughts which, as indicated by Rudolf Steiner, stretches as far as the fixed stars that represent in our world the great Imagination of Eternity, reflected microcosmically in the inner structure of the human head (III, 2).[45]

Thus, after the call 'Soul of Man!' in the five lines of the first three parts of the *Meditation* (lines 2–6 of each part), there is revealed to us the secret of our physical, etheric and astral bodies, as well as the path to a knowledge of them. Then, into these sheaths formed during the course of evolution, there descends the human 'I' as the great gift of the Spirits of Form. In the next five lines of the first three parts (lines 7–11) we have the path of the 'I' from unfreedom to freedom. In the first part the lines speak to us of the human 'I' that 'comes to being' still fully within the 'I' of God. This is an image of the 'I' as it rests hidden within the sentient-soul, still bound up completely with the 'World-Creator-Existence'. The 'I' first awakens in the intellectual and mind soul, which for this reason is marked by the fundamental polarity between the emerging 'I' and the nature of the rest of the world. This chasm which has been present in human development ever since—as the division between outer and inner, matter and spirit, science and religion, etc.—can only be overcome by the soul uniting itself with Christ. For Christ through the Mystery of Golgotha, was able to give true meaning to the primordial 'Deeds of the World's Becoming', and to give to each individual soul the possibility of uniting itself again in the future with those divine-spiritual worlds from which it had fallen during the course of evolution, and thus to incorporate itself once again in the universal oneness of the cosmos. It is of this that lines 7–11 speak.

Finally, in the consciousness soul the human 'I' is fully revealed and comes to true freedom (lines 7–11 of Part III). To this individual 'I', to this 'free willing', there can now be sent down the 'eternal aims of Gods'. And their first rays on Earth are, as we have seen, the impulses of 'moral imagination', by virtue of which the human being can for the first time approach an understanding of what it means—in the whole being of man consisting of spirit, soul and body—truly to *think*, truly to *feel*, and truly to *live*.

But the human being can go still further in this direction. Into his 'I' that has become individually free he can consciously receive the Being of Christ. In the *Meditation* this occurs by adding the fourth part with its inner culmination—the direct call to Christ—to Parts I–III:★

O Light Divine,
O sun of Christ!
Warm Thou
Our Hearts
Enlighten Thou
Our Heads . . .

★ The *Meditation* must be regarded here in the sequence and rhythm in which Rudolf Steiner read it for the first time at the Christmas Conference, on 25 December 1923.

We call on Christ in these words to enter into our 'I', which in free self-offering strives towards Him, so that we may be led not only by our 'I', but by Christ Himself:

> That good may become
> What from our Hearts we would found
> And from our Heads direct
> With single purpose.*

We have already spoken above of these aims to which Christ, having united Himself with our 'I', will lead us. Rudolf Steiner refers to these aims as the sublime religion of the Gods in the spiritual world, as the divine Ideal of Man—of man who has evolved to the fullness of his cosmic existence and who has awakened in himself the three higher spiritual members of his nature: Spirit Self, Life Spirit and Spirit Man.

And this lofty Ideal of world development, the goal of all Earth evolution, has become attainable for us only through the Mystery of Golgotha, in which the great Archetype of divine Man became visible to all humanity.[46] And in the subsequent union of Christ with the Earth there was finally given the possibility of realizing this Ideal. For Christ who alone of all the Gods of the cosmos descended from the macrocosm into microcosmic existence, and knew death there and overcame it—only He can lead us to a conscious reascent into the macrocosm. It is He alone who can guide us to the realization of the goals of the divine Hierarchies, to the development in us of the higher trinity of our being.

Only by actively receiving the Christ into ourselves in a gesture of offering, in the fourth part of the *Meditation*, is it possible to unite with the 'microcosmic' sections of the first three parts the corresponding 'macrocosmic' sections, each of which consists of seven lines (lines 14–20 of Parts I–III) and begins with the word 'For' (*Denn*).

Looking at these sections now in reverse order, we see that the last one (Section 2 of Part III) awakens us in our first macrocosmic principle carried by the Third Hierarchy—the principle of Spirit Self, which is a seed in us from the sphere of the Holy Spirit. The second section of Part II awakens us in our second macrocosmic principle, borne by the Second Hierarchy—our Life Spirit, which is a reflection of the divine sphere of the Son. And finally, the second section of Part I awakens our highest cosmic principle, borne by the First Hierarchy—Spirit Man, the true Son of God in us, a scion of the highest sphere of the Father.[47]

---

* Translator's note: This last line—in German, *Zielvoll führen wollen*—could be rendered in prose as, 'direct with full consciousness of the *aims*'.

Thus the Christ-impulse that is spoken of in the fourth part leads us step by step into the great macrocosmic existence of the Spirit, the Son and the Father. And this is the great cosmic proclamation of Truth which:

The Elemental Spirits hear...
in East and West and North and South:
May human beings hear it!

In this sense the *Foundation Stone Meditation* is the earthly-cosmic image of sevenfold[48] man[49] *who is permeated through and through with Christ*—of man who proceeds from cosmic past to cosmic future and who on the path in the cosmic present can find the Christ!

ANTHROPOSOPHY:
THE PROCLAMATION
OF WORLD PENTECOST

7. The Michael Age and the New Grail Event

From our considerations of the path of Rudolf Steiner's life we were able to see how exceptionally significant it is for us to penetrate into the spiritual foundations of this great human life. It is impossible to walk the anthroposophical path in the right way without seeing in the life of its founder that guiding thread which alone can help us fulfil the aims and tasks of spiritual science. For the picture of *this* life is itself the most convincing evidence that it is possible today in the twentieth century, in the century of technology and materialism, to tread the new Christian path of initiation in full accord with its cosmic Archetype. This, indeed, is truly possible in our time! In this, humanity has been given an example of exceptional power and, in truth, one of invaluable significance.

Rudolf Steiner mentions repeatedly in his lectures that every new element that serves the rightful progress of humanity is brought into the world through specific individuals. And only after this new element has been completely experienced and carried out by and become a part of *one* individual, can it then be incorporated by the Hierarchies into the general life of all humanity, as a new potential won for its further development and progression towards perfection.

This is governed by a strict cosmic law. What the Gods create and prepare for the good of mankind can be brought into general human life only through the sacrificial deed of a single human individuality who opens himself to divine inspiration, or expressed more traditionally, to 'the grace of God'.

As an example of this bringing of new spiritual impulses into earthly development, we can look to the life of Buddha. While characterizing this, Rudolf Steiner indicated that the great teaching of compassion and love which is expressed in the 'Eightfold Path' appeared on the Earth *for the first time* through the great founder of Buddhism, and he particularly emphasizes that before Buddha no one on Earth would have been able to tread this path. By realizing it, by living it for the first time in his own life, however, Gautama Buddha made the Eightfold Path the absolute property of all humanity.[1] Since that time thousands upon thousands have been able to tread this path, thus bringing humanity another step forward in its evolution.

However, in so far as the life of the universe is permeated by cosmic laws which are manifest at all levels of existence, one would also be justified in

303

looking at the course of Rudolf Steiner's life from this point of view. And we can say: in this life the Christian-Rosicrucian path of initiation in its modern form was fully realized by a human individuality for the first time in the age of the consciousness soul, and through this the possibility was given to all humanity whereby *every* individual human being, out of his own free will, can henceforth follow this path.

We can also try now to view the significance of this fact in its historical aspect. In order to do this, we must look at the present forms of spiritual life within humanity, of which the three principal ones are: the ecclesiastic-exoteric form, represented today by many different churches; the Masonic form, living in traditions and symbols that are today hardly understood at all; and thirdly, all the shades of Eastern esotericism founded on fading atavistic faculties that were characteristic of the soul in long-past epochs of human development. If we look at these three streams in the course of their historical development, we see that the church arises in the Graeco-Roman cultural epoch and is founded on the forces of the intellectual or mind soul; that Freemasonry originates in the Egypto-Chaldean epoch, the age of the sentient soul; and lastly, that Eastern occultism stems from even more ancient historical epochs, when forces were at work in humanity having still less affinity with the present time.

The fundamental question of our time, upon whose answer depends the future that has been preordained for humanity by the divine-spiritual Hierarchies, is: Will it be possible in contemporary humanity for a spiritual life to arise which is appropriate to our present cycle of development?

In other words: Will it be possible to inaugurate a new spiritual life within humanity arising completely out of the consciousness soul—that is, from that member of the human being in which for the first time in human evolution there arises the self-aware individual human 'I', which is then capable of effecting a transition from the consciousness soul to Spirit Self, from the physical world to the spiritual?

Two dangers, however, threaten humanity on this path. On the one hand Ahriman seeks to chain human thinking to the material world so as to prevent any spirituality from entering the consciousness soul, and thus hold the human 'I' emerging within it eternally captive in matter.

Even if the soul does not wish to remain the prisoner of its lower inclinations and instincts, there is another temptation awaiting it. For the forces of Ahriman in our time can seem so powerful and terrifying and human thinking so enmeshed in matter that the soul either begins to despair of ever being able to spiritualize itself, or considers the task too difficult. It may then seem that the only way out is to turn to the traditional forms of spirituality—to the church, Freemasonry, or Eastern esotericism. But waiting here for the soul that refuses to participate consciously in the battle of Michael with the Dragon is Lucifer, who is ever lurking there where an attempt is made to preserve unchanged in later epochs the forms of spiritual life that were appropriate only in the past.[2]

These are the two fundamental dangers threatening the human soul today. And if in all its seriousness we bear this in mind in the right way, we will be better able to understand what it was that Rudolf Steiner accomplished for humanity. He opened the way, through the redemption of thinking, for the spiritualizing of the consciousness soul, and showed how the now free human 'I' by offering itself to the Christ-impulse can bring about the transition to Spirit Self and eventually to the still higher members of the being of man. It was necessary, however, if this historical transition was to become the possession of all humanity, that it be realized initially by one human being acting completely out of the present stage of development—acting, that is, not out of the forces of the etheric or the astral body, nor out of the forces of the sentient or the intellectual souls, but out of the purest forces of the individual 'I' rooted in the consciousness soul.

Christ wishes today to enter for the first time since the Mystery of Golgotha directly into the conscious human 'I', into the free 'I' as it has developed only since the fifteenth century, the beginning of the epoch of the consciousness soul. What occurred as it were naturally during the epoch of the intellectual soul—as with St Paul on the road to Damascus[3]— has today, in the epoch of the consciousness soul, been accomplished consciously and freely by one human being. And an archetype was thereby given by which every human being today can find the Christ in his 'I'.

Thus, by the great deed of his life, Rudolf Steiner opened for all humanity the new *conscious* path to Christ—the path of the essential principle of the free 'I'. But it also follows from this that everything we have to do with in the anthroposophical movement and the Anthroposophical Society is something *principally new*, which could not have appeared in any preceding epoch. It is the creative work of completely new forces of consciousness that have been won in our epoch for all human development and illumined by a new light, by the 'Day-radiant Light' (IV, 6) that has shone in the world since the beginning of the 'Age of Light' and the epoch of the Sun Spirit, the Archangel Michael. It is particularly important for anthroposophists to be aware of precisely *this* nature of modern spiritual science. 'Behold, I make all things new.'[4] These words, in our epoch, are particularly applicable to Anthroposophy, for we must work today to meet the future out of completely new forces of consciousness.

This unique position of Anthroposophy in relation to all other occult streams is made evident above all by the fundamental, principal difference between the New Mysteries—founded by Rudolf Steiner at the Christmas

Conference of 1923–24 and in the months that followed this—and the old. As Rudolf Steiner has said, this difference was already indicated in the fifteenth to sixteenth centuries by the Archangel Michael in his lofty supersensible School: 'Then they too [in the supersensible School] pointed to the future, to what was to become the new life of the Mysteries. They pointed to all that was to come, though not in the way of the old Mysteries, which had come to human beings who did not yet possess the Intelligence on Earth and who, accordingly, still had a dreamlike experience of supersensible worlds. They pointed to that new life of the Mysteries which we must now begin to understand in the realm of Anthroposophy, and which is absolutely compatible with the full intelligence of man—the clear, light-filled intelligence.'[5]

It is precisely this fundamental difference between the New and the old Mysteries that shows us how, in a certain sense, nothing that comes from the past can be of real service or help to us in the present. For the soul forces lying at the basis of the New Mysteries today did not yet exist in the past development of humanity. Every anthroposophist can, of course, to a certain extent rightly say to himself: 'I was once connected with this or that Mystery tradition', and this is the foundation upon which rests the karma of *every* human being who comes to Anthroposophy today out of the deepest impulses of his soul. Nevertheless, although without this meeting with the Mysteries in the past we would not be able today to find the way to Anthroposophy, this wisdom of the past that is preserved in our sub-conscious—from no matter how significant a series of past incarnations—*cannot* protect us from mistakes and errors in the present. For the only thing that can help us to avoid these mistakes is what we attain in *this life* out of 'clear, light-filled intelligence' on the path to new initiation.

If in the right way we can approach this fundamental task of the *present*, we shall then also be able to lay a foundation for the 'rightful' reunion of our past with our future; for we are not called upon today to reinstate old impulses but, in self-offering, to create new ones. And in this sense we will always find before our inner gaze, like a guiding star, the path of Rudolf Steiner's life—our Teacher and the greatest pupil of Christ Jesus—in all its crystal clarity, its inner beauty and tragic greatness.

Let us turn once more to the cosmic law governing the entry of spiritual impulses into the Earth-sphere, of which we spoke at the beginning of this chapter. A particularly important aspect of this is characterized by Rudolf Steiner—again in the example of the last Bodhisattva to become a Buddha. 'He [the Bodhisattva] thus placed before humanity that *human form* which human beings must strive to resemble, so that they too *out of themselves* find the teaching of the Eightfold Path, just as the Bodhisattva found it out of

306

himself while under the Bodhi-tree.'[6] From these words we see that the creation of such a 'human form' can ever after serve as an archetype for all humanity only when it conforms to this fundamental law whereby something attained by one individuality can become the possession of all human development. If we apply this law to Rudolf Steiner's life, the question arises: in what sense are we to understand that during the course of his life Rudolf Steiner created that 'human form' towards which we may strive, and which is the archetype of something completely new?

In order to answer this question, we must again call to mind the spiritual foundations of the path of Rudolf Steiner's life, beginning with his emergence as a Teacher of occultism at the beginning of our century.

In Chapter 3 we have already mentioned in some detail how the three seven-year periods of Rudolf Steiner's activity as a Teacher were connected with those periods in the development of each individual human being during which he is successively overshone by the light of his higher spiritual members: from the age of 42 to 49 by the activity of Spirit Self; from 49 to 56 by Life Spirit; and from 56 to 63 by Spirit Man. These higher spiritual members, which overshine ordinary human beings only in their subconsciousness, are fully awake in an initiate and, connected as they are with certain cosmic realms, become higher organs for the perception of these realms. In Rudolf Steiner's case this development was also connected with something else.

We saw that in the first period—the period of Spirit Self—the dominant influence was that of the Bodhisattva Being and extended into his astral body. The Bodhisattva himself, however, who is already passing through a cosmic evolution, is in essence not of a human but rather of an angelic nature. In the period of Life Spirit, it was the celestial Being of the Nathan Soul, which is archangelic in nature, that became increasingly dominant. This worked down into the etheric body of Rudolf Steiner (see Chapter 3).

And during the period of Spirit Man, the influence of Michael, the guiding Time Spirit, came particularly powerfully to the fore and worked in Rudolf Steiner right down to his physical body. This does not of course mean that Michael was not active in him *before* this, for the whole of Rudolf Steiner's spiritual path was founded on a constant connection with the sphere of Michael. The possibility, however, of working as far as the *physical body* of Rudolf Steiner was opened to Michael only at the beginning of this last complete seven-year span of Rudolf Steiner's life on Earth, and only this conscious experience of the deepest connection with the Being of Michael could give him the inner forces necessary to fulfil the offering up of his own physical body at the Christmas Conference.

From that moment onwards the second revelation of Michael became a reality in the life of Rudolf Steiner, so that we can say: his physical body had become Word. This Mystery of the path of his life is connected with the arising of what we mentioned above as that 'human form' which he was to 'place before' men and towards which 'they were to aspire'.

In a lecture in Dornach on 3 August 1924, Rudolf Steiner himself points to this secret of the 'new human form', and says there: 'But Michael's impulses are strong and powerful. Taking their start from the spiritual, they work through man's entire nature. *They work into the spiritual, thence into the soul-nature, and thence into the bodily nature of man..*'[7] For in the Michael-impulse '. . . the spiritual works even into the physical organism.' And he follows this thought through many pages: 'Now [the Michaelic] Intelligence is on the Earth, now it strikes far deeper, it strikes down even into the earthly element of man. *For the first time, the spiritual is preparing to become a race-creating force.* The time will come when one will no longer be able to say: the man looks as if he belonged to this or that country—he is a Turk or an Arab, an Englishman, a Russian or a German—but one will have to say what will amount to this: "In a former life on Earth this man felt impelled to turn towards the spirit in the sense of Michael." Thus, that which is influenced by Michael will appear as an immediate, physically creative, physically formative power.' 'The Michael impulses show themselves as race-creating forces.'

These race-forming impulses had already been prepared by Michael since his former period of rulership but, in order that they could find a way into the Earth-sphere, into humanity, so as to develop there further and gradually come to realization, they had first—in accord with the laws given to our evolution by the guiding spiritual powers—to be realized *once*, even if by only *one* human being, and, moreover, entirely out of his own inner forces. This then is like a portal or gateway through which the spiritual impulses can enter into the Earth-sphere and become there the possession of *all* humanity.

Thus did Buddha at a certain time open the gates for the spiritual impulse of the Eightfold Path. And thus did Aristotle bring into the development of all mankind the faculty of logical thinking.[8] And a *human* gateway had now to be established, through which the 'race-forming impulse' of Michael could reach those human souls who through their karma are connected in one way or another with the Michael Stream.

By taking upon himself at the Christmas Conference the karma of the Anthroposophical Society and the anthroposophical movement and by uniting these two thereby into a single whole, Rudolf Steiner gave the Michaelic impulses supersensibly guiding the anthroposophical movement the possibility of flowing directly into the Earth-sphere and into the Anthroposophical Society active within it. A new stream of esotericism thus flowed into the Society, expressed above all in the founding of the First Class of the esoteric School of Michael, as a direct continuation of the fundamental impulse of the Christmas Conference. The fact that Rudolf Steiner took upon himself the karma of the Society had the spiritual consequence that 'the race-forming impulse of Michael' could now work in the members of the Anthroposophical Society, even into their physical bodies. And the beginnings were thus established for a Michael-community on the Earth. To speak of such a community in an *earthly* sense was not possible before the Christmas Conference, for the Michael-forces worked in the anthroposophical movement until that time only super-sensibly.

In this way, what was being prepared in the supersensible worlds from the sixteenth century onwards in the Michael School, and in the great imaginative cultus at the beginning of the nineteenth century, was able finally to 'incarnate' on the Earth and become, in the newly founded General Anthroposophical Society, historical *fact*. Since the Christmas Conference, therefore, we have *on the physical plane* a Michael-community that is radically different from all other communities of the past or present. It is a community that is united not only as a spiritual but as a spiritual-*physical* whole, which will develop more and more in the future to the point of outwardly perceptible 'racial' features. With the Christmas Conference the gates have indeed opened for *the emergence of a 'Michaelic race' in the world*. Herein also lies the reason why Rudolf Steiner did not begin to speak of these 'race-forming impulses' of Michael until *after* the Christmas Conference, for until then they had not worked directly into the sphere of the Earth.

From this standpoint we can now look again at the history of the gradual arising of the anthroposophical-Michaelic impulse within humanity, as it unfolded during the course of three seven-year periods from the founding of the German Section of the Theosophical Society in 1902 to a completion and culmination in 1923–24 at the Christmas Conference.

However, as we have already seen in the first chapters of this book, Rudolf Steiner's own path of initiation was inseparably entwined with the development of this impulse. This begins with his first seven-year Sun period (1882) and continued until 1899, when in his personal meeting with the Christ he reached the culmination of the Christian-Rosicrucian path of initiation, whose goal we can best express in the words: 'Not I, but Christ in me'. In his spiritual development during these three seven-year Sun periods, Rudolf Steiner was able so to develop and purify the forces of his individual 'I' that at the end of this time it was within his strength to sacrifice these forces to the central Being of our Cosmos, to the Christ Being. Rudolf Steiner referred so often to these Mystery-words in his lectures, because behind them lay his own experience—the greatest spiritual event of his life.

But what was the outcome, esoterically, of this event? It was that Rudolf Steiner's 'I' became the gateway through which not only the will of an individual human being, but the will and wisdom of the divine-spiritual cosmos itself, could now begin to flow into the sphere of man. And this sacrifice was then the point of entry into the earthly world for the anthroposophical-Michaelic impulse.

In the time following one can already discern three basic periods of realization or 'incarnation' of this anthroposophical-Michaelic impulse. The first period (from 1902 to 1909) was primarily concerned with the incarnation of Anthroposophy into the astral element, for it was during this time that the foundations were worked through in a conceptual form for a new science of the spirit. This is the period of Anthroposophy's genesis, in which it is grasped completely individually from person to person.

In the second period (from 1910 to 1916) it reaches the etheric element. The result of this is that it ceases to be only the private affair of the individual and incarnates now also in social, in joint activities.[9] For it is the etheric element that unites people with one another—as is indicated too in the lines relating to the human etheric body in the microcosmic Our Father. Thus there arise from this impulse the Mystery Dramas, eurythmy and the Goetheanum.

The third period (from 1917 to 1923) sees the beginning of Anthroposophy's gradual incarnation into the physical realm. From this there arise the 'daughter-movements'—the threefold social order, education, medicine, etc.—through which the anthroposophical-Michaelic impulse can now work directly into earthly culture and permeate all areas of human life.

Thus we see how the anthroposophical-Michaelic impulse descends by way of the 'I' of Rudolf Steiner from the lofty Sun-sphere to the Earth, passing in the process through three stages of incarnation. And just as in the development of each human being the individual 'I' was able to light up and shine out only through contact with the physical plane, so too the esoteric centre of the Being of Anthroposophy, its 'I', could enter and show itself fully in earthly development only when the anthroposophical-Michaelic impulse had united itself completely with the earthly world at the Christmas Conference—when, that is, the anthroposophical movement and the Anthroposophical Society became a unified whole. At that moment, in the twenty-first year of the movement's life (from 1902 to 1923) the *group-'I'* of the new community of Michaelites was truly *born*. This was its unifying spiritual foundation, working as a completely new 'race-forming' principle, even into the physical body of every anthroposophist.

This birth in the Earth-sphere of the new group-'I' of the Michaelites is one of the most profound Mysteries of the Christmas Conference. And we should ask what occult reality lies behind the words: 'A new race will arise on Earth.' It can only mean that in an occult sense there exists in the supersensible world a centre whose forces work even into the earthly sphere. In other words, the emergence of a new race *on the physical plane* presupposes, of necessity, a group-'I'. This is its very centre, its forming, organizing and unifying principle from which the race-forming forces can work into the physical nature of each individual being and thus constitute the 'body' of the race. For it is in the *harmony* of the race-forming features in the separate individuals that the group-'I' which unites them comes to physical expression. This, according to spiritual science, can only be a *Being* of the spiritual world.

If we now ask which *Being* are we to connect with what has been called here the group-'I' of the Michael community, then we must answer: this birth in the Earth-sphere during the Christmas Conference of the new group-'I', as the supersensible foundation of the Community of Michaelites, is the result of the Michael-forces penetrating directly into this sphere. As Rudolf Steiner indicated very definitely, this came to expression in the founding of the First Class of the esoteric School, which stands under the direct guidance of Michael. Thus we can say with conviction that *Michael himself, the guiding Spirit of our time, works today as the group-'I' of the Michael-community, which was born on the Earth during the Christmas Conference.*

In this spiritual deed of Michael, which was carried out on the Earth by his greatest pupil, is hidden the secret of the new Michael Mysteries—the secret that is connected with the future emergence of a new race of Michaelites.*

From many of Rudolf Steiner's statements we know that through the Mystery of Golgotha the Christ Being gave human development on the Earth its true meaning, and there were brought before humanity again in new form those sublime goals which had once stood before the Gods as they created man. Without the intervention of the Christ Being these aims

* To avoid possible misunderstandings, it is necessary to note that what is meant here in the words 'race' or 'race-forming principle' is a purely occult fact, namely, that today for the first time on the physical plane a community is arising which has as its group-'I' not an Archangel working into the human etheric body but a Being of the Hierarchy of the Archai working into the human *physical* body. One can also say that the word 'race' signifies here such a strong and conscious receiving of a spiritual impulse into the human 'I' that this is then able to work down through all the sheaths as far as the physical body, whose spiritualization can now begin. Thus we are dealing here with a completely new concept of 'race' which has nothing analogous with the past. It would be a gross mistake to confuse this esoteric concept of race with the usual exoteric one.

would have remained eternally unattainable for man, due to his having succumbed to the forces of Lucifer during the Lemurian epoch, and to those of Ahriman during the Atlantean.

In this sense everything which was accomplished on the Earth by Christ Jesus is the *full* and intrinsic realization of the great cosmic aims of the Gods which through the Mystery of Golgotha became visible once more for all humanity. Now, however, they stand before us in a still more sublime form as the divine Ideal of all future evolution.

Proceeding from this we can say: to the degree that the path of Rudolf Steiner's life was able to reflect microcosmically the great macrocosmic path of Christ Jesus, so was he able to receive into himself the 'World-Being's Light' (III, 8), the Light of the Holy Spirit showing thus the beginning of the free and conscious realization of 'the eternal aims of Gods' (III, 7). This realization, however, is a true imitation of Christ in a form appropriate to our time, as it has been given us in the modern Christian-Rosicrucian path of initiation. And 'the World-Being's Light', of 'the eternal aims of Gods' that were at work in Rudolf Steiner's life, reached its culmination in the Christmas Conference. For there this Light of the higher worlds was able for the first time in the age of the consciousness soul, the age of human freedom, to pour itself through the portal of the human 'I' into the realm of the Earth, into the consciousness of individual human beings who wish, in freedom, to follow the impulses of the spiritual world (III, 7–11):

> Where the eternal aims of Gods
> World-Being's Light
> *On thine own I*
> Bestow
> *For thy free Willing.*

And this never-fading Light of the Christmas Conference in which the 'eternal aims of Gods' are working, which has poured itself out for more than half a century into mankind, so that since that time it can live in the consciousness of every individual human 'I' in free will—this Light is present and active among us.

A true knowledge of the connection of Rudolf Steiner's life with the essence of the Christmas Conference can shed light for us on the future development of the anthroposophical-Michaelic impulse in the world, in all its immeasurable significance for humanity and, above all, for those souls who by destiny are connected with this spiritual stream. For going deeply into the essence of the path of Rudolf Steiner's life, into this most significant Mystery of the twentieth century, leads us step by step not only into the secrets of the past and present, but also of the future. In this sense, in the spirit of the fundamental anthroposophical *Meditation*, we can speak of the *eternal aspect* of Rudolf Steiner's life. The *Foundation Stone Meditation* leads us from 'recollection' to 'mindfulness' to 'vision'—to vision of that all-encompassing Spirit of the Cosmos who reveals Himself to us in the 'World-Being's Light' and bestows on us a true knowledge of the 'eternal aims of Gods'. If we take the fundamental impulse of the Christmas Conference into our hearts and souls we can take part in realizing these aims; and an understanding of the path of Rudolf Steiner's life can be of decisive help in this.

We have already seen how deep is the Christian Mystery behind this life, and we have been able to draw a little closer to it only by recognizing Rudolf Steiner's life path as one of imitation of Christ Jesus, in whom is to be found the archetype of all initiation that wishes to proceed from the rightful forces of the times. For just as in the archetypal plant (*Urpflanze*) is contained the intrinsic idea of all plants, each of which is the more perfect the more completely it reflects the fundamental idea of its archetypal form, so too was it the guiding thought in our survey of Rudolf Steiner's life that the more closely the life of the Christian initiate resembles the macro-cosmic path of Christ Jesus, the heavenly archetype of every true spiritual path, the higher does he stand.

Only by looking at it in this way were we able to come closer to the secrets that are connected with the founding and the burning of the First Goetheanum, and also with the Christmas Conference. We were then able also to touch upon the spiritual significance of Rudolf Steiner's illness and his tragic passing. The secret of his death has for more than half a century stood before every anthroposophist as a tormenting problem demanding a solution.

Looking at it in this way also enabled us to experience the path of Rudolf Steiner's life as a process of unbroken spiritual ascent, and to recognize the Christmas Conference as its indisputable culmination. For the supersensible could now flow directly into the earthly forms of the Society, which themselves took on thereby an occult-esoteric nature. One can therefore say: during the Christmas Conference the Society as a unified organism was led to the threshold of the spiritual world, and from that moment onwards the supersensible element entered directly into the process of its further development.

This was possible only by virtue of Rudolf Steiner uniting his own destiny at the Christmas Conference with the destiny of the Society, so that from that time onwards the spiritual path of the Teacher became inseparable from that of his individual pupils. For the esoteric stream of the anthroposophical movement—whose representative was Rudolf Steiner—

313

was united with the Anthroposophical Society, that is, with the Society of *pupils* which was now required to be the bearer and instrument of the anthroposophical movement. And the paths thus united of the Teacher and his pupils became a spiritual unity whose macrocosmic archetype is to be found in the relation of Christ Jesus to his pupil-Apostles. In other words: we have every reason to look for *the archetype of the relation of Rudolf Steiner to the Anthroposophical Society—which means, of Rudolf Steiner to his pupils after the Christmas Conference—in that of Christ Jesus to his Apostles.*

Only a true understanding of what once took place in the time from the night in the Garden of Gethsemane to the Mystery of Pentecost, as a macrocosmic process between Christ Jesus and His Apostles, can give us the clue to the history of the Anthroposophical Society in the past, the present and the future. For the Anthroposophical Society, having itself become at the Christmas Conference an *esoteric* society, must now seek knowledge of its future laws where for all future time is to be found the cosmic archetype of that community which is based on the esoteric principle. Thus we must now immerse ourselves in that great cosmic-human drama of the history of the relation of Christ Jesus and His Apostles, as this is related in *The Fifth Gospel*. And what we are shown thereby is *the archetype of the relation of Teacher and pupil in the new initiation.*

In Chapter 3 we spoke of how the macrocosmic Christ Being, having entered with his 'I' into the three bodily sheaths of Jesus of Nazareth, gradually united Himself with them after the Baptism in the Jordan and of how, in sacrifice, He relinquished his own cosmic forces, in the course of three years descending from Son of God to Son of Man. This deeply tragic process of God becoming man was also in a certain sense to be experienced by the Apostles, by those closest to Christ Jesus. But what for the Christ was a 'descent' was for the Apostles an ascent, for the sacrifices made by the Christ Being in entering ever more deeply into the sheaths of Jesus awoke forces in the Apostles which brought them to ever higher states of consciousness. Thus by experiencing the astral sacrifice of Christ, the Apostles were able to lift their consciousness into the astral plane and, by virtue of His etheric sacrifice, to extend it even into the sphere of Devachan.[10] This means that the first two stages of Christ Jesus' path of sacrifice could be experienced *consciously* by His disciples. They were still able here *in full consciousness* to accompany their Teacher. At the Last Supper, however, and at the event in the Garden of Gethsemane, this was no longer the case.

During the Last Supper, Christ spoke to His disciples of the nature of His last and greatest sacrifice—of His union with the physical body of Jesus of Nazareth,[11] of death at Golgotha and of the overcoming of death. In these prophetic words Christ Jesus strove to prepare His disciples for the future so that they should be able to follow Him consciously—be able, that is, to accompany Him spiritually to the very end of the way of the Cross. For the disciples this meant having to raise themselves in their spiritual consciousness above the Devachan sphere.[12] As the four earthly Gospels and especially the celestial Fifth Gospel bear witness, however, the forces of their consciousness could not extend to these heights, and they sank into 'sleep' ... And since then the call of Christ has sounded through the centuries: 'What, could ye not watch with me one hour? Watch and pray that ye enter not into temptation: the spirit indeed is willing, but the flesh is weak.'[13] Three times Christ calls to the Apostles, and three times they sink into sleep. They were not able to maintain that state of consciousness which could have opened to them the deepest understanding of the Christ Being and the cosmic significance of the Mystery of Golgotha.

In the ninth lecture of *The Gospel of St Mark*, Rudolf Steiner says concerning this: 'It is clearly indicated in the Gospel that Christ Jesus asks for this degree of understanding from them ... What could then have happened? Two things could have happened. The first would have been that the chosen disciples could have accompanied Christ Jesus through everything that was then accomplished as the Mystery of Golgotha, *that the bond between the disciples and Christ could have remained intact even up to the Mystery of Golgotha*. That is one thing which could have happened.'[14] And he continues: 'We can see particularly clearly from the Gospel of St Mark, however, that it was not this but the other possibility which then actually occurred.' One can sense from these words that the whole development of humanity after Christ would have run its course differently had not the connection of Christ with His closest disciples been severed. But world karma was hovering over this event. It could have been that the Apostles did not fall asleep, and yet they *had* to fall asleep. For in His last and greatest sacrifice, Christ Jesus had to stand alone ... He knew this, yet nevertheless the Apostles' falling asleep caused him immeasurable pain.

Rudolf Steiner describes the experience of Christ Jesus in the Garden of Gethsemane in the following way: 'Why did Christ become sorrowful? He did not tremble at the prospect of the Cross. That goes without saying. He trembled at the question: "Will those whom I have brought with me here be able to bear this moment in which is to be decided whether it is their will to go with me in soul, to experience everything with me even to the Cross?" What hung in the balance, then, was the question: would their state of consciousness remain so awake as to be able to experience everything with Christ even to the Cross? This is the "cup" that approaches Him. And He leaves them alone so that they can remain "awake", that is, in a condition of consciousness in which they can experience with Him what He is to experience. Then He goes and prays, "Father, let this cup pass from me. Nevertheless not my will but thine be done." This means: Let me not experience that I stand absolutely alone as Son of Man, but that the others accompany me. And He returns, and they are asleep. They have not been able to maintain that state of consciousness. And He tries a second time, and again they have not maintained it. And He tries yet again, and again they sleep. Then it became plain to Him that He now stood alone, that they could not participate in that which led to the Cross. The cup had not passed from Him! He was destined to fulfil the deed alone and in loneliness of soul. The world did indeed receive the Mystery of Golgotha, but at the time when it took place had as yet no understanding for it. Even the most select, most highly chosen had not the strength to go so far.'[15]

Thus the first possibility of a true *understanding* of the Mystery of Golgotha was not realized. And since that time the experience of 'cosmic loneliness' has been an inseparable part of the new initiation.

The Apostles fell into sleep. And this sleep, as *The Fifth Gospel* bears testimony, became deeper and deeper—neither the Mystery of Golgotha, nor the Resurrection after three days, nor the teachings of the Risen One during the following 40 days—none of this was experienced by the disciples in full consciousness. Their 'sleep' was as though filled with wondrous dreams.[16] But their situation became particularly tragic after the Ascension, when they felt themselves *forsaken* by Christ. And in their pain they now experienced in an infinitely weaker and human form what Christ had experienced when left by them in utter loneliness in the Garden of Gethsemane. During the ten days between Ascension and Pentecost they themselves felt the suffering of Christ in Gethsemane. Thus does world karma hold sway. In Christiania (Oslo), on 17 May 1923, Rudolf Steiner says the following about this: 'And now, having experienced this [the Ascension], there came over the disciples of Christ a great sorrow, a sorrow that is beyond comparison with any that can be found on the Earth ... During the time that is indicated to us in the ten days after the Ascension, the disciples of Christ suffered immeasurably because the countenance of Christ had vanished from among them. And from this pain, from this infinite sadness, there arose that which we call the secret of Whitsun. The disciples of Christ, having lost the vision of Him from their outer, instinctive clairvoyance, found Him again within, in the feeling, *in the experience of sorrow and pain.*'[17] 'And the disciples of Christ, ten days after they had lost the outer countenance of Christ, now said: "We have seen the Mystery of Golgotha. And this gives us the strength to experience once again our immortal being." This was expressed symbolically in the tongues of fire.'

According to *The Fifth Gospel*, these were the fundamental experiences of the Apostles in the time from the events in the Garden of Gethsemane to the day of Pentecost. The culmination of these experiences was the inner enlightenment of Whitsun-day: from the greatest pain and deepest suffering there arose the *World Festival of Knowledge*. In the same lecture Rudolf Steiner speaks of these experiences of the Apostles which led to the World Whitsun, to the search for knowledge on the anthroposophical path of the spirit: 'All true, all great understanding is born of pain and sorrow. If one seeks to follow the path into higher worlds by those means of knowledge that are described in the anthroposophical science of the spirit, one can only reach one's goal through an experience of pain. Without suffering, without suffering a great deal and having thereby become free from that element in pain which drags one down, one cannot come to know and understand the spiritual world.' These words, spoken by Rudolf Steiner from experience of modern initiation, in order to shed light on the inner condition of the disciples between Ascension and the day of Pentecost, enable us to see in the experience of pain a definite stage in the spiritual path. And we find this stage likewise reflected in the history of the Anthroposophical Society as a truly esoteric community.

If now we take the events related in *The Fifth Gospel* as cosmic archetypes, and in the sense of Rudolf Steiner's words quoted above try to understand the laws governing the development of the modern esoteric community, the following picture emerges.

After the burning of the First Goetheanum, the consciousness of the members was severely dulled. This blow proved too great for most of them even though the main brunt and burden of it rested on the shoulders of Rudolf Steiner. Having let the possibility of saving the 'House of the Word' through wakefulness and inner activity slip by, the Anthroposophical Society was unable to recover from the terrible blow of the fire. The consequence of this was its continuing disintegration, resulting finally in the split in the German Society in 1923. Thus in his opening lecture of the Christmas Conference, Rudolf Steiner pointed to the fact that the ruins of the First Goetheanum, which could be seen through the window, were also a picture of the state of the Anthroposophical Society on the eve of the Conference. The true inner cause of its disintegration, however, was the fact that the members had fallen ever deeper into sleep. And this led finally to Rudolf Steiner finding himself utterly alone, despite his enormous efforts during the whole of 1923 to bring about a change, until—a few weeks before the beginning of the Conference—he made his decision concerning the anthroposophical movement and the Anthroposophical Society. The night of the Garden of Gethsemane had descended upon him: 'Could you not watch one hour with me?'[18] Rudolf Steiner had come to his final decision in complete inner loneliness. Of the weight of this 'prayer concerning the cup' we can have only the faintest intimation.

317

But even the Christmas Conference could not sufficiently halt this process of falling asleep. Understanding for its impulses and, above all, active work to realize them—which means, esoterically, working to balance the shared karma—proved inadequate. And this was the real reason why Rudolf Steiner could not remain longer with the anthroposophists on the physical plane to fulfil his task further for, despite all his stupendous work after the Christmas Conference, the necessary awakening in the Society did not occur.

One cannot say, however, there were no personalities around Rudolf Steiner who were unable to awaken—there were of course such individuals. These were pupils who, like John, stood consciously 'at the Cross', but there were many who, like Peter after his three denials, sank still deeper into sleep. And there were those like Thomas . . . Altogether however, that which right to the last moment Rudolf Steiner hoped for when he spoke of his recovery did not come about. The consequence was the sudden and—for the majority of anthroposophists—completely unexpected passing of Rudolf Steiner from the physical plane. For over everything does world karma hold sway!

Ita Wegman relates in her memoirs concerning the last months of Rudolf Steiner's life on Earth that the decisive turning-point came only in the very last days.

And now, when the Teacher had left his pupils, the anthroposophists had to experience something of the loneliness and forsakenness that Rudolf Steiner had undergone before the Christmas Conference. And for the cosmic archetype of this we can again look to the experience and suffering of the esoteric community of the Apostles after the Ascension, when they too felt themselves bereft of their celestial Teacher.

But for the Apostles something else could occur. The hour came when from their profound loneliness they could say: 'We have seen the Mystery of Golgotha. And this gives us the strength to feel again our immortal being. This is expressed symbolically in the tongues of fire (Pentecost).'[19] Thus, 50 days after the Mystery of Golgotha and ten days after Christ had disappeared from them out of profound pain and sorrow the Apostles were able—through memory ('we have seen . . .') of the Mystery of Golgotha and through taking up its impulses ('This gives us the strength')—to come to an experience of their own 'immortal being': that is, of the Christ-Spirit in them! For the path of Whitsun leads from 'recollection/memory' to 'contemplation/mindfulness' to 'vision'. And if we bear in mind that in occult events time has a completely different significance, then we can say: *from Rudolf Steiner's death up to the present, the Anthroposophical Society has experienced a time corresponding to the period undergone by the Apostles between Ascension and Pentecost.* And it is our task today to work from the best forces of our being and from faithfulness to Anthroposophy towards a greater and greater *understanding* of the Christmas Conference—by nurturing remembrance of it. We must take up its impulses—which, however, is only possible by laying the 'dodecahedral *Stone of Love*' of the New Mysteries in our hearts and souls. For these impulses are the origin and fount of the true, living supersensible forces with whose help alone we, as anthroposophists, can fulfil those lofty tasks which stand before us in the modern world.

If we truly dedicate all our strength to work in this direction, we can hope that from the event of Ascension—which, in the above sense, we can compare with Rudolf Steiner's passing from the physical plane—there will follow a *World Festival of Knowledge*. Rudolf Steiner indicated this in many instances in his Karma lectures. He spoke of how Anthroposophy at the end of this century will attain a *culmination*, and will likewise receive a new impulse for its further development. This, however, will be possible *only if the fundamental anthroposophical impulse, the impulse of the Christmas Conference, is understood, and taken up and implemented.*

In this sense the full experience of the Christmas Conference in all its spiritual reality reveals itself as the true Whitsun for anthroposophists. For Whitsun is the festival of the spiritual knowledge of what once occurred *as fact* on the physical plane but which, at that time, could not yet be comprehended in the depths of its hidden essence.

The Christmas Conference is with us! And we must struggle through to an experience of it, there where it exists as an unshakable reality. It is to this that the three fundamental exercises of the *Foundation Stone Meditation* can lead us. 'Practise Spirit-recollection'—remembrance of the Spirit of the Christmas Conference can bring us to a true understanding of it. 'Practise Spirit-mindfulness/contemplation'—contemplation of the Spirit of the Christmas Conference can help us to take up its impulses, to take them up, above all, as a pledge to the 'good Spirit of the Goetheanum' of which Rudolf Steiner spoke with such feeling on 1 January 1924. 'Practise Spirit-vision'—vision of the Spirit of the Christmas Conference will give us the possibility of realizing its impulses in the world, for it is indeed through this that:

the eternal aims of Gods
World-Being's Light
On thine own I
Bestow
For thy free Willing.

Thus the development of the anthroposophical movement and the

Anthroposophical Society, proceeding from those spiritual wellsprings that are revealed to us in Rudolf Steiner's Karma lectures, call us to unfold the mystery of Whitsun. This will bring the *culmination* of the anthroposophical stream. 'Thus we behold a mighty cosmic and earthly call, addressed to the deep karmic relationship of the members of the Anthroposophical Society. We heard [in the previous lecture] how this call will continue *throughout the twentieth century*, and how the *culmination* will come at the end of this century.'[20]

In order to look more closely at what Rudolf Steiner means by this culmination of anthroposophical development at the end of our century, we must turn once again to those Mysteries that are connected with the anthroposophical-Michaelic impulse.

We have already pointed to the four most fundamental stages in the realizing of this impulse, and were able to compare them with the four members of the human being—the 'I', the astral, and the etheric and physical bodies. The anthroposophical-Michaelic impulse as such stems from the higher worlds, where it was prepared in three supersensible events.

Firstly, the Beings of the First Hierarchy sent the Cosmic Intelligence down into the heads of human beings. Man was thereby changed from a heart-being to a head-being, who brings forth his thoughts independently out of himself.[21] This took place at the beginning of the fifteenth century, when esoteric Rosicrucian schools were founded on the Earth.[22] The second event was the founding in the fifteenth century of the supersensible Michael School, which was active for more than three hundred years. It was also at this time that the members of that School in the Sun-sphere experienced the first event, the descent of the Cosmic Intelligence. Thirdly, the great imaginative cultus was performed at the turning-point of the eighteenth and nineteenth centuries in the supersensible sphere bordering on the Earth.[23] Rudolf Steiner says of this: 'What lives in Anthroposophy was awakened, in the first place, by the Michael School in the fifteenth to sixteenth centuries, and by the cultus which took place supersensibly at the end of the eighteenth and beginning of the nineteenth centuries.'[24]

This anthroposophical-Michaelic impulse, formed in this threefold way, then entered into humanity at the transition from the nineteenth to the twentieth century, so that after a development of 21 years it could finally incarnate on the physical plane at the Christmas Conference. This fact is expressed in the founding of the new Michael Mysteries. We must see in this founding the beginning of the realization of that which Michael had indicated to the souls around him in the supersensible School as being the most important task of his future period of rulership on Earth. This task has already been spoken of frequently in this book, and it is, essentially, that the Cosmic Intelligence that has fallen from Michael is to be returned to him in the souls of those human beings who remain true to his sphere. This can happen today through the impulse of the New Mysteries, which is to permeate all realms of human culture and activity.

Rudolf Steiner points to another important aspect of this task in a lecture in Torquay on 21 August 1924. He speaks here of the two fundamental esoteric streams of western spiritual life, the Arthur stream and the Grail stream. He describes these streams in such a way that their connection with the Michael-event in the world becomes evident and relates in detail how, in the Arthur stream, we are dealing with the influence of the still-Cosmic Intelligence of Michael which inspired the Arthurian knights from heavenly heights. The Grail stream on the other hand points prophetically to a time when the Cosmic Intelligence will be grasped and spiritualized on Earth by human souls permeated with the Christ-impulse. After describing these two streams in this way, as the two polarities that have determined the development of western spiritual life, Rudolf Steiner formulates the greatest problem of the Michael-epoch as follows: 'Study of these two streams brings to light the great problem arising from the historical situation at that time. Men are confronted with the after-effects of the Arthur-principle and the after-effects of the Grail-principle. The problem is: how does Michael—not a human being like Parsifal—but how does Michael himself find the path leading from his Arthurian knights, who strive to ensure his cosmic sovereignty, to his Grail knights, who strive to prepare the way for him into the hearts and minds of men in order that therein he may again take hold of the Intelligence? And now the greatest problem of our age takes shape: how shall the Michael rulership bring about a deeper understanding of Christianity? . . . Between these two castles [Tintagel and the Grail castle] looms the great question: how can Michael become the giver of the impulse which will lead to a deeper understanding of the truths of Christianity?'[25]

In order to prepare souls for the solving of this problem—which at the beginning of the new Michael rulership in 1879 was to stand before all humanity—there arose in the lofty Sun-sphere the supersensible School of Michael in which Michael revealed the inner esoteric nature of these two streams: 'A Michael host gathered together in supersensible realms, receiving in the spiritual world the teachings which had been imparted by the Michael Teachers in the old Alexander time, in the time of the Grail tradition, and which had also taken effect in impulses such as had gone out from Arthur's Round Table.'[26]

From these words by Rudolf Steiner we can see that extraordinarily many and diverse representatives of the most differing streams connected with the cosmic Michael-event took part in the supersensible School. For alongside the Platonists of the School of Chartres, the Aristotelian-Dominicans, and those two groups of souls who had a great longing for Anthroposophy—of whom Rudolf Steiner speaks on many occasions in the Karma lectures—there were also the representatives of the Arthur and Grail streams, as well as those of true Rosicrucianism—for in their spiritual work, according to Rudolf Steiner, all strove to meet Michael in the spiritual world.[27] And to this host of souls, whose common element was a devotion to the Michael-sphere and the shared goal of founding on Earth a new Michaelic Christianity, this great task of Michael was given. These souls were to bring about conditions in the new Michael-epoch whereby *something* could occur in the human soul that would enable not only the human being, Parsifal, but Michael himself to find the path from the Arthur stream to that of the Grail—the path to the mastering of his Intelligence in the hearts and souls of human beings.

This 'something' is the great Grail Imagination which must appear again today amongst humanity in a new Michaelic form—the great Imagination of the Chalice holding the Substance of Christ and radiating divine Light in which appears the Holy Spirit in the form of a dove. We may understand this Imagination in its new Michaelic aspect in the following way.

In the fifth post-Atlantean epoch, humanity is experiencing the development of the consciousness soul. It is in this that the independent human 'I' emerges for the first time in the course of humanity's spiritual development. If today the human being takes up into his 'I', in full freedom, the new wisdom of man—Anthropos-Sophia—then, as is indicated in the last chapter of *Occult Science*, he is able to transform this wisdom into love, which thereby becomes the real substance of soul in which Christ can live and work. But man must also become conscious of the presence of Christ in the soul, and the first step towards this is the strengthening of the consciousness soul, which according to Rudolf Steiner 'occurs when having first permeated itself with intellectuality the consciousness soul allows to flow into this coldest element of the soul the warmth of love.'[28] The next step forward lies in transforming the consciousness soul into the imaginative soul,[29] which is able to give form to the substance of Love that now fills the soul more and more.

It is in the union of the substance of Love with the formative forces of Imagination—through which this substance can be *recognized* by the soul as the Substance of Christ—that the Christ-impulse enters the human consciousness. And forces grow in the human being which thereby give him the possibility of coming gradually to a complete spiritualization of his inner world, to a true redemption of the Michaelic Intelligence. And this redeemed Intelligence begins to ray out from the Holy Chalice as divine, life-giving Light. Its substance is Love, its form, Imagination. And this radiating Intelligence, redeemed by the force of the Christ-impulse in the consciousness soul, can be received again and taken up by Michael. And bearing witness to this is the Holy Spirit that appears in the radiant Light of the Chalice of the Grail and, as related by Emil Bock, has henceforth no longer the old character of Mary, but that of Michael.[30]

Thus can the new Michaelic Grail Imagination arise in the human soul: a Holy Chalice whose substance is Love, whose form is Imagination, and whose Light of Thought which it radiates is redeemed Michaelic Intelligence. It is in this Light of Thought that the new Michaelic Spirit can be found.[31]

In our time Michael should be able to find this Grail experience in its Michaelic form in every human soul, for it is only in this way that he can find the path to 'his Grail-knights who wish to pave the way for him to the hearts and souls of human beings, so that he may there take hold of the Intelligence'. But it is to those human beings on Earth who are called upon to participate in realizing these great aims that first and foremost anthroposophists belong. Thus their task is above all to take into their souls the wisdom of man (Anthropos-Sophia) which is none other than the new 'Knowledge of the Grail' that is entering today into humanity. For in the present epoch of the consciousness soul this 'Knowledge of the Grail' must cease to be hidden and must become manifest. In *Occult Science*—the only book in which, as Rudolf Steiner said, a complete summary of Anthroposophy is given[32]—he writes: 'And as the cultural evolution of mankind absorbs the knowledge of the Grail, in the same measure will the spiritual impulse of the Christ-event become effective; its true significance will be revealed and it will grow from strength to strength. The more external development of Christianity as hitherto will increasingly be supplemented by the inner, esoteric aspect. What man can come to know by dint of Imagination, Inspiration and Intuition of the higher worlds in unison with the Mystery of Christ will permeate people's thinking, their feeling and their willing—ever increasingly as time goes on. The "hidden knowledge of the Grail" will become manifest and grow to be a power in man's life, entering ever more fully into all the ways and walks of man.'[33]

We see from these words how through an anthroposophically-orientated spiritual science the new 'Knowledge of the Grail' can gradually come to life among humanity, whereby the impulse 'that was given through the Christ-event can grow ever stronger in significance'. And this is the answer to the question, 'How can Michael become the giver of the impulse which will lead to a deeper understanding of the truths of Christianity?' At the same time, however, the solution becomes evident 'to the great problem of our time': the problem 'that, through the rulership of Michael, Christianity must be grasped in a deeper sense.'[34]

But this deeper understanding of Christianity, which from our time onwards must also gradually unite with its outer, its exoteric stream, is that path of the new Christian Mysteries in which the 'Grail Mysteries', in the form renewed by the guiding Time Spirit, are to arise again today among humanity.

Emil Bock, in his lecture 'The Battle for the Holy Spirit' given on 26 December 1952, says of this new Grail stream today: 'Now not only the exponents of external history in the ninth century have returned [in our time]—the Grail stream too, in a different form, has returned. This means that it is meant to be here ... Today the Grail Lance, which in earlier times brought sickness—in thinking that had become sick—must be transformed into the spear of Michael, transformed into the thought-forms that are open to us through Anthroposophy.'[35] Two groups of human souls in particular are to work on realizing this task in the twentieth century. Rudolf Steiner characterizes them as belonging to the Platonic stream and the Aristotelian stream.

The Platonists had their last decisive incarnation in the twelfth century. They grouped themselves in the main around the School of Chartres or schools like it, and bore within them impulses connected with the most ancient Mystery-wisdom—a wisdom that had come under the influence of the Cosmic Intelligence of Michael. It is possible to say that the School of Chartres was the last oasis in Europe in which this Cosmic Intelligence was still cultivated in the right way. In this sense it belonged esoterically to the Arthur stream.[36] On the other hand, the School of Chartres was closely related to the early history of Christianity. Taken fully into account here was the fact that the Christ-impulse is present on the Earth and is at work in the hearts and souls of human beings. And its connection with the Grail stream thereby comes to light. Rudolf Steiner says of this special position: 'The School of Chartres is placed in a remarkable fashion midway between the northern Arthur-principle and the Christ-principle of the south.'[37] Thus in the School of Chartres and particularly in its leading representatives, there was achieved as early as the twelfth century, like an anticipation of the Christian Mysteries of the future, a certain harmonious synthesis of the Christ-impulse and the deepest essence of the ancient Mysteries of historical and cosmic Christianity—achieved albeit in a pre-intellectual way.*

---

* We must draw attention here to the more imaginative-pictorial nature of the soul activity of the Platonists in comparison with the more intellectual thought activity of the Aristotelians. This difference is clear when one compares the *Anticlaudian* by Alanus ab Insulis with the works of Thomas Aquinas.

Already then, in the following century, a completely new epoch was to begin. For in the thirteenth century it became necessary to prepare the ushering in of a new intellectual age in which was to be laid the foundation of the future epoch of human freedom. Thus the Platonists were now to hand the guidance of earthly affairs into the care of the Aristotelians, who from late classical antiquity had been connected with the sphere of Michael. Being in the spiritual world at the time of the Mystery of Golgotha, the Aristotelians were able to behold Christ's departure from the Sun. They beheld likewise, in the last century, the descent of the Cosmic Intelligence to Earth, and by virtue of this experience were able to receive into themselves the strongest impulse to cultivate this Intelligence in future on the Earth as the individual power of reason of each human being.

Thus we have before us the transition from pre-intellectual to intellectual development, which in the thirteenth century was brought about by the Aristotelians. The majority of these belonged to the Dominican Order and therefore to that stream of Scholasticism which by cultivating individual human intelligence was to prepare for the approaching age of the consciousness soul which began in 1413. And although the Cosmic Intelligence had already begun to penetrate into the Earth-sphere in the eighth to the ninth centuries in a *spiritual-historical* sense, the transition from the cosmic to the earthly impulses occurred at the turning-point of the twelfth and thirteenth centuries when the spiritual guidance of earthly affairs passed from the Platonists to the Aristotelians.

Rudolf Steiner describes in detail how the initiative was handed over from the one stream to the other. It happened in a lofty supersensible council in which both Platonists from the School of Chartres, who were ascending into the spiritual world, and future Dominican-Scholastics, who were about to descend to the Earth in order to fulfil their mission there in the thirteenth century, took part. 'And now, for the time being, the teachers of Chartres handed over to the Aristotelians the administration and ordering of the affairs of the spiritual life on Earth. Those who were now to descend and were by nature fitted to direct the earthly, *personal* intelligence, took over the guidance of the spiritual life on Earth from the Platonists, who could work truly only when the intelligence was being administered *"from Heaven"* [38]—thus does Rudolf Steiner describe this event, so significant for the historical development of humanity. We must note particularly here that this meeting of the two streams took place at that time *not on the Earth*, but *in the spiritual world*.

This supersensible council had another particularly important consequence. Not only was a decision made that the still completely cosmic working of the Intelligence in the Scholastic stream of the School of Chartres should become purely human (through this transition from the

Platonists to the Aristotelians, in order to attain freedom for humanity in the future epoch of the consciousness soul) but also at this celestial council in the thirteenth century there was 'discussed' the future spiritualization, during the new epoch of Michael's rulership, of the Cosmic Intelligence that had sunk to the Earth.

This spiritualization is vital, for since the beginning of the epoch of the consciousness soul the Cosmic Intelligence of Michael has been exposed to the great danger of falling prey completely to the forces of Ahriman on Earth, which at this time reach a particular intensity. Were this to happen it would become impossible for the human 'I'—which is meant in this epoch to come to full inner freedom by directing the Intelligence towards the spirit—to find its way to the higher 'I' of the human being, to Spirit Self. The consequence of this would be that human development would ever after be deflected onto an ahrimanic course. In order, therefore, to prevent this, it was decided at the supersensible council at the beginning of the thirteenth century to work in a joint effort on the Earth at the end of the twentieth century to spiritualize human intelligence—that is, to return it to Michael. 'For this was the agreement reached in that heavenly conference at the beginning of the thirteenth century, that the Aristotelians and the Platonists were to appear together, working for the ever-growing prosperity of the anthroposophical movement in the twentieth century, in order that at the end of this century, with Platonists and Aristotelians in unison, Anthroposophy may reach a certain *culmination* in earthly civilization.'[39] For the sake of this goal these two streams must *first* unite on the Earth or, as Rudolf Steiner says, 'So that before the end of the twentieth century—if civilization is not to fall into complete decadence—the Platonists of Chartres and the Aristotelians who came later must work together ... It is towards this goal that the anthroposophical movement is directed—to the union within it of these two streams.'[40]

But the final union of these two streams had to be preceded by something else. Already in the thirteenth century when the Aristotelians were active on the Earth principally as Dominicans and the majority of the Platonists were in the spiritual world, they were working constantly together in an earthly-heavenly way: 'Then again, when the Aristotelians were teaching in the Dominican Order, the Platonic souls, who were now once more in the spiritual world, were the inspiring genii.'[41]

This interaction and co-operation of Heaven and Earth at that time proved a counterbalance against the fact that, around the year 1250, not even the highest initiates could penetrate clairvoyantly into the spiritual world. This interaction also served as the source of that particular spiritual atmosphere in which alone the foundation and expansion of the Rosicrucian stream was possible.[42] For 'initiation-wisdom, Rosicrucian wis-

326

dom, in the form in which it then spread, consisted in having a certain clarity concerning these conditions.'[43]

If now we bear in mind that precisely in the Grail stream there was, in the words of Rudolf Steiner, 'an endeavour to take into account the fact that the Intelligence would have to be found in future on the Earth, that it no longer streamed down from Heaven',[44] then we can feel with what intensity the Grail-principle was at work in the depths of the souls of the Dominican Scholastics. Nevertheless, in accordance with the will of world karma, the Scholastics could not yet find *direct* access to the esoteric Grail stream,[45] for at this time they had to work more exoterically and completely in the open. Thus the question that so concerned later Scholasticism reached its full height at the death of Thomas Aquinas:[46] How can Christ enter human thinking, enter the Michaelic Cosmic Intelligence that has fallen to the Original Sin of the Earth? In essence, however, this was Parsifal's question in its Michaelic aspect: how can Michael find the way from the Arthur stream to the new Grail stream (see pages 321–22). How can he once again attain sovereignty over the Intelligence. How can the transition be brought about from the epoch of the consciousness soul to that of Spirit Self? In the thirteenth century, six centuries before the beginning of the Michael-epoch, this question had to be raised. But humanity was not yet able to answer it.[47]

At the beginning of the fourteenth century the Aristotelians were united again with the Platonists in the spiritual world. The former were led by Thomas Aquinas, the latter by Alanus ab Insulis. These two spiritual streams, which were responsible for the further destiny of the Cosmic Intelligence between the fifteenth and seventeenth centuries, took part in the supersensible Michael School in the sphere of Intuition, and in the great cultus at the beginning of the nineteenth century in the sphere of Imagination. Thus in supersensible realms and under the guidance of Michael, there was prepared through *both* streams that which on the Earth was to become Anthroposophy.

The preparation for the realization of these aims on the Earth lay in the first place with the Aristotelians. For already in the thirteenth century they had experience in the use of earthly Intelligence. They had played a leading role in the transition from the heavenly to the earthly Intelligence and also asked the fundamental question of the future Michael-epoch—the Parsifal-Michael question. And now as a direct consequence of their work at that time, when individual freedom had been won to a sufficient degree by humanity in the first third of the epoch of the consciousness soul, it was their mission to take the first step in the opposite direction: they were to pave the way for a new spiritualization of earthly Intelligence. Rudolf Steiner did this at the beginning of the twentieth century, at first in a more thought-orientated way in his *Philosophy of Freedom* and then purely occultly in *Occult Science*. He said of this book, however, that it brings again to humanity the 'knowledge of the Grail', whose origins stretch back into the twelfth and thirteenth centuries. Thus on Earth was prepared for Michael the way from his Arthurian knights to his Grail knights.

During this time the Platonists, in accordance with the supersensible agreement of the twelfth to the thirteenth centuries, were in the spiritual world. For they did not have such wide experience of working with the *earthly* Intelligence as had the Aristotelians. In their last incarnations the Platonists were still completely guided by the fact that 'the Intelligence was administered and ordered from Heaven.'[48] They had now to wait until *at the end* of the twentieth century, in the epoch of intellectualism, the Aristotelians would have prepared anew the way to the Spirit, would have laid the foundations for the spiritualization of the Intelligence, so that the Platonists could then bring into this stream of development all the immeasurable wealth of their souls. For they bore within them a great synthesis of Christianity and the ancient Mysteries, a synthesis that had been transformed in the Michael School into the impulse of the New Mysteries.

Although this first stage towards the spiritualizing of human Intelligence on its path of reascent into the Michael-sphere was realized on Earth primarily by the Aristotelians, in the supersensible sphere the Platonists too participated spiritually in this work. Rudolf Steiner characterizes this interaction of the two streams at the *beginning* of the twentieth century as follows: 'Here upon Earth, striving honestly towards Anthroposophy, there are numbers of souls who have always stood near the stream of Michael. Added to these, in the supersensible world, are numbers of souls who have remained behind, among them the teachers of Chartres. And between those who are here in the world of sense and those who are above in the spiritual world, there is a decided tendency to unite their work with one another.'[49] In another lecture, he points to this still more clearly: 'And today, those who were working in the great School of Chartres in the twelfth century, and those who were united with them at the beginning of the thirteenth century in one of the greatest spiritual communities—albeit in the supersensible world—*today* again they are working together. The great spirits of Chartres are working with those who in unison with them subsequently cultivated Aristotelianism on the Earth. It matters not that some of them are working here on the Earth, while others cannot yet descend to the Earth. They are working together now, preparing a new spiritual epoch in earthly evolution. And their great purpose now is to collect the souls who for a long time have been united with them—to gather together the souls with whose help a new spiritual age can then be founded. Their purpose is, in one way or another and within a comparatively short time, in the midst of an otherwise decadent civilization, to make possible a renewed co-operation in earthly life between the spirits of Chartres from the twelfth century and the spirits of the thirteenth century who are united with them. Their purpose is to prepare, so that they will be able to work together in an earthly life, cultivating spirituality once more within the civilization which, apart from this, is sailing on into destruction and disintegration. Intentions that are being cherished *today*, not upon Earth but as *between Earth and Heaven*, such intentions I have wanted to explain to you.'[50]

And inasmuch as the Christmas Conference of 1923–24 was the culmination of anthroposophical development, so there took part in it and were present supersensibly not only the teachers of Chartres but also many other individualities. For the Christmas Conference was the realization on the physical plane of that event whose *archetype* we must seek in the supersensible Michael School of the fifteenth–sixteenth centuries, when Michael first revealed to the souls related to him the secrets of the ancient Mysteries, and then pointed prophetically to the New Mysteries that are connected with the esoteric renewal of Christianity and which were to come to the Earth in his future epoch of rulership, beginning in 1879. The earthly reflection of this process came at the Christmas Conference when Rudolf Steiner first revealed to those anthroposophists present the secrets of the ancient Mysteries,[51] and then laid the Foundation Stone of the New Mysteries. But as in the rhythms of the Christmas Conference there is contained the soul's path between two incarnations, so Rudolf Steiner turned through these rhythms to all souls who are connected with the Michael-event in humanity and gave them the possibility of taking part spiritually in the Conference, no matter what realm of the after-death journey they might be in at that moment. How otherwise could the union have come about of the two spiritual streams of which Bernard Lievegoed writes in his book,[52] if their representatives had not been able to participate spiritually in the Christmas Conference; if they had not been able to be present at the beginnings of the fulfilment amongst mankind of what these representatives of the different streams had once prepared under the guidance of Michael in his supersensible School? Rudolf Steiner describes this as follows: 'And there developed in the supersensible world the most intense preparation for the Michael-impulse, which in our time is, in a certain sense, brought to Earth from Heaven ... And with the consciousness of the present time one must find a connection with what has been taking place supersensibly in the last centuries.'[53]

This special character of the Christmas Conference—that it had the same great significance for *both* worlds and was indeed carried out in *both*—was sensed by many at the time. Looking back on the event, Zeylmans van

Emmichoven writes: 'One had an intimation at the time that those who were not present, and perhaps human beings not alive on the physical plane, also took part in this laying of the Foundation Stone; certainly there were just as many souls in the spiritual world who heard it—souls of both those who had died and those who were not yet born.'[54]

Rudolf Steiner also indicates: 'In all that is happening spiritually there are not only those souls at work who are incarnated today on the Earth but also other souls who are at present between death and a new birth, and who send the rays of their influence down to the Earth. *In our own deeds there lie the impulses of such souls.* For all these things work together, just as deeds on Earth in turn reach up into the realm of Heaven and work on there.'[55] And as a concrete example of this influence of the spiritual world in earthly events, Rudolf Steiner refers in particular to the individuality of Brunetto Latini, the great teacher of Dante, who participated most intensively in the supersensible preparation for Anthroposophy.[56] 'Indeed, in many respects someone like Brunetto Latini is involved in a very great deal of what is happening on the Earth today even though he is not incarnated on it.'[57] And he continues: 'Thus you will see how intimately united the earthly life is with the supersensible. We cannot speak at all of a supersensible world separated from the earthly world of sense. For everything that is of the senses is permeated at the same time supersensibly, *and everything that is supersensible is revealed somewhere or at some time in the world of sense.* Moreover we can only truly receive and understand earthly life if we recognize that these things are behind it. This, my dear friends, is to be the future of the anthroposophical movement since the Christmas Foundation Meeting. We must treat of the supersensible facts openly and without reserve, confessing them in fullness of knowledge. This should be the esoteric trait permeating the anthroposophical movement. Thus alone will it be possible to give it its real spiritual content.'

Bearing this in mind, we can say with conviction that the Christmas Conference was also a sign for the spiritual world that the spiritualization of earthly intelligence and its transformation into a Michaelic Intelligence can be attained in humanity. This in turn is a *renewal* of the agreement in Heaven in the thirteenth century, and the beginning of its realization. *All* the younger members of the Anthroposophical Society, therefore, who feel their deep connection with the anthroposophical movement, can awaken a memory of their participation in the earthly events of the first quarter of this century. For *all* of them took part spiritually or physically in bringing about the anthroposophical-Michaelic impulse on the Earth, and participated likewise in the Christmas Conference. Coming now to the Earth, they must seek to understand it and to realize its impulses in humanity.

In this renewal of the agreement of the thirteenth century and in the fact that in the Christmas Conference the decision made by Aristotle and Alexander in the supersensible council of 869 was realized, there lies the deeper reason why, during the conference and subsequently, Rudolf Steiner spoke again and again of how from that moment onwards a completely new impulse had entered the anthroposophical movement by means of which it was possible to speak of a real 'beginning'.[58] For had this not been so, had it not yet been possible to spiritualize human intelligence on the Earth to a definite degree, the Christmas Conference would not have been possible.[59]

By means of what we have looked at above, we have prepared ourselves now to approach the question that touches upon the central mystery of the Christmas Conference itself. It is connected with the problem mentioned earlier which, according to Rudolf Steiner, can be formulated thus: How can not only the human being Parsifal but Michael himself find the way from the continuing influence (*Nachwirkung*) of the Arthur-principle to the continuing effects (*Nachwirkung*) of the Grail-principle?[60] How can he find the way from his administration of the Intelligence in the Cosmos to guiding it in the hearts and souls of human beings? This is the old Parsifal-question in a new form, having now become the fundamental Michaelic question of our time, and pointing to the esoteric connection between the Christmas Conference and the Grail Mystery.

In our study of the rhythms of the Christmas Conference in Chapter 5, we were able to draw out two fundamental aspects. The first was the complete cycle of the soul's life after death, between two incarnations, and the second was the seven stages of the Christian-Rosicrucian path of initiation as described in *Occult Science*. But in a remarkable way these two aspects point to the Grail Mystery. On 7 January 1913, Rudolf Steiner said concerning this: 'And this Mystery of the Holy Grail can give the modern human being that which leads him to an understanding, right for our time, of the life between death and a new birth.'[61] And in *Occult Science* he writes: 'The path into supersensible worlds, which is described in its first stages in this book, leads to "knowledge of the Grail".'[62]

Thus the two fundamental aspects of the seven rhythms of the Christmas Conference show themselves as the path that leads us to 'knowledge of the Grail'. And the 21-year development of the Anthroposophical Society in the world, with its culmination in the Christmas Conference, is a picture of how under the influence of Michael 'the hidden knowledge of the Grail' became manifest. For today it is no longer the Spirit of Mary but the Michaelic Spirit that appears in the light radiating from the Holy Chalice. Furthermore, these new Michael Mysteries are, in their deepest esoteric essence, none other than the Grail Mysteries renewed by the Time Spirit.

Rudolf Steiner refers particularly to this interrelation in his Michael Letter 'Gnosis and Anthroposophy', of February 1925. Six weeks before his departure from earthly life, he speaks there for the last time on the theme of the Grail. In describing the history of Gnosticism he shows how it originated in the third post-Atlantean epoch, the epoch of the sentient soul. Esoteric Gnosis—in contrast to exoteric Gnosis, whose writings were destroyed in the early centuries of Christianity—was cultivated only in strictly secret 'Gnosis Mysteries' closed to the world, which were preserved on Earth until the beginning of the era of Christendom and, in a changed form, even until the Middle Ages. (In this changed form he refers to them as the 'Divine Mysteries'.)

Rudolf Steiner points to the uninterrupted existence in humanity of these hidden Mysteries, which extend back to the time of the sentient soul, as a profound secret of human development. In the letter mentioned above, he connects these Mysteries with the coming into being of the Grail stream[63] and characterizes their initiates as being individuals who, in the fourth post-Atlantean epoch—the epoch of the intellectual or mind soul— were still able to awaken in themselves the forces of the sentient soul, so that 'the individuals who experienced this were also those who, when it took place, saw clearly into the Mystery of Golgotha in its profound cosmic interconnections'.[64] Thus one can say of these initiates that they bore within them, as it were, two fully developed souls: the sentient soul and the intellectual or mind soul. This means that through the intellectual or mind soul they were connected directly with their historical epoch, but through the sentient soul were connected with the cosmic wisdom of the 'Divine Mysteries'. To these initiates who 'saw clearly into the Mystery of Golgotha in its profound interconnections' belonged Joseph of Arimathea. And he was the first protector of the Grail, the protector of the Holy Chalice which, in the words of Rudolf Steiner, 'held the secret of Golgotha'.[65]

When subsequently there were no longer enough individuals able to bring to life in themselves the sentient soul and thus find a way to the cosmic content of the Grail Mystery, the Grail was taken from the Earth and given into the care of certain spiritual beings. It was intended that later they should return it to man, but then not so much as an impulse of knowledge but as an impulse of feeling, of soul experiences that were suited to prepare human beings for the transition from the intellectual or mind soul to the consciousness soul. And this transition was accomplished esoterically by Parsifal who had developed in himself both the intellectual or mind soul and the consciousness soul.[66] The former corresponds to the epoch in which he had to fulfil his tasks, and the latter points prophetically to the future development of mankind. After Parsifal, the Grail was transferred for protection into the realm of the priest-king Prester John. This realm, however, cannot be found on the Earth, only in the spiritual world.[67] Thus the Grail was taken once again from the Earth until that moment when in the epoch of Michael its Mysteries were to appear anew on Earth, at the time when the foundation must be laid for the transition from the consciousness soul to Spirit Self.[68] This was accomplished in the initiation and subsequent work of Rudolf Steiner. In him the Michaelic Imagination of the Grail, containing as it does the new cosmic Christ-knowledge, became reality. He could prepare the way for the freeing of the Cosmic Intelligence that had fallen to Earth, and was able to lay the foundation for the transition from the consciousness soul to Spirit Self. The beginning of this path in our epoch is made by those souls who receive and take up the new Michaelic Christianity which comes before us today in Anthroposophy.

In a very subtle way Rudolf Steiner points to this development at the end of the Letter 'Gnosis and Anthroposophy'. He brings before us here an image of the Grail which contains 'universal images' in which live 'the secrets of Golgotha'.[69] These secrets of the cosmic Christ-knowledge were taken from the Earth into the spiritual world soon after the Mystery of Golgotha. In the epoch destined to prepare the development of the consciousness soul, it was brought to the Earth again but this time only as a 'content of feeling'. And in our epoch, in which the principle of Spirit Self is to be prepared, this cosmic Christ-knowledge that is held in the divine Chalice has come once again to the Earth. For the content of the Chalice—a content which was first taken up by the forces of the sentient soul, then by those of the intellectual or mind soul as it rose towards the consciousness soul—can be received and taken up today by the purest forces of the consciousness soul as it develops towards Spirit Self, 'so that in our age there may develop out of the consciousness soul a completely new understanding of the Mystery of Golgotha in the light of Michael's activity. It is to this new understanding that Anthroposophy is striving.' If we place these words beside those spoken in Berlin on 7 January 1913, we have before us the whole sequence of spiritual events. 'Everything that is to contribute to spreading this understanding of the Christ-impulse in our time is contained for the Occident in that which one can call the Mystery of the Holy Grail.'[70]

Thus the Grail-impulse arises three times, corresponding each time to one of three successive epochs in world development, and each time it is connected with three historical personalities: with Joseph of Arimathaea, Parsifal, and Rudolf Steiner.[71]

And now we can pose the question which arises directly from our previous considerations: How is the occult event of the Christmas Conference related to the Grail Mystery, which must become today a true Michael Mystery in order that Michael may receive again the Intelligence in the hearts and souls of human beings? This question can only be answered if we are truly conscious that *at the very basis of the New Mysteries, which began with the Christmas Conference, there lies that which is the very heart of the Grail Mystery*.

The renewed image of the Holy Grail, as described above, must arise today in man out of the depths of Michaelic esotericism. It must arise from the depths of the new revelation of Anthropos-Sophia—the Wisdom of the Holy Spirit concerning man. And in this new image of the Grail we can already discern three formative, fundamental elements.

The first of these is the *substance of Love*, which is born in every human 'I' that receives into itself in freedom the new anthroposophical wisdom of the world and of man. However, in order that this substance of Love which fills the human 'I' may also become Christ-substance, it must find its way also to the origin and fount of World Love, which has come into the Earth-sphere by virtue of the Mystery of Golgotha. Thus we can say: only a human love striving towards the Mystery of Golgotha can unite itself with the Cosmic Love, which since the events of Palestine has flowed through our world like a mighty cosmic stream. For 'the event of Golgotha is a free cosmic deed stemming from Cosmic Love; and it is only through the Love in man that the Mystery of Golgotha can be comprehended'.[72] Therefore, in order that our human love be fructified by Cosmic Love and enabled thereby to receive into itself the Christ-impulse, the substance of the new Grail must consist of Cosmic-human Love.

The second element is that which makes it possible for the Christ-impulse working in the substance of Cosmic-human Love to be recognized by human beings. To this end, step by step on the inner path of development, the consciousness soul is to be transformed into the imaginative soul. This imaginative soul will then be able to give form to the Cosmic-human Love which flows through the 'I' or, which is the same, will be able to hold it back within the human being as though in a Chalice. This will be possible because, through the forces of the Michael rulership in our epoch, 'the force of Imagination will enter into the general intellectual consciousness of humanity'.[73] But these at first purely human Imaginations arising through the new faculty of Imagination must, if they are truly to transform the consciousness soul into the imaginative soul, be carried out into the cosmos so as to find there the path to the Cosmic Imaginations. Rudolf Steiner describes this as follows: 'What man experiences from the force of conscious imagining becomes at the same time world-content. The fact that this is possible is a result of the Mystery of Golgotha. The

Christ-force imprints human Imaginations into the Cosmos.'[74] Thus human Imaginations are united with Cosmic Imaginations. And it is from these Cosmic-human Imaginations that the human being can form in his soul a vessel for the stream of Cosmic-human Love that flows through his 'I' bearing the substance of Christ. But this Cosmic-human Love, in which the Christ-substance is concealed, can be held in the soul as though in a chalice; in this way it is brought to consciousness, thus enabling the human being to experience it in his inner being like a true spiritual Sun. This must become the fundamental experience of the new Michael-epoch: 'The Sun-quality (*das Sonnenhafte*), which through many long ages the human being has received only from the cosmos, will begin to shine in the innermost recesses of the soul. Man will learn to speak of an "inner Sun". He will not, however, because of this feel himself in his life between birth and death to be any less an Earth-being, but will see his own being which walks on the Earth as *guided by the Sun*.'[75]

And here we touch upon the deep secret of our time: the possibility *of meeting the Etheric Christ* in the spiritual world immediately bordering the Earth.

This conscious experience in the human soul of the Christ-impulse which lives in the substance of Cosmic-human Love and is gathered as though into a chalice, in the form of Cosmic-human Imaginations—this experience is able to spiritualize once again the divine Intelligence of Michael that has descended to Earth and fallen to earthly forces. This spiritualization would enable the earthly thoughts of human beings to find a path to the World Thoughts of the cosmos, to the Cosmic Intelligence which they can now experience in their hearts as the new organ of knowing. For Michael 'frees thoughts from the realm of the head; he frees for them, opens for them, the path to the heart; he releases glowing enthusiasm from the seat of the feelings (*Gemüt*) so that the human being can live in reverent devotion of soul towards everything that can be experienced in the *Light of thought*.'[76] This 'thought-Light', consisting as it does of the purest Cosmic-human Thoughts, brings forth that shining raying-out of the divine Chalice, that celestial Light of the redeemed Intelligence which, like the *radiance* of the Spiritual Sun, can unite into a single whole with the spiritual substance of Love that is held in the imaginative form of the chalice.

And when in this way human love unites in the soul with Cosmic Love, human imagination with Cosmic Imagination, human thoughts with Cosmic Thoughts, then in truth we have before us the Holy Grail—the Grail whose substance is Cosmic-human Love, whose form is Cosmic-human Imagination, and whose outpoured Light of thinking is Cosmic-human Intelligence, Cosmic-human Thoughts.

This is the *Michaelic Grail* that descended to Earth at the Christmas

Conference of 1923–24 and was laid in the hearts and souls of human beings as 'the dodecahedral imaginative Form of Love' '... which has its substance from Cosmic-human Love, its shape and configuration from Cosmic-human Imagination, and from Cosmic-human Thoughts has that shining *Light* which, in every instance when we remember this moment, can radiate a warm Light to us that spurs on our deed, our thinking, our feeling and our willing'.[77] This Light streaming towards us is the glistening spiritualized Intelligence in which the Spirit can live—the new Michaelic Spirit which then appears in the 'Light of thoughts' radiating from the 'dodecahedral imaginative Form of Love' in our souls, just as in ages past the Spirit appeared in the form of a white dove in the brilliant Light of the Holy Chalice.

Rudolf Steiner speaks of this deeply significant event at the close of the most important meeting of the Christmas Conference—the laying of the Foundation Stone of the Anthroposophical Society in the hearts and souls of human beings: 'Hear it, my dear friends, thus ringing forth in your own hearts! Then you will found here a true union of human beings for Anthroposophia, and will carry the Spirit that prevails in the radiant *Light of Thought* around the dodecahedral Stone of Love forth into the world, where it will shed light and warmth for the true progress of the souls of men, for the progress of the world.'[78]

Thus the Foundation Stone of the Christmas Conference which, on 25 December 1923, was laid in the form of a 'dodecahedral Stone of Love' into the hearts and souls of human beings, shows itself in its most hidden essence to be the true expression of the esoteric being of the Grail as renewed out of the present age of Michael.[79] In a very special way, therefore, the Christmas Conference becomes for us a *Grail-event*, an event belonging not to the sphere of time but to Eternity. For the Grail-experience can be found today by every soul on Earth who wishes out of free will and true devotion to Anthroposophy to lay this Foundation Stone in his or her own heart. And then will the soul be able to join the circle of Michaelic Grail-knights, the community of the new guardians of the Holy Chalice, the Holy Stone.[80]

Immeasurable spiritual horizons are in truth opened up through an awareness of the inner essence of the Christmas Conference which, taken historically, *is the greatest spiritual event of the twentieth century on the physical plane.*

From all the indications of the esoteric nature of the Christmas Conference we have considered in this chapter, it can also be seen that beginnings were laid at the Conference for a path that reunites human and Cosmic Intelligence. A first step was thereby made towards freeing the heavenly Intelligence of Michael from the bonds of Ahriman.

But these beginnings were a direct challenge to Ahriman, and from that moment on, therefore, the battle for the Michaelic Intelligence in humanity became particularly intense and will enter a decisive final phase at the end of the century: 'This is the time above all [the end of the century], which the ahrimanic spirits wish to use most strongly. This is the time they want to use, because human beings are so completely wrapped up in the Intelligence that has come over them. They have become so unbelievably clever. Why, we are quite nervous today about the cleverness of the people we shall meet! We can scarcely ever escape from this anxiety, for nearly all of them are clever. Really we cannot escape from this anxiety about the cleverness of people. But it is indeed so that the cleverness which is thus cultivated is used by Ahriman. And when moreover the bodies are especially adapted to a possible lowering or diminution of consciousness, it may happen that Ahriman himself emerges, incorporated in human form.'[81]

Thus we must also take into account today that beside the Grail stream, which has been present in humanity since the Christmas Conference, there also runs the stream of Klingsor. In Klingsor we have not an incarnation but an *incorporation* of Ahriman into the intellectual or mind soul in the ninth century. However, the consequences of this embodiment could not yet work so destructively on the general course of development because the human being at that time was only just approaching the time of individual Intelligence, the full mastery of which is possible only in the age of the consciousness soul. In our epoch, therefore, for the first time in world history Ahriman has the possibility, as he embodies himself in the consciousness soul, to contend against Michael for the Intelligence in human souls. Rudolf Steiner describes this activity of Ahriman in the consciousness soul as a 'cold hatred'[82] of everything that unfolds as spirituality in the human being out of individual freedom. And we experience the threat of this today ever more strongly. These spiritual 'successors of Klingsor' often appear today almost openly in their endeavours to bring about conditions within humanity that are most propitious for an embodiment of Ahriman in the largest possible number of human souls. For they wish to prevent from taking place that which, at the end of our century, by the will of the spiritual powers who serve the Christ-impulse, *is intended to* occur as the culmination of anthroposophical development in the world, and hence to prepare the *incarnation* of Ahriman at the beginning of the next millennium.[83]

Every anthroposophist should be as wide awake as possible to the seriousness of the situation, and to the fact that in this most difficult of battles—the battle of Michael with the Dragon that is referred to in many prophecies and legends of the past—the combined work of the Platonists and the Aristotelians at the end of the twentieth century will be of the greatest significance. For it is through their activity that the impulses and goals of the Christmas Conference—this true Grail event—are to be fully realized in the world.[84]

'Those who receive Anthroposophy in a sincere way at the present time [1924] are preparing their souls to shorten as far as possible the life between death and a new birth, and to appear again [on Earth] at the end of the twentieth century, united with the teachers of Chartres who have remained behind [in the spiritual world] ... The anthroposophical movement is called upon to work on and on and to appear again [on the Earth] not only in its most important but *in nearly all its souls* at the end of the twentieth century. For then *a great impulse and impetus is to be given for the spiritual life on Earth*, without which earthly civilization would finally be drawn into that decadence, the character of which is only too apparent.'[85]

And Rudolf Steiner continues, referring to the end of our century in the sense indicated above as a 'great epoch': 'Out of such foundations, my dear friends, I would wish to set aflame in your hearts something of the fire that we need in order to make the spiritual life so strong already within the anthroposophical movement that we will appear properly prepared *in that great epoch*—[at whose beginning] we shall work again on Earth after a shortened life in the spiritual worlds—*when, for the salvation of the Earth in its most essential elements, one will look to what anthroposophists are able to do.'*

In these words, which stir the soul so deeply we, the anthroposophists of the end of the century, can hear a call from the spiritual cosmos—a call which began, as has been often stated by Rudolf Steiner, at the Christmas Conference and in which is proclaimed to us that in all humility, but also in full consciousness, we are to take up the aims that have been set before us; and that the guiding powers of humanity look to us, *and we must prove worthy of their trust.* 'The true anthroposophist must be aware that it is a matter today of actively participating in the battle between Ahriman and Michael—a matter of seeing into it and of co-operating in it with Michael.'[86]

And Rudolf Steiner continues to speak of the task of anthroposophists in connection with the approaching end of the century, and of the *culmination* of anthroposophical development in the world through the combined efforts of the two spiritual streams united on Earth: 'Up to [the end of the century] there will be prepared through anthroposophical spirituality that which will then be realized out of the joint activity [of the Platonists and Aristotelians] as the *complete revelation* of what has been prepared by these two streams ... The anthroposophist ... must be aware of how even now [1924] he is called upon to prepare that which is to spread out more and more as spirituality until the *culmination* comes when the true anthroposophists will be present on Earth again, united with the others [the

Platonists], at the end of the century.' This union will be necessary 'so as to attain at the time of the culmination the greatest possible extension of the anthroposophical movement';[87] 'in order to bring to *culmination*, to full expression [at the transition from the twentieth to the twenty-first century], that which [anthroposophists] are able to do now in the service of the Michael rulership ... in order to contemplate that which Anthroposophy is striving for';[88] in order, 'with a far greater spiritual strength, to carry the anthroposophical movement ever further.'[89] 'For what today shines in as it were through many tiny windows must, through the bond between the leaders of the School of Chartres and the leaders of Scholasticism, become in the future a unity, when the spiritual renewal which raises the intellectual into the spiritual enters upon the scene at the end of the twentieth century.'[90] In these words Rudolf Steiner indicates quite clearly how the essential *culmination* of anthroposophical development at the end of the century is directly dependent on the co-operation, on the common efforts of the representatives of the two streams mentioned above.

For this reason the Aristotelians, who have returned to the Earth, and the Platonists must start working *together*. The Aristotelians are those souls who were involved at the beginning of our century in the first stage of the spiritualizing of human intelligence, who were able at that time to open up the way from the Earth to the cosmos and who are to continue this work still more intensively today. And the Platonists are those who, in accordance with the heavenly agreement of the thirteenth century, are also returning to the Earth today, bringing with them their rich experience of the ancient Mysteries. This experience, however, is now deeply united in their souls with the Christ-impulse and is permeated through and through with the experience of the Cosmic Intelligence of Michael. Thus on the basis of what the Aristotelians have already accomplished, the Platonists are now to work in unison with them on the final spiritualization of human intelligence and on the founding of the new Michaelic culture, 'so that the Cosmic Intelligence, which in accordance with the ordering of the world rightfully fell from Michael, can be found again by him within humanity on Earth.'[91]

In this connection we must look on the Christmas Conference as a confirmation and strengthening of the union between the Aristotelians and the Platonists, and as a firm foundation of their common task in the next decades—particularly the 1990s.[92] This joint work, however, will only be possible through the realization within the Anthroposophical Society of the Whitsun festival, the cosmic festival of *knowledge* and of the *union* of spiritually striving human beings. The basis of this union of human beings will be an awareness of their common karma, from which will arise their common mission within humanity. And the fulfilment of this mission is to bring about a situation whereby the centre of the New Mysteries, founded more than 60 years ago as the core of the anthroposophical movement, may now be completed!

Rudolf Steiner talks of this completion as follows: 'And in accordance with this agreement [between the Platonists and the Aristotelians] something must arise from the anthroposophical movement that must find its completion before the end of this century,'[93] 'so as to give them, under the guidance of these two types of spiritual beings [the leaders of the School of Chartres and the leaders of the Scholastics], the last hallowed impulse for the further development of the spiritual life on the Earth.'[94]

Pointing to the connection between the Christmas Conference and the culmination of anthroposophical development at the end of the century is the fact that Rudolf Steiner was not able to speak openly of the secrets of the heavenly and earthly destiny of the Aristotelians and the Platonists in the past, present and the future, nor of their union on the Earth from our time onwards, in accordance with the supersensible agreement, until *after* the Christmas Conference, 'when the demons [the opponents of Michael] that had previously prevented such things from being spoken of [had] now to be silent.'[95]

In this way it is only through the Mystery of the Christmas Conference that the most important secret of the future development of the anthroposophical movement was revealed to anthroposophists. For the Christmas Conference shows us how *that which in the light of the Michael-impulse was laid at that time like a seed in the soul must bear fruit at the end of the century as the culmination of anthroposophical development in the world.* This in turn will find expression in the completion of the New Mysteries which are already in existence on the Earth. The inner nature of these Mysteries, moreover, is 'absolutely compatible with the full, clear and light-filled intelligence of man'.[96]

If now we compare this description of the New Mysteries with what Rudolf Steiner writes in the last chapter of *Occult Science* concerning the modern 'knowledge of the Grail', we see what profound continuity and consistency is governing the development of the anthroposophical movement: 'The pathway into spiritual worlds, the first stages of which were set forth in the preceding chapter, culminates in the "Science of the Grail". It is a characteristic of this new Initiation Knowledge that while its facts can only be investigated with higher faculties of cognition (the methods of attaining which have been described), once investigated and discovered they are well able to be comprehended precisely by the faculties of mind and soul which the fifth epoch has developed'[97]—that is, can be understood with the help of that individual intelligence which in the New Mysteries is to be spiritualized, is to become 'a clear spiritualized intelli-

340

gence filled with bright intelligence-light' and able, in turn, to be the bearer of the cosmic impulse of Michael. For it is in the 'Light of Thought' of this impulse that the union of the two streams can take place. In the Karma lectures Rudolf Steiner speaks of this union as a 'Michael Prophecy'[98] whose fulfilment must play a decisive role today in the great battle of Michael with the Dragon.

'Decisive indeed will be what human hearts do with this Michael-impulse in the world in the course of the twentieth century. And in the course of the twentieth century, when the first century after Kali Yuga has elapsed, humanity will either stand at the grave of all civilization—or at the beginning of that age when in the souls of men, who *in their hearts unite intelligence with spirituality*, Michael's battle will be fought out to victory.'[99] 'For humanity stands today before a great alternative: it can either watch all that is civilization fall into the abyss, or it can raise it up through spirituality, can take it further in the spirit of what lies in the Michael-impulse, which stands before the Christ impulse.'[100]

But this spiritualization of civilization in the sense of 'the Michael-impulse which stands before the Christ-impulse' can happen only when, in the words of Rudolf Steiner, there are on the Earth a sufficient number of souls who take up the Michael-impulse working in the 'Light of Thought'—the 'Michael Thought'—and 'hold it faithfully in their hearts in inner love', so that from such a heart dedicated to Michael, the Michael Thought can pour into the world, penetrating, enlivening and spiritualizing anthroposophical work. Thus does the call from the spiritual world sound out through the twentieth century, addressing itself directly to the will of the anthroposophists: 'Take up the Michael Thought which overcomes the forces of Ahriman, the Thought which gives the strength to acquire here on Earth knowledge of the spirit, so that you may overcome the forces of death.'[101] And it is the greatest task of every anthroposophist today to take up the 'Michael Thought', which since the Christmas Conference has stood before us in all its fullness, revealed in the cosmic-human rhythms of the *Foundation Stone Meditation*, in the Karma lectures, in the Leading Thoughts, and finding its highest embodiment in the First Class of the Free School for Spiritual Science. It is our task to take up this Michael Thought not only into our hearts and souls but to let it permeate all our *actions*, so that they may become truly esoteric. On this will depend the destiny of the New Mysteries, and that means the destiny of all human culture.

Thus the last chapter of this book cannot be completed by the author, for its content in many respects depends on the near future. It can only be finished by turning to all anthroposophists, on whom it rests to play an essential role in the decisive events at the end of the century, and who must inwardly recognize themselves to be representatives of the Aristotelians who have returned *anew* to the Earth, or of the Platonists who now descend with them. It rests upon these two groups of souls to work *together* on the Earth in the spirit of the fundamental impulse of our time, in the spirit of the Michael-Christ impulse, to work in remembrance of their *shared* cosmic past, of their common supersensible-Michaelic karma, the secret of which is indissolubly bound up with the profound spiritual nature of the Christmas Conference, through which alone it can become a *conscious* force in our souls.

May we be able to bring the 'Michael Thought' to life in ourselves so that it will become in us the sounding Cosmic Word that pours forth from Michael's raiment of light—the raiment in which he comes before us as the great Guide of the New Mysteries and by his 'wise beckoning' and gesture calls us, who have laid in our souls the dodecahedral Stone of Love, to experience anew the festival of Whitsun as the cosmic proclamation of Anthroposophy, calls us to receive into our souls the 'Word of Love', so that the 'sacred Will of Worlds'—in which lives *the Will of the Etheric Christ*—may be realized on Earth.

This is the *culmination* of Anthroposophy which is to come at the end of this century as a World Whitsun, as the true festival of the Holy Spirit that is so deeply connected with the revelation of the secrets of the Michaelic Grail, the Imagination of which must today become reality in human souls.

We are called upon to participate consciously in this culmination, in the certainty that the intentions of Michael-Christ will thereby be realized.

The Michael Revelation can guide and nourish us on our journey, awakening us to watchfulness and responsibility. It is the Revelation which, on the eve of Michael's Day 1924, sounded out from the transformed etheric sphere of the Earth, in which in the twentieth century the Etheric Christ is at work—sounded out through Rudolf Steiner, his greatest earthly pupil: 'May the words so speak to your souls *today* that you receive this Michael Thought in the sense of what a faithful follower of Michael may feel when, clothed in the light rays of the Sun, Michael appears and indicates to us *what must now take place*: that this Michael garment, this garment of light, becomes the cosmic waves that are the Christ words—those cosmic words which can transform the Cosmic Logos into the Logos of mankind. Therefore let my words to you *today* be these:

Springing from the Powers of the Sun,
Radiant Spirit-powers, blessing all Worlds!
For Michael's garment of rays
Ye are predestined by Thought Divine.

342

He, the Christ-messenger, revealeth in you—
Bearing mankind aloft—the sacred Will of Worlds.
Ye, the radiant Beings of Aether-Worlds,
Bear the Christ-Word to Man.

Thus shall the Herald of Christ appear
To the thirstily waiting souls,
To whom your Word of Light shines forth
In cosmic age of Spirit-Man.

Ye, the disciples of Spirit-Knowledge,
Take Michael's Wisdom beckoning,
Take the Word of Love of the Will of Worlds
Into your souls' aspiring, actively!'

(Translation of G. & M. Adams)

APPENDICES

Foundation Stone Meditation

(*I, 1*)   Soul of Man!   (1)
Thou livest in the Limbs
Which bear thee through the world of Space
Into the ocean-being of the Spirit.
Practise *Spirit-recollection*   (5)
In depths of soul,
Where in the wielding
World-Creator-Life
Thine own I
Comes to being
Within the I of God.   (11)
Then in the All-World-Being of Man
Thou wilt truly *live*.

(*I, 2*)   For the Father-Spirit of the Heights holds sway
In Depths of Worlds, begetting Life.   (15)
Seraphim, Cherubim, Thrones!
(Spirits of Strength!)
Let there ring out from the Heights
What in the Depths is echoed,
Speaking:
Ex Deo nascimur.   (20)
(From God, Mankind has Being.)
The Elemental Spirits hear it
In East and West and North and South:
May human beings hear it!

(*II, 1*)   Soul of Man!   (1)
Thou livest in the beat of Heart and Lung
Which leads thee through the rhythmic tides of Time
Into the feeling of thine own Soul-being.
Practise *Spirit-mindfulness*   (5)
In balance of the soul,
Where the surging
Deeds of the World's Becoming
Do thine own I

Unite
Unto the I of the World.   (11)
Then 'mid the weaving of the Soul of Man
Thou wilt truly *feel*.

(*II, 2*)   For the Christ-Will in the encircling Round holds sway
In the Rhythms of Worlds, blessing the Soul.   (15)
Kyriotetes, Dynamis, Exusiai!
(Spirits of Light!)
Let there be fired from the East
What through the West is formed,
Speaking:
In Christo morimur.   (20)
(In Christ, Death becomes Life.)
The Elemental Spirits hear it
In East and West and North and South:
May human beings hear it!

(*III, 1*)   Soul of Man!   (1)
Thou livest in the resting Head
Which from the ground of the Eternal
Opens to thee the Thoughts of Worlds.
Practise *Spirit-vision*   (5)
In quietness of Thought,
Where the eternal aims of Gods
World-Being's Light
On thine own I
Bestow
For thy free Willing.   (11)
Then from the ground of the Spirit of Man
Thou wilt truly *think*.

(*III, 2*)   For the Spirit's Universal Thoughts hold sway
In the Being of all Worlds, beseeching Light.   (15)
Archai, Archangeloi, Angeloi!
(Spirits of Soul!)
Let there be prayed in the Depths
What from the Heights is answered,
Speaking:
Per Spiritum Sanctum reviviscimus.   (20)
(In the Spirit's Universal Thoughts, the Soul awakens.)
The Elemental Spirits hear it

In East and West and North and South:
May human beings hear it!

(*IV*, 1)   At the Turning-point of Time   (1)
The Spirit-Light of the World
Entered the stream of Earthly Being.
Darkness of Night
Had held its sway;   (5)
Day-radiant Light
Poured into the souls of men:
Light
That gives warmth
To simple Shepherds' Hearts,   (10)
Light
That enlightens
The wise Heads of Kings.

(*IV*, 2)   O Light Divine,
O Sun of Christ!   (15)
Warm Thou
Our Hearts,
Enlighten Thou
Our Heads,
That good may become   (20)
What from our Hearts we would found
And from our Heads direct
With single purpose.

Grundstein-Meditation

(*I, 1*)   Menschenseele!   (1)
Du lebest in den Gliedern,
Die dich durch die Raumeswelt
In das Geistesmeereswesen tragen:
Übe *Geist-Erinnern*   (5)
In Seelentiefen,
Wo in waltendem
Weltenschöpfer-Sein
Das eigne Ich
Im Gottes-Ich   (10)
Erweset;
Und du wirst wahrhaft *leben*
Im Menschen-Welten-Wesen.

(*I, 2*)   Denn es waltet der Vater-Geist der Höhen
In den Weltentiefen Sein-erzeugend.   (15)
Seraphim, Cherubim, Throne,
(Ihr Kräfte-Geister)
Lasset aus den Höhen erklingen,
Was in den Tiefen das Echo findet;
Dieses spricht:
Ex Deo nascimur.   (20)
(Aus dem Göttlichen weset die Menschheit.)
Das hören die Elementargeister
Im Osten, Westen, Norden, Süden:
Menschen mögen es hören.

(*II, 1*)   Menschenseele!   (1)
Du lebest in dem Herzens-Lungen-Schlage,
Der dich durch den Zeitenrhythmus
Ins eigne Seelenwesensfühlen leitet:
Übe *Geist-Besinnen*   (5)
Im Seelengleichgewichte,
Wo die wogenden
Welten-Werde-Taten
Das eigne Ich

Dem Welten-Ich   (10)
Vereinen;
Und du wirst wahrhaft *fühlen*
Im Menschen-Seelen-Wirken.

(*II, 2*)   Denn es waltet der Christus-Wille im Umkreis
In den Weltenrhythmen Seelen-begnadend.   (15)
Kyriotetes, Dynamis, Exusiai,
(Ihr Lichtes-Geister)
Lasset vom Osten befeuern,
Was durch den Westen sich gestaltet;
Dieses spricht:
In Christo morimur.   (20)
(In dem Christus wird Leben der Tod.)
Das hören die Elementargeister
Im Osten, Westen, Norden, Süden:
Menschen mögen es hören.

(*III, 1*)   Menschenseele!   (1)
Du lebest im ruhenden Haupte,
Das dir aus Ewigkeitsgründen
Die Weltgedanken erschließet:
Übe *Geist-Erschauen*   (5)
In Gedanken-Ruhe,
Wo die ew'gen Götterziele
Welten-Wesens-Licht
Dem eignen Ich
Zu freiem Wollen   (10)
Schenken;
Und du wirst wahrhaft *denken*
In Menschen-Geistes-Gründen.

(*III, 2*)   Denn es walten des Geistes Weltgedanken
Im Weltenwesen Licht-erflehend.   (15)
Archai, Archangeloi, Angeloi,
(Ihr Seelen-Geister)
O lasset aus den Tiefen erbitten,
Was in den Höhen erhöret wird;
Dieses spricht:
Per Spiritum Sanctum reviviscimus.   (20)
(In des Geistes Weltgedanken erwachet die Seele.)
Das hören die Elementargeister

Im Osten, Westen, Norden, Süden:
Menschen mögen es hören.

(IV, 1)   In der Zeiten Wende   (1)
Trat das Welten-Geistes-Licht
In den irdischen Wesensstrom;
Nacht-Dunkel
Hatte ausgewaltet,   (5)
Taghelles Licht
Erstrahlte in Menschenseelen;
Licht,
Das erwärmet
Die armen Hirtenherzen;   (10)
Licht,
Das erleuchtet
Die weisen Königshäupter.

(IV, 2)   Göttliches Licht,
Christus-Sonne,   (15)
Erwärme
Unsere Herzen;
Erleuchte
Unsere Häupter;
Daß gut werde,   (20)
Was wir
Aus Herzen gründen,
Aus Häuptern
Zielvoll führen wollen.

Afterword to the Second Edition

In preparing the second edition of this book, the author did not consider it necessary to make any significant changes. Apart from some finer details and additions, its content has essentially remained the same. This also corresponds to the author's conviction as to the validity of the ideas expressed in the book and that its standpoint is fitting and well-grounded.

Two points of clarification shall alone be added. They appear to the author to be of importance for the understanding of certain questions raised in the book and of its general orientation.

The first point concerns the concept of 'sacrifice', its significance in man's spiritual development and the question as to how this concept is applied in the present work. The principal issue here is that the readiness to make sacrifices on the spiritual path is the capacity which, from the standpoint of the Masters of Wisdom and of the Harmony of Feelings, is from the very outset the most important for the pupil. 'They [the white occultists] value *selfless devotion and readiness for sacrifice* above all other attributes,' writes Rudolf Steiner at the end of his book *Knowledge of the Higher Worlds. How is it Achieved?* This demand of the teachers of the White Lodge can, however, be traced back to a still higher source, to the Greater Guardian of the Threshold, of whom Rudolf Steiner says: 'If he [the initiate] resolves to fulfil the demands of the higher Being of Light, he will be able to contribute to the liberation of the human race. *He offers up his gifts on the altar of humanity.*' These words are applicable above all to Rudolf Steiner himself, who writes in the Foreword to the fifth edition of his book: 'There is *no part* of what has been communicated with which the soul of the writer does not continue to be intimately connected and which does not contain something which still works upon his soul.' In other words: there is no portion of this book which has not been directly *experienced* by the author.

If we recall that, according to *Occult Science—An Outline*, the Christ Himself—whom Rudolf Steiner in one of his lectures characterizes as the 'great sacrifice' (GA 102, 27.1.1908)—gradually reveals Himself to the initiate in the figure of the Greater Guardian of the Threshold, the demand of the Guardian that he 'offer up his gifts on the altar of humanity' becomes for us an indication of the true path of 'imitation of Christ' as it has been described in the present work.

What can the initiate offer up as 'his gifts' on the altar of humanity? Only what is his own, for only such a sacrifice can be a true one.

And what is it that truly belongs to a human being? One thing only: the spiritual content of his ego, together with what he has been able to bring forth from the spiritual content of his ego into his sheaths, that is, transform within them. This transformed part of his sheaths is also his own. Everything else within him is a gift of the Gods.

Thus the initiate can offer up as *his gift* on the altar of humanity only the spiritual forces of his ego and the parts of his sheaths that he has already transformed. However, he can only make this high sacrifice—which is the beginning of the occult path of the imitation of Christ—if the experience of the 'true ego' has become an immediate reality for him *in Intuition*.

For coming to know the true ego in Intuition—which means to *unite* with it (this being the nature of intuitive knowledge)—is for the initiate only possible through the sacrificial dedication of all that his earthly ego, his earthly personality, has been hitherto. (Rudolf Steiner also speaks about such a sacrifice and its relationship to the sacrificial path of Christ Jesus in the lecture of 13.11.1921, GA 208.) In this deed we have, in truth, a kind of 'leap over the cosmic abyss' which lies between the two pronouncements of Christ that rang forth from the Cross on Golgotha: 'My God, my God, why hast thou forsaken me?' (Mark 15: 34) and 'Father, into thy hands I commend my spirit' (Luke 23: 46). But as man has a direct experience of union with the Christ Being only in his true ego, everything which was said becomes for him in the deepest, esoteric sense a fulfilment of the words 'Not I, but Christ in me'. And in the moment when these words have become a spiritual reality for the initiate, the Christ allows his blotted out earthly ego-consciousness, his earthly personality, to resurrect (of course, we should not imagine that this process takes place in time), just as at the Turning-point of Time the Christ awakened the consciousness of Jesus of Nazareth in the spiritual world after the crucifixion on Golgotha.

In this way, the Christ re-endows man's ego with life, though in such a way that all that is best and most spiritual in his personality can ascend to the spiritual world already during his incarnation on Earth. This is to a certain extent a picture of what every human individual experiences after death, when his ego is first taken away and then restored once again, though now endowed with the capacity of living consciously in the spiritual worlds (see pages 220–21). But the initiate receives his earthly ego back from the Christ Being Himself. A real act of death and resurrection is accomplished in his soul when the forces of his earthly ego-consciousness are reawakened through the power of his true ego, so that he is enabled to dwell in both his higher and his ordinary ego. Although he is still an earthly human being like all others, he has henceforth the capacity of entering in full consciousness as a spirit-researcher into the spiritual worlds in every moment of his life. What were formerly two mutually exclusive soul-conditions—beholding the spiritual worlds and thinking in crystal-clear concepts—now become possible *at the same time*. For because of the union that has been made with the Christ Being, not the smallest 'part' of human consciousness, of the concrete human personality, can be lost: 'That is precisely the step forward that has been taken through Christianity, that the *personality*, too, enters into eternity' (GA 264).

This process is repeated within the sheaths of the initiate. Through the sacrifice of the spiritual forces that have been gathered together in them, through the fact they 'have been offered up on the altar of humanity', the Christ-impulse—springing from the ego—also penetrates into them. As a result, the sheaths of the initiate become, as it were, 'spiritually transparent', and the most diverse beings of the spiritual world—including even the highest Hierarchies—are able to speak through them, while his own ego-consciousness, the character of his whole personality in all its individual uniqueness, is preserved in its entirety. For however high the spheres to which such an initiate may penetrate henceforth and however sublime the spiritual Beings who may be revealed through him, his ego-consciousness will be maintained on all planes of cosmic being once this direct relationship to the Christ Being has been won. Rudolf Steiner alludes to this circumstance in the following way: 'When the higher self has wholly taken possession of a human individual and the veil of the personality has fallen away, the *whole choir of the higher Spirits can speak* through him, as did formerly the voice of the sense-world...' (GA 264).

Rudolf Steiner also characterizes this state of affairs in the final words of a mantram which, as he testified on several occasions in esoteric lessons, stems directly from the Masters of Wisdom and of the Harmony of Feelings '...so that through me the Spirits may work/And I become the *self-conscious* instrument/Of their deeds...' (GA 245). The meaning of both quotations becomes clear if we make ourselves aware that, of all the higher beings of the spiritual world, *only the Christ* is able to work within the human ego without extinguishing its power or causing it harm. The other spiritual beings can work for the salvation of the world and of men only through the *sheaths* of human beings.

All this could be experienced to a very high degree in Rudolf Steiner himself. Those who at the beginning of our century had the good fortune to meet him on the physical plane were able to confirm this entirely: the singular warmth and humanity of his earthly personality and its complete transformation—not its disappearance, but its high degree of spiritualization—at the moment when the true ego lit up within it, opening up the possibility for 'the whole choir of the higher Spirits', from the Master individualities to hierarchic Beings, to speak and to act through his sheaths.

(At the beginning of the lecture of 18.12.1913, GA 148, Rudolf Steiner himself alludes to the 'sacrifice' of sheaths described in this book.)

In this sense we should with full clarity distinguish the personality of Rudolf Steiner from those spiritual Beings who worked *through* him. Such a distinction is utterly necessary here. For a confusion of this kind would in this case be a sign that the way in which the Christ-impulse works in *modern* initiation has not been understood.

The difficulties that stand in the way of such an understanding today are connected with the fact that, in the personality of Rudolf Steiner, a kind of initiation which as such only became possible at the end of Kali-Yuga and the beginning of the new age of Michael was accomplished *for the first time* amongst and on behalf of mankind. For certain highly important qualities of modern initiation were in former centuries not yet attainable for even the most sublime teachers of humanity (see GA 233a, 13.1.1924). Thus it would be a serious mistake if one were to seek to judge the initiation of Rudolf Steiner on the basis of notions derived from the former kind of initiation.

The second point concerns a question that may be formulated as follows: was the author familiar with the various difficulties associated with the fulfilment of the Christmas Conference on Earth during the life and after the death of Rudolf Steiner when he was writing his book? The author can answer this question clearly in the affirmative. However, the fact that he has barely touched upon (or, to be more exact, has touched upon only from a particular aspect) the *earthly* difficulties associated with the fulfilment of the impulse of the Christmas Conference—the fundamental anthroposophical impulse—has a deep foundation. For the standpoint from which the author has considered this theme in his book is not of an outwardly historical but of an *occult* nature. This means that from the outset the principal point of emphasis had to be the reality of the actual spiritual impulse and not the physical appearances surrounding it, just as a 'historical' study of the events of Palestine which does not penetrate to the spiritual reality lying behind them could never lead to a true understanding of its place and significance for human evolution as a whole.

Thus the whole complex of the problems associated with the fulfilment of the impulses of the Christmas Conference is from the outset viewed from a sphere where the exoteric concept of 'success' or 'failure' wholly loses its significance, and where the sole *reality* is the 'mystical fact' of the ongoing *living spiritual impulse*, which has its origin in what happened in Dornach at Christmas 1923 and which can only be understood as a process of becoming. For this event is not of the 'past' but something *spiritually present* to which every anthroposophist can gain access in *every* moment of his life, if he does but safeguard the occult standpoint regarding this question which is in this case uniquely correct.

Rudolf Steiner himself writes about this occult standpoint in *Knowledge of the Higher Worlds. How is it Achieved?* 'The pupil must learn not to despair over failure. He must be capable of the thought: "I will forget that I have once more failed in this matter and will try again as if nothing had happened." In this way he struggles through to the conviction that the sources of strength in the world upon which he can draw are inexhaustible. He struggles ever onwards to the spirit which will uplift and support him, however weak and feeble his earthly nature may have proved to be. He must be able to press on into the future, undismayed by any experiences of the past.' For when a human being is in incarnation he can never be absolutely sure that every spiritual impulse which he has inwardly taken hold of can be adequately 'incarnated' *at once* in the corresponding physical reality. Thus the spiritual world does not expect a speedy and complete fulfilment but a constant *endeavour* to reach this goal and an unbreakable *faithfulness* towards it. Rudolf Steiner speaks about this in the lecture on Michaelmas Eve 1923, where he characterizes this inner attitude as the only one that is in accordance with the will of Michael.

'This ability to rise to the point where thoughts about spirit can grip us as powerfully as anything in the physical world, this is Michael power! To have confidence in the ideas of spirit—given the capacity to receive them at all—in such a way as to know: I have received a spiritual impulse of one kind or another. I give myself up to it, I make myself the instrument for its execution. First failure—never mind! Second failure—never mind! Even if there are a hundred failures, what does it matter? For no failure is ever a decisive factor in judging the truth of a spiritual impulse whose effect has been inwardly grasped and understood. We have full confidence in a spiritual impulse which we have grasped at a particular moment only when we can say to ourselves: I have failed a hundred times, but this can at most prove that the conditions for bringing this impulse to realization have not been given to me in this incarnation. However, I know from its own nature that this impulse is right. And although I may have to wait a hundred incarnations for the power to enable this impulse to grow within me, nothing but its own nature can convince me of the efficacy or impotence of any spiritual impulse.

'If you can imagine this thought as developed in the human mind into a great confidence in something of a spiritual nature, if you can conceive that man will cling with rock-like certainty to something that he has seen to be spiritually victorious, so firmly that he refuses to relinquish it even if the outer world vents its opposition against it, you will have an idea of what the Michael power, the being of Michael, is really asking of us; for only then will you comprehend what it is to have full confidence in the spirit ... And when confidence in the spirit has in this way established a disposition of

357

soul such that we are enabled to experience the spirit to be as real as the ground under our feet (of which we know that if it were not there we could not take a step at all), we shall have developed a true awareness of what Michael really wants of us' (GA 223).

The author sees in the spirit of these words of Rudolf Steiner the substantiation and the need for the standpoint that he has adopted. For this book does not wish to speak of faithfulness in the abstract sense but of faithfulness towards an *actual living Spirit* who is working within the anthroposophical movement and who seeks to become manifest through the Christmas Conference in the General Anthroposophical Society. And the future of Anthroposophy on Earth, and—with it—the future of the whole spiritual culture of mankind, depends on *this Spirit* becoming a reality in the modern world.

The new generation of anthroposophists, who bring with them a completely different *experience* from their participation in the anthroposophical movement *before* birth, can find the right path into the future— and the possibility of bringing the impulse which they brought from the spiritual world to fulfilment—only in the sense of Rudolf Steiner's words quoted above. For these words, which bring to expression *his* will, which was grounded by him in the hearts of this new generation, are at the same time the revelation of the will of Michael, who turns to us, the anthroposophists of the end of the century, and whose intentions can become a reality on Earth only through us.

Sergei O. Prokofieff
Stuttgart, December 1985

Notes

All works by Rudolf Steiner are referred to by the *Gesamtausgabe* (GA) volume number from the catalogue of the collected edition of Rudolf Steiner's works in the original German (published by *Rudolf Steiner Verlag*, Dornach, Switzerland). For information on the published English language translations see the list on pages 455–59.

Chapter 1. The Years of Apprenticeship

1 Gospel of St Matthew 3: 2. Emil Bock's translation.
2 Friedrich Rittelmeyer, *Rudolf Steiner Enters My Life*.
3 GA 26, No. 1, 17.2.1924.
4 GA 243, 16.8.1924.
5 See Note 53, Chapter 3.
6 GA 262, the *Notes of Barr*.
7 GA 243, 16.8.1924.
8 Ibid.
9 GA 240, Vol. VI, 1.6.1924.
10 GA 34.
11 GA 28, Chapter 1.
12 A lecture given to a Russian audience in Helsinki, 11.4.1912, GA 158.
13 GA 102.
14 GA 148, 2.10.1913.
15 'Self-Education. Rudolf Steiner's Childhood and Youth up to the Weimar Period', 4.2.1913.
16 Ibid.
17 GA 28, Chapter 1.
18 Compare GA 136 with GA 110.
19 GA 28, Chapter 1.
20 GA 235, Vol. I, 23.3.1924.
21 GA 28, Chapter 2.
22 GA 235, Vol. I, 23.3.1924.
23 See Note 15.
24 GA 28, Chapter 1.
25 GA 174a, 17.2.1918.
26 In GA 99, Lecture 9, Rudolf Steiner describes the Beings of the Archai Hierarchy as consisting of the following seven bodily members: 'I', Spirit Self, Life Spirit and Spirit Man as a 'lower' fourfoldness, and the Holy Spirit, the Son (Logos) and the Father as a higher threefoldness.

27　Rudolf Steiner spoke on many occasions of how, of all the four kingdoms of nature, only man by virtue of his 'I' belongs directly to the Earth-sphere. (This is also the cause of his individualization.) The animals belong with their 'I'—as group-'I'—to the astral plane, and the plants and minerals have their 'I' on the Lower and Upper Devachanic planes respectively. GA 93a, 30.10.1905.

28　GA 28, Chapter 3.

29　GA 262 (Part 1).

30　GA 28, Chapter 3.

31　GA 262 (Part 1).

32　GA 28,　Chapter 3, also for the following quotations.

33　GA 262 (Part 1).

34　Ibid.

35　Rudolf Steiner speaks in some detail of Schröer in GA 238, Vol. IV, 23.9.1924. See also Emil Bock, *Rudolf Steiner, Studien*, Lecture 2.

36　GA 262 (Part 1).

37　GA 28, Chapter 5, and also for the following quotations.

38　GA 148, 2.10.1913.

39　See Edouard Schuré's Foreword to his French translation of Rudolf Steiner's GA 8, written in 1907 on the basis of a personal conversation with Rudolf Steiner in Barr in Alsace.

40　Rudolf Steiner speaks about the luciferic nature of public opinion in GA 141, 12.1.1913.

41　GA 28, Chapter 3.

42　See Note 39.

Chapter 2. The Great Sun Period

1　GA 262 (Part 1).

2　Ibid.

3　GA 28, Chapter 23.

4　GA 107.

5　GA 171, 17.9.1916.

6　GA 262 (Part 1).

7　GA 28, Chapter 5.

8　Ibid., Chapter 11.

9　Ibid., Chapter 7.

10　Ibid., Chapter 11—also for the following quotations.

11　Ibid., Chapter 8.

12　Ibid., Chapter 5.

13　Ibid., Chapter 8.

14　Ibid., Chapter 10.

15　The significance of the year 1888 in Rudolf Steiner's inner development, when the first significant blow was struck against the forces of Ahriman, is mentioned by Rudolf Steiner in his notebook in 1924. The pages in question are published in Rudolf Grosse, *The Christmas Foundation*, pp. 119–21.

16   GA 28, Chapter 7.
17   GA 240, Vol. VI, 18.7.1924.
18   GA 28, Chapter 8.
19   Ibid., Chapter 19.
20   Ibid., Chapter 17.
21   GA 184.
22   GA 174a, 17.2.1918.
23   GA 240, Vol. VIII, 12.8.1924.
24   GA 174a, 17.2.1918.
25   GA 103, Lecture 12.
26   GA 240, Vol. VI, 19.7.1924.
27   Ibid.
28   GA 28, Chapter 17.
29   GA 240, Vol. VIII, 12.8.1924.
30   GA 28, Chapter 16.
31   Ibid., Chapter 22.
32   Ibid., Chapter 23.
33   Ibid., Chapter 24.
34   GA 262 (Part 1).
35   Ibid.
36   GA 28, Chapter 30.
37   Ibid., Chapter 27.
38   Ibid., Chapter 26.
39   GA 13, pp. 296–97.
40   One can establish this date primarily on the basis that during the winter of 1900–01 Rudolf Steiner gave a lecture in the salon of Count Brockdorff in Berlin, in which the results of his most recent experience of the nature of Christianity are fully presented. These lectures were then worked through again into the book *Mysticism at the Dawn of the Modern Age* (GA 7).
41   GA 233a.
42   GA 130.
43   See GA 13. In the first four (German) editions, one of the sections of Chapter 5 ended with the words: 'And yet every true Intuition is "work with the Stone of the Wise".' For every Intuition directly affects those forces which work from the supersensible world right down into the world of sense.' (Translated from the fourth German edition, Leipzig 1913.)
44   GA 112, 7.6.1909.
45   GA 152, 27.5.1914.
46   GA 130.
47   Ibid.
48   F. Rittelmeyer, *Rudolf Steiner Enters My Life*.
49   GA 130, 18.12.1912.
50   See Note 48.

51   GA 129, 24.8.1911.
52   The spiritual sum of the connections between the two great teachers of humanity was subsequently brought to expression by Rudolf Steiner himself in the Imagination that he gave after the Christmas Conference in response to the question regarding his relationship to Christian Rosenkreutz. See Note 148 in Chapter 3.
53   GA 152, 7.3.1914.
54   Continuation of a lecture on 20.5.1923 (GA 226).
55   One must particularly emphasize here that Rudolf Steiner always spoke not so much of an imitation of Christ but primarily of *service* to Christ. (The former took place in traditional Christian initiation.) The reasons for this were connected with the profound secret whereby that which has once been attained by humanity in spiritual development is never lost but lives on, unfolding and ascending according to the laws of living metamorphosis into ever higher spheres of existence. In Chapter 1 it was shown that the Christian-Rosicrucian path of initiation is, in certain respects, divided into two halves. The pupil first undergoes a development, the aim of which is to bring him to a personal supersensible meeting with Christ. The second half is the realization of the consequences of this meeting. In this sense it is possible to speak of the first half of the path as being true *service* to Christ, leading finally to a conscious experience of His Being in the spiritual world, and expressing itself then in the fulfilment of the words 'Not I, but Christ in me'. In these words in turn is contained a true knowledge of the relation of macrocosm and microcosm, of the macrocosmic 'I' of Christ and the microcosmic 'I' of man. At this moment the initiate reaches the summit of his *path of service*, and by consciously experiencing in the microcosm of himself the macrocosmic principle of Christ is now able to make of his life a free reflection of the life of Christ. The path of service continues from then onwards in its highest form: it becomes, step by step, a path of imitation. Thus what we have here is a spiritual metamorphosis in which the traditional Christian path of initiation is repeated at a higher level and in a different form, related now to the epoch of human freedom. And the particular significance of Rudolf Steiner's words in Lecture 14, GA 112, becomes clear; he said that in traditional Christian initiation the *direct* perception of the Mystery of Golgotha was revealed only at the beginning of the fourth stage, which in turn, in the Christian-Rosicrucian path of initiation, corresponds to the experiencing of the Christ Being in the sphere of Intuition (i.e. also the fourth stage). This latter stage is described by Rudolf Steiner in Chapter 6, GA 28. Here, however, one can refer to these interconnections only fleetingly.
      In the traditional Christian initiation, however, the pupil began at once with the imitation that presupposed, as an essential condition, that the pupil withdraw from the world. In the modern Christian-Rosicrucian initiation, in contrast, the pupil begins with conscious *service* stemming from a genuine understanding of the Christ Being as this is revealed to us in spiritual science.

362

In this sense, service of this kind, stemming from understanding, is possible in the present time for *every* human being of good will, and is possible in this form only when arising from full individual freedom. Only at higher levels, when the pupil has attained the stage of Teacher, can his service to Christ become true imitation of Him, revealing itself in this as the highest manifestation of human freedom from which the initiate can then act in the spirit of the cosmic principle of love and self-offering. In this way the path of service gives the pupil the possibility of gathering those spiritual forces that are essential for him, in order that at a higher stage he may then be able to sacrifice them for the good of the world. In the last chapter of *Knowledge of the Higher Worlds*, Rudolf Steiner speaks of this sacrifice of forces that are acquired through individual development at the higher stages of initiation as being the most important principle of the new spiritual path. By virtue of this book, service to Christ becomes in a completely natural way the imitation of Him, for even the great macrocosmic path of Christ is nothing other than a path of continual cosmic sacrifice, fulfilled out of the purest love and compassion for the world. (In conclusion one can add that a similar metamorphosis was also undergone in the Christian-Rosicrucian initiation, and with the fundamental principles of the esoteric regulation of the breathing as practised, for example, in eastern Yoga. In Yoga, work on the conscious experience of the breath comes at the beginning of the path; in the Christian-Rosicrucian initiation it belongs to the inner meditative exercise that is introduced only at the fourth stage of Intuition, when work of this nature is able to contribute to the transformation of the earthly physical body into Spirit Man.)

56   GA 15.
57   GA 148.

Chapter 3. The Path of the Teacher of Humanity

1   GA 28, Chapter 27.
2   This division of the development of the anthroposophical movement into three seven-year periods, often taken in anthroposophical literature as corresponding to the last three full seven-year periods of Rudolf Steiner's life (see *Awakening to Community*, GA 257, 6.2.1923), can be deepened further by a comparison of these periods with the three systems of the human organism and the three faculties of the soul, as follows:

1902–09	Head system	Thinking
1910–16	Rhythmic system	Feeling
1917–23	Limb system	Willing

3   GA 28, Chapters 30 and 31.
4   GA 262, *Notes of Barr*, Part III.
5   Ibid.
6   The term 'Anthroposophy' for the spiritual direction headed by Rudolf

Steiner (as distinct from 'Theosophy') appears at the very beginning of his lecturing activity. As early as the autumn of 1902 Rudolf Steiner gave a cycle of lectures in Berlin entitled *From Zarathustra to Nietzsche: The history of the development of humanity on the basis of the world-view from the most ancient oriental ages up to the present or Anthroposophy.* At the beginning of the following year Rudolf Steiner completed his forty-second year.

7   GA 28, Chapter 31.

8   GA 110.

9   A lecture given to a Russian audience in Helsinki on 11.4.1912 (GA 158).

10   GA 112, 30.6.1909.

11   GA 110.

12   According to Rudolf Steiner (GA 28, Chapter 31), his expulsion was a result of his refusal to accept members of the 'Order of the Star in the East' into the German section of the Theosophical Society. This Order saw its task in proclaiming the reincarnation of Christ in the person of a Hindu boy, Krishnamurti. This absurd affair of the 'new Messiah' was, in a spiritual sense, primarily an attempt by certain occult circles of the East to work against the new Christian occultism arising in the West. In a letter in 1913, Schuré writes the following, founded on facts that were known to him: 'In reality this affair was nothing other than the answer of Adyar to the birth of Christian esotericism, and I am convinced that without this esotericism we would never have heard of the future prophet (i.e. Krishnamurti).' (Quoted from Rihouet Coroze's book *Biographie de Rudolf Steiner,* p. 220, Triades, Paris 1973.) And yet this affair had a still deeper background. Edouard Schuré says in the letter quoted above that even in 1908 there was still no mention whatever within the Theosophical Society of any appearance of the Messiah, and yet he immediately became known in all the branches of the Theosophical Society after he had been officially presented in *October 1909* to a full assembly in Benares and recognized unanimously as the Messiah. If now we compare this with what, in a completely different context, Rudolf Steiner said concerning the significance of the year 1909, the real occult background of all these events becomes clear. Thus in a lecture on 6.2.1917 in GA 175 he says: 'and the occultist can point directly to how, since about 1909, in a clearly perceptible way there has been in preparation that which is to come; that since 1909 we live inwardly in very special times. And it is possible today—one has only to try—to be very close to Christ, to find Christ in a completely different way than was possible in earlier times.' Thus in the year of the appearance of the Etheric Christ in the *supersensible* sphere closest to the physical world, the attempt was made on Earth by certain occult circles to counterfeit this most important spiritual event of the twentieth century.

13   In the nineteenth century only a few of the representatives of occultism could find the forces in themselves to penetrate to the new revelation. To these few belonged, for example, Edouard Schuré. Perhaps this is why, at the start, Rudolf Steiner valued his work so highly.

14 GA 28, Chapter 36.

15 GA 116, 25.10.1909.

16 Ibid.

17 GA 28, Chapter 30.

18 If one does not bear in mind what has been said above, it seems quite incomprehensible why Rudolf Steiner should devote his two first and longest purely occult cycles to shedding light on the relation of the Christ Being to the being of the Buddha, since up to that point he had never mentioned the Buddha in an occult sense. In this connection it is barely necessary to remark that a real understanding of the Buddha is impossible without full knowledge of his mission as a Bodhisattva.

19 Rudolf Steiner speaks of this connection of the Bodhisattvas with the Hierarchy of Angels, that is, with the Moon-sphere, in his lecture on 29.8.1923 in Penmaenmawr (GA 227) and refers there to the Bodhisattvas as 'Moon-emissaries'. And he says further: '...so that ... it was through the Moon-emissaries, who in the Orient are called Bodhisattvas, that the Sun Being also was able to come to the human beings on the Earth.'

20 Rudolf Steiner speaks of the Inspiration received by the Bodhisattva from the Archangel, on 16.4.1909: 'The personalities who are ensouled even into their etheric body, who in post-Atlantean times bear within them an Archangel—these are called Bodhisattvas' (GA 110).

21 In the lecture of 20.9.1909 (GA 114), Rudolf Steiner says the following: 'The transition from Bodhisattva to Buddha meant that for the first time there existed a body into which the Bodhisattva could *fully descend* and within which his powers could develop.' (See also the lecture of 16.9.1909.)

22 Ibid., 16.9.1909.

23 Rudolf Steiner speaks of this departure of the Angel from the Bodhisattva on the latter's attaining to the last stage of Buddhahood (the stage of Spirit Self), on 20.5.1913: 'The individual guidance of human beings rests upon the Angeloi, the Angel Beings. When a *human being* rises from a Bodhisattva to become a Buddha, his Angel becomes as it were freed. It is Angel Beings of this nature which then, having fulfilled their mission, ascend into the realm of the Archangel Beings' (GA 152).

24 In his lecture on 18.4.1909, Rudolf Steiner defines the body of the Nirmanakaya as the astral body that has been purified and transformed into Spirit Self. He says there: 'In short, we have thereby depicted a particularly high being who has attained to this advanced stage by fully developing Spirit Self. This being, in eastern teachings, is called Nirmanakaya...' (GA 110).

25 Here originates the term 'Buddha-Mercury', which is known in occultism and can also be found in Blavatsky. We can perhaps come to some comprehension of what it means by looking at what Rudolf Steiner said in a lecture on 12.4.1909: 'Had one been able to understand the connection between what was seen by Dionysius the Areopagite and what was seen by

the ancient holy Rishis, one would have heard, so to speak, the Moon named on the one hand, and from the other Mysteries the world of the Angels named on the other hand, and one would have known that these were one and the same thing. One would have heard the word Mercury on the one hand, and the word Archangel on the other, and known that these were the same thing' (GA 110).

26 Lecture by Adolf Arenson, given in Stuttgart on 30.3.1930. *Fruits of Earnest Study*, Vol. I.

27 GA 131, 14.10.1911.

28 GA 113, 31.8.1909.

29 This circumstance in Rudolf Steiner's inner development corresponds fully to the tradition of esoteric Christianity, in which the most important result of the conscious meeting with Christ is an experience of the Holy Spirit who is sent by Him. This in turn leads to contact with the sphere of the Bodhisattvas, who in their twelvefoldness form in the World of Foreknowledge (the World of Providence) the 'body of the Holy Spirit'. GA 93a.

30 GA 107, 22.3.1909.

31 See for example GA 116, 25.10.1909.

32 Rudolf Steiner also speaks of this as follows: 'And to the extent that the human being purifies, cleanses and ennobles the astral body (that is, transforms it into Spirit Self), to that extent, in esoteric Christianity, is the Holy Spirit said to be present in him. Using a theosophical expression one could also say: that part of the astral body which has been purified by the "I" is called in esoteric Christianity the part of the astral body that is embraced (*ergriffen*) by the Holy Spirit.' GA 117, 25.3.1907.

33 GA 103, 13.5.1908.

34 'The Spirit of Christmas' in GA 117, 26.12.1909.

35 GA 42/245.

36 GA 113, 31.8.1909.

37 We can have a feeling of his outstanding position in this assembly when Rudolf Steiner calls the Buddha 'the most intimate pupil and friend of Christian Rosenkreutz' (GA 130, 18.12.1912). See also GA 141, 22.12.1912.

38 GA 123, 10.9.1910.

39 GA 28, Chapter 37.

40 GA 262, the comments for Letter No. 28.

41 Because of the beginning of the Russo-Japanese war, this journey did not take place at that time. Later, in 1912–13, it was cancelled again. Because of pressure from the Orthodox Synod, Rudolf Steiner was refused an entry permit into Russia.

42 These words should not be understood to mean that all the content of anthroposophical teachings is derived from inspirations from this Bodhisattva. The Bodhisattva worked then primarily through Rudolf Steiner's astral body. Other cosmic forces were at work through his other bodies.

Likewise, the influences from the Michael-sphere and the sphere of Christian Rosenkreutz do not cease for a moment. Thus in the separate epochs of Rudolf Steiner's life these different spiritual Beings work within him with varying degrees of intensity. This means that in each period a *dominant* influence can arise, or sometimes a number of influences at the same time. These changing influences can be distinguished in acquainting oneself with the development of the fundamental themes running through all Rudolf Steiner's lecturing activity. One must, however, also stress here that *all* these lofty Guides of humanity draw their wisdom from one Source, from the Cosmic Wisdom of the Holy Spirit, but each represents only one aspect of it.

43 In what has been said here we should not be surprised that such different and lofty spiritual forces and leaders of humanity worked through Rudolf Steiner. In this case it was not only possible but also absolutely essential. We have to picture to ourselves the full compass and magnitude of spiritual wisdom which came into the world by virtue of the earthly work of Rudolf Steiner. Where, in all the external history of humanity's development, do we find anything similar? 'Already in just an aesthetic sense the panorama of this all-encompassing picture of the world, embracing as it does both matter and spirit, is something immensely powerful and magnificent. And knowing something of the spiritual history of humanity one must ask: where has humanity ever experienced anything similar? Aristotle, Thomas Aquinas—here there was more...' (F. Rittelmeyer, Stuttgart 1980, loc. cit.). These words by Rittelmeyer point to Rudolf Steiner's place in the spiritual and cultural life of western humanity. All the fundamental aspirations of western humanity—the problem concerning the Christ, the individual 'I', free will, the nature of thinking, science, art, religion—all these problems are to be found focused in Rudolf Steiner as though in an all-encompassing central point; and from him they radiate out again into the world in 6,000 lectures, in dozens of books and articles. A whole picture comes before us of the spiritual life of humanity and of the cosmos. This comes into the world *for the first time*. And we must ask: where can it come from if not from those who guide the spiritual life of humanity, who realize and direct it? Inwardly we cannot consider ourselves anthroposophists to the last fibre of our being if we are not fully aware that when in his lectures Rudolf Steiner spoke, for example, about a Bodhisattva, the Bodhisattva was beside him; that when he spoke of Christian Rosenkreutz, of Manes, Skythianos, Zarathustra, Buddha, all these great Teachers of mankind stood before his spiritual gaze, blessing him in his service to them and to humanity, and opening before him the revelation of their own nature and being. This is a *spiritual reality* which it is essential that every anthroposophist recognizes fully. But there also follows from this the great *responsibility* of those who now continue Rudolf Steiner's work on Earth—the responsibility of *every* anthroposophist before the spiritual world, and above all before those lofty spiritual Beings

who through their great representative sent down to the Earth the new spiritual revelation. The destiny of this revelation is now indissolubly bound with the destiny of all humanity.

44 GA 175, 6.2.1917.

45 Rudolf Steiner often indicated in his later statements concerning the Fifth Gospel that the beginning of these statements was made in the Basle cycle, GA 114.

46 GA 113, 31.8.1909.

47 Adolf Arenson, a lecture given in Stuttgart on 30.3.1930. In *Fruits of Earnest Study*, Vol. I.

48 GA 130, 4.11.1911.

49 GA 118, 25.1.1910.

50 Another important fact is that precisely in 1910, when the Inspirations from the Bodhisattvas were particularly strong, Rudolf Steiner gave the lecture cycle *Occult History* in Stuttgart in which he openly indicates for the first time something of his own past. This theme appears again (and essentially unchanged) in the cycle that he gave during the Christmas Conference and in the Karma lectures.

51 GA 120, 28.5.1910.

52 We can come to a conception of this concord also from Rudolf Steiner's words in his lecture on 20.11.1911 (GA 130) after he had indicated the necessity in our time of finding new sources of Christianity: 'And towards this goal we see the coming-together of the spiritual stream flowing from Jeshu ben Pandira and that stream which at the beginning of the thirteenth century united with Christian Rosenkreutz... Thus there work together the stream of the Maitreya Buddha and the western stream connected with Christian Rosenkreutz.'

53 Occupying an important place in the path of Rudolf Steiner's life is also that cosmic rhythm of which he speaks in a lecture on 18.5.1924 (GA 236). In this lecture he refers to two exceptionally important periods in the life of a human being which he calls the periods of 'karmic challenges' and of 'karmic fulfilment'. The first period extends from birth to the age of 21, and the second from 28 to 49. If now we turn our attention particularly to the beginning, middle and end of these two periods, we find the following rhythm in Rudolf Steiner's life:

Karmic Challenges

1861 His birth on the border between East and West, the 5th and 6th cultural epochs. Thus already by the place of his birth his mission was preordained, namely, to lay the foundations for humanity's gradual transition from the culture of the consciousness soul to the culture of Spirit Self.

1872 He enters the *Realschule* and not the *Gymnasium* in Wiener-Neustadt, which later determined the whole way in which he approached Christianity (see GA 240, 18.7.1924).

368

(Around)
1881 His meeting with his Teacher, whose envoy was the herb-gatherer.

Karmic Fulfilments

1889 His journey to Germany, in which he visits three cities: Weimar, Berlin and Munich. All these cities play a particular role in his destiny. The whole of his fifth seven-year period, which was so important for his inner development, was spent in Weimar. Berlin and Munich later became two important centres of anthroposophical activity (GA 28 Chapter 38).

(Around)
1899 The experience of the Christ in the sphere of Intuition (GA 28, Chapter 26).

1910 The beginning of the proclamation of the Second Coming of Christ in the etheric world.

54 Already from the descriptions Rudolf Steiner gives of this fact one can see that Goethe, who in his artistic work anticipated many of the ideas of Anthroposophy (for example, his Fairy Tale served as the foundation for the first Mystery Drama), prepared his incarnation as Goethe in the sphere of Jupiter (GA 239, 9.6.1924).

55 GA 123, 2.8.1910.

56 Most important too is the fact that these lectures were given in Basle, i.e. close to Dornach, where at the laying of the Foundation Stone of the First Goetheanum the words 'Fifth Gospel' were used for the first time, and the macrocosmic 'Our Father' was read, which according to Rudolf Steiner is the beginning of that Gospel.

57 GA 114, 18.9.1909.

58 GA 175, 6.2.1917.

59 GA 142, 1.1.1913.

60 For the three pre-Christian sacrifices of the Nathan Soul, see GA 152, 7.3.1914.

61 What is meant here is the *whole* participation of Zarathustra in the events of Palestine as described in the Gospel of St Matthew, bearing in mind that Zarathustra's *direct* participation in the preparation of the sheaths for the incarnation of Christ spanned only 18 years, i.e. from the time onwards of his union with the Nathan Jesus child, as indicated in the Gospel of St Luke 2: 42–50.

62 Luke 1: 2.

63 I Corinthians 15: 45 et seq.

64 GA 114, 18.9.1909.

65 This tradition is supported in the third lecture (6.7.1909) of GA 112, in which it is said that in a certain way St Luke gave humanity, in a form compatible with its stage of development at that time, the Gospel of St Paul himself. Apart from this, and pointing to this particular connection of St Luke with St Paul, there is the fact that it was Luke who wrote the Acts of

the Apostles, in which the majority of events touch first and foremost on the life of the Apostle Paul.

66 It should not be a hindrance to an understanding of these words of the Gospel that the Nathan Soul is spoken of in them in the plural: 'even as they delivered them unto us', for as becomes clear from the lecture on 30.12.1913, in GA 149, it is also possible to address the Nathan Soul in the plural; this in turn bears out its role in our cosmos, in which it appears as the archetype of all humanity. (In this connection one can also remember that in the Gospel the shepherds in the fields saw the Nirmanakaya of Buddha as a host of Angels.)

67 GA 114, 16.9.1909.

68 From a lecture on 19.9.1914 quoted in Rudolf Grosse, *The Christmas Foundation*, p. 45.

69 The speech at the laying of the Foundation Stone of the Goetheanum. See GA 42/245.

70 This particular relationship between the Gospel of St Luke and that of St John is also expressed in the [previous] title of the lecture cycle, i.e. *The Gospel of St John in Relation to the Other Three Gospels*, particularly to the Gospel of St Luke. It seems that before the revealing of the secrets of the Fifth Gospel it was necessary to throw light on the relation between these two Gospels.

71 See GA 148, 2.10.1913.

72 See GA 104, 30.6.1908.

73 GA 42/245.

74 Here we have taken primarily two Gospels—that of St Luke and St John—as the Gospel of Jesus and the Gospel of Christ. These together encompass the *whole* evolution of the Earth from Moon to Jupiter, from the Old to the New Adam, from the planet of wisdom to the planet of love. But in this polarity are also included the other two Gospels. The Gospel of St Matthew is also connected in the sense above with the past, but not such a distant past; its genealogy only reaches back to Abraham. The Gospel of St Mark points in the same way to the future, but not quite as far as Jupiter. For this reason the Fifth Gospel, as the Gospel of Eternity, encompasses all four Gospels.

75 In a lecture on 1.1.1913 in GA 142, Rudolf Steiner speaks of how the soul of the Nathan Jesus was not only the bearer of Love and Sacrifice, but also of the *Cosmic Wisdom* of all humanity's evolution. He says there: 'Thus this soul still has all the wisdom which could be experienced through the Saturn, Sun and Moon time...' And he continues: 'This Luke Jesus child had no special human knowledge, but bore within him divine wisdom and the divine ability for sacrifice.' And he relates in the same lecture that from ancient times, those who had been initiated into the Mysteries were always able to communicate with the Being of the Nathan Soul, who was at that time in the spiritual worlds. Later, when this soul incarnated in the Nathan Jesus child and at the age of 12 received the Zarathustra ego into him, all the wisdom which could be gathered on Earth by the ego of the most

important initiate in the course of the Earth's development was united with the Wisdom of the Cosmos. In this way a vessel was created on Earth for the Being of the Christ, for the Representative of the cosmic principle of Love, which contained all the cosmic and earthly wisdom of human development.

76 GA 13.

77 GA 42/245.

78 The following study presupposes that the reader is acquainted with the spiritual-scientific exegesis on the Lord's Prayer—the fundamental Christian Prayer (see *The Structure of the Lord's Prayer*, GA 97)—and with the description of the three pre-Christian sacrifices of Christ through the Nathan Soul.

79 In a lecture in Basle on 1.6.1914 in GA 152, Rudolf Steiner speaks of these three pre-Christian sacrifices of Christ through the Nathan Soul as follows: 'And in a certain way there are three Mysteries of Golgotha which, we must say, did not occur on the physical plane. The fourth was enacted on the physical plane and is the one that is proclaimed to us in the four Gospels and in the Letters of St Paul.'

80 Rudolf Steiner also points to this drawing-near, while speaking of how the three pre-Christian sacrifices occurred through the Nathan Soul on different levels of existence: 'thus did the Christ gradually draw nearer the Earth. The first and second preliminary stages were in the Devachanic world, the third in the astral world, and the Event of Golgotha in the physical world' (GA 152, 30.3.1914).

81 Rudolf Steiner speaks of the archangelic nature of the Nathan Soul on many occasions in different lectures. In the lectures of the first half of 1914 (which are collected in GA 152), he speaks of this, but particularly clearly perhaps in the beginning of a lecture in Pforzheim on 7.3.1914 as follows: 'And in these preparatory events for the Mystery of Golgotha it was once again the same Being, who was then born as the Nathan Jesus child and who was permeated by the Christ Being. This is the important thing about the Mystery of Golgotha, that the Jesus Being who grew up as the Nathan child was permeated through and through by the Christ Being. But this Being, who later became the Jesus Being, was also involved in the three earlier events, but was not incarnated as a human being. He lived as a spiritual, *archangelic-like* Being in the spiritual worlds. And in the spiritual worlds, the preliminary stages to the Mystery of Golgotha, he was permeated by the Christ Being: once in the Lemurian epoch and twice during the Atlantean.' Later, in Basle on 1.6.1914, Rudolf Steiner *particularly stressed* in this lecture the *archangelic-like* nature of the Being who had participated in the three cosmic preliminary stages of the Mystery of Golgotha. And finally, his frequent indications—particularly in GA 114, 18.9.1909—are a further confirmation of the archangelic nature of the Nathan Soul. He points here to the particular connection of this Soul with those cosmic *etheric* forces which in the Lemurian epoch were held back by the Guiding Powers of the Cosmos from falling to the luciferic influences of temptation, and were

preserved in the Mother Lodge for the future development of humanity. In this sense the Nathan Soul is the representative of these purest cosmic *etheric* forces in the cosmos. This in particular shows his *archangelic* nature; that is, the nature of a hierarchical Being that possesses Life Spirit, the transformed *etheric* body. In this connection it is of especial significance that in the Gospel of St Luke it is an Archangel that appears to Mary at the Annunciation.

82 To be exact, Rudolf Steiner describes this process as follows: 'Then tormented humanity's cry of pain penetrated to the heights of that spiritual being of the Nathan Soul. The cry drove that being to the Sun Spirit, so that it was able to be permeated by the Christ.' (5.3.1914, GA 152.)

83 John 1: 18.

84 See GA 233, 25.12.1923.

85 See GA 110, 17.4.1909.

86 See GA 201, 18.4.1920.

87 See GA 122, 22.8.1910.

88 For Christ as the bearer of the macrocosmic principle of the Cosmic-'I', see particularly the lecture in Munich on 9.1.1912 and also the notes to the lecture in Stuttgart on 28.11.1911 (both in GA 130).

89 GA 123, 12.9.1910.

90 In connection with the relation of Jehovah to the Holy Spirit, see the lecture of 1.4.1907 in GA 96.

91 Rudolf Steiner speaks in detail of these three stages of Christ's drawing near the Earth on 24.6.1909 in GA 112.

92 For the relation of the principles of Father, Son and Spirit to the past conditions of our cosmos in the epochs of Saturn, Sun and Moon, see 2.6.1907 in GA 99.

93 It is necessary to emphasize here that the Nathan Soul also has an 'I' which, it is true, is of a completely different nature from the human 'I'; for the human 'I' has become as we know it only by virtue of the experiences of many lives on Earth, through which the Nathan Soul did not go. The Nathan Soul's 'I' in this sense is a purest spark of the divine substance of the Spirits of Form. Rudolf Steiner expresses it thus: 'So what we are dealing with is purely an "I"-like soul, which as it penetrates into the body of Jesus functions naturally like an "I"' (GA 142, 1.1.1913).
    But he speaks more definitely of this: 'The substance which was poured down by the Spirits of Form flowed on but, one could say, something was retained—one could say, one "I" was retained which was exempt from entering into a body of flesh and blood—an "I" which, if we want to express it in biblical terms, continued in the condition of the "I" of Adam before its first earthly embodiment. Such an "I" always existed' (GA 131, 12.10.1911).

94 GA 148, 5.10.1912.

95 From a somewhat different point of view it is possible to connect the four stages of ascent in the second part of the macrocosmic 'Our Father'—ascent from physical body to etheric body to astral body to the 'I'—with the

following description given by Rudolf Steiner in Milan on 21.9.1911 (in GA 130): 'That individuality which was the Christ-Individuality was on the Earth in the body of Jesus of Nazareth for only three years, and will not come again in a physical body. He will come in the fifth cultural epoch in the etheric body, in the sixth cultural epoch in the astral body, and in the seventh epoch in a great Cosmic "I" that is like a great group-soul of all humanity.' On 4.11.1911 in Leipzig Rudolf Steiner brings this higher appearance of the Christ in future epochs into connection with the different spheres of the cosmos. Thus in our time Christ reveals Himself in etheric form on the astral plane; in the sixth epoch He will appear in astral form in the sphere of Lower Devachan, and finally, in the seventh epoch, in the form of the great macrocosmic 'I' in the sphere of Upper Devachan.

96 A lecture on 22.9.1913, *Schicksalszeichen auf dem Entwicklungswege der Anthroposophischen Gesellschaft.*

97 From memoirs of Marie Steiner, published in *Was in der anthroposophischen Gesellschaft vorgeht* on 16.8.1925, p. 28.

98 From the memoirs of Nelly Grosheintz-Laval, of a conversation between Rudolf Steiner and her husband, Dr Grosheintz, in Basle after the first visit to Dornach. (See Rudolf Grosse, *The Christmas Foundation.*)

99 GA 148, 4.10.1913.

100 The speech given at the laying of the Foundation Stone of the Goetheanum (GA 42/245).

101 Ibid.

102 22.9.1913, quoted in Rudolf Grosse, *The Christmas Foundation.*

103 In his book *The Foundation Stone*, Zeylmans van Emmichoven also speaks about this mysterious 'connection between the building and the builder': 'Rudolf Steiner had brought down from exalted spiritual realms the formative forces for this Goetheanum Being, built as it was on the frontier of the physical and the etheric worlds. One may also say that the forces of his own etheric sheath were built into it. When the building met its fiery death, not only Rudolf Steiner's work but his own life-forces were affected.'

104 GA 262, Letter 210. See also Note 142.

105 Perhaps this is the reason why, exactly four months before the laying of the Foundation Stone, Rudolf Steiner gave two lectures in Stuttgart on 18 and 20 May entitled 'The Michael Impulse and the Mystery of Golgotha' (in GA 152).

106 The Mystery of the laying of the Foundation Stone of the First Goetheanum on 20.9.1913 in Dornach. The text, taken in shorthand, was printed for the first time in Rudolf Grosse, *The Christmas Foundation* pp. 30–36 (see Note 96).

107 Rudolf Steiner's words from an article of 18.3.1923 (GA 36).

108 At the end of 1914 Andrei Belyi was working with his wife, the artist Assya Turgeniev, on the capital of the Jupiter column, and at the beginning of 1915 on the capital of the Mars column in the larger cupola of the Goetheanum; at the time described these forms were already fixed on the

columns; the final carving work was done on scaffolding directly under the cupola.

109 Andrei Belyi, *Epopeya Ya*, Part 1, 'Return to the Motherland', quoted in the literary miscellany *Zapiski Mechtateley*, No. 1, Alkonost, St Petersburg 1919.

110 Rudolf Steiner says this, for example, about the spiritual impulse of Leo Tolstoy in GA 197, 8.11.1920 and of Vladimir Soloviev in GA 177, 14.10.1917.

111 GA 260.

112 In connection with the division of the course of life into nine seven-year periods corresponding to the nine fundamental cosmic rhythms, it is also important to note that all these seven-year periods are likewise connected among themselves by profound inner laws which, nevertheless, are related to cosmic laws. This is expressed in the fact that certain periods (of seven years) are related particularly closely to certain others, as though a repetition of them but on a higher level. Basically, it is possible to trace three kinds of such interrelations. Thus certain laws of the first seven-year period reappear, in a certain way, in the sixth period, and again at a still higher level in the ninth. In the same way, the second, fifth and eighth seven-year periods belong together; and finally, the third, fourth and seventh. In presenting these laws in connection with Rudolf Steiner's life, we have tried (although, at present only in a very tentative way) to note these interrelations, even though with closer acquaintance with the separate periods of his life they stand out fairly clearly. A more detailed description is not possible for the time being, since this would require a completely separate investigation which would go beyond the range of this book.

113 GA 240, 20.7.1924.

114 This new interrelation between the Gods and human beings in the epoch of freedom was expressed as early as the seventeenth century by Angelus Silesius. He said: 'There is nothing but I and Thou; and if we two were not, God would not be God, and Heaven would tumble down'—'Without me, God cannot create the smallest worm: if I did not maintain it with Him, it would instantly shatter to pieces.'—'I know that without me God cannot live one moment: if I became nothing, He would of necessity have to give up the ghost.' (See *Mysticism at the Dawn of the Modern Age*, GA 7.)

115 Matthew 18: 20.

116 Luke 22: 46.

117 Matthew 22: 37–39, and Mark 12: 29–31.

118 See, for example, the lecture of 3.11.1905, the notes of the esoteric lesson of 9.10.1907 (GA 42/245) and especially of the esoteric lesson of 5.12.1907.

119 In the lecture of 2.4.1923 (GA 223/229), Rudolf Steiner speaks of how the 'Michael Thought' forms the foundation for a true knowledge of the principle of the Trinity.

120 GA 194, 22.11.1919. See further in the lectures of 22, 23 and 30.11.1919.

121 One must note here that Rudolf Steiner perceived this second revelation of Michael significantly earlier (in 1911). He perceived it at that time, how-

ever, not yet directly from the sphere of Michael but through the Bodhi-sattva working in his astral body. He says of this in GA 130, 21.9.1911: 'And if there were for him [the Maitreya Buddha] a "John the Evangelist", he would have to speak differently from the way in which John the Evangelist spoke of Christ. John wrote, "And the Word became flesh"; the "John the Evangelist" of the Maitreya Buddha would have to say, "and the Flesh became Word".'

From a comparison of these two quotations, taken from lectures in 1911 and 1919, the stages can be clearly seen of that ascending path of inner development which Rudolf Steiner himself underwent at this time.

122   GA 120, 28.5.1910.

123   Rudolf Steiner speaks of how the impulse for the realization of the threefold social organism in modern humanity stems directly from the Michael-sphere, on 2.4.1923 (GA 223/229).

124   In connection with the year 1921, as the year of preparation for the founding of the Christian Community, it is necessary to make the following observations. If we take as our starting point the year 1910—the year of the first appearance in humanity of the Etheric Christ, the most important event of the twentieth century—and subtract eleven years, we get 1899, of which much has already been said in connection with the path of Rudolf Steiner's life; and if we add eleven years, we get 1921, in the summer and autumn of which Rudolf Steiner gave two of his first lecture cycles for priests. The basis was thereby laid for the founding of the Christian Community in Dornach in September 1922.

125   GA 260a, 12.4.1924 and 16.4.1924.

126   Quoted from Rudolf Grosse, *The Christmas Foundation*, p. 62.

127   An article by Rudolf Steiner of 18.3.1923 (GA 36).

128   In a lecture on 20.9.1918 (GA 184) Rudolf Steiner speaks of how, above all, the Goetheanum needs from anthroposophists an inner defence which is created from an ability to stand up fully for anthroposophical affairs on the Earth. He says there: 'How I should like to put it is to say that, really, we should have no joy, no satisfaction in the building if, at the same time, we do not engage all our strength to stand for Anthroposophy itself (*für die anthroposophische Sache*). For the building would become a reason for the destruction of what concerns us if sufficient defensive strength were not found.'

129   In *Rudolf Steiner und die Zivilisationsaufgaben der Anthroposophie—ein Rückblick auf das Jahr 1923*. Speeches and answers to questions (GA 259, augsgabe 1943, pp. 15–16).

130   Assya Turgeniev, *Erinnerungen an Rudolf Steiner und die Entstehungszeit des Dornacher Baues*, Stuttgart, 1972, p. 101.

131   From Rudolf Steiner's speech at the opening of the Christmas Conference on 24.12.1923 (see GA 260). In another context, Rudolf Steiner expresses this thought in the following way: 'Now we are confronted by this terrible misfortune of ours, the heart-breaking sight of the Goetheanum ruins in

Dornach; and we have before us too the Anthroposophical Society, which—even though it has recently acquired a good deal more members— lacks inner stability and is also something of a ruin' (GA 157, 23.1.1923).

132 Zeylmans van Emmichoven, *The Foundation Stone*. In the lecture of 4.3.1923 (GA 257), Rudolf Steiner himself subsequently spoke 'of this possibility of parting company from the Anthroposophical Society and finding other ways of bringing the anthroposophical impulse to fulfilment in the world'—something that was considered particularly seriously at the Delegates' Meeting in Stuttgart (February 1923).

133 GA 260.

134 GA 229, 15.10.1923.

135 The impulses for the opening up of the ancient Mysteries were given through Rudolf Steiner directly from the Michael School. He speaks about this as follows: 'In a magnificent and vivid way there was described in supersensible Inspirations [in the Michael School] that which I was often able to give a glimmer of in describing the ancient life of the Mysteries.' GA 237, 1.8.1924.

136 GA 240, 20.7.1924.

137 Just as once in the lofty supersensible Michael School the ancient initiation wisdom, the basis of the great teachings of the initiates, was 'gone through' once more at the beginning, so too at the Christmas Conference the nature of the old Mysteries was first depicted (see *Mystery Knowledge and Mystery Centres*, GA 232), and then the Foundation Stone laid for the *New*. Thus is the Christmas Conference the true earthly reflection of the spiritual events of the supersensible Michael School.

138 GA 240, 18.7.1924.

139 Genesis 1.

140 GA 260, Marie Steiner's Foreword.

141 See the two Easter lectures given by Rudolf Steiner in Berlin on 25.3 and 1.4.1907 in GA 96, and the lecture of 2.12.1906 (GA 97).
In her article 'In Memory of the Christmas Foundation Meeting' (26.4.1925), Ita Wegman writes the following about Rudolf Steiner's ill-ness: 'Then the master fell ill. At first it was merely physical exhaustion, but then it became apparent that the illness had deeper causes, that karma was taking its toll. From January 1925 onwards he did not speak any longer about exhaustion but rather of the workings of karma' (*An die Freunde*, Arleshem 1960). See also the words with which Rudolf Steiner answered a question posed by some anthroposophists regarding his illness in July 1924 in Arnhem (reported by Pieter de Haan, published in the book by Hans Peter van Manen *Twin Roads to the New Millennium*).

142 All that has been said above does not contradict the fact that at the beginning of Rudolf Steiner's illness physical poisoning may also have played a part. What indicates this particularly are the final words in the following excerpt from a letter from Rudolf Steiner to Marie Steiner on 15.10.1924 (i.e. written exactly ten and a half months after the close of the

Christmas Conference): 'M[y] d[ear] M[arie], I told you some time ago that, since January 1923, the connection of the higher members of my being with its physical body was no longer complete; living in the spirit I lost to a certain extent the immediate connection with my physical organization. Not with the physical world: on the contrary, a healthy discernment of this has become ever stronger and more encompassing. But the adversary forces are now trying to get at my physical body, because spiritually, everything— also in so far as the physical world was concerned—proceeded without hindrance' (GA 262, Letter No. 210). To these words of Rudolf Steiner may be added the description of the beginning of his illness on the last day of the Christmas Conference (1.1.1924) which Ilona Schubert, who personally witnessed this tragic event, gives in her book *Reminiscences of Rudolf Steiner and Marie Steiner-von Sivers*; and also the poetic conclusion of Marie Steiner's Afterword to the first edition of Rudolf Steiner's autobiography. One must particularly stress here that it was the need to put the karma of the Society in order and to improve it, and the inability of the members to work on this task with sufficient intensity, which made such a thing *possible* in the first place. In consequence of this inability, the physical body of Rudolf Steiner was, after the Christmas Conference, defenceless in the face of the forces of darkness constantly lying in wait for him. And for such a situation we have a macrocosmic archetype: Christ, allowing Himself to be betrayed, and around Him His sleeping disciples.

143 When it is said that 'Rudolf Steiner took upon himself the karma of the Anthroposophical Society' or that 'he took upon himself the consequences of the errors of its individual members', what is meant—and this must be emphasized very clearly indeed—is not the personal karma of anthroposophists but their karma with respect to the Michael stream which came into the world in the twentieth century as the anthroposophical movement. We have a macrocosmic archetype for this relationship in the relation— described in the lecture of 15.7.1914 (GA 155)—between the principle of personal karma and the objective process of the redemption of the whole of mankind through Christ Jesus. For Christ, in passing through the Mystery of Golgotha, does not take upon Himself the personal karma of individual human beings (which they must balance out over the course of their incarnations in accordance with the law of cosmic justice) but the *objective* consequences of human deeds for the spiritual macrocosm as a whole.

144 Characterizing this synthesis from the standpoint of esoteric Rosicrucian tradition, we must say: Rudolf Steiner succeeded in the Christmas Conference in uniting on the *social-historic* plane the stream of Cain and the stream of Abel into one stream.

145 We are not talking here of those earthly difficulties that arose in the *Vorstand* after Rudolf Steiner's death or of their consequences for all the further development of the Anthroposophical Society and the anthroposophical movement in the world. At the basis of these difficulties lay that complicated and as yet unresolved individual karma of anthroposophists of which

Rudolf Steiner spoke in his Karma lectures. What we are talking about here is the founding of the *Vorstand* and the Sections as a spiritual reality of a higher order. Although the earthly and the spiritual develop side by side, they must never be confused. Thus without bearing in mind, above all, the purely esoteric character of these institutions, it is not possible to understand why during and after the Christmas Conference Rudolf Steiner gave so much time and energy to their organization as well as to increasing a right understanding among anthroposophists of their character and the inner nature of their mutual relationship. (see GA 240.)

146   In his personal development Rudolf Steiner also attained at that time to that stage of initiation which, albeit in a form corresponding with his time, was attained by Christian Rosenkreutz in the fifteenth century, and which was later described in a more pictorial way in the book by Valentin Andreae, *The Chymical Wedding of Christian Rosenkreutz, anno 1459*. This also sheds light on the fact that in response to a question asked of Rudolf Steiner concerning the relationship of Anthroposophy to the Rosicrucian stream, he gave the following Imagination: on the left there stands Christian Rosenkreutz in a blue stole, and on the right Rudolf Steiner in a red stole. In this Imagination they stand *side by side*. (See B.C.J. Lievegoed, *Mystery Streams in Europe and the New Mysteries*.)

147   Rudolf Grosse, *The Christmas Foundation*, pp. 137–38.

148   GA 260a, 23.5.1924.

149   Ibid., 22.6.1924.

150   Ibid., 18.7.1924.

151   Ibid., 12.8.1924.

152   Ibid., 24.8.1924. Alluding for the last time to the Christmas Conference in the lecture of 5.9.1924 in Dornach, Rudolf Steiner sums up the developments over the past eight months as follows: 'Now that we have been living for many months under the influences stemming from the Christmas Conference and *have been endeavouring to remain true to what we intended in spiritually laying the Foundation Stone of the Anthroposophical Society*, we may rightly say that what has been streaming in [by way of spiritual revelation] is continuing to flow in ever greater measure. And we can also say that hearts have become increasingly open wherever the more esoteric impulse which has been streaming into anthroposophical work since the Christmas Conference is in evidence.

'My dear friends, take into your hearts the full significance of what I have to say out of my experiences of the last few months!'

153   GA 240, Vol. VI, 12.8.1924.

154   GA 194, 22.11.1919.

155   One must note here that the true peculiarity of the sculptural architectural forms of the First Goetheanum lay in the fact that just looking at them was intended to bring human beings gradually to a real perception of karmic relations. In a lecture on 27.4.1924 (GA 236), Rudolf Steiner says: 'And amongst everything else that has been emphasized, this Goetheanum

building, together with the way in which Anthroposophy would have been fostered in it, was in itself an education towards karmic perception. This education towards a perception of karma must come into modern civilization.'

156 Concerning the necessity of balancing out the karma within the Anthroposophical Society, Rudolf Steiner says: 'But how is it, then, that there are also forces which work in such a way that human beings today find their way together under purely spiritual principles when in the ordinary everyday world they are otherwise complete strangers to one another? In what do the forces consist which lead men to find one another? They consist in that through the onset of the Michael rulership a force is brought by Michael which, in those who have followed him, is to bring order into karma once again. So that we can say: What is it that unites the members of the Anthroposophical Society? What unites them is this: they are called upon to put their karma in order!' (GA 237, 8.8.1924).

157 From everything that has been said here, it follows that the decision to join the Anthroposophical Society is of a serious karmic nature, even though in the Statutes of the Society almost nothing is required for this step except a recognition of the legitimate right of the impulse of the Christmas Conference; nevertheless, in an occult sense, this is a serious decision that deeply influences the destiny of an individual if, of course, it is made completely consciously. Rudolf Steiner himself says of this: 'one cannot join the Anthroposophical Society, or at least one cannot join in a completely honest way that deeply engages the soul, without one's destiny becoming essentially and deeply influenced' (GA 237, 3.8.1924). In this sense there is a deep misunderstanding of the Christmas Conference, and consequently of the essence and core of all Anthroposophy, in the position of those who are intensively engaged in Anthroposophy but prefer not to join the Anthroposophical Society. Without doubt the karma of the Anthroposophical Society is a difficult one, but the anthroposophist who understands the inner essence of the Christmas Conference knows that since that time it is Rudolf Steiner above all who bears this karma in the spiritual world. And if we do not wish to share this with him, we can scarcely call ourselves his true pupils or servants of those spiritual powers which through him have called Anthroposophy into life.

158 GA 227, 29.8.1923.

159 In the following words Rudolf Steiner is speaking about the fact that the New Mysteries have been on the Earth *already* since the Christmas Conference, for the Christmas impulse is also the impulse of the New Mysteries (GA 233a, 22.4.1924): 'We must say that it is indeed the case that when that impulse which flowed out from the Goetheanum through the Christmas Conference really establishes itself and lives in the Anthroposophical Society then, by leading on to the Classes which are still to be introduced (which, in part, has begun already), the Anthroposophical Society will form the foundation for further Mystery-life. The further Mystery-life must be

consciously planted through the Anthroposophical Society.' From these words one can also have the feeling that Rudolf Steiner himself could only lay the foundation for the New Mysteries. The possible completion, however, did not only depend on him but also on the members of the Anthroposophical Society, and thus it has remained up to the present time.

160 A sad symptom, and clear evidence of the unpreparedness of some anthroposophists today for Rudolf Steiner's coming again, is the widespread 'seeking' for his next incarnation. Facts of this kind speak of a fundamental misunderstanding of the real situation and also point to a tendency, not yet fully worked out in some anthroposophists, to certain forms of materialism. The question of Rudolf Steiner's activity at the end of the century is a deeply mysterious one, but one must be aware that, in this event, his *outer* activity cannot continue in the same form as occurred at the beginning of the century. In his books and in almost 6,000 lectures, Rudolf Steiner left a spiritual wealth whose proper assimilation in a sufficiently wide circle of anthroposophists is still far from complete. As far as the truly esoteric impulse is concerned, in the sense of the founding of the new Mystery-centre in 1923–24, this can be realized in *wider circles* of the Anthroposophical Society only to the extent that the impulse given in the Christmas Conference and in the First Class of the Free School for Spiritual Science that arose from it is understood and fulfilled.

If, however, at the end of the century there is still too little understanding, then one must have in view that in speaking of the possibility of founding a Second Class Rudolf Steiner limited the number of its participants to 36 (GA 260a—Rudolf Steiner's conversation with Count Polzer-Hoditz, 11.11.1924). In this context the following words of Rudolf Steiner can serve as a real basis for a proper approach to this question:

> Whoever strives constantly towards the Spirit
> Can hope undaunted
> That at the right time
> He will not be without the Guidance of the Spirit.
>
> (From *Truth-Wrought Words*)

In the spirit of these words it is surely not our task to guess at the possible forms of this guidance, but to 'strive towards the Spirit' with all the strength of our souls. And if this, our task, is realized sufficiently, then we can be certain that we will 'not be without the Guidance of the Spirit'.

161 Rudolf Steiner speaks about this continued working of the Christmas Conference in, for example, the following words: 'It [the Christmas Conference] acquires its content solely from the life in the various regions of the Society; it is a reality only because of what continued to happen through it in the life of the Anthroposophical Society. The Christmas Conference only becomes real through what subsequently emerges from it ... Whether

as a Christmas Conference it will be an effective influence upon life depends on whether it is taken further' (GA 260a, 6.2.1924).

162   Rudolf Steiner speaks in the following words about this 'new covenant' that was made at the Christmas Conference with the spiritual powers which guide the anthroposophical movement in the spiritual world, indicating at the same time that this 'new covenant' is a *real source of strength* which is able to ward off the ever-intensifying assaults of the opposing forces on the anthroposophical movement in the wake of the Christmas Conference: 'But it is greatly to be hoped that *the strength of the covenant which we have been allowed to make with good spiritual powers through the Christmas Conference* will in the future be capable of driving from the field all those opposing powers on the spiritual plane which make use of human beings on Earth in order to bring their activities to fulfilment' (GA 260a, 23.5.1924).

163   See Mark 14: 51–52 and 15: 34; and also GA 139, 23.9.1912.

164   GA 211, 2.4.1922 in Dornach; 13.4.1922 in the Hague; 15 and 24.4.1922 in London.

Chapter 4. The Earthly and the Supersensible Goetheanum

1   *The Lord's Prayer* (GA 96), 28.1.1907.

2   We can find a reference to Rudolf Steiner's first sacrifice in Chapter 26 of his autobiography. References to the second sacrifice occur in various lectures given in the period from 1910 to 1913 and are dealt with, in part, in Chapter 3 of this book. They are also brought together in the lecture given by Adolf Arenson in Stuttgart on 30.3.1930, the fifth anniversary of Rudolf Steiner's death (see *Fruits of Earnest Study*, Vol. I).

3   In his opening speech of the Christmas Conference, Rudolf Steiner says: 'We wish today to link up with that which we would have gladly joined together with, even as early as 1913. Here, my dear friends, we desire to take up the thread again, and desire to inscribe in our souls as the prime and most fundamental axiom for the anthroposophical movement, which is to have its vessel (*Hülle*) in the Anthroposophical Society, that everything in it is willed by the spirit, that it seeks to be a fulfilment of what the signs of the time speak to human hearts in glowing letters' (GA 260). These words which refer primarily to the founding of the independent Anthroposophical Society on 3.2.1913, can in their more inner content also be related to the laying of the Foundation Stone of the first Goetheanum in Dornach on 20.9.1913.

4   See also Daniel van Bemmelen's *Das erste Goetheanum als Menschheitsbau*, Dornach 1975.

5   F.W. Zeylmans van Emmichoven, *The Foundation Stone*.

6   In a lecture on 6.9.1918 Rudolf Steiner also calls the Mysteries of Birth and Death the Mysteries of the Moon and the Sun: the Moon is connected with the impulses of heredity which work through birth, and the Sun with the

awakening of individual consciousness which is constantly bound up with the processes of death. In this connection the penetration of ancient Judaism into the Moon Mysteries was particularly profound, since it was its mission to prepare the earthly sheath for the future incarnation of the Christ (see GA 123, 4.9.1910). The initiates of the ancient Jewish people were inspired by Jehovah, the Moon-god. However, herein lies also the reason why the Christ, when He descended into the prepared bodily sheaths of Jesus and thus brought to the Earth a true knowledge of the Mysteries of Death, was understood least of all by the Jewish people, for up to that time they had only nurtured the Mysteries of Birth!

7   In the lecture of 15.4.1922 (GA 211), Rudolf Steiner speaks at some length of how the Gods of the higher Hierarchies themselves had no knowledge of the Mystery of Death but only of the Mystery of Birth, which they communicated to mankind in the Mysteries. Rudolf Steiner puts this as follows: 'These divine-spiritual Teachers of humanity had knowledge of birth but not of death . . . It was as though the Gods, who had hitherto only been able to speak to earthly men of the Mystery of Birth, saw that the Earth was gradually growing away from those forces which they had themselves incorporated into it and that *death would take hold of the soul.*'

8   In this connection, Rudolf Steiner's words in his lecture on 27.8.1924 (GA 240) take on a particular significance, when he speaks of how Christ descended to the Earth with His Spirit Self (see Note 130 of Chapter 5), which is also indicated in the image of the dove (symbol of the Holy Spirit) at the Baptism in the Jordan.

9   In the lecture of 6.7.1909 (GA 112), Rudolf Steiner describes—with particularly meaningful words—this revelation of the true countenance of death through Christ Jesus as the Mystery of union with the highest cosmic life, that is, with the cosmic realm of the Father of All Being.

10 That Christ brought the true impulse of time from the Sun to the Earth, see 4.6.1924, GA 236.

11 See Lecture 12 in GA 103, and 'The Mystery of Golgotha' in GA 96, 25.3.1907.

12 This indicates the metamorphosis of thinking that is imprinted in the forms of the Goetheanum. We can come to an understanding of the resurrection of thinking from its dead and ossified state into a quickened, living form, if we bear the following in mind. In a lecture on 28.6.1914 (GA 286) Rudolf Steiner describes the nature of the fundamental artistic architectural idea which lies at the foundation of this building: 'We enter with reverence into [the sphere of] the Spirit, so that we become one with the Spirit that pours itself out around us in the forms—because all around us are the Spirits of Form—and that comes into movement, because behind the Spirits of Form stand the Spirits of Movement. This is the *new* artistic, architectural thought!'

One must now compare these words with the content of the lecture given on 20.1.1914 in *Human and Cosmic Thought* (GA 151) entitled 'The ascent from rigid to mobile thought as ascent from the realm of the Spirits of Form to the realm of the Spirits of Movement'. In some detail in this lecture Rudolf Steiner points to Goethe as being the first in the modern age to attempt, in his teaching on the archetypal plant (*Urpflanze*) and the archetypal animal, to cross from the static thought to the mobile. If in this context we now remember that in his Foreword to the *Kürschner* edition of Goethe's scientific writings Rudolf Steiner wrote his epoch-making words: 'Perceiving the Idea as it is in reality is the true communion of man' (in *Goethe the Scientist*, GA 1), and if we are aware that 'perceiving the Idea' is only possible in one who has attained a living, mobile thinking, then we come one step nearer to an understanding of what, in its sculptural architectural forms, the Goetheanum was to reveal to humanity.

13   The correspondence adduced here between the large cupola and the macrocosmic 'I' of man and between the small cupola and his microcosmic 'I' is as seen from an *exoteric* standpoint. In an *esoteric* sense we find the opposite correspondence, with the large cupola being associated with man's earthly 'I' and the small with his higher 'I'. This 'esoteric' relationship is, moreover, indicated through the spatial orientation of the Foundation Stone of the First Goetheanum, consisting as it does of two interconnected copper dodecahedra, one smaller and one larger, the latter of which was placed in the direction of the small cupola and the former in the direction of the large cupola.

14   In some detail in a lecture on 18.5.1924 (GA 236), Rudolf Steiner says that we can come to a real understanding of eternity only through studying *together* the two most important principles that are connected with the spiritual existence of the human being: 'unbornness' (*Ungeborenheit*) and immortality. The first forms the hidden core of the Mysteries of Birth, and the second that of the Mysteries of Death. But a study of both these together leads us directly to the inner nature of the Mysteries of Eternity.

15   St Paul, First Epistle to the Corinthians, 3: 16 and 6: 9.

16   From *The Christmas Conference for the Foundation of the General Anthroposophical Society 1923/1924* (GA 260). The evening lecture on 31.12.1923, entitled 'The Envy of Gods—the Envy of Men'.

17   The two side wings of the rose South window—in which is portrayed the metamorphosis of the West door of the First Goetheanum in the countenance of the 'ideal human being' who bears within him the forces of the Sun—point to the Goetheanum as a building that reveals in its forms the celestial archetype of man.

18   GA 286, 7.6.1914.

19   Ibid., 17.6.1914.

20   GA 232, 2.12.1923.

21   Rudolf Grosse, *The Christmas Foundation*, p. 64.

22   12.12.1911 in *And the Temple Becomes Man*—quoted here from Daniel van Bemmelen's *Das erste Goetheanum als Menschheitsbau*, Dornach 1975, p. 8.

23   30.12.1914, in *Art as Seen in the Light of Mystery Wisdom* (GA 275).

24 See Note 17 of this chapter. It is also important to mention here that in the countenance which arose on the right side wing of the window out of a metamorphosis of the West door of the Goetheanum, a form resembling an opening blossom is depicted at the spot of the two-petalled lotus flower— that is, at the point where the etheric body unites with the physical body in the human being. This is a picture of the etheric body which, in our time, is to begin to detach itself again from the physical body, in the region of the head. This will eventually lead to a natural etheric clairvoyance in wide circles of humanity. That which is revealed more than anything else to the human being through this natural awakening of imaginative vision is portrayed in the central theme of the window.

25 For the fact that the human etheric body manifests itself primarily in the fluid element, see the lecture of 1.2.1924 in GA 234, and see also Note 50 of Chapter 5. In a lecture on 31.12.1922 in GA 219 Rudolf Steiner says of this, 'That which allows the blood in us to circulate, which brings the other fluids in us into movement, is the etheric organism.'

26 In the lecture of 31.12.1922 in GA 219, Rudolf Steiner says concerning this: 'To the extent that the world of stars is of a still, a fixed nature which, for example, in the pictures of the zodiac relates in a motionless way in space to the Earth, to that extent is man connected in his physical organism with these form-images (*Formgebilde*) of cosmic space.' However, for the nature of this connection of the human physical body with the twelve signs of the zodiac, see the central theme of the blue South window in the Goetheanum. This connection was also described by Rudolf Steiner from a slightly different angle on 7.6.1912, in GA 137.

27 This connection of the etheric body with the seven main planets is revealed by Rudolf Steiner in his lecture on 21.4.1924 in GA 233. He speaks there of how in the Moon-sphere immediately before the incarnation of the human being onto the Earth, the Moon Teachers of Wisdom form his etheric body from the forces of the seven planets. See Note 93 of Chapter 5.

28 For the fact that the fundamental laws of the etheric body are related to time, see Note 44 of Chapter 6.

29 For the deeper interrelation of the numbers 12 and 7, see particularly the last lecture in GA 113. Here, however, it can only be mentioned that the laws lying at the basis of the number 7 are connected more with the Mysteries of Time (the Sun), and those at the basis of the number 12 more with the Mysteries of Space (the Moon).

30 See also Andrey Belyi's *Epopeya Ya*, Note 109 of Chapter 3.

31 Daniel van Bemmelen, loc. cit. the chapter entitled *Das erste Goetheanum als Haus der Anthroposophie.*

32 See Notes 87 and 88 of Chapter 3.

33 Such an architectural, sculptural, artistic solution [to the problem] of the space of the small cupola, where everything is built and based on a twelvefoldness into which, as the Thirteenth, the Christ enters from the macrocosmic sphere of the 'I', opens up to us also the secret of the twelve

thrones that encircle the central figure of the 'Representative of Man'. For it is in this mighty sensible-supersensible Imagination that there is revealed before us the picture of the lofty Lodge of the twelve Bodhisattvas, whose common mission encompasses all Earth development (depicted in the paintings of the small cupola), and who sit in state on the twelve thrones and contemplate unceasingly the Thirteenth in the centre; that is, the Christ Himself. If we now bear in mind that on the outer periphery of the circle formed on the east side by the twelve columns and the twelve thrones there was situated the speaker's podium from which Anthroposophia, the Wisdom of the Holy Spirit, was to have been proclaimed, we come one step closer to an understanding of the profound Mystery of humanity which was hidden in the First Goetheanum, the true 'Temple of the New Spiritual Life'.

34 It remains here to show that this principle of 12 and 7 is, as has already been mentioned by Zeylmans van Emmichoven, also contained in the *Foundation Stone Meditation*. The first sections of Parts I–III consist of twelve lines (not counting the initial address to the human soul); and the second sections of these parts consist of seven lines to which the three references to the elemental spirits are then added.

35 See GA 180, 6.1.1918.

36 GA 245.

37 The complete text in Rudolf Steiner's notebook (in GA 286) reads as follows:

> People need at first only to *will*
> while moving from column to column.
> A feeling for life awakens in the right way
> when they understand the columns.
> In the cupola: the soul.
> In the forms: the body.
> Will—moving forward
> Feeling—ascending
> Thinking—rounding off.

38 See GA 180, 6.1.1918.

39 It could also be said that in the First Goetheanum the attempt was made to anticipate a *new kingdom of nature*, which in the course of natural evolution is only gradually to arise with the fifth round (the fifth kingdom) of the Earth and attain its true completion only on Jupiter. Rudolf Steiner speaks about this in the lecture of 26.10.1905, in the course of characterizing the task of man in the fourth and fifth rounds: 'Man redeems the mineral kingdom in the fourth round by making it into a work of art. Then everything goes through a pralaya. After this there is no longer a mineral kingdom at all, and the whole Earth has become a plant. Man will have risen half a stage higher, and everything else with him; for example, Cologne Cathedral will emerge

in the fifth round as a plant ... Cologne Cathedral will henceforth grow as part of the plant world out of what will then form the soil' (GA 93a).

40   Quoted in Rudolf Grosse, *The Christmas Foundation*, p. 30.

41   In all its basic elements one can also sense a connection here between this document and the *Foundation Stone Meditation*, given by Rudolf Steiner at the Christmas Conference of 1923–24. Thus we have at the centre of the document the twelvefold image of man, which with the addition of the first letters of the Rosicrucian saying divides into three distinct parts, so that the letters E.D.N. relate primarily to the limb-man who bears the soul through the world of Space into the ocean-being of the Spirit. The letters P.S.S.R. relate to the human head, which opens to the soul from the ground Eternal the World-Thoughts of the Gods. And the letters of the middle realm represent a connecting link between the realm of the head and the realm of the limbs—in it is the intersection of the two circles that one can draw in thought around the two dodecahedra. The letters I.C.M. belong to the human heart and lungs which lead the soul through the rhythmic tides of Time into the feeling of its own Soul-being, in whose depths is realized the meeting of man with Christ.

The Cosmic Word, which in the second sections of Parts I–III of the *Meditation* sounds out here through the spheres of all nine Hierarchies, finds its imaginative expression in these wonderful, musical-sculptural, strong etheric lines. They surround the cosmic archetype of man in the centre, in whose three systems the Cosmic Word—spoken forth by the Hierarchies from the spheres of the Father, the Son and the Spirit—imprints the words: *Ex Deo nascimur; In Christo morimur; Per Spiritum Sanctum reviviscimus*. Thus does the Cosmic Word transform the image of the human soul into the image of the human being of the future who, having realized these words within, fulfils in this way the mission of the Earth and of humanity in the cosmos.

The next words of the document, inasmuch as they are connected with the will, the Cosmic Soul and the Cosmic 'I', direct us clearly to the first three parts of the *Foundation Stone Meditation*, and the fact that the realm of the elements is referred to at the end directs us to the last three lines of Parts I, II and III of the *Meditation*: 'The [elemental] Spirits hear it ...' etc. It is not possible here to go deeply into this document, and for this reason we are obliged to confine ourselves to these brief remarks which can only point the reader in a certain direction for further thoughts of his own. With regard to the fourth part of the *Meditation*, however, we do not find it reflected directly in the document, and there is a profound reason behind this. For the first three parts of the *Meditation* are a call of the Gods of the cosmos to the human soul, in which they proclaim what they have laid down in the human being in the past epochs of world development. But the fourth part is connected with the answer to this of man himself, and this answer of the human soul consists of taking up, in absolute freedom, the impulse of Christ that is contained in Part IV.

In this sense the building of the Goetheanum was only the first step; the second was to be that which the Goetheanum could awaken in the human soul. Right from the beginning this could not have been a part of the building as something *inevitable*, but only as an impulse which was to awaken in the soul in freedom. Looking at and contemplating the Goetheanum, and working to realize its mission in the world, was to bring to birth in the human soul that impulse which was later implanted in the fourth part of the *Meditation*. (It is expressed artistically and sculpturally in the carved Group which was to have been placed in the East of the completed Goetheanum.)

42 GA 153, 14.4.1914.

43 These words are taken from a letter of Margarita Voloshina (Sobashnikova) to Russia from Dornach, written in 1914, and which is in the possession of the author. Margarita Voloshina was present at Rudolf Steiner's talk in Vienna on 14.4.1914 (GA 153), and his words at that time concerning the Goetheanum (see GA 153, 14.4.1914) read in her letter as follows: 'It [the Goetheanum] is in truth the embodiment of the Being whom we serve.'

44 *The Christmas Conference for the Foundation of the General Anthroposophical Society, 1923/1924* (GA 260).

45 GA 260, 1.1.1924, Rudolf Steiner's closing words.

46 GA 219, 31.12.1922.

47 GA 194, 22.11.1919.

48 See GA 153, 14.4.1914.

49 See GA 194, 22.11.1919.

50 In this deed of Rudolf Steiner, we also have—realized at the highest level—the fundamental principle of true Manichaeism: to transform evil into good.

51 *The Christmas Conference for the Foundation of the General Anthroposophical Society, 1923/1924* (GA 260), from the lecture on 31.12.1923, entitled 'The Envy of Gods—The Envy of Men'.

52 In the evening lecture in Düsseldorf on 12.4.1909 (in GA 110), Rudolf Steiner speaks in detail of the nature of the fire or warmth element as the foundation of the visible world and as the mediator between the 'world of bodies and the world of souls'. In particular he expresses this as follows: 'This is why ancient spiritual science—and with it modern spiritual science—said: *warmth* and *fire* is that element in which the material element starts to become soul-element.'

53 See Note 51.

54 See Assya Turgeniev's *Erinnerungen an Rudolf Steiner in die Entstehungszeit des Goetheanums*, Stuttgart 1972, the chapter on New Year's Eve 1922.

55 Matthew, 3: 11.

56 In order to avoid misunderstandings, it should be mentioned here that while giving the lecture Rudolf Steiner was in the process of spiritual investigation on the other side of the threshold, and saw the fire 'with the consciousness of the Angels' in its supersensible aspect, which cannot be pictured by our earthly imagination. However, in accordance with the strict

law of the spiritual world, about which Rudolf Steiner often spoke in his lectures, something experienced in this way in the higher worlds cannot be conveyed directly into everyday human consciousness, for in the present cycle of evolution this consciousness must be directed by the laws of the earthly world and not by those of the spiritual. But for the earthly world on this side of the threshold the fire at the Goetheanum was the greatest tragedy, and was also experienced as such by Rudolf Steiner in his 'human consciousness' during that terrible night of New Year's Eve.

57   In his lecture on 31.12.1922 in GA 219, Rudolf Steiner says: 'Thus is spiritual knowledge a true communion, the beginning of a Cosmic Cultus appropriate to humanity of the present ...'

58   GA 219, 31.12.1922.

59   GA 232, 2.12.1923.

60   *The Christmas Conference for the Foundation of the General Anthroposophical Society 1923/1924* (GA 260), 31.12.1923.

61   GA 232, 2.12.1923.

62   GA 233, 26.12.1923.

63   Rudolf Steiner gave a particularly intimate description of the Ephesian Mysteries in his lecture on 14.8.1924 (GA 243). From this description one can sense the very atmosphere that prevailed at this place which was so important for the whole development of humanity.

64   GA 233, 29.12.1923.

65   Ibid., 26, 27 and 28.12.1923.

66   GA 232, 14.12.1923.

67   See GA 233, 29.12.1923.

68   GA 8, the chapter 'Plato as a Mystic'.

69   This difference in the nature of the philosophies of Plato and of Aristotle is depicted in a wonderful way in Raphael's fresco *The School of Athens* at the Stanza della Segnatura. It is shown in the hand gesture of the old philosopher who is stepping into the middle of the picture, pointing as it does upward to the etheric expanses of the cosmos, and in that of his younger companion, pointing towards the Earth. It is shown also in the works that each of them carry: the one, the *Timaeus*, one of the most profound of Plato's dialogues, being almost an entire encyclopaedia of ancient Mystery-wisdom, in which is discussed, above all, the spiritual origin and evolution of our cosmos; and the other, Aristotle's *Ethics*, a work that deals particularly with the right actions of the wise man in earthly life. For one possible interpretation of this fresco, relating its content to the pre-Christian (classical) epoch of humanity's development, see the lecture of 5.5.1909 (GA 284/285).

70   GA 187, 25.12.1918.

71   Plato sets forth his teaching on reincarnation in particular detail in his dialogues *Phaedrus* (246a–249d) and the *Republic* (614–621b). From his description it is clear that we are dealing with an ancient form of this teaching. However, the idea of the pre-existence of the soul as the basis of

the teaching of reincarnation is developed by Plato most completely in the *Meno* (81b–86b) and the *Phaedo* (72e–77d), in which he tries to confirm this idea by showing that all earthly knowledge has its origins in the soul's *memory* of its pre-earthly existence.

It must be mentioned here, however, that the characteristic peculiarity of this ancient teaching on reincarnation was the absence of any clear conception of the individual 'I', which as the immortal core of the human being is that which passes through various incarnations. From this absence comes the possibility—also affirmed by Plato (see the *Republic*, 620a–620d)—of a human being's incarnating in the next life as an animal. In the East this peculiarity of the ancient teaching on reincarnation appears even more strongly. In Buddhism, for example, we find generally no reference at all to the individual 'I', and from this has arisen the negative relationship of Buddhism to the earthly world as a whole—to the world, that is, in which alone the consciousness of the individual 'I' can develop.

On the other hand, it is in Aristotle that we have the appearance of a real interest in the physical world. For this reason he is not only the father of earthly thinking (logic) but in a certain sense is also the founder of the physical sciences. In this respect Aristotle was the true forerunner and herald of the coming Christianity. For Christ was to descend to the Earth and kindle in every human being the light of the eternal, immortal 'I'; then through His subsequent union with the Earth He was to bring to it its true meaning and reveal its infinite importance for humanity. This lay in the fact that since the Mystery of Golgotha the Earth has become the cosmic body of Christ, which in the course of time must become spiritualized through the activity of the human 'I' that is permeated through and through with Christ. However, in order that such a relationship with the Earth could arise, it was essential to prepare for it before the onset of the Christian era. And this was possible only through a rejection of the teaching of reincarnation in its old form with its inevitable disregard for all earthly things, for 'it is indeed the case that it was necessary for the development of humanity that for a time consciousness of repeated lives on Earth should withdraw, so that the human being could become accustomed to taking seriously and intensely just one life on Earth' (GA 187, 1.1.1919).

72   GA 187, 28.12.1918.
73   Ibid., 25.12.1918.
74   GA 18. This quote is from GA 115.
75   Aristotle refutes Plato's fundamental argument for the pre-existence of the soul ('Earthly knowledge is a memory of pre-earthly existence'—see Note 71 of this chapter) in his *Prior Analytics* (67a 21) and in the *Topics* (111b 27). In this way Aristotle dismisses the teaching of pre-existence altogether.
76   GA 115, 12.12.1911.
77   In his book *The Riddles of Philosophy* (GA 18) Rudolf Steiner says of this: 'That the soul has an existence prior to earthly life is accepted by Plato but not by Aristotle.'

78 GA 187, 1.1.1919. Rudolf Steiner often expresses this thought—also in other lectures.

79 GA 115, 12.12.1911.

80 Ibid., 13.12.1911.

81 GA 131, 14.10.1911, GA 130, 2.12.1911, and also Note 27 of Chapter 6.

82 In the fact that Aristotle had at that time to bring about the disappearance of the teaching of reincarnation in its ancient, pre-Christian form from the esoteric tradition of the West, and that in the twentieth century it was Rudolf Steiner who had then to introduce this teaching anew into all the cultural life of humanity, but now in a new and profoundly Christian form—in this fact we see a true fulfilment of the great cosmic law, according to which each individual who accomplishes something in the service of the Guiding Powers of the world must, after a certain time, perform a similar deed in consequence of it, but in such a way now that it appears like the opposite pole of the first. Rudolf Steiner throws light on the nature of the working of this great cosmic law in the example of the mission of Abraham: 'In the same way that in the past epoch up to our time [the second millennium after Christ] the spirit of Moses held sway, so now [the 3rd millennium AD] the spirit of Abraham is beginning to reign in order that, having led humanity in past times [3rd millennium BC] into a consciousness of God within the physical world, he may now lead humanity out of it again. For it is an eternal ancient law of the cosmos that every individual who performs a particular deed must carry it out more than once: that is, at least in two periods, the second deed appearing as the opposite of the first. What Abraham brought down to humanity, into its physical consciousness, he will carry up again into the spiritual world' (in GA 118, 6.3.1910). The 'cosmic law' referred to here also throws a quite particular light on what Rudolf Steiner said to W.J. Stein in the Hague in the year 1922 about his mission in this life being that of giving practical form to the teaching of reincarnation and karma. See *W.J. Stein/Rudolf Steiner, Dokumentation*, Dornach, 1985, p. 295, and also the words with which Rudolf Steiner supplements this theme in Note 164 (ibid.). Rudolf Steiner speaks especially clearly about the significance of the knowledge of reincarnation and karma for the anthroposophical view of the world in the lecture of 5.3.1912 (GA 135).

83 *Reincarnation and Karma: Their Significance in Modern Culture* (GA 135). 21.2.1912 and 5.3.1912.

84 For the luciferic nature of the ancient Greek culture see GA 120, 28.5.1910.

85 Also characteristic in this connection is Aristotle's definition of tragedy as a moral catharsis of the soul, which consists of overcoming egoism (in which Lucifer is at work) through compassion, and overcoming fear (in which Ahriman works) through fearlessness.

86 GA 240, 19.7.1924.

87 Ibid., 20.7.1924.

88 Albert Stöckel, *Lehrbuch der Geschichte der Philosophie*, Mainz, 1889.

89   GA 237, 1.8.1924.

90   This denial by Aristotle of the teaching of reincarnation, the influence of which played an intrinsic part in the subsequent disappearance of this teaching from the external, exoteric culture of Europe, does not mean, however, that it was also completely withdrawn from the secret, esoteric tradition of the West. However, this process developed to the extent that even the pupils of the Rosicrucian schools in the Middle Ages knew nothing of reincarnation but rather that knowledge of it belonged at that time only to the *highest* stages of initiation and was kept strictly secret (see GA 131, 6.10.1911). An interesting example in this connection is the first great work of H.P. Blavatsky, *Isis Unveiled*, which was written out of Rosicrucian inspiration but in which the idea of reincarnation is altogether absent.

91   Rudolf Steiner says in a number of his lectures that the psychic constitution of the ancient Greeks was based on their particular faculty of *memory*. See in this context the lecture of 10.12.1912 in GA 141.

92   GA 126, 1.1.1911.

93   GA 240, 14.8.1924.

94   Before his incarnation as Thomas Aquinas in the thirteenth century, the individuality of Aristotle had a short incarnation at the beginning of the ninth century AD. Rudolf Steiner reminds us of this in his lecture in Torquay on 14.8.1924 (GA 240). For greater detail of this see the lecture by Emil Bock on 27.2.1952 entitled *Ephesus und die Gralsburg*, loc. cit.

95   GA 240, 18.7.1924.

96   To avoid misunderstandings here it must be stressed that in the personalities of Alexander the Great and Albertus Magnus we are dealing with two different individualities, both of whom, in completely different epochs, were connected particularly closely with the individuality to whom this chapter is devoted—to Aristotle-Thomas Aquinas. This is why Rudolf Steiner usually mentions Alexander when speaking of Aristotle, and often refers to Albertus Magnus in connection with Thomas Aquinas.

97   GA 237, 8.8.1924.

98   GA 240, 19.7.1924.

99   The German word *Besinnen* is derived from the noun *Sinn* which means, among other things, meaning or sense, feeling, perception, and sense organ. Thus the word *Besinnen* points to that inner process whereby thinking experiences and senses itself through the thinking subject, and serves the subject at the same time as a sense organ, an organ of perception that arises in its purest form in the conscious 'thinking about thinking' of which Thomas Aquinas often speaks in his works.

100   GA 240, 19.7.1924.

101   Ibid., 27.8.1924.

102   In a lecture in Torquay on 14.8.1924 (in GA 240) Rudolf Steiner characterizes the meeting in AD 869 in the spiritual world between Aristotle and

Alexander on the one side and Harun al Rashid and his counsellor on the other as a spiritual battle (*Geisteskampf*).

103 In the lecture of 8.8.1924 (GA 237), Rudolf Steiner speaks of a further important event which took place around the year 869 in the spiritual world. This event was associated with the fall of a number of Beings belonging to the Hierarchy of the Angels from the sphere of Michael. The consequences of this separation into 'Michaelic' and 'anti-Michaelic' Angels also came to expression in the antithesis between Aristotle and Alexander on the one hand and Harun-al-Rashid and his counsellor on the other, when they met in the spiritual world in 869; for Aristotle and Harun-al-Rashid, together with the human souls connected with them, were working out of the inspiration of Angels who had adopted a contrary position with regard to the sphere of Michael.

104 GA 240, 14.8.1924.

105 Between these came one other, somewhat shorter incarnation in the ninth century AD, which was of very special significance—see Note 94 of this chapter.

106 GA 240, 19.7.1924.

107 Ibid.

108 GA 74, 23.5.1920.

109 In connection with the year 1250, which was of exceptional importance for all earthly development and of which Rudolf Steiner speaks on many occasions in the most varied contexts in his lectures and in GA 15, it is essential to indicate, if only very briefly, something of the complex spiritual-physical constellation of that year. One of its peculiarities has already been discussed: 1250 was the year in which for a short time it was absolutely impossible, even for the highest initiates, to receive on the physical plane any enlightenment from the spiritual worlds. Rudolf Steiner speaks of this as follows: 'In the middle of the thirteenth century there was suddenly no more clairvoyance. On all human beings there descended a spiritual darkness. For even the most illumined minds (*Geister*), for the most highly developed personalities and also the initiates, there was no longer any access to the spiritual worlds ... for a short while even they could not directly perceive the spiritual world' (GA 130, 27.9.1911).

However, directly *after* this short period of darkness there follows the epoch of a new spiritual life for western humanity. 'As the year 1250 drew near, there began a new type of guidance to the supersensible worlds' (GA 15). This is why Rudolf Steiner connects with this time the founding of the 'new culture' in humanity, which was being prepared then in two ways: exoterically, in the blossoming of Scholasticism in the second half of the thirteenth century, and esoterically, in the founding of the Rosicrucian stream through the initiation of Christian Rosenkreutz shortly after 1250. (See GA 130, 27.9.1911.)

All these events were in turn connected with significant supersensible happenings relating to the year 1250 and which proceeded directly from the

Hierarchies, from the cosmos. From this we distinguish two types of influence on humanity on Earth: the first is connected with the spiritual evolution of the Archai (the Spirits of Personality) to whom, around the fourth century, the Spirits of Form (the Exusiai) transferred the responsibility for the Cosmic World Thoughts. By virtue of this transference the thought world of human beings began gradually to take on more and more of an individual, personal character. Thoughts now gradually become the property of man. According to Rudolf Steiner, this cosmic process—which had begun in the last centuries before Christ and reached a kind of culmination in the fourth century AD—was not fully completed until the thirteenth century (see GA 222, 16.3.1923). As a result of this—even if only for a short period beginning around 1250—the Archai were able to influence not only the thought-world of human beings but were also able to give direct impulses for the shaping of the individual human *personality*— a process which was later expressed outwardly in the European Renaissance. They then withdrew from the direct guidance of humanity, giving over the field of action into the care of the Archangels (GA 130, 29.1.1911). However, as a result of their participation in the spiritual guidance of humanity, the Archai themselves were able to advance so far in their own development that, around the beginning of the twentieth century, they began to ascend from the rank of Spirits of Personality to that of Exusiai or Spirits of Form. As Spirits of Form they send down to the Earth a new revelation which we find, above all, in the anthroposophically-orientated spiritual science of the present. 'And let us take it up in a living and lively way, this spiritual science, which I have spoken of as the revelation of the Spirits of Personality, who as Creators intervene and act anew; let us take it up for our times not simply as the work of men but, as I have said, as something revealed from the heights of Heaven ... Redemption [for our times] can come only if human souls can be found who turn to meet the Spirit that wishes to reveal itself in a new way through the Spirits of Personality, who from the lesser state of Time Spirits wish to become Creators. There is no other way' (GA 187, 31.12.1918).

Thus we have here one type of influence where the Hierarchies work from the cosmos on the events on Earth and which has its beginning around the time of Aristotle. On 16.4.1923 (GA 306), Rudolf Steiner says: 'There were long periods of time involved in this transference [of the Cosmic Thoughts]. It was prepared for even in pre-Christian times and was completed only in the twelfth, thirteenth and fourteenth centuries after Christ; the fourth century is, so to speak, only the *middle* of this span of time' (GA 222). If the fourth century is the 'middle' of this process, the beginning of it must lie in the fifth–fourth century before Christ, that is, around the time of Aristotle. And from then onwards the process develops further, through the fourth century AD and the time around 1250, and then, after a pause, it continues with the appearance on Earth at the beginning of the twentieth century of anthroposophically-orientated spiritual science.

The second type of spiritual influence on the Earth around 1250 was of a different nature. It concerns Beings of a still higher Hierarchy—the Spirits of Form. In a lecture on 31.12.1910 (in GA 126), Rudolf Steiner speaks of how the influence of these Spirits works particularly strongly on the physical evolution of the Earth (and least strongly on the inner being of man) during the epoch of the great Atlantean catastrophe, and that such an unusual constellation of this kind must at some point find its opposite pole in the history of humanity. A time would have to come when these Spirits would be able to work more strongly on the inner development of human beings and only very slightly on the physical evolution of the Earth, and this occurred around the year 1250. It was precisely because of this that that time was particularly favourable for the initiation of Christian Rosenkreutz, which was thus carried out during a period of the maximum activity of the Spirits of the Sun (the Exusiai) in the inner being of man.

To all that has been said above one must add that around the time of 1250 there was also an intrinsic shift in the Earth's axis (Rudolf Steiner speaks of this in his lectures on 29.1.1911 in GA 130 and on 31.12.1911 in GA 126). And to conclude this study, it is essential to draw attention to the fact that in his descriptions of all these events relating to the year 1250, Rudolf Steiner stressed particularly their inner connection with the two streams within humanity that have already been indicated: the streams of Scholasticism and Rosicrucianism, which have their beginning at this time. For in these streams we have the two fundamental poles of the 'new culture' of all humanity—poles which in our time, with the beginning of the new Age of Michael, must become one within modern humanity and above all within the Anthroposophical Society itself.

110 For the nature of this profoundly dramatic battle of the representatives of Scholasticism with Arabized Aristotelianism, see particularly the lecture on 1.7.1924 in GA 237.

111 For the task of the fifth post-Atlantean epoch as being a confrontation with evil in connection with the development of the consciousness soul, see Lectures 4 and 5 of GA 185.

112 GA 137, 6.6.1912.

113 On 12.10.1918 (in GA 184) Rudolf Steiner indicates that the ahrimanic impulse which worked in Roger Bacon had its origins in the Academy of Gondishapur.

114 GA 74, 25.5.1920.

115 In a lecture in Dornach on 1.7.1924 (GA 237) Rudolf Steiner speaks of the significance of the work of the teachers of Scholasticism for the preparation of the approaching age of the consciousness soul: 'The European people were, as a whole, quite unable in the tenth, eleventh and twelfth centuries to let an outlook like that of these personalities [i.e. the Arabian philosophers] pass over them without their reacting to it, for [had they done so] the development of the consciousness soul would not have taken place. Even though it was decreed, so to speak, in a decision of the Gods that this

consciousness soul should develop, it was nevertheless the case that it could not have developed out of European humanity's own activity as a totality but that an impulse had to be given which worked towards its particular development.' From the content further on in the lecture, it becomes clear that this impulse 'which had been given towards developing the consciousness soul in accordance with the decision of the Gods' was the impulse of Scholasticism.

116 GA 26, 12.10.1924.

117 What is referred to here are the two paths along which the Aristotelian teaching was later spread. One path was taken primarily by those works of Aristotle connected with a knowledge of nature. Alexander the Great spread these in Asia and Africa, whence from the eleventh century onwards they returned again to Europe, mainly as a result of the Crusades. These Aristotelian works then provided the basis of medieval alchemy. The second path was taken principally by Aristotle's works on logic. His pupil Theophrastus spread them in Southern and Central Europe where they played a decisive part in the emergence of Scholasticism. If, however, we look at the two principal representatives of that Scholasticism, Thomas Aquinas and Albertus Magnus, we see how, even by the thirteenth century, they were able to unite the two streams to a considerable degree, for both were occupied not only with the writings on logic but also with those on a philosophy of nature, as far as these were available at that time. In other words, they devoted themselves not only to activity in thought but also to alchemy. (F.W. Zeylmans van Emmichoven, *The Foundation Stone*, the chapter 'From the Philosophers' Stone to the Stone of Love'.)

118 GA 233, 29.12.1923.

119 In this sense the following words of Rudolf Steiner point in a particularly profound way to the inner nature of the new Michaelic Christianity: 'This is why, from the standpoint of our spiritual science, one emphasizes the Christ-impulse so often—because the Christ-impulse lies in the straight line of formative, ordering thinking' (1.1.1919, GA 187).

120 GA 240, 19.7.1924.

121 See Note 146 of Chapter 3.

122 It was for this reason—and this must be understood in the right way by anthroposophists—that the full title of the lecture cycle given by Rudolf Steiner during the Christmas Conference, in which he spoke of this secret to the whole Anthroposophical Society, was called *World History in the Light of Anthroposophy and as a Foundation for Knowledge of the Human Spirit*.

123 In this context it is also significant that especially in his lecture cycle in *Cologne* (GA 142) Rudolf Steiner speaks particularly incisively about the spiritual task of Thomas Aquinas—the task of bringing about a harmonious union of Christianity and Aristotelianism; in other words, a union of the Christ-impulse with that extract of the ancient Mystery-wisdom which was contained in the philosophy of Aristotle (GA 142, 28.12.1912).

124 GA 233, 31.12.1923.

125 GA 233a, 22.4.1924.

126 From the nature of the whole lecture (in GA 233a, 13.1.1924) one can have the feeling that this 'lofty spirit' was the Archangel Michael himself.

127 GA 233a, 13.1.1924.

128 One must also note here that everything which with the help of the warmth-ether is inscribed into the astral light later returns, as has been said above, from the sphere beyond the zodiac. This sphere, however, is also the macrocosmic 'I'-sphere, the sphere from which Christ once came to the Earth (see p. 146).

129 If we also remember here that, as Rudolf Steiner has said (see Note 155 of Chapter 3), it was the forms themselves of the First Goetheanum that were meant to make possible, in the human being who gazed upon them, the development of a true experiencing of and penetration into the inner nature of karma, then we understand that it was the *Spirit of the Goetheanum*, resurrected and returned from the far distances of the cosmos, that made possible those karmic investigations in particular, which Rudolf Steiner undertook after the Christmas Conference. And the fact that, as Rudolf Steiner has said, these karmic investigations were connected with the uncovering of profound secrets of the Michael-sphere, is in full accord with the participation of Michael himself (which we have already looked at) in the cosmic destiny of the First Goetheanum after the fire.

130 GA 233a, 13.1.1924.

131 GA 233a, 22.4.1924.

132 Ibid.

133 Rudolf Steiner's speech at the laying of the Foundation Stone (GA 245).

134 *The Christmas Conference for the Foundation of the General Anthroposophical Society 1923/1924* (GA 260), 1.1.1924, Rudolf Steiner's concluding words.

Chapter 5. The Christmas Conference of 1923–24

1 GA 260.

2 The following words of Rudolf Steiner, spoken on the day of the laying of the Foundation Stone of the 'General Anthroposophical Society', also point to this relation of Michael's guidance to the inner nature of the Christmas Conference: 'The Greeks could still grasp the nature of man as a whole, according to spirit, soul and body, when they allowed the ancient words to resound, the primeval words of the Sun, the words of Apollo: "Know Thyself". But we must word it differently today when we renew it out of the *signs of our time* in the right way. We must say: O soul of man, know thyself in thy living being and weaving (*in Deinem wesenden Weben*) in spirit, soul and body.' (*The Christmas Conference for the Foundation of the General Anthroposophical Society 1923/1924*, GA 260). Firstly, in these words we are

directed to the inner, esoteric nature of the Sun Mysteries of ancient Greece, which once received their revelations directly from the Sun-sphere of Michael. (This is also why they flowered precisely in the previous epoch of Michael's rulership.) Secondly, these words direct us to a renewal of these ancient Mysteries through 'the signs of our time'. This expression 'the signs of our time' accords with a lecture given by Rudolf Steiner in Munich on 17 February 1918, entitled 'Signs of the Times, Michael's Battle and Its Reflection on Earth' (GA 174a); it is an occult term connected with the present Mystery of Michael. In the addition to the ancient Mystery-saying 'Know Thyself' of the words 'in thy living being and weaving', this also points to the direct inspiration of Michael. For it is Michael who awakens the human being in our epoch to the threefold experiences of him in accordance with spirit, soul and body. (See GA 223/229, 2.4.1923, and GA 194, 30.11.1919.)

3 F.W. Zeylmans van Emmichoven, *The Foundation Stone*, p. 36.

4 GA 260.

5 The connection of the four words which characterize the esoteric content of the Christmas Conference with the four parts of the *Foundation Stone Meditation* corresponds to the sections of the *Meditation* as given on p. 347.

6 In a lecture in Arnhem on 18.7.1924 (GA 240), while speaking of the union, through the Christmas Conference, of the anthroposophical movement and the Anthroposophical Society, Rudolf Steiner describes their inner nature as follows: 'Up to the time of the Christmas Foundation Meeting I was always able to make a distinction between the anthroposophical movement and the Anthroposophical Society. The latter represented as it were the earthly projection of something that exists in the spiritual worlds in a certain stream of the spiritual life. What was taught here on Earth and communicated as anthroposophical wisdom—this was the reflection of the stream flowing in spiritual worlds through the present phase of the evolution of mankind. The Anthroposophical Society was then a kind of "administrative organ" for the anthroposophical knowledge flowing through the anthroposophical movement.'

7 GA 260a, 7.6.1924.

8 GA 260a, 6.2.1924.

9 GA 260.

10 Ibid.

11 GA 103, 22.5.1908.

12 Entry into the higher worlds in the *right way*—that is, for the good of earthly development—was *always* attained by initiates in the Mysteries only by uniting themselves with the Christ-impulse. Up to the Mystery of Golgotha this occurred by the initiates ascending into the Sun-sphere, for this alone gave them the possibility of using for the good of earthly development that cosmic wisdom which, in ancient pre-Christian times, could be attained only from the hands of Lucifer. Rudolf Steiner speaks of this as follows: 'When one goes back to the origins of humanity one finds that the sources

of pagan wisdom are always to be found in luciferic beings . . . The luciferic beings inculcated their wisdom into man but their desire was that it would make him turn away from the Earth, without passing through earthly evolution. Lucifer wants to abandon the Earth to its fate, to win mankind for a kingdom alien to the kingdom of Christ. The wise men of olden times who received the primeval wisdom from the hands of Lucifer had, as I said, to pledge themselves not to yield to his wishes but to use the wisdom for the good of Earth-evolution. And that, in essence, was what was accomplished through the pre-Christian Mysteries' (GA 191, 15.11.1919).This, as mentioned above, would be attained by the initiates in these Mysteries only by uniting themselves with the Christ-impulse in the Sun-sphere.

13   In GA 233a, 13.1.1924, Rudolf Steiner speaks of how the most important challenge of the new Michael epoch is to include among the fundamental principles of contemporary civilization the principle of initiation (which in itself is possible only through the realization of an esotericism that works socially amongst mankind). He says there: 'The world must reach a point once again where it is able to accept the principle of initiation as such among the principles of civilization. For only through this can it come about that, here on Earth, the human being can gather into his soul something with which he can come before Michael and meet his consenting gaze that says: this is right before the world (*Weltgerecht*). Then the will is strengthened by this and the human being incorporated into the spiritual progression of the world. The human being will thereby become a co-worker in that which, beginning now in the epoch of Michael, is to be brought into human and Earth development by Michael.'

14   See GA 158.

15   We can remind ourselves here that in his lecture on 13.1.1924 (GA 233a) Rudolf Steiner says that prior to the beginning of the new epoch of Michael, even Christian Rosenkreutz was not able to receive from the cosmos the reflected rays inscribed in the astral light by the warmth ether, except through a dulled consciousness; and only since 1879 has it been possible to experience this in full waking consciousness, through a conscious meeting with Michael in the spiritual world.

16   GA 233, 29.12.1923.

17   It was said above (p. 199) that an important task of anthroposophists since the Christmas Conference is to create the conditions for a working together in the Anthroposophical Society of both the incarnated and the non-incarnated human beings who are united through a common karmic bond with Anthroposophy and Michael (see further regarding the participation of the non-incarnated souls at the Christmas Conference in chapter 7). This aspect is also discernible in the initiation of Lazarus. For according to Rudolf Steiner, in the course of his initiation his being was permeated 'from above' as far as the intellectual soul by the entelechy of John the Baptist in the spiritual worlds, which was at that time working supersensibly in the circle of the Apostles as their group-soul (see the lecture of 28.9.1924, and also the

explanation that Rudolf Steiner gave to Ludwig Noll, GA 238; and the lecture of 20.9.1912, GA 139).

18   *The Christmas Conference for the Foundation of the General Anthroposophical Society, 1923/1924* (GA 260), 1.1.1924, the closing lecture.

19   GA 260a, 18.1.1924.

20   GA 10, the chapter 'The Guardian of the Threshold'.

21   Rudolf Steiner speaks of this transition from the Soul-world into the Spirit-land as being an ascent from the Moon-sphere into that of the Sun. 'Now when we have completed this backward review [through the experiences during Kamaloka of our previous life on Earth], when we then arrive back at our starting point, we must find that transition which I mention in my *Theosophy* as the transition from the Soul-world into the Spirit-land. Connected with this, however, is the fact that we leave the Moon-realm and move within the cosmos into the realm of the Sun.' (GA 226, 17.5.1923.)

22   Only the earlier editions of *Occult Science* contain the fourth and seventh stage formulated in this way. (See also GA 99, 6.6.1907.) In the last edition (1925) the fourth stage is described as 'Living into the spiritual surroundings (corresponding to Intuition)', and the seventh as 'Experiencing as a fundamental mood of soul the totality of the previous stages.'

23   The correlation spoken of here between the first four stages of the Christian-Rosicrucian path of initiation and the four lower members of the human being can also be considered from a somewhat different point of view, namely, when one looks at the process of the spiritual pupil's ascent to a true knowledge of his higher 'I' which is normally separate from the three bodies. In this case the first level of the Christian-Rosicrucian path corresponds to a knowledge of the 'I' in its reflection in the *physical body*, through the astral and etheric sheaths. On attaining to imaginative consciousness on the astral plane (in the world of Elements) the pupil is able to experience his higher 'I' in its reflection in the *etheric body*, through the astral sheath. Later, having ascended into Lower Devachan (the world of the planets) and having reached the stage of inspirational consciousness, he is able to experience his higher 'I' reflected in the *astral body*. And finally, having risen in Intuition to Upper Devachan (the world of the fixed stars), he is able to experience his higher 'I' as it were 'face to face', and to recognize in it the Christ, working there since the Mystery of Golgotha. (For this reason also the word 'intuition', even in ordinary usage, is always connected with something very intimate in the human being, just as in spiritual knowledge it is only in Intuition that the true countenance of the *higher 'I'* is revealed—the holy of holies.) This sequence of the relationship of the initiation stages with the sheaths of the human being corresponds completely with the order in which these are given in the gradual ascent from the lower to the higher (physical body—etheric body—astral body—'I'...), as conveyed, for example, in *Theosophy*. The sequence, given in Chapter 5, however ('I'—astral body—etheric body—physical body) corresponds to that of the

399

'transformation' of the sheaths *during the course of occult development*, which is described in Chapter 5 of *Occult Science*—and we must bear in mind here that in both cases we are dealing with different aspects of one and the same process. In the first case we are looking at it from the point of view of the development of the pupil, who as the *subject* of knowledge works towards the gradual awakening of consciousness in the corresponding bodily sheaths. In the second case (described above) the description is made from the point of view of the *object* of this knowledge—the higher 'I' of the human being—to the direct perception of which every pupil must gradually rise, being the higher goal of his spiritual path. One can find a particularly detailed description of this ascent of the pupil during the course of the new initiation, from the physical body through the etheric and astral bodies to the higher 'I', in the fourth and fifth lectures of the cycle GA 234. Here Rudolf Steiner describes how in ordinary thinking we comprehend only the solid constituents of the human organism; how in imaginative knowledge we comprehend our etheric body, working in the so-called 'fluid-man' (that is, in the fluid element of our organism); in inspirational knowledge we comprehend the astral body, working in the 'air-man'; and finally, in intuitive knowledge there is revealed to us the inner nature of our true 'I', which finds its outer expression in the 'warmth-man'. See also in this connection the initiation, often described by Rudolf Steiner, similar to that undergone by Brunetto Latini, e.g. in GA 237, 13.7.1924, and also in the lecture on 28.7.1922 (GA 214). See also Note 95, Chapter 3.

24 For this connection of the principles of the Spirit, the Son and the Father with the higher members of the human being, see the lecture of 25.3.1907 in GA 96.

25 GA 110, 16.4.1909.

26 GA 260.

27 GA 13.

28 GA 260.

29 Ibid.

30 GA 243, 22.8.1924.

31 We must also note here that in pre-Christian times the soul of one who had died could not experience the great macrocosmic Man that arises from the working of all nine Hierarchies without the help of the Christ who dwelt at that time in the Sun. Thus what Christ once gave to human beings in the Sun-sphere as their self-experience in the great macrocosmic human being can now through His sacrificial union with the Earth also be attained by human beings while incarnated in a physical body, through a completely *free* union on Earth with the Christ-impulse (see GA 239, 25.5.1924). This possibility, which was won by Christ for all future development and which will be realized only very gradually within humanity, proceeding from freedom, also directs us to the stupendous goal of all Earth evolution. This will become evident later through our study of the concluding 7th rhythm of the Christmas Conference.

32　GA 260.

33　Ibid.

34　See also in GA 239, 14.6.1924.

35　The composition of the rhythm of the first day also gives us a picture of how through the Christ-impulse in the new initiation (in Part IV) the two principal Mystery-paths of antiquity are united: the path of sinking deeply into one's own soul (the path of the Buddha, who appears to the shepherds), which is connected more to the first sections of the first three parts; and the path of sinking meditatively into the secrets of the macrocosm (the path of Zarathustra, represented by his pupils, the Magi of the East), which is connected more with the second sections of the same parts.

36　The call to the elemental spirits cited here can also be connected with that passage in the new Isis legend (GA 180, 6.1.1918), where it is related how Isis receives back her son, whom Typhon had torn to pieces, in his true form. Rudolf Steiner describes this as follows: 'But the day came when she was able to receive him back in his true and genuine form from the hands of a group of spirits who were *elemental spirits* of nature . . .' And he says further that thanks to this wonderful return of her son, a clairvoyance was suddenly enkindled in Isis which then revealed to her 'the most profound significance . . . of that which in St John's Gospel is called the Logos; there was revealed to her the Johannine significance of the Mystery of Golgotha. By this force the power of the cowhorns took hold of her paper crown and transformed it into a true crown of gold, of genuine wisdom.'

37　See Note 88, Chapter 3.

38　GA 40, 'Credo, the Individual and the Universe'.

39　One must note here that although the process of the birth of the higher 'I' takes place in every human being after death, different souls, depending on their inner structure, pass through this event with different degrees of consciousness so that, for example, a soul which through the whole course of its earthly life had nurtured almost exclusively materialistic thoughts can experience this birth in almost total unconsciousness.

40　GA 112, 24.6.1909.

41　*Occult Science* (GA 13).

42　GA 112, 24.6.1909. Rudolf Steiner also speaks in this lecture of the connection between the Grail stream and the Rosicrucian stream: 'Those who called themselves Johannine Christians and had as their symbol the Rose-Cross, said: What has been reborn for humanity in the events of Palestine as the secret of humanity's higher "I" has been preserved. It has been preserved by that small community which has its origin in Rosicrucianism. This continuity is shown in a symbol: that holy Chalice, called the "Holy Grail", from which Christ Jesus ate and drank with his disciples, and in which the blood that flowed from the wounds was caught by Joseph of Arimathaea. As is related, this Chalice was brought to Europe by an Angel. A temple was built for it and the Rosicrucians became the keepers of what was in the vessel—keepers, that is, of what amounted to the true being of the God reborn. The Mystery of the reborn God held sway within humanity—it is the Mystery of the Grail.'

Also, the following words of Rudolf Steiner on the Mystery of the Holy Grail are exceptionally important, both for a deeper penetration into the inner nature of the interrelation between the Grail stream and the Rosicrucian stream, as well as a real awareness in particular of the true role of the Grail Mystery in the revelation of the supersensible life of the soul between death and a new birth, as is contained in the seven fundamental rhythms of the Christmas Conference: 'Everything which is to contribute in our times to the spreading of an understanding of the Christ-impulse is encompassed for the Occident in that which can be called the Mystery of the Holy Grail. And the Mystery of the Holy Grail is intimately connected with such things as have already been spoken about: with the conferring on Buddha of the mission for Mars by Christian Rosenkreutz [GA 141, 22.12.1912, and GA 130, 18.12.1912]. *And this Mystery of the Holy Grail can give the modern human being that which brings him to an understanding, right for our time, of the life between death and a new birth*' (GA 141, 7.1.1913).

In connection with these last words one can also call to mind that on 23.7.1922 (in GA 214) Rudolf Steiner describes how the real keepers of the Grail in the supersensible world are chosen souls of the dead.

43   GA 234, 10.2.1924.

44   These three stages of the gradual ascent of the human being into the sphere of freedom were already fully described in Chapter 9 of Rudolf Steiner's *The Philosophy of Freedom*.

45   GA 260.

46   GA 227, 29.8.1923; GA 231, 14.11.1923, and in particular GA 239, 31.3.1924 and 9.6.1924.

47   GA 13, Chapter 6.

48   In connection with the first three rhythms we must note the following. The three fundamental anthroposophical exercises as formulated in the *Foundation Stone Meditation* (I, II, III, 5) only appear in the rhythm of the third day. They are entirely absent in the rhythm of the second day and are given in the rhythm of the first day not in the form of exercises but as a description of the three different aspects of human soul activity which find expression in 'Spirit-recollection', 'Spirit-mindfulness' and 'Spirit-vision'. The abbreviation of these lines of the *Meditation* in the first rhythm and their complete absence in the second rhythm is of deep significance. As will be shown later, the first rhythm relates to the *first stage* of the Christian-Rosicrucian path of initiation, the stage of studying modern spiritual science beginning from one's ordinary faculty of human understanding. This stage *precedes* the commencement of actual esoteric practice (concentration, meditation and contemplation). These lines, therefore, in the first rhythm of the *Meditation*, are given not in the form of soul-exercises as in the *Meditation* itself (I, II, III, 5) but in a form which depicts those aspects of human soul-activity (soul-processes) which gradually lead the student of the spirit to a direct

experience of the spiritual worlds. As said, in the second rhythm there is no reference at all to these lines, but they appear again in their complete form in the third rhythm. This is connected with the fact that the second rhythm already leads us into the world of Inspiration. In his lectures Rudolf Steiner frequently speaks of the fact that, from the twentieth century onwards, imaginative perception will begin to emerge naturally in people without the preparatory exercises carried out in an occult training. This will occur in three ways: as perception of the aura and the elemental world; as perception of the karmic consequences of an action done in the present; and as a meeting with the Etheric Christ.The absence of the exercises from the rhythm of the second day points directly to this in a remarkable way. And their appearance in the rhythm of the third day also relates to indications by Rudolf Steiner that even though it may be possible to receive true Imaginations through certain conditions without undergoing a proper occult development, it is not possible to receive true Inspirations in this way in the sphere into which the student enters at the third stage. For what is perceived without occult preparation as 'spiritual hearing' cannot be properly interpreted by one who has not entered the path of spiritual training (see the lecture of 18.7.1923, GA 350). For the existence of the soul after death this absence of the exercises in the rhythm of the second day points to the fact that a proper entry after death into the sphere of the Sun, whose lowest realms of spiritual activity are found in the World of Imaginations, i.e. the World of Souls (see the lecture of 1.4.1913 in GA 141), is not possible at the present cycle of development for human forces alone, without the help of the Christ-impulse taken up on Earth (see GA 239, 31.3.1924).

49   In *Occult Science* we read: 'To the eye of the spirit, life is a flowing essence, like seas and rivers pervading the Spirit-land. Better still is the comparison with the circulation of the blood in the human body. For while the seas and rivers in external nature appear as though distributed irregularly, there is a certain regularity in the distribution of the flowing life in the Spirit-land, even as in the circulation of the blood.'

50   In reference to these two interconnections, on the one hand between the realm of 'seas and rivers' of Lower Devachan, which contains all the archetypes of the etheric (life) elements, and the organization of our blood circulation (the heart)—i.e. the 'liquid-man' in us—and on the other hand between the airy sphere or 'atmosphere' of Lower Devachan, which contains the archetypes of the astral (feeling) element and the organization of our lungs—i.e. the 'air-man' in us—Rudolf Steiner says the following: 'All this is what was able to lead us to the threefold nature of the human being— to the physical body, etheric body and astral body, which express themselves through the "air-man", the "fluid-man" and the "solid-man", which in turn have their counterparts in the structures of the solid man, in the changing forms of the liquid-man, and in that which permeates the human being as an inner music that can be experienced in feeling' (GA 234,

403

1.2.1924); and 'thus in matter, in solid earthly matter, one can really see the physical element; and in the fluid element, in the way this has effect in the human being, one can see the etheric; and in the airy element, the astral' (GA 234, 2.2.1924).

51   The actual words in *Occult Science* of this description of the second region of Lower Devachan read: 'And this "flowing life" is experienced at the same time as spiritual musical sound.'

52   In *Occult Science* Rudolf Steiner describes the four realms of the Spirit-land as follows: 'One should imagine the thought, such as it is in man, lifted out of him and as an active being endowed with an inner life of its own. In this way, one has a faint picture of what fills the Spirit-land.' See also Note 33, Chapter 6.

53   In *Occult Science* Rudolf Steiner writes: 'What one finds in the fifth region can be compared to physical light. It is wisdom manifested in the form that is most truly its own.'

54   GA 260.

55   GA 13, Chapter 6.

56   Regarding Christ as the leader of souls from the Moon-sphere to that of the Sun in after-death existence, see, for example, the lectures of 14.9.1922 (GA 215) and 28.8.1923 (GA 227).

57   GA 239, 31.3.1924.

58   In a lecture in Breslau on 8.6.1924 (GA 239), Rudolf Steiner says the following concerning the participation of *all* nine Hierarchies in the forming of karma: 'In human destiny we can perceive, firstly the working of the Angeloi, Archangeloi, Archai; then of still loftier Sun Beings, Exusiai, Dynamis, Kyriotetes; then of the Thrones who are concerned mainly with the elaboration of karma in the Mars-sphere; then of the Cherubim who elaborate the karma belonging to the Jupiter-sphere; and then of the Seraphim who work together with man on the elaboration of karma in the Saturn-sphere—Saturn karma. In man's destiny, in his karma, we behold the working of the higher Hierarchies. This karma, at first, is like a veil, a curtain. If we look behind this veil we gaze at the weaving deeds and influences of Angeloi, Archangeloi, Archai, Exusiai, Dynamis, Kyriotetes, Thrones, Cherubim, Seraphim.'

59   This awesome picture of the work of all nine Hierarchies at the hour of Cosmic Midnight, as is perceived by the initiate at the moment of his beholding the Midnight Sun, is described by Rudolf Steiner in particular detail in his lecture on 27.6.1924 in GA 236.

60   See GA 231, 13.11.1923; and Note 63 of this chapter (and compare also the lecture of 2.3.1924 in GA 235).

61   See, for example, GA 13.

62   The expression 'face to face' is used by Rudolf Steiner in his description of the soul's existence in the sphere of Intuition (Upper Devachan) when it is one with the spiritual Hierarchies. See the lecture of 17.5.1923 in GA 226.

63   This enumeration of the names of all nine Hierarchies in the rhythm of the

day in question speaks also of the fact that this rhythm leads us up into the sphere of Intuition. For as is borne witness by Rudolf Steiner in a lecture in Dornach on 23.7.1922 (GA 214), imaginative knowledge opens the way into the sphere of the Third Hierarchy, inspirational knowledge the way into the sphere of the Second Hierarchy, and only intuitive knowledge leads into the sphere of the First Hierarchy. It follows from this that an overall perception of *all nine* Hierarchies together is only possible in intuitive knowledge—that is, from the sphere of Intuition. We are also directed to this sphere, in the rhythm in question, by the description of the activity in the cosmos of the Cosmic Word which, as Rudolf Steiner says in his *Theosophy*, is revealed to the initiate only at his passing from Lower Devachan into Upper Devachan, and leads him to the 'border of the three worlds' (see *Theosophy*—the last two paragraphs of the chapter 'The Spirit-land'). In his lecture on 13.11.1923 (in GA 231), Rudolf Steiner speaks of this transition from the Cosmic Music (Cosmic Rhythm) to the Cosmic Word as also being a transition from the sphere of Inspiration into that of Intuition. He says there: 'Now we proceed further, from Inspiration to Intuition. And now something quite extraordinary arises out of the Cosmic Music: ... the Cosmic Music changes into the speech of the whole cosmos. That which should be comprehended under the words "Cosmic Speech" becomes audible. In earlier times this was understood as the "Cosmic Word". The Cosmic Word becomes audible.'

And later in this lecture, while describing the nature of the sphere of Intuition, he continues: 'If we then manage to move on (out of the sphere of Inspiration) to Intuition and perceive how the human muscular and skeletal system is woven out of the formation of the world of the Cosmic Word, Cosmic Speech, we come to the First Hierarchy, to the Cherubim, Seraphim and Thrones. And we have then arrived approximately at the mid-point between death and a new birth, the moment which I describe in my *Mystery Dramas* as the "Midnight-hour of Existence".' (In a lecture in Paris on 25.5.1924—in GA 239—Rudolf Steiner also calls the 'Midnight Hour of Existence' the 'Height of Midnight'.) And he completes in this lecture the description of the great picture of the combined activity of all nine Hierarchies: 'Thus we are able to describe how the hierarchic order ascends from the Third to the Second, up to the First Hierarchy. When we describe what is working there, what is contained there beyond the Earth but which works down into the earthly—as we look upon the deeds of these Hierarchies, a remarkable picture takes shape before us. We gaze upon the hierarchical order, see below the working Beings of the Third Hier-archy, the Angels, Archangels and Archai, and we see the Beings of the Second Hierarchy, the Exusiai, Kyriotetes and Dynamis, and we see how they all work and act together in the cosmos. Then we gaze upon the Beings of the First Hierarchy, on the Cherubim, Seraphim and Thrones. And only now does there arise for us a comprehensible picture of the human body: on the one side is the order of the Hierarchies, whom we follow right to their deeds, and we allow these deeds to come before our spiritual eyes—and there before us is *man*.'

64 GA 130.

65 GA 227, 30.8.1923. One should note here, however, that the experience in question of the past, which reaches its climax in the knowledge of Old Saturn in the sphere of Intuition, occurs during the *whole* of the first half of the life after death. And in the preceding stages of Inspiration and Imagination (Lower Devachan and astral plane) there is revealed a knowledge of Old Sun and Old Moon respectively. Rudolf Steiner often points in his lectures to this connection of existence after death with the past development of the Earth. For example, in a lecture in Milan on 27.10.1912 (in GA 140) he says: 'If you look at the description which we have often given as the life of Saturn, Sun and Moon, you will have there the course of the path that one actually experiences after death. But the remarkable thing is that one does not experience it in the sequence in which it arises in the cosmos—Saturn, Sun, Moon—but experiences the Moon-existence first, then the Sun-existence, and lastly the Saturn-existence. If you read through the description of this which I give in *Cosmic Memory*, and go farther back from the Moon, you have that world which the soul experiences on its path after death.'

66 GA 13, Chapter 6.

67 The fourth Mystery Drama, *The Souls' Awakening*, Scene VI, the first monologue of the Guardian of the Threshold.

68 Further confirmation of this may be gleaned from the fact that, according to Rudolf Steiner, the human soul after death in the spiritual world gradually clothes itself with first the Spirit Self, then the Life Spirit and finally, during Cosmic Midnight, with Spirit Man (see GA 168, 18.2.1916, and GA 208, 21.10.1921), with the sheaths whose first rudiments were laid down in the epochs of Old Saturn, Old Sun and Old Moon by the higher Hierarchies (GA 11). A similar process also takes place in the path of initiation. For by consciously entering the higher worlds, the spirit-pupil is enabled to come in contact with these three higher members of man's being and in this way to receive a real imagination of the future conditions of the Earth, Jupiter, Venus and Vulcan—as was described in connection with the rhythms of 27, 28 and 29 December.

69 One can also establish a connection between what has been said here and the following: in a lecture in Vienna on 10.4.1914 (in GA 153), Rudolf Steiner speaks of how it is during the *second half* of existence after death—that is, after the Cosmic Midnight (the period which corresponds to the 5th, 6th and 7th rhythms of the Christmas Conference)—that the soul of the one who has died perceives, while being guided on its downward path to the Earth by the Holy Spirit, the Ideal of Man in the spiritual world as the great cosmic aim of the Gods (see Rudolf Steiner's words on pp. 288–89). This Ideal is also the highest religion of the Gods in the spiritual world, and is the first thing that Christ brought to the Earth. In this sense we have in the

7th rhythm a reference to the realization of this Ideal of Man which, in Rudolf Steiner's words, represents 'the reflection of divine existence in human form' (p. 289); and the path leading to this is given in the 5th and 6th rhythms (see the study of these three rhythms further on in this chapter).

70   GA 107, 22.3.1909.

71   Rudolf Steiner refers to the profoundly sacrificial nature of the Baptism in the Jordan in Lecture 10, GA 112.

72   This state of being 'overshone' by the Holy Spirit is described by Rudolf Steiner in detail in GA 236, 4.6.1924.

73   GA 240, 27.8.1924, and Note 130 of this chapter.

74   This state of being 'overshone' by the Holy Spirit (see GA 236, 4.6.1924) is a true anticipation of the Jupiter-existence, to which Rudolf Steiner's representation of the seventh seal of the Apocalypse also points (see GA 284/285). In this seal a transparent cube is portrayed below, symbolizing the future Jupiter condition which was once beheld by John the Evangelist in the image of the 'New Jerusalem' (compare Revelation 21: 2 with Lectures 12 and 16, GA 104). And above is the form of the Holy Chalice which arises from the human being's transformation of his astral body (of the snake around the cube below) into Spirit Self, which then becomes the true vessel of the Holy Spirit (the image of the dove).

75   GA 240, 19.7.1924.

76   One must bear in mind here that in the rhythm of this day, which speaks of the descent of the Sun Spirit, Christ, from the Sun to the Earth and of His entry 'into the stream of Earthly Being', we also have a reference to the descent into the earthly sphere of the Cosmic Intelligence of Michael, inasmuch as Christ and the Cosmic Intelligence are connected with one another. Rudolf Steiner speaks of this as follows: 'Now this too was connected with the descent of Christ to the Earth; Michael and his hosts witnessed not only the departure of Christ from the Sun, but above all they saw how Michael himself was gradually losing his dominion over the Cosmic Intelligence' (GA 237). And elsewhere he says: 'But after the Mystery of Golgotha something of deep significance took place in that Michael's dominion over the Cosmic Intelligence gradually fell away from him, fell from his grasp ... And if we look into the spiritual world we see that the descent of the Intelligence from the Sun to the Earth is accomplished by about the eighth century AD' (GA 240, 21.8.1924).

If we now turn to the fourth part of the *Meditation*, which was read on this day in its entirety, we find in its first five lines a reference to the descent of the Christ-impulse to Earth, and in the next two lines (6 and 7), a reference to the subsequent descent into human souls of the Intelligence of Michael. In particular, as has been pointed out by Zeylmans van Emmichoven in *The Foundation Stone*, the words 'Day-radiant Light' relate to the Archangel Michael. (See the chapter 'The Pentagram and the Sun of Christ'.)

77   GA 120, 28.5.1910.

78   GA 123, 5.9.1910.

79   Ibid., 4.9.1910.

80   Rudolf Steiner speaks of this great cosmic awaiting of the Christ in GA 130, and on 9.1.1912 (GA 130).

81   GA 226, 17.5.1923.

82   That the concept of heredity is applicable not only to the qualities of the physical body but *to a certain extent* also to those of the etheric body may be found expressed in the lecture of 5.6.1909 (GA 112). However, the concept of heredity is wholly inapplicable to the astral body.

83   GA 231, 17.11.1923.

84   The following words of Rudolf Steiner speak of how Zarathustra perceived Christ above all in the manifestation of the forces of His macrocosmic *astral* body in the image of the great Astral Aura of the Sun. 'And understanding Zarathustra, one could say that this is what he taught to those who were his pupils: you must be fully aware that behind the physical sunlight there is a spiritual light. Just as behind the physical human being there is his astral element, the aura, so too behind the sun is the great Aura' (GA 123, 12.9.1910). 'This is how [the legend] speaks when it speaks of the astral body of the sun, of Ahura Mazdao.'

85   GA 227, 28.8.1923.

86   GA 136, 11.4.1912.

87   GA 103, 20.5.1908.

88   See GA 26, the article for New Year 1925.

89   In this rhythm we are directed by its connection with the Being of the Sun Mysteries to the supersensible School of Michael in the fourteenth to sixteenth centuries. The content of these Sun-Mysteries, as related by Rudolf Steiner in his lecture on 28.7.1924, came to life again in this School: 'And there was revived [in the supersensible School of Michael] all that which had once lived as Michael Wisdom in the Sun-Mysteries' (GA 237). And in the same lecture he continues: 'My dear friends, those who were in that supersensible School of Michael partook in the teachings which I have outlined so very briefly. The teachings they heard were a repetition of what had been taught in the *Sun-Mysteries* since ancient time.' And in a lecture on 1.8.1924 (in GA 237), he speaks of how a particularly intimate teaching in the supersensible School was the content of the teaching of the 'Fall of Man'. And in this connection a wonderful picture is given us by the fourth part of the *Meditation*—read on this day in its entirety—with its reference, in its sixth and seventh lines, to the descent of the Cosmic Intelligence of Michael into the souls of men (see GA 26, the article for New Year 1925). For an understanding of this aspect of Part IV of the *Meditation*, however, we should remember that, as Rudolf Steiner has said, since the beginning of the fourteenth century this Cosmic Intelligence which had fallen from the sphere of Michael and already entered human souls was, to a significant extent, in the clutches of ahrimanic forces. Thus our prime task in this time of the new rulership of Michael (and Michael pointed to this prophetically in his supersensible School), is to spiritualize the Intelligence, to redeem it

from the sphere of the 'Fall' into which it entered on descending into the souls of human beings (see also GA 74). This task, however, can only be fulfilled by permeating our hearts and heads with the Light of the Christ-Sun (14–19). This alone can then serve as a basis for that which is given us directly in the rhythm of this day, where the three exercises are spoken of which in the new initiation lead the pupil to a true redemption of the now earthbound Michaelic Intelligence—lead to its raising-up out of the sphere of the Fall into the realm of spiritual life. And in the hearts and heads of human beings, the Intelligence can thereby become that which flows out into the world as the true *good*:

> That good may become
> What from our Hearts we would found
> And from our Heads direct
> With single purpose.

In the fulfilment of these words there opens before us the path that awakens the will to truly overcome in humanity the consequences of the Fall. And this is the true realization on the Earth of the intentions of Michael, who turns now not only to human perception but above all to the human will, and calls man to what Rudolf Steiner speaks of as follows: 'Take up in your heart the Michael Thought which conquers the ahrimanic forces, the Thought which gives you the strength to gain spiritual knowledge here on Earth so that you can conquer the forces of death' (GA 223, 1.4.1923). And he explains, further on, that '. . . to take up the Michael-force means to take up the force of spiritual knowledge into our will, into that which we direct "with single purpose".' Finally, a reference must be made to what was said by Rudolf Steiner in a lecture on 28.7.1924 concerning the fact that during the time of the activity of the Michael School in the supersensible world, the souls of those present there 'took part . . . in a stupendous event that could only appear within the evolution of our cosmos after long, long epochs of time' (GA 237). He describes this 'stupendous event' as follows: '. . . in that age [the first third of the fifteenth century] the Earth appeared to the spirits in the supersensible worlds, surrounded by mighty lightnings and thunderclaps. The Seraphim, Cherubim and Thrones were carrying over the Cosmic Intelligence into that member of man's organization which we call the system of nerves and senses, the head-organization.' According to Rudolf Steiner, the Second Hierarchy—the Exusiai, Dynamis, Kyriotetes—also participated at that time in this great event, and all this was beheld by the members of the supersensible School in which 'all the Beings of the Hierarchy of the Angeloi, Archangeloi and Archai who belonged to the Michael stream also took part' (GA 240, 27.8.1924).

Thus we see that the human souls connected with the stream of Michael were able from the sphere of the Sun to experience in the lightning and thunder the activity of *all* nine Hierarchies in connection with this great

409

cosmic event—an event which was an essential condition for the genesis of celestial Anthroposophy. In a certain sense this event also preceded the first stage of Anthroposophy's preparation, taking place as it did in the super-sensible School. It is of this stupendous event that the preceding 4th rhythm of the Christmas Conference speaks, in which all nine Hierarchies come before us, so that every anthroposophist who immerses himself inwardly in the essence of this rhythm can recall this awe-inspiring picture, beheld by him at that time in the thunder and lightning. And Rudolf Steiner speaks as follows of the necessity for anthroposophists of awakening this memory: 'This should be understood, for these thunders and lightnings, my dear friends, are to become enthusiasm in the hearts and minds of anthroposophists!' (GA 137).

90   This birth of new elemental spirits in the Earth's surroundings after 1899, at the turning-point between the nineteenth and twentieth centuries, is spoken of by Rudolf Steiner in a lecture on 19.9.1911 (GA 130). Farther on in this lecture he speaks of how all these events, both the natural ones (the birth of new elemental spirits) and the moral ones (whereby from the twentieth century onwards people will begin to perceive the karmic consequences of their actions)—'all these events will group themselves around the future Christ-event'. And we are guided by these words to the direct connection that exists between the birth of these new elemental spirits of nature and the appearance of Christ in the twentieth century in the etheric.

91   GA 96, 1.4.1907.

92   See Note 110 of this chapter.

93   In a lecture at Dornach on 21.4.1924 (GA 233a), Rudolf Steiner presents the following relationship between the days of the week (i.e. the planetary spheres) and the faculties imprinted into the etheric body which forms itself anew:

(Moon)	(Monday)	
Mars	Tuesday	Speech
Mercury	Wednesday	Movement
Jupiter	Thursday	Wisdom
Venus	Friday	Love, Beauty
Saturn	Saturday	Inner warmth of soul
Sun	Sunday	Protective forces

(The names of the planets corresponding to the days of the week are added here by the present author.) If it is now borne in mind that the faculties of the etheric body in this diagram relate to the planets, then—beginning with Mars which is particularly active on Tuesdays, that is, on that day of the week on which the actual Mystery part of the Christmas Conference began, and going on to the Sun (Sunday)—it is possible to see a correspondence between them and the first seven days of the Christmas Conference. Reference to this correspondence can be made here only very fleetingly, since an investigation into its deeper connections would take us too far from the aim we have set ourselves in this chapter. However, from this point of view the Christmas Conference can also be seen as a path towards a gradual transformation of the human etheric body out of the forces of the whole planetary cosmos, so that into the etheric body may enter the Etheric Christ!

94   GA 227, 19.8.1923.

95   GA 233a, 21.4.1924.

96   Without actually mentioning the second concept, Rudolf Steiner also speaks in the lecture of 27.12.1918 (GA 187) about the difference between the stage of 'Christ-bearer' (Christophorus) in the old Mysteries and that of 'Christ-receiver' in the New. What he says is that in the old initiation, albeit somewhat unclearly, man experienced that he was overshone 'from above' by his higher 'I'. When ascending into the macrocosm he was able to take this experience with him, so as there to become a Christophoros, a bearer of the Cosmic Christ. At the time of the events of Palestine, however, even this dim experience of the higher 'I' was finally lost. Man became inwardly empty, as was an absolute necessity if there was to be an awareness of individual freedom.

An altogether new impulse for the whole of subsequent evolution was then given through the Mystery of Golgotha as a result of which it became for the first time possible for man to unite himself with his higher 'I' on the Earth. This can come about through a conscious receiving of the Christ-impulse by virtue of the fact that—through filling the 'void' of the 'I'—the Christ-impulse makes it possible for man gradually to attain the goal of the New Mysteries: that he should become a 'Christ-receiver'.

97   See the Mystery-words spoken by Rudolf Steiner in Dornach on 20.9.1913 at the laying of the Foundation Stone of the First Goetheanum, published for the first time in Rudolf Grosse, *The Christmas Foundation*.

98   GA 142, 1.1.1913.

99   F.W. Zeylmans van Emmichoven, *The Foundation Stone*, the chapter 'The Pentagram and the Sun of Christ'.

100 All the thoughts presented here in our commentary follow in the most direct way from the rhythm of the day in question, in which the union of the Christ-Sun with the sphere of the Earth's elemental spirits is spoken of. Thus, on the one hand, the elemental spirits of the Earth, as the keepers in the Earth-sphere of all the wisdom of Old Moon, are also the keepers of the Moon Logos which, in the rhythm of the day under consideration, is transformed by the Christ-Sun—that is, by the Sun Logos. On the other hand there is revealed to us here the secret of the redemption of the elemental spirits: by virtue of Christ's activity in the etheric realm of the Earth the elemental spirits in the sphere of nature have, from this moment, received the Christ into themselves. Both these deeply significant events, already accomplished in the elemental world, must, through a conscious understanding of them, become for human beings the archetypes of their

own development—to which the *Meditation* directs us in the words: 'May human beings hear it!'

101 From a comparison of the 4th, 5th and 6th rhythms of the Christmas Conference (the rhythms of the Saturday, Sunday and Monday) with the description of the life of the soul after death—as given by Rudolf Steiner in the second lecture of GA 226—there arises a particularly exact presentation of that period during the soul's sojourn in the spiritual world between death and rebirth which comes after the experience of the Midnight Hour of existence. In this lecture Rudolf Steiner depicts in particular the following *three* very different stages of the soul's gradual descent from spiritual heights to a new physical incarnation:

1. To begin with, the soul dwells in the highest spiritual realm (in Upper Devachan), in which it experiences itself together with spirits of the higher Hierarchies as a spirit among spirits, beholding them as it were 'face to face'. In this sphere the soul works together with these Beings—and also with other human souls—on the creation of the cosmic archetype of its physical body and on the elaboration of its future karma. This condition of the soul after death corresponds exactly with the fourth rhythm of the Christmas Conference, given on a Saturday—the day of Saturn.

2. Thereafter the soul descends into the next sphere—the Sun-sphere proper (or more exactly the lower sphere of the Sun-realm—corresponding to existence in Lower Devachan). Here the soul's perception of separate beings of the divine-spiritual Hierarchies gradually dissolves into the perception of a single Sun spirituality. Rudolf Steiner calls this condition the 'manifestation' of the spiritual Beings (as opposed to the direct experience of them in the preceding stage). Due to this partial darkening of the spiritual horizon the soul's experience of itself becomes stronger, and as a result of this there awakens for the first time an interest in the earthly world. This comes to expression in the fact that 'when the spiritual world only manifests itself' the soul 'becomes strangely interested in certain successions of generations'. Thus in this second stage the soul gazes down from the Sun-sphere onto a sequence of generations 'at the end of which come those who will be one's parents when one descends again to the Earth'. The soul then stands at the point of crossing over from the realm of the Sun into that of the Moon and, as Rudolf Steiner has said, it is during this transition that the Christ Being plays a most important role.

Thus the description of the experiences of this stage corresponds exactly to the 5th rhythm of the Christmas Conference—the rhythm given on the day of the *Sun*.

3. And finally, at the third stage, the soul descends into the Moon-sphere proper (the Soul-land or astral plane), in which it unites with the moral result of its past life on Earth; in conformity with this it must now form its own new etheric body from the substance of the cosmic ether. These experiences of the soul in the Moon-sphere correspond to the 6th rhythm of the Christmas Conference—the rhythm given on the Monday, the day of the Moon.

The 7th rhythm, given on a Tuesday, corresponds to the Mystery of the soul's incarnation into the earthly physical body in which the forces of Mars are particularly active. These forces are connected with the element of iron in human blood, which in turn constitutes the physiological basis for the human 'I'—the centre of the incarnated human being.

102   The connection of the rhythm in question with the supersensible cultus, as the second phase of the celestial preparation of Anthroposophy, is referred to by Rudolf Steiner particularly in the following statements concerning the content of the cultus. In a lecture on 8.7.1924 (in GA 237), describing what was experienced in connection with its participation in the imaginative cultus by one of the two groups of human souls which later took part in the anthroposophical movement, Rudolf Steiner says: 'Then it was that these souls among others found themselves face to face with a great supersensible cult or ritual, consisting of mighty Imaginations. And in the sublime Imaginations of that supersensible ritual there was enacted before their spiritual vision, above all other things, the great Sun-Mystery of Christ.' We see from these words that the most important content of this cultus was the Sun-Mystery of Christ. This is supported by the following words of Rudolf Steiner concerning the supersensible cultus: 'And all that the Michael-pupils had learned before in the supersensible School was elaborated there in mighty pictures' (GA 237, 28.7.1924).

And as has already been shown in Note 89 of this chapter, what the pupils of Michael learnt above all in the supersensible School were the secrets of the Sun-Mystery, at the centre of which was always the Sun-Mystery of Christ. One must add to this the following words of Rudolf Steiner: 'At the end of the eighteenth century and the beginning of the nineteenth century there hovers in the immediate neighbourhood of the physical world of sense a great supersensible event, consisting in supersensible acts of ritual, an unfolding of mighty pictures of the spiritual life, of beings of the universe, of the Beings of the Hierarchies in connection with the great ether-workings of the universe and the human workings on Earth' (GA 238, 16.9.1924). Thus, from all Rudolf Steiner's statements quoted here we see, firstly, that this imaginative cultus took place in the supersensible surroundings closest to the Earth (i.e. in the sphere of the elemental spirits), and secondly, that its central point is the 'Sun-Mystery of Christ'. We are thus dealing here with those two attributes corresponding exactly with the rhythm of this day.

103   GA 15.

104   Reference is made here to Saturn because it is this planet as the remnant of Old Saturn that has a particular relation to the creation of the human physical body.

105   GA 260.

106   GA 131, 11.11.1911.

107   Ibid., 12.11.1911.

108   GA 148, 3.10.1913.

109   GA 139, 23.9.1912.

110 In *Occult Science* Rudolf Steiner writes about the processes whereby the soul forms the etheric and physical bodies before birth, and which are considered in the last two rhythms as follows: 'Consciously to partake in the last two events—this re-equipment with an etheric and with a physical body—would only be possible for an 'I' which by its own spiritual activity had developed the hidden creative forces of these bodies, in other words, Life Spirit and Spirit Man. So long as man has not yet reached this stage Beings more advanced in evolution than himself have to direct the process.' Concerning the conscious work in this respect of the pupil of the spirit, Rudolf Steiner said the following in Berlin on 24.10.1905 (which has been preserved only in part): 'Through the work of our higher 'I' we transform the transient body given us by the Gods and create for ourselves immortal bodies. The Chela who ennobles his etheric body (so that it remains in existence) gradually renounces the Maharajas. The Master whose physical body also remains in existence can renounce the Lipikas. He stands above karma. This fact we must describe as the progress of man in his inner life' (GA 93a).

111 Zeymans van Emmichoven describes this path in the last chapter of *The Foundation Stone*.

112 For the New Isis sunk in sleep, see GA 180, 6.1.1918.

113 The activity of Lucifer and Ahriman in the cosmos and in the bodily sheaths of the human being is exceptionally complex and many-sided. Here we have taken only one aspect, described by Rudolf Steiner in a lecture on 23.11.1919 in GA 194.

114 GA 194, 28.11.1919. An imaginative picture of the beings which Lucifer and Ahriman want to make man resemble can be found in the lecture of 15.7.1923 (GA 225).

115 GA 180, 6.1.1918.

116 Ibid.

117 When here and earlier on in this chapter reference is made to the past, present and future in connection with the first three parts of the *Foundation Stone Meditation* and certain of its individual lines, the following should be taken into consideration. The *Foundation Stone Meditation*, like every true meditation, has the task of leading man exclusively to an experience of spiritual life in the present. So when we speak in connection with the *Foundation Stone Meditation* of past and future, what is meant is their supersensible radiation into the spirit-present; in other words, that higher condition in which past and future become *spirit-present* in the immediate supersensible environment.

118 From this description, based as it is on the overall composition of the *Foundation Stone Meditation*, there arises the relation of the limb-system to the past, the rhythmical system to the present, and the head-system to the future. To complete this we can also note that the connection of the limb-system with the past is based on earthly forces that work particularly strongly here and which, in their present form, are the outcome of the past

development of our cosmos. The head-system, in contrast, is more connected with the future, for the thoughts, the images of the external world which arise in it when the human being has passed through the portal of death, will later become the seeds of the future cosmos (see lecture of 24.5.1915, GA 162). The middle system on the other hand is connected with the present, bringing about through rhythm the harmonious interaction of past and future in the human organism. It should be added that Rudolf Steiner also indicates another way of looking at these relationships. If one recalls, for example, that man's head in the one incarnation is the metamorphosis of his limbs in the previous incarnation, the head system can be associated more with the past and the limb system with the future. Such a way of looking at it is absolutely correct, but it is significantly different from that of the *Foundation Stone Meditation*, and in the present context it is the latter which is of particular importance.

119   GA 131, 11.10.1911.

120   The three stages of the soul's experience as it descends to earthly incarnation, which are set out in Note 101 on the basis of indications given by Rudolf Steiner in a lecture on 17.5.1923 in GA 226, are connected by him at the end of that lecture with the three prime faculties won by the child in the time *prior* to the full awakening of the individual 'I': walking upright, speaking and thinking. The first faculty here is the physical reflection of the higher supersensible experiences of the first stage, in which the soul lives as a spiritual being among other Beings in the sphere of Upper Devachan. The second faculty corresponds to the second stage in which the soul, descending now into the sphere of Lower Devachan, perceives only the manifestations of spiritual Beings. And the third faculty is the result of the reflection in the physical world of all that was experienced by the soul in the Moon-sphere (i.e. the astral plane) immediately prior to birth. One should bear in mind here, however, that the carrying over of these lofty supersensible experiences of the soul between death and a new birth into the physical sphere, where they appear as upright posture, speech and thinking, occurs in the present cycle of development, as Rudolf Steiner has said, not through the human being alone but through the Beings of the Hierarchy closest to him: through the Archai, Archangeloi and Angeloi (see GA 226, 18.5.1923).

On the other hand, in a lecture on 7.3.1914 (in GA 152), Rudolf Steiner speaks of the three faculties of the child, mentioned above, as being a reflection of the three pre-Christian deeds of Christ accomplished on the physical plane through the Nathan Soul; for 'in Lemuria the physical body was in danger, and later, in Atlantis, it was the etheric and astral organs' (30.3.1914, GA 152). And it is only by virtue of the fact that the Christ, by means of the etheric forces sacrificially put at His disposal by the Nathan Soul, was able to avert this danger from the physical body, enabling the child today to learn to walk upright. Because, through the Nathan Soul, the Christ in ancient times turned aside the danger to the etheric organs, the child today learns to speak. And through the healing of the astral organs in the primeval past, the child today learns to think (for although the spiritual aspect of speech is rooted in the etheric body, thinking is rooted in the astral body).

We can now consider that there are also expressed in these three 'pre-Christian' deeds of Christ in the supersensible spheres the three stages of His drawing near to the Earth. Rudolf Steiner speaks of this as follows: 'Thus the Christ approached the Earth gradually. The first and second stages were in the world of Devachan; the third, in the astral world; and in the physical world came the Event of Golgotha.' From all that has been said above, a natural connection arises on the one hand between the three stages of the soul's after-death existence in the spheres of Upper and Lower Devachan and on the astral plane (or Moon-sphere) respectively; and on the other hand the three celestial sacrifices of Christ through the Nathan Soul, which were once fulfilled in the same spiritual spheres. Moreover, just like the experiences of the soul between death and rebirth, so too do the three sacrifices of Christ through the Nathan Soul find their expression in the physical world in one and the same phenomenon: in the child's mastery, in the first three years of life, of the ability to walk upright, to speak and to think.

And just as for the Christ Being these three sacrifices are the three stages of His drawing near to the Earth, so too do we find here yet another con-firmation that in its descent to a new birth the path of the soul is the microcosmic re-enactment of the macrocosmic path of Christ towards the Earth and the fulfilment of the Mystery of Golgotha. For this reason, in the 4th, 5th and 6th rhythms of the Christmas Conference, we are also able to speak of a reflection of the inner essence of each of the three celestial sacrifices fulfilled by Christ through the Nathan Soul. Thus in the 4th rhythm, which leads us into the sphere of Upper Devachan, we have a reference at the same time to the first sacrificial deed of Christ accomplished through the Nathan Soul from this lofty sphere, and by virtue of which, during the Lemurian epoch, the physical body of man was saved. The archetype of the physical body is to be found in Upper Devachan, but its rudimentary foundations were laid down by the Hierarchies during the time of Old Saturn. This is why the rhythm of this day is given on the day of Saturn—a Saturday. Thereafter, in the 5th rhythm, corresponding as it does to Lower Devachan (the Sun-sphere proper), we are directed to the second of Christ's deeds of sacrifice, accomplished through the Nathan Soul from this second spiritual sphere. This sacrifice at the beginning of the Atlantean epoch saved the 'life-organs' of the human being, the archetype of which is to be found in Lower Devachan, but whose first elements were established at the time of Old Sun. Again, therefore, this rhythm was given on the day of the Sun—on Sunday. And lastly, in the rhythm of the 6th day, relating to the spiritual surroundings closest to the Earth (the Moon-sphere), we are directed to the third sacrificial deed of Christ accomplished through the Nathan Soul. It is by this deed that the human 'organs of soul', the

416

archetype of which exists on the astral plane and whose foundation was laid down on Old Moon, were saved. Thus the rhythm of this day is given under the sign of the Moon, that is on a Monday. In conclusion, the 7th rhythm gives us a picture of the fourth and most important sacrifice of Christ through the Nathan Soul, who at the beginning of our era incarnated as Jesus of Nazareth and with whose physical, etheric and astral sheaths the high Sun Being of the Christ united in his thirtieth year in order—in the name of the salvation of the human 'I'—to create a physical body of such a nature that, in its three fundamental systems of head, rhythmic system and limbs, it was able to become the purest expression of the Father, the Son and the Spirit. This in turn created necessary preconditions, so that for the first time on the Earth a human being could arise from whose astral, etheric and physical bodies the forces of Lucifer and Ahriman had been completely driven out. For it is only an astral body evolved to the state of Spirit Self that can make of the head-organization of man a pure expression of the cosmic principle of the Spirit. And only an etheric body that has developed to Life Spirit can make of the human rhythmic system a pure reflection of the macrocosmic principle of the Son. And lastly, it is only the physical body transformed into Spirit Man that can become, right into its limb-system, the pure reflection of the macrocosmic forces of the Father.

Thus, having entered as the most sublime macrocosmic 'I' into the three bodily sheaths of Jesus of Nazareth, and having driven from them both Lucifer and Ahriman, the Christ in the course of three years gradually transformed through His 'I' the astral body of Jesus into Spirit Self, his etheric body into Life Spirit, and his physical body into Spirit Man—into the body of the Resurrection. By this He brought to *every* human 'I' that force by which, in the course of all the future aeons of Jupiter, Venus and Vulcan, it may develop ever upwards from the human 'I' of Earth to the final Resurrection in Spirit Man. Thus, although the 'I'-principle is not named directly in the 7th rhythm, its ascending and transforming activity— *even into the physical body*—lies, nevertheless, at the basis of this last rhythm of the Christmas Conference. (Concerning the connection of the body of the Resurrection [the phantom] with the principle of the 'I', see the cycle GA 131, 10.10.1911.) And surveying in one glance the whole future evolution of the Earth, we add inwardly to this rhythm the words of Christ: 'Verily, verily I say unto you, he that believeth in me, the works that I do shall he do also' (John 14: 12).

121　The term 'Anthroposophy' appeared as early as 1903, i.e. right at the beginning of Rudolf Steiner's open activity as a teacher (see Note 6, Chapter 3).

122　In connection with the main stages—contained in the seven rhythms—of the soul's journey through the spheres of the spiritual cosmos between death and rebirth, we must add the following. Rudolf Steiner often speaks in his lectures of the influence on man in his after-death existence of the luciferic and ahrimanic forces. These work in such a way that soon after passing through the portal of death the human being is approached particularly by Lucifer, and directly before a new incarnation on the Earth by Ahriman (see particularly 24.11.1923 in GA 232). We find the reflection of this connection in the first and last two rhythms of the Christmas Conference respectively, which speak of a true overcoming in the Earth's evolution of the luciferic and ahrimanic forces of temptation. Thus the 1st rhythm directs us to the inescapable necessity of setting ourselves against the forces of Lucifer at work in the soul. This rhythm speaks of a knowledge of the Mysteries of the 'I' gained through occult exercises and, more exactly, of the development of the 'I' from unfreedom to freedom—that development, in other words, over which the luciferic spirits are constantly at pains to gain influence. These luciferic spirits, which are seated above all in the *astral body* of the human being, seek to influence the human 'I' from there in two ways. They appear first of all as irreconcilable opponents of human freedom. Against this freedom they do battle by awakening 'the wishes, desires and passions which well up from within' the human being through the dark veil of which, in the astral body, the 'I' is not able to penetrate to real inner freedom. Man must work against this luciferic temptation through his own *moral development*, by working to overcome his lower, sensual nature. In his commentary on the 1st rhythm, Rudolf Steiner points to this moral development as the principal weapon in the battle with Lucifer, and speaks there of the need for 'moral feeling' in the ascent from 'coming into being' (I, 10) to 'union' (II, 10) and to 'bestowing' (III, 10). This is also the golden rule of true spiritual science, as spoken of in *Knowledge of the Higher Worlds*: 'For every one step that you take in pursuit of higher knowledge, take three steps in the perfecting of your own character.' Once these luciferic forces, in that form in which they most commonly tempt all humanity (including, that is, those individuals who have not taken the path of occult development) have been overcome to a certain extent by the pupil of the spirit, they then approach him with temptations of a far stronger and more subtle nature. An idea of what is involved here can only be gained by one who has already entered upon the path of occult development. Lucifer emerges here no longer as the opponent of freedom, but as the great tempter of freedom who seeks to entice human beings to use freedom in an evil way, to use it for their own egotistical ends. This is the temptation of pride (lack of reverence) which, in an esoteric sense, is rooted in a want of true self-knowledge, to which in every way Lucifer seeks to prevent the pupil from coming. This purely occult temptation is portrayed in the scene of Christ Jesus's temptation in the desert, which in accordance with the Fifth Gospel Rudolf Steiner describes as follows: 'First, in his solitude, the Christ Being in the body of Jesus of Nazareth confronted Lucifer—Lucifer as he wields and works, Lucifer who approaches human beings when they over-value the self, when they have too little humility and *self-knowledge*' (5.10.1913, GA 148). It is to the overcoming of this second form of luciferic temptation that the 2nd rhythm of the Christmas

Conference points, and which again concerns knowledge of the Mysteries of the human 'I'. Here, however, this knowledge is significantly deepened and becomes not only a foundation for moral development (as was the case in the preceding rhythm) but also for true self-knowledge, which Rudolf Steiner speaks of in his commentary. This 2nd rhythm gradually leads the pupil of the spirit to a real overcoming of all the wrongful forces of Lucifer working in him—that is, of that spirit who is ever leading the human being into illusions regarding his inner nature. By attaining in this way, through true self-knowledge in the sense of the 2nd rhythm, the possibility truly to think, to feel, and to live (I, II, III, 13 [12]) the pupil reaches a specific stage in the purifying of his astral body (that is, in its transformation into Spirit Self (see the description of this in the present chapter), which effects in him the final overcoming of the luciferic forces of temptation.

In the 6th and 7th rhythms of the Christmas Conference, however (insofar as these speak of the experiences of the human soul immediately before its descent to the Earth), we are directed to the path of overcoming the forces of Ahriman in the Earth's development. Here one must take into account that whereas Lucifer tempts man from within, from the depths of his own soul, Ahriman works more from without—through the surrounding world of nature or directly through the physical body. Also from this point of view, the 6th and 7th rhythms of the Conference give us an all-embracing picture of that path on which it is possible to truly conquer all the wrongfully working forces of Ahriman. However, while in our present cycle of development the human being alone, working out of his own soul-forces, can overcome the temptation of Lucifer, he can overcome Ahriman only with the help of the Christ-impulse taken up in his own soul. Not we ourselves but only the Christ in us can, in the last analysis, conquer Ahriman. It is not yet possible for the human being using his own (human) forces alone to conquer Ahriman completely. Rudolf Steiner describes this situation as follows: 'For the time being—for the rest of Earth evolution up to Vulcan—Ahriman, through the activity of the higher Hierarchies, cannot be expelled entirely from the scene. It will never be impossible, through purely spiritual efforts, to conquer the inner temptation of Lucifer—the wants, desires and passions which rise up from within, and what rises up as pride, arrogance, self-exaltation. Lucifer, if he alone attacks the human being, can be conquered by spiritual means. Even when Lucifer and Ahriman together assail the human being from within, it is possible to gain victory by spiritual means. But when Ahriman is alone, his influence penetrates down into the material events of earthly evolution. And being there, he cannot be expelled from the scene. Ahriman, Mephisto, Mammon—these are identical—are concealed in money, in everything that has to do with natural external egotism. Since it is always necessary for an element of what is externally materialistic to mix in with human life, man has always to reckon with Ahriman' (18.12.1913, GA 148). In this sense the 6th rhythm gives us the possibility of overcoming the forces of Ahriman in our etheric body. This is achieved through a real experience of how, since the

419

Mystery of Golgotha, the forces of the Christ-Sun have held sway in the realms of the elements—in that spiritual sphere, that is, which until the Mystery of Golgotha was seized to the greatest extent by Ahriman. Only thus can we contribute to a true spiritualization of our Earth, to its gradual transformation from planet to star. In his commentary on this rhythm, Rudolf Steiner speaks about this great future of the Earth as being 'the meaning of all Earth evolution'. By taking up the Christ-impulse into ourselves we must learn anew to see all nature around us as permeated with the spirit. In every stone, every cloud, in every plant, we must learn to see how, since the time of the Mystery of Golgotha, the Christ-substance is at work in it. For only such a perception of external nature, seeing it as permeated through and through with the Christ, can fetter the forces of Ahriman working in our etheric body. With this in view, Ahriman is at pains to present the whole of nature to us as a soulless and dead machine; and this correspondingly finds expression in Ahriman's endeavour to bring the impulse of death into the human etheric body and to prevent its future transformation into Life Spirit.

The 7th rhythm directs us to the *final and conclusive* overcoming in Earth evolution of the wrongfully working forces of Ahriman. In the normal flow of evolution this will take place only on Vulcan when, at the stage of Spirit Man reached by all humanity, it will be possible to possess a physical body whose three systems are the pure reflection of the macrocosmic forces of the Father, the Son and the Spirit. Anyone, however, who takes up into himself the forces of Resurrection contained in the Christ-impulse, anyone who participates inwardly in 'eternal Life', in the life resurrected from the Grave of Golgotha, anyone who raises up in himself that 'picture of the spiritual origins' of which Rudolf Steiner speaks in his commentary on the 7th rhythm, will be able now, in our times, to work on the transformation of the distorting forces of Ahriman in the physical body.

If we recall that the 4th rhythm of the Christmas Conference speaks, in the first place, of the Cosmic Christ whom the pupil at this stage of his initiation experiences 'face to face' as his true 'I', and in the second place of the all-encompassing working of Christ in the cosmos as the 'Cosmic Word' (which Rudolf Steiner speaks of in his commentary to the 4th rhythm), then the overall composition of all seven rhythms of the Christmas Conference reveals itself as being connected with the esoteric essence of the 'Group' sculpture, with the image of the New Isis, the Divine Wisdom (see the description of the 7th rhythm), and with the content of the north-facing rose window of the Goetheanum.

From this point of view, therefore, one can also trace the significant connections between the seven rhythms of the Christmas Conference and the seven apocalyptic seals given by Rudolf Steiner at the Congress in Munich. It is not possible, however, to give time to this here. With regard to the 3rd and 5th rhythms, the following can be borne in mind: in the 3rd rhythm the direct reference to counteraction against the forces of Lucifer is absent, for in this realm, which is united with the cosmic rhythm permeating our cosmos, the Archangel Michael rules. In our epoch he brings out of the high Sun-sphere the 'inner rhythm in the soul' in accordance with the 'cosmic rhythm', by awakening through the three occult exercises an awareness for the Trinity that holds sway in the Cosmic All. In this way there is revealed to us the '... experience of the Spirit-world which has as its sphere the *cosmic rhythm within and outside man,* just as man has the earthly world with its physical beings and processes. To this Spirit-world there belongs everything that takes place through Michael in the present cosmic moment. A Spirit such as Michael brings what would otherwise reside in Lucifer's realm into the realm of purely human evolution—which is not influenced by Lucifer—by *choosing the world of rhythm for his dwelling-place*' (GA 26; see also Note 129). This Michaelic aspect is also present in the two previous rhythms. The first rhythm speaks of what the soul 'rhythmicizes out of the cosmic rhythm' so that the soul's own 'inner rhythm' arises as the reflection of the cosmic rhythm, as 'a rhythm which ascending from "comes into being" to "unite" to "bestow" ... makes the transition to the moral feeling' which fills man's thinking, feeling and will with a new light. In the 2nd rhythm the Michaelic aspect comes to expression in that it speaks not only of ordinary self-knowledge but of the 'self-knowledge necessitated by the signs of the times'. (Regarding the connection of the 'signs of the times' with the Michael impulse, see Note 2.) The 5th rhythm, which is connected with the 'Turning-point of Time', speaks also of how, through the Mystery of Golgotha, Christ overcame that darkening of the higher consciousness induced through the power of Ahriman, the Sun-demon, and in which the soul until the event of the Mystery of Golgotha had lived in the spiritual world after death. In *Occult Science* we find in this context the following description: 'And when the Mystery of Golgotha had been accomplished, when the death on the Cross had been suffered, then did the Christ appear in that world where human souls sojourn after death and set limits to the power of Ahriman. From this moment on, that region which the Greeks had called the 'realm of the Shades' was suddenly shot through with spiritual lightning, announcing to the beings there that Light was to come again into that realm. What was achieved by the Mystery of Golgotha for the physical world shed its light also into the spiritual world.'

In the *Foundation Stone Meditation* the following words in particular correspond to this event:

Darkness of Night
Had held its sway;
Day-radiant Light
Poured into the souls of men.

If now we take into account that the ahrimanic forces work predominantly in the human will, we shall understand that it is only by receiving the Christ-

Sun into ourselves that we can be guided as far as this sphere—to the true overcoming of the forces of the Sun-demon. This must find expression in true deeds of goodness; and we find the impulse for this in the 5th rhythm:

That good may become
What from our Hearts we would found
And from our Heads direct
With single purpose.

If man is indeed able to fill himself with the revelation of the 'Cosmic Word' contained in the fourth rhythm, it becomes possible for him to take hold of the other six rhythms in a completely new way. Then his 'moral feeling' (1st rhythm), when taken hold of by the 'Cosmic Word', can gradually lead him to an experience of the 'spiritual picture of man's origins' (7th rhythm); a true 'self-knowledge' (2nd rhythm) can, under the influence of the 'Cosmic Word', reveal to him the 'meaning of Earth-evolution' (6th rhythm); and finally, life in the 'cosmic rhythm' (3rd rhythm), when imbued with the sounding of the 'Cosmic Word', can lead him to a beholding of the Mystery of the 'Turning-point of Time' (5th rhythm).

Altogether one can summarize the thoughts presented above as follows:

4th Rhythm

Cosmic Word
The Cosmic Christ; in Him the
activity of all nine Hierarchies—who
form in the Cosmos the great
macrocosmic Man, the Anthropos—
becomes a unity

3rd Rhythm	5th Rhythm
Cosmic Rhythm	*Turning-point of Time*
Sun-sphere	Sun-sphere
(Michael)	(Christ)

2nd Rhythm	6th Rhythm
Self-Knowledge	*The Meaning of Earth-evolution*
(Overcoming the influences of the	The spiritualization of one's
luciferic forces on the human 'I')	experience of the Earth, which
	thereby becomes a star.
	Overcoming of the ahrimanic forces
	in the human etheric body through
	the Christ-impulse.

1st Rhythm	7th Rhythm
Moral feeling	*The spiritual picture of man's origins*
(Overcoming the forces of Lucifer in the human astral body)	(Overcoming of the forces of Ahriman in the human physical body through the Christ-impulse)

123   If we take the whole 21-year path of Anthroposophy's emergence in the world—from the founding of the German section of the Theosophical Society in 1902 to the Christmas Conference in 1923—and divide this into seven parts, we get seven three-year periods, each of which, in a certain sense, corresponds to the seven stages of Anthroposophy's development up to the Christmas Conference. If we take the middle year of each of these three-year periods, and the main event which occurred in it, we find the following picture:

1904—The beginning of the esoteric work proper in the German section of the Theosophical Society, directed towards the future founding in western humanity of the new Mysteries of the 'I'.

1907—The Munich Congress. The beginning of the permeation of Rudolf Steiner's astral body by the guiding Bodhisattva of our time.

1910—The beginning of the proclamation through Rudolf Steiner of the Etheric Christ. The first Mystery Drama, 'The Portal of Initiation'.

1913—The laying of the Foundation Stone of the First Goetheanum. Lectures on the Fifth Gospel.

1916—The beginning in Rudolf Steiner's lecturing work on the social theme, which can be headed as 'Christ and the twentieth century'.

1919—The beginning of the development of the 'daughter' movements of Anthroposophy, and primarily of the movement for a threefold social organism as the only means of saving Europe from impending catastrophe.

1922—The Congresses in Stuttgart, Vienna, Dornach and Berlin. The death of the First Goetheanum and its resurrection as the Spirit which then shed its radiance over the whole of the Christmas Conference of 1923–24.

124   GA 260.

125   One ought really to talk here of ten sessions, if with the nine described above one also includes the day of the opening of the Christmas Conference on 24.12.1923. Since, however, the Mystery part proper of the Christmas Conference began with the laying of the Foundation Stone *through* Rudolf Steiner on 25 December and proceeded subsequently with the rhythms of the anthroposophical *Meditation*, it was therefore these nine sessions that we took as the basis of our study, during each of which there sounded out the words of the *Foundation Stone Meditation*.

126   GA 231, 17.11.1923.

127   Ibid.

128 GA 99, 4.6.1907.

129 GA 229, the lecture on 15.10.1923. What has been said here is also an answer to the question: Why was the *Foundation Stone Meditation* given every day *throughout* the Christmas Conference in a particular *rhythm?* The possibility was thereby created *for Michael himself to participate directly in it,* since 'Michael's realm is that which is revealed in rhythm' (GA 26). This indication by Rudolf Steiner can also shed a new light upon what he said on 18.1.1924 about the Christmas Conference: '...if you think back to the Christmas Conference, you will feel bound to say that something which originated from the spiritual world came into being there.' And '...an event such as our Christmas Conference is not to be thought of as some-thing that takes place within the earthly realm' (GA 260a).

130 If to these three last rhythms—given in the course of the days of the Sun, the Moon, and of Mars (Sunday, Monday, Tuesday)—one adds that which Rudolf Steiner presents in his lecture in London on 27.8.1924 (see GA 240), in which he described in detail how on the path of His descent to Earth the Christ left his Spirit Man in the Sun-sphere, His Life Spirit in the surroundings of the Earth (i.e. in the Moon-sphere), and through the Baptism in the Jordan entered the bodily sheaths of Jesus of Nazareth with His Spirit Self, then we can also connect with these last three rhythms of the Christmas Conference the idea of the higher trinity of the human being—Spirit Man, Life Spirit and Spirit Self. We find a link in this way with what from a slightly different point of view is said by Zeylmans van Emmichoven in connection with these rhythms, i.e. that it is possible in the totality of the seven rhythms of the Christmas Conference as a whole to experience both the macrocosmic and the microcosmic Our Father, of which we spoke in more detail in Chapter 3.

131 See GA 139, 23.9.1912, and also Chapter 7.

132 This connection of the Bodhisattva with the astral body and that of the Buddha with the etheric body in the process of working on Spirit Self and Life Spirit respectively is also indicated in the two following statements by Rudolf Steiner: 'All other great guiding beings (apart from Christ) incar-nated in such a way that their spiritual being united with the astral body. When we attempt to understand the beings of the Bodhisattvas, we find that their spiritual part, which worked on Earth, rose into the higher worlds and was united only with the astral body' (18.4.1910 in 'The Return of Christ' in GA 118) and: 'At the end of his lofty path a Bodhisattva becomes a Buddha and no longer needs to take on a physical body. The stage of Buddha completes his cycle of incarnations and he enters into a new and higher evolution. The lowest member of his being is then no longer a physical body but an etheric body, and he is visible henceforth only to the clairvoyant eye' (13.4.1910, GA 118).

133 Rudolf Steiner speaks of the Dhyani-Buddhas on 16.4.1909 in GA 110.

134 The nature of the cosmic evolution in which these beings are already to be

found expresses itself in the fact that they have a direct connection with the Christ on quite other levels of existence. (See GA 137, 12.6.1912.)

135 We need not be surprised here that such different beings at such different stages of their development can be working on one and the same higher principle of their being. Thus for example, the pupil begins to work consciously on the development of the principle of Spirit Self from the second stage onwards of the Christian-Rosicrucian path of initiation (imaginative knowledge), and goes over to the *actual* development of it at the fifth stage (knowledge of the relation of the macrocosm and microcosm). The Bodhisattva on the other hand elaborates his Spirit Self at a still higher level, but the full development of this principle is attained only by Beings of the Hierarchy of Angels. The possibility of so many stages of this principle's development is connected with the fact that, for its *complete* realization, a *whole cosmic aeon* is necessary—the aeon of Jupiter. (All that has been said here applies also to the other two higher principles: Life Spirit and Spirit Man.)

136 The difference (similar to the one in the Christian-Rosicrucian path of initiation) between the first four stages, which are of a more cognitive character, and the following three which are already connected with the *actual* transformation of the sheaths, is also to be found in the seven fundamental stages of the after-death journey of the soul between two incarnations. Thus the first four stages are connected more with the experience of the spiritual results of the last earthly life, whereas the final three are connected predominantly with the actual formation, on the basis of the experience gleaned in the spiritual world during the first four stages, of the new sheaths (astral body, etheric body, physical body) for the new incarnation.

137 For more detail or this see Chapter 6.

138 See Note 43, Chapter 2.

139 GA 13.

140 One must particularly stress in connection with these words by Rudolf Steiner that the only thing that can help the pupil to preserve his 'separate consciousness' at this stage of initiation is his connection with the Christ-impulse.

141 In connection with this fundamental difference between the eastern and western paths of initiation, one can also remember the numerous descriptions of this state by ancient and contemporary eastern writers who always posited, as the most essential condition for the union of the human being with the macrocosm, the complete dissolution of the higher 'I', of 'separate consciousness' as the bearer of individual existence (compare, for example, the descriptions of the ecstasies of Ramakrishna, etc).

142 The enumeration here of the seven stages of the Christian-Rosicrucian path of initiation is given in the sixth edition (1916) but not in the last edition (1925) of *Occult Science* (see Note 22 of this chapter for more detail concerning this).

143 For this reason every anthroposophist who brings these seven fundamental rhythms of the Christmas Conference inwardly to life can resurrect in himself the Christmas Conference as the true path of initiation of the present, as willed in our time by Michael himself. And just as Olaf Åsteson once experienced—albeit in a dreamlike state of consciousness—the opening up of the spiritual world during the days of Christmas, and just as many other initiates, who according to Rudolf Steiner belonged to the same Mystery-stream, also underwent similar experiences during the days of Christmastide, so we too—but now in *full waking consciousness*—can renew at *every* Christmastide that path of initiation which was given to us in these seven rhythms, until it becomes fully alive in us and opens to us the true door to the Temple of the New Mysteries. In this sense the Christmas Conference can be realized in the soul of *every* anthroposophist, at *every* Christmastide, if only there is alive in us the will towards true sacrificial service and inner development.

144 GA 28, Chapter 8.

145 The inspirational nature of *The Philosophy of Freedom* is also expressed in its connection with the etheric body, out of the *transformed* forces of which it was written. Rudolf Steiner indicates this in detail in a lecture to the workmen at the Goetheanum on 28.7.1923 (GA 350). He says there: 'In order to have any thoughts at all of the kind that are in this book, a person must right from the start and page for page get used to resorting to his etheric body.' He shows in these words that the thoughts presented by him in *The Philosophy of Freedom* arise from a conscious experience of the self in the etheric body, which is only possible on having attained the stage of Inspiration. A good deal earlier, in a lecture on 9.2.1905, he also points to *The Philosophy of Freedom* as being a spiritual path leading the pupil from his earthly 'I' to his higher 'I'—to consciousness of Manas—and also through this to the even higher consciousness of Buddhi. In other words, from ordinary object consciousness to imaginative and inspirational consciousness: 'You will find what I have just described expressed there [in *The Philosophy of Freedom*] in the concepts of western philosophy. You will find the development there of the soul (*Seelische*) from Kama to the life of Manas! I have called Ahamkara the "I" and Manas "higher thinking", pure thinking, and Buddhi—without yet pointing to its origins—I have called "moral fantasy". These are just different expressions for one and the same thing' (GA 53, 9.2.1905). And finally, in Chapter 22, GA 28, looking back over his inner development during the Weimar period (the second seven-year Sun period), Rudolf Steiner speaks of the three stages of knowledge attained by him at that time, in the description of which there clearly follow the stages of scientific, imaginative and inspirational knowledge. In this sense one can also define *The Philosophy of Freedom* as a book written out of 'inspired Imagination', inasmuch as the Imaginations of the first seven-year Sun period contained in it are enriched and permeated by Inspirations from the second seven-year period.

146   See, for example, *Occult Science*, and also Note 60 of this chapter.

147   GA 28, Chapter 22.

148   One must particularly emphasize here that the connection between the passage through the spheres of Imagination, Inspiration and Intuition and the three seven-year Sun periods of Rudolf Steiner's life does not have to be taken in an absolute sense. Thus, for example, in his first seven-year Sun period, Rudolf Steiner definitely had certain Inspirations and even Intuitions. What we are speaking of here are only the cosmic tendencies that are present in certain periods of *every* human life, and which are particularly propitious for the development of a certain kind of spiritual knowledge on the path of initiation. Rudolf Steiner speaks about the possibility of passing through the various stages of initiation not only in strict succession in the penultimate chapter of *Occult Science—An Outline*. He says there: 'One should not, however, suppose that these stages are to be passed through one after the other . . . For example, it may well happen that one has come to no more than a few Imaginations with a certain surety and yet is already carrying out exercises that draw Inspiration, Intuition or the knowledge of the relationship between microcosm and macrocosm into the sphere of one's experience.'

149   GA 260.

Chapter 6. The Foundation Stone Meditation

1   GA 260.

2   GA 240, 18.7.1924.

3   GA 260.

4   Ibid.

5   This revelation of Christ from the sphere of the Father is also referred to in words from the New Testament, 'No man hath seen God at any time; the only begotten Son, which is in the bosom of the Father, he hath declared Him' (John 1: 18).

6   In the lecture of 14.11.1909 (GA 117), Rudolf Steiner speaks from a quite particular standpoint about initiations of will, feeling and thinking, associating them directly with the sources of the Gospels. Thus St Mark's Gospel was written out of the revelation of a will initiation, St Luke's Gospel out of the revelation of a feeling initiation and St John's Gospel out of a thinking (Sophia) initiation. And in St Matthew's Gospel all three initiations are harmoniously combined though in a 'diluted' form (GA 117, 2.11.1909). For the attention of the Evangelist Matthew is directed particularly towards the lineal descent of the *physical body* of Jesus of Nazareth (GA 123, 12.9.1910) and, hence, to a certain extent reflects the *past* of human evolution; whereas the Fifth Gospel—in the Akashic Record—is associated with the future evolution of mankind, which because of the retrograde flow of time in the

spiritual world also constantly permeates the present. Thus we have the following relationship of the Gospels to the *Foundation Stone Meditation*:

Part I	— Gospel of St Mark
Part II	— Gospel of St Luke
Part III	— Gospel of St John
Part IV (lines 1–13)	— Gospel of St Matthew
Part IV (lines 14–25)	— Fifth Gospel (Akashic Record)

In this way we see that the content of the *Foundation Stone Meditation* as a whole not only derives from the same regions of the spiritual world out of which the four Evangelists drew their inspiration but is also directly connected with the cosmic sphere of the Akashic Record, the great primal source of all supersensible knowledge of the events in Palestine.

7 Rudolf Steiner spoke frequently of how a true knowledge of thinking, feeling and willing leads the human being up into the spheres of Imagination, Inspiration and Intuition respectively. In this sense the sphere of Intuition also corresponds to the sphere of the working of Cosmic Will. In the lecture of 3.7.1921 (GA 205), Rudolf Steiner alludes to this fact with particular clarity in connection with his description of the life of the soul after death as a process of its gradual ascent from the sphere of Imagination, through the sphere of Inspiration to that of Intuition. Abiding in the sphere of Intuition ('in the sounding of the Cosmic Word') corresponds to the experience of 'Cosmic Midnight'. The soul's path back to the Earth then begins by Intuition becoming—as Rudolf Steiner says in the lecture referred to— permeated by *Cosmic Will*. This will impulse thrusts its way—to the extent that the soul is in a process of descent—into the soul's inspirative and imaginative existence, thus preparing it for a new incarnation. It follows from this that the 'Will' that is pronounced in Part II of the *Meditation*—which is here the Cosmic Will of Christ—belongs to this high sphere of spiritual existence, that of Intuition.

8 Rudolf Steiner describes the reappearance of Christ in the etheric in the twentieth century as resulting from Christ's experiencing in the spiritual world 'a renewal of the Mystery of Golgotha' (GA 152, 20.5.1913). However, he speaks in particularly significant words about this 'repetition of the Mystery of Golgotha' in the twentieth century in a lecture on 2.5.1913 (GA 152). Here he describes how, as a result of the spiritual consequences of the materialism of the nineteenth century, the consciousness of Christ underwent a kind of 'spiritual death' in the sphere of the Angels, a suspension (*Aufhebung*) of consciousness, to arise then anew as the new Christ-awareness in the souls of human beings at the beginning of the twentieth century. He also says in this lecture: 'Twice has the Christ been crucified: once physically, in the physical world at the beginning of our age, and a second time, spiritually, in the nineteenth century, in the way I have described. It is possible to say that humanity experienced the resurrection

428

of His body at that time, and from the twentieth century onwards will experience the resurrection of His consciousness.' This latter event is described by Rudolf Steiner as the human being's experiencing of the reappearance of Christ in the etheric.

9   These two ways in which the Christ Being may be experienced—in the sphere of Intuition through initiation and 'naturally' in the etheric sphere bordering on the Earth—are depicted in the two rose (actually peach-blossom coloured) windows of the First Goetheanum. Thus in the South window we have the experiences of the modern path of initiation: in the left part man's ascent into the world of Imagination, on the right into the world of Inspiration and in the middle into that of Intuition. In the latter part a human being is portrayed who, deeply immersed in meditation, is experiencing Cosmic Midnight in Intuition. Below him we see a picture of the death-forces working in matter. Man rises up out of their domain in order to experience his true 'I', which is where the forces of the Cosmic Christ are working.

In the North window, the meeting with the Etheric Christ is portrayed in its central part (the plantlike forms are an indication of the etheric world bordering on the Earth). Man attains to this experience not through occult development but through the faculty of etheric clairvoyance which is naturally made available to him. The figure of his Guardian Angel (standing *behind* the human figure) leads man to this experience, the karmic preconditions of which Rudolf Steiner describes in the lecture of 14.4.1914 (GA 153). This central part is flanked by a portrayal of the consequences of the earthly and etheric Mystery of Golgotha for the future evolution of the world (see GA 145, 28.3.1913).

10   GA 130, 28.9.1911.

11   GA 131, 10.10.1911.

12   This relation of the threefold social organism to the threefold organism of the human being is referred to by Rudolf Steiner in his lecture on 24.6.1920 (GA 197). It should be noted that in comparing the *Foundation Stone Meditation* with the Threefold Social Order we have hitherto been considering the *first sections* of Parts I, II and III. However, an analogous comparison can also be made on the basis of the *second sections*. The references which they contain to the sphere of the Father, the Son and the Spirit in association with the three Rosicrucian dicta will then lead to other relationships (see the lecture of 25.12.1918, GA 187).

13   In connection with this realization of the great ideal of true Rosicrucianism, which consists in a real synthesis of science, art and religion, we must note that the path to this synthesis also shows us the *Foundation Stone Meditation* in its entirety. Here, in its first three parts, these three most important spheres of human activity first go through a process of inner spiritualization after which, in the fourth part, they attain to their highest synthesis through the fundamental spiritual impulse of Earth evolution—through the impulse of Christ. Thus in the third part we are dealing with a science which becomes spiritual

429

science, speaking to the human being of the great *Wisdom* of the world. The second part sees the spiritualization of art, which through a co-experience of the divine *Beauty* of the world then becomes the awakener in the human being of true *Love*. And through the first part religion regains its primal meaning; it becomes *religio*, a direct *connection* with the higher worlds from which man then receives the impulses for truly moral deeds ('And you will truly *live*...'), the stimulus towards the free creation of the truly *good*. By passing in this way through this process of inner spiritualization, these fundamental spheres of human activity—science, art and religion—find in the fourth part their highest synthesis in the impulse of Christ. In the first 13 lines spiritual science attains its highest level by revealing to humanity the great Wisdom concerning the Christ (Christosophy). The next six lines (14–19), speak of a spiritualized art which, having absorbed in the working of Christ the mightiest principle for the transformation and spiritualization of matter, rises to the loftiest revelation of the new Beauty of the world which is permeated by the divine radiance of the Christ-Sun. And in the last lines (20–24) we have the highest principle of religion which transforms the will of man even to the point of his being able to offer himself up on the altar of the world in the name of realizing in the world the great aims of the divine-spiritual cosmos that were brought to the Earth through Christ Jesus.

Thus does the fourth part of the *Meditation* lead to a real awakening in us of Christ-Wisdom, Christ-Love and the Christian capacity of self-offering as the true foundation for a renewal of science, art and religion.

14   Regarding the correspondence between human and cosmic rhythm, see GA 175, 13.2.1917, and GA 201, 16.4.1920.

15   GA 236, 4.6.1924.

16   This connection of breathing (lungs) and thinking (head) is referred to by Rudolf Steiner in some detail in a lecture on 10.5.1924 in GA 236, in which he indicates that thinking, in a certain sense, is a refined form of breathing.

17   The relationship of Lucifer and Ahriman to love and wisdom as presented here is based on Rudolf Steiner's observations in the lecture of 28.5.1910 (GA 120). There is, however, another relationship to be considered, if one bears in mind that Lucifer distorts the principle of the Holy Spirit (the principle of wisdom) and Ahriman the principle of the Son (that of love). See also the Christmas Study of 1924 in GA 26.

18   B.C.J. Lievegoed, *Mystery Streams in Europe and the New Mysteries*, Chapter 6, 'The Merging of the Four Great Mystery Streams in the Christmas Foundation Meeting'.

19   Rudolf Steiner speaks of this in his commentary to the text of the *Foundation Stone Meditation* on 25.12.1923 (GA 260).

20   Rudolf Steiner says in connection with this: 'Such a Being as the Christ is surrounded by twelve Bodhisattvas; we cannot speak of more than twelve because when the twelve Bodhisattvas have fulfilled their mission our time of Earth existence will be at an end' (25.10.1909, GA 116).

21   Pointing to the essential secret in this context is also the fact that in the

ancient philosophy of India the same term was used for this sixth member of the human being (the transformed etheric body) as for the higher, super-Devachanic sphere which is the sphere of the substance of Life Spirit; for both of these the term *Buddhi* was used (the Buddhi-body and the Buddhi-sphere).

22 GA 119, 26.3.1910.

23 The fact that in the second element of the *Foundation Stone Meditation* (Parts II and IV) the working of the Christ is viewed from the spiritual sphere closest to the Earth right up to the sphere of the Bodhisattvas or the Buddhi-world simply indicates that in the present cycle of world development it is these four supersensible worlds above all which participate in the evolution of humanity: the astral or elemental world, Lower Devachan (Spiritual World), Upper Devachan (the World of Reason) and the World of Providence (which is the World of Archetypes)—see 26.3.1910 in GA 119. The Being of Christ is in no way exhausted in these last-mentioned worlds, for it descended into them from higher worlds still. This descent of Christ from worlds beyond the sphere of Providence, and also from beyond the sphere of Nirvana, is spoken about by Rudolf Steiner at the end of a lecture on 25.10.1909, in which he also reveals the whole difference between the microcosmic being of the Bodhisattva and the Buddhas who in accordance with their rank ascend into these two worlds from below, and the macrocosmic Being of Christ who descends into these spheres from above, from cosmic heights which are already far beyond our imagination (GA 116).

24 The essential nature of this process becomes clearer if we remember that the stream permeating man from the Buddhi-world, the World of Providence, is the stream of the Holy Spirit (see the description of the 4th rhythm of the Christmas Conference in Chapter 5). As a result of undergoing an etheric Golgotha in the twentieth century, Christ gives to all humanity the possibility of arresting, in a natural way, the stream of the Holy Spirit and of gradually bringing it to the point where, in the course of the next 2,500 years, more and more individuals, through the outpouring of the Spirit, will be able to grow into the World of Imaginations. Thereby will be prepared for all humanity that which the Apostles, anticipating our epoch, experienced at Pentecost through the enlightenment of their *heads* by the 'individualized Holy Spirit' (see 15.5.1910, GA 118, and 7.5.1910, 'The Whitsun Mystery and its Connection with the Ascension' in GA 224).

We can try and deepen our understanding of this process from yet another angle by looking at what is said by Rudolf Steiner in a lecture on 14.4.1914 in GA 153. He describes there how the human being's existence on Earth and after death must proceed in order that in the next incarnation he may be found worthy to have the natural ability of seeing into the world of Imagination and to meet there the Etheric Christ. He speaks in detail in this lecture of how the human being who during life takes up the Christ-impulse so strongly that the words *In Christo morimur* become an absolutely real experience for him will then also be able to carry this impulse of Christ through the portals of death. After death Christ accompanies the soul through the whole course of its subsequent ascent into the spiritual worlds, and accompanies it in such a way that at the moment of its greatest distance from the Earth, at the time of the World Midnight when the soul rises to the highest limits of Upper Devachan and is overshone by the Holy Spirit from the sphere of Buddhi, the Christ-impulse unites with the stream of the Spirit which will now accompany the soul on its Earthward journey to a new incarnation. Furthermore, this Christ-impulse strengthens the stream of the Spirit to such an extent that it is then able to enter with the human being at birth into earthly existence. By virtue of this, such a human being is already born as though secretly overshone by the Holy Spirit, through whose working he is led, sooner or later, to a perception of the imaginative sphere and to a direct meeting within it with the Etheric Christ. Thus we see here also the Christ-impulse, which encompasses our whole cosmos from the spiritual sphere nearest the Earth right to the world of Buddhi. From there it strengthens the stream of the spirit in man in such a way that it can be arrested in human consciousness on Earth and thus arise in it as the world of true Imaginations.

25 This is why, in his commentary on 25 December, the first day of the Conference, Rudolf Steiner connects this second part of the *Meditation* with the *archetypes* of cosmic existence (i.e. directly with the World of Archetypes or Buddhi) on the one hand, and with the Cosmic Imaginations on the other. In particular he says: '... thus one will grasp the archetypes of world existence when one feels within oneself the mysterious transition between world rhythm and heart rhythm, and through this again the human rhythm which plays itself out mysteriously in a soul-spiritual way between heart and lung' (GA 260). He then goes on to characterize this second part again—particularly the human rhythmic system in it—and connects this with the 'Cosmic Imagination' which is to come to life again in human imagination. He even uses here the expression 'the Archetype of Imagination' (*das Urbild der Imagination*). We need only compare this with what was said by him in the cycle GA 119 concerning the relation of the World of Archetypes (Buddhi) with imaginative knowledge (see quotations from this cycle on pp. 284–85 of this chapter).

26 The new Bodhisattva has to fulfil on Earth only *part* of the 'Christ-Will' from the world of Fore-knowledge, for this 'Christ-Will' can be brought to fulfilment on the Earth in its *entirety* only when the mission of the last of the twelve Bodhisattvas has come to an end: 'And only when the last Bodhisattva—who belongs to Christ—has accomplished his work will mankind have a feeling of what Christ is; for it will then be ensouled by a *will in which the Christ Himself lives*' (GA 116, 25.10.1909; see Note 20).

27 'Faith, Love, Hope', 2.12.1911 (GA 130). The nature of the working of Christ as the Lord of Karma is characterized by Rudolf Steiner in this lecture as follows: 'Christ will work in such a way on the balancing, the rectification, of the karma of individual human beings that this will then be able to make

the best possible contribution to the progress of *all* humanity' (see 14.11.1911 in GA 131). However, a direct influence of this nature is possible, as he says at the end of a lecture on 22.10.1906 (GA 55/96), only from the sphere of Buddhi or *Providence* (Fore-knowledge). For the role of Providence in the world is to incorporate individual deeds in the right way into the totality of the cosmos for the good of its further development. In this sense, beginning in the twentieth century, the Christ-Will, which is spoken of in the second part of the *Meditation*, works in the surroundings of the Earth as true Providence in the world of humanity. It gives every human being, in the process of rectifying his own individual karma, the possibility of furthering in the best possible way the good of all humanity.

28 That Christ from the twentieth century onwards becomes the Lord of Karma is directly associated with the emergence of a natural imaginative clairvoyance, and this in turn is able to arise because Christ makes it possible for present-day human beings to arrest within their souls the stream of the Holy Spirit from the world of Providence (see Note 24). The connection between these two events is further confirmed through the fact that one of the first experiences of the new clairvoyance will be that of one's own karma and above all the karmic consequences of one's own deeds (see the lecture of 14.10.1911, GA 131). In order that we may further deepen our understanding of this deeply significant Mystery of our time, we shall turn to the fourth rhythm of the Christmas Conference as considered in Chapter 5, where it was described how during Cosmic Midnight the soul beholds the way in which its own karma is fashioned through the activity of all nine Hierarchies, which is revealed to it in the unified sounding of the Cosmic Word (see Note 58 to Chapter 5). This process, which extends throughout the second half of life after death, unfolds in such a way that the karma which has been prepared in the sphere of the First Hierarchy passes over into the sphere of the Second Hierarchy and finally into that of the Third. In this sphere the human soul, in the course of preparing for incarnation on Earth, passes in turn through the domains of the Archai, Archangeloi and Angeloi, who incorporate the karma which has been forged by the higher Hierarchies in the four members of man's being (see further in the lectures of 18 and 25.1.1925, GA 26). The Beings of the Hierarchy of the Angeloi are the last to participate in this sublime work. They are the mediators between the macrocosmic weaving of karma and the human individual. Their special position also comes to expression in that they do not only bring the process of the embodiment of karma in the human being to a culmination but accomplish something even greater: they accompany the human individual in the course of his earthly life as 'Guardian Angels'.

But it was precisely in this 'last member' of the great hierarchic whole in connection with human karma that 'in the period between the founding of Christianity and the age of the consciousness soul' (whose high point came in the year 869) a fateful division took place. What happened was that a significant number of Angels left the sphere of Michael—that is, the sphere of the 'good' Hierarchies—and entered into opposition against it (see Note 103 to Chapter 4 and the lecture of 8.8.1924, GA 237). For this reason, the karmic relations of human beings have from the year 869 until our own time entered into ever greater disorder. In other words: the karma that had been prepared by the higher Hierarchies in common has—because of the 'split' within the last member of the Hierarchies (in the domain of the Angels)—been prevented from being lived out in the right way among mankind.

Into this deeply tragic situation there now enters the Etheric Christ. As the bearer of the entire fullness of the Cosmic Word (see the description of the fourth rhythm), He is through the Mystery of Golgotha connected with the karma of the whole of mankind. Today, however, He works as the Etheric Christ in the supersensible world bordering upon the Earth in the 'outward form' of an *Angel* (see the lecture of 2.5.1913, GA 152), thus gaining access to the karmic relationships of every *single* human individual. (In the third chapter of *The Spiritual Guidance of Man* (GA 15), Rudolf Steiner also speaks of how the Christ works in our time through the *entire* Hierarchy of the Angels *as a whole*.) Thus, as the Lord of Karma, Christ appears in the present epoch of Michael's rulership pre-eminently where karmic relationships have become particularly chaotic, that is, in the domain of the Angels. And so through His healing influence He enables human individuals from our time onwards to work upon bringing their karma into balance by gradually acquiring a conscious relationship to Him. Anthroposophy represents a way in which such a *conscious* relationship to karma can be achieved.

29   GA 153, 10.4.1914.

30   The ideal of man as a being who has developed Spirit Self, Life Spirit and Spirit Man in himself is sent down today primarily from the cosmic sphere of Michael; for Michael, as the guiding Spirit of our time (Archai), who has himself developed these three higher members completely, is at the same time also directly concerned with human freedom (GA 233a, 13.1.1924).

31   GA 233a, 13.1.1924.

32   GA 240, 19.7.1924.

33   In speaking of 'cosmic thoughts' or 'Cosmic Intelligence', we must not imagine something abstract, but a working-together, a sum total of real spiritual Beings (see the lecture on 8.8.1924 in GA 237).

34   The Rosicrucian sayings contained in the first three parts of the *Foundation Stone Meditation* can also be connected with the three great cosmic calls or revelations given to humanity on Earth, of which Rudolf Steiner speaks on 30.11.1911 (GA 127), and on 2.12.1911 (GA 130). The first revelation or call was the voice heard by Moses on Sinai when the great secrets of the Father-sphere were revealed to him—in particular the history of creation, i.e. the origin of humanity in the bosom of God. It was this revelation that was then set down by Moses in the book of Genesis, and of which the Rosicrucian saying speaks: *Ex Deo nascimur*. The second call was the call of John the Baptist who proclaimed the coming of Christ who would conquer death and thereby bring the Light of True Life into the darkness of Earth existence. It is

of this that the second Rosicrucian saying speaks: *In Christo morimur*. And the third call is the revelation to all humanity of modern spiritual science. As the new proclamation of the spirit today, this reveals the true knowledge of the Christ Being which is vital for the whole future development of the Earth. However, this new knowledge of Christ is connected above all in our epoch with the activity of Michael, the guiding Spirit of our age; for it is from him, the 'Countenance of Christ', that the new understanding of the Mystery of Golgotha descends to humanity today and leads us directly to the Sun-Mystery of the Living Christ. Rudolf Steiner speaks of this as follows: 'Michael is essentially a Sun Spirit. He is therefore the Spirit whose task in our epoch is to bring about a deeper, more esoteric understanding of the truths of Christianity. Christ came from the Sun. Christ, the Sun Being, dwelt on the Earth in the body of Jesus and has lived since then in supersensible communion with the world of men. But before the whole Mystery connected with Christ can reveal itself to the soul, mankind must become sufficiently mature and the necessary deepening will to a great extent have to be achieved during the present Age of Michael' (21.8.1924, GA 240). This deepening, however, is only possible through the spiritualization of the thought-life of modern human beings which is attained through Anthroposophy and leads to a gradual awakening of man in the spiritual world, that is, in 'the Spirit's Universal Thoughts' that bear within them 'the eternal aims of Gods'. And it is to this that the third Rosicrucian saying directs us: *Per Spiritum Sanctum reviviscimus*.

The fourth part speaks directly of the Christ-Sun itself, which is at work as the fundamental force in all three calls or revelations. Thus, in ancient times, from the heights of the Sun-sphere Christ sent the first revelation to Moses through his Moon-servant, Jahve. Thereafter the great Sun-Spirit Himself descended to Earth and in the Mystery of Golgotha, by overcoming death, realized the second revelation which had been proclaimed by John the Baptist. And now in our age of the rulership of Michael and at the end of the dark age of Kali Yuga, Christ sends to the Earth through spiritual science the new proclamation of the Spirit which, as the true Light of the Spiritual Sun, brings a real knowledge of Christ and of the Mystery of Golgotha.

35 GA 240, 18.7.1924.

36 In connection with the study of the *Foundation Stone Meditation* presented here, we must add that the three elements described, comprising all four parts, also have a direct relation to the three Christian festivals of Christmas, Easter and Whitsun. In order to feel this connection one has only to recall certain statements by Rudolf Steiner concerning the festivals. In a lecture on 15.5.1910 (in GA 118) he characterizes Christmas as the festival for remembrance of the past, from which hope for the present and the future is born. He describes Easter as the festival which through the Mystery of Golgotha enables us in the present to awaken inwardly in the Spirit. And Whitsun speaks to us of the future, when through our union with the Christ-impulse we shall be able to rise to an inner perception of the Spirit, which as

'the individualized Holy Spirit' will then in turn not only be able to reveal to us a new knowledge of Christ but to make the Christ-impulse the fundamental force at work in our soul. In this sense, in characterizing these three festivals he explains how in the course of the year there is revealed to us what as human beings we were, are, and may become. He connects Christmas with the Earth, Easter with the world of the planets, with Sun and Moon, and Whitsun with the fixed stars and the sphere of the free 'I' which lies beyond them. Then, in a lecture on 4.6.1924 (GA 236) he relates Christmas with the world of space, which is born from the forces of the Father; Easter with the sphere of time, the cosmic sphere of the Son, from which Christ descended to the Earth; and Whitsun with the sphere of Eternity from which the forces of the Spirit work. And lastly, in the same lecture he points directly to the fact that the most profound essence of these Christian festivals is also contained in the three Rosicrucian sayings which speak of birth from the Father, the overcoming of death in Christ, and the future awakening in the Spirit.

If now we compare all these facts with the first three parts of the *Meditation*, we find the following picture. The first part, the 'Christmas' part, concerns the sphere of the Earth. This relates in the human organism to the limb-system (line 2), which in each new incarnation is the first to arise. Further on, this part speaks of earthly space (3), which is born of the Father (14–15). Here, in a downward direction from above, there appears the Representative of man (20), the Nathan Soul which, by uniting itself with the Christ Being, will find the true life (13 [12]). And the fact that the festival relating to this part is immovable is indicated especially in the words 'comes to being' (*erweset*) (10 [11]).

The second part, the 'Easter' part, concerns the sphere of the moving stars (planets)—which is mirrored in our rhythmic system (2)—and above all the sphere of the Sun (17–18) as the great cosmic sphere of time (3); for Easter, as a movable feast, is dependent on the position of the heavenly bodies. And in this festival of the descent of Cosmic Love (14), by virtue of the sacrifice on Golgotha which brought about a reunion of man and world (9–11) through overcoming death (20), is also contained the fulfilment of all the Sun Mysteries of antiquity.

The third part, the 'Whitsun' part, concerns the eternal sphere of the Spirit (3) which is mirrored in the human head (2), and also concerns our ascent into this sphere by developing a true thinking (13 [12]) through which the soul can awaken in 'the Spirit's Universal Thoughts' (20) and experience the 'Eternal aims of Gods' sent down into them for humanity. And this is the true Whitsun experience, the festival of the 'free individuality' (9–11). However, the reference in this part to the two cosmic directions—from below upwards (17–18) in the macrocosmic section and from above downwards (7–11) in the microcosmic section—also directs us to two particularly closely related festivals, to Ascension and Whitsun. Thus in these three parts of the *Meditation* we have the three principal festivals of Christianity. And it is through an experience of these in the cycle of the year that humanity as a whole on its path of evolution is prepared for the initiation of all mankind, for the gradual growing into the spiritual world through a rhythmical experience of the Mysteries of Birth, Death and Resurrection. The reason why the festivals of the ascending half of the year are shown to us here, that is, in the time 'when the Sun moves northwards', is explained by Rudolf Steiner in a lecture on 4.6.1924 as follows: 'If one understands the relation of the physical to the soul-element of the human being and to the superphysical element that encompasses freedom within it, and which man partakes of on Earth, then one understands, in the relation between the festivals of Christmas, Easter and Whitsun, *the free human being on Earth*' ('Ascension and Pentecost', GA 236). The other half of the year—connected as it is in this lecture with human karma, in the shaping of which all the divine-spiritual Hierarchies take part— is also concealed in the *Meditation* in the reference in the second elements of the first three parts to the joint working of all nine Hierarchies in our cosmos. The fourth part ('At the Turning-point . . .') is, in this connection, of a somewhat different nature. For from the standpoint we have adopted, this part speaks not of the general but of the *individual* path of initiation which is connected neither with the rhythm of the year nor with the general process of evolution. We will be able to mention this only very briefly. Just as the starting-point of the new times is revealed as the entry of the Spirit-Light of the World into 'the stream of Earthly Being', the union of the Sun-Being of Christ with the dark sphere of the Earth, so the new Christian initiation too has its foundation in this greatest event of all Earth evolution, which is spoken of in the first seven lines of Part 4. These lines refer to the most profound *knowledge* of the nature of the Christ-Sun Mysteries, the Christmas Mystery (1–3), the Easter Mystery (4–5) and the Whitsun Mystery (6–7). Thus, on the basis of this all-encompassing knowledge of the Christ-impulse in its working in the cosmos, on Earth and in humanity, we then begin to work towards a union of the two principal Mystery-streams—a union of the stream of the Shepherds (inwardly) and the stream of the Kings (outwardly). It is of this that the next six lines (8–13) speak.

For the same Light of Christ which poured into the souls of men at the Turning-point of Time also permeated the hearts of Shepherds as well as the heads of Kings (Magi). The inner work, on one initiation path, of uniting these two streams into a single higher synthesis gradually prepares us for, and gives us the hope of, a direct personal meeting with the Christ in the Spiritual World. This meeting, as the inner culmination of the whole spiritual path, is spoken of in the next six lines of Part 4 (14–19). And when this has taken place, the fruits of such an individual experience of the Christ can be carried out into the world and become socially active forces there, working towards the progress of all humanity through the Christ-impulse which permeates them. This potential for a socially healing effect of the Christ-impulse amongst humanity is indicated to us in the last lines of Part 4:

That good may become
What from our Hearts we would found
And from our Heads direct
With single purpose.

Moreover, the realization of these words works right into the karma of each individual human being as well as into that of all humanity.

37   GA 112, 24.6.1909.

38   GA 155, 30.5.1912.

39   GA 26, 22.3.1925, p. 201.

40   GA 130, 2.12.1911.

41   GA 194, 23.11.1919.

42   GA 55, 30.5.1914.

43   We must note here that the synthesis of the general and the individual referred to above (p. 296), which is contained in the *Foundation Stone Meditation*, is also the synthesis of two fundamental Christian Mystery-principles that are expressed in the words of Christ, 'For where two or three are gathered together in my name, there am I in the midst of them' (Matthew 18: 20), and in the words of Paul, 'Not I, but Christ in me' (Galations 2: 20). Of these two principles, the first concerns all humanity and finds its highest realization in the process already considered by us, of creating the 'immortal individuality'; the second on the other hand is connected with individual initiation which culminates in a direct experience of the Christ in the human 'I'. (A study of this individual path of initiation as contained in the *Meditation* follows on in this chapter.) In this sense, the most important and distinct feature of the Christmas Conference as a whole lies in the fact that it creates a foundation and reveals the true archetype for a higher synthesis in humanity of the two Mystery-principles mentioned above. The path to the attainment of this synthesis lies, above all, in the *joint* work of anthroposophists on the *Meditation*. This, however, is only possible by means of a true understanding of the Christmas Conference itself. (This was spoken of in greater detail in the preceding chapter.)

44   GA 226, 16.5.1923. On 2.2.1924 (in GA 234) Rudolf Steiner says: 'The etheric body is a time-organism. The physical body is a space-organism.'

45   This interrelation of the physical, etheric and astral bodies with the first sections of Parts I–III of the *Meditation* can be strengthened by the references there to the three systems of the human organism—the limb-system, the heart/lung-system (rhythm) and the head-system (I, II, III, 2)—which in turn are the physiological basis of human will, feeling and thinking (I, II, III, 13 [12]). These, however, as we know from numerous references by Rudolf Steiner (for example, on 1.10.1911 in GA 130), draw their impulses from Upper Devachan, Lower Devachan and the astral world respectively, that is, from those cosmic spheres from which the forces flow for the formation of our physical, etheric and astral bodies (see 26.5.1907, GA 99, and 20.11.1907, GA 100).

It is possible to feel this interrelation by immersing oneself in the first section of Parts I–III separately. Thus the first section of Part I refers to the limb-system and the metabolism—that is, to that area of the human organism with which to a high degree the essence of the 'phantom' of the human physical body is connected. For those processes of ash formation and salt dissolution, which on 11.10.1911 in GA 131 Rudolf Steiner describes as being the fundamental processes that arise in the 'phantom', clearly belong to the limb-system and to the metabolism. This connection between the 'phantom' of the human physical body and the first section of Part I of the *Meditation* is also referred to in lines 12–13 (which have already been discussed on p. 275 of this chapter).

The connection between the etheric body and the first section of Part II is indicated there by the reference to the rhythm of 'the beat of heart and lung' (2). This rhythm, described by Rudolf Steiner on a number of occasions (see for example GA 175 and GA 201), is in complete correspondence with cosmic rhythms, and in particular with the motion of the Sun. The basis of this correspondence between the rhythms of the cosmos and the rhythms of the human organism is rooted in the etheric body. In an article in 1925 Rudolf Steiner wrote of this: 'In the etheric body there is constant move-ment that is a reflection of the changing constellations during the human life on Earth. The etheric body configures itself even in relation to the changes in the heavens of day and night—that is, to the motion of the movement of the Sun' (GA 26). In the *Meditation* these changing constellations of the stars are referred to in lines 3 and 7–8. In a lecture on 7.5.1923 Rudolf Steiner speaks further about the etheric body: 'The etheric body is actually something that is striving constantly not towards the Earth but always upwards to the Sun. As human beings we are so constituted that our physical body has earthly weight [this is primarily expressed in our limb-system; just as the system of the heart and lungs overcomes gravity through rhythm, so the head-system, the brain, overcomes gravity by floating in cerebral fluid] and our etheric body strives constantly towards the Sun.' And he adds: 'The etheric body of man, by striving Sunwards, strives towards Christ' (GA 224, 7.5.1923). And inasmuch as the first section of the *Meditation* points to the etheric body, so the second part too speaks of this profound secret. The etheric body strives constantly towards the cosmos, to the sphere of the Sun, to Christ—that is, in the sense of the *Meditation*, to the second section of Part II, which speaks of both the Sun (17–18) and of Christ (14). This special connection of the human etheric body with the Sun is also pointed to in Rudolf Steiner's words from the last lecture of the cycle GA 123: 'In this etheric body there also lives something that is of the Sun. There sounds into the etheric body something which was alive as the Harmony of the Spheres and which is perceptible behind mere physicality as coming from the Gods. Thus we can say: lofty Gods live in the etheric body, and precisely such Gods as are related to the Sun Gods,' i.e. the Second Hierarchy, the Spirits of Light (16), who are the leading spirits in the sphere of the Sun and the planets. Corresponding to this realm is the world of

Inspiration or the Harmony of the Spheres.

And lastly, the first section of Part III speaks of the astral body, which in the words of Rudolf Steiner (19.5.1908, GA 103) is the 'Light-body'; we are particularly directed to this in the *Meditation* by line 8 (compare also p. 290 of this chapter).

46 GA 13.

47 See Note 24 of Chapter 5.

48 If we bear in mind that, as contained in the *Foundation Stone Meditation*, the sevenfold nature of the human being is itself also an image of the whole of Earth-evolution from Saturn to Vulcan, and if we remember all that has been said in this book concerning the relation of the *Meditation* to the existence of the soul after death and to the new sevenfold Christian-Rosicrucian path of initiation, then we shall really be able to sense how, in this all-encompassing text, is contained the quintessence of the three fundamental anthroposophical works, *Occult Science, Theosophy* and *Knowledge of the Higher Worlds*. Together these represent the three fundamental aspects of Anthroposophy: spiritual evolution, the being of man and the path of knowledge which, in turn, give new impulses for the development of human thinking, feeling and willing. This is why, in truth, the *Meditation* reveals to us the very essence of all Anthroposophy as *Anthropos-Sophia*, as the most profound wisdom of man.

49 It follows from what has been presented here that the *Foundation Stone Meditation* also yields us a picture of the ninefold human being whose individual members are connected in the following way with the corresponding lines of the *Meditation*:

I. Physical body	Part I	⎫
II. Etheric body	Part II	⎬ Lines 2–6
III. Astral body	Part III	⎭
IV. Sentient soul	Part I	⎫
V. Intellectual and Mind soul	Part II	⎬ Lines 7–11
VI. Consciousness soul	Part III	⎭
Product of fully developed Sentient soul	Part I	⎫
Product of fully developed Intellectual and Mind soul	Part II	⎬ Lines 12–13
Product of fully developed Consciousness soul	Part III	⎭
VII. Spirit Self	Part III	⎫
VIII. Life Spirit	Part II	⎬ Lines 14–20
IX. Spirit Man	Part I	⎭

Part IV contains the hidden essence of the human 'I' into which Christ enters, thereby uniting cosmic past and cosmic future in the cosmic present.

1   GA 114, 16 and 17.9.1909.

2   We must note here that in speaking of the three fundamental forms of the spiritual life that exist in contemporary humanity as the legacy of past epochs—the ecclesiastical, the masonic and the eastern—we have in mind the 'purer forms' of their manifestation. This means those forms which from the spiritual wellsprings of Anthroposophy Rudolf Steiner tried during his lifetime to renew. In the so-called Esoteric Lessons, especially in the early ones, he endeavoured to transform the eastern occultism as it was practised in the Theosophical Society into Christian esotericism. The same was attempted for 'Masonic symbolism' in a ceremonial ritual (see GA 28, Chapter 36), and also for the sacrament and ritual of the Church by the founding of the Christian Community in 1921–22.

In our time, however, these 'pure forms' of inherited spirituality are degenerating increasingly into something completely different. The Church succumbs ever more to Jesuitism, and is thus transformed into the opposite of its true nature (see 22.9.1918, GA 184). Freemasonry, pursuing political goals, degenerates increasingly into an occult materialism of the darkest kind (see 20 and 22.1.1917, GA 174). And in the East, private occult interests are developing more and more which are profoundly hostile to Christianity (see the *Notes of Barr*, Part III (GA 262), and the lecture of 18.11.1917 in GA 178): for universal human interests can exist only where the central point is the impulse of Christ.

3   In GA 112, Lecture 14, and GA 123, Lecture 10, Rudolf Steiner says that the awakening of clairvoyance in the Apostle Paul at the time of the event of Damascus was only possible because he had been born prematurely, that is, had entered the physical world earlier than is usual for a human being. St Paul himself speaks of this in the First Letter to the Corinthians, 15: 8.

4   Revelation 21: 5.

5   GA 237, 1.8.1924.

6   GA 114, 20.9.1909.

7   GA 237, 3.8.1924.

8   In the third lecture of GA 114, Rudolf Steiner gives the example of Buddha as well as that of Aristotle, for these individualities both represent two *opposite* streams in human development (see GA 139, Lecture 4, and Note 71 of Chapter 4). Together these two examples illustrate particularly clearly the *universality* of that cosmic law by which spiritual impulses can enter into the sphere of the Earth. Rudolf Steiner also speaks about this law in the lecture of 13.4.1910 (GA 118): 'The view tends to predominate that the same faculties have always been present in a greater or lesser degree. However, this is by no means the case. There has been a constant flow of new faculties in the course of evolution and, whenever mankind has become mature enough to be endowed with a new gift, the new faculty has

first *had to be incorporated in a great human individual.* It was manifested firstly in him, and he then sowed seeds in those souls that were ready for it.'

9   Concerning the relation of the astral element and the 'I' with man's individual development on the one hand and that of the etheric element with the social development on the other, see GA 123, 12.9.1910.

10 GA 123, Lecture 10. Rudolf Steiner says here that the first two stages of the Apostles' supersensible experience corresponded to the imaginative (the Feeding of the Five Thousand and the Walking on the Water) and the inspirational (the Transfiguration) states of consciousness.

11 Christ reveals to His disciples this Mystery of His union with the physical body of Jesus of Nazareth through the Mystery of the Communion during the Last Supper, where the bread and wine are an allusion to Christ's union with the body and blood of Jesus. For only through the latter can the Christ unite Himself after the Mystery of Golgotha with the 'body' of the Earth (John 13–18) and also with the body and blood of every human being dwelling on it.

12 Now, at the third stage, the Apostles had to attain to intuitive consciousness in order to ascend to the Buddhi-sphere and experience there the eternal cosmic archetype of the Twelve who surround the Thirteenth.

13 Matthew 26: 40–41.

14 GA 139, 23.9.1912.

15 Ibid.

16 GA 148, 2.10.1913.

17 GA 226, 17.5.1923.

18 Matthew 26: 40.

19 GA 226, 17.5.1923.

20 GA 237, 1.8.1924.

21 Rudolf Steiner speaks in detail of this supersensible event in the lecture of 28.7.1924 in GA 237 (see also Note 89 of Chapter 5).

22 In his lecture in Dornach on 28.7.1924, Rudolf Steiner says this event 'took place in the first third of the fifteenth century, in that time when, behind the scenes of the development of the new age, the Rosicrucian School was founded' (GA 237). This founding occurred at that time under the guidance of Christian Rosenkreutz himself, who after his initiation around 1250 incarnated again in 1378 and was active in a physical body until 1484 (see also the *Notes of Barr*, Part II, GA 262).

23 See the description of the 5th and 6th rhythms of the Christmas Conference in Chapter 5 and also Notes 89 and 102 of Chapter 5. In this way we can follow the *entire* cosmic–earthly path of Anthroposophy's genesis, consisting as it does of seven great stages which correspond to the seven members of man's being. Thus the supersensible event at the beginning of the fifteenth century which occurred in the sphere of the First Hierarchy, i.e. in the sphere of Intuition (Upper Devachan), corresponds to Spirit Man; the Sun School of Michael in the fifteenth to sixteenth centuries, which took place in the sphere of Inspiration (Lower Devachan), corresponds to Life Spirit;

and thirdly the imaginative cultus on the astral plane at the end of the eighteenth and the beginning of the nineteenth century corresponds to Spirit Self. Thus the three higher, celestial stages of Anthroposophy's preparation correspond to the three higher members of man's being. The four stages of its earthly development (considered from p. 309 onwards in this chapter) correspond to the four lower members of the human being: to the 'I', the astral, etheric and physical bodies. In this way, *all* of Anthroposophy's development—from the cosmic event at the beginning of the fifteenth century to the Christmas Conference of 1923–24, presenting as it does the successive descent of a spiritual impulse from the sphere of Upper Devachan to its final embodiment on the Earth—thus comes before us as a complete sevenfold whole, revealing itself as a *living being* which, through the working on Earth of the New Mysteries, must gradually enter upon a path of ascendant development. Rudolf Steiner speaks in the following way about Anthroposophy not only as a living being but as an 'invisible *human being*' (i.e. a being consisting of *seven* principles: 'Anthroposophy is essentially an invisible human being who walks among visible men and towards whom ... one has the greatest conceivable responsibility, who must indeed be accepted as an invisible human being, as someone truly present, to whom one must go for advice concerning life's individual actions ... It is absolutely necessary that everything that happens comes about on the advice of the *human being, Anthroposophy*. It is a part of life's realities to envisage Anthroposophy as a living being' (GA 258, 16.6.1923).

24 GA 238, 16.9.1924. Nothing is mentioned here of the supersensible event in the sphere of the First Hierarchy at the beginning of the fifteenth century because, as is implied, this event is essentially to be regarded as the hidden heart of the supersensible School of Michael.

25 GA 240, 21.8.1924.

26 Ibid.

27 For more on this connection of the Michael-impulse with the essence of Rosicrucianism, see the lecture in Dornach on 13.1.1924 (GA 233a), and also the article 'Hindrances and Helps to the Michael Forces in the Dawn of the Age of the Spiritual Soul' in GA 26, 14.12.1924.

28 'A Christmas Study: The Mystery of the Logos', GA 26, 28.12.1924.

29 GA 145, 29.3.1913. Rudolf Steiner speaks here of how, in occult development, the consciousness soul must gradually be transformed into the imaginative soul, the intellectual or mind soul into the inspirational soul, and the sentient soul into the intuitive soul. See also the second lecture of GA 99 in which he says that Spirit Self arises in the consciousness soul, Life Spirit in the intellectual or mind soul and Spirit Man in the sentient soul (compare also what is said in Note 49 of Chapter 6).

30 See Emil Bock, *Rudolf Steiner. Studien zu seinem Lebensgang und Lebenswerk*, a lecture for members of the Anthroposophical Society on 26.12.1952. For the relation between the Michael-principle and the principle of the Holy

Spirit, see also what is said in Chapter 6 of this book concerning the third part of the *Foundation Stone Meditation*.

31   This picture of the Michaelic Grail can become even clearer if we compare it with what is said by Rudolf Steiner in his lecture *The Etherization of the Blood* in GA 130. Two fundamental spiritual streams are spoken of here which penetrate the human organism in two directions. The first is the microcosmic stream (Rudolf Steiner also calls it the 'intellectual' stream), which flows from the heart to the head. This is the stream of etherized human blood. The second is the macrocosmic stream (which he calls the moral-will stream). This flows from the head to the heart, penetrating into the human head from the cosmos during sleep. In the first, the microcosmic stream, the etheric blood of Christ, too, has been working *as substance* ever since the Mystery of Golgotha. This, however, according to Rudolf Steiner can only unite with the etherized blood of human beings (that means enter their consciousness) if they take up modern spiritual science. If this occurs, the human being comes gradually into the *imaginative* world and can experience there a meeting with the Etheric Christ. This meeting in turn illumines and spiritualizes the intellectual, microcosmic stream in such a way that it begins to radiate the purest *Light of thoughts* in which intelligence is redeemed. And then towards this Light radiating from below upwards—a Light issuing from the *substance of the etheric blood of Christ*, which is made conscious to human beings through *their formative force of Imagination*— through the second, the macrocosmic stream, of the Michaelic *Spirit*-impulse, which flows from head to heart, there can flow into the being of man the impulse of Michael himself. For Michael 'frees thoughts from the realm of the head; he opens the way for them into the heart' (GA 26). Thus in the human being there is the meeting of the Michael-impulse coming from outside, from the macrocosm, and the Christ-impulse rising from the depths of the human soul, and the human being can feel how his 'gaze into the outer world [into the macrocosm] falls spiritually on Michael, and how [his] gaze into the inner depths of the soul [into the microcosm] falls spiritually on Christ (GA 26). In this union of the Christ-impulse with the impulse of Michael we also have the harmonious union of the Arthurian and Grail principles in the human soul. All in all, the above description makes us aware of the deep connection that exists between the Grail stream and the preparation for Christ's appearance in the etheric realm. After all, the beginning of the Grail Mysteries is itself intimately connected with the Mysteries of the etheric cosmos. Rudolf Steiner speaks about this in the following words from the lecture of 1.10.1922 (GA 216): 'For the visions which also included the conception of the Mystery of Golgotha—in the way that I have just characterized it [with regard to the Grail stream]—were related to the etheric cosmos.' And in the lecture of 1.10.1911 referred to above, this Mystery is spoken of from the other aspect: that of the influence of the etherized blood of Christ within man (see the characterization of the Grail stream in the lecture of 27.8.1924, GA 240). Thus the Grail Mysteries

444

first lead man to become conscious of the etherized blood of Christ within himself (this comes to expression in the legends through the fact that beholding the Grail enlivens and strengthens the physical forces), and later to beholding the Mysteries of the etheric cosmos. This latter aspect enables human individuals *in our time* to gain access to an experience of the Etheric Christ.

32   *Occult Science*, preface written on 10.1.1925 to the 1925 edition.

33   *Occult Science*, the chapter 'Present and Future Evolution of the World and of Mankind'. If we also bear in mind here that the path into the super-sensible worlds described in *Occult Science* is the *Rosicrucian* path appropriate to our time, then we can feel the wonderful harmony and continuity that exists in the spiritual life of the West between the Rosicrucian stream and the stream of the Grail. (See also the last lecture in GA 99.)

34   GA 240, 21.8.1924.

35   Emil Bock, *Rudolf Steiner, Studien zu seine, Lebensgang und Lebenswerk*, p. 346.

36   Rudolf Steiner speaks about this inner connection between the School of Chartres and the Arthurian stream, as follows: 'And it was for this reason also that there still hovered over the School of Chartres something of that Sun-Christianity which the Knights of Arthur's Round Table, as Knights of Michael, tried to establish as impulses in the world.' (GA 240.)

37   GA 240, 21.8.1924.

38   Ibid., 19.7.1924.

39   Ibid.

40   Ibid., 18.7.1924.

41   GA 238, 12.9.1924. Rudolf Steiner speaks in this lecture of how something similar took place in the twelfth century when the Platonists of the School of Chartres, who were then living on the Earth, were inspired by the Aristotelians from the spiritual world.

42   On 13.7.1924, in GA 237, Rudolf Steiner says: 'Only genuine Rosicrucianism could work into the spiritual atmosphere.'

43   GA 237, 18.7.1924.

44   GA 240, 21.8.1924.

45   Rudolf Steiner speaks as follows concerning the impossibility for the Dominican Schoolmen in the thirteenth century to approach the Grail Mystery *consciously*: 'Many significant happenings were connected with what was here taking place. For example: when one of the Schoolmen had come down from the spiritual world to work for the spread of Christianity in an Aristotelian form he had not, to begin with, been able fully to grasp the essential import of the Grail-principle. Karma had willed it so' (21.8.1924, GA 240).

46   A karmic constellation such as this (see GA 74, 23.5.1920) can also shed light on the very special significance of the previous incarnation of the individuality of Thomas Aquinas in the ninth century, at a time in which he was to become acquainted with both the Arthurian and the Grail streams,

445

but *before* their union through the working of Parsifal, which took place a little later in that same century (see Note 94 of Chapter 4). Because of this experience of the inner nature of these two streams *before* their union, Thomas Aquinas was then able to receive the necessary spiritual impulse to formulate later, in the thirteenth century, the fundamental question of medieval Scholasticism.

47 See *Occult Science*, the chapter 'Present and Future Evolution of the World and of Mankind'.

48 GA 240, 19.7.1924.

49 GA 238, 16.9.1924.

50 GA 237, 13.7.1924.

51 See GA 232, which was given immediately prior to the Christmas Conference, and the cycle GA 233, given during the Conference.

52 B.C.J. Lievegoed, *Mystery Streams in Europe and the New Mysteries*, concerning the union during the Christmas Conference of the four principal Mystery streams: the Michaelic (North), the Rosicrucian (South), the Arthurian (West), and the Grail stream (East).

53 GA 238, 12.9.1924.

54 F.W. Zeylmans van Emmichoven, *The Foundation Stone*.

55 GA 238, 12.9.1924.

56 In a lecture on 19.7.1924 (in GA 240), Rudolf Steiner points, among other things, to the participation of Brunetto Latini in the imaginative cultus at the end of the eighteenth and beginning of the nineteenth centuries. When speaking of such a participation of souls in the spiritual world in earthly affairs (i.e. in the development of Anthroposophy on Earth in the first quarter of the twentieth century), Rudolf Steiner lays particular emphasis on the supersensible influence of the individuality of Julian the Apostate (in the lecture of 16.9.1924) and of Novalis (in the lecture of 28.9.1924). (Both lectures are in GA 238.)

57 Ibid. Rudolf Steiner refers remarkably often in the Karma lectures to the individuality of Brunetto Latini (1220–94), and frequently speaks about the true consequence of his sunstroke—an initiation into world secrets, which occurred under the influence of the supersensible radiance of the School of Chartres that was still active at that time in the spiritual atmosphere of Europe (see for example 18.7.1924 in GA 240 and 12.9.1924 in GA 243). In a lecture on 16.8.1924 in GA 243 Rudolf Steiner also refers to his direct meeting, during his spiritual investigations, with Brunetto Latini in the spiritual world. All these facts can acquire a very different significance for us if we bear in mind that Brunetto Latini, the great teacher of Dante, who had attained his initiation completely in the spirit of the School of Chartres, lived in the thirteenth century and was thus a contemporary, not of the teachers of the School of Chartres, but of the Dominican Schoolmen and above all of Thomas Aquinas (1225–74). In this context one should not exclude the possibility that the great Dominican and the last representative of the School of Chartres may have met in Paris. Thomas Aquinas taught

there for many years at the university, and Brunetto Latini lived there in exile for seven years. Thomas Aquinas' lectures enjoyed great success in Paris, and Brunetto Latini could certainly have been present on a number of occasions. It is also interesting to note that Dante, having based his *Divine Comedy* on the knowledge he had received from Brunetto Latini, tried also, in an original way, to unite it with the teachings of Thomas Aquinas, as though prophetically anticipating the possibility of uniting Platonism and Aristotelianism on the Earth—a union which was to take place in the future.

58 In describing the nature of the supersensible Council in AD 869 at which there occurred the meeting between Aristotle and Alexander and Harun-al-Rashid and his counsellor, Rudolf Steiner points to the significant fact that also involved in this meeting on the side of Aristotle were many of the Knights of King Arthur, who at that time were in the spiritual world. As regards the influence of this Council on the subsequent development of European spiritual life, one can trace it right to the teaching of the School of Chartres and then even further, through Brunetto Latini, to Dante's *Divine Comedy*. For in all these teachings, as we learn from Rudolf Steiner (10.9.1924 in GA 238), there were working those inspiring rays of that spiritual council of 869 (see Note 57 of this chapter).

59 One must remember here that Zeylmans van Emmichoven in *The Foundation Stone* characterizes the transition accomplished by Rudolf Steiner at the Christmas Conference from 'the Stone of the Wise' to 'the Stone of Love' as a transition from the principle of the hexagram to that of the pentagram, and also refers to it as a transition from the principle of the working of man's 'I' from outside his being to the working of the human 'I' from within. (See the chapter in *The Foundation Stone* 'From the Philosopher's Stone to the Stone of Love'.) A definition such as this, taken in its microcosmic aspect, can also be understood as the transition from the Cosmic Intelligence, once governed in the cosmos by Michael, to human intelligence which is governed by every individual himself in his own inner being. However, Rudolf Steiner characterizes the Foundation Stone not as a simple pentagram but as a 'dodecahedron', a form consisting of twelve pentagons, i.e. the pentagram in its macrocosmic aspect related to the twelve directions of cosmic space. Thus we are no longer dealing here with the experience of Intelligence alone in the inner nature of human beings (the pentagram) but with its gradual reascent back into the macrocosm, into the Sun-sphere of Michael, i.e. with its genuine spiritualization.

On the other hand, on the basis of Rudolf Steiner's words quoted on p. 321 of this chapter, we are also dealing here with the beginning of the microcosmic transition from the Arthurian principle to that of the Grail. In this connection, however, there is still another aspect of these two principles, on the basis of which it is possible to talk of their synthesis—a synthesis whose foundation was laid at the Christmas Conference. Thus in Lecture 9 of the cycle GA 185, Rudolf Steiner characterizes these two streams as being connected with both the social and the individual element respectively. Further, one can also find these two elements—albeit in a somewhat different form—in the fundamental soul-mood of the Platonists and Aristotelians. For this reason, precisely through the joint work of these two streams, the social and individual principles must by the end of the century find their higher and final synthesis. This is a vital condition for the further development of contemporary humanity.

60   Concerning the true 'influence of the Grail principle in our time' (see Rudolf Steiner's words quoted on p. 321 of this chapter), he says the following: 'This [taking up of spiritual knowledge into the consciousness soul] is one of the results of the new Mysteries; these are the most important, most significant results which must today be taken up from the present Mysteries which are *a fruit of the influence of the Grail Mysteries*' (7.2.1913, GA 144).

61   GA 141, 7.1.1913.

62   *Occult Science*, the chapter 'Present and Future Evolution of the World and of Mankind'.

63   In a lecture on 7.2.1913 Rudolf Steiner refers to the original connection of the Grail Mysteries with the wisdom of the third post-Atlantean epoch (the epoch of the sentient soul): 'In the ascent of the Grail it is possible to sense that which became submerged in ancient Egypt. In this ascent of the Holy Grail we have before us everything that is the Christian renewal of the life of the ancient Mysteries' (GA 144).

64   GA 26, 'Gnosis and Anthroposophy', 15.2.1925.

65   Ibid.

66   Parsifal lived in the fourth post-Atlantean epoch and had thus fully developed within himself the intellectual or mind soul. At that time, however, he was prophetically also the bearer—and herein lies the unique quality of his initiation—of the consciousness soul. Rudolf Steiner indicates this, for example, in the following words: 'And what must run its course in the consciousness soul is expressed in everything which crystallized around the figure of Parsifal' (GA 144).

67   GA 149, 2.1.1914.

68   In his lectures Rudolf Steiner frequently says that it is precisely in our time that the foundations are being laid for the future epoch of Spirit Self (the sixth post-Atlantean epoch), i.e. a start must be made for the transition from the consciousness soul to the next highest member of the human being. In a lecture on 7.2.1913 he says the following concerning this: 'What today has already become more spiritualized, by having been transformed into a wisdom which can be spread everywhere—because we are now already at the transition to the sixth cultural epoch, in which these things are no longer bound to a particular place—that was, in those medieval times [the epoch of Parsifal] ... still tied down to certain localities' (GA 144).

69   GA 26.

70   GA 141, 7.1.1913.

71 In the last lecture of the cycle *Christ and the Spiritual World* (GA 149) are the words: '...that each time a Grail King, a truly appointed Guardian of the Grail, dies the name of his worthy successor appears on the Holy Grail. *There it is to be read, which means that it will be necessary to learn to read the stellar script again in a new form. Let us, my dear friends, try to make ourselves worthy to do this.* Let us endeavour to learn to read it in the form in which it must be given us today. For in fact it is nothing other than a reading of the stellar script when we try to explain human evolution in terms of the development of Saturn, Sun, Moon and Earth, up to Vulcan ... Let us look upon what it is our privilege to nurture in Anthroposophy as a renewed quest for the Grail ...' In these profoundly significant words we must be aware, above all, of the fact that they are speaking of the necessity in our time of reading in the stellar script the *name of the new Guardian of the Grail*. Moreover, this new name can definitely not be that of Parsifal, for this has already been read *long ago*. We are concerned here with a *new name* which *has still to be read*. To this question, posed as it was at that time from the innermost development of Anthroposophy in the course of twice seven years, there could not yet, in 1914, be given a conclusive answer. But the answer could be given nine years later at the Christmas Conference of 1923–24 when, as a result of the lowering of the 'dodecahedral Stone of Love' into the hearts and souls of anthroposophists, the secret of the *new Name* could become manifest. Thus we may say: the three names mentioned above correspond to three completely *different* spiritual individualities. And the citing of the name of Rudolf Steiner in this connection points to the fact that it is this name which can be read in the signs of the occult or stellar script on the 'Ganganda Greida', the 'itinerant source of sustenance', as is said in the lecture-cycle referred to above with regard to Parsifal and his initiation in the ninth century. What Parsifal accomplished for the ninth century Rudolf Steiner achieved for the twentieth century as his spiritual successor. And in this way is an answer given to the question as to the true *Mystery-name* of Rudolf Steiner. For the Mystery-name is not the name of the individuality of some lofty teacher or other but stands for a *spiritual quality*!

The Imagination that Albert Steffen describes in his 'Memorial address'— published in the book *In Memoriam Rudolf Steiner* (Dornach 1925)—also points towards the Mystery-name of Rudolf Steiner as being the new guardian of the Michaelic Grail.

72 GA 26, No. 143.

73 Ibid., 'The Freedom of Man and the Age of Michael', 22.2.1925.

74 Ibid.

75 Ibid., 'The Condition of the Human Soul Before the Dawn of the Michael Age'.

76 Ibid., 'At the Dawn of the Michael Age'.

77 GA 260. At this point, perhaps the author could be allowed a more personal comment. It is his conviction that it is impossible in the words of human speech to give a more exact or more profound definition of the inner nature

of the Holy Grail than that given by Rudolf Steiner in his words characterizing the 'dodecahedral imaginative Stone of Love'. By virtue of this, two world secrets become, in truth, at once unusually concrete and infinitely close to the soul; the inner nature of the Grail becomes understandable and attainable, and the being of the 'dodecahedral Stone of Love' takes on the nature of almost palpable reality, revealing itself as an exceptionally significant content for inner meditation.

78   GA 260.

79   Seen from this angle, the Mystery cultus-act of the laying of the Foundation Stone takes on a very particular significance. It is possible also here to distinguish four ascending stages, but we shall be able to consider these at this point only very briefly. Thus the first stage begins with the reading of the first sections of Parts I, II and III of the *Foundation Stone Meditation*, in which is revealed the esoteric nature of the three systems constituting the physical being of man. In addition, for the microcosmically working forces of the Spirit, the Son (Christ) and the Father in these three systems, through their conscious union in the 'form-giving substance' of the human soul, there arises an image of the new Michaelic Grail as the 'dodecahedral imaginative Stone of Love' radiating the 'Thought-Light' of spiritualized Intelligence. There follows, at the second stage, the turning to the 'original Christmas', to the great 'Turning-point of Time', and the fourth part of the *Meditation* sounds out. In this act we have the process of 'sanctification' of the Grail, its direct union with the Impulse of the Christ-Sun, which in our time works from the etheric sphere of the Earth. Because of this, at the third stage, the forces working microcosmically in the three systems of the human organism can be united with the macrocosmic forces which correspond to them in the cosmos. Concerning this, Rudolf Steiner says: '... Let it [the working of these forces] be placed ... *in the way in which it works through the cosmos, on to our Stone* which we have now laid in the ground of our hearts...' And then there sounds out each of the first three parts of the *Meditation*, in which we have the complete union of the microcosm (the three systems of the human organism) with the macrocosm (the forces of the Father, the Son—Christ— and the Spirit, as well as the nine Hierarchies which serve them). And finally, at the fourth stage, as the climax of the entire Mystery cultus-act, we have in the 'Thought Light' issuing from the 'dodecahedral Stone of Love', the appearance of that Spirit who is to be carried out into the world by anthroposophists 'there where it is to shed light and warmth for the progress of human souls, for the progress of the world'.

     In these four Mystery-stages it is also possible to perceive a gradual ascent from the spiritual-physical to the etheric, to the astral, and finally to the principle of the 'I'.

80   The medieval authors, who were still connected with the true tradition of the Grail stream, characterized in their works dedicated to this theme this mysterious 'thing' in different ways. Chretien de Troyes defines the Grail as a 'Chalice'; Wolfram von Eschenbach describes it as a 'Stone'; and Robert

de Boron, as a 'sign'. It is significant that Rudolf Steiner also characterizes the Foundation Stone as a 'sign': 'And from these three forces—from the Spirit of the heights, from the Christ power of the circumference, and from the working of the Father, the creative Father-activity that streams upwards from the depths—we *will*, at this moment, to form in our soul the dodecahedral Foundation Stone, which we sink in the ground of our souls, so that it may there be a steadfast *sign* in the vigorous foundation of our soul-nature, and so that in the future working of the Anthroposophical Society we may stand on this firm Foundation Stone' (GA 260).

Still another aspect of the Christmas Conference points us directly to the Grail event as its deeper content. To understand this aspect one must bear in mind Rudolf Steiner's statement, quoted in Note 71, that—so to speak—the key to the hidden secrets of the Holy Grail can be found in our times only by reading the stellar script. One must then compare these words with what is said on the last day of the Christmas Conference: 'If I write for you in this way the rhythms in their harmony, it is because there really lies within them a replica of the starry constellations' (GA 260). From what is said by Rudolf Steiner here, it is clear that all seven fundamental rhythms of the Christmas Conference present nothing other than *a new reading of the stellar script*, attainable today on the modern path of Christian initiation. However, the fact that these words, which characterize the inner nature of all seven rhythms, were spoken by Rudolf Steiner to explain the 7th directs us to the very particular relation of just this 7th rhythm to the secret of the new Michaelic Grail. For just as the 'dodecahedral imaginative Stone of Love' was created from the forces working *microcosmically* in the three systems of the human organism—the forces of the Spirit, the Son (Christ) and the Father (see the description of the rhythm given on 25.12.23)—so too, in the 7th rhythm, expressing as it does the seventh and highest stage of both cosmic and individual development, we have the *macrocosmic* activity of the forces of the Father, the Son (Christ) and the Spirit in the three systems of the human organism (see the rhythm given on 1.1.1924) as the completion and goal of all Earth-evolution. (Also compare here with the seventh seal of the Apocalypse, as the culmination of the sevenfold initiations, in which there is given the new 'Rosicrucian' Imagination of the Grail.)

81 GA 237, 4.8.1924.
82 GA 26.
83 See GA 191, 1.11.1919.
84 We must look here to another profound mystery connected with the Christmas Conference as a Grail event. It can come before us in all clarity by bringing together two lectures of 1909 in which the question of 'spiritual economy' is considered. In a lecture on 7.3.1909 (GA 109/11), Rudolf Steiner says that just as in past centuries numerous replicas preserved in the spiritual world of the etheric body and astral body of Christ Jesus have been at work in humanity, so too, beginning with our time, a certain number of people by taking up into their souls the new knowledge of Christ that is

open to humanity today through anthroposophically-orientated spiritual science are gradually to prepare themselves to receive into their own 'I' an imprint of the living images, preserved in the supersensible world, of the 'I' of Christ Jesus. It is just in this preparation that spiritual science has an important task. Rudolf Steiner says: 'It belongs to the inner mission of the spiritual world-stream [Anthroposophy] to prepare people to reach such a stage of inner maturity that an ever greater number of human beings can now also receive into themselves an image, a reflection of the "I"-nature of Christ Jesus.' For 'these imprinted images of the Christ Jesus Individuality are waiting to be received by human souls—they are waiting!' ('Spiritual Bells of Easter' in GA 109/111). In the lecture on 11.4.1909, Rudolf Steiner says that these images, derived from the imprint of the 'I' of Christ in the bodily sheaths of Jesus, are preserved in the spiritual world as the holiest centre of the Grail Mystery, the secrets of which in our time must become the property of a wider circle of appropriately prepared people. And he continues in this context: 'If human souls open themselves to be enkindled by spiritual science to an understanding of secrets such as these [i.e. secrets of the Grail Mysteries, as the Mysteries of the divine blood, the bearers of the living images of the Christ-"I"], if our souls live into such as understanding, then they attain the maturity to recognize, when gazing on that Holy Chalice, the Mystery of the Christ-"I", of the eternal "I" which every human "I" can become. This is that secret—people have only to allow themselves to be called upon by spiritual science to understand this secret as a fact, in order, in the sight of the Holy Grail, to receive the "I" of Christ.' In this sense we can also characterize the Mystery of the laying of the 'dodecahedral Stone of Love' of the General Anthroposophical Society into the hearts and souls of the people at the Christmas Conference as the beginning of fully conscious work towards the future we have described. For by uniting in our soul human love with Cosmic Love, human imagination with Cosmic Imagination, human thoughts with Cosmic Thoughts, we prepare ourselves so that at a definite moment of our life (be it in this incarnation or the next) we shall be worthy to take up into our own 'I' a reflection, a 'counter-image' of the macrocosmic 'I' of Christ. And this is the very real path upon which every anthroposophist today can enter, who has laid in his heart and soul the 'dodecahedral imaginative Form of Love' and who works in the spirit of the impulse of the Christmas Conference, the fundamental Christian impulse of our time (compare with what is said in Note 79 of this chapter).

85   GA 238, 16.9.1924.
86   GA 237, 28.7.1924.
87   Ibid., 8.8.1924.
88   GA 240, 14.8.1924.
89   Ibid., 27.8.1924.
90   Ibid., 18.7.1924.
91   Ibid., 19.7.1924.

92 In his book *The Christmas Foundation*, in the chapter 'The Rhythmic Sequences of the year 869', Rudolf Grosse points to the two streams of time that are particularly relevant for the twentieth century. On the one hand is the rhythm connected with the year 869 in which the 8th Ecumenical Council abolished the spirit. If one takes as the turning-point the beginning of the fifth post-Atlantean epoch, then with equal intervals we get the following sequence, 869–1413–1957. The year 1957 was that in which, in a spiritual sense, the consequences of 869 had to fall. However, working against this potential outbreak of dark forces was the impulse of the Christmas Conference that had taken place exactly 33 years before. If we now take 1957 as our turning-point, from a rhythm of 33 years we get that point in time from which the Christmas Conference must gradually find its spiritual fulfilment, 1924–1957–1990. It follows from this that at the beginning of the last decade of the twentieth century there must be a possibility given to the new impulse of Light to enter into the development of the Earth.
93 GA 240, 18.7.1924.
94 Ibid., 20.7.1924.
95 Ibid., 12.8.1924.
96 GA 237, 1.8.1924.
97 *Occult Science*, the chapter 'Present and Future Evolution of the World and of Mankind'.
98 GA 240, 27.8.1924.
99 Ibid., 19.7.1924.
100 Ibid., 27.8.1924.
101 GA 223, 1.4.1923.

Bibliographical References

List of Works by Rudolf Steiner Referred to in the Present Book

The English title is given only in cases where a similar (though not always identical) volume to the original German edition from the collected works—the *Gesamtausgabe* (abbreviated as 'GA')—has been published in English translation. In many cases, lectures are available in typescript or in print as single lectures or compilations from the collected works. For information on these contact Rudolf Steiner House Library, 35 Park Road, London NW1 6XT, or similar anthroposophical libraries around the world.

Publishers:

AP:	Anthroposophic Press (New York)
APC:	Anthroposophical Publishing Company (London)
GAR:	Garber Communications, Inc. (New York), Imprint: Spiritual Science Library
MER:	Mercury Press (Spring Valley, New York)
RSP:	Rudolf Steiner Press (England)

GA

1	*Einleitungen zu Goethes Naturwissenschaftlichen Schriften*
4	*The Philosophy of Freedom* (RSP, 1988)
7	*Mysticism at the Dawn of the Modern Age* (GAR, 1980)
8	*Christianity as Mystical Fact* (RSP, 1972)
9	*Theosophy* (RSP, 1989)
10	*Knowledge of the Higher Worlds* (RSP, 1989)
11	*Cosmic Memory* (GAR, 1990)
13	*Occult Science* (RSP, 1962)
15	*The Spiritual Guidance of Humanity* (AP, 1992)
18	*The Riddles of Philosophy* (AP, 1973)
21	*Von Seelenrätseln*. Some articles appear in *The Case for Anthroposophy* (RSP, 1970)
23	*Towards Social Renewal* (RSP, 1977)
24	*The Renewal of the Social Organism* (AP, 1985)
26	*Anthroposophical Leading Thoughts* (RSP, 1985)
28	*The Course of My Life* (AP, 1980)
34	*Lucifer-Gnosis*
40	*Wahrspruchworte*
53	*Ursprung und Ziel des Menschen*

245	*Anweisungen für eine esoterische Schülung.* Extracts from this volume translated as *Guidance in Esoteric Training* (RSP, 1972)

245   *Anweisungen für eine esoterische Schülung.* Extracts from this volume translated as *Guidance in Esoteric Training* (RSP, 1972)

257   *Awakening to Community* (AP, 1974)

258   *The Anthroposophic Movement* (RSP, 1993)

260   *The Christmas Conference Proceedings* (AP, 1990)

260a   *Die Konstitution der Allgemeinen Anthroposophischen Gesellschaft und der Freien Hochschule für Geisteswissenschaft.* Some material appears in *The Life, Nature and Cultivation of Anthroposophy* (RSP, 1963)

262   *Correspondence and Documents* (1901–25) (RSP, 1988)

275   *Kunst im Lichte der Mysterienweisheit.* Some lectures appear in *Art as Seen in the Light of Mystery Wisdom* (RSP, 1984)

284/5   *Bilder okkulter Siegel und Säulen*

286   *Wege zu einem neuen Baustil.* Some lectures appear in *Ways to a New Style in Architecture* (APC, 1927)

330   *Neugestaltung des sozialen Organismus*

331   *Betriebsräte und Sozialisierung*

350   *Rhythmen in Kosmos und im Menschenwesen. Wie kommt man zum Schauen der geistigen Welt?* Some lectures appear in *Learning to See into the Spiritual World* (AP, 1990)

Books by other Authors

Arenson, Adolf. *Fruits of Earnest Study, Volume 1* (London: Harry Collison, 1931)

Bock, Emil. *Rudolf Steiner, Studien zu seinem Lebensgang und Lebenswerk* (Stuttgart: 1961)

Grosse, Rudolf. *The Christmas Foundation: Beginning of a New Cosmic Age* (North Vancouver: Steiner Book Centre, 1984)

Lievegoed, B.C.J. *Mystery Streams in Europe and the New Mysteries* (New York: Anthroposophic Press, 1982)

Rittelmeyer, Friedrich. *Rudolf Steiner Enters My Life* (Edinburgh: Floris Books, 1963)

Schubert, Ilona. *Reminiscences of Rudolf Steiner and Marie Steiner von Sivers* (London: Temple Lodge Press, 1991)

Stein, W.J./Steiner, Rudolf. *Dokumentation eines wegweisenden Zussammenwirkens* (Dornach: Verlag am Goetheanum, 1985)

Turgeniev, Assya. *Erinnerungen an Rudolf Steiner* (Stuttgart: Verlag Freies Geistesleben, 1972)

Van Bemmelen, Daniel. *Das erste Goetheanum als Menschheitsbau* (Dornach: Verlag am Goetheanum, 1975)

Van Emmichoven, Zeylmans. *The Foundation Stone* (London: Rudolf Steiner Press, 1963)

Van Manen, Hans Peter. *Twin Roads to the New Millennium* (London: Rudolf Steiner Press, 1988)

Wegman, Ita. *An die Freunde* (Arlesheim: Edition Natura Verlag, 1960). See also *Esoteric Studies. The Michael Impulse* (London: Temple Lodge Publishing, 1993)

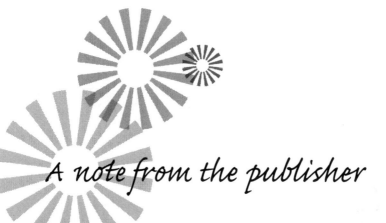

A note from the publisher

For more than a quarter of a century, **Temple Lodge Publishing** has made available new thought, ideas and research in the field of spiritual science.

Anthroposophy, as founded by Rudolf Steiner (1861-1925), is commonly known today through its practical applications, principally in education (Steiner-Waldorf schools) and agriculture (biodynamic food and wine). But behind this outer activity stands the core discipline of spiritual science, which continues to be developed and updated. True science can never be static and anthroposophy is living knowledge.

Our list features some of the best contemporary spiritual-scientific work available today, as well as introductory titles. So, visit us online at **www.templelodge.com** and join our emailing list for news on new titles.

If you feel like supporting our work, you can do so by buying our books or making a direct donation (we are a non-profit/charitable organisation).

office@templelodge.com

TEMPLE LODGE

For the finest books of Science and Spirit